# Data Mining Techniques
## For Marketing, Sales, and Customer Relationship Management

## Second Edition

Michael J.A. Berry
Gordon S. Linoff

WILEY

Wiley Publishing, Inc.

**Vice President and Executive Group Publisher:** Richard Swadley
**Vice President and Executive Publisher:** Bob Ipsen
**Vice President and Publisher:** Joseph B. Wikert
**Executive Editorial Director:** Mary Bednarek
**Executive Editor:** Robert M. Elliott
**Editorial Manager:** Kathryn A. Malm
**Senior Production Editor:** Fred Bernardi
**Development Editor:** Emilie Herman, Erica Weinstein
**Production Editor:** Felicia Robinson
**Media Development Specialist:** Laura Carpenter VanWinkle
**Text Design & Composition:** Wiley Composition Services

*Library of Congress Cataloging-in-Publication Data:*

Berry, Michael J. A.
 Data mining techniques : for marketing, sales, and customer
relationship management / Michael J.A. Berry, Gordon Linoff.— 2nd ed.
  p. cm.
Includes index.
 ISBN 0-471-47064-3 (paper/website)
 1. Data mining. 2. Marketing—Data processing. 3. Business—Data
processing. I. Linoff, Gordon. II. Title.
HF5415.125 .B47 2004
658.8′02—dc22

                              2003026693

ISBN: 0-471-47064-3

Printed in the United States of America

10  9  8  7  6

*To Stephanie, Sasha, and Nathaniel. Without your patience and understanding, this book would not have been possible.*

*— Michael*

*To Puccio. Grazie per essere paziente con me.*

*Ti amo.*

*— Gordon*

# Contents

# About the Authors

Michael J. A. Berry and Gordon S. Linoff are well known in the data mining field. They have jointly authored three influential and widely read books on data mining that have been translated into many languages. They each have close to two decades of experience applying data mining techniques to business problems in marketing and customer relationship management.

Michael and Gordon first worked together during the 1980s at Thinking Machines Corporation, which was a pioneer in mining large databases. In 1996, they collaborated on a data mining seminar, which soon evolved into the first edition of this book. The success of that collaboration gave them the courage to start Data Miners, Inc., a respected data mining consultancy, in 1998. As data mining consultants, they have worked with a wide variety of major companies in North America, Europe, and Asia, turning customer databases, call detail records, Web log entries, point-of-sale records, and billing files into useful information that can be used to improve the customer experience. The authors' years of hands-on data mining experience are reflected in every chapter of this extensively updated and revised edition of their first book, *Data Mining Techniques*.

When not mining data at some distant client site, Michael lives in Cambridge, Massachusetts, and Gordon lives in New York City.

And, of course, all the people we thanked in the first edition are still deserving of acknowledgement:

| | | |
|---|---|---|
| Bob Flynn | Jim Flynn | Paul Berry |
| Bryan McNeely | Kamran Parsaye | Rakesh Agrawal |
| Claire Budden | Karen Stewart | Ric Amari |
| David Isaac | Larry Bookman | Rich Cohen |
| David Waltz | Larry Scroggins | Robert Groth |
| Dena d'Ebin | Lars Rohrberg | Robert Utzschnieder |
| Diana Lin | Lounette Dyer | Roland Pesch |
| Don Peppers | Marc Goodman | Stephen Smith |
| Ed Horton | Marc Reifeis | Sue Osterfelt |
| Edward Ewen | Marge Sherold | Susan Buchanan |
| Fred Chapman | Mario Bourgoin | Syamala Srinivasan |
| Gary Drescher | Prof. Michael Jordan | Wei-Xing Ho |
| Gregory Lampshire | Patsy Campbell | William Petefish |
| Janet Smith | Paul Becker | Yvonne McCollin |
| Jerry Modes | | |

# Acknowledgments

We are fortunate to be surrounded by some of the most talented data miners anywhere, so our first thanks go to our colleagues at Data Miners, Inc. from whom we have learned so much: Will Potts, Dorian Pyle, and Brij Masand. There are also clients with whom we work so closely that we consider them our colleagues as well: Harrison Sohmer and Stuart E. Ward, III are in that category. Our Editor, Bob Elliott, Editorial Assistant, Erica Weinstein, and Development Editor, Emilie Herman, kept us (more or less) on schedule and helped us maintain a consistent style. Lauren McCann, a graduate student at M.I.T. and intern at Data Miners, prepared the census data used in some examples and created some of the illustrations.

We would also like to acknowledge all of the people we have worked with in scores of data mining engagements over the years. We have learned something from every one of them. The many whose data mining projects have influenced the second edition of this book include:

| | | |
|---|---|---|
| Al Fan | Herb Edelstein | Nick Gagliardo |
| Alan Parker | Jill Holtz | Nick Radcliffe |
| Anne Milley | Joan Forrester | Patrick Surry |
| Brian Guscott | John Wallace | Ronny Kohavi |
| Bruce Rylander | Josh Goff | Sheridan Young |
| Corina Cortes | Karen Kennedy | Susan Hunt Stevens |
| Daryl Berry | Kurt Thearling | Ted Browne |
| Daryl Pregibon | Lynne Brennen | Terri Kowalchuk |
| Doug Newell | Mark Smith | Victor Lo |
| Ed Freeman | Mateus Kehder | Yasmin Namini |
| Erin McCarthy | Michael Patrick | Zai Ying Huang |

# Why and What Is Data Mining?

In the first edition of this book, the first sentence of the first chapter began with the words "Somerville, Massachusetts, home to one of the authors of this book, . . ." and went on to tell of two small businesses in that town and how they had formed learning relationships with their customers. In the intervening years, the little girl whose relationship with her hair braider was described in the chapter has grown up and moved away and no longer wears her hair in cornrows. Her father has moved to nearby Cambridge. But one thing has not changed. The author is still a loyal customer of the Wine Cask, where some of the same people who first introduced him to cheap Algerian reds in 1978 and later to the wine-growing regions of France are now helping him to explore Italy and Germany.

After a quarter of a century, they still have a loyal customer. That loyalty is no accident. Dan and Steve at the Wine Cask learn the tastes of their customers and their price ranges. When asked for advice, their response will be based on their accumulated knowledge of that customer's tastes and budgets as well as on their knowledge of their stock.

The people at The Wine Cask know a lot about wine. Although that knowledge is one reason to shop there rather than at a big discount liquor store, it is their intimate knowledge of each customer that keeps people coming back. Another wine shop could open across the street and hire a staff of expert oenophiles, but it would take them months or years to achieve the same level of customer knowledge.

Well-run small businesses naturally form learning relationships with their customers. Over time, they learn more and more about their customers, and they use that knowledge to serve them better. The result is happy, loyal customers and profitable businesses. Larger companies, with hundreds of thousands or millions of customers, do not enjoy the luxury of actual personal relationships with each one. These larger firms must rely on other means to form learning relationships with their customers. In particular, they must learn to take full advantage of something they have in abundance—the data produced by nearly every customer interaction. This book is about analytic techniques that can be used to turn customer data into customer knowledge.

## Analytic Customer Relationship Management

It is widely recognized that firms of all sizes need to learn to emulate what small, service-oriented businesses have always done well—creating one-to-one relationships with their customers. Customer relationship management is a broad topic that is the subject of many books and conferences. Everything from lead-tracking software to campaign management software to call center software is now marketed as a customer relationship management tool. The focus of this book is narrower—the role that data mining can play in improving customer relationship management by improving the firm's ability to form learning relationships with its customers.

In every industry, forward-looking companies are moving toward the goal of understanding each customer individually and using that understanding to make it easier for the customer to do business with them rather than with competitors. These same firms are learning to look at the value of each customer so that they know which ones are worth investing money and effort to hold on to and which ones should be allowed to depart. This change in focus from broad market segments to individual customers requires changes throughout the enterprise, and nowhere more than in marketing, sales, and customer support.

Building a business around the customer relationship is a revolutionary change for most companies. Banks have traditionally focused on maintaining the spread between the rate they pay to bring money in and the rate they charge to lend money out. Telephone companies have concentrated on connecting calls through the network. Insurance companies have focused on processing claims and managing investments. It takes more than data mining to turn a product-focused organization into a customer-centric one. A data mining result that suggests offering a particular customer a widget instead of a gizmo will be ignored if the manager's bonus depends on the number of gizmos sold this quarter and not on the number of widgets (even if the latter are more profitable).

In the narrow sense, data mining is a collection of tools and techniques. It is one of several technologies required to support a customer-centric enterprise. In a broader sense, data mining is an attitude that business actions should be based on learning, that informed decisions are better than uninformed decisions, and that measuring results is beneficial to the business. Data mining is also a process and a methodology for applying the tools and techniques. For data mining to be effective, the other requirements for analytic CRM must also be in place. In order to form a learning relationship with its customers, a firm must be able to:

- *Notice* what its customers are doing
- *Remember* what it and its customers have done over time
- *Learn* from what it has remembered
- *Act* on what it has learned to make customers more profitable

Although the focus of this book is on the third bullet—learning from what has happened in the past—that learning cannot take place in a vacuum. There must be transaction processing systems to capture customer interactions, data warehouses to store historical customer behavior information, data mining to translate history into plans for future action, and a customer relationship strategy to put those plans into practice.

## The Role of Transaction Processing Systems

A small business builds relationships with its customers by noticing their needs, remembering their preferences, and learning from past interactions how to serve them better in the future. How can a large enterprise accomplish something similar when most company employees may never interact personally with customers? Even where there is customer interaction, it is likely to be with a different sales clerk or anonymous call-center employee each time, so how can the enterprise notice, remember, and learn from these interactions? What can replace the creative intuition of the sole proprietor who recognizes customers by name, face, and voice, and remembers their habits and preferences?

In a word, nothing. But that does not mean that we cannot try. Through the clever application of information technology, even the largest enterprise can come surprisingly close. In large commercial enterprises, the first step—noticing what the customer does—has already largely been automated. Transaction processing systems are everywhere, collecting data on seemingly everything. The records generated by automatic teller machines, telephone switches, Web servers, point-of-sale scanners, and the like are the raw material for data mining.

These days, we all go through life generating a constant stream of transaction records. When you pick up the phone to order a canoe paddle from L.L.

Bean or a satin bra from Victoria's Secret, a call detail record is generated at the local phone company showing, among other things, the time of your call, the number you dialed, and the long-distance company to which you have been connected. At the long-distance company, similar records are generated recording the duration of your call and the exact routing it takes through the switching system. This data will be combined with other records that store your billing plan, name, and address in order to generate a bill. At the catalog company, your call is logged again along with information about the particular catalog from which you ordered and any special promotions you are responding to. When the customer service representative that answered your call asks for your credit card number and expiration date, the information is immediately relayed to a credit card verification system to approve the transaction; this too creates a record. All too soon, the transaction reaches the bank that issued your credit card, where it appears on your next monthly statement. When your order, with its item number, size, and color, goes into the cataloger's order entry system, it spawns still more records in the billing system and the inventory control system. Within hours, your order is also generating transaction records in a computer system at UPS or FedEx where it is scanned about a dozen times between the warehouse and your home, allowing you to check the shipper's Web site to track its progress.

These transaction records are not generated with data mining in mind; they are created to meet the operational needs of the company. Yet all contain valuable information about customers and all can be mined successfully. Phone companies have used call detail records to discover residential phone numbers whose calling patterns resemble those of a business in order to market special services to people operating businesses from their homes. Catalog companies have used order histories to decide which customers should be included in which future mailings—and, in the case of Victoria's secret, which models produce the most sales. Federal Express used the change in its customers' shipping patterns during a strike at UPS in order to calculate their share of their customers' package delivery business. Supermarkets have used point-of-sale data in order to decide what coupons to print for which customers. Web retailers have used past purchases in order to determine what to display when customers return to the site.

These transaction systems are the customer touch points where information about customer behavior first enters the enterprise. As such, they are the eyes and ears (and perhaps the nose, tongue, and fingers) of the enterprise.

## The Role of Data Warehousing

The customer-focused enterprise regards every record of an interaction with a client or prospect—each call to customer support, each point-of-sale transaction, each catalog order, each visit to a company Web site—as a learning opportunity. But learning requires more than simply gathering data. In fact, many companies gather hundreds of gigabytes or terabytes of data from and about their customers without learning anything! Data is gathered because it is needed for some operational purpose, such as inventory control or billing. And, once it has served that purpose, it languishes on disk or tape or is discarded.

For learning to take place, data from many sources—billing records, scanner data, registration forms, applications, call records, coupon redemptions, surveys—must first be gathered together and organized in a consistent and useful way. This is called *data warehousing*. Data warehousing allows the enterprise to remember what it has noticed about its customers.

**TIP** Customer patterns become evident over time. Data warehouses need to support accurate historical data so that data mining can pick up these critical trends.

One of the most important aspects of the data warehouse is the capability to track customer behavior over time. Many of the patterns of interest for customer relationship management only become apparent over time. Is usage trending up or down? How frequently does the customer return? Which channels does the customer prefer? Which promotions does the customer respond to?

A number of years ago, a large catalog retailer discovered the importance of retaining historical customer behavior data when they first started keeping more than a year's worth of history on their catalog mailings and the responses they generated from customers. What they discovered was a segment of customers that only ordered from the catalog at Christmas time. With knowledge of that segment, they had choices as to what to do. They could try to come up with a way to stimulate interest in placing orders the rest of the year. They could improve their overall response rate by not mailing to this segment the rest of the year. Without some further experimentation, it is not clear what the right answer is, but without historical data, they would never have known to ask the question.

A good data warehouse provides access to the information gleaned from transactional data in a format that is much friendlier than the way it is stored in the operational systems where the data originated. Ideally, data in the warehouse has been gathered from many sources, cleaned, merged, tied to particular customers, and summarized in various useful ways. Reality often falls short of this ideal, but the corporate data warehouse is still the most important source of data for analytic customer relationship management.

## The Role of Data Mining

The data warehouse provides the enterprise with a memory. But, memory is of little use without intelligence. Intelligence allows us to comb through our memories, noticing patterns, devising rules, coming up with new ideas, figuring out the right questions, and making predictions about the future. This book describes tools and techniques that add intelligence to the data warehouse. These techniques help make it possible to exploit the vast mountains of data generated by interactions with customers and prospects in order to get to know them better.

Who is likely to remain a loyal customer and who is likely to jump ship? What products should be marketed to which prospects? What determines whether a person will respond to a certain offer? Which telemarketing script is best for this call? Where should the next branch be located? What is the next product or service this customer will want? Answers to questions like these lie buried in corporate data. It takes powerful data mining tools to get at them.

The central idea of data mining for customer relationship management is that data from the past contains information that will be useful in the future. It works because customer behaviors captured in corporate data are not random, but reflect the differing needs, preferences, propensities, and treatments of customers. The goal of data mining is to find patterns in historical data that shed light on those needs, preferences, and propensities. The task is made difficult by the fact that the patterns are not always strong, and the signals sent by customers are noisy and confusing. Separating signal from noise—recognizing the fundamental patterns beneath seemingly random variations—is an important role of data mining.

This book covers all the most important data mining techniques and the strengths and weaknesses of each in the context of customer relationship management.

## The Role of the Customer Relationship Management Strategy

To be effective, data mining must occur within a context that allows an organization to change its behavior as a result of what it learns. It is no use knowing that wireless telephone customers who are on the wrong rate plan are likely to cancel their subscriptions if there is no one empowered to propose that they switch to a more appropriate plan as suggested in the sidebar. Data mining should be embedded in a corporate customer relationship strategy that spells out the actions to be taken as a result of what is learned through data mining. When low-value customers are identified, how will they be treated? Are there programs in place to stimulate their usage to increase their value? Or does it make more sense to lower the cost of serving them? If some channels consistently bring in more profitable customers, how can resources be shifted to those channels?

Data mining is a tool. As with any tool, it is not sufficient to understand how it works; it is necessary to understand how it will be used.

> ### DATA MINING SUGGESTS, BUSINESSES DECIDE
>
> This sidebar explores the example from the main text in slightly more detail. An analysis of attrition at a wireless telephone service provider often reveals that people whose calling patterns do not match their rate plan are more likely to cancel their subscriptions. People who use more than the number of minutes included in their plan are charged for the extra minutes—often at a high rate. People who do not use their full allotment of minutes are paying for minutes they do not use and are likely to be attracted to a competitor's offer of a cheaper plan.
>
> This result suggests doing something proactive to move customers to the right rate plan. But this is not a simple decision. As long as they don't quit, customers on the wrong rate plan are more profitable if left alone. Further analysis may be needed. Perhaps there is a subset of these customers who are not price sensitive and can be safely left alone. Perhaps any intervention will simply hand customers an opportunity to cancel. Perhaps a small "rightsizing" test can help resolve these issues. Data mining can help make more informed decisions. It can suggest tests to make. Ultimately, though, the business needs to make the decision.

## What Is Data Mining?

Data mining, as we use the term, is the exploration and analysis of large quantities of data in order to discover meaningful patterns and rules. For the purposes of this book, we assume that the *goal* of data mining is to allow a corporation to improve its marketing, sales, and customer support operations through a better understanding of its customers. Keep in mind, however, that the data mining techniques and tools described here are equally applicable in fields ranging from law enforcement to radio astronomy, medicine, and industrial process control.

In fact, hardly any of the data mining algorithms were first invented with commercial applications in mind. The commercial data miner employs a grab bag of techniques borrowed from statistics, computer science, and machine learning research. The choice of a particular combination of techniques to apply in a particular situation depends on the nature of the data mining task, the nature of the available data, and the skills and preferences of the data miner.

Data mining comes in two flavors—directed and undirected. Directed data mining attempts to explain or categorize some particular target field such as income or response. Undirected data mining attempts to find patterns or similarities among groups of records without the use of a particular target field or collection of predefined classes. Both these flavors are discussed in later chapters.

Data mining is largely concerned with building models. A model is simply an algorithm or set of rules that connects a collection of inputs (often in the form of fields in a corporate database) to a particular target or outcome. Regression, neural networks, decision trees, and most of the other data mining techniques discussed in this book are techniques for creating models. Under the right circumstances, a model can result in insight by providing an explanation of how outcomes of particular interest, such as placing an order or failing to pay a bill, are related to and predicted by the available facts. Models are also used to produce *scores*. A score is a way of expressing the findings of a model in a single number. Scores can be used to sort a list of customers from most to least loyal or most to least likely to respond or most to least likely to default on a loan.

The data mining process is sometimes referred to as *knowledge discovery* or KDD (knowledge discovery in databases). We prefer to think of it as *knowledge creation*.

## What Tasks Can Be Performed with Data Mining?

Many problems of intellectual, economic, and business interest can be phrased in terms of the following six tasks:

- Classification
- Estimation
- Prediction
- Affinity grouping
- Clustering
- Description and profiling

The first three are all examples of directed data mining, where the goal is to find the value of a particular target variable. Affinity grouping and clustering are undirected tasks where the goal is to uncover structure in data without respect to a particular target variable. Profiling is a descriptive task that may be either directed or undirected.

### Classification

Classification, one of the most common data mining tasks, seems to be a human imperative. In order to understand and communicate about the world, we are constantly classifying, categorizing, and grading. We divide living things into phyla, species, and general; matter into elements; dogs into breeds; people into races; steaks and maple syrup into USDA grades.

Classification consists of examining the features of a newly presented object and assigning it to one of a predefined set of classes. The objects to be classified are generally represented by records in a database table or a file, and the act of classification consists of adding a new column with a class code of some kind.

The classification task is characterized by a well-defined definition of the classes, and a training set consisting of preclassified examples. The task is to build a model of some kind that can be applied to unclassified data in order to classify it.

Examples of classification tasks that have been addressed using the techniques described in this book include:

- Classifying credit applicants as low, medium, or high risk
- Choosing content to be displayed on a Web page
- Determining which phone numbers correspond to fax machines
- Spotting fraudulent insurance claims
- Assigning industry codes and job designations on the basis of free-text job descriptions

In all of these examples, there are a limited number of classes, and we expect to be able to assign any record into one or another of them. Decision trees (discussed in Chapter 6) and nearest neighbor techniques (discussed in Chapter 8) are techniques well suited to classification. Neural networks (discussed in Chapter 7) and link analysis (discussed in Chapter 10) are also useful for classification in certain circumstances.

## Estimation

Classification deals with discrete outcomes: yes or no; measles, rubella, or chicken pox. Estimation deals with continuously valued outcomes. Given some input data, estimation comes up with a value for some unknown continuous variable such as income, height, or credit card balance.

In practice, estimation is often used to perform a classification task. A credit card company wishing to sell advertising space in its billing envelopes to a ski boot manufacturer might build a classification model that put all of its cardholders into one of two classes, skier or nonskier. Another approach is to build a model that assigns each cardholder a "propensity to ski score." This might be a value from 0 to 1 indicating the estimated probability that the cardholder is a skier. The classification task now comes down to establishing a threshold score. Anyone with a score greater than or equal to the threshold is classed as a skier, and anyone with a lower score is considered not to be a skier.

The estimation approach has the great advantage that the individual records can be rank ordered according to the estimate. To see the importance of this, imagine that the ski boot company has budgeted for a mailing of 500,000 pieces. If the classification approach is used and 1.5 million skiers are identified, then it might simply place the ad in the bills of 500,000 people selected at random from that pool. If, on the other hand, each cardholder has a propensity to ski score, it can send the ad to the 500,000 most likely candidates.

Examples of estimation tasks include:

- Estimating the number of children in a family
- Estimating a family's total household income
- Estimating the lifetime value of a customer
- Estimating the probability that someone will respond to a balance transfer solicitation.

Regression models (discussed in Chapter 5) and neural networks (discussed in Chapter 7) are well suited to estimation tasks. Survival analysis (Chapter 12) is well suited to estimation tasks where the goal is to estimate the time to an event, such as a customer stopping.

## Prediction

Prediction is the same as classification or estimation, except that the records are classified according to some predicted future behavior or estimated future value. In a prediction task, the only way to check the accuracy of the classification is to wait and see. The primary reason for treating prediction as a separate task from classification and estimation is that in predictive modeling there are additional issues regarding the temporal relationship of the input variables or predictors to the target variable.

Any of the techniques used for classification and estimation can be adapted for use in prediction by using training examples where the value of the variable to be predicted is already known, along with historical data for those examples. The historical data is used to build a model that explains the current observed behavior. When this model is applied to current inputs, the result is a prediction of future behavior.

Examples of prediction tasks addressed by the data mining techniques discussed in this book include:

- Predicting the size of the balance that will be transferred if a credit card prospect accepts a balance transfer offer
- Predicting which customers will leave within the next 6 months
- Predicting which telephone subscribers will order a value-added service such as three-way calling or voice mail

Most of the data mining techniques discussed in this book are suitable for use in prediction so long as training data is available in the proper form. The choice of technique depends on the nature of the input data, the type of value to be predicted, and the importance attached to explicability of the prediction.

## Affinity Grouping or Association Rules

The task of affinity grouping is to determine which things go together. The prototypical example is determining what things go together in a shopping cart at the supermarket, the task at the heart of *market basket analysis*. Retail chains can use affinity grouping to plan the arrangement of items on store shelves or in a catalog so that items often purchased together will be seen together.

Affinity grouping can also be used to identify cross-selling opportunities and to design attractive packages or groupings of product and services.

Affinity grouping is one simple approach to generating rules from data. If two items, say cat food and kitty litter, occur together frequently enough, we can generate two *association rules*:

- People who buy cat food also buy kitty litter with probability P1.
- People who buy kitty litter also buy cat food with probability P2.

Association rules are discussed in detail in Chapter 9.

## Clustering

Clustering is the task of segmenting a heterogeneous population into a number of more homogeneous subgroups or *clusters*. What distinguishes clustering from classification is that clustering does not rely on predefined classes. In classification, each record is assigned a predefined class on the basis of a model developed through training on preclassified examples.

In clustering, there are no predefined classes and no examples. The records are grouped together on the basis of self-similarity. It is up to the user to determine what meaning, if any, to attach to the resulting clusters. Clusters of symptoms might indicate different diseases. Clusters of customer attributes might indicate different market segments.

Clustering is often done as a prelude to some other form of data mining or modeling. For example, clustering might be the first step in a market segmentation effort: Instead of trying to come up with a one-size-fits-all rule for "what kind of promotion do customers respond to best," first divide the customer base into clusters or people with similar buying habits, and then ask what kind of promotion works best for each cluster. Cluster detection is discussed in detail in Chapter 11. Chapter 7 discusses self-organizing maps, another technique sometimes used for clustering.

## Profiling

Sometimes the purpose of data mining is simply to describe what is going on in a complicated database in a way that increases our understanding of the people, products, or processes that produced the data in the first place. A good enough *description* of a behavior will often suggest an *explanation* for it as well. At the very least, a good description suggests where to start looking for an explanation. The famous gender gap in American politics is an example of how a simple description, "women support Democrats in greater numbers than do men," can provoke large amounts of interest and further study on the part of journalists, sociologists, economists, and political scientists, not to mention candidates for public office.

Decision trees (discussed in Chapter 6) are a powerful tool for profiling customers (or anything else) with respect to a particular target or outcome. Association rules (discussed in Chapter 9) and clustering (discussed in Chapter 11) can also be used to build profiles.

# Why Now?

Most of the data mining techniques described in this book have existed, at least as academic algorithms, for years or decades. However, it is only in the last decade that commercial data mining has caught on in a big way. This is due to the convergence of several factors:

- The data is being produced.
- The data is being warehoused.
- Computing power is affordable.
- Interest in customer relationship management is strong.
- Commercial data mining software products are readily available.

Let's look at each factor in turn.

## Data Is Being Produced

Data mining makes the most sense when there are large volumes of data. In fact, most data mining algorithms *require* large amounts of data in order to build and train the models that will then be used to perform classification, prediction, estimation, or other data mining tasks.

A few industries, including telecommunications and credit cards, have long had an automated, interactive relationship with customers that generated many transaction records, but it is only relatively recently that the automation of everyday life has become so pervasive. Today, the rise of supermarket point-of-sale scanners, automatic teller machines, credit and debit cards, pay-per-view television, online shopping, electronic funds transfer, automated order processing, electronic ticketing, and the like means that data is being produced and collected at unprecedented rates.

## Data Is Being Warehoused

Not only is a large amount of data being produced, but also, more and more often, it is being extracted from the operational billing, reservations, claims processing, and order entry systems where it is generated and then fed into a data warehouse to become part of the corporate memory.

Data warehousing brings together data from many different sources in a common format with consistent definitions for keys and fields. It is generally not possible (and certainly not advisable) to perform computer- and input/output (I/O)–intensive data mining operations on an operational system that the business depends on to survive. In any case, operational systems store data in a format designed to optimize performance of the operational task. This format is generally not well suited to decision-support activities like data mining. The data warehouse, on the other hand, should be designed exclusively for decision support, which can simplify the job of the data miner.

## Computing Power Is Affordable

Data mining algorithms typically require multiple passes over huge quantities of data. Many are computationally intensive as well. The continuing dramatic decrease in prices for disk, memory, processing power, and I/O bandwidth has brought once-costly techniques that were used only in a few government-funded laboratories into the reach of ordinary businesses.

The successful introduction of parallel relational database management software by major suppliers such as Oracle, Teradata, and IBM, has brought the power of parallel processing into many corporate data centers for the first time. These parallel database server platforms provide an excellent environment for large-scale data mining.

## Interest in Customer Relationship Management Is Strong

Across a wide spectrum of industries, companies have come to realize that their customers are central to their business and that customer information is one of their key assets.

### *Every Business Is a Service Business*

For companies in the service sector, information confers competitive advantage. That is why hotel chains record your preference for a nonsmoking room and car rental companies record your preferred type of car. In addition, companies that have not traditionally thought of themselves as service providers are beginning to think differently. Does an automobile dealer sell cars or transportation? If the latter, it makes sense for the dealership to offer you a loaner car whenever your own is in the shop, as many now do.

Even commodity products can be enhanced with service. A home heating oil company that monitors your usage and delivers oil when you need more, sells a better product than a company that expects you to remember to call to arrange a delivery before your tank runs dry and the pipes freeze. Credit card companies, long-distance providers, airlines, and retailers of all kinds often compete as much or more on service as on price.

### *Information Is a Product*

Many companies find that the information they have about their customers is valuable not only to themselves, but to others as well. A supermarket with a loyalty card program has something that the consumer packaged goods industry would love to have—knowledge about who is buying which products. A credit card company knows something that airlines would love to know—who is buying a lot of airplane tickets. Both the supermarket and the credit card company are in a position to be knowledge brokers or *infomediaries*. The supermarket can charge consumer packaged goods companies more to print coupons when the supermarkets can promise higher redemption rates by printing the right coupons for the right shoppers. The credit card company can charge the airlines to target a frequent flyer promotion to people who travel a lot, but fly on other airlines.

Google knows what people are looking for on the Web. It takes advantage of this knowledge by selling sponsored links. Insurance companies pay to make sure that someone searching on "car insurance" will be offered a link to their site. Financial services pay for sponsored links to appear when someone searches on the phrase "mortgage refinance."

In fact, any company that collects valuable data is in a position to become an information broker. The *Cedar Rapids Gazette* takes advantage of its dominant position in a 22-county area of Eastern Iowa to offer direct marketing services to local businesses. The paper uses its own obituary pages and wedding announcements to keep its marketing database current.

## Commercial Data Mining Software Products Have Become Available

There is always a lag between the time when new algorithms first appear in academic journals and excite discussion at conferences and the time when commercial software incorporating those algorithms becomes available. There is another lag between the initial availability of the first products and the time that they achieve wide acceptance. For data mining, the period of widespread availability and acceptance has arrived.

Many of the techniques discussed in this book started out in the fields of statistics, artificial intelligence, or machine learning. After a few years in universities and government labs, a new technique starts to be used by a few early adopters in the commercial sector. At this point in the evolution of a new technique, the software is typically available in source code to the intrepid user willing to retrieve it via FTP, compile it, and figure out how to use it by reading the author's Ph.D. thesis. Only after a few pioneers become successful with a new technique, does it start to appear in real products that come with user's manuals and help lines.

Nowadays, new techniques are being developed; however, much work is also devoted to extending and improving existing techniques. All the techniques discussed in this book are available in commercial software products, although there is no single product that incorporates all of them.

# How Data Mining Is Being Used Today

This whirlwind tour of a few interesting applications of data mining is intended to demonstrate the wide applicability of the data mining techniques discussed in this book. These vignettes are intended to convey something of the excitement of the field and possibly suggest ways that data mining could be profitably employed in your own work.

## A Supermarket Becomes an Information Broker

Thanks to point-of-sale scanners that record every item purchased and loyalty card programs that link those purchases to individual customers, supermarkets are in a position to notice a lot about their customers these days.

Safeway was one of the first U.S. supermarket chains to take advantage of this technology to turn itself into an information broker. Safeway purchases address and demographic data directly from its customers by offering them discounts in return for using loyalty cards when they make purchases. In order to obtain the card, shoppers voluntarily divulge personal information of the sort that makes good input for actionable customer insight.

From then on, each time the shopper presents the discount card, his or her transaction history is updated in a data warehouse somewhere. With every trip to the store, shoppers teach the retailer a little more about themselves. The supermarket itself is probably more interested in aggregate patterns (what items sell well together, what should be shelved together) than in the behavior of individual customers. The information gathered on individuals is of great interest to the *manufacturers* of the products that line the stores' aisles.

Of course, the store assures the customers that the information thus collected will be kept private and it is. Rather than selling Coca-Cola a list of frequent Pepsi buyers and vice versa, the chain sells *access* to customers who, based on their known buying habits and the data they have supplied, are likely prospects for a particular supplier's product. Safeway charges several cents per name to suppliers who want their coupon or special promotional offer to reach just the right people. Since the coupon redemption also becomes an entry in the shopper's transaction history file, the precise response rate of the targeted group is a matter of record. Furthermore, a particular customer's response or lack thereof to the offer becomes input data for future predictive models.

American Express and other charge card suppliers do much the same thing, selling advertising space in and on their billing envelopes. The price they can charge for space in the envelope is directly tied to their ability to correctly identify people likely to respond to the ad. That is where data mining comes in.

## A Recommendation-Based Business

Virgin Wines sells wine directly to consumers in the United Kingdom through its Web site, www.virginwines.com. New customers are invited to complete a survey, "the wine wizard," when they first visit the site. The wine wizard asks each customer to rate various styles of wines. The ratings are used to create a profile of the customer's tastes. During the course of building the profile, the wine wizard makes some trial recommendations, and the customer has a chance to agree or disagree with them in order to refine the profile. When the wine wizard has been completed, the site knows enough about the customer to start making recommendations.

Over time, the site keeps track of what each customer actually buys and uses this information to update his or her customer profile. Customers can update their profiles by redoing the wine wizard at any time. They can also browse through their own past purchases by clicking on the "my cellar" tab. Any wine a customer has ever purchased or rated on the site is in the cellar. Customers may rate or rerate their past purchases at any time, providing still more feedback to the recommendation system. With these recommendations, the web site can offer customers new wines that they should like, emulating the way that stores like the Wine Cask have built loyal customer relationships.

## Cross-Selling

USAA is an insurance company that markets to active duty and retired military personnel and their families. The company attributes information-based marketing, including data mining, with a doubling of the number of products held by the average customer. USAA keeps detailed records on its customers and uses data mining to predict where they are in their life cycles and what products they are likely to need.

Another company that has used data mining to improve its cross-selling ability is Fidelity Investments. Fidelity maintains a data warehouse filled with information on all of its retail customers. This information is used to build data mining models that predict what other Fidelity products are likely to interest each customer. When an existing customer calls Fidelity, the phone representative's screen shows exactly where to lead the conversation.

In addition to improving the company's ability to cross-sell, Fidelity's retail marketing data warehouse has allowed the financial services powerhouse to build models of what makes a loyal customer and thereby increase customer retention. Once upon a time, these models caused Fidelity to retain a marginally profitable bill-paying service that would otherwise have been cut. It turned out that people who used the service were far less likely than the average customer to take their business to a competitor. Cutting the service would have encouraged a profitable group of loyal customers to shop around.

A central tenet of customer relationship management is that it is more profitable to focus on "wallet share" or "customer share," the amount of business you can do with each customer, than on market share. From financial services to heavy manufacturing, innovative companies are using data mining to increase the value of each customer.

## Holding on to Good Customers

Data mining is being used to promote customer retention in any industry where customers are free to change suppliers at little cost and competitors are eager to lure them away. Banks call it attrition. Wireless phone companies call it churn. By any name, it is a big problem. By gaining an understanding of *who* is likely to leave and *why*, a retention plan can be developed that addresses the right issues and targets the right customers.

In a mature market, bringing in a new customer tends to cost more than holding on to an existing one. However, the incentive offered to retain a customer is often quite expensive. Data mining is the key to figuring out which customers should get the incentive, which customers will stay without the incentive, and which customers should be allowed to walk.

## Weeding out Bad Customers

In many industries, some customers cost more than they are worth. These might be people who consume a lot of customer support resources without buying much. Or, they might be those annoying folks who carry a credit card they rarely use, are sure to pay off the full balance when they do, but must still be mailed a statement every month. Even worse, they might be people who owe you a lot of money when they declare bankruptcy.

The same data mining techniques that are used to spot the most valuable customers can also be used to pick out those who should be turned down for a loan, those who should be allowed to wait on hold the longest time, and those who should always be assigned a middle seat near the engine (or is that just our paranoia showing?).

## Revolutionizing an Industry

In 1988, the idea that a credit card issuer's most valuable asset is the information it has about its customers was pretty revolutionary. It was an idea that Richard Fairbank and Nigel Morris shopped around to 25 banks before Signet Banking Corporation decided to give it a try.

Signet acquired behavioral data from many sources and used it to build predictive models. Using these models, it launched the highly successful balance transfer program that changed the way the credit card industry works. In 1994, Signet spun off the card operation as Capital One, which is now one of the top 10 credit card issuers. The same aggressive use of data mining technology that fueled such rapid growth is also responsible for keeping Capital One's loan loss rates among the lowest in the industry. Data mining is now at the heart of the marketing strategy of all the major credit card issuers.

Credit card divisions may have led the charge of banks into data mining, but other divisions are not far behind. At Wachovia, a large North Carolina-based bank, data mining techniques are used to predict which customers are likely to be moving soon. For most people, moving to a new home in another town means closing the old bank account and opening a new one, often with a different company. Wachovia set out to improve retention by identifying customers who are about to move and making it easy for them to transfer their business to another Wachovia branch in the new location. Not only has retention improved markedly, but also a profitable relocation business has developed. In addition to setting up a bank account, Wachovia now arranges for gas, electricity, and other services at the new location.

## And Just about Anything Else

These applications should give you a feel for what is possible using data mining, but they do not come close to covering the full range of applications. The data mining techniques described in this book have been used to find quasars, design army uniforms, detect second-press olive oil masquerading as "extra virgin," teach machines to read aloud, and recognize handwritten letters. They will, no doubt, be used to do many of the things your business will require to grow and prosper for the rest of the century. In the next chapter, we turn to how businesses make effective use of data mining, using the virtuous cycle of data mining.

# Lessons Learned

Data Mining is an important component of analytic customer relationship management. The goal of analytic customer relationship management is to recreate, to the extent possible, the intimate, learning relationship that a well-run small business enjoys with its customers. A company's interactions with its customers generates large volumes of data. This data is initially captured in transaction processing systems such as automatic teller machines, telephone switch records, and supermarket scanner files. The data can then be collected, cleaned, and summarized for inclusion in a customer data warehouse. A well-designed customer data warehouse contains a historical record of customer interactions that becomes the memory of the corporation. Data mining tools can be applied to this historical record to learn things about customers that will allow the company to serve them better in the future. The chapter presented several examples of commercial applications of data mining such as better targeted couponing, making recommendations, cross selling, customer retention, and credit risk reduction.

Data mining itself is the process of finding useful patterns and rules in large volumes of data. This chapter introduced and defined six common data mining tasks: classification, estimation, prediction, affinity grouping, clustering, and profiling. The remainder of the book examines a variety of data mining algorithms and techniques that can be applied to these six tasks. To be successful, these techniques must become integral parts of a larger business process. That integration is the subject of the next chapter, *The Virtuous Cycle of Data Mining*.

CHAPTER

# 2

# The Virtuous Cycle
# of Data Mining

In the first part of the nineteenth century, textile mills were the industrial success stories. These mills sprang up in the growing towns and cities along rivers in England and New England to harness hydropower. Water, running over water wheels, drove spinning, knitting, and weaving machines. For a century, the symbol of the industrial revolution was water driving textile machines.

The business world has changed. Old mill towns are now quaint historical curiosities. Long mill buildings alongside rivers are warehouses, shopping malls, artist studios and computer companies. Even manufacturing companies often provide more value in services than in goods. We were struck by an ad campaign by a leading international cement manufacturer, Cemex, that presented concrete as a service. Instead of focusing on the quality of cement, its price, or availability, the ad pictured a bridge over a river and sold the idea that "cement" is a service that connects people by building bridges between them. Concrete as a service? A very modern idea.

Access to electrical or mechanical power is no longer the criterion for success. For mass-market products, data about customer interactions is the new waterpower; knowledge drives the turbines of the service economy and, since the line between service and manufacturing is getting blurry, much of the manufacturing economy as well. Information from data focuses marketing efforts by segmenting customers, improves product designs by addressing real customer needs, and improves allocation of resources by understanding and predicting customer preferences.

Data is at the heart of most companies' core business processes. It is generated by transactions in operational systems regardless of industry—retail, telecommunications, manufacturing, utilities, transportation, insurance, credit cards, and banking, for example. Adding to the deluge of internal data are external sources of demographic, lifestyle, and credit information on retail customers, and credit, financial, and marketing information on business customers. The promise of data mining is to find the interesting patterns lurking in all these billions and trillions of bytes. Merely finding patterns is not enough. *You must respond to the patterns and act on them, ultimately turning data into information, information into action, and action into value.* This is the virtuous cycle of data mining in a nutshell.

To achieve this promise, data mining needs to become an essential business process, incorporated into other processes including marketing, sales, customer support, product design, and inventory control. The virtuous cycle places data mining in the larger context of business, shifting the focus away from the discovery mechanism to the actions based on the discoveries. Throughout this chapter and this book, we will be talking about *actionable* results from data mining (and this usage of "actionable" should not be confused with its definition in the legal domain, where it means that some action has grounds for legal action).

Marketing literature makes data mining seem so easy. Just apply the automated algorithms created by the best minds in academia, such as neural networks, decision trees, and genetic algorithms, and you are on your way to untold successes. Although algorithms are important, the data mining solution is more than just a set of powerful techniques and data structures. The techniques have to be applied in the right areas, on the right data. The virtuous cycle of data mining is an iterative learning process that builds on results over time. Success in using data will transform an organization from reactive to proactive. This is the virtuous cycle of data mining, used by the authors for extracting maximum benefit from the techniques described later in the book.

This chapter opens with a brief case history describing an actual example of the application of data mining techniques to a real business problem. The case study is used to introduce the virtuous cycle of data mining. Data mining is presented as an ongoing activity within the business with the results of one data mining project becoming inputs to the next. Each project goes through four major stages, which together form one trip around the virtuous cycle. Once these stages have been introduced, they are illustrated with additional case studies.

## A Case Study in Business Data Mining

Once upon a time, there was a bank that had a business problem. One particular line of business, home equity lines of credit, was failing to attract good customers. There are several ways that a bank can attack this problem.

The bank could, for instance, lower interest rates on home equity loans. This would bring in more customers and increase market share at the expense of lowered margins. Existing customers might switch to the lower rates, further depressing margins. Even worse, assuming that the initial rates were reasonably competitive, lowering the rates might bring in the worst customers—the disloyal. Competitors can easily lure them away with slightly better terms. The sidebar "Making Money or Losing Money" talks about the problems of retaining loyal customers.

In this example, Bank of America was anxious to expand its portfolio of home equity loans after several direct mail campaigns yielded disappointing results. The National Consumer Assets Group (NCAG) decided to use data mining to attack the problem, providing a good introduction to the virtuous cycle of data mining. (We would like to thank Larry Scroggins for allowing us to use material from a Bank of America Case Study he wrote. We also benefited from conversations with Bob Flynn, Lounette Dyer, and Jerry Modes, who at the time worked for Hyperparallel.)

## Identifying the Business Challenge

BofA needed to do a better job of marketing home equity loans to customers. Using common sense and business consultants, they came up with these insights:

- People with college-age children want to borrow against their home equity to pay tuition bills.
- People with high but variable incomes want to use home equity to smooth out the peaks and valleys in their income.

---

**MAKING MONEY OR LOSING MONEY?**

Home equity loans generate revenue for banks from interest payments on the loans, but sometimes companies grapple with services that lose money. As an example, Fidelity Investments once put its bill-paying service on the chopping block because this service consistently lost money. Some last-minute analysis saved it, though, by showing that Fidelity's most loyal and most profitable customers used the bill paying service; although the bill paying service lost money, Fidelity made much more money on these customers' other accounts. After all, customers that trust their financial institution to pay their bills have a very high level of trust in that institution.

Cutting such value-added services may inadvertently exacerbate the profitability problem by causing the best customers to look elsewhere for better service.

Marketing literature for the home equity line product reflected this view of the likely customer, as did the lists drawn up for telemarketing. These insights led to the disappointing results mentioned earlier.

## Applying Data Mining

BofA worked with data mining consultants from Hyperparallel (then a data mining tool vendor that has since been absorbed into Yahoo!) to bring a range of data mining techniques to bear on the problem. There was no shortage of data. For many years, BofA had been storing data on its millions of retail customers in a large relational database on a powerful parallel computer from NCR/Teradata. Data from 42 *systems of record* was cleansed, transformed, aligned, and then fed into the corporate data warehouse. With this system, BofA could see all the relationships each customer maintained with the bank.

This historical database was truly worthy of the name—some records dating back to 1914! More recent customer records had about 250 fields, including demographic fields such as income, number of children, and type of home, as well as internal data. These customer attributes were combined into a customer signature, which was then analyzed using Hyperparallel's data mining tools.

A decision tree derived rules to classify existing bank customers as likely or unlikely to respond to a home equity loan offer. The decision tree, trained on thousands of examples of customers who had obtained the product and thousands who had not, eventually learned rules to tell the difference between them. Once the rules were discovered, the resulting model was used to add yet another attribute to each prospect's record. This attribute, the "good prospect" flag, was generated by a data mining model.

Next, a sequential pattern-finding tool was used to determine *when* customers were most likely to want a loan of this type. The goal of this analysis was to discover a sequence of events that had frequently preceded successful solicitations in the past.

Finally, a clustering tool was used to automatically segment the customers into groups with similar attributes. At one point, the tool found 14 clusters of customers, many of which did not seem particularly interesting. One cluster, however, was very interesting indeed. This cluster had two intriguing properties:

- 39 percent of the people in the cluster had both business and personal accounts.

- This cluster accounted for over a quarter of the customers who had been classified by the decision tree as likely responders to a home equity loan offer.

This data suggested to inquisitive data miners that people might be using home equity loans to start businesses.

## Acting on the Results

With this new understanding, NCAG teamed with the Retail Banking Division and did what banks do in such circumstances: they sponsored market research to talk to customers. Now, the bank had one more question to ask: "Will the proceeds of the loan be used to start a business?" The results from the market research confirmed the suspicions aroused by data mining, so NCAG changed the message and targeting on their marketing of home equity loans.

Incidentally, market research and data mining are often used for similar ends—to gain a better understanding of customers. Although powerful, market research has some shortcomings:

- Responders may not be representative of the population as a whole. That is, the set of responders may be biased, particularly by where past marketing efforts were focused, and hence form what is called an *opportunistic sample*.

- Customers (particularly dissatisfied customers and former customers) have little reason to be helpful or honest.

- For any given action, there may be an accumulation of reasons. For instance, banking customers may leave because a branch closed, the bank bounced a check, and they had to wait too long at ATMs. Market research may pick up only the proximate cause, although the sequence is more significant.

Despite these shortcomings, talking to customers and former customers provides insights that cannot be provided in any other way. This example with BofA shows that the two methods are compatible.

**TIP** When doing market research on existing customers, it is a good idea to use data mining to take into account what is already known about them.

## Measuring the Effects

As a result of the new campaign, Bank of America saw the response rate for home equity campaigns jump from 0.7 percent to 7 percent. According to Dave McDonald, vice president of the group, the strategic implications of data mining are nothing short of the transformation of the retail side of the bank from a mass-marketing institution to a learning institution. "We want to get to the point where we are *constantly* executing marketing programs—not just quarterly mailings, but *programs* on a consistent basis." He has a vision of a closed-loop marketing process where operational data feeds a rapid analysis process that leads to program creation for execution and testing, which in turn generates additional data to rejuvenate the process. In short, the virtuous cycle of data mining.

## What Is the Virtuous Cycle?

The BofA example shows the virtuous cycle of data mining in practice. Figure 2.1 shows the four stages:

1. Identifying the business problem.
2. Mining data to transform the data into actionable information.
3. Acting on the information.
4. Measuring the results.

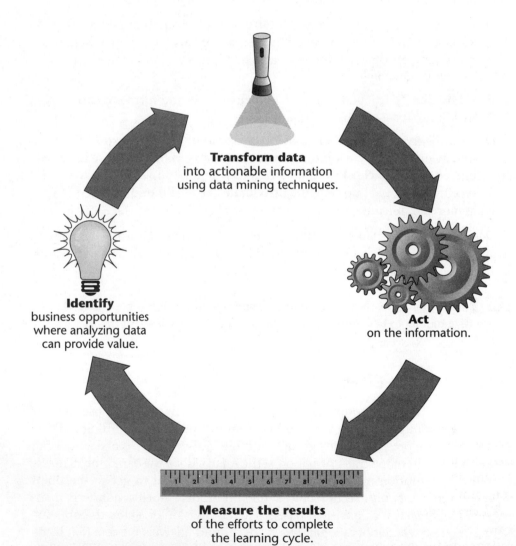

**Transform data**
into actionable information
using data mining techniques.

**Act**
on the information.

**Identify**
business opportunities
where analyzing data
can provide value.

**Measure the results**
of the efforts to complete
the learning cycle.

**Figure 2.1** The virtuous cycle of data mining focuses on business results, rather than just exploiting advanced techniques.

As these steps suggest, the key to success is incorporating data mining into business processes and being able to foster lines of communication between the technical data miners and the business users of the results.

## Identify the Business Opportunity

The virtuous cycle of data mining starts with identifying the right business opportunities. Unfortunately, there are too many good statisticians and competent analysts whose work is essentially wasted because they are solving problems that don't help the business. Good data miners want to avoid this situation.

Avoiding wasted analytic effort starts with a willingness to act on the results. Many normal business processes are good candidates for data mining:

- Planning for a new product introduction
- Planning direct marketing campaigns
- Understanding customer attrition/churn
- Evaluating results of a marketing test

These are examples of where data mining can enhance existing business efforts, by allowing business managers to make more informed decisions—by targeting a different group, by changing messaging, and so on.

To avoid wasting analytic effort, it is also important to measure the impact of whatever actions are taken in order to judge the value of the data mining effort itself. If we cannot measure the results of mining the data, then we cannot learn from the effort and there is no virtuous cycle.

Measurements of past efforts and ad hoc questions about the business also suggest data mining opportunities:

- What types of customers responded to the last campaign?
- Where do the best customers live?
- Are long waits at automated tellers a cause of customers' attrition?
- Do profitable customers use customer support?
- What products should be promoted with Clorox bleach?

Interviewing business experts is another good way to get started. Because people on the business side may not be familiar with data mining, they may not understand how to act on the results. By explaining the value of data mining to an organization, such interviews provide a forum for two-way communication.

We once participated in a series of interviews at a telecommunications company to discuss the value of analyzing call detail records (records of completed calls made by each customer). During one interview, the participants were slow in understanding how this could be useful. Then, a colleague pointed out that lurking inside their data was information on which customers used fax machines at home (the details of this are discussed in Chapter 10 on Link Analysis). Click! Fax machine usage would be a good indicator of who was working from home. And to make use of that information, there was a specific product bundle for the work-at-home crowd. Without our prodding, this marketing group would never have considered searching through data to find this information. Joining the technical and the business highlighted a very valuable opportunity.

**TIP** When talking to business users about data mining opportunities, make sure they focus on the business problems and not technology and algorithms. Let the technical experts focus on the technology and the business experts focus on the business.

## Mining Data

Data mining, the focus of this book, transforms data into actionable results. Success is about making business sense of the data, not using particular algorithms or tools. Numerous pitfalls interfere with the ability to use the results of data mining:

- Bad data formats, such as not including the zip code in the customer address in the results

- Confusing data fields, such as a delivery date that means "planned delivery date" in one system and "actual delivery date" in another system

- Lack of functionality, such as a call-center application that does not allow annotations on a per-customer basis

- Legal ramifications, such as having to provide a legal reason when rejecting a loan (and "my neural network told me so" is not acceptable)

- Organizational factors, since some operational groups are reluctant to change their operations, particularly without incentives

- Lack of timeliness, since results that come too late may no longer be actionable

Data comes in many forms, in many formats, and from multiple systems, as shown in Figure 2.2. Identifying the right data sources and bringing them together are critical success factors. Every data mining project has data issues: inconsistent systems, table keys that don't match across databases, records overwritten every few months, and so on. Complaints about data are the number one excuse for not doing anything. The real question is "What can be done with available data?" This is where the algorithms described later in this book come in.

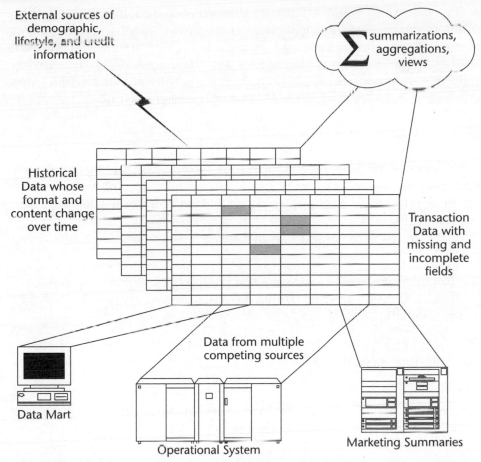

External sources of demographic, lifestyle, and credit information

Σ summarizations, aggregations, views

Historical Data whose format and content change over time

Transaction Data with missing and incomplete fields

Data from multiple competing sources

Data Mart

Operational System

Marketing Summaries

**Figure 2.2**   Data is never clean. It comes in many forms, from many sources both internal and external.

A wireless telecommunications company once wanted to put together a data mining group after they had already acquired a powerful server and a data mining software package. At this late stage, they contacted Data Miners to help them investigate data mining opportunities. In the process, we learned that a key factor for churn was overcalls: new customers making too many calls during their first month. Customers would learn about the excess usage when the first bill arrived, sometime during the middle of the second month. By that time, the customers had run up more large bills and were even more unhappy. Unfortunately, the customer service group also had to wait for the same billing cycle to detect the excess usage. There was no lead time to be proactive.

However, the nascent data mining group had resources and had identified appropriate data feeds. With some relatively simple programming, it was possible to identify these customers within days of their first overcall. With this information, the customer service center could contact at-risk customers and move them onto appropriate billing plans even before the first bill went out. This simple system was a big win for data mining, simply because having a data mining group—with the skills, hardware, software, and access—was the enabling factor for putting together this triggering system.

## Take Action

Taking action is the purpose of the virtuous cycle of data mining. As already mentioned, action can take many forms. Data mining makes business decisions more informed. Over time, we expect that better-informed decisions lead to better results.

Actions are usually going to be in line with what the business is doing anyway:

- Sending messages to customers and prospects via direct mail, email, telemarketing, and so on; with data mining, different messages may go to different people
- Prioritizing customer service
- Adjusting inventory levels
- And so on

The results of data mining need to feed into business processes that touch customers and affect the customer relationship.

## Measuring Results

The importance of measuring results has already been highlighted. Despite its importance, it is the stage in the virtuous cycle most likely to be overlooked. Even though the value of measurement and continuous improvement is widely acknowledged, it is usually given less attention than it deserves. How many business cases are implemented, with no one going back to see how well reality matched the plans? Individuals improve their own efforts by comparing and learning, by asking questions about why plans match or do not match what really happened, by being willing to learn that earlier assumptions were wrong. What works for individuals also works for organizations.

The time to start thinking about measurement is at the beginning when identifying the business problem. How can results be measured? A company that sends out coupons to encourage sales of their products will no doubt measure the coupon redemption rate. However, coupon-redeemers may have purchased the product anyway. Another appropriate measure is increased sales in particular stores or regions, increases that can be tied to the particular marketing effort. Such measurements may be difficult to make, because they require more detailed sales information. However, if the goal is to increase sales, there needs to be a way to measure this directly. Otherwise, marketing efforts may be all "sound and fury, signifying nothing."

Standard reports, which may arrive months after interventions have occurred, contain summaries. Marketing managers may not have the technical skills to glean important findings from such reports, even if the information is there. Understanding the impact on customer retention, means tracking old marketing efforts for even longer periods of time. Well-designed Online Analytic Processing (OLAP) applications, discussed in Chapter 15, can be a big help for marketing groups and marketing analysts. However, for some questions, the most detailed level is needed.

It is a good idea to think of every data mining effort as a small business case. Comparing expectations to actual results makes it possible to recognize promising opportunities to exploit on the next round of the virtuous cycle. We are often too busy tackling the next problem to devote energy to measuring the success of current efforts. This is a mistake. Every data mining effort, whether successful or not, has lessons that can be applied to future efforts. The question is what to measure and how to approach the measurement so it provides the best input for future use.

As an example, let's start with what to measure for a targeted acquisition campaign. The canonical measurement is the response rate: How many people targeted by the campaign actually responded? This leaves a lot of information lying on the table. For an acquisition effort, some examples of questions that have future value are:

- Did this campaign reach and bring in profitable customers?

- Were these customers retained as well as would be expected?

- What are the characteristics of the most loyal customers reached by this campaign? Demographic profiles of known customers can be applied to future prospective customers. In some circumstances, such profiles should be limited to those characteristics that can be provided by an external source so the results from the data mining analysis can be applied purchased lists.

- Do these customers purchase additional products? Can the different systems in an organization detect if one customer purchases multiple products?

- Did some messages or offers work better than others?

- Did customers reached by the campaign respond through alternate channels?

All of these measurements provide information for making more informed decisions in the future. Data mining is about connecting the past—through learning—to future actions.

One particular measurement is *lifetime customer value*. As its name implies, this is an estimate of the value of a customer during the entire course of his or her relationship. In some industries, quite complicated models have been developed to estimate lifetime customer value. Even without sophisticated models, shorter-term estimates, such as value after 1 month, 6 months, and 1 year, can prove to be quite useful. Customer value is discussed in more detail in Chapter 4.

## Data Mining in the Context of the Virtuous Cycle

A typical large regional telephone company in the United States has millions of customers. It owns hundreds or thousands of switches located in central offices, which are typically in several states in multiple time zones. Each switch can handle thousands of calls simultaneously—including advanced features such as call waiting, conference calling, call-forwarding, voice mail, and digital services. Switches, among the most complex computing devices yet developed, are available from a handful of manufacturers. A typical telephone company has multiple versions of several switches from each of the vendors. Each of these switches provides volumes of data in its own format on every call and attempted call—volumes measured in tens of gigabytes each day. In addition, each state has its own regulations affecting the industry, not to mention federal laws and regulations that are subject to rather frequent changes. And, to add to the confusion, the company offers thousands of different billing plans to its customers, which range from occasional residential users to Fortune 100 corporations.

How does this company—or any similar large corporation—manage its billing process, the bread and butter of its business, responsible for the majority of its revenue? The answer is simple: Very carefully! Companies have developed detailed processes for handling standard operations; they have policies and procedures. These processes are robust. Bills go out to customers, even when the business reorganizes, even when database administrators are on vacation, even when computers are temporarily down, even as laws and regulations change, and switches are upgraded. If an organization can manage a process as complicated as getting accurate bills out every month to millions of residential, business, and government customers, surely incorporating data mining into decision processes should be fairly easy. Is this the case?

Large corporations have decades of experience developing and implementing mission-critical applications for running their business. Data mining is different from the typical operational system (see Table 2.1). The skills needed for running a successful operational system do not necessarily lead to successful data mining efforts.

**Table 2.1**   Data Mining Differs from Typical Operational Business Processes

| TYPICAL OPERATIONAL SYSTEM | DATA MINING SYSTEM |
| --- | --- |
| Operations and reports on historical data | Analysis on historical data often applied to most current data to determine future actions |
| Predictable and periodic flow of work, typically tied to calendar | Unpredictable flow of work depending on business and marketing needs |
| Limited use of enterprise-wide data | The more data, the better the results (generally) |
| Focus on line of business (such as account, region, product code, minutes of use, and so on), not on customer | Focus on actionable entity, such as product, customer, sales region |
| Response times often measured in seconds/milliseconds (for interactive systems) while waiting weeks/months for reports | Iterative processes with response times often measured in minutes or hours |
| System of record for data | Copy of data |
| Descriptive and repetitive | Creative |

First, problems being addressed by data mining differ from operational problems—*a data mining system does not seek to replicate previous results exactly.* In fact, replication of previous efforts can lead to disastrous results. It may result in marketing campaigns that market to the same people over and over. You do not want to learn from analyzing data that a large cluster of customers fits the profile of the customers contacted in some previous campaign. Data mining processes need to take such issues into account, unlike typical operational systems that want to reproduce the same results over and over— whether completing a telephone call, sending a bill, authorizing a credit purchase, tracking inventory, or other countless daily operations.

*Data mining is a creative process.* Data contains many obvious correlations that are either useless or simply represent current business policies. For example, analysis of data from one large retailer revealed that people who buy maintenance contracts are also very likely to buy large household appliances. Unless the retailer wanted to analyze the effectiveness of sales of maintenance contracts with appliances, such information is worse than useless—the maintenance contracts in question are only sold with large appliances. Spending millions of dollars on hardware, software, and analysts to find such results is a waste of resources that can better be applied elsewhere in the business. Analysts need to understand what is of value to the business and how to arrange the data to bring out the nuggets.

*Data mining results change over time.* Models expire and become less useful as time goes on. One cause is that data ages quickly. Markets and customers change quickly as well.

*Data mining provides feedback into other processes that may need to change.* Decisions made in the business world often affect current processes and interactions with customers. Often, looking at data finds imperfections in operational systems, imperfections that should be fixed to enhance future customer understanding.

The rest of this chapter looks at some more examples of the virtuous cycle of data mining in action.

# A Wireless Communications Company Makes the Right Connections

The wireless communications industry is fiercely competitive. Wireless phone companies are constantly dreaming up new ways to steal customers from their competitors and to keep their own customers loyal. The basic service offering is a commodity, with thin margins and little basis for product differentiation, so phone companies think of novel ways to attract new customers.

This case study talks about how one mobile phone provider used data mining to improve its ability to recognize customers who would be attracted to a new service offering. (We are indebted to Alan Parker of Apower Solutions for many details in this study.)

## The Opportunity

This company wanted to test market a new product. For technical reasons, their preliminary roll-out tested the product on a few hundred subscribers —a tiny fraction of the customer base in the chosen market.

The initial problem, therefore, was to figure out who was likely to be interested in this new offering. This is a classic application of data mining: finding the most cost-effective way to reach the desired number of responders. Since fixed costs of a direct marketing campaign are constant by definition, and the cost per contact is also fairly constant, the only practical way to reduce the total cost of the campaign is to reduce the number of contacts.

The company needed a certain number of people to sign up in order for the trial to be valid. The company's past experience with new-product introduction campaigns was that about 2 to 3 percent of existing customers would respond favorably. So, to reach 500 responders, they would expect to contact between about 16,000 and 25,000 prospects.

How should the targets be selected? It would be handy to give each prospective customer a score from, say, 1 to 100, where 1 means "is very likely to purchase the product" and 100 means "very unlikely to purchase the product." The prospects could then be sorted according to this score, and marketing could work down this list until reaching the desired number of responders. As the cumulative gains chart in Figure 2.3 illustrates, contacting the people most likely to respond achieves the quota of responders with fewer contacts, and hence at a lower cost.

The next chapter explains cumulative gains charts in more detail. For now, it is enough to know that the curved line is obtained by ordering the scored prospects along the X-axis with those judged most likely to respond on the left and those judged least likely on the right. The diagonal line shows what would happen if prospects were selected at random from all prospects. The chart shows that good response scores lower the cost of a direct marketing campaign by allowing fewer prospects to be contacted.

How did the mobile phone company get such scores? By data mining, of course!

## How Data Mining Was Applied

Most data mining methods learn by example. The neural network or decision tree generator or what have you is fed thousands and thousands of training examples. Each of the training examples is clearly marked as being either a responder or a nonresponder. After seeing enough of these examples, the tool comes up with a model in the form of a computer program that reads in unclassified records and updates each with a response score or classification.

In this case, the offer in question was a new product introduction, so there was no training set of people who had already responded. One possibility would be to build a model based on people who had ever responded to *any* offer in the past. Such a model would be good for discriminating between people who refuse all telemarketing calls and throw out all junk mail, and those who occasionally respond to some offers. These types of models are called *nonresponse models* and can be valuable to mass mailers who really do want their message to reach a large, broad market. The AARP, a non-profit organization that provides services to retired people, saved millions of dollars in mailing costs when it began using a nonresponse model. Instead of mailing to every household with a member over 50 years of age, as they once did, they discard the bottom 10 percent and still get almost all the responders they would have.

However, the wireless company only wanted to reach a few hundred responders, so a model that identified the top 90 percent would not have served the purpose. Instead, they formed a training set of records from a similar new product introduction in another market.

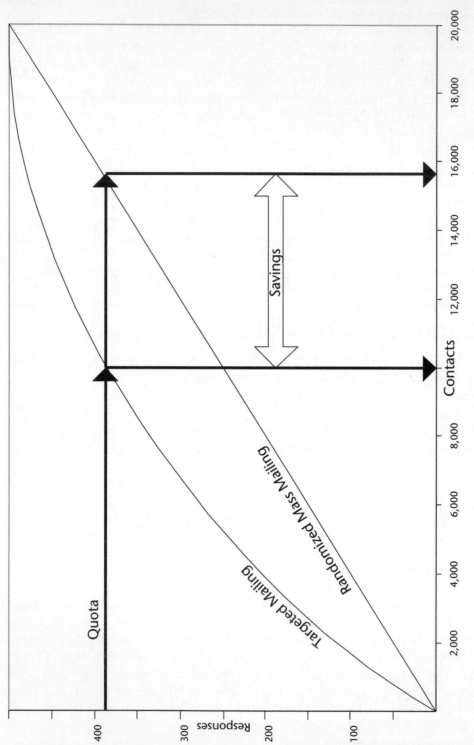

**Figure 2.3** Ranking prospects, using a response model, makes it possible to save money by targeting fewer customers and getting the same number of responders.

## Defining the Inputs

The data mining techniques described in this book automate the central core of the model building process. Given a collection of input data fields, and a target field (in this case, purchase of the new product) they can find patterns and rules that explain the target in terms of the inputs. For data mining to succeed, there must be some relationship between the input variables and the target.

In practice, this means that it often takes much more time and effort to identify, locate, and prepare input data than it does to create and run the models, especially since data mining tools make it so easy to create models. It is impossible to do a good job of selecting input variables without knowledge of the business problem being addressed. This is true even when using data mining tools that claim the ability to accept *all* the data and figure out automatically which fields are important. Information that knowledgeable people in the industry expect to be important is often not represented in raw input data in a way data mining tools can recognize.

The wireless phone company understood the importance of selecting the right input data. Experts from several different functional areas including marketing, sales, and customer support met together with outside data mining consultants to brainstorm about the best way to make use of available data. There were three data sources available:

A marketing customer information file

A call detail database

A demographic database

The call detail database was the largest of the three by far. It contained a record for each call made or received by every customer in the target market. The marketing database contained summarized customer data on usage, tenure, product history, price plans, and payment history. The third database contained purchased demographic and lifestyle data about the customers.

## Derived Inputs

As a result of the brainstorming meetings and preliminary analysis, several summary and descriptive fields were added to the customer data to be used as input to the predictive model:

Minutes of use

Number of incoming calls

Frequency of calls

Sphere of influence

Voice mail user flag

Some of these fields require a bit of explanation. Minutes of use (MOU) is a standard measure of how good a customer is. The more minutes of use, the better the customer. Historically, the company had focused on MOU almost to the exclusion of all other variables. But, MOU masks many interesting differences: 2 long calls or 100 short ones? All outgoing calls or half incoming? All calls to the same number or calls to many numbers? The next items in the above list are intended to shed more light on these questions.

Sphere of influence (SOI) is another interesting measure because it was developed as a result of an earlier data mining effort. A customer's SOI is the number of people with whom she or he had phone conversations during a given time period. It turned out that high SOI customers behaved differently, as a group, than low SOI customers in several ways including frequency of calls to customer service and loyalty.

## The Actions

Data from all three sources was brought together and used to create a data mining model. The model was used to identify likely candidates for the new product. Two direct mailings were made: one to a list based on the results of the data mining model and one to control group selected using business-as-usual methods. As shown in Figure 2.4, 15 percent of the people in the target group purchased the new product, compared to only 3 percent in the control group.

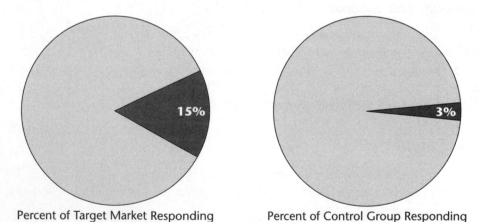

Percent of Target Market Responding          Percent of Control Group Responding

**Figure 2.4**   These results demonstrate a very successful application of data mining.

## Completing the Cycle

With the help of data mining, the right group of prospects was contacted for the new product offering. That is not the end of the story, though. Once the results of the new campaign were in, data mining techniques could help to get a better picture of the actual responders. Armed with a buyer profile of the buyers in the initial test market, and a usage profile of the first several months of the new service, the company was able to do an even better job of targeting prospects in the next five markets where the product was rolled out.

# Neural Networks and Decision Trees Drive SUV Sales

In 1992, before any of the commercial data mining tools available today were on the market, one of the big three U.S. auto makers asked a group of researchers at the Pontikes Center for Management at Southern Illinois University in Carbondale to develop an "expert system" to identify likely buyers of a particular sport-utility vehicle. (We are grateful to Wei-Xiong Ho who worked with Joseph Harder of the College of Business and Administration at Southern Illinois on this project.)

Traditional expert systems consist of a large database of hundreds or thousands of rules collected by observing and interviewing human experts who are skilled at a particular task. Expert systems have enjoyed some success in certain domains such as medical diagnosis and answering tax questions, but the difficulty of collecting the rules has limited their use.

The team at Southern Illinois decided to solve these problems by generating the rules directly from historical data. In other words, they would replace expert interviews with data mining.

## The Initial Challenge

The initial challenge that Detroit brought to Carbondale was to improve response to a direct mail campaign for a particular model. The campaign involved sending an invitation to a prospect to come test-drive the new model. Anyone accepting the invitation would find a free pair of sunglasses waiting at the dealership. The problem was that very few people were returning the response card or calling the toll-free number for more information, and few of those that did ended up buying the vehicle. The company knew it could save itself a lot of money by not sending the offer to people unlikely to respond, but it didn't know who those were.

## How Data Mining Was Applied

As is often the case when the data to be mined is from several different sources, the first challenge was to integrate data so that it could tell a consistent story.

### The Data

The first file, the "mail file," was a mailing list containing names and addresses of about a million people who had been sent the promotional mailing. This file contained very little information likely to be useful for selection.

The mail file was appended with data based on zip codes from the commercially available PRIZM database. This database contains demographic and "psychographic" characterizations of the neighborhoods associated with the zip codes.

Two additional files contained information on people who had sent back the response card or called the toll-free number for more information. Linking the response cards back to the original mailing file was simple because the mail file contained a nine-character key for each address that was printed on the response cards. Telephone responders presented more of a problem since their reported name and address might not exactly match their address in the database, and there is no guarantee that the call even came from someone on the mailing list since the recipient may have passed the offer on to someone else.

Of 1,000,003 people who were sent the mailing, 32,904 responded by sending back a card and 16,453 responded by calling the toll-free number for a total initial response rate of 5 percent. The auto maker's primary interest, of course, was in the much smaller number of people who both responded to the mailing and bought the advertised car. These were to be found in a sales file, obtained from the manufacturer, that contained the names, addresses, and model purchased for all car buyers in the 3-month period following the mailing.

An automated name-matching program with loosely set matching standards discovered around 22,000 apparent matches between people who bought cars and people who had received the mailing. Hand editing reduced the intersection to 4,764 people who had received the mailing and bought a car. About half of those had purchased the advertised model. See Figure 2.5 for a comparison of all these data sources.

### Down the Mine Shaft

The experimental design called for the population to be divided into exactly two classes—success and failure. This is certainly a questionable design since it obscures interesting differences. Surely, people who come into the dealership to test-drive one model, but end up buying another should be in a different class than nonresponders, or people who respond, but buy nothing. For that matter, people who weren't considered good enough prospects to be sent a mailing, but who nevertheless bought the car are an even more interesting group.

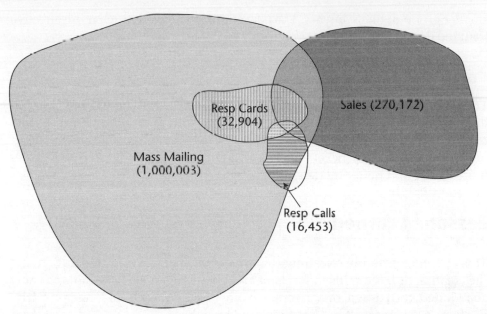

**Figure 2.5**  Prospects in the training set have overlapping relationships.

Be that as it may, success was defined as "received a mailing and bought the car" and failure was defined as "received the mailing, but did not buy the car." A series of trials was run using decision trees and neural networks. The tools were tested on various kinds of training sets. Some of the training sets reflected the true proportion of successes in the database, while others were enriched to have up to 10 percent successes—and higher concentrations might have produced better results.

The neural network did better on the sparse training sets, while the decision tree tool appeared to do better on the enriched sets. The researchers decided on a two-stage process. First, a neural network determined who was likely to buy a car, any car, from the company. Then, the decision tree was used to predict which of the likely car buyers would choose the advertised model. This two-step process proved quite successful. The hybrid data mining model combining decision trees and neural networks missed very few buyers of the targeted model while at the same time screening out many more nonbuyers than either the neural net or the decision tree was able to do.

## The Resulting Actions

Armed with a model that could effectively reach responders the company decided to take the money saved by mailing fewer pieces and put it into improving the lure offered to get likely buyers into the showroom. Instead of sunglasses for the masses, they offered a nice pair of leather boots to the far smaller group of likely buyers. The new approach proved much more effective than the first.

## Completing the Cycle

The university-based data mining project showed that even with only a limited number of broad-brush variables to work with and fairly primitive data mining tools, data mining could improve the effectiveness of a direct marketing campaign for a big-ticket item like an automobile. The next step is to gather more data, build better models, and try again!

# Lessons Learned

This chapter started by recalling the drivers of the industrial revolution and the creation of large mills in England and New England. These mills are now abandoned, torn down, or converted to other uses. Water is no longer the driving force of business. It has been replaced by data.

The virtuous cycle of data mining is about harnessing the power of data and transforming it into actionable business results. Just as water once turned the wheels that drove machines throughout a mill, data needs to be gathered and disseminated throughout an organization to provide value. If data is water in this analogy, then data mining is the wheel, and the virtuous cycle spreads the power of the data to all the business processes.

The virtuous cycle of data mining is a learning process based on customer data. It starts by identifying the right business opportunities for data mining. The best business opportunities are those that will be acted upon. Without action, there is little or no value to be gained from learning about customers.

Also very important is measuring the results of the action. This completes the loop of the virtuous cycle, and often suggests further data mining opportunities.

# CHAPTER 3

# Data Mining Methodology and Best Practices

The preceding chapter introduced the virtuous cycle of data mining as a business process. That discussion divided the data mining process into four stages:

1. Identifying the problem
2. Transforming data into information
3. Taking action
4. Measuring the outcome

Now it is time to start looking at data mining as a technical process. The high-level outline remains the same, but the emphasis shifts. Instead of identifying a business problem, we now turn our attention to translating business problems into data mining problems. The topic of transforming data into information is expanded into several topics including hypothesis testing, profiling, and predictive modeling. In this chapter, taking action refers to technical actions such as model deployment and scoring. Measurement refers to the testing that must be done to assess a model's stability and effectiveness before it is used to guide marketing actions.

Because the entire book is based on this methodology, the best practices introduced here are elaborated upon elsewhere. The purpose of this chapter is to bring them together in one place and to organize them into a methodology.

The best way to avoid breaking the virtuous cycle of data mining is to understand the ways it is likely to fail and take preventative steps. Over the years, the authors have encountered many ways for data mining projects to go wrong. In response, we have developed a useful collection of habits—things we do to smooth the path from the initial statement of a business problem to a stable model that produces actionable and measurable results. This chapter presents this collection of best practices as the orderly steps of a data mining methodology. Don't be fooled—data mining is a naturally iterative process. Some steps need to be repeated several times, but none should be skipped entirely.

The need for a rigorous approach to data mining increases with the complexity of the data mining approach. After establishing the need for a methodology by describing various ways that data mining efforts can fail in the absence of one, the chapter starts with the simplest approach to data mining—using ad hoc queries to test hypotheses—and works up to more sophisticated activities such as building formal profiles that can be used as scoring models and building true predictive models. Finally, the four steps of the virtuous cycle are translated into an 11-step data mining methodology.

# Why Have a Methodology?

Data mining is a way of learning from the past so as to make better decisions in the future. The best practices described in this chapter are designed to avoid two undesirable outcomes of the learning process:

- Learning things that aren't true
- Learning things that are true, but not useful

These pitfalls are like the rocks of Scylla and the whirlpool of Charybdis that protect the narrow straits between Sicily and the Italian mainland. Like the ancient sailors who learned to avoid these threats, data miners need to know how to avoid common dangers.

## Learning Things That Aren't True

Learning things that aren't true is more dangerous than learning things that are useless because important business decisions may be made based on incorrect information. Data mining results often seem reliable because they are based on actual data in a seemingly scientific manner. This appearance of reliability can be deceiving. The data itself may be incorrect or not relevant to the question at hand. The patterns discovered may reflect past business decisions or nothing at all. Data transformations such as summarization may have destroyed or hidden important information. The following sections discuss some of the more common problems that can lead to false conclusions.

## Patterns May Not Represent Any Underlying Rule

It is often said that figures don't lie, but liars can figure. When it comes to finding patterns in data, figures don't have to actually lie in order to suggest things that aren't true. There are so many ways to construct patterns that any random set of data points will reveal one if examined long enough. Human beings depend so heavily on patterns in our lives that we tend to see them even when they are not there. We look up at the nighttime sky and see not a random arrangement of stars, but the Big Dipper, or, the Southern Cross, or Orion's Belt. Some even see astrological patterns and portents that can be used to predict the future. The widespread acceptance of outlandish conspiracy theories is further evidence of the human need to find patterns.

Presumably, the reason that humans have evolved such an affinity for patterns is that patterns often do reflect some underlying truth about the way the world works. The phases of the moon, the progression of the seasons, the constant alternation of night and day, even the regular appearance of a favorite TV show at the same time on the same day of the week are useful because they are stable and therefore predictive. We can use these patterns to decide when it is safe to plant tomatoes and how to program the VCR. Other patterns clearly do not have any predictive power. If a fair coin comes up heads five times in a row, there is still a 50-50 chance that it will come up tails on the sixth toss.

The challenge for data miners is to figure out which patterns are predictive and which are not. Consider the following patterns, all of which have been cited in articles in the popular press as if they had predictive value:

- The party that does not hold the presidency picks up seats in Congress during off-year elections.
- When the American League wins the World Series, Republicans take the White House.
- When the Washington Redskins win their last home game, the incumbent party keeps the White House.
- In U.S. presidential contests, the taller man usually wins.

The first pattern (the one involving off-year elections) seems explainable in purely political terms. Because there is an underlying explanation, this pattern seems likely to continue into the future and therefore has predictive value. The next two alleged predictors, the ones involving sporting events, seem just as clearly to have no predictive value. No matter how many times Republicans and the American League may have shared victories in the past (and the authors have not researched this point), there is no reason to expect the association to continue in the future.

What about candidates' heights? At least since 1945 when Truman (who was short, but taller than Dewey) was elected, the election in which Carter beat

Ford is the only one where the shorter candidate won. (So long as "winning" is defined as "receiving the most votes" so that the 2000 election that pitted 6'1" Gore against the 6'0" Bush still fits the pattern.) Height does not seem to have anything to do with the job of being president. On the other hand, height is positively correlated with income and other social marks of success so consciously or unconsciously, voters may perceive a taller candidate as more presidential. As this chapter explains, the right way to decide if a rule is stable and predictive is to compare its performance on multiple samples selected at random from the same population. In the case of presidential height, we leave this as an exercise for the reader. As is often the case, the hardest part of the task will be collecting the data—even in the age of Google, it is not easy to locate the heights of unsuccessful presidential candidates from the eighteenth, nineteenth, and twentieth centuries!

The technical term for finding patterns that fail to generalize is *overfitting*. Overfitting leads to unstable models that work one day, but not the next. Building stable models is the primary goal of the data mining methodology.

### The Model Set May Not Reflect the Relevant Population

The model set is the collection of historical data that is used to develop data mining models. For inferences drawn from the model set to be valid, the model set must reflect the population that the model is meant to describe, classify, or score. A sample that does not properly reflect its parent population is *biased*. Using a biased sample as a model set is a recipe for learning things that are not true. It is also hard to avoid. Consider:

- Customers are not like prospects.
- Survey responders are not like nonresponders.
- People who read email are not like people who do not read email.
- People who register on a Web site are not like people who fail to register.
- After an acquisition, customers from the acquired company are not necessarily like customers from the acquirer.
- Records with no missing values reflect a different population from records with missing values.

Customers are not like prospects because they represent people who responded positively to whatever messages, offers, and promotions were made to attract customers in the past. A study of current customers is likely to suggest more of the same. If past campaigns have gone after wealthy, urban consumers, then any comparison of current customers with the general population will likely show that customers tend to be wealthy and urban. Such a model may miss opportunities in middle-income suburbs. The consequences of using a biased sample can be worse than simply a missed marketing opportunity.

In the United States, there is a history of "redlining," the illegal practice of refusing to write loans or insurance policies in certain neighborhoods. A search for patterns in the historical data from a company that had a history of redlining would reveal that people in certain neighborhoods are unlikely to be customers. If future marketing efforts were based on that finding, data mining would help perpetuate an illegal and unethical practice.

Careful attention to selecting and sampling data for the model set is crucial to successful data mining.

## Data May Be at the Wrong Level of Detail

In more than one industry, we have been told that usage often goes down in the month before a customer leaves. Upon closer examination, this turns out to be an example of learning something that is not true. Figure 3.1 shows the monthly minutes of use for a cellular telephone subscriber. For 7 months, the subscriber used about 100 minutes per month. Then, in the eighth month, usage went down to about half that. In the ninth month, there was no usage at all.

This subscriber appears to fit the pattern in which a month with decreased usage precedes abandonment of the service. But appearances are deceiving. Looking at minutes of use by day instead of by month would show that the customer continued to use the service at a constant rate until the middle of the month and then stopped completely, presumably because on that day, he or she began using a competing service. The putative period of declining usage does not actually exist and so certainly does not provide a window of opportunity for retaining the customer. What appears to be a leading indicator is actually a trailing one.

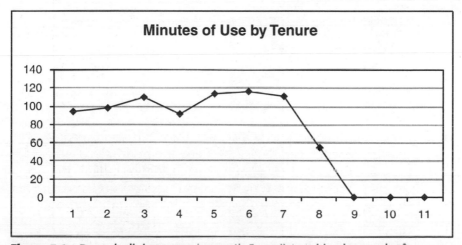

**Figure 3.1** Does declining usage in month 8 predict attrition in month 9?

Figure 3.2 shows another example of confusion caused by aggregation. Sales appear to be down in October compared to August and September. The picture comes from a business that has sales activity only on days when the financial markets are open. Because of the way that weekends and holidays fell in 2003, October had fewer trading days than August and September. That fact alone accounts for the entire drop-off in sales.

In the previous examples, aggregation led to confusion. Failure to aggregate to the appropriate level can also lead to confusion. In one case, data provided by a charitable organization showed an inverse correlation between donors' likelihood to respond to solicitations and the size of their donations. Those more likely to respond sent smaller checks. This counterintuitive finding is a result of the large number of solicitations the charity sent out to its supporters each year. Imagine two donors, each of whom plans to give $500 to the charity. One responds to an offer in January by sending in the full $500 contribution and tosses the rest of the solicitation letters in the trash. The other sends a $100 check in response to each of five solicitations. On their annual income tax returns, both donors report having given $500, but when seen at the individual campaign level, the second donor seems much more responsive. When aggregated to the yearly level, the effect disappears.

## Learning Things That Are True, but Not Useful

Although not as dangerous as learning things that aren't true, learning things that aren't useful is more common.

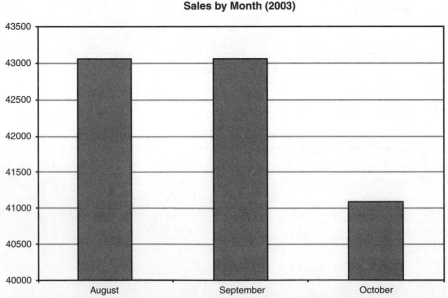

**Figure 3.2**    Did sales drop off in October?

### Learning Things That Are Already Known

Data mining should provide new information. Many of the strongest patterns in data represent things that are already known. People over retirement age tend not to respond to offers for retirement savings plans. People who live where there is no home delivery do not become newspaper subscribers. Even though they may respond to subscription offers, service never starts. For the same reason, people who live where there are no cell towers tend not to purchase cell phones.

Often, the strongest patterns reflect business rules. If data mining "discovers" that people who have anonymous call blocking also have caller ID, it is perhaps because anonymous call blocking is only sold as part of a bundle of services that also includes caller ID. If there are no sales of certain products in a particular location, it is possible that they are not offered there. We have seen many such discoveries. Not only are these patterns uninteresting, their strength may obscure less obvious patterns.

Learning things that are already known does serve one useful purpose. It demonstrates that, on a technical level, the data mining effort is working and the data is reasonably accurate. This can be quite comforting. If the data and the data mining techniques applied to it are powerful enough to discover things that are known to be true, it provides confidence that other discoveries are also likely to be true. It is also true that data mining often uncovers things that ought to have been known, but were not; that retired people do not respond well to solicitations for retirement savings accounts, for instance.

### Learning Things That Can't Be Used

It can also happen that data mining uncovers relationships that are both true and previously unknown, but still hard to make use of. Sometimes the problem is regulatory. A customer's wireless calling patterns may suggest an affinity for certain land-line long-distance packages, but a company that provides both services may not be allowed to take advantage of the fact. Similarly, a customer's credit history may be predictive of future insurance claims, but regulators may prohibit making underwriting decisions based on it.

Other times, data mining reveals that important outcomes are outside the company's control. A product may be more appropriate for some climates than others, but it is hard to change the weather. Service may be worse in some regions for reasons of topography, but that is also hard to change.

> **TIP** Sometimes it is only a failure of imagination that makes new information appear useless. A study of customer attrition is likely to show that the strongest predictors of customers leaving is the way they were acquired. It is too late to go back and change that for existing customers, but that does not make the information useless. Future attrition can be reduced by changing the mix of acquisition channels to favor those that bring in longer-lasting customers.

The data mining methodology is designed to steer clear of the Scylla of learning things that aren't true and the Charybdis of not learning anything useful. In a more positive light, the methodology is designed to ensure that the data mining effort leads to a stable model that successfully addresses the business problem it is designed to solve.

## Hypothesis Testing

Hypothesis testing is the simplest approach to integrating data into a company's decision-making processes. The purpose of hypothesis testing is to substantiate or disprove preconceived ideas, and it is a part of almost all data mining endeavors. Data miners often bounce back and forth between approaches, first thinking up possible explanations for observed behavior (often with the help of business experts) and letting those hypotheses dictate the data to be analyzed. Then, letting the data suggest new hypotheses to test.

Hypothesis testing is what scientists and statisticians traditionally spend their lives doing. A hypothesis is a proposed explanation whose validity can be tested by analyzing data. Such data may simply be collected by observation or generated through an experiment, such as a test mailing. Hypothesis testing is at its most valuable when it reveals that the assumptions that have been guiding a company's actions in the marketplace are incorrect. For example, suppose that a company's advertising is based on a number of hypotheses about the target market for a product or service and the nature of the responses. It is worth testing whether these hypotheses are borne out by actual responses. One approach is to use different call-in numbers in different ads and record the number that each responder dials. Information collected during the call can then be compared with the profile of the population the advertisement was designed to reach.

> **TIP** Each time a company solicits a response from its customers, whether through advertising or a more direct form of communication, it has an opportunity to gather information. Slight changes in the design of the communication, such as including a way to identify the channel when a prospect responds, can greatly increase the value of the data collected.

By its nature, hypothesis testing is ad hoc, so the term "methodology" might be a bit strong. However, there are some identifiable steps to the process, the first and most important of which is generating good ideas to test.

## Generating Hypotheses

The key to generating hypotheses is getting diverse input from throughout the organization and, where appropriate, outside it as well. Often, all that is needed to start the ideas flowing is a clear statement of the problem itself—especially if it is something that has not previously been recognized as a problem.

It happens more often than one might suppose that problems go unrecognized because they are not captured by the metrics being used to evaluate the organization's performance. If a company has always measured its sales force on the number of new sales made each month, the sales people may never have given much thought to the question of how long new customers remain active or how much they spend over the course of their relationship with the firm. When asked the right questions, however, the sales force may have insights into customer behavior that marketing, with its greater distance from the customer, has missed.

## Testing Hypotheses

Consider the following hypotheses:

- Frequent roamers are less sensitive than others to the price per minute of cellular phone time.
- Families with high-school age children are more likely to respond to a home equity line offer than others.
- The save desk in the call center is saving customers who would have returned anyway.

Such hypotheses must be transformed in a way that allows them to be tested on real data. Depending on the hypotheses, this may mean interpreting a single value returned from a simple query, plowing through a collection of association rules generated by market basket analysis, determining the significance of a correlation found by a regression model, or designing a controlled experiment. In all cases, careful critical thinking is necessary to be sure that the result is not biased in unexpected ways.

Proper evaluation of data mining results requires both analytical and business knowledge. Where these are not present in the same person, it takes cross-functional cooperation to make good use of the new information.

# Models, Profiling, and Prediction

Hypothesis testing is certainly useful, but there comes a time when it is not sufficient. The data mining techniques described in the rest of this book are all designed for learning *new* things by creating models based on data.

In the most general sense, a model is an explanation or description of how something works that reflects reality well enough that it can be used to make inferences about the real world. Without realizing it, human beings use models all the time. When you see two restaurants and decide that the one with white tablecloths and real flowers on each table is more expensive than the one with Formica tables and plastic flowers, you are making an inference based on a model you carry in your head. When you set out to walk to the store, you again consult a mental model of the town.

Data mining is all about creating models. As shown in Figure 3.3, models take a set of inputs and produce an output. The data used to create the model is called a *model set*. When models are applied to new data, this is called the *score set*. The model set has three components, which are discussed in more detail later in the chapter:

- The *training set* is used to build a set of models.

- The *validation set*[1] is used to choose the best model of these.

- The *test set* is used to determine how the model performs on unseen data.

Data mining techniques can be used to make three kinds of models for three kinds of tasks: descriptive profiling, directed profiling, and prediction. The distinctions are not always clear.

Descriptive models describe what is in the data. The output is one or more charts or numbers or graphics that explain what is going on. Hypothesis testing often produces descriptive models. On the other hand, both *directed profiling* and *prediction* have a goal in mind when the model is being built. The difference between them has to do with time frames, as shown in Figure 3.4. In profiling models, the target is from the same time frame as the input. In predictive models, the target is from a later time frame. *Prediction* means finding patterns in data from one period that are capable of explaining outcomes in a later period. The reason for emphasizing the distinction between profiling and prediction is that it has implications for the modeling methodology, especially the treatment of time in the creation of the model set.

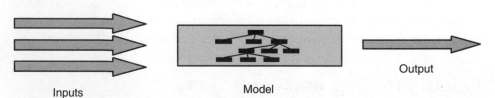

Inputs          Model          Output

**Figure 3.3**  Models take an input and produce an output.

1 The first edition called the three partitions of the model set the training set, the test set, and the evaluation set. The authors still like that terminology, but standard usage in the data mining community is now training/validation/test. To avoid confusion, this edition adopts the training/validation/test nomenclature.

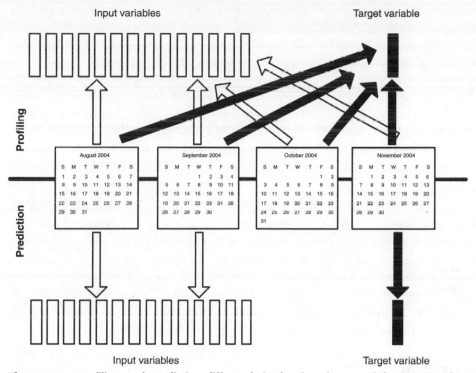

**Figure 3.4** Profiling and prediction differ only in the time frames of the input and target variables.

## Profiling

Profiling is a familiar approach to many problems. It need not involve any sophisticated data analysis. Surveys, for instance, are one common method of building customer profiles. Surveys reveal what customers and prospects look like, or at least the way survey responders answer questions.

Profiles are often based on demographic variables, such as geographic location, gender, and age. Since advertising is sold according to these same variables, demographic profiles can turn directly into media strategies. Simple profiles are used to set insurance premiums. A 17-year-old male pays more for car insurance than a 60-year-old female. Similarly, the application form for a simple term life insurance policy asks about age, sex, and smoking—and not much more.

Powerful though it is, profiling has serious limitations. One is the inability to distinguish cause and effect. So long as the profiling is based on familiar demographic variables, this is not noticeable. If men buy more beer than women, we do not have to wonder whether beer drinking might be the cause of maleness. It seems safe to assume that the link is from men to beer and not vice versa.

With behavioral data, the direction of causality is not always so clear. Consider a couple of actual examples from real data mining projects:

- People who have purchased certificates of deposit (CDs) have little or no money in their savings accounts.

- Customers who use voice mail make a lot of short calls to their own number.

Not keeping money in a savings account is a common behavior of CD holders, just as being male is a common feature of beer drinkers. Beer companies seek out males to market their product, so should banks seek out people with no money in savings in order to sell them certificates of deposit? Probably not! Presumably, the CD holders have no money in their savings accounts because they used that money to buy CDs. A more common reason for not having money in a savings account is not having any money, and people with no money are not likely to purchase certificates of deposit. Similarly, the voice mail users call their own number so much because in this particular system that is one way to check voice mail. The pattern is useless for finding prospective users.

## Prediction

Profiling uses data from the past to describe what happened in the past. Prediction goes one step further. Prediction uses data from the past to predict what is likely to happen in the future. This is a more powerful use of data. While the correlation between low savings balances and CD ownership may not be useful in a profile of CD holders, it is likely that having a *high* savings balance is (in combination with other indicators) a predictor of *future* CD purchases.

Building a predictive model requires separation in time between the model inputs or predictors and the model output, the thing to be predicted. If this separation is not maintained, the model will not work. This is one example of why it is important to follow a sound data mining methodology.

## The Methodology

The data mining methodology has 11 steps.

1. Translate the business problem into a data mining problem.
2. Select appropriate data.
3. Get to know the data.
4. Create a model set.
5. Fix problems with the data.

6. Transform data to bring information to the surface.

7. Build models.

8. Asses models.

9. Deploy models.

10. Assess results.

11. Begin again.

As shown in Figure 3.5, the data mining process is best thought of as a set of nested loops rather than a straight line. The steps do have a natural order, but it is not necessary or even desirable to completely finish with one before moving on to the next. And things learned in later steps will cause earlier ones to be revisited.

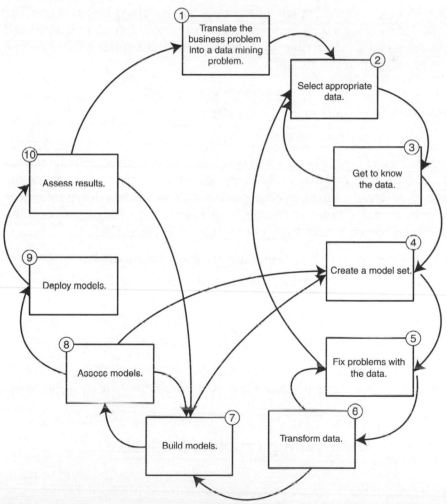

**Figure 3.5** Data mining is not a linear process.

## Step One: Translate the Business Problem into a Data Mining Problem

A favorite scene from *Alice in Wonderland* is the passage where Alice asks the Cheshire cat for directions:

> *"Would you tell me, please, which way I ought to go from here?"*
> *"That depends a good deal on where you want to get to," said the Cat.*
> *"I don't much care where—" said Alice.*
> *"Then it doesn't matter which way you go," said the Cat.*
> *"—so long as I get somewhere," Alice added as an explanation.*
> *"Oh, you're sure to do that," said the Cat, "if you only walk long enough."*

The Cheshire cat might have added that without some way of recognizing the destination, you can never tell whether you have walked long enough! The proper destination for a data mining project is the solution of a well-defined business problem. Data mining goals for a particular project should not be stated in broad, general terms, such as:

- Gaining insight into customer behavior
- Discovering meaningful patterns in data
- Learning something interesting

These are all worthy goals, but even when they have been achieved, they are hard to measure. Projects that are hard to measure are hard to put a value on. Wherever possible, the broad, general goals should be broken down into more specific ones to make it easier to monitor progress in achieving them. Gaining insight into customer behavior might turn into concrete goals:

- Identify customers who are unlikely to renew their subscriptions.
- Design a calling plan that will reduce churn for home-based business customers.
- Rank order all customers based on propensity to ski.
- List products whose sales are at risk if we discontinue wine and beer sales.

Not only are these concrete goals easier to monitor, they are easier to translate into data mining problems as well.

## What Does a Data Mining Problem Look Like?

To translate a business problem into a data mining problem, it should be reformulated as one of the six data mining tasks introduced in Chapter One:

- Classification
- Estimation
- Prediction
- Affinity Grouping
- Clustering
- Description and Profiling

These are the tasks that can be accomplished with the data mining techniques described in this book (though no single data mining tool or technique is equally applicable to all tasks).

The first three tasks, classification, estimation, and prediction are examples of *directed* data mining. Affinity grouping and clustering are examples of *undirected* data mining. Profiling may be either directed or undirected. In directed data mining there is always a target variable—something to be classified, estimated, or predicted. The process of building a classifier starts with a predefined set of classes and examples of records that have already been correctly classified. Similarly, the process of building an estimator starts with historical data where the values of the target variable are already known. The modeling task is to find rules that explain the known values of the target variable.

In undirected data mining, there is no target variable. The data mining task is to find overall patterns that are not tied to any one variable. The most common form of undirected data mining is clustering, which finds groups of similar records without any instructions about which variables should be considered as most important. Undirected data mining is descriptive by nature, so undirected data mining techniques are often used for profiling, but directed techniques such as decision trees are also very useful for building profiles. In the machine learning literature, directed data mining is called *supervised learning* and undirected data mining is called *unsupervised learning*.

## How Will the Results Be Used?

This is one of the most important questions to ask when deciding how best to translate a business problem into a data mining problem. Surprisingly often, the initial answer is "we're not sure." An answer is important because, as the cautionary tale in the sidebar illustrates, different intended uses dictate different solutions.

For example, many of our data mining engagements are designed to improve customer retention. The results of such a study could be used in any of the following ways:

- Proactively contact high risk/high value customers with an offer that rewards them for staying.

- Change the mix of acquisition channels to favor those that bring in the most loyal customers.

- Forecast customer population in future months.

- Alter the product to address defects that are causing customers to defect.

Each of these goals has implications for the data mining process. Contacting existing customers through an outbound telemarketing or direct mail campaign implies that in addition to identifying customers at risk, there is an understanding of *why* they are at risk so an attractive offer can be constructed, and *when* they are at risk so the call is not made too early or too late. Forecasting implies that in addition to identifying which current customers are likely to leave, it is possible to determine how many new customers will be added and how long they are likely to stay. This latter problem of forecasting new customer starts is typically embedded in business goals and budgets, and is not usually a predictive modeling problem.

## How Will the Results Be Delivered?

A data mining project may result in several very different types of deliverables. When the primary goal of the project is to gain insight, the deliverable is often a report or presentation filled with charts and graphs. When the project is a one-time proof-of-concept or pilot project, the deliverable may consist of lists of customers who will receive different treatments in a marketing experiment. When the data mining project is part of an ongoing analytic customer relationship management effort, the deliverable is likely to be a computer program or set of programs that can be run on a regular basis to score a defined subset of the customer population along with additional software to manage models and scores over time. The form of the deliverable can affect the data mining results. Producing a list of customers for a marketing test is not sufficient if the goal is to dazzle marketing managers.

## The Role of Business Users and Information Technology

As described in Chapter 2, the only way to get good answers to the questions posed above is to involve the owners of the business problem in figuring out how data mining results will be used and IT staff and database administrators in figuring out how the results should be delivered. It is often useful to get input from a broad spectrum within the organization and, where appropriate, outside it as well. We suggest getting representatives from the various constituencies within the enterprise together in one place, rather than interviewing them separately. That way, people with different areas of knowledge and expertise have a chance to react to each other's ideas. The goal of all this consultation is a clear statement of the business problem to be addressed. The final

---

**MISUNDERSTANDING THE BUSINESS PROBLEM: A CAUTIONARY TALE**

Data Miners, the consultancy started by the authors, was once called upon to analyze supermarket loyalty card data on behalf of a large consumer packaged goods manufacturer. To put this story in context, it helps to know a little bit about the supermarket business. In general, a supermarket does not care whether a customer buys Coke or Pepsi (unless one brand happens to be on a special deal that temporarily gives it a better margin), so long as the customer purchases soft drinks. Product manufacturers, who care very much which brands are sold, vie for the opportunity to manage whole categories in the stores. As category managers, they have some control over how their own products and those of their competitors are merchandised. Our client wanted to demonstrate its ability to utilize loyalty card data to improve category management. The category picked for the demonstration was yogurt because by supermarket standards, yogurt is a fairly high-margin product.

As we understood it, the business goal was to identify yogurt lovers. To create a target variable, we divided loyalty card customers into groups of high, medium, and low yogurt affinity based on their total yogurt purchases over the course of a year and into groups of high, medium, and low users based on the proportion of their shopping dollars spent on yogurt. People who were in the high category by both measures were labeled as yogurt lovers.

The transaction data had to undergo many transformations to be turned into a customer signature. Input variables included the proportion of trips and of dollars spent at various times of day and in various categories, shopping frequency, average order size, and other behavioral variables.

Using this data, we built a model that gave all customers a yogurt lover score. Armed with such a score, it would be possible to print coupons for yogurt when likely yogurt lovers checked out, even if they did not purchase any yogurt on that trip. The model might even identify good prospects who had not yet gotten in touch with their inner yogurt lover, but might if prompted with a coupon.

The model got good lift, and we were pleased with it. The client, however, was disappointed. "But, who *is* the yogurt lover?" asked the client. "Someone who gets a high score from the yogurt lover model" was not considered a good answer. The client was looking for something like "The yogurt lover is a woman between the ages of $X$ and $Y$ living in a zip code where the median home price is between $M$ and $N$." A description like that could be used for deciding where to buy advertising and how to shape the creative content of ads. Ours, based on shopping behavior rather than demographics, could not.

---

statement of the business problem should be as specific as possible. "Identify the 10,000 gold-level customers most likely to defect within the next 60 days" is better than "provide a churn score for all customers."

The role of the data miner in these discussions is to ensure that the final statement of the business problem is one that can be translated into a data mining problem. Otherwise, the best data mining efforts in the world may be addressing the wrong business problem.

Data mining is often presented as a technical problem of finding a model that explains the relationship of a target variable to a group of input variables. That technical task is indeed central to most data mining efforts, but it should not be attempted until the target variable has been properly defined and the appropriate input variables identified. That, in turn, depends on a good understanding of the business problem to be addressed. As the story in the sidebar illustrates, failure to properly translate the business problem into a data mining problem leads to one of the dangers we are trying to avoid— learning things that are true, but not useful.

For a complete treatment of turning business problems into data mining problems, we recommend the book *Business Modeling and Data Mining* by our colleague Dorian Pyle. This book gives detailed advice on how to find the business problems where data mining provides the most benefit and how to formulate those problems for mining. Here, we simply remind the reader to consider two important questions before beginning the actual data mining process: How will the results be used? And, in what form will the results be delivered? The answer to the first question goes a long way towards answering the second.

## Step Two: Select Appropriate Data

Data mining requires data. In the best of all possible worlds, the required data would already be resident in a corporate data warehouse, cleansed, available, historically accurate, and frequently updated. In fact, it is more often scattered in a variety of operational systems in incompatible formats on computers running different operating systems, accessed through incompatible desktop tools.

The data sources that are useful and available vary, of course, from problem to problem and industry to industry. Some examples of useful data:

- Warranty claims data (including both fixed-format and free-text fields)
- Point-of-sale data (including ring codes, coupons proffered, discounts applied)
- Credit card charge records
- Medical insurance claims data
- Web log data
- E-commerce server application logs
- Direct mail response records
- Call-center records, including memos written by the call-center reps
- Printing press run records

- Motor vehicle registration records
- Noise level in decibels from microphones placed in communities near an airport
- Telephone call detail records
- Survey response data
- Demographic and lifestyle data
- Economic data
- Hourly weather readings (wind direction, wind strength, precipitation)
- Census data

Once the business problem has been formulated, it is possible to form a wish list of data that would be nice to have. For a study of existing customers, this should include data from the time they were acquired (acquisition channel, acquisition date, original product mix, original credit score, and so on), similar data describing their current status, and behavioral data accumulated during their tenure. Of course, it may not be possible to find everything on the wish list, but it is better to start out with an idea of what you would like to find.

Occasionally, a data mining effort starts without a specific business problem. A company becomes aware that it is not getting good value from the data it collects, and sets out to determine whether the data could be made more useful through data mining. The trick to making such a project successful is to turn it into a project designed to solve a specific problem. The first step is to explore the available data and make a list of candidate business problems. Invite business users to create a lengthy wish list which can then be reduced to a small number of achievable goals—the data mining problem.

## What Is Available?

The first place to look for data is in the corporate data warehouse. Data in the warehouse has already been cleaned and verified and brought together from multiple sources. A single data model hopefully ensures that similarly named fields have the same meaning and compatible data types throughout the database. The corporate data warehouse is a historical repository; new data is appended, but the historical data is never changed. Since it was designed for decision support, the data warehouse provides detailed data that can be aggregated to the right level for data mining. Chapter 15 goes into more detail about the relationship between data mining and data warehousing.

The only problem is that in many organizations such a data warehouse does not actually exist or one or more data warehouses exist, but don't live up to the promises. That being the case, data miners must seek data from various departmental databases and from within the bowels of operational systems.

These operational systems are designed to perform a certain task such as claims processing, call switching, order entry, or billing. They are designed with the primary goal of processing transactions quickly and accurately. The data is in whatever format best suits that goal and the historical record, if any, is likely to be in a tape archive. It may require significant political and programming effort to get the data in a form useful for knowledge discovery.

In some cases, operational procedures have to be changed in order to supply data. We know of one major catalog retailer that wanted to analyze the buying habits of its customers so as to market differentially to new customers and long-standing customers. Unfortunately, anyone who hadn't ordered anything in the past six months was routinely purged from the records. The substantial population of people who loyally used the catalog for Christmas shopping, but not during the rest of the year, went unrecognized and indeed were *unrecognizable*, until the company began keeping historical customer records.

In many companies, determining what data is available is surprisingly difficult. Documentation is often missing or out of date. Typically, there is no one person who can provide all the answers. Determining what is available requires looking through data dictionaries, interviewing users and database administrators, and examining existing reports.

**WARNING** Use database documentation and data dictionaries as a guide but do not accept them as unalterable fact. The fact that a field is defined in a table or mentioned in a document does not mean the field exists, is actually available for all customers, and is correctly loaded.

## How Much Data Is Enough?

Unfortunately, there is no simple answer to this question. The answer depends on the particular algorithms employed, the complexity of the data, and the relative frequency of possible outcomes. Statisticians have spent years developing tests for determining the smallest model set that can be used to produce a model. Machine learning researchers have spent much time and energy devising ways to let parts of the training set be reused for validation and test. All of this work ignores an important point: In the commercial world, statisticians are scarce, and data is anything but.

In any case, where data *is* scarce, data mining is not only less effective, it is less likely to be useful. Data mining is most useful when the sheer volume of data obscures patterns that might be detectable in smaller databases. Therefore, our advice is to use so much data that the questions about what constitutes an adequate sample size simply do not arise. We generally start with tens of thousands if not millions of preclassified records so that the training, validation, and test sets each contain many thousands of records.

In data mining, more is better, but with some caveats. The first caveat has to do with the relationship between the size of the model set and its *density*. Density refers to the prevalence of the outcome of interests. Often the target variable represents something relatively rare. It is rare for prospects to respond to a direct mail offer. It is rare for credit card holders to commit fraud. In any given month, it is rare for newspaper subscribers to cancel their subscriptions. As discussed later in this chapter (in the section on creating the model set), it is desirable for the model set to be balanced with equal numbers of each of the outcomes during the model-building process. A smaller, balanced sample is preferable to a larger one with a very low proportion of rare outcomes.

The second caveat has to do with the data miner's time. When the model set is large enough to build good, stable models, making it larger is counterproductive because everything will take longer to run on the larger dataset. Since data mining is an iterative process, the time spent waiting for results can become very large if each run of a modeling routine takes hours instead of minutes.

A simple test for whether the sample used for modeling is large enough is to try doubling it and measure the improvement in the model's accuracy. If the model created using the larger sample is significantly better than the one created using the smaller sample, then the smaller sample is not big enough. If there is no improvement, or only a slight improvement, then the original sample is probably adequate.

## How Much History Is Required?

Data mining uses data from the past to make predictions about the future. But how far in the past should the data come from? This is another simple question without a simple answer. The first thing to consider is seasonality. Most businesses display some degree of seasonality. Sales go up in the fourth quarter. Leisure travel goes up in the summer. There should be enough historical data to capture periodic events of this sort.

On the other hand, data from too far in the past may not be useful for mining because of changing market conditions. This is especially true when some external event such as a change in the regulatory regime has intervened. For many customer-focused applications, 2 to 3 years of history is appropriate. However, even in such cases, data about the beginning of the customer relationship often proves very valuable—what was the initial channel, what was the initial offer, how did the customer initially pay, and so on.

## How Many Variables?

Inexperienced data miners are sometimes in too much of a hurry to throw out variables that seem unlikely to be interesting, keeping only a few carefully chosen variables they expect to be important. The data mining approach calls for letting the data itself reveal what is and is not important.

Often, variables that had previously been ignored turn out to have predictive value when used in combination with other variables. For example, one credit card issuer, that had never included data on cash advances in its customer profitability models, discovered through data mining that people who use cash advances only in November and December are highly profitable. Presumably, these are people who are prudent enough to avoid borrowing money at high interest rates most of the time (a prudence that makes them less likely to default than habitual users of cash advances) but who need some extra cash for the holidays and are willing to pay exorbitant interest to get it.

It is true that a final model is usually based on just a few variables. But these few variables are often derived by combining several other variables, and it may not have been obvious at the beginning which ones end up being important.

## What Must the Data Contain?

At a minimum, the data must contain examples of all possible outcomes of interest. In directed data mining, where the goal is to predict the value of a particular target variable, it is crucial to have a model set comprised of preclassified data. To distinguish people who are likely to default on a loan from people who are not, there needs to be thousands of examples from each class to build a model that distinguishes one from the other. When a new applicant comes along, his or her application is compared with those of past customers, either directly, as in memory-based reasoning, or indirectly through rules or neural networks derived from the historical data. If the new application "looks like" those of people who defaulted in the past, it will be rejected.

Implicit in this description is the idea that it is possible to know what happened in the past. To learn from our mistakes, we first have to recognize that we have made them. This is not always possible. One company had to give up on an attempt to use directed knowledge discovery to build a warranty claims fraud model because, although they suspected that some claims might be fraudulent, they had no idea which ones. Without a training set containing warranty claims clearly marked as fraudulent or legitimate, it was impossible to apply these techniques. Another company wanted a direct mail response model built, but could only supply data on people who had responded to past campaigns. They had not kept any information on people who had not responded so there was no basis for comparison.

## Step Three: Get to Know the Data

It is hard to overstate the importance of spending time exploring the data before rushing into building models. Because of its importance, Chapter 17 is devoted to this topic in detail. Good data miners seem to rely heavily on intuition—somehow being able to guess what a good derived variable to try might be, for instance. The only way to develop intuition for what is going on in an unfamiliar dataset is to immerse yourself in it. Along the way, you are likely to discover many data quality problems and be inspired to ask many questions that would not otherwise have come up.

## Examine Distributions

A good first step is to examine a histogram of each variable in the dataset and think about what it is telling you. Make note of anything that seems surprising. If there is a state code variable, is California the tallest bar? If not, why not? Are some states missing? If so, does it seem plausible that this company does not do business in those states? If there is a gender variable, are there similar numbers of men and women? If not, is that unexpected? Pay attention to the range of each variable. Do variables that should be counts take on negative values? Do the highest and lowest values sound like reasonable values for that variable to take on? Is the mean much different from the median? How many missing values are there? Have the variable counts been consistent over time?

**TIP**  As soon as you get your hands on a data file from a new source, it is a good idea to profile the data to understand what is going on, including getting counts and summary statistics for each field, counts of the number of distinct values taken on by categorical variables, and where appropriate, cross-tabulations such as sales by product by region. In addition to providing insight into the data, the profiling exercise is likely to raise warning flags about inconsistencies or definitional problems that could destroy the usefulness of later analysis.

Data visualization tools can be very helpful during the initial exploration of a database. Figure 3.6 shows some data from the 2000 census of the state of New York. (This dataset may be downloaded from the companion Web site at www.data-miners.com/companion where you will also find suggested exercises that make use of it.) The red bars indicate the proportion of towns in the county where more than 15 percent of homes are heated by wood. (In New York, a town is a subdivision of a county that may or may not include any incorporated villages or cities. For instance, the *town* of Cortland is in West-chester county and includes the *village* of Croton-on-Hudson, whereas the *city* of Cortland is in Cortland County, in another part of the state.) The picture, generated by software from Quadstone, shows at a glance that wood-burning stoves are not much used to heat homes in the urbanized counties close to New York City, but are popular in rural areas upstate.

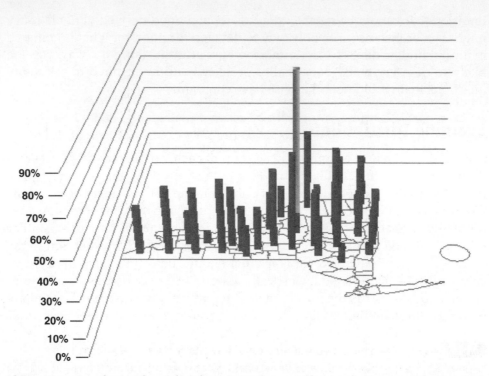

90% —
80% —
70% —
60% —
50% —
40% —
30% —
20% —
10% —
0% —

**Figure 3.6**    Prevalence of wood as the primary source of heat varies by county in New York state.

## Compare Values with Descriptions

Look at the values of each variable and compare them with the description given for that variable in available documentation. This exercise often reveals that the descriptions are inaccurate or incomplete. In one dataset of grocery purchases, a variable that was labeled as being an item count had many noninteger values. Upon further investigation, it turned out that the field contained an item count for products sold by the item, but a weight for items sold by weight. Another dataset, this one from a retail catalog company, included a field that was described as containing total spending over several quarters. This field was mysteriously capable of predicting the target variable—whether a customer had placed an order from a particular catalog mailing. Everyone who had not placed an order had a zero value in the mystery field. Everyone who had placed an order had a number greater than zero in the field. We surmise that the field actually contained the value of the customer's order from the mailing in question. In any case, it certainly did not contain the documented value.

## Validate Assumptions

Using simple cross-tabulation and visualization tools such as scatter plots, bar graphs, and maps, validate assumptions about the data. Look at the target variable in relation to various other variables to see such things as response by channel or churn rate by market or income by sex. Where possible, try to match reported summary numbers by reconstructing them directly from the base-level data. For example, if reported monthly churn is 2 percent, count up the number of customers that cancel one month and see if it is around 2 percent of the total.

**TIP** Trying to recreate reported aggregate numbers from the detail data that supposedly goes into them is an instructive exercise. In trying to explain the discrepancies, you are likely to learn much about the operational processes and business rules behind the reported numbers.

## Ask Lots of Questions

Wherever the data does not seem to bear out received wisdom or your own expectations, make a note of it. An important output of the data exploration process is a list of questions for the people who supplied the data. Often these questions will require further research because few users look at data as carefully as data miners do. Examples of the kinds of questions that are likely to come out of the preliminary exploration are:

- Why are no auto insurance policies sold in New Jersey or Massachusetts?
- Why were some customers active for 31 days in February, but none were active for more than 28 days in January?
- Why were so many customers born in 1911? Are they really that old?
- Why are there no examples of repeat purchasers?
- What does it mean when the contract begin date is after the contract end date?
- Why are there negative numbers in the sale price field?
- How can active customers have a non-null value in the cancelation reason code field?

These are all real questions we have had occasion to ask about real data. Sometimes the answers taught us things we hadn't known about the client's industry. New Jersey and Massachusetts do not allow automobile insurers much flexibility in setting rates, so a company that sees its main competitive advantage as smarter pricing does not want to operate in those markets. Other times we learned about idiosyncrasies of the operational systems, such as the data entry screen that insisted on a birth date even when none was known, which lead to a lot of people being assigned the birthday November 11, 1911 because 11/11/11 is the date you get by holding down the "1" key and letting it auto-repeat until the field is full (and no other keys work to fill in valid dates). Sometimes we discovered serious problems with the data such as the data for February being misidentified as January. And in the last instance, we learned that the process extracting the data had bugs.

# Step Four: Create a Model Set

The model set contains all the data that is used in the modeling process. Some of the data in the model set is used to find patterns. Some of the data in the model set is used to verify that the model is stable. Some is used to assess the model's performance. Creating a model set requires assembling data from multiple sources to form customer signatures and then preparing the data for analysis.

## Assembling Customer Signatures

The model set is a table or collection of tables with one row per item to be studied, and fields for everything known about that item that could be useful for modeling. When the data describes customers, the rows of the model set are often called *customer signatures*. Assembling the customer signatures from relational databases often requires complex queries to join data from many tables and then augmenting it with data from other sources.

Part of the data assembly process is getting all data to be at the correct level of summarization so there is one value per customer, rather than one value per transaction or one value per zip code. These issues are discussed in Chapter 17.

## Creating a Balanced Sample

Very often, the data mining task involves learning to distinguish between groups such as responders and nonresponders, goods and bads, or members of different customer segments. As explained in the sidebar, data mining algorithms do best when these groups have roughly the same number of members. This is unlikely to occur naturally. In fact, it is usually the more interesting groups that are underrepresented.

Before modeling, the dataset should be made balanced either by sampling from the different groups at different rates or adding a weighting factor so that the members of the most popular groups are not weighted as heavily as members of the smaller ones.

## ADDING MORE NEEDLES TO THE HAYSTACK

In standard statistical analysis, it is common practice to throw out *outliers*—observations that are far outside the normal range. In data mining, however, these outliers may be just what we are looking for. Perhaps they represent fraud, some sort of error in our business procedures, or some fabulously profitable niche market. In these cases, we don't want to throw out the outliers, we want to get to know and understand them!

The problem is that knowledge discovery algorithms learn by example. If there are not enough examples of a particular class or pattern of behavior, the data mining tools will not be able to come up with a model for predicting it. In this situation, we may be able to improve our chances by artificially enriching the training data with examples of the rare event.

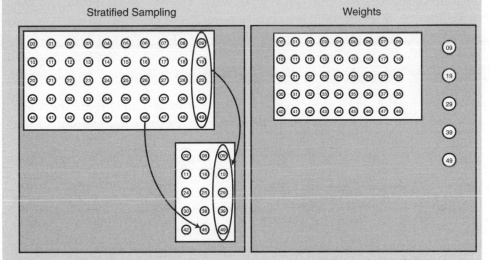

When an outcome is rare, there are two ways to create a balanced sample.

For example, a bank might want to build a model of who is a likely prospect for a private banking program. These programs appeal only to the very wealthiest clients, few of whom are represented in even a fairly large sample of bank customers. To build a model capable of spotting these fortunate individuals, we might create a training set of checking transaction histories of a population that includes 50 percent private banking clients even though they represent fewer than 1 percent of all checking accounts.

Alternately, each private banking client might be given a weight of 1 and other customers a weight of 0.01, so the total weight of the exclusive customers equals the total weight of the rest of the customers (we prefer to have the maximum weight be 1).

## Including Multiple Timeframes

The primary goal of the methodology is creating stable models. Among other things, that means models that will work at any time of year and well into the future. This is more likely to happen if the data in the model set does not all come from one time of year. Even if the model is to be based on only 3 months of history, different rows of the model set should use different 3-month windows. The idea is to let the model generalize from the past rather than memorize what happened at one particular time in the past.

Building a model on data from a single time period increases the risk of learning things that are not generally true. One amusing example that the authors once saw was an association rules model built on a single week's worth of point of sale data from a supermarket. Association rules try to predict items a shopping basket will contain given that it is known to contain certain other items. In this case, all the rules predicted eggs. This surprising result became less so when we realized that the model set was from the week before Easter.

## Creating a Model Set for Prediction

When the model set is going to be used for prediction, there is another aspect of time to worry about. Although the model set should contain multiple timeframes, any one customer signature should have a gap in time between the predictor variables and the target variable. Time can always be divided into three periods: the past, present, and future. When making a prediction, a model uses data from the past to make predictions about the future.

As shown in Figure 3.7, all three of these periods should be represented in the model set. Of course all data comes from the past, so the time periods in the model set are actually the distant past, the not-so-distant past, and the recent past. Predictive models are built be finding patterns in the distant past that explain outcomes in the recent past. When the model is deployed, it is then able to use data from the recent past to make predictions about the future.

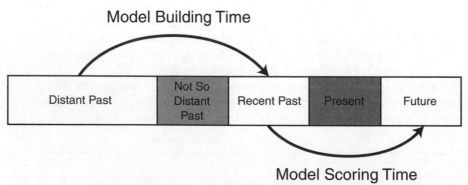

**Figure 3.7**  Data from the past mimics data from the past, present, and future.

It may not be immediately obvious why some recent data—from the not-so-distant past—is not used in a particular customer signature. The answer is that when the model is applied in the present, no data from the present is available as input. The diagram in Figure 3.8 makes this clearer.

If a model were built using data from June (the not-so-distant past) in order to predict July (the recent past), then it could not be used to predict September until August data was available. But when is August data available? Certainly not in August, since it is still being created. Chances are, not in the first week of September either, since it has to be collected and cleaned and loaded and tested and blessed. In many companies, the August data will not be available until mid-September or even October, by which point nobody will care about predictions for September. The solution is to include a month of latency in the model set.

## Partitioning the Model Set

Once the preclassified data has been obtained from the appropriate time-frames, the methodology calls for dividing it into three parts. The first part, the *training set*, is used to build the initial model. The second part, the *validation set1*, is used to adjust the initial model to make it more general and less tied to the idiosyncrasies of the training set. The third part, the *test set*, is used to gauge the likely effectiveness of the model when applied to unseen data. Three sets are necessary because once data has been used for one step in the process, it can no longer be used for the next step because the information it contains has already become part of the model; therefore, it cannot be used to correct or judge.

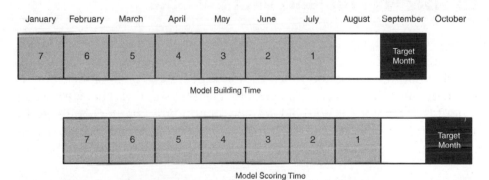

**Figure 3.8**  Time when the model is built compared to time when the model is used.

People often find it hard to understand why the training set and validation set are "tainted" once they have been used to build a model. An analogy may help: Imagine yourself back in the fifth grade. The class is taking a spelling test. Suppose that, at the end of the test period, the teacher asks you to estimate your own grade on the quiz by marking the words you got wrong. You will give yourself a very good grade, but your spelling will not improve. If, at the beginning of the period, you thought there should be an 'e' at the end of "tomato," nothing will have happened to change your mind when you grade your paper. No new information has entered the system. You need a validation set!

Now, imagine that at the end of the test the teacher allows you to look at the papers of several neighbors before grading your own. If they all agree that "tomato" has no final 'e,' you may decide to mark your own answer wrong. If the teacher gives the same quiz tomorrow, you will do better. But how much better? If you use the papers of the very same neighbors to evaluate your performance tomorrow, you may still be fooling yourself. If they all agree that "potatoes" has no more need of an 'e' than "tomato," and you have changed your own guess to agree with theirs, then you will overestimate your actual grade on the second quiz as well. That is why the test set should be different from the validation set.

For predictive models, the test set should also come from a different time period than the training and validation sets. The proof of a model's stability is in its ability to perform well month after month. A test set from a different time period, often called an *out of time* test set, is a good way to verify model stability, although such a test set is not always available.

## Step Five: Fix Problems with the Data

All data is dirty. All data has problems. What is or isn't a problem varies with the data mining technique. For some, such as decision trees, missing values, and outliers do not cause too much trouble. For others, such as neural networks, they cause all sorts of trouble. For that reason, some of what we have to say about fixing problems with data can be found in the chapters on the techniques where they cause the most difficulty. The rest of what we have to say on this topic can be found in Chapter 17 in the section called "The Dark Side of Data."

The next few sections talk about some of the common problems that need to be fixed.

## Categorical Variables with Too Many Values

Variables such as zip code, county, telephone handset model, and occupation code are all examples of variables that convey useful information, but not in a way that most data mining algorithms can handle. The problem is that while where a person lives and what he or she does for work are important predictors, there are so many possible values for the variables that carry this information and so few examples in your data for most of the values, that variables such as zip code and occupation end up being thrown away along with their valuable information content.

Variables like these must either be grouped so that many classes that all have approximately the same relationship to the target variable are grouped together, or they must be replaced by interesting attributes of the zip code, handset model or occupation. Replace zip codes by the zip code's median home price or population density or historical response rate or whatever else seems likely to be predictive. Replace occupation with median salary for that occupation. And so on.

## Numeric Variables with Skewed Distributions and Outliers

Skewed distributions and outliers cause problems for any data mining technique that uses the values arithmetically (by multiplying them by weights and adding them together, for instance). In many cases, it makes sense to discard records that have outliers. In other cases, it is better to divide the values into equal sized ranges, such as deciles. Sometimes, the best approach is to transform such variables to reduce the range of values by replacing each value with its logarithm, for instance.

## Missing Values

Some data mining algorithms are capable of treating "missing" as a value and incorporating it into rules. Others cannot handle missing values, unfortunately. None of the obvious solutions preserve the true distribution of the variable. Throwing out all records with missing values introduces bias because it is unlikely that such records are distributed randomly. Replacing the missing value with some likely value such as the mean or the most common value adds spurious information. Replacing the missing value with an unlikely value is even worse since the data mining algorithms will not recognize that –999, say, is an unlikely value for age. The algorithms will go ahead and use it.

When missing values must be replaced, the best approach is to impute them by creating a model that has the missing value as its target variable.

## Values with Meanings That Change over Time

When data comes from several different points in history, it is not uncommon for the same value in the same field to have changed its meaning over time. Credit class "A" may always be the best, but the exact range of credit scores that get classed as an "A" may change from time to time. Dealing with this properly requires a well-designed data warehouse where such changes in meaning are recorded so a new variable can be defined that has a constant meaning over time.

## Inconsistent Data Encoding

When information on the same topic is collected from multiple sources, the various sources often represent the same data different ways. If these differences are not caught, they add spurious distinctions that can lead to erroneous conclusions. In one call-detail analysis project, each of the markets studied had a different way of indicating a call to check one's own voice mail. In one city, a call to voice mail from the phone line associated with that mailbox was recorded as having the same origin and destination numbers. In another city, the same situation was represented by the presence of a specific nonexistent number as the call destination. In yet another city, the actual number dialed to reach voice mail was recorded. Understanding apparent differences in voice mail habits between cities required putting the data in a common form.

The same data set contained multiple abbreviations for some states and, in some cases, a particular city was counted separately from the rest of the state. If issues like this are not resolved, you may find yourself building a model of calling patterns to California based on data that excludes calls to Los Angeles.

# Step Six: Transform Data to Bring Information to the Surface

Once the data has been assembled and major data problems fixed, the data must still be prepared for analysis. This involves adding derived fields to bring information to the surface. It may also involve removing outliers, binning numeric variables, grouping classes for categorical variables, applying transformations such as logarithms, turning counts into proportions, and the like. Data preparation is such an important topic that our colleague Dorian Pyle has written a book about it, *Data Preparation for Data Mining* (Morgan Kaufmann 1999), which should be on the bookshelf of every data miner. In this book, these issues are addressed in Chapter 17. Here are a few examples of such transformations.

## Capture Trends

Most corporate data contains time series. Monthly snapshots of billing information, usage, contacts, and so on. Most data mining algorithms do not understand time series data. Signals such as "three months of declining revenue" cannot be spotted treating each month's observation independently. It is up to the data miner to bring trend information to the surface by adding derived variables such as the ratio of spending in the most recent month to spending the month before for a short-term trend and the ratio of the most recent month to the same month a year ago for a long-term trend.

## Create Ratios and Other Combinations of Variables

Trends are one example of bringing information to the surface by combining multiple variables. There are many others. Often, these additional fields are derived from the existing ones in ways that might be obvious to a knowledgeable analyst, but are unlikely to be considered by mere software. Typical examples include:

```
obesity_index = height² / weight
PE = price / earnings
pop_density = population / area
rpm = revenue_passengers * miles
```

Adding fields that represent relationships considered important by experts in the field is a way of letting the mining process benefit from that expertise.

## Convert Counts to Proportions

Many datasets contain counts or dollar values that are not particularly interesting in themselves because they vary according to some other value. Larger households spend more money on groceries than smaller households. They spend more money on produce, more money on meat, more money on packaged goods, more money on cleaning products, more money on everything. So comparing the dollar amount spent by different households in any one category, such as bakery, will only reveal that large households spend more. It is much more interesting to compare the *proportion* of each household's spending that goes to each category.

The value of converting counts to proportions can be seen by comparing two charts based on the NY State towns dataset. Figure 3.9 compares the count of houses with bad plumbing to the prevalence of heating with wood. A relationship is visible, but it is not strong. In Figure 3.10, where the count of houses with bad plumbing has been converted into the proportion of houses with bad plumbing, the relationship is much stronger. Towns where many houses have bad plumbing also have many houses heated by wood. Does this mean that wood smoke destroys plumbing? It is important to remember that the patterns that we find determine correlation, not causation.

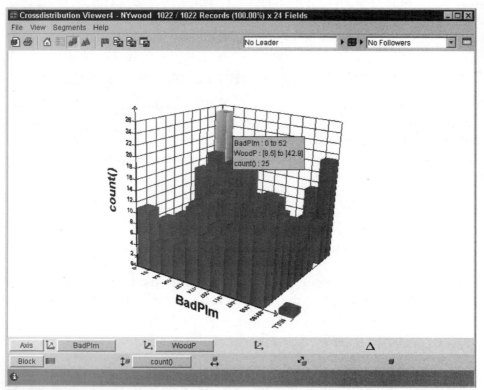

**Figure 3.9** Chart comparing count of houses with bad plumbing to prevalence of heating with wood.

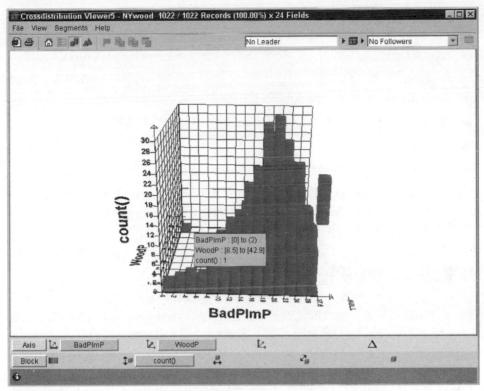

**Figure 3.10** Chart comparing proportion of houses with bad plumbing to prevalence of heating with wood.

# Step Seven: Build Models

The details of this step vary from technique to technique and are described in the chapters devoted to each data mining method. In general terms, this is the step where most of the work of creating a model occurs. In directed data mining, the training set is used to generate an explanation of the independent or target variable in terms of the independent or input variables. This explanation may take the form of a neural network, a decision tree, a linkage graph, or some other representation of the relationship between the target and the other fields in the database. In undirected data mining, there is no target variable. The model finds relationships between records and expresses them as association rules or by assigning them to common clusters.

Building models is the one step of the data mining process that has been truly automated by modern data mining software. For that reason, it takes up relatively little of the time in a data mining project.

# Step Eight: Assess Models

This step determines whether or not the models are working. A model assessment should answer questions such as:

- How accurate is the model?
- How well does the model describe the observed data?
- How much confidence can be placed in the model's predictions?
- How comprehensible is the model?

Of course, the answer to these questions depends on the type of model that was built. Assessment here refers to the technical merits of the model, rather than the measurement phase of the virtuous cycle.

## Assessing Descriptive Models

The rule, If (state='MA)' then heating source is oil, seems more descriptive than the rule, If (area=339 OR area=351 OR area=413 OR area=508 OR area=617 OR area=774 OR area=781 OR area=857 OR area=978) then heating source is oil. Even if the two rules turn out to be equivalent, the first one seems more expressive.

Expressive power may seem purely subjective, but there is, in fact, a theoretical way to measure it, called the *minimum description length* or MDL. The minimum description length for a model is the number of bits it takes to encode both the rule and the list of all exceptions to the rule. The fewer bits required, the better the rule. Some data mining tools use MDL to decide which sets of rules to keep and which to weed out.

## Assessing Directed Models

Directed models are assessed on their accuracy on previously unseen data. Different data mining tasks call for different ways of assessing performance of the model as a whole and different ways of judging the likelihood that the model yields accurate results for any particular record.

Any model assessment is dependent on context; the same model can look good according to one measure and bad according to another. In the academic field of machine learning—the source of many of the algorithms used for data mining—researchers have a goal of generating models that can be understood in their entirety. An easy-to-understand model is said to have good "mental fit." In the interest of obtaining the best mental fit, these researchers often prefer models that consist of a few simple rules to models that contain many such rules, even when the latter are more accurate. In a business setting, such explicability may not be as important as performance—or may be more important.

Model assessment can take place at the level of the whole model or at the level of individual predictions. Two models with the same overall accuracy may have quite different levels of variance among the individual predictions. A decision tree, for instance, has an overall classification error rate, but each branch and leaf of the tree also has an error rate as well.

## Assessing Classifiers and Predictors

For classification and prediction tasks, accuracy is measured in terms of the error rate, the percentage of records classified incorrectly. The classification error rate on the preclassified test set is used as an estimate of the expected error rate when classifying new records. Of course, this procedure is only valid if the test set is representative of the larger population.

Our recommended method of establishing the error rate for a model is to measure it on a test dataset taken from the same population as the training and validation sets, but disjointed from them. In the ideal case, such a test set would be from a more recent time period than the data in the model set; however, this is not often possible in practice.

A problem with error rate as an assessment tool is that some errors are worse than others. A familiar example comes from the medical world where a false negative on a test for a serious disease causes the patient to go untreated with possibly life-threatening consequences whereas a false positive only leads to a second (possibly more expensive or more invasive) test. A *confusion matrix* or *correct classification matrix*, shown in Figure 3.11, can be used to sort out false positives from false negatives. Some data mining tools allow costs to be associated with each type of misclassification so models can be built to minimize the cost rather than the misclassification rate.

## Assessing Estimators

For estimation tasks, accuracy is expressed in terms of the difference between the predicted score and the actual measured result. Both the accuracy of any one estimate and the accuracy of the model as a whole are of interest. A model may be quite accurate for some ranges of input values and quite inaccurate for others. Figure 3.12 shows a linear model that estimates total revenue based on a product's unit price. This simple model works reasonably well in one price range but goes badly wrong when the price reaches the level where the elasticity of demand for the product (the ratio of the percent change in quantity sold to the percent change in price) is greater than one. An elasticity greater than one means that any further price increase results in a decrease in revenue because the increased revenue per unit is more than offset by the drop in the number of units sold.

Percent of Row Frequency

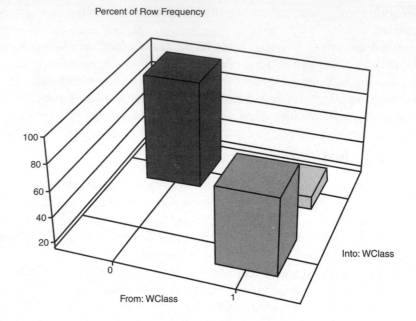

**Figure 3.11**    A confusion matrix cross-tabulates predicted outcomes with actual outcomes.

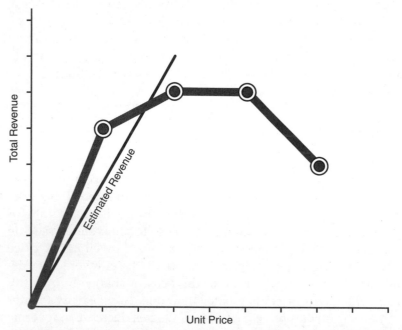

**Figure 3.12**    The accuracy of an estimator may vary considerably over the range of inputs.

The standard way of describing the accuracy of an estimation model is by measuring how far off the estimates are *on average*. But, simply subtracting the estimated value from the true value at each point and taking the mean results in a meaningless number. To see why, consider the estimates in Table 3.1.

The average difference between the true values and the estimates is zero; positive differences and negative differences have canceled each other out. The usual way of solving this problem is to sum the squares of the differences rather than the differences themselves. The average of the squared differences is called the *variance*. The estimates in this table have a variance of 10.

$$(-5^2 + 2^2 + -2^2 + 1^2 + 4^2)/5 = (25 + 4 + 4 + 1 + 16)/5 = 50/5 = 10$$

The smaller the variance, the more accurate the estimate. A drawback to variance as a measure is that it is not expressed in the same units as the estimates themselves. For estimated prices in dollars, it is more useful to know how far off the estimates are in dollars rather than *square* dollars! For that reason, it is usual to take the square root of the variance to get a measure called the *standard deviation*. The standard deviation of these estimates is the square root of 10 or about 3.16. For our purposes, all you need to know about the standard deviation is that it is a measure of how widely the estimated values vary from the true values.

## Comparing Models Using Lift

Directed models, whether created using neural networks, decision trees, genetic algorithms, or Ouija boards, are all created to accomplish some task. Why not judge them on their ability to classify, estimate, and predict? The most common way to compare the performance of classification models is to use a ratio called *lift*. This measure can be adapted to compare models designed for other tasks as well. What lift actually measures is the change in concentration of a particular class when the model is used to select a group from the general population.

```
lift = P(class_t | sample) / P(class_t | population)
```

**Table 3.1**  Countervailing Errors

| TRUE VALUE | ESTIMATED VALUE | ERROR |
|---|---|---|
| 127 | 132 | -5 |
| 78 | 76 | 2 |
| 120 | 122 | -2 |
| 130 | 129 | 1 |
| 95 | 91 | 4 |

An example helps to explain this. Suppose that we are building a model to predict who is likely to respond to a direct mail solicitation. As usual, we build the model using a preclassified training dataset and, if necessary, a preclassified validation set as well. Now we are ready to use the test set to calculate the model's lift.

The classifier scores the records in the test set as either "predicted to respond" or "not predicted to respond." Of course, it is not correct every time, but if the model is any good at all, the group of records marked "predicted to respond" contains a higher proportion of actual responders than the test set as a whole. Consider these records. If the test set contains 5 percent actual responders and the sample contains 50 percent actual responders, the model provides a lift of 10 (50 divided by 5).

Is the model that produces the highest lift necessarily the best model? Surely a list of people half of whom will respond is preferable to a list where only a quarter will respond, right? Not necessarily—not if the first list has only 10 names on it!

The point is that lift is a function of sample size. If the classifier only picks out 10 likely respondents, and it is right 100 percent of the time, it will achieve a lift of 20—the highest lift possible when the population contains 5 percent responders. As the confidence level required to classify someone as likely to respond is relaxed, the mailing list gets longer, and the lift decreases.

Charts like the one in Figure 3.13 will become very familiar as you work with data mining tools. It is created by sorting all the prospects according to their likelihood of responding as predicted by the model. As the size of the mailing list increases, we reach farther and farther down the list. The X-axis shows the percentage of the population getting our mailing. The Y-axis shows the percentage of all responders we reach.

If no model were used, mailing to 10 percent of the population would reach 10 percent of the responders, mailing to 50 percent of the population would reach 50 percent of the responders, and mailing to everyone would reach all the responders. This mass-mailing approach is illustrated by the line slanting upwards. The other curve shows what happens if the model is used to select recipients for the mailing. The model finds 20 percent of the responders by mailing to only 10 percent of the population. Soliciting half the population reaches over 70 percent of the responders.

Charts like the one in Figure 3.13 are often referred to as *lift charts*, although what is really being graphed is cumulative response or *concentration*. Figure 3.13 shows the actual lift chart corresponding to the response chart in Figure 3.14. The chart shows clearly that lift decreases as the size of the target list increases.

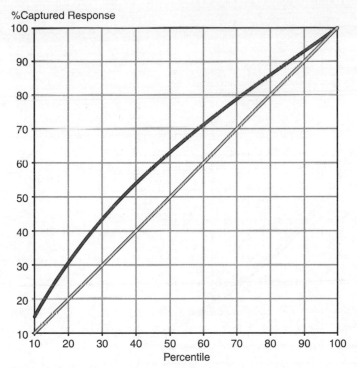

**Figure 3.13** Cumulative response for targeted mailing compared with mass mailing.

## Problems with Lift

Lift solves the problem of how to compare the performance of models of different kinds, but it is still not powerful enough to answer the most important questions: Is the model worth the time, effort, and money it cost to build it? Will mailing to a segment where lift is 3 result in a profitable campaign?

These kinds of questions cannot be answered without more knowledge of the business context, in order to build costs and revenues into the calculation. Still, lift is a very handy tool for comparing the performance of two models applied to the same or comparable data. Note that the performance of two models can only be compared using lift when the tests sets have the same density of the outcome.

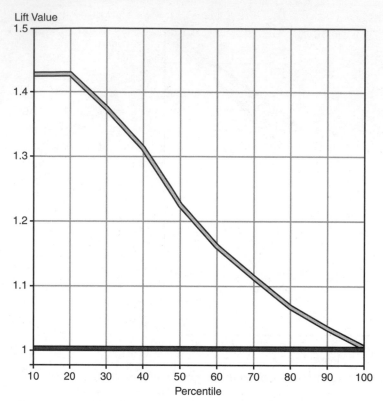

**Figure 3.14** A lift chart starts high and then goes to 1.

## Step Nine: Deploy Models

Deploying a model means moving it from the data mining environment to the scoring environment. This process may be easy or hard. In the worst case (and we have seen this at more than one company), the model is developed in a special modeling environment using software that runs nowhere else. To deploy the model, a programmer takes a printed description of the model and recodes it in another programming language so it can be run on the scoring platform.

A more common problem is that the model uses input variables that are not in the original data. This should not be a problem since the model inputs are at least derived from the fields that were originally extracted to from the model set. Unfortunately, data miners are not always good about keeping a clean, reusable record of the transformations they applied to the data.

The challenging in deploying data mining models is that they are often used to score very large datasets. In some environments, every one of millions of customer records is updated with a new behavior score every day. A score is simply an additional field in a database table. Scores often represent a probability or likelihood so they are typically numeric values between 0 and 1, but by no means necessarily so. A score might also be a class label provided by a clustering model, for instance, or a class label with a probability.

## Step Ten: Assess Results

The response chart in Figure 3.14compares the number of responders reached for a given amount of postage, with and without the use of a predictive model. A more useful chart would show how many dollars are brought in for a given expenditure on the marketing campaign. After all, if developing the model is very expensive, a mass mailing may be more cost-effective than a targeted one.

- What is the fixed cost of setting up the campaign and the model that supports it?
- What is the cost per recipient of making the offer?
- What is the cost per respondent of fulfilling the offer?
- What is the value of a positive response?

Plugging these numbers into a spreadsheet makes it possible to measure the impact of the model in dollars. The cumulative response chart can then be turned into a cumulative profit chart, which determines where the sorted mailing list should be cut off. If, for example, there is a high fixed price of setting up the campaign and also a fairly high price per recipient of making the offer (as when a wireless company buys loyalty by giving away mobile phones or waiving renewal fees), the company loses money by going after too few prospects because, there are still not enough respondents to make up for the high fixed costs of the program. On the other hand, if it makes the offer to too many people, high variable costs begin to hurt.

Of course, the profit model is only as good as its inputs. While the fixed and variable costs of the campaign are fairly easy to come by, the predicted value of a responder can be harder to estimate. The process of figuring out what a customer is worth is beyond the scope of this book, but a good estimate helps to measure the true value of a data mining model.

In the end, the measure that counts the most is return on investment. Measuring lift on a test set helps choose the right model. Profitability models based on lift will help decide how to apply the results of the model. But, it is very important to measure these things in the field as well. In a database marketing application, this requires always setting aside control groups and carefully tracking customer response according to various model scores.

## Step Eleven: Begin Again

Every data mining project raises more questions than it answers. This is a good thing. It means that new relationships are now visible that were not visible before. The newly discovered relationships suggest new hypotheses to test and the data mining process begins all over again.

## Lessons Learned

Data mining comes in two forms. Directed data mining involves searching through historical records to find patterns that explain a particular outcome. Directed data mining includes the tasks of classification, estimation, prediction, and profiling. Undirected data mining searches through the same records for interesting patterns. It includes the tasks of clustering, finding association rules, and description.

Data mining brings the business closer to data. As such, hypothesis testing is a very important part of the process. However, the primary lesson of this chapter is that data mining is full of traps for the unwary and following a methodology based on experience can help avoid them.

The first hurdle is translating the business problem into one of the six tasks that can be solved by data mining: classification, estimation, prediction, affinity grouping, clustering, and profiling.

The next challenge is to locate appropriate data that can be transformed into actionable information. Once the data has been located, it should be thoroughly explored. The exploration process is likely to reveal problems with the data. It will also help build up the data miner's intuitive understanding of the data. The next step is to create a model set and partition it into training, validation, and test sets.

Data transformations are necessary for two purposes: to fix problems with the data such as missing values and categorical variables that take on too many values, and to bring information to the surface by creating new variables to represent trends and other ratios and combinations.

Once the data has been prepared, building models is a relatively easy process. Each type of model has its own metrics by which it can be assessed, but there are also assessment tools that are independent of the type of model. Some of the most important of these are the lift chart, which shows how the model has increased the concentration of the desired value of the target variable and the confusion matrix that shows that misclassification error rate for each of the target classes. The next chapter uses examples from real data mining projects to show the methodology in action.

# Data Minin...
## Marketi...
## Relationsl...

comes from traditional mining...
oil. As a noun, a prospect is s...
fields to be pumped and...
is someone who mi...
approached in the...
using data min...
valuable cu...
For m...
are a...
to...

Some people find data mining techniques interesting from a technical per-spective. However, for most people, the techniques are interesting as a means to an end. The techniques do not exist in a vacuum; they exist in a business context. This chapter is about the business context.

This chapter is organized around a set of business objectives that can be addressed by data mining. Each of the selected business objectives is linked to specific data mining techniques appropriate for addressing the problem. The business topics addressed in this chapter are presented in roughly ascending order of complexity of the customer relationship. The chapter starts with the problem of communicating with potential customers about whom little is known, and works up to the varied data mining opportunities presented by ongoing customer relationships that may involve multiple products, multiple communications channels, and increasingly individualized interactions.

In the course of discussing the business applications, technical material is introduced as appropriate, but the details of specific data mining techniques are left for later chapters.

## Prospecting

Prospecting seems an excellent place to begin a discussion of business appli-cations of data mining. After all, the primary definition of the verb *to prospect* where it means *to explore for mineral deposits or* omething with possibilities, evoking images of oil nineral deposits to be mined. In marketing, a prospect ght reasonably be expected to become a customer if right way. Both noun and verb resonate with the idea of ng to achieve the business goal of locating people who will be tomers in the future.

ost businesses, relatively few of Earth's more than six billion people tually prospects. Most can be excluded based on geography, age, ability pay, and need for the product or service. For example, a bank offering home equity lines of credit would naturally restrict a mailing offering this type of loan to homeowners who reside in jurisdictions where the bank is licensed to operate. A company selling backyard swing sets would like to send its catalog to households with children at addresses that seem likely to have backyards. A magazine wants to target people who read the appropriate language and will be of interest to its advertisers. And so on.

Data mining can play many roles in prospecting. The most important of these are:

- Identifying good prospects
- Choosing a communication channel for reaching prospects
- Picking appropriate messages for different groups of prospects

Although all of these are important, the first—identifying good prospects— is the most widely implemented.

## Identifying Good Prospects

The simplest definition of a good prospect—and the one used by many companies—is simply someone who might at least express interest in becoming a customer. More sophisticated definitions are more choosey. Truly good prospects are not only *interested* in becoming customers; they can afford to become customers, they will be profitable to have as customers, they are unlikely to defraud the company and likely to pay their bills, and, if treated well, they will be loyal customers and recommend others. No matter how simple or sophisticated the definition of a prospect, the first task is to target them.

Targeting is important whether the message is to be conveyed through advertising or through more direct channels such as mailings, telephone calls, or email. Even messages on billboards are targeted to some degree; billboards for airlines and rental car companies tend to be found next to highways that lead to airports where people who use these services are likely to be among those driving by.

Data mining is applied to this problem by first defining what it means to be a good prospect and then finding rules that allow people with those characteristics to be targeted. For many companies, the first step toward using data mining to identify good prospects is building a response model. Later in this chapter is an extended discussion of response models, the various ways they are employed, and what they can and cannot do.

## Choosing a Communication Channel

Prospecting requires communication. Broadly speaking, companies intentionally communicate with prospects in several ways. One way is through public relations, which refers to encouraging media to cover stories about the company and spreading positive messages by word of mouth. Although highly effective for some companies (such as Starbucks and Tupperware), public relations are not directed marketing messages.

Of more interest to us are advertising and direct marketing. Advertising can mean anything from matchbook covers to the annoying pop-ups on some commercial Web sites to television spots during major sporting events to product placements in movies. In this context, advertising targets groups of people based on common traits; however, advertising does not make it possible to customize messages to individuals. A later section discusses choosing the right place to advertise, by matching the profile of a geographic area to the profile of prospects.

Direct marketing does allow customization of messages for individuals. This might mean outbound telephone calls, email, postcards, or glossy color catalogs. Later in the chapter is a section on differential response analysis, which explains how data mining can help determine which channels have been effective for which groups of prospects.

## Picking Appropriate Messages

Even when selling the same basic product or service, different messages are appropriate for different people. For example, the same newspaper may appeal to some readers primarily for its sports coverage and to others primarily for its coverage of politics or the arts. When the product itself comes in many variants, or when there are multiple products on offer, picking the right message is even more important.

Even with a single product, the message can be important. A classic example is the trade-off between price and convenience. Some people are very price sensitive, and willing to shop in warehouses, make their phone calls late at night, always change planes, and arrange their trips to include a Saturday night. Others will pay a premium for the most convenient service. A message based on price will not only fail to motivate the convenience seekers, it runs the risk of steering them toward less profitable products when they would be happy to pay more.

This chapter describes how simple, single-campaign response models can be combined to create a best next offer model that matches campaigns to customers. Collaborative filtering, an approach to grouping customers into like-minded segments that may respond to similar offers, is discussed in Chapter 8.

## Data Mining to Choose the Right Place to Advertise

One way of targeting prospects is to look for people who resemble current customers. For instance, through surveys, one nationwide publication determined that its readers have the following characteristics:

- 59 percent of readers are college educated.
- 46 percent have professional or executive occupations.
- 21 percent have household income in excess of $75,000/year.
- 7 percent have household income in excess of $100,000/year.

Understanding this profile helps the publication in two ways: First, by targeting prospects who match the profile, it can increase the rate of response to its own promotional efforts. Second, this well-educated, high-income readership can be used to sell advertising space in the publication to companies wishing to reach such an audience. Since the theme of this section is targeting prospects, let's look at how the publication used the profile to sharpen the focus of its prospecting efforts. The basic idea is simple. When the publication wishes to advertise on radio, it should look for stations whose listeners match the profile. When it wishes to place "take one" cards on store counters, it should do so in neighborhoods that match the profile. When it wishes to do outbound telemarketing, it should call people who match the profile. The data mining challenge was to come up with a good definition of what it means to match the profile.

## Who Fits the Profile?

One way of determining whether a customer fits a profile is to measure the similarity—which we also call distance—between the customer and the profile. Several data mining techniques use this idea of measuring similarity as a distance. Memory-based reasoning, discussed in Chapter 8, is a technique for classifying records based on the classifications of known records that are "in the same neighborhood." Automatic cluster detection, the subject of Chapter 11, is another data mining technique that depends on the ability to calculate a distance between two records in order to find clusters of similar records close to each other.

For this profiling example, the purpose is simply to define a distance metric to determine how well prospects fit the profile. The data consists of survey results that represent a snapshot of subscribers at a particular time. What sort of measure makes sense with this data? In particular, what should be done about the fact that the profile is expressed in terms of percentages (58 percent are college educated; 7 percent make over $100,000), whereas an individual either is or is not college educated and either does or does not make more than $100,000?

Consider two survey participants. Amy is college educated, earns $80,000/year, and is a professional. Bob is a high-school graduate earning $50,000/year. Which one is a better match to the readership profile? The answer depends on how the comparison is made. Table 4.1 shows one way to develop a score using only the profile and a simple distance metric.

This table calculates a score based on the proportion of the audience that agrees with each characteristic. For instance, because 58 percent of the readership is college educated, Amy gets a score of 0.58 for this characteristic. Bob, who did not graduate from college, gets a score of 0.42 because the other 42 percent of the readership presumably did not graduate from college. This is continued for each characteristic, and the scores are added together. Amy ends with a score of 2.18 and Bob with the higher score of 2.68. His higher score reflects the fact that he is more similar to the profile of current readers than is Amy.

**Table 4.1** Calculating Fitness Scores for Individuals by Comparing Them along Each Demographic Measure

|  | READER-SHIP | YES SCORE | NO SCORE | AMY | BOB | AMY SCORE | BOB SCORE |
|---|---|---|---|---|---|---|---|
| College educated | 58% | 0.58 | 0.42 | YES | NO | 0.58 | 0.42 |
| Prof or exec | 46% | 0.46 | 0.54 | YES | NO | 0.46 | 0.54 |
| Income >$75K | 21% | 0.21 | 0.79 | YES | NO | 0.21 | 0.79 |
| Income >$100K | 7% | 0.07 | 0.93 | NO | NO | 0.93 | 0.93 |
| Total |  |  |  |  |  | 2.18 | 2.68 |

The problem with this approach is that while Bob looks more like the profile than Amy does, Amy looks more like the audience the publication has *targeted*—namely, college-educated, higher-income individuals. The success of this targeting is evident from a comparison of the readership profile with the demographic characteristics of the U.S. population as a whole. This suggests a less naive approach to measuring an individual's fit with the publication's audience by taking into account the characteristics of the general population in addition to the characteristics of the readership. The approach measures the extent to which a prospect differs from the general population in the same ways that the readership does.

Compared to the population, the readership is better educated, more professional, and better paid. In Table 4.2, the "Index" columns compare the readership's characteristics to the entire population by dividing the percent of the readership that has a particular attribute by the percent of the population that has it. Now, we see that the readership is almost three times more likely to be college educated than the population as a whole. Similarly, they are only about half as likely not to be college educated. By using the indexes as scores for each characteristic, Amy gets a score of 8.42 (2.86 + 2.40 + 2.21 + 0.95) versus Bob with a score of only 3.02 (0.53 + 0.67 + 0.87 + 0.95). The scores based on indexes correspond much better with the publication's target audience. The new scores make more sense because they now incorporate the additional information about how the target audience differs from the U.S. population as a whole.

**Table 4.2**  Calculating Scores by Taking the Proportions in the Population into Account

|  | YES | | | NO | | |
|  | READER-SHIP | US POP | INDEX | READER-SHIP | US POP | INDEX |
| --- | --- | --- | --- | --- | --- | --- |
| College educated | 58% | 20.3% | 2.86 | 42% | 79.7% | 0.53 |
| Prof or exec | 46% | 19.2% | 2.40 | 54% | 80.8% | 0.67 |
| Income >$75K | 21% | 9.5% | 2.21 | 79% | 90.5% | 0.87 |
| Income >$100K | 7% | 2.4% | 2.92 | 93% | 97.6% | 0.95 |

**TIP** When comparing customer profiles, it is important to keep in mind the profile of the population as a whole. For this reason, using indexes is often better than using raw values.

Chapter 11 describes a related notion of similarity based on the difference between two angles. In that approach, each measured attribute is considered a separate dimension. Taking the average value of each attribute as the origin, the profile of current readers is a vector that represents how far he or she differs from the larger population and in what direction. The data representing a prospect is also a vector. If the angle between the two vectors is small, the prospect differs from the population in the same direction.

## Measuring Fitness for Groups of Readers

The idea behind index-based scores can be extended to larger groups of people. This is important because the particular characteristics used for measuring the population may not be available for each customer or prospect. Fortunately, and not by accident, the preceding characteristics are all demographic characteristics that are available through the U.S. Census and can be measured by geographical divisions such as census tract (see the sidebar, "Data by Census Tract").

The process here is to rate each census tract according to its fitness for the publication. The idea is to estimate the proportion of each census tract that fits the publication's readership profile. For instance, if a census tract has an adult population that is 58 percent college educated, then everyone in it gets a fitness score of 1 for this characteristic. If 100 percent are college educated, then the score is still 1—a perfect fit is the best we can do. If, however, only 5.8 percent graduated from college, then the fitness score for this characteristic is 0.1. The overall fitness score is the average of the individual scores for each characteristic.

Figure 4.1 provides an example for three census tracts in Manhattan. Each tract has a different proportion of the four characteristics being considered. This data can be combined to get an overall fitness score for each tract. Note that everyone in the tract gets the same score. The score represents the proportion of the population in that tract that fits the profile.

## DATA BY CENSUS TRACT

The U.S. government is constitutionally mandated to carry out an enumeration of the population every 10 years. The primary purpose of the census is to allocate seats in the House of Representatives to each state. In the process of satisfying this mandate, the census also provides a wealth of information about the American population.

The U.S. Census Bureau (www.census.gov) surveys the American population using two questionnaires, the *short form* and the *long form* (not counting special purposes questionnaires, such as the one for military personnel). Most people get the short form, which asks a few basic questions about gender, age, ethnicity, and household size. Approximately 2 percent of the population gets the long form, which asks much more detailed questions about income, occupation, commuting habits, spending patterns, and more. The responses to these questionnaires provide the basis for demographic profiles.

The Census Bureau strives to keep this information up to date between each decennial census. The Census Bureau does not release information about individuals. Instead, it aggregates the information by small geographic areas. The most commonly used is the *census tract*, consisting of about 4,000 individuals. Although census tracts do vary in size, they are much more consistent in population than other geographic units, such as counties and postal codes.

The census does have smaller geographic units, *blocks* and *block groups*; however, in order to protect the privacy of residents, some data is not made available below the level of census tracts. From these units, it is possible to aggregate information by county, state, metropolitan statistical area (MSA), legislative districts, and so on. The following figure shows some census tracts in the center of Manhattan:

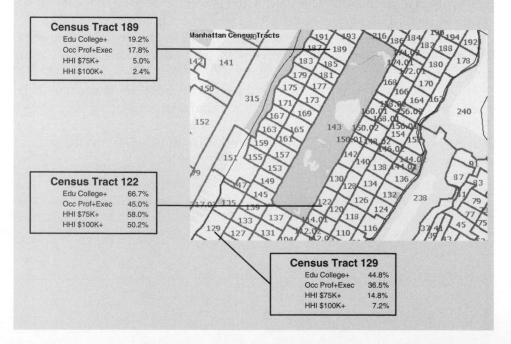

| Census Tract 189 | |
| --- | --- |
| Edu College+ | 19.2% |
| Occ Prof+Exec | 17.8% |
| HHI $75K+ | 5.0% |
| HHI $100K+ | 2.4% |

| Census Tract 122 | |
| --- | --- |
| Edu College+ | 66.7% |
| Occ Prof+Exec | 45.0% |
| HHI $75K+ | 58.0% |
| HHI $100K+ | 50.2% |

| Census Tract 129 | |
| --- | --- |
| Edu College+ | 44.8% |
| Occ Prof+Exec | 36.5% |
| HHI $75K+ | 14.8% |
| HHI $100K+ | 7.2% |

**DATA BY CENSUS TRACT** *(continued)*

One philosophy of marketing is based on the old proverb "birds of a feather flock together." That is, people with similar interests and tastes live in similar areas (whether voluntarily or because of historical patterns of discrimination). According to this philosophy, it is a good idea to market to people where you already have customers and in similar areas. Census information can be valuable, both for understanding where concentrations of customers are located and for determining the profile of similar areas.

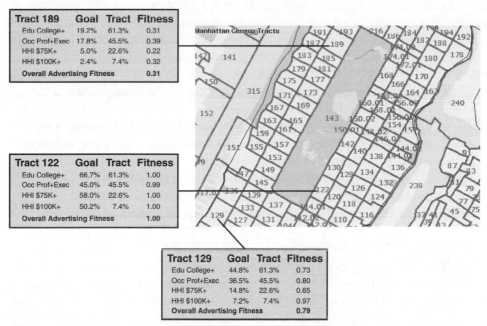

| Tract 189 | Goal | Tract | Fitness |
|---|---|---|---|
| Edu College+ | 19.2% | 61.3% | 0.31 |
| Occ Prof+Exec | 17.8% | 45.5% | 0.39 |
| HHI $75K+ | 5.0% | 22.6% | 0.22 |
| HHI $100K+ | 2.4% | 7.4% | 0.32 |
| Overall Advertising Fitness | | | 0.31 |

| Tract 122 | Goal | Tract | Fitness |
|---|---|---|---|
| Edu College+ | 66.7% | 61.3% | 1.00 |
| Occ Prof+Exec | 45.0% | 45.5% | 0.99 |
| HHI $75K+ | 58.0% | 22.6% | 1.00 |
| HHI $100K+ | 50.2% | 7.4% | 1.00 |
| Overall Advertising Fitness | | | 1.00 |

| Tract 129 | Goal | Tract | Fitness |
|---|---|---|---|
| Edu College+ | 44.8% | 61.3% | 0.73 |
| Occ Prof+Exec | 36.5% | 45.5% | 0.80 |
| HHI $75K+ | 14.8% | 22.6% | 0.65 |
| HHI $100K+ | 7.2% | 7.4% | 0.97 |
| Overall Advertising Fitness | | | 0.79 |

**Figure 4.1**  Example of calculating readership fitness for three census tracts in Manhattan.

# Data Mining to Improve Direct Marketing Campaigns

Advertising can be used to reach prospects about whom nothing is known as individuals. Direct marketing requires at least a tiny bit of additional information such as a name and address or a phone number or an email address. Where there is more information, there are also more opportunities for data mining. At the most basic level, data mining can be used to improve targeting by selecting which people to contact.

Actually, the first level of targeting does not require data mining, only data. In the United States, and to a lesser extent in many other countries, there is quite a bit of data available about a large proportion of the population. In many countries, there are companies that compile and sell household-level data on all sorts of things including income, number of children, education level, and even hobbies. Some of this data is collected from public records. Home purchases, marriages, births, and deaths are matters of public record that can be gathered from county courthouses and registries of deeds. Other data is gathered from product registration forms. Some is imputed using models. The rules governing the use of this data for marketing purposes vary from country to country. In some, data can be sold by address, but not by name. In others data may be used only for certain approved purposes. In some countries, data may be used with few restrictions, but only a limited number of households are covered. In the United States, some data, such as medical records, is completely off limits. Some data, such as credit history, can only be used for certain approved purposes. Much of the rest is unrestricted.

**WARNING** The United States is unusual in both the extent of commercially available household data and the relatively few restrictions on its use. Although household data is available in many countries, the rules governing its use differ. There are especially strict rules governing transborder transfers of personal data. Before planning to use houshold data for marketing, look into its availability in your market and the legal restrictions on making use of it.

Household-level data can be used directly for a first rough cut at segmentation based on such things as income, car ownership, or presence of children. The problem is that even after the obvious filters have been applied, the remaining pool can be very large relative to the number of prospects likely to respond. Thus, a principal application of data mining to prospects is targeting—finding the prospects most likely to actually respond to an offer.

## Response Modeling

Direct marketing campaigns typically have response rates measured in the single digits. Response models are used to improve response rates by identifying prospects who are more likely to respond to a direct solicitation. The most useful response models provide an actual estimate of the likelihood of response, but this is not a strict requirement. Any model that allows prospects to be ranked by likelihood of response is sufficient. Given a ranked list, direct marketers can increase the percentage of responders reached by campaigns by mailing or calling people near the top of the list.

The following sections describe several ways that model scores can be used to improve direct marketing. This discussion is independent of the data mining techniques used to generate the scores. It is worth noting, however, that many of the data mining techniques in this book can and have been applied to response modeling.

According to the Direct Marketing Association, an industry group, a typical mailing of 100,000 pieces costs about $100,000 dollars, although the price can vary considerably depending on the complexity of the mailing. Of that, some of the costs, such as developing the creative content, preparing the artwork, and initial setup for printing, are independent of the size of the mailing. The rest of the cost varies directly with the number of pieces mailed. Mailing lists of known mail order responders or active magazine subscribers can be purchased on a price per thousand names basis. Mail shop production costs and postage are charged on a similar basis. The larger the mailing, the less important the fixed costs become. For ease of calculation, the examples in this book assume that it costs one dollar to reach one person with a direct mail campaign. This is not an unreasonable estimate, although simple mailings cost less and very fancy mailings cost more.

## Optimizing Response for a Fixed Budget

The simplest way to make use of model scores is to use them to assign ranks. Once prospects have been ranked by a propensity-to-respond score, the prospect list can be sorted so that those most likely to respond are at the top of the list and those least likely to respond are at the bottom. Many modeling techniques can be used to generate response scores including regression models, decision trees, and neural networks.

Sorting a list makes sense whenever there is neither time nor budget to reach all prospects. If some people must be left out, it makes sense to leave out the ones who are least likely to respond. Not all businesses feel the need to leave out prospects. A local cable company may consider every household in its town to be a prospect and it may have the capacity to write or call every one of those households several times a year. When the marketing plan calls for making identical offers to every prospect, there is not much need for response modeling! However, data mining may still be useful for selecting the proper messages and to predict how prospects are likely to behave as customers.

A more likely scenario is that the marketing budget does not allow the same level of engagement with every prospect. Consider a company with 1 million names on its prospect list and $300,000 to spend on a marketing campaign that has a cost of one dollar per contact. This company, which we call the Simplifying Assumptions Corporation (or SAC for short), can maximize the number of responses it gets for its $300,000 expenditure by scoring the prospect list with a response model and sending its offer to the prospects with the top 300,000 scores. The effect of this action is illustrated in Figure 4.2.

## ROC CURVES

Models are used to produce scores. When a cutoff score is used to decide which customers to include in a campaign, the customers are, in effect, being classified into two groups—those likely to respond, and those not likely to respond. One way of evaluating a classification rule is to examine its error rates. In a binary classification task, the overall misclassification rate has two components, the false positive rate, and the false negative rate. Changing the cutoff score changes the proportion of the two types of error. For a response model where a higher score indicates a higher liklihood to respond, choosing a high score as the cutoff means fewer false positive (people labled as responders who do not respond) and more false negatives (people labled as nonresponders who would respond).

An ROC curve is used to represent the relationship of the false-positive rate to the false-negative rate of a test as the cutoff score varies. The letters ROC stand for "Receiver Operating Characteristics" a name that goes back to the curve's origins in World War II when it was developed to assess the ability of radar operators to identify correctly a blip on the radar screen , whether the blip was an enemy ship or something harmless. Today, ROC curves are more likely to used by medical researchers to evaluate medical tests. The false positive rate is plotted on the X-axis and one minus the false negative rate is plotted on the Y-axis. The ROC curve in the following figure

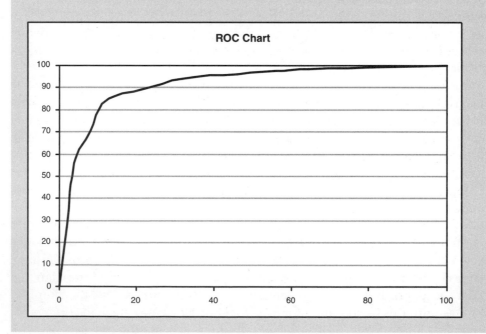

## ROC CURVES (continued)

Reflects a test with the error profile represented by the following table:

| FN | 0 | 2 | 4 | 8 | 12 | 22 | 32 | 46 | 60 | 80 | 100 |
|---|---|---|---|---|---|---|---|---|---|---|---|
| FP | 100 | 72 | 44 | 30 | 16 | 11 | 6 | 4 | 2 | 1 | 0 |

Choosing a cutoff for the model score such that there are very few false positives, leads to a high rate of false negatives and vice versa. A good model (or medical test) has some scores that are good at discriminating between outcomes, thereby reducing both kinds of error. When this is true, the ROC curve bulges towards the upper-left corner. The area under the ROC curve is a measure of the model's ability to differentiate between two outcomes. This measure is called *discrimination.* A perfect test has discrimination of 1 and a useless test for two outcomes has discrimination 0.5 since that is the area under the diagonal line that represents no model.

ROC curves tend to be less useful for marketing applications than in some other domains. One reason is that the false positive rates are so high and the false negative rates so low that even a large change in the cutoff score does not change the shape of the curve much.

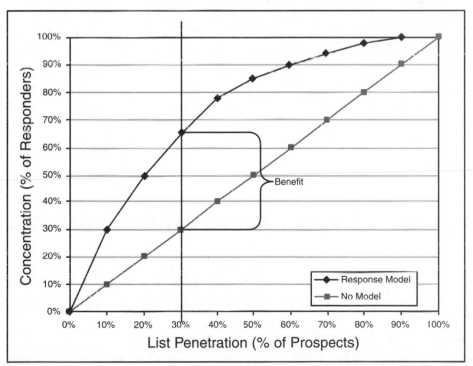

**Figure 4.2** A cumulative gains or concentration chart shows the benefit of using a model.

The upper, curved line plots the *concentration*, the percentage of all responders captured as more and more of the prospects are included in the campaign. The straight diagonal line is there for comparison. It represents what happens with no model so the concentration does not vary as a function of penetration. Mailing to 30 percent of the prospects chosen at random would find 30 percent of the responders. With the model, mailing to the top 30 percent of prospects finds 65 percent of the responders. The ratio of concentration to penetration is the lift. The difference between these two lines is the *benefit*. Lift was discussed in the previous chapter. Benefit is discussed in a sidebar.

The model pictured here has lift of 2.17 at the third decile, meaning that using the model, SAC will get twice as many responders for its expenditure of $300,000 than it would have received by mailing to 30 percent of its one million prospects at random.

## Optimizing Campaign Profitability

There is no doubt that doubling the response rate to a campaign is a desirable outcome, but how much is it actually worth? Is the campaign even profitable? Although lift is a useful way of comparing models, it does not answer these important questions. To address profitability, more information is needed. In particular, calculating profitability requires information on revenues as well as costs. Let's add a few more details to the SAC example.

The Simplifying Assumptions Corporation sells a single product for a single price. The price of the product is $100. The total cost to SAC to manufacture, warehouse and distribute the product is $55 dollars. As already mentioned, it costs one dollar to reach a prospect. There is now enough information to calculate the value of a response. The gross value of each response is $100. The net value of each response takes into account the costs associated with the response ($55 for the cost of goods and $1 for the contact) to achieve net revenue of $44 per response. This information is summarized in Table 4.3.

**Table 4.3**   Profit/Loss Matrix for the Simplifying Assumptions Corporation

| MAILED | RESPONDED | |
|---|---|---|
| | Yes | No |
| Yes | $44 | $–1 |
| No | $0 | $0 |

**BENEFIT**

Concentration charts, such as the one pictured in Figure 4.2, are usually discussed in terms of lift. Lift measures the relationship of concentration to penetration and is certainly a useful way of comparing the performance of two models at a given depth in the prospect list. However, it fails to capture another concept that seems intuitively important when looking at the chart—namely, how far apart are the lines, and at what penetration are they farthest apart?

Our colleague, the statistician Will Potts, gives the name *benefit* to the difference between concentration and penetration. Using his nomenclature, the point where this difference is maximized is the *point of maximum benefit*. Note that the point of maximum benefit does not correspond to the point of highest lift. Lift is always maximized at the left edge of the concentration chart where the concentration is highest and the slope of the curve is steepest.

The point of maximum benefit is a bit more interesting. To explain some of its useful properties this sidebar makes reference to some things (such ROC curves and KS tests) that are not explained in the main body of the book. Each bulleted point is a formal statement about the maximum benefit point on the concentration curve. The formal statements are followed by informal explanations.

◆ The maximum benefit is proportional to the maximum distance between the cumulative distribution functions of the probabilities in each class.

What this means is that the model score that cuts the prospect list at the penetration where the benefit is greatest is also the score that maximizes the Kolmogorov-Smirnov (KS) statistic. The KS test is popular among some statisticians, especially in the financial services industry. It was developed as a test of whether two distributions are different. Splitting the list at the point of maximum benefit results in a "good list" and a "bad list" whose distributions of responders are maximally separate from each other and from the population. In this case, the "good list" has a maximum proportion of responders and the "bad list" has a minimum proportion.

◆ The maximum benefit point on the concentration curve corresponds to the maximum perpendicular distance between the corresponding ROC curve and the no-model line.

The ROC curve resembles the more familiar concentration or cumulative gains chart, so it is not surprising that there is a relationship between them. As explained in another sidebar, the ROC curve shows the trade-off between two types of misclassification error. The maximum benefit point on the cumulative gains chart corresponds to a point on the ROC curve where the separation between the classes is maximized.

◆ The maximum benefit point corresponds to the decision rule that maximizes the unweighted average of sensitivity and specificity.

*(continued)*

---

**BENEFIT** *(continued)*

As used in the medical world, *sensitivity* is the proportion of true positives among people who get a positive result on a test. In other words, it is the true positives divided by the sum of the true positives and false positives. Sensitivity measures the likelihood that a diagnosis based on the test is correct. *Specificity* is the proportion of true negatives among people who get a negative result on the test. A good test should be both sensitive and specific. The maximum benefit point is the cutoff that maximizes the average of these two measures. In Chapter 8, these concepts go by the names *recall* and *precision*, the terminology used in information retrieval. Recall measures the number of articles on the correct topic returned by a Web search or other text query. Precision measures the percentage of the returned articles that are on the correct topic.

◆ The maximum benefit point corresponds to a decision rule that minimizes the expected loss assuming the misclassification costs are inversely proportional to the prevalence of the target classes.

One way of evaluating classification rules is to assign a cost to each type of misclassification and compare rules based on that cost. Whether they represent responders, defaulters, fraudsters, or people with a particular disease, the rare cases are generally the most interesting so missing one of them is more costly than misclassifying one of the common cases. Under that assumption, the maximum benefit picks a good classification rule.

---

This table says that if a prospect is contacted and responds, the company makes forty-four dollars. If a prospect is contacted, but fails to respond, the company loses $1. In this simplified example, there is neither cost nor benefit in choosing not to contact a prospect. A more sophisticated analysis might take into account the fact that there is an opportunity cost to not contacting a prospect who would have responded, that even a nonresponder may become a better prospect as a result of the contact through increased brand awareness, and that responders may have a higher lifetime value than indicated by the single purchase. Apart from those complications, this simple profit and loss matrix can be used to translate the response to a campaign into a profit figure. Ignoring campaign overhead fixed costs, if one prospect responds for every 44 who fail to respond, the campaign breaks even. If the response rate is better than that, the campaign is profitable.

**WARNING** If the cost of a failed contact is set too low, the profit and loss matrix suggests contacting everyone. This may not be a good idea for other reasons. It could lead to prospects being bombarded with innapropriate offers.

## How the Model Affects Profitability

How does the model whose lift and benefit are characterized by Figure 4.2 affect the profitability of a campaign? The answer depends on the start-up cost for the campaign, the underlying prevalence of responders in the population and on the cutoff penetration of people contacted. Recall that SAC had a budget of $300,000. Assume that the underlying prevalence of responders in the population is 1 percent. The budget is enough to contact 300,000 prospects, or 30 percent of the prospect pool. At a depth of 30 percent, the model provides lift of about 2, so SAC can expect twice as many responders as they would have without the model. In this case, twice as many means 2 percent instead of 1 percent, yielding 6,000 (2% * 300,000) responders each of whom is worth $44 in net revenue. Under these assumptions, SAC grosses $600,000 and nets $264,000 from responders. Meanwhile, 98 percent of prospects or 294,000 do not respond. Each of these costs a dollar, so SAC loses $30,000 on the campaign.

Table 4.4 shows the data used to generate the concentration chart in Figure 4.2. It suggests that the campaign could be made profitable by spending less money to contact fewer prospects while getting a better response rate. Mailing to only 10,000 prospects, or the top 10 percent of the prospect list, achieves a lift of 3. This turns the underlying response rate of 1 percent into a response rate of 3 percent. In this scenario, 3,000 people respond yielding revenue of $132,000. There are now 97,000 people who fail to respond and each of them costs one dollar. The resulting profit is $35,000. Better still, SAC has $200,000 left in the marketing budget to use on another campaign or to improve the offer made in this one, perhaps increasing response still more.

**Table 4.4**  Lift and Cumulative Gains by Decile

| PENETRATION | GAINS | CUMULATIVE GAINS | LIFT |
|---|---|---|---|
| 0% | 0% | 0% | 0 |
| 10% | 30% | 30% | 3.000 |
| 20% | 20% | 50% | 2.500 |
| 30% | 15% | 65% | 2.167 |
| 40% | 13% | 78% | 1.950 |
| 50% | 7% | 85% | 1.700 |
| 60% | 5% | 90% | 1.500 |
| 70% | 4% | 94% | 1.343 |
| 80% | 4% | 96% | 1.225 |
| 90% | 2% | 100% | 1.111 |
| 100% | 0% | 100% | 1.000 |

A smaller, better-targeted campaign can be more profitable than a larger and more expensive one. Lift increases as the list gets smaller, so is smaller always better? The answer is no because the absolute revenue decreases as the number of responders decreases. As an extreme example, assume the model can generate lift of 100 by finding a group with 100 percent response rate when the underlying response rate is 1 percent. That sounds fantastic, but if there are only 10 people in the group, they are still only worth $440. Also, a more realistic example would include some up-front fixed costs. Figure 4.3 shows what happens with the assumption that there is a $20,000 fixed cost for the campaign in addition to the cost of $1 per contact, revenue of $44 per response, and an underlying response rate of 1 percent. The campaign is only profitable for a small range of file penetrations around 10 percent.

Using the model to optimize the profitability of a campaign seems more attractive than simply using it to pick whom to include on a mailing or call list of predetermined size, but the approach is not without pitfalls. For one thing, the results are dependent on the campaign cost, the response rate, and the revenue per responder, none of which are known prior to running the campaign. In the example, these were known, but in real life, they can only be estimated. It would only take a small variation in any one of these to turn the campaign in the example above completely unprofitable or to make it profitable over a much larger range of deciles.

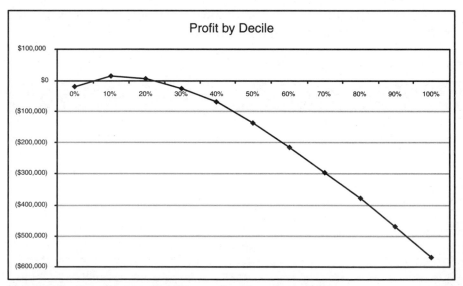

**Figure 4.3** Campaign profitability as a function of penetration.

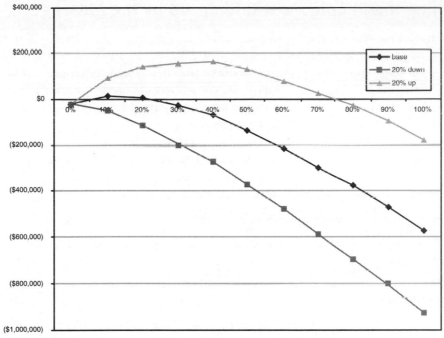

**Figure 4.4** A 20 percent variation in response rate, cost, and revenue per responder has a large effect on the profitability of a campaign.

Figure 4.4 shows what would happen to this campaign if the assumptions on cost, response rate, and revenue were all off by 20 percent. Under the pessimistic scenario, the best that can be achieved is a loss of $20,000. Under the optimistic scenario, the campaign achieves maximum profitability of $161,696 at 40 percent penetration. Estimates of cost tend to be fairly accurate since they are based on postage rates, printing charges, and other factors that can be determined in advance. Estimates of response rates and revenues are usually little more than guesses. So, while optimizing a campaign for profitability sounds appealing, it is unlikely to be possible in practice without conducting an actual test campaign. Modeling campaign profitability in advance is primarily a what-if analysis to determine likely profitability bounds based on various assumptions. Although optimizing a campaign in advance is not particularly useful, it can be useful to measure the results of a campaign after it has been run. However, to do this effectively, there need to be customers included in the campaign with a full range of response scores—even customers from lower deciles.

**WARNING** The profitability of a campaign depends on so many factors that can only be estimated in advance that the only reliable way to do it is to use an actual market test.

## Reaching the People Most Influenced by the Message

One of the more subtle simplifying assumptions made so far is that when a model with good lift is identifying people who respond to the offer. Since these people receive an offer and proceed to make purchases at a higher rate than other people, the assumption seems to be confirmed. There is another possibility, however: The model could simply be identifying people who are likely to buy the product with or without the offer.

This is not a purely theoretical concern. A large bank, for instance, did a direct mail campaign to encourage customers to open investment accounts. Their analytic group developed a model for response for the mailing. They went ahead and tested the campaign, using three groups:

- *Control group*: A group chosen at random to receive the mailing.

- *Test group*: A group chosen by modeled response scores to receive the mailing.

- *Holdout group*: A group chosen by model scores who did not receive the mailing.

The models did quite well. That is, the customers who had high model scores did indeed respond at a higher rate than the control group and customers with lower scores. However, customers in the holdout group also responded at the same rate as customers in the test group.

What was happening? The model worked correctly to identify people interested in such accounts. However, every part of the bank was focused on getting customers to open investment accounts—broadcast advertising, posters in branches, messages on the Web, training for customer service staff. The direct mail was drowned in the noise from all the other channels, and turned out to be unnecessary.

**TIP** To test whether both a model and the campaign it supports are effective, track the relationship of response rate to model score among prospects in a holdout group who are not part of the campaign as well as among prospects who are included in the campaign.

The goal of a marketing campaign is to change behavior. In this regard, reaching a prospect who is going to purchase anyway is little more effective than reaching a prospect who will not purchase despite having received the offer. A group identified as likely responders may also be less likely to be influenced by a marketing message. Their membership in the target group means that they are likely to have been exposed to many similar messages in the past from competitors. They are likely to already have the product or a close substitute or to be firmly entrenched in their refusal to purchase it. A marketing message may make more of a difference with people who have not heard it all before. Segments with the highest scores might have responded anyway, even without the marketing investment. This leads to the almost paradoxical conclusion that the segments with the highest scores in a response model may not provide the biggest return on a marketing investment.

## Differential Response Analysis

The way out of this dilemma is to directly model the actual goal of the campaign, which is not simply reaching prospects who then make purchases. The goal should be reaching prospects who are more likely to make purchases because of having been contacted. This is known as *differential response analysis*.

Differential response analysis starts with a treated group and a control group. If the treatment has the desired effect, overall response will be higher in the treated group than in the control group. The object of differential response analysis is to find segments where the difference in response between the treated and untreated groups is greatest. Quadstone's marketing analysis software has a module that performs this differential response analysis (which they call "uplift analysis") using a slightly modified decision tree as illustrated in Figure 4.5.

The tree in the illustration is based on the response data from a test mailing, shown in Table 4.5. The data tabulates the take-up rate by age and sex for an advertised service for a treated group that received a mailing and a control group that did not.

It doesn't take much data mining to see that the group with the highest response rate is young men who received the mailing, followed by old men who received the mailing. Does that mean that a campaign for this service should be aimed primarily at men? Not if the goal is to maximize the number of new customers who would not have signed up without prompting. Men included in the campaign do sign up for the service in greater numbers than women, but men are more likely to purchase the service in any case. The differential response tree makes it clear that the group most affected by the campaign is old women. This group is not at all likely (0.4 percent) to purchase the service without prompting, but with prompting they experience a more than tenfold increase in purchasing.

**Table 4.5**  Response Data from a Test Mailing

| | CONTROL GROUP | | TREATED (MAILED TO) GROUP | |
| --- | --- | --- | --- | --- |
| | YOUNG | OLD | YOUNG | OLD |
| women | 0.8% | 0.4% | 4.1% (↑3.3) | 4.6% (↑4.2) |
| men | 2.8% | 3.3% | 6.2% (↑3.4) | 5.2% (↑1.9) |

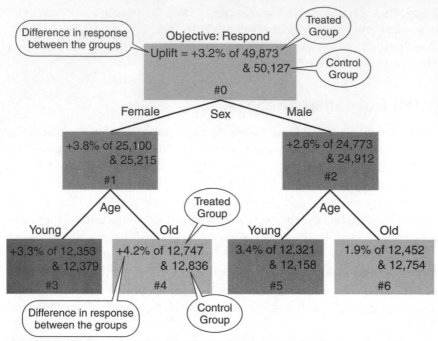

**Figure 4.5** Quadstone's differential response tree tries to maximize the difference in response between the treated group and a control group.

# Using Current Customers to Learn About Prospects

A good way to find good prospects is to look in the same places that today's best customers came from. That means having some of way of determining who the best customers are today. It also means keeping a record of how current customers were acquired and what they looked like at the time of acquisition.

Of course, the danger of relying on current customers to learn where to look for prospects is that the current customers reflect past marketing decisions. Studying current customers will not suggest looking for new prospects anyplace that hasn't already been tried. Nevertheless, the performance of current customers is a great way to evaluate the existing acquisition channels. For prospecting purposes, it is important to know what current customers looked like back when they were prospects themselves. Ideally you should:

- Start tracking customers before they become customers.
- Gather information from new customers at the time they are acquired.
- Model the relationship between acquisition-time data and future outcomes of interest.

The following sections provide some elaboration.

## Start Tracking Customers before They Become Customers

It is a good idea to start recording information about prospects even before they become customers. Web sites can accomplish this by issuing a cookie each time a visitor is seen for the first time and starting an anonymous profile that remembers what the visitor did. When the visitor returns (using the same browser on the same computer), the cookie is recognized and the profile is updated. When the visitor eventually becomes a customer or registered user, the activity that led up to that transition becomes part of the customer record.

Tracking responses and responders is good practice in the offline world as well. The first critical piece of information to record is the fact that the prospect responded at all. Data describing who responded and who did not is a necessary ingredient of future response models. Whenever possible, the response data should also include the marketing action that stimulated the response, the channel through which the response was captured, and when the response came in.

Determining which of many marketing messages stimulated the response can be tricky. In some cases, it may not even be possible. To make the job easier, response forms and catalogs include identifying codes. Web site visits capture the referring link. Even advertising campaigns can be distinguished by using different telephone numbers, post office boxes, or Web addresses.

Depending on the nature of the product or service, responders may be required to provide additional information on an application or enrollment form. If the service involves an extension of credit, credit bureau information may be requested. Information collected at the beginning of the customer relationship ranges from nothing at all to the complete medical examination sometimes required for a life insurance policy. Most companies are somewhere in between.

## Gather Information from New Customers

When a prospect first becomes a customer, there is a golden opportunity to gather more information. Before the transformation from prospect to customer, any data about prospects tends to be geographic and demographic. Purchased lists are unlikely to provide anything beyond name, contact information, and list source. When an address is available, it is possible to infer other things about prospects based on characteristics of their neighborhoods. Name and address together can be used to purchase household-level information about prospects from providers of marketing data. This sort of data is useful for targeting broad, general segments such as "young mothers" or "urban teenagers" but is not detailed enough to form the basis of an individualized customer relationship.

Among the most useful fields that can be collected for future data mining are the initial purchase date, initial acquisition channel, offer responded to, initial product, initial credit score, time to respond, and geographic location. We have found these fields to be predictive a wide range of outcomes of interest such as expected duration of the relationship, bad debt, and additional purchases. These initial values should be maintained as is, rather than being overwritten with new values as the customer relationship develops.

## Acquisition-Time Variables Can Predict Future Outcomes

By recording everything that was known about a customer at the time of acquisition and then tracking customers over time, businesses can use data mining to relate acquisition-time variables to future outcomes such as customer longevity, customer value, and default risk. This information can then be used to guide marketing efforts by focusing on the channels and messages that produce the best results. For example, the survival analysis techniques described in Chapter 12 can be used to establish the mean customer lifetime for each channel. It is not uncommon to discover that some channels yield customers that last twice as long as the customers from other channels. Assuming that a customer's value per month can be estimated, this translates into an actual dollar figure for how much more valuable a typical channel A customer is than a typical channel B customer—a figure that is as valuable as the cost-per-response measures often used to rate channels.

# Data Mining for Customer Relationship Management

Customer relationship management naturally focuses on established customers. Happily, established customers are the richest source of data for mining. Best of all, the data generated by established customers reflects their actual individual behavior. Does the customer pay bills on time? Check or credit card? When was the last purchase? What product was purchased? How much did it cost? How many times has the customer called customer service? How many times have we called the customer? What shipping method does the customer use most often? How many times has the customer returned a purchase? This kind of behavioral data can be used to evaluate customers' potential value, assess the risk that they will end the relationship, assess the risk that they will stop paying their bills, and anticipate their future needs.

## Matching Campaigns to Customers

The same response model scores that are used to optimize the budget for a mailing to prospects are even more useful with existing customers where they can be used to tailor the mix of marketing messages that a company directs to its existing customers. Marketing does not stop once customers have been acquired. There are cross-sell campaigns, up-sell campaigns, usage stimulation campaigns, loyalty programs, and so on. These campaigns can be thought of as competing for access to customers.

When each campaign is considered in isolation, and all customers are given response scores for every campaign, what typically happens is that a similar group of customers gets high scores for many of the campaigns. Some customers are just more responsive than others, a fact that is reflected in the model scores. This approach leads to poor customer relationship management. The high-scoring group is bombarded with messages and becomes irritated and unresponsive. Meanwhile, other customers never hear from the company and so are not encouraged to expand their relationships.

An alternative is to send a limited number of messages to each customer, using the scores to decide which messages are most appropriate for each one. Even a customer with low scores for every offer has higher scores for some then others. In *Mastering Data Mining* (Wiley, 1999), we describe how this system has been used to personalize a banking Web site by highlighting the products and services most likely to be of interest to each customer based on their banking behavior.

## Segmenting the Customer Base

Customer segmentation is a popular application of data mining with established customers. The purpose of segmentation is to tailor products, services, and marketing messages to each segment. Customer segments have traditionally been based on market research and demographics. There might be a "young and single" segment or a "loyal entrenched segment." The problem with segments based on market research is that it is hard to know how to apply them to all the customers who were not part of the survey. The problem with customer segments based on demographics is that not all "young and singles" or "empty nesters" actually have the tastes and product affinities ascribed to their segment. The data mining approach is to identify behavioral segments.

### Finding Behavioral Segments

One way to find behavioral segments is to use the undirected clustering techniques described in Chapter 11. This method leads to clusters of similar customers but it may be hard to understand how these clusters relate to the business. In Chapter 2, there is an example of a bank successfully using automatic cluster detection to identify a segment of small business customers that were good prospects for home equity credit lines. However, that was only one of 14 clusters found and others did not have obvious marketing uses.

More typically, a business would like to perform a segmentation that places every customer into some easily described segment. Often, these segments are built with respect to a marketing goal such as subscription renewal or high spending levels. Decision tree techniques described in Chapter 6 are ideal for this sort of segmentation.

Another common case is when there are preexisting segment definition that are based on customer behavior and the data mining challenge is to identify patterns in the data that correspond to the segments. A good example is the grouping of credit card customers into segments such as "high balance revolvers" or "high volume transactors."

One very interesting application of data mining to the task of finding patterns corresponding to predefined customer segments is the system that AT&T Long Distance uses to decide whether a phone is likely to be used for business purposes.

AT&T views anyone in the United States who has a phone and is not already a customer as a potential customer. For marketing purposes, they have long maintained a list of phone numbers called the Universe List. This is as complete as possible a list of U.S. phone numbers for both AT&T and non-AT&T customers flagged as either business or residence. The original method of obtaining non-AT&T customers was to buy directories from local phone companies, and search for numbers that were not on the AT&T customer list. This was both costly and unreliable and likely to become more so as the companies supplying the directories competed more and more directly with AT&T. The original way of determining whether a number was a home or business was to call and ask.

In 1995, Corina Cortes and Daryl Pregibon, researchers at Bell Labs (then a part of AT&T) came up with a better way. AT&T, like other phone companies, collects call detail data on every call that traverses its network (they are legally mandated to keep this information for a certain period of time). Many of these calls are either made or received by noncustomers. The telephone numbers of non-customers appear in the call detail data when they dial AT&T 800 numbers and when they receive calls from AT&T customers. These records can be analyzed and scored for likelihood to be businesses based on a statistical model of businesslike behavior derived from data generated by known businesses. This score, which AT&T calls "bizocity," is used to determine which services should be marketed to the prospects.

Every telephone number is scored every day. AT&T's switches process several hundred million calls each day, representing about 65 million distinct phone numbers. Over the course of a month, they see over 300 million distinct phone numbers. Each of those numbers is given a small profile that includes the number of days since the number was last seen, the average daily minutes of use, the average time between appearances of the number on the network, and the bizocity score.

The bizocity score is generated by a regression model that takes into account the length of calls made and received by the number, the time of day that calling peaks, and the proportion of calls the number makes to known businesses. Each day's new data adjusts the score. In practice, the score is a weighted average over time with the most recent data counting the most.

Bizocity can be combined with other information in order to address particular business segments. One segment of particular interest in the past is home businesses. These are often not recognized as businesses even by the local phone company that issued the number. A phone number with high bizocity that is at a residential address or one that has been flagged as residential by the local phone company is a good candidate for services aimed at people who work at home.

### Tying Market Research Segments to Behavioral Data

One of the big challenges with traditional survey-based market research is that it provides a lot of information about a few customers. However, to use the results of market research effectively often requires understanding the characteristics of all customers. That is, market research may find interesting segments of customers. These then need to be projected onto the existing customer base using available data. Behavioral data can be particularly useful for this; such behavioral data is typically summarized from transaction and billing histories. One requirement of the market research is that customers need to be identified so the behavior of the market research participants is known.

Most of the directed data mining techniques discussed in this book can be used to build a classification model to assign people to segments based on available data. All that is needed is a training set of customers who have already been classified. How well this works depends largely on the extent to which the customer segments are actually supported by customer behavior.

## Reducing Exposure to Credit Risk

Learning to avoid bad customers (and noticing when good customers are about to turn bad) is as important as holding on to good customers. Most companies whose business exposes them to consumer credit risk do credit screening of customers as part of the acquisition process, but risk modeling does not end once the customer has been acquired.

### Predicting Who Will Default

Assessing the credit risk on existing customers is a problem for any business that provides a service that customers pay for in arrears. There is always the chance that some customers will receive the service and then fail to pay for it.

Nonrepayment of debt is one obvious example; newspapers subscriptions, telephone service, gas and electricity, and cable service are among the many services that are usually paid for only after they have been used.

Of course, customers who fail to pay for long enough are eventually cut off. By that time they may owe large sums of money that must be written off. With early warning from a predictive model, a company can take steps to protect itself. These steps might include limiting access to the service or decreasing the length of time between a payment being late and the service being cut off.

Involuntary churn, as termination of services for nonpayment is sometimes called, can be modeled in multiple ways. Often, involuntary churn is considered as a binary outcome in some fixed amount of time, in which case techniques such as logistic regression and decision trees are appropriate. Chapter 12 shows how this problem can also be viewed as a survival analysis problem, in effect changing the question from "Will the customer fail to pay next month?" to "How long will it be until half the customers have been lost to involuntary churn?"

One of the big differences between voluntary churn and involuntary churn is that involuntary churn often involves complicated business processes, as bills go through different stages of being late. Over time, companies may tweak the rules that guide the processes to control the amount of money that they are owed. When looking for accurate numbers in the near term, modeling each step in the business processes may be the best approach.

### Improving Collections

Once customers have stopped paying, data mining can aid in collections. Models are used to forecast the amount that can be collected and, in some cases, to help choose the collection strategy. Collections is basically a type of sales. The company tries to sell its delinquent customers on the idea of paying its bills instead of some other bill. As with any sales campaign, some prospective payers will be more receptive to one type of message and some to another.

## Determining Customer Value

Customer value calculations are quite complex and although data mining has a role to play, customer value calculations are largely a matter of getting financial definitions right. A seemingly simple statement of customer value is the total revenue due to the customer minus the total cost of maintaining the customer. But how much revenue should be attributed to a customer? Is it what he or she has spent in total to date? What he or she spent this month? What we expect him or her to spend over the next year? How should indirect revenues such as advertising revenue and list rental be allocated to customers?

Costs are even more problematic. Businesses have all sorts of costs that may be allocated to customers in peculiar ways. Even ignoring allocated costs and looking only at direct costs, things can still be pretty confusing. Is it fair to blame customers for costs over which they have no control? Two Web customers order the exact same merchandise and both are promised free delivery. The one that lives farther from the warehouse may cost more in shipping, but is she really a less valuable customer? What if the next order ships from a different location? Mobile phone service providers are faced with a similar problem. Most now advertise uniform nationwide rates. The providers' costs are far from uniform when they do not own the entire network. Some of the calls travel over the company's own network. Others travel over the networks of competitors who charge high rates. Can the company increase customer value by trying to discourage customers from visiting certain geographic areas?

Once all of these problems have been sorted out, and a company has agreed on a definition of *retrospective* customer value, data mining comes into play in order to estimate *prospective* customer value. This comes down to estimating the revenue a customer will bring in per unit time and then estimating the customer's remaining lifetime. The second of these problems is the subject of Chapter 12.

## Cross-selling, Up-selling, and Making Recommendations

With existing customers, a major focus of customer relationship management is increasing customer profitability through cross-selling and up-selling. Data mining is used for figuring out what to offer to whom and when to offer it.

### Finding the Right Time for an Offer

Charles Schwab, the investment company, discovered that customers generally open accounts with a few thousand dollars even if they have considerably more stashed away in savings and investment accounts. Naturally, Schwab would like to attract some of those other balances. By analyzing historical data, they discovered that customers who transferred large balances into investment accounts usually did so during the first few months after they opened their first account. After a few months, there was little return on trying to get customers to move in large balances. The window was closed. As a results of learning this, Schwab shifted its strategy from sending a constant stream of solicitations throughout the customer life cycle to concentrated efforts during the first few months.

A major newspaper with both daily and Sunday subscriptions noticed a similar pattern. If a Sunday subscriber upgrades to daily and Sunday, it usually happens early in the relationship. A customer who has been happy with just the Sunday paper for years is much less likely to change his or her habits.

### Making Recommendations

One approach to cross-selling makes use of association rules, the subject of Chapter 9. Association rules are used to find clusters of products that usually sell together or tend to be purchased by the same person over time. Customers who have purchased some, but not all of the members of a cluster are good prospects for the missing elements. This approach works for retail products where there are many such clusters to be found, but is less effective in areas such as financial services where there are fewer products and many customers have a similar mix, and the mix is often determined by product bundling and previous marketing efforts.

# Retention and Churn

Customer attrition is an important issue for any company, and it is especially important in mature industries where the initial period of exponential growth has been left behind. Not surprisingly, churn (or, to look on the bright side, retention) is a major application of data mining. We use the term churn as it is generally used in the telephone industry to refer to all types of customer attrition whether voluntary or involuntary; churn is a useful word because it is one syllable and easily used as both a noun and a verb.

## Recognizing Churn

One of the first challenges in modeling churn is deciding what it is and recognizing when it has occurred. This is harder in some industries than in others. At one extreme are businesses that deal in anonymous cash transactions. When a once loyal customer deserts his regular coffee bar for another down the block, the barista who knew the customer's order by heart may notice, but the fact will not be recorded in any corporate database. Even in cases where the customer is identified by name, it may be hard to tell the difference between a customer who has churned and one who just hasn't been around for a while. If a loyal Ford customer who buys a new F150 pickup every 5 years hasn't bought one for 6 years, can we conclude that he has defected to another brand?

Churn is a bit easier to spot when there is a monthly billing relationship, as with credit cards. Even there, however, attrition might be silent. A customer stops using the credit card, but doesn't actually cancel it. Churn is easiest to define in subscription-based businesses, and partly for that reason, churn modeling is most popular in these businesses. Long-distance companies, mobile phone service providers, insurance companies, cable companies, financial services companies, Internet service providers, newspapers, magazines, and some retailers all share a subscription model where customers have a formal, contractual relationship which must be explicitly ended.

## Why Churn Matters

Churn is important because lost customers must be replaced by new customers, and new customers are expensive to acquire and generally generate less revenue in the near term than established customers. This is especially true in mature industries where the market is fairly saturated—anyone likely to want the product or service probably already has it from somewhere, so the main source of new customers is people leaving a competitor.

Figure 4.6 illustrates that as the market becomes saturated and the response rate to acquisition campaigns goes down, the cost of acquiring new customers goes up. The chart shows how much each new customer costs for a direct mail acquisition campaign given that the mailing costs $1 and it includes an offer of $20 in some form, such as a coupon or a reduced interest rate on a credit card. When the response rate to the acquisition campaign is high, such as 5 percent, the cost of a new customer is $40. (It costs $100 dollars to reach 100 people, five of whom respond at a cost of $20 dollars each. So, five new customers cost $200 dollars.) As the response rate drops, the cost increases rapidly. By the time the response rate drops to 1 percent, each new customer costs $200. At some point, it makes sense to spend that money holding on to existing customers rather than attracting new ones.

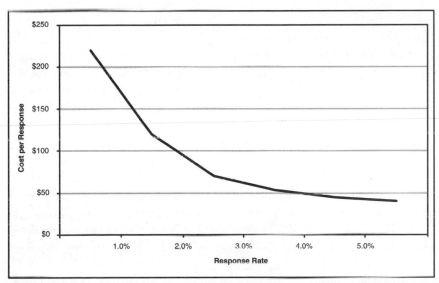

**Figure 4.6** As the response rate to an acquisition campaign goes down, the cost per customer acquired goes up.

Retention campaigns can be very effective, but also very expensive. A mobile phone company might offer an expensive new phone to customers who renew a contract. A credit card company might lower the interest rate. The problem with these offers is that any customer who is made the offer will accept it. Who wouldn't want a free phone or a lower interest rate? That means that many of the people accepting the offer would have remained customers even without it. The motivation for building churn models is to figure out who is most at risk for attrition so as to make the retention offers to high-value customers who might leave without the extra incentive.

## Different Kinds of Churn

Actually, the discussion of why churn matters assumes that churn is voluntary. Customers, of their own free will, decide to take their business elsewhere. This type of attrition, known as *voluntary churn*, is actually only one of three possibilities. The other two are *involuntary churn* and *expected churn*.

Involuntary churn, also known as *forced attrition*, occurs when the company, rather than the customer, terminates the relationship—most commonly due to unpaid bills. *Expected churn* occurs when the customer is no longer in the target market for a product. Babies get teeth and no longer need baby food. Workers retire and no longer need retirement savings accounts. Families move away and no longer need their old local newspaper delivered to their door.

It is important not to confuse the different types of churn, but easy to do so. Consider two mobile phone customers in identical financial circumstances. Due to some misfortune, neither can afford the mobile phone service any more. Both call up to cancel. One reaches a customer service agent and is recorded as voluntary churn. The other hangs up after ten minutes on hold and continues to use the phone without paying the bill. The second customer is recorded as forced churn. The underlying problem—lack of money—is the same for both customers, so it is likely that they will both get similar scores. The model cannot predict the difference in hold times experienced by the two subscribers.

Companies that mistake forced churn for voluntary churn lose twice—once when they spend money trying to retain customers who later go bad and again in increased write-offs.

Predicting forced churn can also be dangerous. Because the treatment given to customers who are not likely to pay their bills tends to be nasty—phone service is suspended, late fees are increased, dunning letters are sent more quickly. These remedies may alienate otherwise good customers and increase the chance that they will churn voluntarily.

In many companies, voluntary churn and involuntary churn are the responsibilities of different groups. Marketing is concerned with holding on to good customers and finance is concerned with reducing exposure to bad customers.

From a data mining point of view, it is better to address both voluntary and involuntary churn together since all customers are at risk for both kinds of churn to varying degrees.

## Different Kinds of Churn Model

There are two basic approaches to modeling churn. The first treats churn as a binary outcome and predicts which customers will leave and which will stay. The second tries to estimate the customers' remaining lifetime.

### Predicting Who Will Leave

To model churn as a binary outcome, it is necessary to pick some time horizon. If the question is "Who will leave tomorrow?" the answer is hardly anyone. If the question is "Who will have left in 100 years?" the answer, in most businesses, is nearly everyone. Binary outcome churn models usually have a fairly short time horizon such as 60 or 90 days. Of course, the horizon cannot be too short or there will be no time to act on the model's predictions.

Binary outcome churn models can be built with any of the usual tools for classification including logistic regression, decision trees, and neural networks. Historical data describing a customer population at one time is combined with a flag showing whether the customers were still active at some later time. The modeling task is to discriminate between those who left and those who stayed.

The outcome of a binary churn model is typically a score that can be used to rank customers in order of their likelihood of churning. The most natural score is simply the probability that the customer will leave within the time horizon used for the model. Those with voluntary churn scores above a certain threshold can be included in a retention program. Those with involuntary churn scores above a certain threshold can be placed on a watch list.

Typically, the predictors of churn turn out to be a mixture of things that were known about the customer at acquisition time, such as the acquisition channel and initial credit class, and things that occurred during the customer relationship such as problems with service, late payments, and unexpectedly high or low bills. The first class of churn drivers provides information on how to lower future churn by acquiring fewer churn-prone customers. The second class of churn drivers provides insight into how to reduce the churn risk for customers who are already present.

### Predicting How Long Customers Will Stay

The second approach to churn modeling is the less common method, although it has some attractive features. In this approach, the goal is to figure out how much longer a customer is likely to stay. This approach provides more information than simply whether the customer is expected to leave within 90 days. Having an estimate of remaining customer tenure is a necessary ingredient for a customer lifetime value model. It can also be the basis for a customer loyalty score that defines a loyal customer as one who will remain for a long time in the future rather than one who has remained a long time up until now.

One approach to modeling customer longevity would be to take a snapshot of the current customer population, along with data on what these customers looked like when they were first acquired, and try to estimate customer tenure directly by trying to determine what long-lived customers have in common besides an early acquisition date. The problem with this approach, is that the longer customers have been around, the more different market conditions were back when they were acquired. Certainly it is not safe to assume that the characteristics of someone who got a cellular subscription in 1990 are good predictors of which of today's new customers will keep their service for many years.

A better approach is to use survival analysis techniques that have been borrowed and adapted from statistics. These techniques are associated with the medical world where they are used to study patient survival rates after medical interventions and the manufacturing world where they are used to study the expected time to failure of manufactured components.

Survival analysis is explained in Chapter 12. The basic idea is to calculate for each customer (or for each group of customers that share the same values for model input variables such as geography, credit class, and acquisition channel) the probability that having made it as far as today, he or she will leave before tomorrow. For any one tenure this *hazard*, as it is called, is quite small, but it is higher for some tenures than for others. The chance that a customer will survive to reach some more distant future date can be calculated from the intervening hazards.

## Lessons Learned

The data mining techniques described in this book have applications in fields as diverse as biotechnology research and manufacturing process control. This book, however, is written for people who, like the authors, will be applying these techniques to the kinds of business problems that arise in marketing and customer relationship management. In most of the book, the focus on customer-centric applications is implicit in the choice of examples used to illustrate the techniques. In this chapter, that focus is more explicit.

Data mining is used in support of both advertising and direct marketing to identify the right audience, choose the best communications channels, and pick the most appropriate messages. Prospective customers can be compared to a profile of the intended audience and given a fitness score. Should information on individual prospects not be available, the same method can be used to assign fitness scores to geographic neighborhoods using data of the type available form the U.S. census bureau, Statistics Canada, and similar official sources in many countries.

A common application of data mining in direct modeling is response modeling. A response model scores prospects on their likelihood to respond to a direct marketing campaign. This information can be used to improve the response rate of a campaign, but is not, by itself, enough to determine campaign profitability. Estimating campaign profitability requires reliance on estimates of the underlying response rate to a future campaign, estimates of average order sizes associated with the response, and cost estimates for fulfillment and for the campaign itself. A more customer-centric use of response scores is to choose the best campaign for each customer from among a number of competing campaigns. This approach avoids the usual problem of independent, score-based campaigns, which tend to pick the same people every time.

It is important to distinguish between the ability of a model to recognize people who are interested in a product or service and its ability to recognize people who are moved to make a purchase based on a particular campaign or offer. Differential response analysis offers a way to identify the market segments where a campaign will have the greatest impact. Differential response models seek to maximize the difference in response between a treated group and a control group rather than trying to maximize the response itself.

Information about current customers can be used to identify likely prospects by finding predictors of desired outcomes in the information that was known about current customers before they became customers. This sort of analysis is valuable for selecting acquisition channels and contact strategies as well as for screening prospect lists. Companies can increase the value of their customer data by beginning to track customers from their first response, even before they become customers, and gathering and storing additional information when customers are acquired.

Once customers have been acquired, the focus shifts to customer relationship management. The data available for active customers is richer than that available for prospects and, because it is behavioral in nature rather than simply geographic and demographic, it is more predictive. Data mining is used to identify additional products and services that should be offered to customers based on their current usage patterns. It can also suggest the best time to make a cross-sell or up-sell offer.

One of the goals of a customer relationship management program is to retain valuable customers. Data mining can help identify which customers are the most valuable and evaluate the risk of voluntary or involuntary churn associated with each customer. Armed with this information, companies can target retention offers at customers who are both valuable and at risk, and take steps to protect themselves from customers who are likely to default.

From a data mining perspective, churn modeling can be approached as either a binary-outcome prediction problem or through survival analysis. There are advantages and disadvantages to both approaches. The binary outcome approach works well for a short horizon, while the survival analysis approach can be used to make forecasts far into the future and provides insight into customer loyalty and customer value as well.

# CHAPTER 5

# The Lure of Statistics: Data Mining Using Familiar Tools

For statisticians (and economists too), the term "data mining" has long had a pejorative meaning. Instead of finding useful patterns in large volumes of data, data mining has the connotation of searching for data to fit preconceived ideas. This is much like what politicians do around election time—search for data to show the success of their deeds; this is certainly not what we mean by data mining! This chapter is intended to bridge some of the gap between statisticians and data miners.

The two disciplines are very similar. Statisticians and data miners commonly use many of the same techniques, and statistical software vendors now include many of the techniques described in the next eight chapters in their software packages. Statistics developed as a discipline separate from mathematics over the past century and a half to help scientists make sense of observations and to design experiments that yield the reproducible and accurate results we associate with the scientific method. For almost all of this period, the issue was not too much data, but too little. Scientists had to figure out how to understand the world using data collected by hand in notebooks. These quantities were sometimes mistakenly recorded, illegible due to fading and smudged ink, and so on. Early statisticians were practical people who invented techniques to handle whatever problem was at hand. Statisticians are still practical people who use modern techniques as well as the tried and true.

What is remarkable and a testament to the founders of modern statistics is that techniques developed on tiny amounts of data have survived and still prove their utility. These techniques have proven their worth not only in the original domains but also in virtually all areas where data is collected, from agriculture to psychology to astronomy and even to business.

Perhaps the greatest statistician of the twentieth century was R. A. Fisher, considered by many to be the father of modern statistics. In the 1920s, before the invention of modern computers, he devised methods for designing and analyzing experiments. For two years, while living on a farm outside London, he collected various measurements of crop yields along with potential explanatory variables—amount of rain and sun and fertilizer, for instance. To understand what has an effect on crop yields, he invented new techniques (such as analysis of variance—ANOVA) and performed perhaps a million calculations on the data he collected. Although twenty-first-century computer chips easily handle many millions of calculations in a second, each of Fisher's calculations required pulling a lever on a manual calculating machine. Results trickled in slowly over weeks and months, along with sore hands and calluses.

The advent of computing power has clearly simplified some aspects of analysis, although its bigger effect is probably the wealth of data produced. Our goal is no longer to extract every last iota of possible information from each rare datum. Our goal is instead to make sense of quantities of data so large that they are beyond the ability of our brains to comprehend in their raw format.

The purpose of this chapter is to present some key ideas from statistics that have proven to be useful tools for data mining. This is intended to be neither a thorough nor a comprehensive introduction to statistics; rather, it is an introduction to a handful of useful statistical techniques and ideas. These tools are shown by demonstration, rather than through mathematical proof.

The chapter starts with an introduction to what is probably the most important aspect of applied statistics—the skeptical attitude. It then discusses looking at data through a statistician's eye, introducing important concepts and terminology along the way. Sprinkled through the chapter are examples, especially for confidence intervals and the chi-square test. The final example, using the chi-square test to understand geography and channel, is an unusual application of the ideas presented in the chapter. The chapter ends with a brief discussion of some of the differences between data miners and statisticians—differences in attitude that are more a matter of degree than of substance.

## Occam's Razor

William of Occam was a Franciscan monk born in a small English town in 1280—not only before modern statistics was invented, but also before the Renaissance and the printing press. He was an influential philosopher, theologian, and professor who expounded many ideas about many things, including church politics. As a monk, he was an ascetic who took his vow of poverty very seriously. He was also a fervent advocate of the power of reason, denying the existence of universal truths and espousing a modern philosophy that was quite different from the views of most of his contemporaries living in the Middle Ages.

What does William of Occam have to do with data mining? His name has become associated with a very simple idea. He himself explained it in Latin (the language of learning, even among the English, at the time), "*Entia non sunt multiplicanda sine necessitate.*" In more familiar English, we would say "the simpler explanation is the preferable one" or, more colloquially, "Keep it simple, stupid." Any explanation should strive to reduce the number of causes to a bare minimum. This line of reasoning is referred to as Occam's Razor and is William of Occam's gift to data analysis.

The story of William of Occam had an interesting ending. Perhaps because of his focus on the power of reason, he also believed that the powers of the church should be separate from the powers of the state—that the church should be confined to religious matters. This resulted in his opposition to the meddling of Pope John XXII in politics and eventually to his own excommunication. He eventually died in Munich during an outbreak of the plague in 1349, leaving a legacy of clear and critical thinking for future generations.

## The Null Hypothesis

Occam's Razor is very important for data mining and statistics, although statistics expresses the idea a bit differently. The *null hypothesis* is the assumption that differences among observations are due simply to chance. To give an example, consider a presidential poll that gives Candidate A 45 percent and Candidate B 47 percent. Because this data is from a poll, there are several sources of error, so the values are only approximate estimates of the popularity of each candidate. The layperson is inclined to ask, "Are these two values different?" The statistician phrases the question slightly differently, "What is the probability that these two values are really the same?"

Although the two questions are very similar, the statistician's has a bit of an attitude. This attitude is that the difference may have no significance at all and is an example of using the null hypothesis. There is an observed difference of 2 percent in this example. However, this observed value may be explained by the particular sample of people who responded. Another sample may have a difference of 2 percent in the other direction, or may have a difference of 0 percent. All are reasonably likely results from a poll. Of course, if the preferences differed by 20 percent, then sampling variation is much less likely to be the cause. Such a large difference would greatly improve the confidence that one candidate is doing better than the other, and greatly reduce the probability of the null hypothesis being true.

> **TIP**  The simplest explanation is usually the best one—even (or especially) if it does not prove the hypothesis you want to prove.

This skeptical attitude is very valuable for both statisticians and data miners. Our goal is to demonstrate results that work, and to discount the null hypothesis. One difference between data miners and statisticians is that data miners are often working with sufficiently large amounts of data that make it unnecessary to worry about the mechanics of calculating the probability of something being due to chance.

## P-Values

The null hypothesis is not merely an approach to analysis; it can also be quantified. The *p-value* is the probability that the null hypothesis is true. Remember, when the null hypothesis is true, nothing is really happening, because differences are due to chance. Much of statistics is devoted to determining bounds for the p-value.

Consider the previous example of the presidential poll. Consider that the p-value is calculated to be 60 percent (more on how this is done later in the chapter). This means that there is a 60 percent likelihood that the difference in the support for the two candidates as measured by the poll is due strictly to chance and not to the overall support in the general population. In this case, there is little evidence that the support for the two candidates is different.

Let's say the p-value is 5 percent, instead. This is a relatively small number, and it means that we are 95 percent *confident* that Candidate B is doing better than Candidate A. Confidence, sometimes called the *q-value*, is the flip side of the p-value. Generally, the goal is to aim for a confidence level of at least 90 percent, if not 95 percent or more (meaning that the corresponding p-value is less than 10 percent, or 5 percent, respectively).

These ideas—null hypothesis, p-value, and confidence—are three basic ideas in statistics. The next section carries these ideas further and introduces the statistical concept of distributions, with particular attention to the normal distribution.

## A Look at Data

A *statistic* refers to a measure taken on a sample of data. Statistics is the study of these measures and the samples they are measured on. A good place to start, then, is with such useful measures, and how to look at data.

## Looking at Discrete Values

Much of the data used in data mining is discrete by nature, rather than continuous. Discrete data shows up in the form of products, channels, regions, and descriptive information about businesses. This section discusses ways of looking at and analyzing discrete fields.

### Histograms

The most basic descriptive statistic about discrete fields is the number of times different values occur. Figure 5.1 shows a *histogram* of stop reason codes during a period of time. A histogram shows how often each value occurs in the data and can have either absolute quantities (204 times) or percentage (14.6 percent). Often, there are too many values to show in a single histogram such as this case where there are over 30 additional codes grouped into the "other" category.

In addition to the values for each category, this histogram also shows the cumulative proportion of stops, whose scale is shown on the left-hand side. Through the cumulative histogram, it is possible to see that the top three codes account for about 50 percent of stops, and the top 10, almost 90 percent. As an aesthetic note, the grid lines intersect both the left- and right-hand scales at sensible points, making it easier to read values off of the chart.

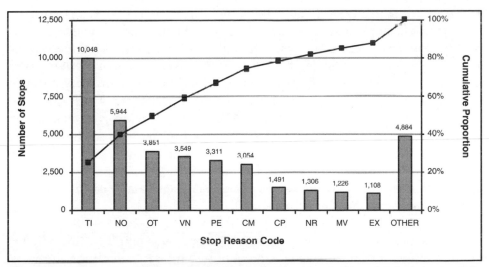

**Figure 5.1**   This example shows both a histogram (as a vertical bar chart) and cumulative proportion (as a line) on the same chart for stop reasons associated with a particular marketing effort.

## Time Series

Histograms are quite useful and easily made with Excel or any statistics package. However, histograms describe a single moment. Data mining is often concerned with what is happening over time. A key question is whether the frequency of values is constant over time.

Time series analysis requires choosing an appropriate time frame for the data; this includes not only the units of time, but also when we start counting from. Some different time frames are the beginning of a customer relationship, when a customer requests a stop, the actual stop date, and so on. Different fields belong in different time frames. For example:

- Fields describing the beginning of a customer relationship—such as original product, original channel, or original market—should be looked at by the customer's original start date.

- Fields describing the end of a customer relationship—such as last product, stop reason, or stop channel—should be looked at by the customer's stop date or the customer's tenure at that point in time.

- Fields describing events during the customer relationship—such as product upgrade or downgrade, response to a promotion, or a late payment—should be looked at by the date of the event, the customer's tenure at that point in time, or the relative time since some other event.

The next step is to plot the time series as shown in Figure 5.2. This figure has two series for stops by stop date. One shows a particular stop type over time (price increase stops) and the other, the total number of stops. Notice that the units for the time axis are in days. Although much business reporting is done at the weekly and monthly level, we prefer to look at data by day in order to see important patterns that might emerge at a fine level of granularity, patterns that might be obscured by summarization. In this case, there is a clear up and down wiggling pattern in both lines. This is due to a weekly cycle in stops. In addition, the lighter line is for the price increase related stops. These clearly show a marked increase starting in February, due to a change in pricing.

**TIP** When looking at field values over time, look at the data by day to get a feel for the data at the most granular level.

A time series chart has a wealth of information. For example, fitting a line to the data makes it possible to see and quantify long term trends, as shown in Figure 5.2. Be careful when doing this, because of seasonality. Partial years might introduce inadvertent trends, so include entire years when using a best-fit line. The trend in this figure shows an increase in stops. This may be nothing to worry about, especially since the number of customers is also increasing over this period of time. This suggests that a better measure would be the stop rate, rather than the raw number of stops.

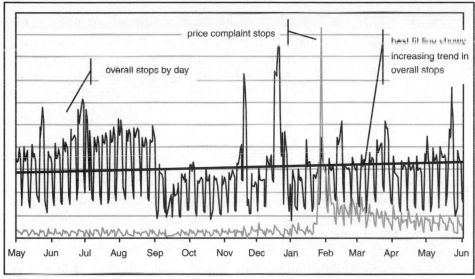

**Figure 5.2**  This chart shows two time series plotted with different scales. The dark line is for overall stops; the light line for pricing related stops shows the impact of a change in pricing strategy at the end of January.

## Standardized Values

A time series chart provides useful information. However, it does not give an idea as to whether the changes over time are expected or unexpected. For this, we need some tools from statistics.

One way of looking at a time series is as a partition of all the data, with a little bit on each day. The statistician now wants to ask a skeptical question: "Is it possible that the differences seen on each day are strictly due to chance?" This is the null hypothesis, which is answered by calculating the p-value—the probability that the variation among values could be explained by chance alone.

Statisticians have been studying this fundamental question for over a century. Fortunately, they have also devised some techniques for answering it. This is a question about *sample variation*. Each day represents a sample of stops from all the stops that occurred during the period. The variation in stops observed on different days might simply be due to an expected variation in taking random samples.

There is a basic theorem in statistics, called the Central Limit Theorem, which says the following:

*As more and more samples are taken from a population, the distribution of the averages of the samples (or a similar statistic) follows the normal distribution. The average (what statisticians call the mean) of the samples comes arbitrarily close to the average of the entire population.*

The Central Limit Theorem is actually a very deep theorem and quite interesting. More importantly, it is useful. In the case of discrete variables, such as number of customers who stop on each day, the same idea holds. The statistic used for this example is the count of the number of stops on each day, as shown earlier in Figure 5.2. (Strictly speaking, it would be better to use a proportion, such as the ratio of stops to the number of customers; this is equivalent to the count for our purposes with the assumption that the number of customers is constant over the period.)

The normal distribution is described by two parameters, the mean and the standard deviation. The mean is the average count for each day. The standard deviation is a measure of the extent to which values tend to cluster around the mean and is explained more fully later in the chapter; for now, using a function such as STDEV() in Excel or STDDEV() in SQL is sufficient. For the time series, the standard deviation is the standard deviation of the daily counts. Assuming that the values for each day were taken randomly from the stops for the entire period, the set of counts should follow a normal distribution. If they don't follow a normal distribution, then something besides chance is affecting the values. Notice that this does not tell us what is affecting the values, only that the simplest explanation, sample variation, is insufficient to explain them.

This is the motivation for *standardizing* time series values. This process produces the number of standard deviations from the average:

- Calculate the average value for all days.
- Calculate the standard deviation for all days.
- For each value, subtract the average and divide by the standard deviation to get the number of standard deviations from the average.

The purpose of standardizing the values is to test the null hypothesis. When true, the standardized values should follow the normal distribution (with an average of 0 and a standard deviation of 1), exhibiting several useful properties. First, the standardized value should take on negative values and positive values with about equal frequency. Also, when standardized, about two-thirds (68.4 percent) of the values should be between minus one and one. A bit over 95 percent of the values should be between –2 and 2. And values over 3 or less than –3 should be very, very rare—probably not visible in the data. Of course, "should" here means that the values are following the normal distribution and the null hypothesis holds (that is, all time related effects are explained by sample variation). When the null hypothesis does not hold, it is often apparent from the standardized values. The aside, "A Question of Terminology," talks a bit more about distributions, normal and otherwise.

Figure 5.3 shows the standardized values for the data in Figure 5.2. The first thing to notice is that the shape of the standardized curve is very similar to the shape of the original data; what has changed is the scale on the vertical dimension. When comparing two curves, the scales for each change. In the previous figure, overall stops were much larger than pricing stops, so the two were shown using different scales. In this case, the standardized pricing stops are towering over the standardized overall stops, even though both are on the same scale.

The overall stops in Figure 5.3 are pretty typically normal, with the following caveats. There is a large peak in December, which probably needs to be explained because the value is over four standard deviations away from the average. Also, there is a strong weekly trend. It would be a good idea to repeat this chart using weekly stops instead of daily stops, to see the variation on the weekly level.

The lighter line showing the pricing related stops clearly does not follow the normal distribution. Many more values are negative than positive. The peak is at over 13—which is way, way too high.

Standardized values, or *z-values* as they are often called, are quite useful. This example has used them for looking at values over time too see whether the values look like they were taken randomly on each day; that is, whether the variation in daily values could be explained by sampling variation. On days when the z-value is relatively high or low, then we are suspicious that something else is at work, that there is some other factor affecting the stops. For instance, the peak in pricing stops occurred because there was a change in pricing. The effect is quite evident in the daily z-values.

The z-value is useful for other reasons as well. For instance, it is one way of taking several variables and converting them to similar ranges. This can be useful for several data mining techniques, such as clustering and neural networks. Other uses of the z-value are covered in Chapter 17, which discusses data transformations.

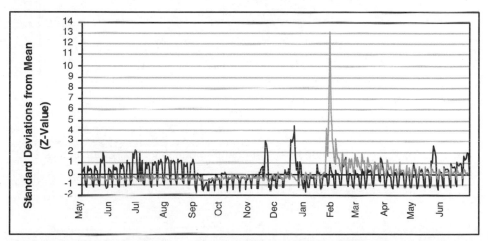

**Figure 5.3**   Standardized values make it possible to compare different groups on the same chart using the same scale; this shows overall stops and price increase related stops.

**A QUESTION OF TERMINOLOGY**

One very important idea in statistics is the idea of a distribution. For a discrete variable, a distribution is a lot like a histogram—it tells how often a given value occurs as a probability between 0 and 1. For instance, a uniform distribution says that all values are equally represented. An example of a uniform distribution would occur in a business where customers pay by credit card and the same number of customers pays with American Express, Visa, and MasterCard.

The normal distribution, which plays a very special role in statistics, is an example of a distribution for a continuous variable. The following figure shows the normal (sometimes called Gaussian or bell-shaped) distribution with a mean of 0 and a standard deviation of 1. The way to read this curve is to look at areas between two points. For a value that follows the normal distribution, the probability that the value falls between two values—for example, between 0 and 1—is the area under the curve. For the values of 0 and 1, the probability is 34.1 percent; this means that 34.1 percent of the time a variable that follows a normal distribution will take on a value within one standard deviation above the mean. Because the curve is symmetric, there is an additional 34.1% probability of being one standard deviation below the mean, and hence 68.2% probability of being within one standard deviation above the mean.

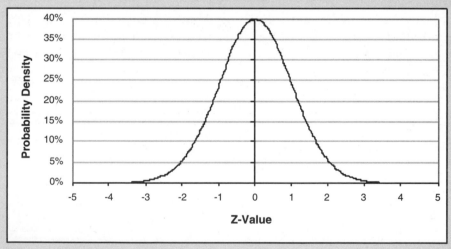

The probability density function for the normal distribution looks like the familiar bell-shaped curve.

The previous paragraph showed a picture of a bell-shaped curve and called it the normal distribution. Actually, the correct terminology is *density function* (or *probability density function*). Although this terminology derives from advanced mathematical probability theory, it makes sense. The density function gives a flavor for how "dense" a variable is. We use a density function by measuring the area under the curve between two points, rather than by reading the individual values themselves. In the case of the normal distribution, the values are densest around the 0 and less dense as we move away.

The following figure shows the function that is properly called the normal distribution. This form, ranging from 0 to 1, is also called a cumulative distribution function. Mathematically, the distribution function for a value $X$ is defined as the probability that the variable takes on a value less than or equal to $X$. Because of the "less than or equal to" characteristic, this function always starts near 0, climbs upward, and ends up close to 1. In general, the density function provides more visual clues to the human about what is going on with a distribution. Because density functions provide more information, they are often referred to as distributions, although that is technically incorrect.

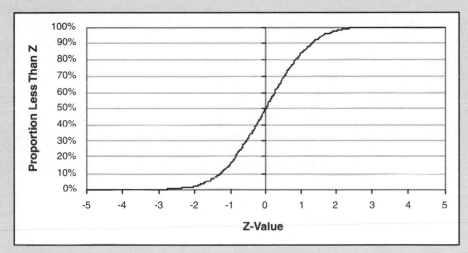

The (cumulative) distribution function for the normal distribution has an S-shape and is antisymmetric around the Y-axis.

## From Standardized Values to Probabilities

Assuming that the standardized value follows the normal distribution makes it possible to calculate the probability that the value would have occurred by chance. Actually, the approach is to calculate the probability that something further from the mean would have occurred—the p-value. The reason the exact value is not worth asking is because any given z-value has an arbitrarily small probability. Probabilities are defined on ranges of z-values as the area under the normal curve between two points.

Calculating something further from the mean might mean either of two things:

- The probability of being more than z standard deviations from the mean.

- The probability of being z standard deviations greater than the mean (or alternatively z standard deviations less than the mean).

The first is called a two-tailed distribution and the second is called a one-tailed distribution. The terminology is clear in Figure 5.4, because the tails of the distributions are being measured. The two-tailed probability is always twice as large as the one-tailed probability for z-values. Hence, the two-tailed p-value is more pessimistic than the one-tailed one; that is, the two-tailed is more likely to assume that the null hypothesis is true. If the one-tailed says the probability of the null hypothesis is 10 percent, then the two-tailed says it is 20 percent. As a default, it is better to use the two-tailed probability for calculations to be on the safe side.

The two-tailed p-value can be calculated conveniently in Excel, because there is a function called NORMSDIST, which calculates the cumulative normal distribution. Using this function, the two-tailed p-value is 2 * NORMSDIST(−ABS(z)). For a value of 2, the result is 4.6 percent. This means that there is a 4.6 percent chance of observing a value more than two standard deviations from the average—plus or minus two standard deviations from the average. Or, put another way, there is a 95.4 percent confidence that a value falling outside two standard deviations is due to something besides chance. For a precise 95 percent confidence, a bound of 1.96 can be used instead of 2. For 99 percent confidence, the limit is 2.58. The following shows the limits on the z-value for some common confidence levels:

- 90% confidence → z-value > 1.64
- 95% confidence → z-value > 1.96
- 99% confidence → z-value > 2.58
- 99.5% confidence → z-value > 2.81
- 99.9% confidence → z-value > 3.29
- 99.99% confidence → z-value > 3.89

The confidence has the property that it is close to 100 percent when the value is unlikely to be due to chance and close to 0 when it is. The signed confidence adds information about whether the value is too low or too high. When the observed value is less than the average, the signed confidence is negative.

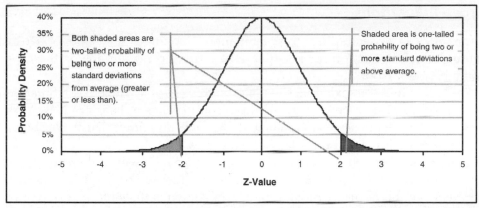

**Figure 5.4** The tail of the normal distribution answers the question: "What is the probability of getting a value of *z* or greater?"

Figure 5.5 shows the signed confidence for the data shown earlier in Figures 5.2 and 5.3, using the two-tailed probability. The shape of the signed confidence is different from the earlier shapes. The overall stops bounce around, usually remaining within reasonable bounds. The pricing-related stops, though, once again show a very distinct pattern, being too low for a long time, then peaking and descending. The signed confidence levels are bounded by 100 percent and –100 percent. In this chart, the extreme values are near 100 percent or –100 percent, and it is hard to tell the difference between 99.9 percent and 99.99999 percent. To distinguish values near the extremes, the z-values in Figure 5.3 are better than the signed confidence.

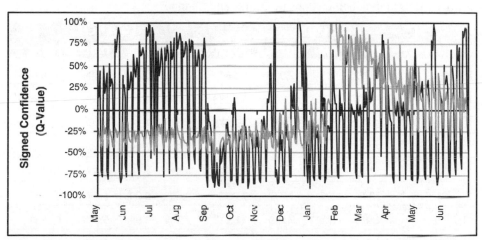

**Figure 5.5** Based on the same data from Figures 5.2 and 5.3, this chart shows the signed confidence (q-values) of the observed value based on the average and standard deviation. This sign is positive when the observed value is too high, negative when it is too low.

## Cross-Tabulations

Time series are an example of cross-tabulation—looking at the values of two or more variables at one time. For time series, the second variable is the time something occurred.

Table 5.1 shows an example used later in this chapter. The cross-tabulation shows the number of new customers from counties in southeastern New York state by three channels: telemarketing, direct mail, and other. This table shows both the raw counts and the relative frequencies.

It is possible to visualize cross-tabulations as well. However, there is a lot of data being presented, and some people do not follow complicated pictures. Figure 5.6 shows a surface plot for the counts shown in the table. A surface plot often looks a bit like hilly terrain. The counts are the height of the hills; the counties go up one side and the channels make the third dimension. This surface plot shows that the other channel is quite high for Manhattan (New York county). Although not a problem in this case, such peaks can hide other hills and valleys on the surface plot.

# Looking at Continuous Variables

Statistics originated to understand the data collected by scientists, most of which took the form of continuous measurements. In data mining, we encounter continuous data less often, because there is a wealth of descriptive data as well. This section talks about continuous data from the perspective of descriptive statistics.

**Table 5.1**  Cross-tabulation of Starts by County and Channel

| | COUNTS | | | | FREQUENCIES | | | |
|---|---|---|---|---|---|---|---|---|
| COUNTY | TM | DM | OTHER | TOTAL | TM | DM | OTHER | TOTAL |
| BRONX | 3,212 | 413 | 2,936 | **6,561** | 2.5% | 0.3% | 2.3% | 5.1% |
| KINGS | 9,773 | 1,393 | 11,025 | **22,191** | 7.7% | 1.1% | 8.6% | 17.4% |
| NASSAU | 3,135 | 1,573 | 10,367 | **15,075** | 2.5% | 1.2% | 8.1% | 11.8% |
| NEW YORK | 7,194 | 2,867 | 28,965 | **39,026** | 5.6% | 2.2% | 22.7% | 30.6% |
| QUEENS | 6,266 | 1,380 | 10,954 | **18,600** | 4.9% | 1.1% | 8.6% | 14.6% |
| RICHMOND | 784 | 277 | 1,772 | **2,833** | 0.6% | 0.2% | 1.4% | 2.2% |
| SUFFOLK | 2,911 | 1,042 | 7,159 | **11,112** | 2.3% | 0.8% | 5.6% | 8.7% |
| WESTCHESTER | 2,711 | 1,230 | 8,271 | **12,212** | 2.1% | 1.0% | 6.5% | 9.6% |
| TOTAL | **35,986** | **10,175** | **81,449** | **127,610** | 28.2% | 8.0% | 63.8% | 100.0% |

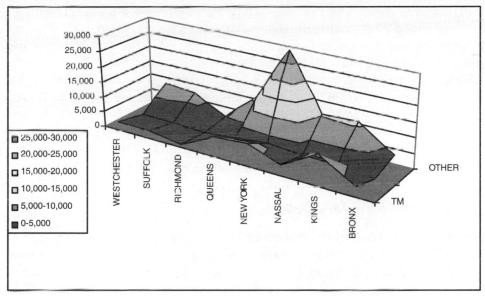

**Figure 5.6**    A surface plot provides a visual interface for cross-tabulated data.

## Statistical Measures for Continuous Variables

The most basic statistical measures describe a set of data with just a single value. The most commonly used statistic is the *mean* or average value (the sum of all the values divided by the number of them). Some other important things to look at are:

**Range.** The range is the difference between the smallest and largest observation in the sample. The range is often looked at along with the minimum and maximum values themselves.

**Mean.** This is what is called an average in everyday speech.

**Median.** The median value is the one which splits the observations into two equally sized groups, one having observations smaller than the median and another containing observations larger than the median.

**Mode.** This is the value that occurs most often.

The median can be used in some situations where it is impossible to calculate the mean, such as when incomes are reported in ranges of $10,000 dollars with a final category "over $100,000." The number of observations are known in each group, but not the actual values. In addition, the median is less affected by a few observations that are out of line with the others. For instance, if Bill Gates moves onto your block, the average net worth of the neighborhood will dramatically increase. However, the median net worth may not change at all.

In addition, various ways of characterizing the range are useful. The range itself is defined by the minimum and maximum value. It is often worth looking at percentile information, such as the 25th and 75th percentile, to understand the limits of the middle half of the values as well.

Figure 5.7 shows a chart where the range and average are displayed for order amount by day. This chart uses a logarithmic (log) scale for the vertical axis, because the minimum order is under $10 and the maximum over $1,000. In fact, the minimum is consistently around $10, the average around $70, and the maximum around $1,000. As with discrete variables, it is valuable to use a time chart for continuous values to see when unexpected things are happening.

### Variance and Standard Deviation

Variance is a measure of the dispersion of a sample or how closely the observations cluster around the average. The range is not a good measure of dispersion because it takes only two values into account—the extremes. Removing one extreme can, sometimes, dramatically change the range. The variance, on the other hand, takes every value into account. The difference between a given observation and the mean of the sample is called its *deviation*. The variance is defined as the average of the squares of the deviations.

Standard deviation, the square root of the variance, is the most frequently used measure of dispersion. It is more convenient than variance because it is expressed in the same units as the observations rather than in terms of those units squared. This allows the standard deviation itself to be used as a unit of measurement. The z-score, which we used earlier, is an observation's distance from the mean measured in standard deviations. Using the normal distribution, the z-score can be converted to a probability or confidence level.

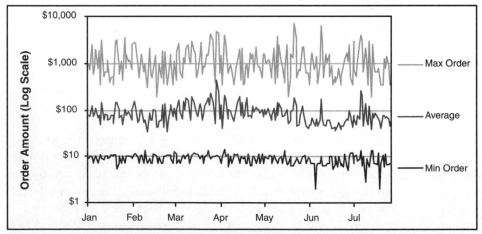

**Figure 5.7**  A time chart can also be used for continuous values; this one shows the range and average for order amounts each day.

## A Couple More Statistical Ideas

*Correlation* is a measure of the extent to which a change in one variable is related to a change in another. Correlation ranges from −1 to 1. A correlation of 0 means that the two variables are not related. A correlation of 1 means that as the first variable changes, the second is guaranteed to change in the same direction, though not necessarily by the same amount. Another measure of correlation is the $R^2$ value, which is the correlation squared and goes from 0 (no relationship) to 1 (complete relationship). For instance, the radius and the circumference of a circle are perfectly correlated, although the latter grows faster than the former. A negative correlation means that the two variables move in opposite directions. For example, altitude is negatively correlated to air pressure.

*Regression* is the process of using the value of one of a pair of correlated variables in order to predict the value of the second. The most common form of regression is linear regression, so called because it attempts to fit a straight line through the observed $X$ and $Y$ pairs in a sample. Once the line has been established, it can be used to predict a value for $Y$ given any $X$ and for $X$ given any $Y$.

# Measuring Response

This section looks at statistical ideas in the context of a marketing campaign. The champion-challenger approach to marketing tries out different ideas against the business as usual. For instance, assume that a company sends out a million billing inserts each month to entice customers to do something. They have settled on one approach to the bill inserts, which is the *champion* offer. Another offer is a *challenger* to this offer. Their approach to comparing these is:

- Send the champion offer to 900,000 customers.
- Send the challenger offer to 100,000 customers.
- Determine which is better.

The question is, how do we know when one offer is better than another? This section introduces the ideas of confidence to understand this in more detail.

## Standard Error of a Proportion

The approach to answering this question uses the idea of a confidence interval. The challenger offer, in the above scenario, is being sent to a random subset of customers. Based on the response in this subset, what is the expected response for this offer for the entire population?

For instance, let's assume that 50,000 people in the original population would have responded to the challenger offer if they had received it. Then about 5,000 would be expected to respond in the 10 percent of the population that received the challenger offer. If exactly this number did respond, then the sample response rate and the population response rate would both be 5.0 percent. However, it is possible (though highly, highly unlikely) that all 50,000 responders are in the sample that receives the challenger offer; this would yield a response rate of 50 percent. On the other hand it is also possible (and also highly, highly unlikely) that none of the 50,000 are in the sample chosen, for a response rate of 0 percent. In any sample of one-tenth the population, the observed response rate might be as low as 0 percent or as high as 50 percent. These are the extreme values, of course; the actual value is much more likely to be close to 5 percent.

So far, the example has shown that there are many different samples that can be pulled from the population. Now, let's flip the situation and say that we have observed 5,000 responders in the sample. What does this tell us about the entire population? Once again, it is possible that these are all the responders in the population, so the low-end estimate is 0.5 percent. On the other hand, it is possible that everyone else was as responder and we were very, very unlucky in choosing the sample. The high end would then be 90.5 percent.

That is, there is a 100 percent confidence that the actual response rate on the population is between 0.5 percent and 90.5 percent. Having a high confidence is good; however, the range is too broad to be useful. We are willing to settle for a lower confidence level. Often, 95 or 99 percent confidence is quite sufficient for marketing purposes.

The distribution for the response values follows something called the binomial distribution. Happily, the binomial distribution is very similar to the normal distribution whenever we are working with a population larger than a few hundred people. In Figure 5.8, the jagged line is the binomial distribution and the smooth line is the corresponding normal distribution; they are practically identical.

The challenge is to determine the corresponding normal distribution given that a sample of size 100,000 had a response rate of 5 percent. As mentioned earlier, the normal distribution has two parameters, the mean and standard deviation. The mean is the observed average (5 percent) in the sample. To calculate the standard deviation, we need a formula, and statisticians have figured out the relationship between the standard deviation (strictly speaking, this is the standard error but the two are equivalent for our purposes) and the mean value and the sample size for a proportion. This is called the standard error of a proportion (SEP) and has the formula:

$$SEP = \sqrt{\frac{p * (1 - p)}{N}}$$

In this formula, $p$ is the average value and $N$ is the size of the population. So, the corresponding normal distribution has a standard deviation equal to the square root of the product of the observed response times one minus the observed response divided by the total number of samples.

We have already observed that about 68 percent of data following a normal distribution lies within one standard deviation. For the sample size of 100,000, the formula is SQRT(5% * 95% / 100,000) is about 0.07 percent. So, we are 68 percent confident that the actual response is between 4.93 percent and 5.07 percent. We have also observed that a bit over 95 percent is within two standard deviations; so the range of 4.86 percent and 5.14 percent is just over 95 percent confident. So, if we observe a 5 percent response rate for the challenger offer, then we are over 95 percent confident that the response rate on the whole population would have been between 4.86 percent and 5.14 percent. Note that this conclusion depends very much on the fact that people who got the challenger offer were selected randomly from the entire population.

## Comparing Results Using Confidence Bounds

The previous section discussed confidence intervals as applied to the response rate of one group who received the challenger offer. In this case, there are actually two response rates, one for the champion and one for the challenger. Are these response rates different? Notice that the observed rates could be different (say 5.0 percent and 5.001 percent), but these could be indistinguishable from each other. One way to answer the question is to look at the confidence interval for each response rate and see whether they overlap. If the intervals do not overlap, then the response rates are different.

This example investigates a range of response rates from 4.5 percent to 5.5 percent for the champion model. In practice, a single response rate would be known. However, investigating a range makes it possible to understand what happens as the rate varies from much lower (4.5 percent) to the same (5.0 percent) to much larger (5.5 percent).

The 95 percent confidence is 1.96 standard deviation from the mean, so the lower value is the mean minus this number of standard deviations and the upper is the mean plus this value. Table 5.2 shows the lower and upper bounds for a range of response rates for the champion model going from 4.5 percent to 5.5 percent.

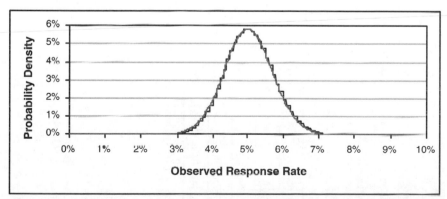

**Figure 5.8**  Statistics has proven that actual response rate on a population is very close to a normal distribution whose mean is the measured response on a sample and whose standard deviation is the standard error of proportion (SEP).

**Table 5.2** The 95 Percent Confidence Interval Bounds for the Champion Group

| RESPONSE | SIZE | SEP | 95% CONF | 95% CONF * SEP | LOWER | UPPER |
|---|---|---|---|---|---|---|
| 4.5% | 900,000 | 0.0219% | 1.96 | 0.0219%*1.96=0.0429% | 4.46% | 4.54% |
| 4.6% | 900,000 | 0.0221% | 1.96 | 0.0221%*1.96=0.0433% | 4.56% | 4.64% |
| 4.7% | 900,000 | 0.0223% | 1.96 | 0.0223%*1.96=0.0437% | 4.66% | 4.74% |
| 4.8% | 900,000 | 0.0225% | 1.96 | 0.0225%*1.96=0.0441% | 4.76% | 4.84% |
| 4.9% | 900,000 | 0.0228% | 1.96 | 0.0228%*1.96=0.0447% | 4.86% | 4.94% |
| 5.0% | 900,000 | 0.0230% | 1.96 | 0.0230%*1.96=0.0451% | 4.95% | 5.05% |
| 5.1% | 900,000 | 0.0232% | 1.96 | 0.0232%*1.96=0.0455% | 5.05% | 5.15% |
| 5.2% | 900,000 | 0.0234% | 1.96 | 0.0234%*1.96=0.0459% | 5.15% | 5.25% |
| 5.3% | 900,000 | 0.0236% | 1.96 | 0.0236%*1.96=0.0463% | 5.25% | 5.35% |
| 5.4% | 900,000 | 0.0238% | 1.96 | 0.0238%*1.96=0.0466% | 5.35% | 5.45% |
| 5.5% | 900,000 | 0.0240% | 1.96 | 0.0240%*1.96=0.0470% | 5.45% | 5.55% |

Response rates vary from 4.5% to 5.5%. The bounds for the 95% confidence level are calculated using 1.96 standard deviations from the mean.

Based on these possible response rates, it is possible to tell if the confidence bounds overlap. The 95 percent confidence bounds for the challenger model were from about 4.86 percent to 5.14 percent. These bounds overlap the confidence bounds for the champion model when its response rates are 4.9 percent, 5.0 percent, or 5.1 percent. For instance, the confidence interval for a response rate of 4.9 percent goes from 4.86 percent to 4.94 percent; this does overlap 4.86 percent—5.14 percent. Using the overlapping bounds method, we would consider these statistically the same.

## Comparing Results Using Difference of Proportions

Overlapping bounds is easy but its results are a bit pessimistic. That is, even though the confidence intervals overlap, we might still be quite confident that the difference is not due to chance with some given level of confidence. Another approach is to look at the *difference* between response rates, rather than the rates themselves. Just as there is a formula for the standard error of a proportion, there is a formula for the standard error of a difference of proportions (SEDP):

$$\text{SEDP} = \sqrt{\frac{p1 * (1 - p1)}{N1} + p2 * \frac{(1 - p2)}{N2}}$$

This formula is a lot like the formula for the standard error of a proportion, except the part in the square root is repeated for each group. Table 5.3 shows this applied to the champion challenger problem with response rates varying between 4.5 percent and 5.5 percent for the champion group.

By the difference of proportions, three response rates on the champion have a confidence under 95 percent (that is, the p-value exceeds 5 percent). If the challenger response rate is 5.0 percent and the champion is 5.1 percent, then the difference in response rates might be due to chance. However, if the champion has a response rate of 5.2 percent, then the likelihood of the difference being due to chance falls to under 1 percent.

> **WARNING** Confidence intervals only measure the likelihood that sampling affected the result. There may be many other factors that we need to take into consideration to determine if two offers are significantly different. Each group must be selected entirely randomly from the whole population for the difference of proportions method to work.

**Table 5.3** The 95 Percent Confidence Interval Bounds for the Difference between the Champion and Challenger groups

| CHALLENGER | | CHAMPION | | DIFFERENCE | | | |
| RESPONSE | SIZE | RESPONSE | SIZE | VALUE | SEDP | Z-VALUE | P-VALUE |
|---|---|---|---|---|---|---|---|
| 5.0% | 100,000 | 4.5% | 900,000 | 0.5% | 0.07% | 6.9 | 0.0% |
| 5.0% | 100,000 | 4.6% | 900,000 | 0.4% | 0.07% | 5.5 | 0.0% |
| 5.0% | 100,000 | 4.7% | 900,000 | 0.3% | 0.07% | 4.1 | 0.0% |
| 5.0% | 100,000 | 4.8% | 900,000 | 0.2% | 0.07% | 2.8 | 0.6% |
| 5.0% | 100,000 | 4.9% | 900,000 | 0.1% | 0.07% | 1.4 | 16.8% |
| 5.0% | 100,000 | 5.0% | 900,000 | 0.0% | 0.07% | 0.0 | 100.0% |
| 5.0% | 100,000 | 5.1% | 900,000 | -0.1% | 0.07% | -1.4 | 16.9% |
| 5.0% | 100,000 | 5.2% | 900,000 | -0.2% | 0.07% | -2.7 | 0.6% |
| 5.0% | 100,000 | 5.3% | 900,000 | -0.3% | 0.07% | -4.1 | 0.0% |
| 5.0% | 100,000 | 5.4% | 900,000 | -0.4% | 0.07% | -5.5 | 0.0% |
| 5.0% | 100,000 | 5.5% | 900,000 | -0.5% | 0.07% | -6.9 | 0.0% |

## Size of Sample

The formulas for the standard error of a proportion and for the standard error of a difference of proportions both include the sample size. There is an inverse relationship between the sample size and the size of the confidence interval: the larger the size of the sample, the narrower the confidence interval. So, if you want to have more confidence in results, it pays to use larger samples.

Table 5.4 shows the confidence interval for different sizes of the challenger group, assuming the challenger response rate is observed to be 5 percent. For very small sizes, the confidence interval is very wide, often too wide to be useful. Earlier, we had said that the normal distribution is an approximation for the estimate of the actual response rate; with small sample sizes, the estimation is not a very good one. Statistics has several methods for handling such small sample sizes. However, these are generally not of much interest to data miners because our samples are much larger.

**Table 5.4**    The 95 Percent Confidence Interval for Difference Sizes of the Challenger Group

| RESPONSE | SIZE | SEP | 95% CONF | LOWER | HIGH | WIDTH |
| --- | --- | --- | --- | --- | --- | --- |
| 5.0% | 1,000 | 0.6892% | 1.96 | 3.65% | 6.35% | 2.70% |
| 5.0% | 5,000 | 0.3082% | 1.96 | 4.40% | 5.60% | 1.21% |
| 5.0% | 10,000 | 0.2179% | 1.96 | 4.57% | 5.43% | 0.85% |
| 5.0% | 20,000 | 0.1541% | 1.96 | 4.70% | 5.30% | 0.60% |
| 5.0% | 40,000 | 0.1090% | 1.96 | 4.79% | 5.21% | 0.43% |
| 5.0% | 60,000 | 0.0890% | 1.96 | 4.83% | 5.17% | 0.35% |
| 5.0% | 80,000 | 0.0771% | 1.96 | 4.85% | 5.15% | 0.30% |
| 5.0% | 100,000 | 0.0689% | 1.96 | 4.86% | 5.14% | 0.27% |
| 5.0% | 120,000 | 0.0629% | 1.96 | 4.88% | 5.12% | 0.25% |
| 5.0% | 140,000 | 0.0582% | 1.96 | 4.89% | 5.11% | 0.23% |
| 5.0% | 160,000 | 0.0545% | 1.96 | 4.89% | 5.11% | 0.21% |
| 5.0% | 180,000 | 0.0514% | 1.96 | 4.90% | 5.10% | 0.20% |
| 5.0% | 200,000 | 0.0487% | 1.96 | 4.90% | 5.10% | 0.19% |
| 5.0% | 500,000 | 0.0308% | 1.96 | 4.94% | 5.06% | 0.12% |
| 5.0% | 1,000,000 | 0.0218% | 1.96 | 4.96% | 5.04% | 0.09% |

## What the Confidence Interval Really Means

The confidence interval is a measure of only one thing, the statistical dispersion of the result. Assuming that everything else remains the same, it measures the amount of inaccuracy introduced by the process of sampling. It also assumes that the sampling process itself is random—that is, that any of the one million customers could have been offered the challenger offer with an equal likelihood. Random means random. The following are examples of what not to do:

- Use customers in California for the challenger and everyone else for the champion.

- Use the 5 percent lowest and 5 percent highest value customers for the challenger, and everyone else for the champion.

- Use the 10 percent most recent customers for the challenger, and everyone else for the champion.

- Use the customers with telephone numbers for the telemarketing campaign; everyone else for the direct mail campaign.

All of these are biased ways of splitting the population into groups. The previous results all assume that there is no such systematic bias. When there is systematic bias, the formulas for the confidence intervals are not correct.

Using the formula for the confidence interval means that there is no systematic bias in deciding whether a particular customer receives the champion or the challenger message. For instance, perhaps there was a champion model that predicts the likelihood of customers responding to the champion offer. If this model were used, then the challenger sample would no longer be a random sample. It would consist of the leftover customers from the champion model. This introduces another form of bias.

Or, perhaps the challenger model is only available to customers in certain markets or with certain products. This introduces other forms of bias. In such a case, these customers should be compared to the set of customers receiving the champion offer with the same constraints.

Another form of bias might come from the method of response. The challenger may only accept responses via telephone, but the champion may accept them by telephone or on the Web. In such a case, the challenger response may be dampened because of the lack of a Web channel. Or, there might need to be special training for the inbound telephone service reps to handle the challenger offer. At certain times, this might mean that wait times are longer, another form of bias.

The confidence interval is simply a statement about statistics and dispersion. It does not address all the other forms of bias that might affect results, and these forms of bias are often more important to results than sample variation. The next section talks about setting up a test and control experiment in marketing, diving into these issues in more detail.

## Size of Test and Control for an Experiment

The champion-challenger model is an example of a two-way test, where a new method (the challenger) is compared to business-as-usual activity (the champion). This section talks about ensuring that the test and control are large enough for the purposes at hand. The previous section talked about determining the confidence interval for the sample response rate. Here, we turn this logic inside out. Instead of starting with the size of the groups, let's instead consider sizes from the perspective of test design. This requires several items of information:

- Estimated response rate for one of the groups, which we call $p$
- Difference in response rates that we want to consider significant (acuity of the test), which we call $d$
- Confidence interval (say 95 percent)

This provides enough information to determine the size of the samples needed for the test and control. For instance, suppose that the business as usual has a response rate of 5 percent and we want to measure with 95 percent confidence a difference of 0.2 percent. This means that if the response of the test group greater than 5.2 percent, then the experiment can detect the difference with a 95 percent confidence level.

For a problem of this type, the first step this is to determine the value of SEDP. That is, if we are willing to accept a difference of 0.2 percent with a confidence of 95 percent, then what is the corresponding standard error? A confidence of 95 percent means that we are 1.96 standard deviations from the mean, so the answer is to divide the difference by 1.96, which yields 0.102 percent. More generally, the process is to convert the p-value (95 percent) to a z-value (which can be done using the Excel function NORMSINV) and then divide the desired confidence by this value.

The next step is to plug these values into the formula for SEDP. For this, let's assume that the test and control are the same size:

$$\frac{0.2\%}{1.96}\sqrt{\frac{p*(1-p)}{N+(p+d)}*\frac{(1-p-d)}{N}}$$

Plugging in the values just described ($p$ is 5% and $d$ is 0.2%) results in:

$$0.102\% = \sqrt{\frac{5\%*95\%}{N}+\frac{5.2\%*94.8\%}{N}} = \sqrt{\frac{0.0963}{N}}$$

$$N = \frac{0.0963}{(0.00102)^2} = 66,875$$

So, having equal-sized groups of of 92,561 makes it possible to measure a 0.2 percent difference in response rates with a 95 percent accuracy. Of course, this does not guarantee that the results will differ by at least 0.2 percent. It merely says that with control and test groups of at least this size, a difference in response rates of 0.2 percent should be measurable and statistically significant.

The size of the test and control groups affects how the results can be interpreted. However, this effect can be determined in advance, before the test. It is worthwhile determining the acuity of the test and control groups before running the test, to be sure that the test can produce useful results.

**TIP** Before running a marketing test, determine the acuity of the test by calculating the difference in response rates that can be measured with a high confidence (such as 95 percent).

# Multiple Comparisons

The discussion has so far used examples with only one comparison, such as the difference between two presidential candidates or between a test and control group. Often, we are running multiple tests at the same time. For instance, we might try out three different challenger messages to determine if one of these produces better results than the business-as-usual message. Because handling multiple tests does affect the underlying statistics, it is important to understand what happens.

## The Confidence Level with Multiple Comparisons

Consider that there are two groups that have been tested, and you are told that difference between the responses in the two groups is 95 percent certain to be due to factors other than sampling variation. A reasonable conclusion is that there is a difference between the two groups. In a well-designed test, the most likely reason would the difference in message, offer, or treatment.

Occam's Razor says that we should take the simplest explanation, and not add anything extra. The simplest hypothesis for the difference in response rates is that the difference is not significant, that the response rates are really approximations of the same number. If the difference is significant, then we need to search for the reason why.

Now consider the same situation, except that you are now told that there were actually 20 groups being tested, and you were shown only one pair. Now you might reach a very different conclusion. If 20 groups are being tested, then you should expect one of them to exceed the 95 percent confidence bound due only to chance, since 95 percent means 19 times out of 20. You can no longer conclude that the difference is due to the testing parameters. Instead, because it is likely that the difference is due to sampling variation, this is the simplest hypothesis.

The confidence level is based on only one comparison. When there are multiple comparisons, that condition is not true, so the confidence as calculated previously is not quite sufficient.

## Bonferroni's Correction

Fortunately, there is a simple correction to fix this problem, developed by the Italian mathematician Carlo Bonferroni. We have been looking at confidence as saying that there is a 95 percent chance that some value is between A and B. Consider the following situation:

- X is between A and B with a probability of 95 percent.
- Y is between C and D with a probability of 95 percent.

Bonferroni wanted to know the probability that both of these are true. Another way to look at it is to determine the probability that one or the other is false. This is easier to calculate. The probability that the first is false is 5 percent, as is the probability of the second being false. The probability that either is false is the sum, 10 percent, minus the probability that both are false at the same time (0.25 percent). So, the probability that both statements are true is about 90 percent.

Looking at this from the p-value perspective says that the p-value of both statements together (10 percent) is approximated by the sum of the p-values of the two statements separately. This is not a coincidence. In fact, it is reasonable to calculate the p-value of any number of statements as the sum of the p values of each one. If we had eight variables with a 95 percent confidence, then we would expect all eight to be in their ranges 60 percent at any given time (because 8 * 5% is a p-value of 40%).

Bonferroni applied this observation in reverse. If there are eight tests and we want an overall 95 percent confidence, then the bound for the p-value needs to be 5% / 8 = 0.625%. That is, each observation needs to be at least 99.375 percent confident. The Bonferroni correction is to divide the desired bound for the p-value by the number of comparisons being made, in order to get a confidence of 1 – p for all comparisons.

## Chi-Square Test

The difference of proportions method is a very powerful method for estimating the effectiveness of campaigns and for other similar situations. However, there is another statistical test that can be used. This test, the chi-square test, is designed specifically for the situation when there are multiple tests and at least two discrete outcomes (such as response and non-response).

The appeal of the chi-square test is that it readily adapts to multiple test groups and multiple outcomes, so long as the different groups are distinct from each other. This, in fact, is about the only important rule when using this test. As described in the next chapter on decision trees, the chi-square test is the basis for one of the earliest forms of decision trees.

## Expected Values

The place to start with chi-square is to lay data out in a table, as in Table 5.5. This is a simple $2 \times 2$ table, which represents a test group and a control group in a test that has two outcomes, say response and nonresponse. This table also shows the total values for each column and row; that is, the total number of responders and nonresponders (each column) and the total number in the test and control groups (each row). The response column is added for reference; it is not part of the calculation.

What if the data were broken up between these groups in a completely unbiased way? That is, what if there really were no differences between the columns and rows in the table? This is a completely reasonable question. We can calculate the expected values, assuming that the number of responders and non-responders is the same, and assuming that the sizes of the champion and challenger groups are the same. That is, we can calculate the expected value in each cell, given that the size of the rows and columns are the same as in the original data.

One way of calculating the expected values is to calculate the proportion of each row that is in each column, by computing each of the following four quantities, as shown in Table 5.6:

- Proportion of everyone who responds
- Proportion of everyone who does not respond

These proportions are then multiplied by the count for each row to obtain the expected value. This method for calculating the expected value works when the tabular data has more columns or more rows.

**Table 5.5** The Champion-Challenger Data Laid out for the Chi-Square Test

|  | RESPONDERS | NON-RESPONDERS | TOTAL | RESPONSE |
|---|---|---|---|---|
| Champion | 43,200 | 856,800 | 900,000 | 4.80% |
| Challenger | 5,000 | 95,000 | 100,000 | 5.00% |
| TOTAL | 48,200 | 951,800 | 1,000,000 | 4.82% |

**Table 5.6**  Calculating the Expected Values and Deviations from Expected for the Data in Table 5.5

|  | ACTUAL RESPONSE | | | EXPECTED RESPONSE | | DEVIATION | |
|  | YES | NO | TOTAL | YES | NO | YES | NO |
|---|---|---|---|---|---|---|---|
| Champion | 43,200 | 856,800 | 900,000 | 43,380 | 856,620 | −180 | 180 |
| Challenger | 5,000 | 95,000 | 100,000 | 4,820 | 95,180 | 180 | −180 |
| TOTAL | 48,200 | 951,800 | 1,000,000 | 48,200 | 951,800 | | |
| OVERALL PROPORTION | 4.82% | 95.18% | | | | | |

The expected value is quite interesting, because it shows how the data would break up if there were no other effects. Notice that the expected value is measured in the same units as each cell, typically a customer count, so it actually has a meaning. Also, the sum of the expected values is the same as the sum of all the cells in the original table. The table also includes the deviation, which is the difference between the observed value and the expected value. In this case, the deviations all have the same value, but with different signs. This is because the original data has two rows and two columns. Later in the chapter there are examples using larger tables where the deviations are different. However, the deviations in each row and each column always cancel out, so the sum of the deviations in each row is always 0.

## Chi-Square Value

The deviation is a good tool for looking at values. However, it does not provide information as to whether the deviation is expected or not expected. Doing this requires some more tools from statistics, namely, the chi-square distribution developed by the English statistician Karl Pearson in 1900.

The chi-square value for each cell is simply the calculation:

$$\text{Chi-square}(x) = \sqrt{\frac{(x - \text{expected}(x))^2}{\text{expected}(x)}}$$

The chi-square value for the entire table is the sum of the chi-square values of all the cells in the table. Notice that the chi-square value is always 0 or positive. Also, when the values in the table match the expected value, then the overall chi-square is 0. This is the best that we can do. As the deviations from the expected value get larger in magnitude, the chi-square value also gets larger.

Unfortunately, chi-square values do not follow a normal distribution. This is actually obvious, because the chi-square value is always positive, and the normal distribution is symmetric. The good news is that chi-square values follow another distribution, which is also well understood. However, the chi-square distribution depends not only on the value itself but also on the size of the table. Figure 5.9 shows the density functions for several chi-square distributions.

What the chi-square depends on is the degrees of freedom. Unlike many ideas in probability and statistics, degrees of freedom is easier to calculate than to explain. The number of degrees of freedom of a table is calculated by subtracting one from the number of rows and the number of columns and multiplying them together. The $2 \times 2$ table in the previous example has 1 degree of freedom. A $5 \times 7$ table would have 24 (4 * 6) degrees of freedom. The aside "Degrees of Freedom" discusses this in a bit more detail.

**WARNING** The chi-square test does not work when the number of expected values in any cell is less than 5 (and we prefer a slightly higher bound). Although this is not an issue for large data mining problems, it can be an issue when analyzing results from a small test.

The process for using the chi-square test is:

- Calculate the expected values.
- Calculate the deviations from expected.
- Calculate the chi-square (square the deviations and divide by the expected).
- Sum for an overall chi-square value for the table.
- Calculate the probability that the observed values are due to chance (in Excel, you can use the CHIDIST function).

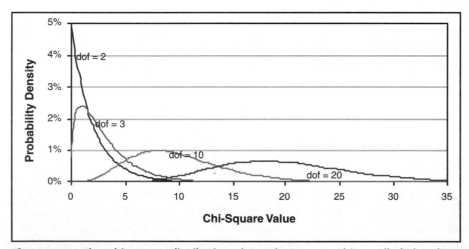

**Figure 5.9** The chi-square distribution depends on something called the degrees of freedom. In general, though, it starts low, peaks early, and gradually descends.

**DEGREES OF FREEDOM**

The idea behind the degrees of freedom is how many different variables are needed to describe the table of expected values. This is a measure of how constrained the data is in the table.

If the table has $r$ rows and $c$ columns, then there are $r * c$ cells in the table. With no constraints on the table, this is the number of variables that would be needed. However, the calculation of the expected values has imposed some constraints. In particular, the sum of the values in each row is the same for the expected values as for the original table, because the sum of each row is fixed. That is, if one value were missing, we could recalculate it by taking the constraint into account by subtracting the sum of the rest of values in the row from the sum for the whole row. This suggests that the degrees of freedom is $r * c - r$. The same situation exists for the columns, yielding an estimate of $r * c - r - c$.

However, there is one additional constraint. The sum of all the row sums and the sum of all the column sums must be the same. It turns out, we have over counted the constraints by one, so the degrees of freedom is really $r * c - r - c + 1$. Another way of writing this is $(r - 1) * (c - 1)$.

The result is the probability that the distribution of values in the table is due to random fluctuations rather than some external criteria. As Occam's Razor suggests, the simplest explanation is that there is no difference at all due to the various factors; that observed differences from expected values are entirely within the range of expectation.

## Comparison of Chi-Square to Difference of Proportions

Chi-square and difference of proportions can be applied to the same problems. Although the results are not exactly the same, the results are similar enough for comfort. Earlier, in Table 5.4, we determined the likelihood of champion and challenger results being the same using the difference of proportions method for a range of champion response rates. Table 5.7 repeats this using the chi-square calculation instead of the difference of proportions. The results from the chi-square test are very similar to the results from the difference of proportions—a remarkable result considering how different the two methods are.

**Table 5.7**  Chi-Square Calculation for Difference of Proportions Example in Table 5.4

| CHALLENGER | | CHAMPION | | OVERALL | CHALLENGER EXP | | CHAMPION EXP | | CHAL CHI-SQUARE | | CHAMP CHI-SQUARE | | CHI-SQUARE | | DIFF PROP |
|---|---|---|---|---|---|---|---|---|---|---|---|---|---|---|---|
| RESP | NON RESP | RESP | NON-RESP | RESP | RESP | NON RESP | RESP | NON RESP | RESP | NON RESP | RESP | NON RESP | VALUE | P-VALUE | P-VALUE |
| 5,000 | 95,000 | 40,500 | 859,500 | 4.55% | 4,550 | 95,450 | 40,950 | 859,050 | 44.51 | 2.12 | 4.95 | 0.24 | 51.81 | 0.00% | 0.00% |
| 5,000 | 95,000 | 41,400 | 858,600 | 4.64% | 4,640 | 95,360 | 41,760 | 858,240 | 27.93 | 1.36 | 3.10 | 0.15 | 32.54 | 0.00% | 0.00% |
| 5,000 | 95,000 | 42,300 | 857,700 | 4.73% | 4,730 | 95,270 | 42,570 | 857,430 | 15.41 | 0.77 | 1.71 | 0.09 | 17.97 | 0.00% | 0.00% |
| 5,000 | 95,000 | 43,200 | 856,800 | 4.82% | 4,820 | 95,180 | 43,380 | 856,620 | 6.72 | 0.34 | 0.75 | 0.04 | 7.85 | 0.51% | 0.58% |
| 5,000 | 95,000 | 44,100 | 855,900 | 4.91% | 4,910 | 95,090 | 44,190 | 855,810 | 1.65 | 0.09 | 0.18 | 0.01 | 1.93 | 16.50% | 16.83% |
| 5,000 | 95,000 | 45,000 | 855,000 | 5.00% | 5,000 | 95,000 | 45,000 | 855,000 | 0.00 | 0.00 | 0.00 | 0.00 | 0.00 | 100.00% | 100.00% |
| 5,000 | 95,000 | 45,900 | 854,100 | 5.09% | 5,090 | 94,910 | 45,810 | 854,190 | 1.59 | 0.09 | 0.18 | 0.01 | 1.86 | 17.23% | 16.91% |
| 5,000 | 95,000 | 46,800 | 853,200 | 5.18% | 5,180 | 94,820 | 46,620 | 853,380 | 6.25 | 0.34 | 0.69 | 0.04 | 7.33 | 0.68% | 0.60% |
| 5,000 | 95,000 | 47,700 | 852,300 | 5.27% | 5,270 | 94,730 | 47,430 | 852,570 | 13.83 | 0.77 | 1.54 | 0.09 | 16.23 | 0.01% | 0.00% |
| 5,000 | 95,000 | 48,600 | 851,400 | 5.36% | 5,360 | 94,640 | 48,240 | 851,760 | 24.18 | 1.37 | 2.69 | 0.15 | 28.39 | 0.00% | 0.00% |
| 5,000 | 95,000 | 49,500 | 850,500 | 5.45% | 5,450 | 94,550 | 49,050 | 850,950 | 37.16 | 2.14 | 4.13 | 0.24 | 43.66 | 0.00% | 0.00% |

# An Example: Chi-Square for Regions and Starts

A large consumer-oriented company has been running acquisition campaigns in the New York City area. The purpose of this analysis is to look at their acquisition channels to try to gain an understanding of different parts of the area. For the purposes of this analysis, three channels are of interest:

**Telemarketing.** Customers who are acquired through outbound telemarketing calls (note that this data was collected before the national do-not-call list went into effect).

**Direct mail.** Customers who respond to direct mail pieces.

**Other.** Customers who come in through other means.

The area of interest consists of eight counties in New York State. Five of these counties are the boroughs of New York City, two others (Nassau and Suffolk counties) are on Long Island, and one (Westchester) lies just north of the city. This data was shown earlier in Table 5.1. This purpose of this analysis is to determine whether the breakdown of starts by channel and county is due to chance or whether some other factors might be at work.

This problem is particularly suitable for chi-square because the data can be laid out in rows and columns, with no customer being counted in more than one cell. Table 5.8 shows the deviation, expected values, and chi-square values for each combination in the table. Notice that the chi-square values are often quite large in this example. The overall chi-square score for the table is 7,200, which is very large; the probability that the overall score is due to chance is basically 0. That is, the variation among starts by channel and by region is not due to sample variation. There are other factors at work.

The next step is to determine which of the values are too high and too low and with what probability. It is tempting to convert each chi-square value in each cell into a probability, using the degrees of freedom for the table. The table is 8 × 3, so it has 14 degrees of freedom. However, this is not an appropriate thing to do. The chi-square result is for the entire table; inverting the individual scores to get a probability does not produce valid results. Chi-square scores are not additive.

An alternative approach proves more accurate. The idea is to compare each cell to everything else. The result is a table that has two columns and two rows, as shown in Table 5.9. One column is the column of the original cell; the other column is everything else. One row is the row of the original cell; the other row is everything else.

**Table 5.8**  Chi-Square Calculation for Counties and Channels Example

| COUNTY | EXPECTED | | | DEVIATION | | | CHI-SQUARE | | |
|---|---|---|---|---|---|---|---|---|---|
| | TM | DM | OTHER | TM | DM | OTHER | TM | DM | OTHER |
| BRONX | 1,850.2 | 523.1 | 4,187.7 | 1,362 | −110 | −1,252 | 1,002.3 | 23.2 | 374.1 |
| KINGS | 6,257.9 | 1,769.4 | 14,163.7 | 3,515 | −376 | −3,139 | 1,974.5 | 80.1 | 695.6 |
| NASSAU | 4,251.1 | 1,202.0 | 9,621.8 | −1,116 | 371 | 745 | 293.0 | 114.5 | 57.7 |
| NEW YORK | 11,005.3 | 3,111.7 | 24,908.9 | −3,811 | −245 | 4,056 | 1,319.9 | 19.2 | 660.5 |
| QUEENS | 5,245.2 | 1,483.1 | 11,871.7 | 1,021 | −103 | −918 | 198.7 | 7.2 | 70.9 |
| RICHMOND | 798.9 | 225.9 | 1,808.2 | −15 | 51 | −36 | 0.3 | 11.6 | 0.7 |
| SUFFOLK | 3,133.6 | 886.0 | 7,092.4 | −223 | 156 | 67 | 15.8 | 27.5 | 0.6 |
| WESTCHESTER | 3,443.8 | 973.7 | 7,794.5 | −733 | 256 | 477 | 155.9 | 67.4 | 29.1 |

**Table 5.9**   Chi-Square Calculation for Bronx and TM

| | EXPECTED | | DEVIATION | | CHI-SQUARE | |
|---|---|---|---|---|---|---|
| COUNTY | TM | NOT_TM | TM | NOT_TM | TM | NOT_TM |
| BRONX | 1,850.2 | 4,710.8 | 1,361.8 | −1,361.8 | 1,002.3 | 393.7 |
| NOT BRONX | 34,135.8 | 86,913.2 | −1,361.8 | 1,361.8 | 54.3 | 21.3 |

The result is a set of chi-square values for the Bronx-TM combination, in a table with 1 degree of freedom. The Bronx-TM score by itself is a good approximation of the overall chi-square value for the $2 \times 2$ table (this assumes that the original cells are roughly the same size). The calculation for the chi-square value uses this value (1002.3) with 1 degree of freedom. Conveniently, the chi-square calculation for this cell is the same as the chi-square for the cell in the original calculation, although the other values do not match anything. This makes it unnecessary to do additional calculations.

This means that an estimate of the effect of each combination of variables can be obtained using the chi-square value in the cell with a degree of freedom of 1. The result is a table that has a set of p-values that a given square is caused by chance, as shown in Table 5.10.

However, there is a second correction that needs to be made because there are many comparisons taking place at the same time. Bonferroni's adjustment takes care of this by multiplying each p-value by the number of comparisons—which is the number of cells in the table. For final presentation purposes, convert the p-values to their opposite, the confidence and multiply by the sign of the deviation to get a signed confidence. Figure 5.10 illustrates the result.

**Table 5.10**   Estimated P-Value for Each Combination of County and Channel, without Correcting for Number of Comparisons

| COUNTY | TM | DM | OTHER |
|---|---|---|---|
| BRONX | 0.00% | 0.00% | 0.00% |
| KINGS | 0.00% | 0.00% | 0.00% |
| NASSAU | 0.00% | 0.00% | 0.00% |
| NEW YORK | 0.00% | 0.00% | 0.00% |
| QUEENS | 0.00% | 0.74% | 0.00% |
| RICHMOND | 59.79% | 0.07% | 39.45% |
| SUFFOLK | 0.01% | 0.00% | 42.91% |
| WESTCHESTER | 0.00% | 0.00% | 0.00% |

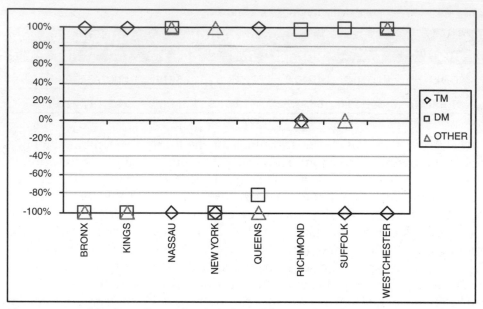

**Figure 5.10**   This chart shows the signed confidence values for each county and region combination; the preponderance of values near 100% and −100% indicate that observed differences are statistically significant.

The result is interesting. First, almost all the values are near 100 percent or −100 percent, meaning that there are statistically significant differences among the counties. In fact, telemarketing (the diamond) and direct mail (the square) are always at opposite ends. There is a direct inverse relationship between the two. Direct mail is high and telemarketing low in three counties—Manhattan, Nassau, and Suffolk. There are many wealthy areas in these counties, suggesting that wealthy customers are more likely to respond to direct mail than telemarketing. Of course, this could also mean that direct mail campaigns are directed to these areas, and telemarketing to other areas, so the geography was determined by the business operations. To determine which of these possibilities is correct, we would need to know who was contacted as well as who responded.

## Data Mining and Statistics

Many of the data mining techniques discussed in the next eight chapters were invented by statisticians or have now been integrated into statistical software; they are extensions of standard statistics. Although data miners and statisticians use similar techniques to solve similar problems, the data mining approach differs from the standard statistical approach in several areas:

- Data miners tend to ignore measurement error in raw data.
- Data miners assume that there is more than enough data and processing power.
- Data mining assumes dependency on time everywhere.
- It can be hard to design experiments in the business world.
- Data is truncated and censored.

These are differences of approach, rather than opposites. As such, they shed some light on how the business problems addressed by data miners differ from the scientific problems that spurred the development of statistics.

## No Measurement Error in Basic Data

Statistics originally derived from measuring scientific quantities, such as the width of a skull or the brightness of a star. These measurements are quantitative and the precise measured value depends on factors such as the type of measuring device and the ambient temperature. In particular, two people taking the same measurement at the same time are going to produce slightly different results. The results might differ by 5 percent or 0.05 percent, but there is a difference. Traditionally, statistics looks at observed values as falling into a confidence interval.

On the other hand, the amount of money a customer paid last January is quite well understood—down to the last penny. The definition of customer may be a little bit fuzzy; the definition of January may be fuzzy (consider 5-4-4 accounting cycles). However, the amount of the payment is precise. There is no measurement error.

There are sources of error in business data. Of particular concern is operational error, which can cause systematic bias in what is being collected. For instance, clock skew may mean that two events that seem to happen in one sequence may happen in another. A database record may have a Tuesday update date, when it really was updated on Monday, because the updating process runs just after midnight. Such forms of bias are systematic, and potentially represent spurious patterns that might be picked up by data mining algorithms.

One major difference between business data and scientific data is that the latter has many continuous values and the former has many discrete values. Even monetary amounts are discrete—two values can differ only by multiples of pennies (or some similar amount)—even though the values might be represented by real numbers.

## There Is a Lot of Data

Traditionally, statistics has been applied to smallish data sets (at most a few thousand rows) with few columns (less than a dozen). The goal has been to squeeze as much information as possible out of the data. This is still important in problems where collecting data is expensive or arduous—such as market research, crash testing cars, or tests of the chemical composition of Martian soil.

Business data, on the other hand, is very voluminous. The challenge is understanding *anything* about what is happening, rather than *every possible thing*. Fortunately, there is also enough computing power available to handle the large volumes of data.

Sampling theory is an important part of statistics. This area explains how results on a subset of data (a *sample*) relate to the whole. This is very important when planning to do a poll, because it is not possible to ask everyone a question; rather, pollsters ask a very small sample and derive overall opinion. However, this is much less important when all the data is available. Usually, it is best to use all the data available, rather than a small subset of it.

There are a few cases when this is not necessarily true. There might simply be too much data. Instead of building models on tens of millions of customers; build models on hundreds of thousands—at least to learn how to build better models. Another reason is to get an *unrepresentative* sample. Such a sample, for instance, might have an equal number of churners and nonchurners, although the original data had different proportions. However, it is generally better to use more data rather than sample down and use less, unless there is a good reason for sampling down.

## Time Dependency Pops Up Everywhere

Almost all data used in data mining has a time dependency associated with it. Customers' reactions to marketing efforts change over time. Prospects' reactions to competitive offers change over time. Comparing results from a marketing campaign one year to the previous year is rarely going to yield exactly the same result. We do not expect the same results.

On the other hand, we do expect scientific experiments to yield similar results regardless of when the experiment takes place. The laws of science are considered immutable; they do not change over time. By contrast, the business climate changes daily. Statistics often considers repeated observations to be independent observations. That is, one observation does not resemble another. Data mining, on the other hand, must often consider the time component of the data.

## Experimentation is Hard

Data mining has to work within the constraints of existing business practices. This can make it difficult to set up experiments, for several reasons:

- Businesses may not be willing to invest in efforts that reduce short-term gain for long-term learning.
- Business processes may interfere with well-designed experimental methodologies.
- Factors that may affect the outcome of the experiment may not be obvious.
- Timing plays a critical role and may render results useless.

Of these, the first two are the most difficult. The first simply says that tests do not get done. Or, they are done so poorly that the results are useless. The second poses the problem that a seemingly well-designed experiment may not be executed correctly. There are always hitches when planning a test; sometimes these hitches make it impossible to read the results.

## Data Is Censored and Truncated

The data used for data mining is often incomplete, in one of two special ways. *Censored* values are incomplete because whatever is being measured is not complete. One example is customer tenures. For active customers, we know the tenure is greater than the current tenure; however, we do not know which customers are going to stop tomorrow and which are going to stop 10 years from now. The actual tenure is greater than the observed value and cannot be known until the customer actually stops at some unknown point in the future.

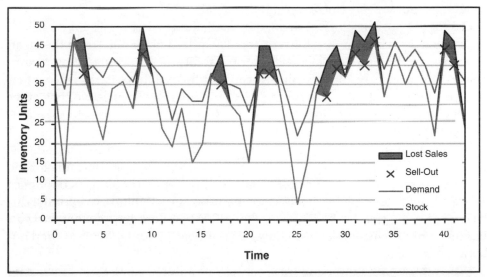

**Figure 5.11** A time series of product sales and inventory illustrates the problem of censored data.

Figure 5.11 shows another situation with the same result. This curve shows sales and inventory for a retailer for one product. Sales are always less than or equal to the inventory. On the days with the Xs, though, the inventory sold out. What were the potential sales on these days? The potential sales are greater than or equal to the observed sales—another example of censored data.

*Truncated* data poses another problem in terms of biasing samples. Truncated data is not included in databases, often because it is too old. For instance, when Company A purchases Company B, their systems are merged. Often, the active customers from Company B are moved into the data warehouse for Company A. That is, all customers active on a given date are moved over. Customers who had stopped the day before are not moved over. This is an example of left truncation, and it pops up throughout corporate databases, usually with no warning (unless the documentation is very good about saying what is not in the warehouse as well as what is). This can cause confusion when looking at when customers started—and discovering that all customers who started 5 years before the merger were mysteriously active for at least 5 years. This is not due to a miraculous acquisition program. This is because all the ones who stopped earlier were excluded.

## Lessons Learned

This chapter talks about some basic statistical methods that are useful for analyzing data. When looking at data, it is useful to look at histograms and cumulative histograms to see what values are most common. More important, though, is looking at values over time.

One of the big questions addressed by statistics is whether observed values are expected or not. For this, the number of standard deviations from the mean (z-score) can be used to calculate the probability of the value being due to chance (the p-value). High p-values mean that the null hypothesis is true; that is, nothing interesting is happening. Low p-values are suggestive that other factors may be influencing the results. Converting z-scores to p-values depends on the normal distribution.

Business problems often require analyzing data expressed as proportions. Fortunately, these behave similarly to normal distributions. The formula for the standard error for proportions (SEP) makes it possible to define a confidence interval on a proportion such as a response rate. The standard error for the difference of proportions (SEDP) makes it possible to determine whether two values are similar. This works by defining a confidence interval for the difference between two values.

When designing marketing tests, the SEP and SEDP can be used for sizing test and control groups. In particular, these groups should be large enough to measure differences in response with a high enough confidence. Tests that have more than two groups need to take into account an adjustment, called Bonferroni's correction, when setting the group sizes.

The chi-square test is another statistical method that is often useful. This method directly calculates the estimated values for data laid out in rows and columns. Based on these estimates, the chi-square test can determine whether the results are likely or unlikely. As shown in an example, the chi-square test and SEDP methods produce similar results.

Statisticians and data miners solve similar problems. However, because of historical differences and differences in the nature of the problems, there are some differences in approaches. Data miners generally have lots and lots of data with few measurement errors. This data changes over time, and values are sometimes incomplete. The data miner has to be particularly suspicious about bias introduced into the data by business processes.

The next eight chapters dive into more detail into more modern techniques for building models and understanding data. Many of these techniques have been adopted by statisticians and build on over a century of work in this area.

# Decision Trees

Decision trees are powerful and popular for both classification and prediction. The attractiveness of tree-based methods is due largely to the fact that decision trees represent rules. Rules can readily be expressed in English so that we humans can understand them; they can also be expressed in a database access language such as SQL to retrieve records in a particular category. Decision trees are also useful for exploring data to gain insight into the relationships of a large number of candidate input variables to a target variable. Because decision trees combine both data exploration and modeling, they are a powerful first step in the modeling process even when building the final model using some other technique.

There is often a trade-off between model accuracy and model transparency. In some applications, the accuracy of a classification or prediction is the only thing that matters; if a direct mail firm obtains a model that can accurately predict which members of a prospect pool are most likely to respond to a certain solicitation, the firm may not care how or why the model works. In other situations, the ability to explain the reason for a decision is crucial. In insurance underwriting, for example, there are legal prohibitions against discrimination based on certain variables. An insurance company could find itself in the position of having to demonstrate to a court of law that it has not used illegal discriminatory practices in granting or denying coverage. Similarly, it is more acceptable to both the loan officer and the credit applicant to hear that an application for credit has been denied on the basis of a computer-generated rule (such as income below some threshold and number of existing revolving accounts greater than some other threshold) than to hear that the decision has been made by a neural network that provides no explanation for its action.

This chapter begins with an examination of what decision trees are, how they work, and how they can be applied to classification and prediction problems. It then describes the core algorithm used to build decision trees and discusses some of the most popular variants of that core algorithm. Practical examples drawn from the authors' experience are used to demonstrate the utility and general applicability of decision tree models and to illustrate practical considerations that must be taken into account.

# What Is a Decision Tree?

A decision tree is a structure that can be used to divide up a large collection of records into successively smaller sets of records by applying a sequence of simple decision rules. With each successive division, the members of the resulting sets become more and more similar to one another. The familiar division of living things into kingdoms, phyla, classes, orders, families, genera, and species, invented by the Swedish botanist Carl Linnaeus in the 1730s, provides a good example. Within the animal kingdom, a particular animal is assigned to the phylum *chordata* if it has a spinal cord. Additional characteristics are used to further subdivide the chordates into the birds, mammals, reptiles, and so on. These classes are further subdivided until, at the lowest level in the taxonomy, members of the same species are not only morphologically similar, they are capable of breeding and producing fertile offspring.

A decision tree model consists of a set of rules for dividing a large heterogeneous population into smaller, more homogeneous groups with respect to a particular target variable. A decision tree may be painstakingly constructed by hand in the manner of Linnaeus and the generations of taxonomists that followed him, or it may be grown automatically by applying any one of several decision tree algorithms to a model set comprised of preclassified data. This chapter is mostly concerned with the algorithms for automatically generating decision trees. The target variable is usually categorical and the decision tree model is used either to calculate the probability that a given record belongs to each of the categories, or to classify the record by assigning it to the most likely class. Decision trees can also be used to estimate the value of a continuous variable, although there are other techniques more suitable to that task.

## Classification

Anyone familiar with the game of Twenty Questions will have no difficulty understanding how a decision tree classifies records. In the game, one player thinks of a particular place, person, or thing that would be known or recognized by all the participants, but the player gives no clue to its identity. The other players try to discover what it is by asking a series of yes-or-no questions. A good player rarely needs the full allotment of 20 questions to move all the way from "Is it bigger than a bread box?" to "the Golden Gate Bridge."

A decision tree represents such a series of questions. As in the game, the answer to the first question determines the follow-up question. The initial questions create broad categories with many members; follow-on questions divide the broad categories into smaller and smaller sets. If the questions are well chosen, a surprisingly short series is enough to accurately classify an incoming record.

The game of Twenty Questions illustrates the process of using a tree for appending a score or class to a record. A record enters the tree at the root node. The root node applies a test to determine which *child node* the record will encounter next. There are different algorithms for choosing the initial test, but the goal is always the same: To choose the test that best discriminates among the target classes. This process is repeated until the record arrives at a *leaf node*. All the records that end up at a given leaf of the tree are classified the same way. There is a unique path from the root to each leaf. That path is an expression of the *rule* used to classify the records.

Different leaves may make the same classification, although each leaf makes that classification for a different reason. For example, in a tree that classifies fruits and vegetables by color, the leaves for apple, tomato, and cherry might all predict "red," albeit with varying degrees of confidence since there are likely to be examples of green apples, yellow tomatoes, and black cherries as well.

The decision tree in Figure 6.1 classifies potential catalog recipients as likely (1) or unlikely (0) to place an order if sent a new catalog.

The tree in Figure 6.1 was created using the SAS Enterprise Miner Tree Viewer tool. The chart is drawn according to the usual convention in data mining circles—with the root at the top and the leaves at the bottom, perhaps indicating that data miners ought to get out more to see how real trees grow. Each node is labeled with a node number in the upper-right corner and the predicted class in the center. The decision rules to split each node are printed on the lines connecting each node to its children. The split at the root node on "lifetime orders"; the left branch is for customers who had six or fewer orders and the right branch is for customers who had seven or more.

Any record that reaches leaf nodes 19, 14, 16, 17, or 18 is classified as likely to respond, because the predicted class in this case is 1. The paths to these leaf nodes describe the rules in the tree. For example, the rule for leaf 19 is *If the customer has made more than 6.5 orders and it has been fewer than 765 days since the last order, the customer is likely to respond.*

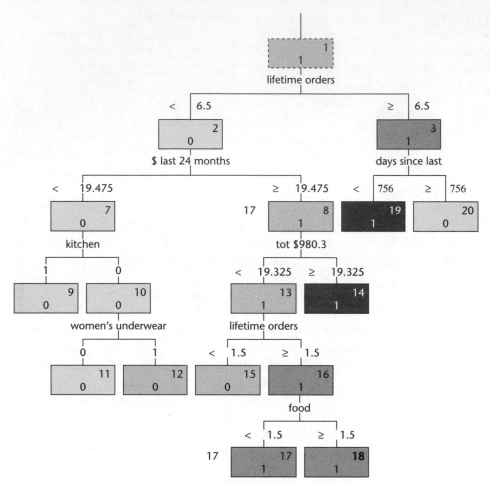

**Figure 6.1** A binary decision tree classifies catalog recipients as likely or unlikely to place an order.

Alert readers may notice that some of the splits in the decision tree appear to make no difference. For example, nodes 17 and 18 are differentiated by the number of orders they have made that included items in the food category, but both nodes are labeled as responders. That is because although the probability of response is higher in node 18 than in node 17, in both cases it is above the threshold that has been set for classifying a record as a responder. As a classifier, the model has only two outputs, one and zero. This binary classification throws away useful information, which brings us to the next topic, using decision trees to produce scores and probabilities.

## Scoring

Figure 6.2 is a picture of the same tree as in Figure 6.1, but using a different tree viewer and with settings modified so that the tree is now annotated with additional information—namely, the percentage of records in class 1 at each node.

It is now clear that the tree describes a dataset containing half responders and half nonresponders, because the root node has a proportion of 50 percent. As described in Chapter 3, this is typical of a training set for a response model with a binary target variable. Any node with more than 50 percent responders is labeled with "1" in Figure 6.1, including nodes 17 and 18. Figure 6.2 clarifies the difference between these nodes. In Node 17, 52.8 percent of records represent responders, while in Node 18, 66.9 percent do. Clearly, a record in Node 18 is more likely to represent a responder than a record in Node 17. The proportion of records in the desired class can be used as a *score*, which is often more useful than just the classification. For a binary outcome, a classification merely splits records into two groups. A score allows the records to be sorted from most likely to least likely to be members of the desired class.

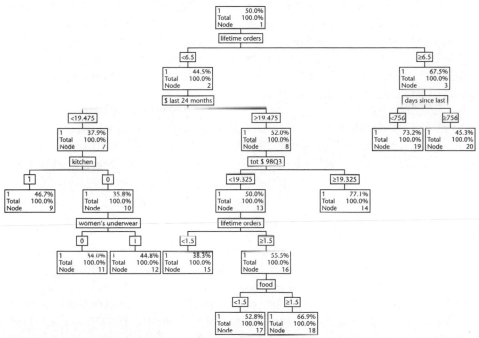

**Figure 6.2**  A decision tree annotated with the proportion of records in class 1 at each node shows the probability of the classification.

For many applications, a score capable of rank-ordering a list is all that is required. This is sufficient to choose the top *N* percent for a mailing and to calculate lift at various depths in the list. For some applications, however, it is not sufficient to know that A is more likely to respond than B; we want to know that actual likelihood of a response from A. Assuming that the prior probability of a response is known, it can be used to calculate the probability of response from the score generated on the oversampled data used to build the tree. Alternatively, the model can be applied to preclassified data that has a distribution of responses that reflects the true population. This method, called *backfitting*, creates scores using the class proportions at the tree's leaves to represent the probability that a record drawn from a similar population is a member of the class. These, and related issues, are discussed in detail in Chapter 3.

## Estimation

Suppose the important business question is not *who will respond* but *what will be the size of the customer's next order*? The decision tree can be used to answer that question too. Assuming that order amount is one of the variables available in the preclassified model set, the average order size in each leaf can be used as the estimated order size for any unclassified record that meets the criteria for that leaf. It is even possible to use a numeric target variable to build the tree; such a tree is called a *regression tree*. Instead of increasing the purity of a categorical variable, each split in the tree is chosen to decrease the variance in the values of the target variable within each child node.

The fact that trees can be (and sometimes are) used to estimate continuous values does not make it a good idea. A decision tree estimator can only generate as many discrete values as there are leaves in the tree. To estimate a continuous variable, it is preferable to use a continuous function. Regression models and neural network models are generally more appropriate for estimation.

## Trees Grow in Many Forms

The tree in Figure 6.1 is a binary tree of nonuniform depth; that is, each nonleaf node has two children and leaves are not all at the same distance from the root. In this case, each node represents a yes-or-no question, whose answer determines by which of two paths a record proceeds to the next level of the tree. Since any multiway split can be expressed as a series of binary splits, there is no real need for trees with higher branching factors. Nevertheless, many data mining tools are capable of producing trees with more than two branches. For example, some decision tree algorithms split on categorical variables by creating a branch for each class, leading to trees with differing numbers of branches at different nodes. Figure 6.3 illustrates a tree that uses both three-way and two-way splits for the same classification problem as the tree in Figures 6.1 and 6.2.

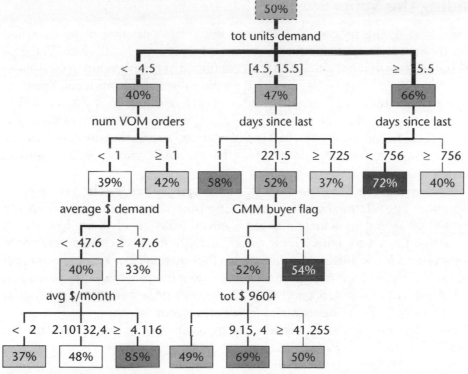

**Figure 6.3** This ternary decision tree is applied to the same the same classification problem as in Figure 6.1.

**TIP** There is no relationship between the number of branches allowed at a node and the number of classes in the target variable. A binary tree (that is, one with two-way splits) can be used to classify records into any number of categories, and a tree with multiway splits can be used to classify a binary target variable.

## How a Decision Tree Is Grown

Although there are many variations on the core decision tree algorithm, all of them share the same basic procedure: Repeatedly split the data into smaller and smaller groups in such a way that each new generation of nodes has greater purity than its ancestors with respect to the target variable. For most of this discussion, we assume a binary, categorical target variable, such as responder/nonresponder. This simplifies the explanations without much loss of generality.

## Finding the Splits

At the start of the process, there is a training set consisting of preclassified records—that is, the value of the target variable is known for all cases. The goal is to build a tree that assigns a class (or a likelihood of membership in each class) to the target field of a new record based on the values of the input variables.

The tree is built by splitting the records at each node according to a function of a single input field. The first task, therefore, is to decide which of the input fields makes the best split. The best split is defined as one that does the best job of separating the records into groups where a single class predominates in each group.

The measure used to evaluate a potential split is *purity*. The next section talks about specific methods for calculating purity in more detail. However, they are all trying to achieve the same effect. With all of them, low purity means that the set contains a representative distribution of classes (relative to the parent node), while high purity means that members of a single class predominate. The best split is the one that increases the purity of the record sets by the greatest amount. A good split also creates nodes of similar size, or at least does not create nodes containing very few records.

These ideas are easy to see visually. Figure 6.4 illustrates some good and bad splits.

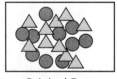

Original Data

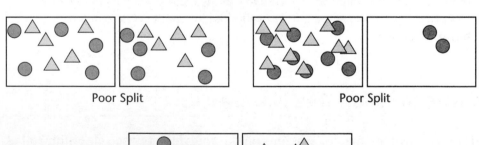

Poor Split                    Poor Split

Good Split

**Figure 6.4**   A good split increases purity for all the children.

The first split is a poor one because there is no increase in purity. The initial population contains equal numbers of the two sorts of dot; after the split, so does each child. The second split is also poor, because all though purity is increased slightly, the pure node has few members and the purity of the larger child is only marginally better than that of the parent. The final split is a good one because it leads to children of roughly same size and with much higher purity than the parent.

Tree-building algorithms are exhaustive. They proceed by taking each input variable in turn and measuring the increase in purity that results from every split suggested by that variable. After trying all the input variables, the one that yields the best split is used for the initial split, creating two or more children. If no split is possible (because there are too few records) or if no split makes an improvement, then the algorithm is finished with that node and the node become a leaf node. Otherwise, the algorithm performs the split and repeats itself on each of the children. An algorithm that repeats itself in this way is called a *recursive algorithm*.

Splits are evaluated based on their effect on node purity in terms of the target variable. This means that the choice of an appropriate splitting criterion depends on the type of the *target* variable, not on the type of the *input* variable. With a categorical target variable, a test such as Gini, information gain, or chi-square is appropriate whether the input variable providing the split is numeric or categorical. Similarly, with a continuous, numeric variable, a test such as variance reduction or the F-test is appropriate for evaluating the split regardless of whether the input variable providing the split is categorical or numeric.

## Splitting on a Numeric Input Variable

When searching for a binary split on a numeric input variable, each value that the variable takes on in the training set is treated as a candidate value for the split. Splits on a numeric variable take the form $X < N$. All records where the value of $X$ (the splitting variable) is less than some constant $N$ are sent to one child and all records where the value of $X$ is greater than or equal to $N$ are sent to the other. After each trial split, the increase in purity, if any, due to the split is measured. In the interests of efficiency, some implementations of the splitting algorithm do not actually evaluate every value; they evaluate a sample of the values instead.

When the decision tree is scored, the only use that it makes of numeric inputs is to compare their values with the split points. They are never multiplied by weights or added together as they are in many other types of models. This has the important consequence that decision trees are not sensitive to outliers or skewed distributions of numeric variables, because the tree only uses the rank of numeric variables and not their absolute values.

## Splitting on a Categorical Input Variable

The simplest algorithm for splitting on a categorical input variable is simply to create a new branch for each class that the categorical variable can take on. So, if color is chosen as the best field on which to split the root node, and the training set includes records that take on the values red, orange, yellow, green, blue, indigo, and violet, then there will be seven nodes in the next level of the tree. This approach is actually used by some software packages, but it often yields poor results. High branching factors quickly reduce the population of training records available at each node in lower levels of the tree, making further splits less reliable.

A more common approach is to group together the classes that, taken individually, predict similar outcomes. More precisely, if two classes of the input variable yield distributions of the classes of the output variable that do not differ *significantly* from one another, the two classes can be merged. The usual test for whether the distributions differ significantly is the chi-square test.

## Splitting in the Presence of Missing Values

One of the nicest things about decision trees is their ability to handle missing values in either numeric or categorical input fields by simply considering null to be a possible value with its own branch. This approach is preferable to throwing out records with missing values or trying to impute missing values. Throwing out records due to missing values is likely to create a biased training set because the records with missing values are not likely to be a random sample of the population. Replacing missing values with imputed values has the risk that important information provided by the fact that a value is missing will be ignored in the model. We have seen many cases where the fact that a particular value is null has predictive value. In one such case, the count of non-null values in appended household-level demographic data was positively correlated with response to an offer of term life insurance. Apparently, people who leave many traces in Acxiom's household database (by buying houses, getting married, registering products, and subscribing to magazines) are more likely to be interested in life insurance than those whose lifestyles leave more fields null.

> **TIP** Decision trees can produce splits based on missing values of an input variable. The fact that a value is null can often have predictive value so do not be hasty to filter out records with missing values or to try to replace them with imputed values.

Although splitting on null as a separate class is often quite valuable, at least one data mining product offers an alternative approach as well. In Enterprise Miner, each node stores several possible splitting rules, each one based on a different input field. When a null value is encountered in the field that yields the best splits, the software uses the *surrogate split* based on the next best available input variable.

## Growing the Full Tree

The initial split produces two or more child nodes, each of which is then split in the same manner as the root node. Once again, all input fields are considered as candidate splitters, even fields already used for splits. However, fields that take on only one value are eliminated from consideration since there is no way that they can be used to create a split. A categorical field that has been used as a splitter higher up in the tree is likely to become single-valued fairly quickly. The best split for each of the remaining fields is determined. When no split can be found that significantly increases the purity of a given node, or when the number of records in the node reaches some preset lower bound, or when the depth of the tree reaches some preset limit, the split search for that branch is abandoned and the node is labeled as a leaf node.

Eventually, it is not possible to find any more splits anywhere in the tree and the full decision tree has been grown. As we will see, this full tree is generally not the tree that does the best job of classifying a new set of records.

Decision-tree-building algorithms begin by trying to find the input variable that does the best job of splitting the data among the desired categories. At each succeeding level of the tree, the subsets created by the preceding split are themselves split according to whatever rule works best for them. The tree continues to grow until it is no longer possible to find better ways to split up incoming records. If there were a completely deterministic relationship between the input variables and the target, this recursive splitting would eventually yield a tree with completely pure leaves. It is easy to manufacture examples of this sort, but they do not occur very often in marketing or CRM applications.

Customer behavior data almost never contains such clear, deterministic relationships between inputs and outputs. The fact that two customers have the exact same description in terms of the available input variables does not ensure that they will exhibit the same behavior. A decision tree for a catalog response model might include a leaf representing females with age greater than 50, three or more purchases within the last year, and total lifetime spending of over $145. The customers reaching this leaf will typically be a mix of responders and nonresponders. If the leaf in question is labeled "responder," than the proportion of nonresponders is the *error rate* for this leaf. The ratio of the proportion of responders in this leaf to the proportion of responders in the population is the *lift* at this leaf.

One circumstance where deterministic rules are likely to be discovered is when patterns in data reflect business rules. The authors had this fact driven home to them by an experience at Caterpillar, a manufacturer of diesel engines. We built a decision tree model to predict which warranty claims would be approved. At the time, the company had a policy by which certain claims were paid automatically. The results were startling: The model was 100 percent accurate on unseen test data. In other words, it had discovered the exact rules used by Caterpillar to classify the claims. On this problem, a neural network tool was less successful. Of course, discovering known business rules may not be particularly useful; it does, however, underline the effectiveness of decision trees on rule-oriented problems.

Many domains, ranging from genetics to industrial processes really do have underlying rules, though these may be quite complex and obscured by noisy data. Decision trees are a natural choice when you suspect the existence of underlying rules.

## Measuring the Effectiveness Decision Tree

The effectiveness of a decision tree, taken as a whole, is determined by applying it to the test set—a collection of records not used to build the tree—and observing the percentage classified correctly. This provides the classification error rate for the tree as a whole, but it is also important to pay attention to the quality of the individual branches of the tree. Each path through the tree represents a rule, and some rules are better than others.

At each node, whether a leaf node or a branching node, we can measure:

- The number of records entering the node
- The proportion of records in each class
- How those records would be classified if this were a leaf node
- The percentage of records classified correctly at this node
- The variance in distribution between the training set and the test set

Of particular interest is the percentage of records classified correctly at this node. Surprisingly, sometimes a node higher up in the tree does a better job of classifying the test set than nodes lower down.

## Tests for Choosing the Best Split

A number of different measures are available to evaluate potential splits. Algorithms developed in the machine learning community focus on the increase in purity resulting from a split, while those developed in the statistics community focus on the statistical significance of the difference between the distributions of the child nodes. Alternate splitting criteria often lead to trees that look quite different from one another, but have similar performance. That is because there are usually many candidate splits with very similar performance. Different purity measures lead to different candidates being selected, but since all of the measures are trying to capture the same idea, the resulting models tend to behave similarly.

## Purity and Diversity

The first edition of this book described splitting criteria in terms of the *decrease in diversity* resulting from the split. In this edition, we refer instead to the *increase in purity*, which seems slightly more intuitive. The two phrases refer to the same idea. A purity measure that ranges from 0 (when no two items in the sample are in the same class) to 1 (when all items in the sample are in the same class) can be turned into a diversity measure by subtracting it from 1. Some of the measures used to evaluate decision tree splits assign the lowest score to a pure node; others assign the highest score to a pure node. This discussion refers to all of them as purity measures, and the goal is to optimize purity by minimizing or maximizing the chosen measure.

Figure 6.5 shows a good split. The parent node contains equal numbers of light and dark dots. The left child contains nine light dots and one dark dot. The right child contains nine dark dots and one light dot. Clearly, the purity has increased, but how can the increase be quantified? And how can this split be compared to others? That requires a formal definition of purity, several of which are listed below.

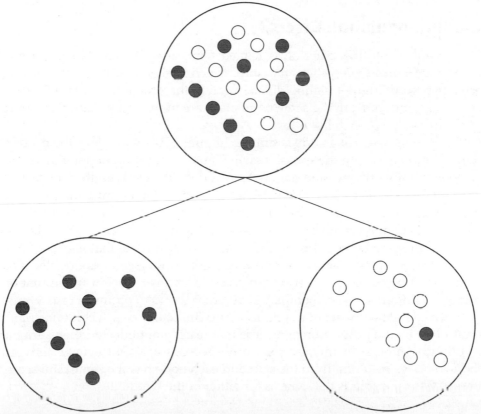

**Figure 6.5**  A good split on a binary categorical variable increases purity.

Purity measures for evaluating splits for categorical target variables include:

- Gini (also called population diversity)
- Entropy (also called information gain)
- Information gain ratio
- Chi-square test

When the target variable is numeric, one approach is to bin the value and use one of the above measures. There are, however, two measures in common use for numeric targets:

- Reduction in variance
- F test

Note that the choice of an appropriate purity measure depends on whether the *target* variable is categorical or numeric. The type of the input variable does not matter, so an entire tree is built with the same purity measure. The split illustrated in 6.5 might be provided by a numeric input variable (AGE > 46) or by a categorical variable (STATE is a member of CT, MA, ME, NH, RI, VT). The purity of the children is the same regardless of the type of split.

## Gini or Population Diversity

One popular splitting criterion is named Gini, after Italian statistician and economist, Corrado Gini. This measure, which is also used by biologists and ecologists studying population diversity, gives the probability that two items chosen at random from the same population are in the same class. For a pure population, this probability is 1.

The Gini measure of a node is simply the sum of the squares of the proportions of the classes. For the split shown in Figure 6.5, the parent population has an equal number of light and dark dots. A node with equal numbers of each of 2 classes has a score of $0.5^2 + 0.5^2 = 0.5$, which is expected because the chance of picking the same class twice by random selection with replacement is one out of two. The Gini score for either of the resulting nodes is $0.1^2 + 0.9^2 = 0.82$. A perfectly pure node would have a Gini score of 1. A node that is evenly balanced would have a Gini score of 0.5. Sometimes the scores is doubled and then 1 subtracted, so it is between 0 and 1. However, such a manipulation makes no difference when comparing different scores to optimize purity.

To calculate the impact of a split, take the Gini score of each child node and multiply it by the proportion of records that reach that node and then sum the resulting numbers. In this case, since the records are split evenly between the two nodes resulting from the split and each node has the same Gini score, the score for the split is the same as for either of the two nodes.

## Entropy Reduction or Information Gain

Information gain uses a clever idea for defining purity. If a leaf is entirely pure, then the classes in the leaf can be easily described—they all fall in the same class. On the other hand, if a leaf is highly impure, then describing it is much more complicated. Information theory, a part of computer science, has devised a measure for this situation called *entropy*. In information theory, *entropy* is a measure of how disorganized a system is. A comprehensive introduction to information theory is far beyond the scope of this book. For our purposes, the intuitive notion is that the number of bits required to describe a particular situation or outcome depends on the size of the set of possible outcomes. Entropy can be thought of as a measure of the number of yes/no questions it would take to determine the state of the system. If there are 16 possible states, it takes $\log_2(16)$, or four bits, to enumerate them or identify a particular one. Additional information reduces the number of questions needed to determine the state of the system, so information gain means the same thing as entropy reduction. Both terms are used to describe decision tree algorithms.

The entropy of a particular decision tree node is the sum, over all the classes represented in the node, of the proportion of records belonging to a particular class multiplied by the base two logarithm of that proportion. (Actually, this sum is usually multiplied by –1 in order to obtain a positive number.) The entropy of a split is simply the sum of the entropies of all the nodes resulting from the split weighted by each node's proportion of the records. When entropy reduction is chosen as a splitting criterion, the algorithm searches for the split that reduces entropy (or, equivalently, increases information) by the greatest amount.

For a binary target variable such as the one shown in Figure 6.5, the formula for the entropy of a single node is

```
-1 * ( P(dark)log₂P(dark) + P(light)log₂P(light) )
```

In this example, $P$(dark) and $P$(light) are both one half. Plugging 0.5 into the entropy formula gives:

```
-1 * (0.5 log₂(0.5) + 0.5 log₂(0.5))
```

The first term is for the light dots and the second term is for the dark dots, but since there are equal numbers of light and dark dots, the expression simplifies to $-1 * \log_2(0.5)$ which is +1. What is the entropy of the nodes resulting from the split? One of them has one dark dot and nine light dots, while the other has nine dark dots and one light dots. Clearly, they each have the same level of entropy. Namely,

```
-1 * (0.1 log₂(0.1) + 0.9 log₂(0.9)) = 0.33 + 0.14 = 0.47
```

To calculate the total entropy of the system after the split, multiply the entropy of each node by the proportion of records that reach that node and add them up to get an average. In this example, each of the new nodes receives half the records, so the total entropy is the same as the entropy of each of the nodes, 0.47. The total entropy reduction or information gain due to the split is therefore 0.53. This is the figure that would be used to compare this split with other candidates.

## Information Gain Ratio

The entropy split measure can run into trouble when combined with a splitting methodology that handles categorical input variables by creating a separate branch for each value. This was the case for ID3, a decision tree tool developed by Australian researcher J. Ross Quinlan in the nineteen-eighties, that became part of several commercial data mining software packages. The problem is that just by breaking the larger data set into many small subsets , the number of classes represented in each node tends to go down, and with it, the entropy. The decrease in entropy due solely to the number of branches is called the *intrinsic information* of a split. (Recall that entropy is defined as the sum over all the branches of the probability of each branch times the log base 2 of that probability. For a random n-way split, the probability of each branch is $1/n$. Therefore, the entropy due solely to splitting from an n-way split is simply $n * 1/n \log (1/n)$ or $\log(1/n)$. Because of the intrinsic information of many-way splits, decision trees built using the entropy reduction splitting criterion without any correction for the intrinsic information due to the split tend to be quite bushy. Bushy trees with many multi-way splits are undesirable as these splits lead to small numbers of records in each node, a recipe for unstable models.

In reaction to this problem, C5 and other descendents of ID3 that once used information gain now use the ratio of the total information gain due to a proposed split to the intrinsic information attributable solely to the number of branches created as the criterion for evaluating proposed splits. This test reduces the tendency towards very bushy trees that was a problem in earlier decision tree software packages.

## Chi-Square Test

As described in Chapter 5, the chi-square ($X^2$) test is a test of statistical significance developed by the English statistician Karl Pearson in 1900. Chi-square is defined as the sum of the squares of the standardized differences between the *expected* and *observed* frequencies of some occurrence between multiple disjoint samples. In other words, the test is a measure of the probability that an observed difference between samples is due only to chance. When used to measure the purity of decision tree splits, higher values of chi-square mean that the variation is more significant, and not due merely to chance.

## COMPARING TWO SPLITS USING GINI AND ENTROPY

Consider the following two splits, illustrated in the figure below. In both cases, the population starts out perfectly balanced between dark and light dots with ten of each type. One proposed split is the same as in Figure 6.5 yielding two equal-sized nodes, one 90 percent dark and the other 90 percent light. The second split yields one node that is 100 percent pure dark, but only has 6 dots and another that that has 14 dots and is 71.4 percent light.

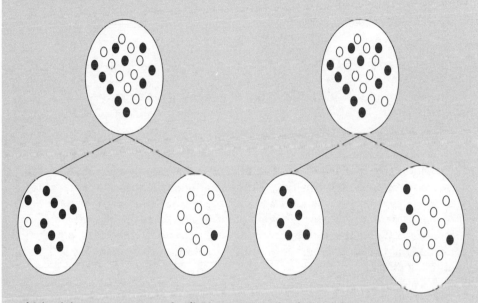

Which of these two proposed splits increases purity the most?

### EVALUATING THE TWO SPLITS USING GINI

As explained in the main text, the Gini score for each of the two children in the first proposed split is $0.1^2 + 0.9^2 = 0.820$. Since the children are the same size, this is also the score for the split.

What about the second proposed split? The Gini score of the left child is 1 since only one class is represented. The Gini score of the right child is

$$\text{Gini}_{right} = (4/14)^2 + (10/14)^2 = 0.082 + 0.510 = 0.592$$

and the Gini score for the split is:

$$(6/20)\text{Gini}_{left} + (14/20)\text{Gini}_{right} = 0.3*1 + 0.7*0.592 = 0.714$$

Since the Gini score for the first proposed split (0.820) is greater than for the second proposed split (0.714), a tree built using the Gini criterion will prefer the split that yields two nearly pure children over the split that yields one completely pure child along with a larger, less pure one.

*(continued)*

**COMPARING TWO SPLITS USING GINI AND ENTROPY** *(continued)*

**EVALUATING THE TWO SPLITS USING ENTROPY**

As calculated in the main text, the entropy of the parent node is 1. The entropy of the first proposed split is also calculated in the main text and found to be 0.47 so the information gain for the first proposed split is 0.53.

How much information is gained by the second proposed split? The left child is pure and so has entropy of 0. As for the right child, the formula for entropy is

```
-(P(dark)log₂P(dark) + P(light)log₂P(light))
```

so the entropy of the right child is:

```
Entropy_right = -((4/14)log₂(4/14) + (10/14)log₂(10/14)) = 0.516 +
0.347 = 0.863
```

The entropy of the split is the weighted average of the entropies of the resulting nodes. In this case,

```
0.3*Entropy_left + 0.7*Entropy_right = 0.3*0 + 0.7*0.863 = 0.604
```

Subtracting 0.604 from the entropy of the parent (which is 1) yields an information gain of 0.396. This is less than 0.53, the information gain from the first proposed split, so in this case, entropy splitting criterion also prefers the first split to the second. Compared to Gini, the entropy criterion does have a stronger preference for nodes that are purer, even if smaller. This may be appropriate in domains where there really are clear underlying rules, but it tends to lead to less stable trees in "noisy" domains such as response to marketing offers.

For example, suppose the target variable is a binary flag indicating whether or not customers continued their subscriptions at the end of the introductory offer period and the proposed split is on acquisition channel, a categorical variable with three classes: direct mail, outbound call, and email. If the acquisition channel had no effect on renewal rate, we would expect the number of renewals in each class to be proportional to the number of customers acquired through that channel. For each channel, the chi-square test subtracts that expected number of renewals from the actual observed renewals, squares the difference, and divides the difference by the expected number. The values for each class are added together to arrive at the score. As described in Chapter 5, the chi-square distribution provide a way to translate this chi-square score into a probability. To measure the purity of a split in a decision tree, the score is sufficient. A high score means that the proposed split successfully splits the population into subpopulations with significantly different distributions.

The chi-square test gives its name to CHAID, a well-known decision tree algorithm first published by John A. Hartigan in 1975. The full acronym stands for Chi-square Automatic Interaction Detector. As the phrase "automatic interaction detector" implies, the original motivation for CHAID was for detecting statistical relationships between variables. It does this by building a decision tree, so the method has come to be used as a classification tool as well. CHAID makes use of the Chi-square test in several ways—first to merge classes that do not have significantly different effects on the target variable; then to choose a best split; and finally to decide whether it is worth performing any additional splits on a node. In the research community, the current fashion is away from methods that continue splitting only as long as it seems likely to be useful and towards methods that involve pruning. Some researchers, however, still prefer the original CHAID approach, which does not rely on pruning.

The chi-square test applies to categorical variables so in the classic CHAID algorithm, input variables must be categorical. Continuous variables must be binned or replaced with ordinal classes such as *high, medium, low*. Some current decision tree tools such as SAS Enterprise Miner, use the chi-square test for creating splits using categorical variables, but use another statistical test, the F test, for creating splits on continuous variables. Also, some implementations of CHAID continue to build the tree even when the splits are not statistically significant, and then apply pruning algorithms to prune the tree back.

## Reduction in Variance

The four previous measures of purity all apply to categorical targets. When the target variable is numeric, a good split should reduce the variance of the target variable. Recall that variance is a measure of the tendency of the values in a population to stay close to the mean value. In a sample with low variance, most values are quite close to the mean; in a sample with high variance, many values are quite far from the mean. The actual formula for the variance is the mean of the sums of the squared deviations from the mean. Although the reduction in variance split criterion is meant for numeric targets, the dark and light dots in Figure 6.5 can still be used to illustrate it by considering the dark dots to be 1 and the light dots to be 0. The mean value in the parent node is clearly 0.5. Every one of the 20 observations differs from the mean by 0.5, so the variance is $(20 * 0.5^2) / 20 = 0.25$. After the split, the left child has 9 dark spots and one light spot, so the node mean is 0.9. Nine of the observations differ from the mean value by 0.1 and one observation differs from the mean value by 0.9 so the variance is $(0.9^2 + 9 * 0.1^2) / 10 = 0.09$. Since both nodes resulting from the split have variance 0.09, the total variance after the split is also 0.09. The reduction in variance due to the split is $0.25 - 0.09 = 0.16$.

## F Test

Another split criterion that can be used for numeric target variables is the F test, named for another famous Englishman—statistician, astronomer, and geneticist, Ronald. A. Fisher. Fisher and Pearson reportedly did not get along despite, or perhaps because of, the large overlap in their areas of interest. Fisher's test does for continuous variables what Pearson's chi-square test does for categorical variables. It provides a measure of the probability that samples with different means and variances are actually drawn from the same population.

There is a well-understood relationship between the variance of a sample and the variance of the population from which it was drawn. (In fact, so long as the samples are of reasonable size and randomly drawn from the population, sample variance is a good estimate of population variance; very small samples—with fewer than 30 or so observations—usually have higher variance than their corresponding populations.) The F test looks at the relationship between two estimates of the population variance—one derived by pooling all the samples and calculating the variance of the combined sample, and one derived from the between-sample variance calculated as the variance of the sample means. If the various samples are randomly drawn from the same population, these two estimates should agree closely.

The F score is the ratio of the two estimates. It is calculated by dividing the between-sample estimate by the pooled sample estimate. The larger the score, the less likely it is that the samples are all randomly drawn from the same population. In the decision tree context, a large F-score indicates that a proposed split has successfully split the population into subpopulations with significantly different distributions.

## Pruning

As previously described, the decision tree keeps growing as long as new splits can be found that improve the ability of the tree to separate the records of the training set into increasingly pure subsets. Such a tree has been optimized for the training set, so eliminating any leaves would only increase the error rate of the tree on the training set. Does this imply that the full tree will also do the best job of classifying new datasets? Certainly not!

A decision tree algorithm makes its best split first, at the root node where there is a large population of records. As the nodes get smaller, idiosyncrasies of the particular training records at a node come to dominate the process. One way to think of this is that the tree finds general patterns at the big nodes and patterns specific to the training set in the smaller nodes; that is, the tree overfits the training set. The result is an unstable tree that will not make good predictions. The cure is to eliminate the unstable splits by merging smaller leaves through a process called pruning; three general approaches to pruning are discussed in detail.

## The CART Pruning Algorithm

CART is a popular decision tree algorithm first published by Leo Breiman, Jerome Friedman, Richard Olshen, and Charles Stone in 1984. The acronym stands for Classification and Regression Trees. The CART algorithm grows binary trees and continues splitting as long as new splits can be found that increase purity. As illustrated in Figure 6.6, inside a complex tree, there are many simpler subtrees, each of which represents a different trade-off between model complexity and training set misclassification rate. The CART algorithm identifies a set of such subtrees as candidate models. These candidate subtrees are applied to the validation set and the tree with the lowest validation set misclassification rate is selected as the final model.

### Creating the Candidate Subtrees

The CART algorithm identifies candidate subtrees through a process of repeated pruning. The goal is to prune first those branches providing the least additional predictive power per leaf. In order to identify these least useful branches, CART relies on a concept called the *adjusted error rate*. This is a measure that increases each node's misclassification rate on the training set by imposing a complexity penalty based on the number of leaves in the tree. The adjusted error rate is used to identify weak branches (those whose misclassification rate is not low enough to overcome the penalty) and mark them for pruning.

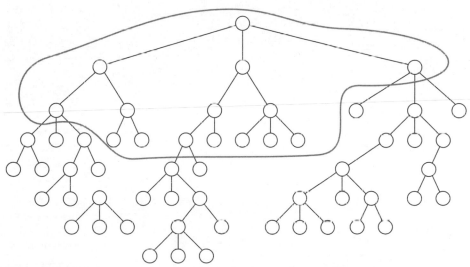

**Figure 6.6**  Inside a complex tree, there are simpler, more stable trees.

## COMPARING MISCLASSIFICAION RATES ON TRAINING AND VALIDATION SETS

The error rate on the validation set should be larger than the error rate on the training set, because the training set was used to build the rules in the model. A large difference in the misclassification error rate, however, is a symptom of an unstable model. This difference can show up in several ways as shown by the following three graphs generated by SAS Enterprise Miner. The graphs represent the percent of records correctly classified by the candidate models in a decision tree. Candidate subtrees with fewer nodes are on the left; with more nodes are on the right. These figures show the percent correctly classified instead of the error rate, so they are upside down from the way similar charts are shown elsewhere in this book.

As expected, the first chart shows the candidate trees performing better and better on the training set as the trees have more and more nodes—the training process stops when the performance no longer improves. On the validation set, however, the candidate trees reach a peak and then the performance starts to decline as the trees get larger. The optimal tree is the one that works on the validation set, and the choice is easy because the peak is well-defined.

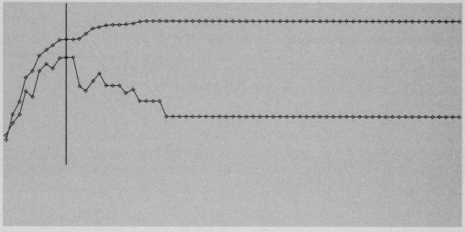

This chart shows a clear inflection point in the graph of the percent correctly classified in the validation set.

**COMPARING MISCLASSIFICAION RATES ON TRAINING AND
VALIDATION SETS** *(continued)*

Sometimes, though, there is not clear demarcation point. That is, the
performance of the candidate models on the validation set never quite reaches
a maximum as the trees get larger. In this case, the pruning algorithm chooses
the entire tree (the largest possible subtree), as shown in the following
illustration:

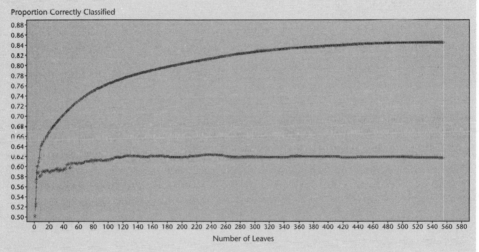

In this chart, the percent correctly classified in the validation set levels off early and
remains far below the percent correctly classified in the training set.

The final example is perhaps the most interesting, because the results on the
validation set become unstable as the candidate trees become larger. The cause
of the instability is that the leaves are too small. In this tree, there is an
example of a leaf that has three records from the training set and all three have
a target value of 1 – a perfect leaf. However, in the validation set, the one
record that falls there has the value 0. The leaf is 100 percent wrong. As the
tree grows more complex, more of these too-small leaves are included,
resulting in the instability seen below:

*(continued)*

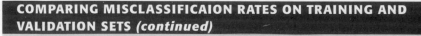

**COMPARING MISCLASSIFICAION RATES ON TRAINING AND VALIDATION SETS** *(continued)*

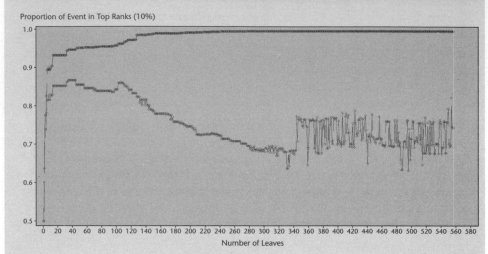

Proportion of Event in Top Ranks (10%)

Number of Leaves

In this chart, the percent correctly classified on the validation set decreases with the complexity of the tree and eventually becomes chaotic.

**The last two figures are examples of unstable models. The simplest way to avoid instability of this sort is to ensure that leaves are not allowed to become too small.**

The formula for the adjusted error rate is:

```
AE(T) = E(T) + αleaf_count(T)
```

Where $\alpha$ is an adjustment factor that is increased in gradual steps to create new subtrees. When $\alpha$ is zero, the adjusted error rate equals the error rate. To find the first subtree, the adjusted error rates for all possible subtrees containing the root node are evaluated as $\alpha$ is gradually increased. When the adjusted error rate of some subtree becomes less than or equal to the adjusted error rate for the complete tree, we have found the first candidate subtree, $\alpha_1$. All branches that are not part of $\alpha_1$ are pruned and the process starts again. The $\alpha_1$ tree is pruned to create an $\alpha_2$ tree. The process ends when the tree has been pruned all the way down to the root node. Each of the resulting subtrees (sometimes called the *alphas*) is a candidate to be the final model. Notice that all the candidates contain the root node and the largest candidate is the entire tree.

## Picking the Best Subtree

The next task is to select, from the pool of candidate subtrees, the one that works best on new data. That, of course, is the purpose of the validation set. Each of the candidate subtrees is used to classify the records in the validation set. The tree that performs this task with the lowest overall error rate is declared the winner. The winning subtree has been pruned sufficiently to remove the effects of overtraining, but not so much as to lose valuable information. The graph in Figure 6.7 illustrates the effect of pruning on classification accuracy. The technical aside goes into this in more detail.

Because this pruning algorithm is based solely on misclassification rate, without taking the probability of each classification into account, it replaces any subtree whose leaves all make the same classification with a common parent that also makes that classification. In applications where the goal is to select a small proportion of the records (the top 1 percent or 10 percent, for example), this pruning algorithm may hurt the performance of the tree, since some of the removed leaves contain a very high proportion of the target class. Some tools, such as SAS Enterprise Miner, allow the user to prune trees optimally for such situations.

## Using the Test Set to Evaluate the Final Tree

The winning subtree was selected on the basis of its overall error rate when applied to the task of classifying the records in the validation set. But, while we expect that the selected subtree will continue to be the best performing subtree when applied to other datasets, the error rate that caused it to be selected may slightly overstate its effectiveness. There are likely to be a large number of subtrees that all perform about as well as the one selected. To a certain extent, the one of these that delivered the lowest error rate on the validation set may simply have "gotten lucky" with that particular collection of records. For that reason, as explained in Chapter 3, the selected subtree is applied to a third preclassified dataset that is disjoint with both the validation set and the training set. This third dataset is called the test set. The error rate obtained on the test set is used to predict expected performance of the classification rules represented by the selected tree when applied to unclassified data.

**WARNING** Do not evaluate the performance of a model by its lift or error rate on the validation set. Like the training set, it has had a hand in creating the model and so will overstate the model's accuracy. Always measure the model's accuracy on a test set that is drawn from the same population as the training and validation sets, but has not been used in any way to create the model.

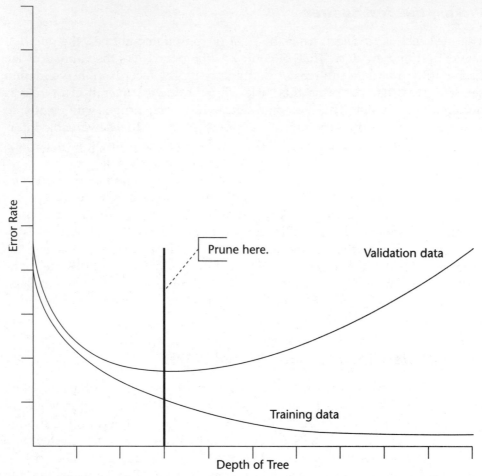

**Figure 6.7** Pruning chooses the tree whose miscalculation rate is minimized on the validation set.

## The C5 Pruning Algorithm

C5 is the most recent version of the decision-tree algorithm that Australian researcher, J. Ross Quinlan has been evolving and refining for many years. An earlier version, ID3, published in 1986, was very influential in the field of machine learning and its successors are used in several commercial data mining products. (The name ID3 stands for "Iterative Dichotomiser 3." We have not heard an explanation for the name C5, but we can guess that Professor Quinlan's background is mathematics rather than marketing.) C5 is available as a commercial product from RuleQuest (www.rulequest.com).

The trees grown by C5 are similar to those grown by CART (although unlike CART, C5 makes multiway splits on categorical variables). Like CART, the C5 algorithm first grows an overfit tree and then prunes it back to create a more stable model. The pruning strategy is quite different, however. C5 does not make use of a validation set to choose from among candidate subtrees; the same data used to grow the tree is also used to decide how the tree should be pruned. This may reflect the algorithm's origins in the academic world, where in the past, university researchers had a hard time getting their hands on substantial quantities of real data to use for training sets. Consequently, they spent much time and effort trying to coax the last few drops of information from their impoverished datasets—a problem that data miners in the business world do not face.

### Pessimistic Pruning

C5 prunes the tree by examining the error rate at each node and assuming that the true error rate is actually substantially worse. If $N$ records arrive at a node, and $E$ of them are classified incorrectly, then the error rate at that node is $E/N$. Now the whole point of the tree-growing algorithm is to minimize this error rate, so the algorithm assumes that $E/N$ is the best than can be done.

C5 uses an analogy with statistical sampling to come up with an estimate of the worst error rate likely to be seen at a leaf. The analogy works by thinking of the data at the leaf as representing the results of a series of trials each of which can have one of two possible results. (Heads or tails is the usual example.) As it happens, statisticians have been studying this particular situation since at least 1713, the year that Jacques Bernoulli's famous binomial formula was posthumously published. So there are well-known formulas for determining what it means to have observed $E$ occurrences of some event in $N$ trials.

In particular, there is a formula which, for a given confidence level, gives the confidence interval—the range of expected values of $E$. C5 assumes that the observed number of errors on the training data is the low end of this range, and substitutes the high end to get a leaf's predicted error rate, $E/N$ on unseen data. The smaller the node, the higher the error rate. When the high-end estimate of the number of errors at a node is less than the estimate for the errors of its children, then the children are pruned.

## Stability-Based Pruning

The pruning algorithms used by CART and C5 (and indeed by all the commercial decision tree tools that the authors have used) have a problem. They fail to prune some nodes that are clearly unstable. The split highlighted in Figure 6.8 is a good example. The picture was produced by SAS Enterprise

Miner using its default settings for viewing a tree. The numbers on the left-hand side of each node show what is happening on the training set. The numbers on the right-hand side of each node show what is happening on the validation set. This particular tree is trying to identify churners. When only the training data is taken into consideration, the highlighted branch seems to do very well; the concentration of churners rises from 58.0 percent to 70.9 percent. Unfortunately, when the very same rule is applied to the validation set, the concentration of churners actually *decreases* from 56.6 percent to 52 percent.

One of the main purposes of a model is to make consistent predictions on previously unseen records. Any rule that cannot achieve that goal should be eliminated from the model. Many data mining tools allow the user to prune a decision tree manually. This is a useful facility, but we look forward to data mining software that provides automatic stability-based pruning as an option. Such software would need to have a less subjective criterion for rejecting a split than "the distribution of the validation set results looks different from the distribution of the training set results." One possibility would be to use a test of statistical significance, such as the chi-Square Test or the difference of proportions. The split would be pruned when the confidence level is less than some user-defined threshold, so only splits that are, say, 99 percent confident on the validation set would remain.

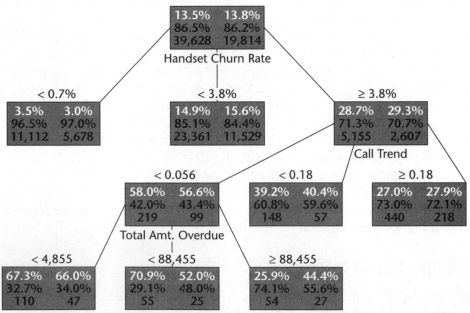

**Figure 6.8** An unstable split produces very different distributions on the training and validation sets.

**WARNING** Small nodes cause big problems. A common cause of unstable decision tree models is allowing nodes with too few records. Most decision tree tools allow the user to set a minimum node size. As a rule of thumb, nodes that receive fewer than about 100 training set records are likely to be unstable.

## Extracting Rules from Trees

When a decision tree is used primarily to generate scores, it is easy to forget that a decision tree is actually a collection of rules. If one of the purposes of the data mining effort is to gain understanding of the problem domain, it can be useful to reduce the huge tangle of rules in a decision tree to a smaller, more comprehensible collection.

There are other situations where the desired output is a set of rules. In *Mastering Data Mining*, we describe the application of decision trees to an industrial process improvement problem, namely the prevention of a certain type of printing defect. In that case, the end product of the data mining project was a small collection of simple rules that could be posted on the wall next to each press.

When a decision tree is used for producing scores, having a large number of leaves is advantageous because each leaf generates a different score. When the object is to generate rules, the fewer rules the better. Fortunately, it is often possible to collapse a complex tree into a smaller set of rules.

The first step in that direction is to combine paths that lead to leaves that make the same classification. The partial decision tree in Figure 6.9 yields the following rules:

Watch the game and home team wins and out with friends then **beer**.

Watch the game and home team wins and sitting at home then **diet soda**.

Watch the game and home team loses and out with friends then **beer**.

Watch the game and home team loses and sitting at home then **milk**.

The two rules that predict beer can be combined by eliminating the test for whether the home team wins or loses. That test is important for discriminating between milk and diet soda, but has no bearing on beer consumption. The new, simpler rule is:

Watch the game and out with friends then **beer**.

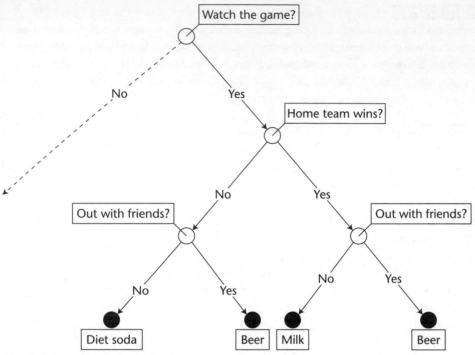

**Figure 6.9**  Multiple paths lead to the same conclusion.

Up to this point, nothing is controversial because no information has been lost, but C5's rule generator goes farther. It attempts to generalize each rule by removing clauses, then comparing the predicted error rate of the new, briefer rule to that of the original using the same pessimistic error rate assumption used for pruning the tree in the first place. Often, the rules for several different leaves generalize to the same rule, so this process results in fewer rules than the decision tree had leaves.

In the decision tree, every record ends up at exactly one leaf, so every record has a definitive classification. After the rule-generalization process, however, there may be rules that are not mutually exclusive and records that are not covered by any rule. Simply picking one rule when more than one is applicable can solve the first problem. The second problem requires the introduction of a *default class* assigned to any record not covered by any of the rules. Typically, the most frequently occurring class is chosen as the default.

Once it has created a set of generalized rules, Quinlan's C5 algorithm groups the rules for each class together and eliminates those that do not seem to contribute much to the accuracy of the set of rules as a whole. The end result is a small number of easy to understand rules.

## Taking Cost into Account

In the discussion so far, the error rate has been the sole measure for evaluating the fitness of rules and subtrees. In many applications, however, the costs of misclassification vary from class to class. Certainly, in a medical diagnosis, a false negative can be more harmful than a false positive; a scary Pap smear result that, on further investigation, proves to have been a false positive, is much preferable to an undetected cancer. A cost function multiplies the probability of misclassification by a weight indicating the cost of that misclassification. Several tools allow the use of such a cost function instead of an error function for building decision trees.

# Further Refinements to the Decision Tree Method

Although they are not found in most commercial data mining software packages, there are some interesting refinements to the basic decision tree method that are worth discussing.

## Using More Than One Field at a Time

Most decision tree algorithms test a single variable to perform each split. This approach can be problematic for several reasons, not least of which is that it can lead to trees with more nodes than necessary. Extra nodes are cause for concern because only the training records that arrive at a given node are available for inducing the subtree below it. The fewer training examples per node, the less stable the resulting model.

Suppose that we are interested in a condition for which both age and gender are important indicators. If the root node split is on age, then each child node contains only about half the women. If the initial split is on gender, then each child node contains only about half the old folks.

Several algorithms have been developed to allow multiple attributes to be used in combination to form the splitter. One technique forms Boolean conjunctions of features in order to reduce the complexity of the tree. After finding the feature that forms the best split, the algorithm looks for the feature which, when combined with the feature chosen first, does the best job of improving the split. Features continue to be added as long as there continues to be a statistically significant improvement in the resulting split.

This procedure can lead to a much more efficient representation of classification rules. As an example, consider the task of classifying the results of a vote according to whether the motion was passed unanimously. For simplicity, consider the case where there are only three votes cast. (The degree of simplification to be made only increases with the number of voters.)

Table 6.1 contains all possible combinations of three votes and an added column to indicate the unanimity of the result.

**Table 6.1** All Possible Combinations of Votes by Three Voters

| FIRST VOTER | SECOND VOTER | THIRD VOTER | UNANIMOUS? |
|---|---|---|---|
| Nay | Nay | Nay | **TRUE** |
| Nay | Nay | Aye | **FALSE** |
| Nay | Aye | Nay | **FALSE** |
| Nay | Aye | Aye | **FALSE** |
| Aye | Nay | Nay | **FALSE** |
| Aye | Nay | Aye | **FALSE** |
| Aye | Aye | Nay | **FALSE** |
| Aye | Aye | Aye | **TRUE** |

Figure 6.10 shows a tree that perfectly classifies the training data, requiring five internal splitting nodes. Do not worry about how this tree is created, since that is unnecessary to the point we are making.

Allowing features to be combined using the logical **and** function to form conjunctions yields the much simpler tree in Figure 6.11. The second tree illustrates another potential advantage that can arise from using combinations of fields. The tree now comes much closer to expressing the notion of unanimity that inspired the classes: "When all voters agree, the decision is unanimous."

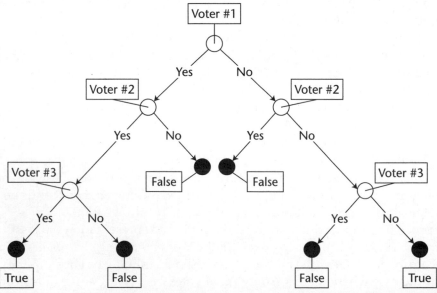

**Figure 6.10** The best binary tree for the unanimity function when splitting on single fields.

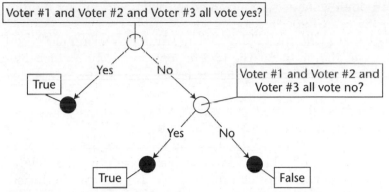

**Figure 6.11**  Combining features simplifies the tree for defining unanimity.

A tree that can be understood all at once is said, by machine learning researchers, to have good "mental fit." Some researchers in the machine learning field attach great importance to this notion, but that seems to be an artifact of the tiny, well-structured problems around which they build their studies. In the real world, if a classification task is so simple that you can get your mind around the entire decision tree that represents it, you probably don't need to waste your time with powerful data mining tools to discover it. We believe that the ability to understand the rule that leads to any particular leaf is very important; on the other hand, the ability to interpret an entire decision tree at a glance is neither important nor likely to be possible outside of the laboratory.

## Tilting the Hyperplane

Classification problems are sometimes presented in geometric terms. This way of thinking is especially natural for datasets having continuous variables for all fields. In this interpretation, each record is a point in a multidimensional space. Each field represents the position of the record along one axis of the space. Decision trees are a way of carving the space into regions, each of which is labeled with a class. Any new record that falls into one of the regions is classified accordingly.

Traditional decision trees, which test the value of a single field at each node, can only form *rectangular* regions. In a two-dimensional space, a test of the form Y less than some constant forms a region bounded by a line perpendicular to the Y-axis and parallel to the X-axis. Different values for the constant cause the line to move up and down, but the line remains horizontal. Similarly, in a space of higher dimensionality, a test on a single field defines a hyperplane that is perpendicular to the axis represented by the field used in the test and parallel to all the other axes. In a two-dimensional space, with only horizontal and vertical lines to work with, the resulting regions are rectangular. In three-dimensional space, the corresponding shapes are rectangular solids, and in any multidimensional space, there are hyper-rectangles.

The problem is that some things don't fit neatly into rectangular boxes. Figure 6.12 illustrates the problem: The two regions are really divided by a diagonal line; it takes a deep tree to generate enough rectangles to approximate it adequately.

In this case, the true solution can be found easily by allowing linear combinations of the attributes to be considered. Some software packages attempt to tilt the hyperplanes by basing their splits on a weighted sum of the values of the fields. There are a variety of hill-climbing approaches for selecting the weights.

Of course, it is easy to come up with regions that are not captured easily even when diagonal lines are allowed. Regions may have curved boundaries and fields may have to be combined in more complex ways (such as multiplying length by width to get area). There is no substitute for the careful selection of fields to be inputs to the tree-building process and, where necessary, the creation of derived fields that capture relationships known or suspected by domain experts. These derived fields may be functions of several other fields. Such derived fields inserted manually serve the same purpose as automatically combining fields to tilt the hyperplane.

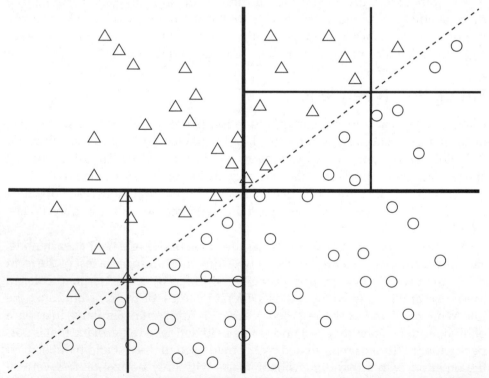

**Figure 6.12**  The upper-left and lower-right quadrants are easily classified, while the other two quadrants must be carved up into many small boxes to approximate the boundary between the regions.

## Neural Trees

One way of combining input from many fields at every node is to have each node consist of a small neural network. For domains where rectangular regions do a poor job describing the true shapes of the classes, neural trees can produce more accurate classifications, while being quicker to train and to score than pure neural networks.

From the point of view of the user, this hybrid technique has more in common with neural-network variants than it does with decision-tree variants because, in common with other neural-network techniques, it is not capable of explaining its decisions. The tree still produces rules, but these are of the form $F(w1x1, w2x2, w3x3, . . .) \leq N$, where $F$ is the combining function used by the neural network. Such rules make more sense to neural network software than to people.

## Piecewise Regression Using Trees

Another example of combining trees with other modelling methods is a form of piecewise linear regression in which each split in a decision tree is chosen so as to minimize the error of a simple regression model on the data at that node. The same method can be applied to logistic regression for categorical target variables.

# Alternate Representations for Decision Trees

The traditional tree diagram is a very effective way of representing the actual structure of a decision tree. Other representations are sometimes more useful when the focus is more on the relative sizes and concentrations of the nodes.

## Box Diagrams

While the tree diagram and Twenty Questions analogy are helpful in visualizing certain properties of decision-tree methods, in some cases, a box diagram is more revealing. Figure 6.13 shows the box diagram representation of a decision tree that tries to classify people as male or female based on their ages and the movies they have seen recently. The diagram may be viewed as a sort of nested collection of two-dimensional scatter plots.

At the root node of a decision tree, the first three-way split is based on which of three groups the survey respondent's most recently seen movie falls. In the outermost box of the diagram, the horizontal axis represents that field. The outermost box is divided into sections, one for each node at the next level of the tree. The size of each section is proportional to the number of records that fall into it. Next, the vertical axis of each box is used to represent the field that is used as the next splitter for that node. In general, this will be a different field for each box.

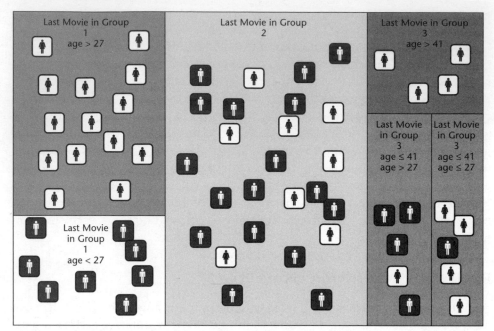

**Figure 6.13**　A box diagram represents a decision tree. Shading is proportional to the purity of the box; size is proportional to the number of records that land there.

There is now a new set of boxes, each of which represents a node at the third level of the tree. This process continues, dividing boxes until the leaves of the tree each have their own box. Since decision trees often have nonuniform depth, some boxes may be subdivided more often than others. Box diagrams make it easy to represent classification rules that depend on any number of variables on a two-dimensional chart.

The resulting diagram is very expressive. As we toss records onto the grid, they fall into a particular box and are classified accordingly. A box chart allows us to look at the data at several levels of detail. Figure 6.13 shows at a glance that the bottom left contains a high concentration of males.

Taking a closer look, we find some boxes that seem to do a particularly good job at classification or collect a large number of records. Viewed this way, it is natural to think of decision trees as a way of drawing boxes around groups of similar points. All of the points within a particular box are classified the same way because they all meet the rule defining that box. This is in contrast to classical statistical classification methods such as linear, logistic, and quadratic discriminants that attempt to partition data into classes by drawing a line or elliptical curve through the data space. This is a fundamental distinction: Statistical approaches that use a single line to find the boundary between classes are weak when there are several very different ways for a record to become part of the target class. Figure 6.14 illustrates this point using two species of dinosaur. The decision tree (represented as a box diagram) has successfully isolated the stegosaurs from the triceratops.

In the credit card industry, for example, there are several ways for customers to be profitable. Some profitable customers have low transaction rates, but keep high revolving balances without defaulting. Others pay off their balance in full each month, but are profitable due to the high transaction volume they generate. Yet others have few transactions, but occasionally make a large purchase and take several months to pay it off. Two very dissimilar customers may be equally profitable. A decision tree can find each separate group, label it, and by providing a description of the box itself, suggest the reason for each group's profitability.

## Tree Ring Diagrams

Another clever representation of a decision tree is used by the Enterprise Miner product from SAS Institute. The diagram in Figure 6.15 looks as though the tree has been cut down and we are looking at the stump.

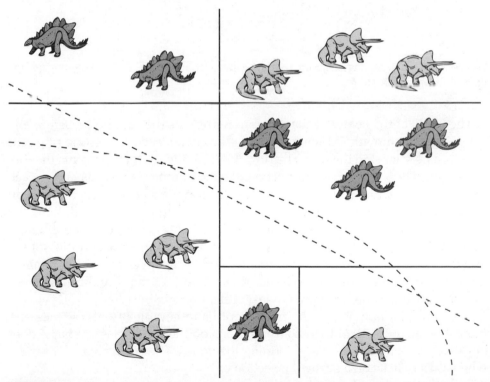

**Figure 6.14** Often a simple line or curve cannot separate the regions and a decision tree does better.

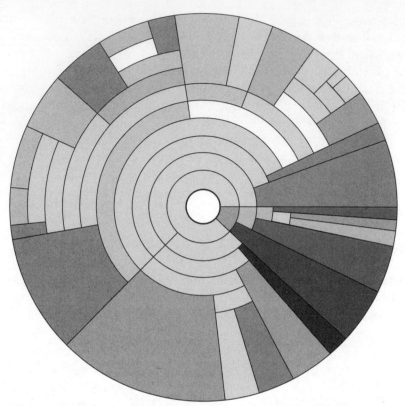

**Figure 6.15** A tree ring diagram produced by SAS Enterprise Miner summarizes the different levels of the tree.

The circle at the center of the diagram represents the root node, before any splits have been made. Moving out from the center, each concentric ring represents a new level in the tree. The ring closest to the center represents the root node split. The arc length is proportional to the number of records taking each of the two paths, and the shading represents the node's purity. The first split in the model represented by this diagram is fairly unbalanced. It divides the records into two groups, a large one where the concentration is little different from the parent population, and a small one with a high concentration of the target class. At the next level, this smaller node is again split and one branch, represented by the thin, dark pie slice that extends all the way through to the outermost ring of the diagram, is a leaf node.

The ring diagram shows the tree's depth and complexity at a glance and indicates the location of high concentrations on the target class. What it does not show directly are the rules defining the nodes. The software reveals these when a user clicks on a particular section of the diagram.

# Decision Trees in Practice

Decision trees can be applied in many different situations.

- To explore a large dataset to pick out useful variables
- To predict future states of important variables in an industrial process
- To form directed clusters of customers for a recommendation system

This section includes examples of decision trees being used in all of these ways.

## Decision Trees as a Data Exploration Tool

During the data exploration phase of a data mining project, decision trees are a useful tool for picking the variables that are likely to be important for predicting particular targets. One of our newspaper clients, *The Boston Globe*, was interested in estimating a town's expected home delivery circulation level based on various demographic and geographic characteristics. Armed with such estimates, they would, among other things, be able to spot towns with untapped potential where the actual circulation was lower than the expected circulation. The final model would be a regression equation based on a handful of variables. But which variables? And what exactly would the regression attempt to estimate? Before building the regression model, we used decision trees to help explore these questions.

Although the newspaper was ultimately interested in predicting the actual number of subscribing households in a given city or town, that number does not make a good target for a regression model because towns and cities vary so much in size. It is not useful to waste modeling power on discovering that there are more subscribers in large towns than in small ones. A better target is the *penetration*—the proportion of households that subscribe to the paper. This number yields an estimate of the total number of subscribing households simply by multiply it by the number of households in a town. Factoring out town size yields a target variable with values that range from zero to somewhat less than one.

The next step was to figure out which factors, from among the hundreds in the town signature, separate towns with high penetration (the "good" towns) from those with low penetration (the "bad" towns). Our approach was to build decision tree with a binary good/bad target variable. This involved sorting the towns by home delivery penetration and labeling the top one third "good" and the bottom one third "bad." Towns in the middle third—those that are not clearly good or bad—were left out of the training set. The screen shot in Figure 6.16 shows the top few levels of one of the resulting trees.

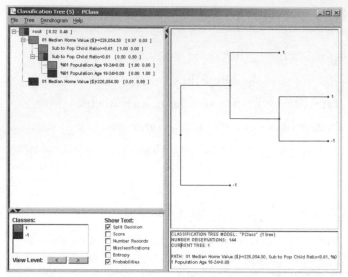

**Figure 6.16**   A decision tree separates good towns from the bad, as visualized by Insightful Miner.

The tree shows that median home value is the best first split. Towns where the median home value (in a region with some of the most expensive housing in the country) is less than $226,000 dollars are poor prospects for this paper. The split at the next level is more surprising. The variable chosen for the split is one of a family of derived variables comparing the subscriber base in the town to the town population as a whole. Towns where the subscribers are similar to the general population are better, in terms of home delivery penetration, than towns where the subscribers are farther from the mean. Other variables that were important for distinguishing good from bad towns included the mean years of school completed, the percentage of the population in blue collar occupations, and the percentage of the population in high-status occupations. All of these ended up as inputs to the regression model.

Some other variables that we had expected to be important such as distance from Boston and household income turned out to be less powerful. Once the decision tree has thrown a spotlight on a variable by either including it or failing to use it, the reason often becomes clear with a little thought. The problem with distance from Boston, for instance, is that as one first drives out into the suburbs, home penetration goes up with distance from Boston. After a while, however, distance from Boston becomes negatively correlated with penetration as people far from Boston do not care as much about what goes on there. Home price is a better predictor because its distribution resembles that of the target variable, increasing in the first few miles and then declining. The decision tree provides guidance about which variables to think about as well as which variables to use.

## Applying Decision-Tree Methods to Sequential Events

Predicting the future is one of the most important applications of data mining. The task of analyzing trends in historical data in order to predict future behavior recurs in every domain we have examined.

One of our clients, a major bank, looked at the detailed transaction data from its customers in order to spot earlier warning signs for attrition in its checking accounts. ATM withdrawals, payroll-direct deposits, balance inquiries, visits to the teller, and hundreds of other transaction types and customer attributes were tracked over time to find *signatures* that allow the bank to recognize that a customer's loyalty is beginning to weaken while there is still time to take corrective action.

Another client, a manufacturer of diesel engines, used the decision tree component of SPSS's Clementine data mining suite to forecast diesel engine sales based on historical truck registration data. The goal was to identify individual owner-operators who were likely to be ready to trade in the engines of their big rigs.

Sales, profits, failure modes, fashion trends, commodity prices, operating temperatures, interest rates, call volumes, response rates, and return rates: People are trying to predict them all. In some fields, notably economics, the analysis of time-series data is a central preoccupation of statistical analysts, so you might expect there to be a large collection of ready-made techniques available to be applied to predictive data mining on time-ordered data. Unfortunately, this is not the case.

For one thing, much of the time-series analysis work in other fields focuses on analyzing patterns in a single variable such as the dollar-yen exchange rate or unemployment *in isolation*. Corporate data warehouses may well contain data that exhibits cyclical patterns. Certainly, average daily balances in checking accounts reflect that rents are typically due on the first of the month and that many people are paid on Fridays, but, for the most part, these sorts of patterns are not of interest because they are neither unexpected nor actionable.

In commercial data mining, our focus is on how a large number of independent variables combine to predict some future outcome. Chapter 9 discusses how time can be integrated into association rules in order to find sequential patterns. Decision-tree methods have also been applied very successfully in this domain, but it is generally necessary to enrich the data with trend information by including fields such as differences and rates of change that explicitly represent change over time. Chapter 17 discusses these data preparation issues in more detail. The following section describes an application that automatically generates these derived fields and uses them to build a tree-based simulator that can be used to project an entire database into the future.

# Simulating the Future

This discussion is largely based on discussions with Marc Goodman and on his 1995 doctoral dissertation on a technique called *projective visualization*. Projective visualization uses a database of snapshots of historical data to develop a simulator. The simulation can be run to project the values of all variables into the future. The result is an extended database whose new records have exactly the same fields as the original, but with values supplied by the simulator rather than by observation. The approach is described in more detail in the technical aside.

## *Case Study: Process Control in a Coffee-Roasting Plant*

Nestlé, one of the largest food and beverages companies in the world, used a number of continuous-feed coffee roasters to produce a variety of coffee products including Nescafé Granules, Gold Blend, Gold Blend Decaf, and Blend 37. Each of these products has a "recipe" that specifies target values for a plethora of roaster variables such as the temperature of the air at various exhaust points, the speed of various fans, the rate that gas is burned, the amount of water introduced to quench the beans, and the positions of various flaps and valves. There are a lot of ways for things to go wrong when roasting coffee, ranging from a roast coming out too light in color to a costly and damaging roaster fire. A bad batch of roasted coffee incurs a big cost; damage to equipment is even more expensive.

To help operators keep the roaster running properly, data is collected from about 60 sensors. Every 30 seconds, this data, along with control information, is written to a log and made available to operators in the form of graphs. The project described here took place at a Nestlé research laboratory in York, England. Nestlé used projective visualization to build a coffee roaster simulation based on the sensor logs.

### Goals for the Simulator

Nestlé saw several ways that a coffee roaster simulator could improve its processes.

- By using the simulator to try out new recipes, a large number of new recipes could be evaluated without interrupting production. Furthermore, recipes that might lead to roaster fires or other damage could be eliminated in advance.

- The simulator could be used to train new operators and expose them to routine problems and their solutions. Using the simulator, operators could try out different approaches to resolving a problem.

## USING DECISION TREES FOR PROJECTIVE VISUALIZATION

Using Goodman's terminology, which comes from the machine learning field, each snapshot of a moment in time is called a *case*. A case is made up of *attributes*, which are the fields in the case record. Attributes may be of any data type and may be continuous or categorical. The attributes are used to form *features*. Features are Boolean (yes/no) variables that are combined in various ways to form the internal nodes of a decision tree. For example, if the database contains a numeric salary field, a continuous attribute, then that might lead to creation of a feature such as salary < 38,500.

For a continuous variable like salary, a feature of the form attribute $\leq$ value is generated for every value observed in the training set. This means that there are potentially as many features derived from an attribute as there are cases in the training set. Features based on equality or set membership are generated for symbolic attributes and literal attributes such as names of people or places.

The attributes are also used to generate *interpretations*; these are new attributes derived from the given ones. Interpretations generally reflect knowledge of the domain and what sorts of relationships are likely to be important. In the current problem, finding patterns that occur over time, the amount, direction, and rate of change in the value of an attribute from one time period to the next are likely to be important. Therefore, for each numeric attribute, the software automatically generates interpretations for the difference and the discrete first and second derivatives of the attribute.

In general, however, the user supplies interpretations. For example, in a credit risk model, it is likely that the ratio of debt to income is more predictive than the magnitude of either. With this knowledge we might add an interpretation that was the ratio of those two attributes. Often, user-supplied interpretations combine attributes in ways that the program would not come up with automatically. Examples include calculating a great-circle distance from changes in latitude and longitude or taking the product of three linear measurements to get a volume.

### FROM ONE CASE TO THE NEXT

The central idea behind projective visualization is to use the historical cases to generate a set of rules for generating case *n+1* from case *n*. When this model is applied to the final observed case, it generates a new projected case. To project more than one time step into the future, we continue to apply the model to the most recently created case. Naturally, confidence in the projected values decreases as the simulation is run for more and more time steps.

The figure illustrates the way a single attribute is projected using a decision tree based on the features generated from all the other attributes and interpretations in the previous case. During the training process, a separate decision tree is grown for each attribute. This entire forest is evaluated in order to move from one simulation step to the next.

*(continued)*

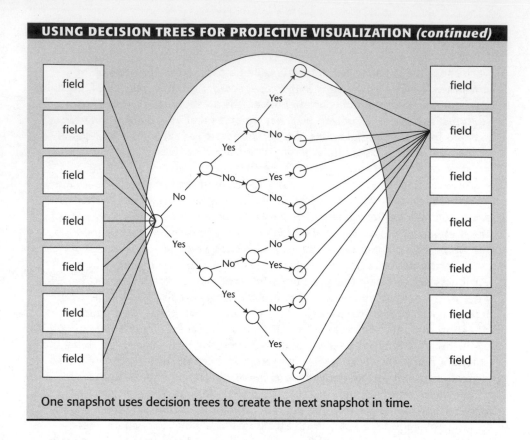

**USING DECISION TREES FOR PROJECTIVE VISUALIZATION *(continued)***

One snapshot uses decision trees to create the next snapshot in time.

■ The simulator could track the operation of the actual roaster and project it several minutes into the future. When the simulation ran into a problem, an alert could be generated while the operators still had time to avert trouble.

### Evaluation of the Roaster Simulation

The simulation was built using a training set of 34,000 cases. The simulation was then evaluated using a test set of around 40,000 additional cases that had not been part of the training set. For each case in the test set, the simulator generated projected snapshots 60 steps into the future. At each step the projected values of all variables were compared against the actual values. As expected, the size of the error increases with time. For example, the error rate for product temperature turned out to be 2/3°C per minute of projection, but even 30 minutes into the future the simulator is doing considerably better than random guessing.

The roaster simulator turned out to be more accurate than all but the most experienced operators at projecting trends, and even the most experienced operators were able to do a better job with the aid of the simulator. Operators enjoyed using the simulator and reported that it gave them new insight into corrective actions.

## Lessons Learned

Decision-tree methods have wide applicability for data exploration, classification, and scoring. They can also be used for estimating continuous values although they are rarely the first choice since decision trees generate "lumpy" estimates—all records reaching the same leaf are assigned the same estimated value. They are a good choice when the data mining task is classification of records or prediction of discrete outcomes. Use decision trees when your goal is to assign each record to one of a few broad categories. Theoretically, decision trees can assign records to an arbitrary number of classes, but they are error-prone when the number of training examples per class gets small. This can happen rather quickly in a tree with many levels and/or many branches per node. In many business contexts, problems naturally resolve to a binary classification such as responder/nonresponder or good/bad so this is not a large problem in practice.

Decision trees are also a natural choice when the goal is to generate understandable and explainable rules. The ability of decision trees to generate rules that can be translated into comprehensible natural language or SQL is one of the greatest strengths of the technique. Even in complex decision trees , it is generally fairly easy to follow any one path through the tree to a particular leaf. So the explanation for any particular classification or prediction is relatively straightforward.

Decision trees require less data preparation than many other techniques because they are equally adept at handling continuous and categorical variables. Categorical variables, which pose problems for neural networks and statistical techniques, are split by forming groups of classes. Continuous variables are split by dividing their range of values. Because decision trees do not make use of the actual values of numeric variables, they are not sensitive to outliers and skewed distributions. This robustness comes at the cost of throwing away some of the information that is available in the training data, so a well-tuned neural network or regression model will often make better use of the same fields than a decision tree. For that reason, decision trees are often used to pick a good set of variables to be used as inputs to another modeling technique. Time-oriented data does require a lot of data preparation. Time series data must be enhanced so that trends and sequential patterns are made visible.

Decision trees reveal so much about the data to which they are applied that the authors make use of them in the early phases of nearly every data mining project even when the final models are to be created using some other technique.

# Artificial Neural Networks

Artificial neural networks are popular because they have a proven track record in many data mining and decision support applications. Neural networks—the "artificial" is usually dropped—are a class of powerful, general-purpose tools readily applied to prediction, classification, and clustering. They have been applied across a broad range of industries, from predicting time series in the financial world to diagnosing medical conditions, from identifying clusters of valuable customers to identifying fraudulent credit card transactions, from recognizing numbers written on checks to predicting the failure rates of engines.

The most powerful neural networks are, of course, the biological kind. The human brain makes it possible for people to generalize from experience; computers, on the other hand, usually excel at following explicit instructions over and over. The appeal of neural networks is that they bridge this gap by modeling, on a digital computer, the neural connections in human brains. When used in well-defined domains, their ability to generalize and learn from data mimics, in some sense, our own ability to learn from experience. This ability is useful for data mining, and it also makes neural networks an exciting area for research, promising new and better results in the future.

There is a drawback, though. The results of training a neural network are internal weights distributed throughout the network. These weights provide no more insight into *why* the solution is valid than dissecting a human brain explains our thought processes. Perhaps one day, sophisticated techniques for probing neural networks may help provide some explanation. In the meantime, neural networks are best approached as black boxes with internal workings as mysterious as the workings of our brains. Like the responses of the Oracle at Delphi worshipped by the ancient Greeks, the answers produced by neural networks are often correct. They have business value—in many cases a more important feature than providing an explanation.

This chapter starts with a bit of history; the origins of neural networks grew out of actual attempts to model the human brain on computers. It then discusses an early case history of using this technique for real estate appraisal, before diving into technical details. Most of the chapter presents neural networks as predictive modeling tools. At the end, we see how they can be used for undirected data mining as well. A good place to begin is, as always, at the beginning, with a bit of history.

## A Bit of History

Neural networks have an interesting history in the annals of computer science. The original work on the functioning of neurons—biological neurons—took place in the 1930s and 1940s, before digital computers really even existed. In 1943, Warren McCulloch, a neurophysiologist at Yale University, and Walter Pitts, a logician, postulated a simple model to explain how biological neurons work and published it in a paper called "A Logical Calculus Immanent in Nervous Activity." While their focus was on understanding the anatomy of the brain, it turned out that this model provided inspiration for the field of artificial intelligence and would eventually provide a new approach to solving certain problems outside the realm of neurobiology.

In the 1950s, when digital computers first became available, computer scientists implemented models called perceptrons based on the work of McCulloch and Pitts. An example of a problem solved by these early networks was how to balance a broom standing upright on a moving cart by controlling the motions of the cart back and forth. As the broom starts falling to the left, the cart learns to move to the left to keep it upright. Although there were some limited successes with perceptrons in the laboratory, the results were disappointing as a general method for solving problems.

One reason for the limited usefulness of early neural networks is that most powerful computers of that era were less powerful than inexpensive desktop computers today. Another reason was that these simple networks had theoretical deficiencies, as shown by Seymour Papert and Marvin Minsky (two professors at the Massachusetts Institute of Technology) in 1968. Because of these deficiencies, the study of neural network implementations on computers slowed down drastically during the 1970s. Then, in 1982, John Hopfield of the California Institute of Technology invented back propagation, a way of training neural networks that sidestepped the theoretical pitfalls of earlier approaches.

This development sparked a renaissance in neural network research. Through the 1980s, research moved from the labs into the commercial world, where it has since been applied to solve both operational problems—such as detecting fraudulent credit card transactions as they occur and recognizing numeric amounts written on checks—and data mining challenges.

At the same time that researchers in artificial intelligence were developing neural networks as a model of biological activity, statisticians were taking advantage of computers to extend the capabilities of statistical methods. A technique called logistic regression proved particularly valuable for many types of statistical analysis. Like linear regression, logistic regression tries to fit a curve to observed data. Instead of a line, though, it uses a function called the logistic function. Logistic regression, and even its more familiar cousin linear regression, can be represented as special cases of neural networks. In fact, the entire theory of neural networks can be explained using statistical methods, such as probability distributions, likelihoods, and so on. For expository purposes, though, this chapter leans more heavily toward the biological model than toward theoretical statistics.

Neural networks became popular in the 1980s because of a convergence of several factors. First, computing power was readily available, especially in the business community where data was available. Second, analysts became more comfortable with neural networks by realizing that they are closely related to known statistical methods. Third, there was relevant data since operational systems in most companies had already been automated. Fourth, useful applications became more important than the holy grails of artificial intelligence. Building tools to help people superseded the goal of building artificial people. Because of their proven utility, neural networks are, and will continue to be, popular tools for data mining.

## Real Estate Appraisal

Neural networks have the ability to learn by example in much the same way that human experts gain from experience. The following example applies neural networks to solve a problem familiar to most readers—real estate appraisal.

Why would we want to automate appraisals? Clearly, automated appraisals could help real estate agents better match prospective buyers to prospective homes, improving the productivity of even inexperienced agents. Another use would be to set up kiosks or Web pages where prospective buyers could describe the homes that they wanted—and get immediate feedback on how much their dream homes cost.

Perhaps an unexpected application is in the secondary mortgage market. Good, consistent appraisals are critical to assessing the risk of individual loans and loan portfolios, because one major factor affecting default is the proportion of the value of the property at risk. If the loan value is more than 100 percent of the market value, the risk of default goes up considerably. Once the loan has been made, how can the market value be calculated? For this purpose, Freddie Mac, the Federal Home Loan Mortgage Corporation, developed a product called Loan Prospector that does these appraisals automatically for homes throughout the United States. Loan Prospector was originally based on neural network technology developed by a San Diego company HNC, which has since been merged into Fair Isaac.

Back to the example. This neural network mimics an appraiser who estimates the market value of a house based on features of the property (see Figure 7.1). She knows that houses in one part of town are worth more than those in other areas. Additional bedrooms, a larger garage, the style of the house, and the size of the lot are other factors that figure into her mental calculation. She is not applying some set formula, but balancing her experience and knowledge of the sales prices of similar homes. And, her knowledge about housing prices is not static. She is aware of recent sale prices for homes throughout the region and can recognize trends in prices over time—fine-tuning her calculation to fit the latest data.

**Figure 7.1**   Real estate agents and appraisers combine the features of a house to come up with a valuation—an example of biological neural networks at work.

The appraiser or real estate agent is a good example of a human expert in a well-defined domain. Houses are described by a fixed set of standard features taken into account by the expert and turned into an appraised value. In 1992, researchers at IBM recognized this as a good problem for neural networks. Figure 7.2 illustrates why. A neural network takes specific inputs—in this case the information from the housing sheet—and turns them into a specific output, an appraised value for the house. The list of inputs is well defined because of two factors: extensive use of the multiple listing service (MLS) to share information about the housing market among different real estate agents and standardization of housing descriptions for mortgages sold on secondary markets. The desired output is well defined as well—a specific dollar amount. In addition, there is a wealth of experience in the form of previous sales for teaching the network how to value a house.

**TIP** Neural networks are good for prediction and estimation problems. A good problem has the following three characteristics:

- *The inputs are well understood*. You have a good idea of which features of the data are important, but not necessarily how to combine them.

- *The output is well understood*. You know what you are trying to model.

- *Experience is available*. You have plenty of examples where both the inputs and the output are known. These known cases are used to train the network.

The first step in setting up a neural network to calculate estimated housing values is determining a set of features that affect the sales price. Some possible common features are shown in Table 7.1. In practice, these features work for homes in a single geographical area. To extend the appraisal example to handle homes in many neighborhoods, the input data would include zip code information, neighborhood demographics, and other neighborhood quality-of-life indicators, such as ratings of schools and proximity to transportation. To simplify the example, these additional features are not included here.

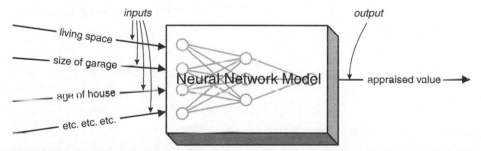

**Figure 7.2** A neural network is like a black box that knows how to process inputs to create an output. The calculation is quite complex and difficult to understand, yet the results are often useful.

**Table 7.1**  Common Features Describing a House

| FEATURE | DESCRIPTION | RANGE OF VALUES |
|---|---|---|
| Num_Apartments | Number of dwelling units | Integer: 1–3 |
| Year_Built | Year built | Integer: 1850–1986 |
| Plumbing_Fixtures | Number of plumbing fixtures | Integer: 5–17 |
| Heating_Type | Heating system type | coded as A or B |
| Basement_Garage | Basement garage (number of cars) | Integer: 0–2 |
| Attached_Garage | Attached frame garage area (in square feet) | Integer: 0–228 |
| Living_Area | Total living area (square feet) | Integer: 714–4185 |
| Deck_Area | Deck / open porch area (square feet) | Integer: 0–738 |
| Porch_Area | Enclosed porch area (square feet) | Integer: 0–452 |
| Recroom_Area | Recreation room area (square feet) | Integer: 0–672 |
| Basement_Area | Finished basement area (square feet) | Integer: 0–810 |

Training the network builds a model which can then be used to estimate the target value for unknown examples. Training presents known examples (data from previous sales) to the network so that it can learn how to calculate the sales price. The training examples need two more additional features: the sales price of the home and the sales date. The sales price is needed as the target variable. The date is used to separate the examples into a training, validation, and test set. Table 7.2 shows an example from the training set.

The process of training the network is actually the process of adjusting weights inside it to arrive at the best combination of weights for making the desired predictions. The network starts with a random set of weights, so it initially performs very poorly. However, by reprocessing the training set over and over and adjusting the internal weights each time to reduce the overall error, the network gradually does a better and better job of approximating the target values in the training set. When the appoximations no longer improve, the network stops training.

**Table 7.2** Sample Record from Training Set with Values Scaled to Range −1 to 1

| FEATURE | RANGE OF VALUES | ORIGINAL VALUE | SCALED VALUE |
|---------|-----------------|----------------|--------------|
| Sales_Price | $103,000–$250,000 | $171,000 | −0.0748 |
| Months_Ago | 0–23 | 4 | −0.6522 |
| Num_Apartments | 1-3 | 1 | −1.0000 |
| Year_Built | 1850–1986 | 1923 | +0.0730 |
| Plumbing_Fixtures | 5–17 | 9 | −0.3077 |
| Heating_Type | coded as A or B | B | +1.0000 |
| Basement_Garage | 0–2 | 0 | −1.0000 |
| Attached_Garage | 0–228 | 120 | +0.0524 |
| Living_Area | 714–4185 | 1,614 | −0.4813 |
| Deck_Area | 0–738 | 0 | −1.0000 |
| Porch_Area | 0–452 | 210 | −0.0706 |
| Recroom_Area | 0–672 | 0 | −1.0000 |
| Basement_Area | 0–810 | 175 | −0.5672 |

This process of adjusting weights is sensitive to the representation of the data going in. For instance, consider a field in the data that measures lot size. If lot size is measured in acres, then the values might reasonably go from about ⅛ to 1 acre. If measured in square feet, the same values would be 5,445 square feet to 43,560 square feet. However, for technical reasons, neural networks restrict their inputs to small numbers, say between −1 and 1. For instance, when an input variable takes on very large values relative to other inputs, then this variable dominates the calculation of the target. The neural network wastes valuable iterations by reducing the weights on this input to lessen its effect on the output. That is, the first "pattern" that the network will find is that the lot size variable has much larger values than other variables. Since this is not particularly interesting, it would be better to use the lot size as measured in acres rather than square feet.

This idea generalizes. Usually, the inputs in the neural network should be smallish numbers. It is a good idea to limit them to some small range, such as −1 to 1, which requires mapping all the values, both continuous and categorical prior to training the network.

One way to map continuous values is to turn them into fractions by subtracting the middle value of the range from the value, dividing the result by the size of the range, and multiplying by 2. For instance, to get a mapped value for

*Year_Built* (1923), subtract (1850 + 1986)/2 = 1918 (the middle value) from 1923 (the year the oldest house was built) and get 7. Dividing by the number of years in the range (1986 – 1850 + 1 = 137) yields a scaled value and multiplying by 2 yields a value of 0.0730. This basic procedure can be applied to any continuous feature to get a value between –1 and 1. One way to map categorical features is to assign fractions between –1 and 1 to each of the categories. The only categorical variable in this data is *Heating_Type*, so we can arbitrarily map B 1 and A to –1. If we had three values, we could assign one to –1, another to 0, and the third to 1, although this approach does have the drawback that the three heating types will seem to have an order. Type –1 will appear closer to type 0 than to type 1. Chapter 17 contains further discussion of ways to convert categorical variables to numeric variables without adding spurious information.

With these simple techniques, it is possible to map all the fields for the sample house record shown earlier (see Table 7.2) and train the network. Training is a process of iterating through the training set to adjust the weights. Each iteration is sometimes called a *generation*.

Once the network has been trained, the performance of each generation must be measured on the validation set. Typically, earlier generations of the network perform better on the validation set than the final network (which was optimized for the training set). This is due to overfitting, (which was discussed in Chapter 3) and is a consequence of neural networks being so powerful. In fact, neural networks are an example of a universal approximator. That is, any function can be approximated by an appropriately complex neural network. Neural networks and decision trees have this property; linear and logistic regression do not, since they assume particular shapes for the underlying function.

As with other modeling approaches, neural networks can learn patterns that exist only in the training set, resulting in overfitting. To find the best network for unseen data, the training process remembers each set of weights calculated during each generation. The final network comes from the generation that works best on the validation set, rather than the one that works best on the training set.

When the model's performance on the validation set is satisfactory, the neural network model is ready for use. It has learned from the training examples and figured out how to calculate the sales price from all the inputs. The model takes descriptive information about a house, suitably mapped, and produces an output. There is one caveat. The output is itself a number between 0 and 1 (for a logistic activation function) or –1 and 1 (for the hyperbolic tangent), which needs to be remapped to the range of sale prices. For example, the value 0.75 could be multiplied by the size of the range ($147,000) and then added to the base number in the range ($103,000) to get an appraisal value of $213,250.

# Neural Networks for Directed Data Mining

The previous example illustrates the most common use of neural networks: building a model for classification or prediction. The steps in this process are:

1. Identify the input and output features.
2. Transform the inputs and outputs so they are in a small range, (–1 to 1).
3. Set up a network with an appropriate topology.
4. Train the network on a representative set of training examples.
5. Use the validation set to choose the set of weights that minimizes the error.
6. Evaluate the network using the test set to see how well it performs.
7. Apply the model generated by the network to predict outcomes for unknown inputs.

Fortunately, data mining software now performs most of these steps automatically. Although an intimate knowledge of the internal workings is not necessary, there are some keys to using networks successfully. As with all predictive modeling tools, the most important issue is choosing the right training set. The second is representing the data in such a way as to maximize the ability of the network to recognize patterns in it. The third is interpreting the results from the network. Finally, understanding some specific details about how they work, such as network topology and parameters controlling training, can help make better performing networks.

One of the dangers with any model used for prediction or classification is that the model becomes stale as it gets older—and neural network models are no exception to this rule. For the appraisal example, the neural network has learned about historical patterns that allow it to predict the appraised value from descriptions of houses based on the contents of the training set. There is no guarantee that current market conditions match those of last week, last month, or 6 months ago—when the training set might have been made. New homes are bought and sold every day, creating and responding to market forces that are not present in the training set. A rise or drop in interest rates, or an increase in inflation, may rapidly change appraisal values. The problem of keeping a neural network model up to date is made more difficult by two factors. First, the model does not readily express itself in the form of rules, so it may not be obvious when it has grown stale. Second, when neural networks degrade, they tend to degrade gracefully making the reduction in performance less obvious. In short, the model gradually expires and it is not always clear exactly when to update it.

The solution is to incorporate more recent data into the neural network. One way is to take the same neural network back to training mode and start feeding it new values. This is a good approach if the network only needs to tweak results such as when the network is pretty close to being accurate, but you think you can improve its accuracy even more by giving it more recent examples. Another approach is to start over again by adding new examples into the training set (perhaps removing older examples) and training an entirely new network, perhaps even with a different topology (there is further discussion of network topologies later). This is appropriate when market conditions may have changed drastically and the patterns found in the original training set are no longer applicable.

The virtuous cycle of data mining described in Chapter 2 puts a premium on measuring the results from data mining activities. These measurements help in understanding how susceptible a given model is to aging and when a neural network model should be retrained.

**WARNING** A neural network is only as good as the training set used to generate it. The model is static and must be explicitly updated by adding more recent examples into the training set and retraining the network (or training a new network) in order to keep it up-to-date and useful.

## What Is a Neural Net?

Neural networks consist of basic units that mimic, in a simplified fashion, the behavior of biological neurons found in nature, whether comprising the brain of a human or of a frog. It has been claimed, for example, that there is a unit within the visual system of a frog that fires in response to fly-like movements, and that there is another unit that fires in response to things about the size of a fly. These two units are connected to a neuron that fires when the combined value of these two inputs is high. This neuron is an input into yet another which triggers tongue-flicking behavior.

The basic idea is that each neural unit, whether in a frog or a computer, has many inputs that the unit combines into a single output value. In brains, these units may be connected to specialized nerves. Computers, though, are a bit simpler; the units are simply connected together, as shown in Figure 7.3, so the outputs from some units are used as inputs into others. All the examples in Figure 7.3 are examples of feed-forward neural networks, meaning there is a one-way flow through the network from the inputs to the outputs and there are no cycles in the network.

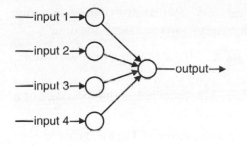

This simple neural network takes four inputs and produces an output. This result of training this network is equivalent to the statistical technique called logistic regression.

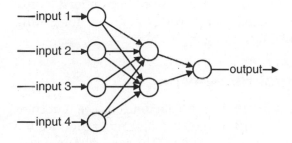

This network has a middle layer called the *hidden layer*, which makes the network more powerful by enabling it to recognize more patterns.

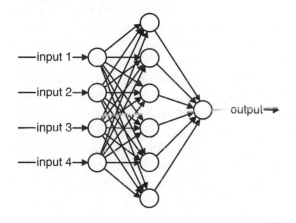

Increasing the size of the hidden layer makes the network more powerful but introduces the risk of overfitting. Usually, only one hidden layer is needed.

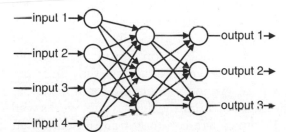

A neural network can produce multiple output values.

**Figure 7.3** Feed-forward neural networks take inputs on one end and transform them into outputs.

Feed-forward networks are the simplest and most useful type of network for directed modeling. There are three basic questions to ask about them:

- What are units and how do they behave? That is, what is the activation function?

- How are the units connected together? That is, what is the topology of a network?

- How does the network learn to recognize patterns? That is, what is back propagation and more generally how is the network trained?

The answers to these questions provide the background for understanding basic neural networks, an understanding that provides guidance for getting the best results from this powerful data mining technique.

## What Is the Unit of a Neural Network?

Figure 7.4 shows the important features of the artificial neuron. The unit combines its inputs into a single value, which it then transforms to produce the output; these together are called the *activation function*. The most common activation functions are based on the biological model where the output remains very low until the combined inputs reach a threshold value. When the combined inputs reach the threshold, the unit is *activated* and the output is high.

Like its biological counterpart, the unit in a neural network has the property that small changes in the inputs, when the combined values are within some middle range, can have relatively large effects on the output. Conversely, large changes in the inputs may have little effect on the output, when the combined inputs are far from the middle range. This property, where sometimes small changes matter and sometimes they do not, is an example of *nonlinear behavior*. The power and complexity of neural networks arise from their nonlinear behavior, which in turn arises from the particular activation function used by the constituent neural units.

The activation function has two parts. The first part is the *combination function* that merges all the inputs into a single value. As shown in Figure 7.4, each input into the unit has its own weight. The most common combination function is the weighted sum, where each input is multiplied by its weight and these products are added together. Other combination functions are sometimes useful and include the maximum of the weighted inputs, the minimum, and the logical AND or OR of the values. Although there is a lot of flexibility in the choice of combination functions, the standard weighted sum works well in many situations. This element of choice is a common trait of neural networks. Their basic structure is quite flexible, but the defaults that correspond to the original biological models, such as the weighted sum for the combination function, work well in practice.

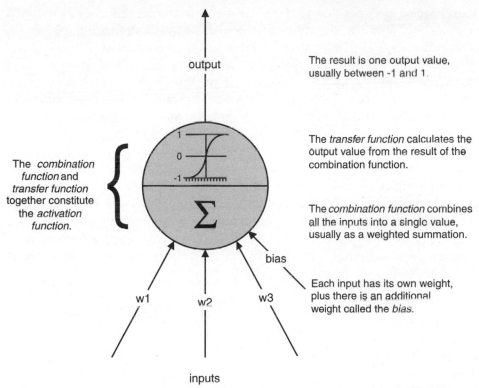

The result is one output value, usually between -1 and 1.

The *transfer function* calculates the output value from the result of the combination function.

The combination function and transfer function together constitute the activation function.

The *combination function* combines all the inputs into a single value, usually as a weighted summation.

Each input has its own weight, plus there is an additional weight called the *bias*.

**Figure 7.4** The unit of an artificial neural network is modeled on the biological neuron. The output of the unit is a nonlinear combination of its inputs.

The second part of the activation function is the *transfer function*, which gets its name from the fact that it transfers the value of the combination function to the output of the unit. Figure 7.5 compares three typical transfer functions: the sigmoid (logistic), linear, and hyperbolic tangent functions. The specific values that the transfer function takes on are not as important as the general form of the function. From our perspective, the linear transfer function is the least interesting. A feed-forward neural network consisting only of units with linear transfer functions and a weighted sum combination function is really just doing a linear regression. Sigmoid functions are S-shaped functions, of which the two most common for neural networks are the logistic and the hyperbolic tangent. The major difference between them is the range of their outputs, between 0 and 1 for the logistic and between –1 and 1 for the hyperbolic tangent.

The logistic and hyperbolic tangent transfer functions behave in a similar way. Even though they are not linear, their behavior is appealing to statisticians. When the weighted sum of all the inputs is near 0, then these functions are a close approximation of a linear function. Statisticians appreciate linear systems, and almost-linear systems are almost as well appreciated. As the magnitude of the weighted sum gets larger, these transfer functions gradually saturate (to 0 and 1 in the case of the logistic; to –1 and 1 in the case of the hyperbolic tangent). This behavior corresponds to a gradual movement from a linear model of the input to a nonlinear model. In short, neural networks have the ability to do a good job of modeling on three types of problems: linear problems, near-linear problems, and nonlinear problems. There is also a relationship between the activation function and the range of input values, as discussed in the sidebar, "Sigmoid Functions and Ranges for Input Values."

A network can contain units with different transfer functions, a subject we'll return to later when discussing network topology. Sophisticated tools sometimes allow experimentation with other combination and transfer functions. Other functions have significantly different behavior from the standard units. It may be fun and even helpful to play with different types of activation functions. If you do not want to bother, though, you can have confidence in the standard functions that have proven successful for many neural network applications.

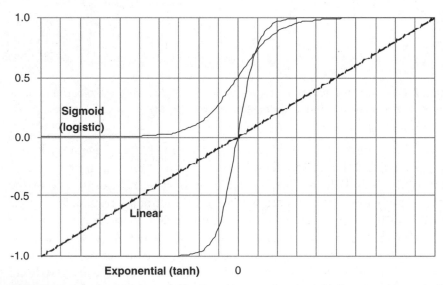

**Figure 7.5** Three common transfer functions are the sigmoid, linear, and hyperbolic tangent functions.

## SIGMOID FUNCTIONS AND RANGES FOR INPUT VALUES

The sigmoid activation functions are S-shaped curves that fall within bounds. For instance, the logistic function produces values between 0 and 1, and the hyperbolic tangent produces values between −1 and 1 for all possible outputs of the summation function. The formulas for these functions are:

$$\text{logistic}(x) = 1/(1 + e^{-x})$$

$$\tanh(x) = (e^x - e^{-x})/(e^x + e^{-x})$$

When used in a neural network, the $x$ is the result of the combination function, typically the weighted sum of the inputs into the unit.

Since these functions are defined for all values of $x$, why do we recommend that the inputs to a network be in a small range, typically from −1 to 1? The reason has to do with how these functions behave near 0. In this range, they behave in an almost linear way. That is, small changes in $x$ result in small changes in the output; changing $x$ by half as much results in about half the effect on the output. The relationship is not exact, but it is a close approximation.

For training purposes, it is a good idea to start out in this quasi-linear area. As the neural network trains, nodes may find linear relationships in the data. These nodes adjust their weights so the resulting value falls in this linear range. Other nodes may find nonlinear relationships. Their adjusted weights are likely to fall in a larger range.

Requiring that all inputs be in the same range also prevents one set of inputs, such as the price of a house—a big number in the tens of thousands— from dominating other inputs, such as the number of bedrooms. After all, the combination function is a weighted sum of the inputs, and when some values are very large, they will dominate the weighted sum. When $x$ is large, small adjustments to the weights on the inputs have almost no effect on the output of the unit making it difficult to train. That is, the sigmoid function can take advantage of the difference between one and two bedrooms, but a house that costs $50,000 and one that costs $1,000,000 would be hard for it to distinguish, and it can take many generations of training the network for the weights associated with this feature to adjust. Keeping the inputs relatively small enables adjustments to the weights to have a bigger impact. This aid to training is the strongest reason for insisting that inputs stay in a small range.

In fact, even when a feature naturally falls into a range smaller than −1 to 1, such as 0.5 to 0.75, it is desirable to scale the feature so the input to the network uses the entire range from −1 to 1. Using the full range of values from −1 to 1 ensures the best results.

Although we recommend that inputs be in the range from −1 to 1, this should be taken as a guideline, not a strict rule. For instance, standardizing variables—subtracting the mean and dividing by the standard deviation—is a common transformation on variables. This results in small enough values to be useful for neural networks.

## Feed-Forward Neural Networks

A feed-forward neural network calculates output values from input values, as shown in Figure 7.6. The topology, or structure, of this network is typical of networks used for prediction and classification. The units are organized into three layers. The layer on the left is connected to the inputs and called the *input layer*. Each unit in the input layer is connected to exactly one source field, which has typically been mapped to the range –1 to 1. In this example, the input layer does not actually do any work. Each input layer unit copies its input value to its output. If this is the case, why do we even bother to mention it here? It is an important part of the vocabulary of neural networks. In practical terms, the input layer represents the process for mapping values into a reasonable range. For this reason alone, it is worth including them, because they are a reminder of a very important aspect of using neural networks successfully.

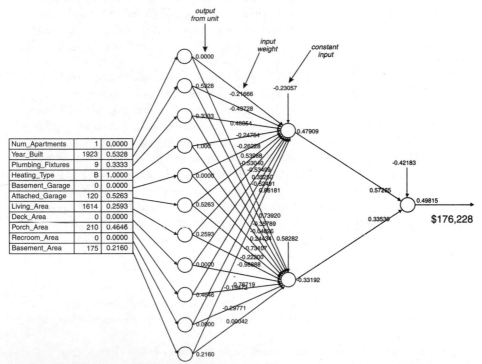

**Figure 7.6** The real estate training example shown here provides the input into a feed-forward neural network and illustrates that a network is filled with seemingly meaningless weights.

The next layer is called the *hidden layer* because it is connected neither to the inputs nor to the output of the network. Each unit in the hidden layer is typically fully connected to all the units in the input layer. Since this network contains standard units, the units in the hidden layer calculate their output by multiplying the value of each input by its corresponding weight, adding these up, and applying the transfer function. A neural network can have any number of hidden layers, but in general, one hidden layer is sufficient. The wider the layer (that is, the more units it contains) the greater the capacity of the network to recognize patterns. This greater capacity has a drawback, though, because the neural network can memorize patterns-of-one in the training examples. *We want the network to generalize on the training set, not to memorize it.* To achieve this, the hidden layer should not be too wide.

Notice that the units in Figure 7.6 each have an additional input coming down from the top. This is the constant input, sometimes called a *bias*, and is always set to 1. Like other inputs, it has a weight and is included in the combination function. The bias acts as a global offset that helps the network better understand patterns. The training phase adjusts the weights on constant inputs just as it does on the other weights in the network.

The last unit on the right is the *output layer* because it is connected to the output of the neural network. It is fully connected to all the units in the hidden layer. Most of the time, the neural network is being used to calculate a single value, so there is only one unit in the output layer and the value. We must map this value back to understand the output. For the network in Figure 7.6, we have to convert 0.49815 back into a value between $103,000 and $250,000. It corresponds to $176,228, which is quite close to the actual value of $171,000. In some implementations, the output layer uses a simple linear transfer function, so the output is a weighted linear combination of inputs. This eliminates the need to map the outputs.

It is possible for the output layer to have more than one unit. For instance, a department store chain wants to predict the likelihood that customers will be purchasing products from various departments, such as women's apparel, furniture, and entertainment. The stores want to use this information to plan promotions and direct target mailings.

To make this prediction, they might set up the neural network shown in Figure 7.7. This network has three outputs, one for each department. The outputs are a propensity for the customer described in the inputs to make his or her next purchase from the associated department.

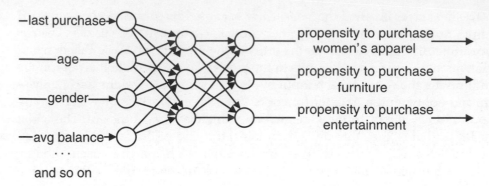

**Figure 7.7** This network has with more than one output and is used to predict the department where department store customers will make their next purchase.

After feeding the inputs for a customer into the network, the network calculates three values. Given all these outputs, how can the department store determine the right promotion or promotions to offer the customer? Some common methods used when working with multiple model outputs are:

- Take the department corresponding to the output with the maximum value.

- Take departments corresponding to the outputs with the top three values.

- Take all departments corresponding to the outputs that exceed some threshold value.

- Take all departments corresponding to units that are some percentage of the unit with the maximum value.

All of these possibilities work well and have their strengths and weaknesses in different situations. There is no one right answer that always works. In practice, you want to try several of these possibilities on the test set in order to determine which works best in a particular situation.

There are other variations on the topology of feed-forward neural networks. Sometimes, the input layers are connected directly to the output layer. In this case, the network has two components. These direct connections behave like a standard regression (linear or logistic, depending on the activation function in the output layer). This is useful building more standard statistical models. The hidden layer then acts as an adjustment to the statistical model.

## How Does a Neural Network Learn Using Back Propagation?

Training a neural network is the process of setting the best weights on the edges connecting all the units in the network. The goal is to use the training set to calculate weights where the output of the network is as close to the desired output as possible for as many of the examples in the training set as possible. Although back propagation is no longer the preferred method for adjusting the weights, it provides insight into how training works and it was the original method for training feed-forward networks. At the heart of back propagation are the following three steps:

1. The network gets a training example and, using the existing weights in the network, it calculates the output or outputs.

2. Back propagation then calculates the error by taking the difference between the calculated result and the expected (actual result).

3. The error is fed back through the network and the weights are adjusted to minimize the error—hence the name back propagation because the errors are sent back through the network.

The back propagation algorithm measures the overall error of the network by comparing the values produced on each training example to the actual value. It then adjusts the weights of the output layer to reduce, but not eliminate, the error. However, the algorithm has not finished. It then assigns the blame to earlier nodes the network and adjusts the weights connecting those nodes, further reducing overall error. The specific mechanism for assigning blame is not important. Suffice it to say that back propagation uses a complicated mathematical procedure that requires taking partial derivatives of the activation function.

Given the error, how does a unit adjust its weights? It estimates whether changing the weight on each input would increase or decrease the error. The unit then adjusts each weight to reduce, but not eliminate, the error. The adjustments for each example in the training set slowly nudge the weights, toward their optimal values. Remember, the goal is to generalize and identify patterns in the input, not to memorize the training set. Adjusting the weights is like a leisurely walk instead of a mad-dash sprint. After being shown enough training examples during enough generations, the weights on the network no longer change significantly and the error no longer decreases. This is the point where training stops; the network has learned to recognize patterns in the input.

This technique for adjusting the weights is called the *generalized delta* rule. There are two important parameters associated with using the generalized delta rule. The first is *momentum*, which refers to the tendency of the weights inside each unit to change the "direction" they are heading in. That is, each weight remembers if it has been getting bigger or smaller, and momentum tries to keep it going in the same direction. A network with high momentum responds slowly to new training examples that want to reverse the weights. If momentum is low, then the weights are allowed to oscillate more freely.

## TRAINING AS OPTIMIZATION

Although the first practical algorithm for training networks, back propagation is an inefficient way to train networks. The goal of training is to find the set of weights that minimizes the error on the training and/or validation set. This type of problem is an optimization problem, and there are several different approaches.

It is worth noting that this is a hard problem. First, there are many weights in the network, so there are many, many different possibilities of weights to consider. For a network that has 28 weights (say seven inputs and three hidden nodes in the hidden layer). Trying every combination of just two values for each weight requires testing $2^{28}$ combinations of values—or over 250 million combinations. Trying out all combinations of 10 values for each weight would be prohibitively expensive.

A second problem is one of symmetry. In general, there is no single best value. In fact, with neural networks that have more than one unit in the hidden layer, there are always multiple optima—because the weights on one hidden unit could be entirely swapped with the weights on another. This problem of having multiple optima complicates finding the best solution.

One approach to finding optima is called hill climbing. Start with a random set of weights. Then, consider taking a single step in each direction by making a small change in each of the weights. Choose whichever small step does the best job of reducing the error and repeat the process. This is like finding the highest point somewhere by only taking steps uphill. In many cases, you end up on top of a small hill instead of a tall mountain.

One variation on hill climbing is to start with big steps and gradually reduce the step size (the Jolly Green Giant will do a better job of finding the top of the nearest mountain than an ant). A related algorithm, called *simulated annealing*, injects a bit of randomness in the hill climbing. The randomness is based on physical theories having to do with how crystals form when liquids cool into solids (the crystalline formation is an example of optimization in the physical world). Both simulated annealing and hill climbing require many, many iterations—and these iterations are expensive computationally because they require running a network on the entire training set and then repeating again, and again for each step.

A better algorithm for training is the conjugate gradient algorithm. This algorithm tests a few different sets of weights and then guesses where the optimum is, using some ideas from multidimensional geometry. Each set of weights is considered to be a single point in a multidimensional space. After trying several different sets, the algorithm fits a multidimensional parabola to the points. A parabola is a U-shaped curve that has a single minimum (or maximum). Conjugate gradient then continues with a new set of weights in this region. This process still needs to be repeated; however, conjugate gradient produces better values more quickly than back propagation or the various hill climbing methods. Conjugate gradient (or some variation of it) is the preferred method of training neural networks in most data mining tools.

The *learning rate* controls how quickly the weights change. The best approach for the learning rate is to start big and decrease it slowly as the network is being trained. Initially, the weights are random, so large oscillations are useful to get in the vicinity of the best weights. However, as the network gets closer to the optimal solution, the learning rate should decrease so the network can fine-tune to the most optimal weights.

Researchers have invented hundreds of variations for training neural networks (see the sidebar "Training As Optimization"). Each of these approaches has its advantages and disadvantages. In all cases, they are looking for a technique that trains networks quickly to arrive at an optimal solution. Some neural network packages offer multiple training methods, allowing users to experiment with the best solution for their problems.

One of the dangers with any of the training techniques is falling into something called a local optimum. This happens when the network produces okay results for the training set and adjusting the weights no longer improves the performance of the network. However, there is some other combination of weights—significantly different from those in the network—that yields a much better solution. This is analogous to trying to climb to the top of a mountain by choosing the steepest path at every turn and finding that you have only climbed to the top of a nearby hill. There is a tension between finding the local best solution and the global best solution. Controlling the learning rate and momentum helps to find the best solution.

## Heuristics for Using Feed-Forward, Back Propagation Networks

Even with sophisticated neural network packages, getting the best results from a neural network takes some effort. This section covers some heuristics for setting up a network to obtain good results.

Probably the biggest decision is the number of units in the hidden layer. The more units, the more patterns the network can recognize. This would argue for a very large hidden layer. However, there is a drawback. The network might end up memorizing the training set instead of generalizing from it. In this case, more is not better. Fortunately, you can detect when a network is overtrained. If the network performs very well on the training set, but does much worse on the validation set, then this is an indication that it has memorized the training set.

How large should the hidden layer be? The real answer is that no one knows. It depends on the data, the patterns being detected, and the type of network. Since overfitting is a major concern with networks using customer data, we generally do not use hidden layers larger than the number of inputs. A good place to start for many problems is to experiment with one, two, and three nodes in the hidden layer. This is feasible, especially since training neural networks now takes seconds or minutes, instead of hours. If adding more nodes improves the performance of the network, then larger may be better. When the network is overtraining, reduce the size of the layer. If it is not sufficiently accurate, increase its size. When using a network for classification, however, it can be useful to start with one hidden node for each class.

Another decision is the size of the training set. The training set must be sufficiently large to cover the ranges of inputs available for each feature. In addition, you want several training examples for each weight in the network. For a network with $s$ input units, $h$ hidden units, and 1 output, there are $h * (s + 1) + h + 1$ weights in the network (each hidden layer node has a weight for each connection to the input layer, an additional weight for the bias, and then a connection to the output layer and its bias). For instance, if there are 15 input features and 10 units in the hidden network, then there are 171 weights in the network. There should be at least 30 examples for each weight, but a better minimum is 100. For this example, the training set should have at least 17,100 rows.

Finally, the learning rate and momentum parameters are very important for getting good results out of a network using the back propagation training algorithm (it is better to use conjugate gradient or similar approach). Initially, the learning should be set high to make large adjustments to the weights. As the training proceeds, the learning rate should decrease in order to fine-tune the network. The momentum parameter allows the network to move toward a solution more rapidly, preventing oscillation around less useful weights.

# Choosing the Training Set

The training set consists of records whose prediction or classification values are already known. Choosing a good training set is critical for all data mining modeling. A poor training set dooms the network, regardless of any other work that goes into creating it. Fortunately, there are only a few things to consider in choosing a good one.

## Coverage of Values for All Features

The most important of these considerations is that the training set needs to cover the full range of values for all features that the network might encounter, including the output. In the real estate appraisal example, this means including inexpensive houses and expensive houses, big houses and little houses, and houses with and without garages. In general, it is a good idea to have several examples in the training set for each value of a categorical feature and for values throughout the ranges of ordered discrete and continuous features.

This is true regardless of whether the features are actually used as inputs into the network. For instance, lot size might not be chosen as an input variable in the network. However, the training set should still have examples from all different lot sizes. A network trained on smaller lot sizes (some of which might be low priced and some high priced) is probably not going to do a good job on mansions.

## Number of Features

The number of input features affects neural networks in two ways. First, the more features used as inputs into the network, the larger the network needs to be, increasing the risk of overfitting and increasing the size of the training set. Second, the more features, the longer is takes the network to converge to a set of weights. And, with too many features, the weights are less likely to be optimal.

This variable selection problem is a common problem for statisticians. In practice, we find that decision trees (discussed in Chapter 6) provide a good method for choosing the best variables. Figure 7.8 shows a nice feature of SAS Enterprise Miner. By connecting a neural network node to a decision tree node, the neural network only uses the variables chosen by the decision tree.

An alternative method is to use intuition. Start with a handful of variables that make sense. Experiment by trying other variables to see which ones improve the model. In many cases, it is useful to calculate new variables that represent particular aspects of the business problem. In the real estate example, for instance, we might subtract the square footage of the house from the lot size to get an idea of how large the yard is.

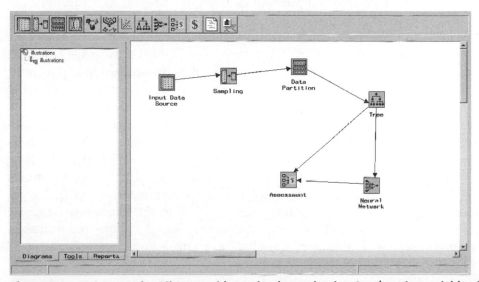

**Figure 7.8** SAS Enterprise Miner provides a simple mechanism for choosing variables for a neural network—just connect a neural network node to a decision tree node.

## Size of Training Set

The more features there are in the network, the more training examples that are needed to get a good coverage of patterns in the data. Unfortunately, there is no simple rule to express a relationship between the number of features and the size of the training set. However, typically a minimum of a few hundred examples are needed to support each feature with adequate coverage; having several thousand is not unreasonable. The authors have worked with neural networks that have only six or seven inputs, but whose training set contained hundreds of thousands of rows.

When the training set is not sufficiently large, neural networks tend to overfit the data. Overfitting is guaranteed to happen when there are fewer training examples than there are weights in the network. This poses a problem, because the network will work very, very well on the training set, but it will fail spectacularly on unseen data.

Of course, the downside of a really large training set is that it takes the neural network longer to train. In a given amount of time, you may get better models by using fewer input features and a smaller training set and experimenting with different combinations of features and network topologies rather than using the largest possible training set that leaves no time for experimentation.

## Number of Outputs

In most training examples, there are typically many more inputs going in than there are outputs going out, so good coverage of the inputs results in good coverage of the outputs. However, it is very important that there be many examples for all possible output values from the network. In addition, the number of training examples for each possible output should be about the same. This can be critical when deciding what to use as the training set.

For instance, if the neural network is going to be used to detect rare, but important events—failure rates in a diesel engines, fraudulent use of a credit card, or who will respond to an offer for a home equity line of credit—then the training set must have a sufficient number of examples of these rare events. A random sample of available data may not be sufficient, since common examples will swamp the rare examples. To get around this, the training set needs to be balanced by oversampling the rare cases. For this type of problem, a training set consisting of 10,000 "good" examples and 10,000 "bad" examples gives better results than a randomly selected training set of 100,000 good examples and 1,000 bad examples. After all, using the randomly sampled training set the neural network would probably assign "good" regardless of the input—and be right 99 percent of the time. This is an exception to the general rule that a larger training set is better.

**TIP** The training set for a neural network has to be large enough to cover all the values taken on by all the features. You want to have at least a dozen, if not hundreds or thousands, of examples for each input feature. For the outputs of the network, you want to be sure that there is an even distribution of values. This is a case where fewer examples in the training set can actually improve results, by not swamping the network with "good" examples when you want to train it to recognize "bad" examples. The size of the training set is also influenced by the power of the machine running the model. A neural network needs more time to train when the training set is very large. That time could perhaps better be used to experiment with different features, input mapping functions, and parameters of the network.

## Preparing the Data

Preparing the input data is often the most complicated part of using a neural network. Part of the complication is the normal problem of choosing the right data and the right examples for a data mining endeavor. Another part is mapping each field to an appropriate range—remember, using a limited range of inputs helps networks better recognize patterns. Some neural network packages facilitate this translation using friendly, graphical interfaces. Since the format of the data going into the network has a big effect on how well the network performs, we are reviewing the common ways to map data. Chapter 17 contains additional material on data preparation.

### Features with Continuous Values

Some features take on continuous values, generally ranging between known minimum and maximum bounds. Examples of such features are:

- Dollar amounts (sales price, monthly balance, weekly sales, income, and so on)
- Averages (average monthly balance, average sales volume, and so on)
- Ratios (debt-to-income, price-to-earnings, and so on)
- Physical measurements (area of living space, temperature, and so on)

The real estate appraisal example showed a good way to handle continuous features. When these features fall into a predefined range between a minimum value and a maximum value, the values can be scaled to be in a reasonable range, using a calculation such as:

mapped_value = 2 * (original_value – min) / (max – min + 1) – 1

This transformation (subtract the min, divide by the range, double and subtract 1) produces a value in the range from –1 to 1 that follows the same distribution as the original value. This works well in many cases, but there are some additional considerations.

The first is that the range a variable takes in the training set may be different from the range in the data being scored. Of course, we try to avoid this situation by ensuring that all variables values are represented in the training set. However, this ideal situation is not always possible. Someone could build a new house in the neighborhood with 5,000 square feet of living space perhaps rendering the real estate appraisal network useless. There are several ways to approach this:

- Plan for a larger range. The range of living areas in the training set was from 714 square feet to 4185 square feet. Instead of using these values for the minimum and maximum value of the range, allow for some growth, using, say, 500 and 5000 instead.

- Reject out-of-range values. Once we start extrapolating beyond the ranges of values in the training set, we have much less confidence in the results. Only use the network for predefined ranges of input values. This is particularly important when using a network for controlling a manufacturing process; wildly incorrect results can lead to disasters.

- Peg values lower than the minimum to the minimum and higher than the maximum to the maximum. So, houses larger than 4,000 square feet would all be treated the same. This works well in many situations. However, we suspect that the price of a house is highly correlated with the living area. So, a house with 20 percent more living area than the maximum house size (all other things being equal) would cost about 20 percent more. In other situations, pegging the values can work quite well.

- Map the minimum value to –0.9 and the maximum value to 0.9 instead of –1 and 1.

- Or, most likely, don't worry about it. It is important that most values are near 0; a few exceptions probably will not have a significant impact.

Figure 7.9 illustrates another problem that arises with continuous features—skewed distribution of values. In this data, almost all incomes are under $100,000, but the range goes from $10,000 to $1,000,000. Scaling the values as suggested maps a $30,000 income to –0.96 and a $65,000 income to –0.89, hardly any difference at all, although this income differential might be very significant for a marketing application. On the other hand, $250,000 and $800,000 become –0.51 and +0.60, respectively—a very large difference, though this income differential might be much less significant. The incomes are highly skewed toward the low end, and this can make it difficult for the neural network to take advantage of the income field. Skewed distributions can prevent a network from effectively using an important field. Skewed distributions affect neural networks but not decision trees because neural networks actually use the values for calculations; decision trees only use the ordering (rank) of the values.

There are several ways to resolve this. The most common is to split a feature like income into ranges. This is called *discretizing* or *binning* the field. Figure 7.9 illustrates breaking the incomes into 10 equal-width ranges, but this is not useful at all. Virtually all the values fall in the first two ranges. Equal-sized quintiles provide a better choice of ranges:

$10,000–$17,999   very low (–1.0)

$18,000–$31,999   low (–0.5)

$32,000–$63,999   middle (0.0)

$64,000–$99,999   high (+0.5)

$100,000 and above   very high (+1.0)

Information is being lost by this transformation. A household with an income of $65,000 now looks exactly like a household with an income of $98,000. On the other hand, the sheer magnitude of the larger values does not confuse the neural network.

There are other methods as well. For instance, taking the logarithm is a good way of handling values that have wide ranges. Another approach is to standardize the variable, by subtracting the mean and dividing by the standard deviation. The standardized value is going to very often be between –2 and +2 (that is, for most variables, almost all values fall within two standard deviations of the mean). Standardizing variables is often a good approach for neural networks. However, it must be used with care, since big outliers make the standard deviation big. So, when there are big outliers, many of the standardized values will fall into a very small range, making it hard for the network to distinguish them from each other.

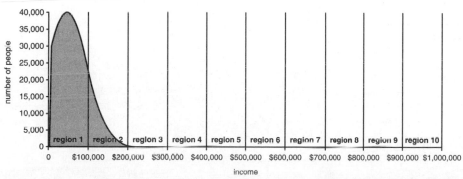

**Figure 7.9** Household income provides an example of a skewed distribution. Almost all the values are in the first 10 percent of the range (income of less than $100,000).

## Features with Ordered, Discrete (Integer) Values

Continuous features can be binned into ordered, discrete values. Other examples of features with ordered values include:

- Counts (number of children, number of items purchased, months since sale, and so on)
- Age
- Ordered categories (low, medium, high)

Like the continuous features, these have a maximum and minimum value. For instance, age usually ranges from 0 to about 100, but the exact range may depend on the data used. The number of children may go from 0 to 4, with anything over 4 considered to be 4. Preparing such fields is simple. First, count the number of different values and assign each a proportional fraction in some range, say from 0 to 1. For instance, if there are five distinct values, then these get mapped to 0, 0.25, 0.50, 0.75, and 1, as shown in Figure 7.10. Notice that mapping the values onto the unit interval like this preserves the ordering; this is an important aspect of this method and means that information is not being lost.

It is also possible to break a range into unequal parts. One example is called *thermometer codes*:

$$0 \;\rightarrow\; 0\,0\,0\,0 \quad = 0/16 = 0.0000$$
$$1 \;\rightarrow\; 1\,0\,0\,0 \quad = 8/16 = 0.5000$$
$$2 \;\rightarrow\; 1\,1\,0\,0 \quad = 12/16 = 0.7500$$
$$3 \;\rightarrow\; 1\,1\,1\,0 \quad = 14/16 = 0.8750$$

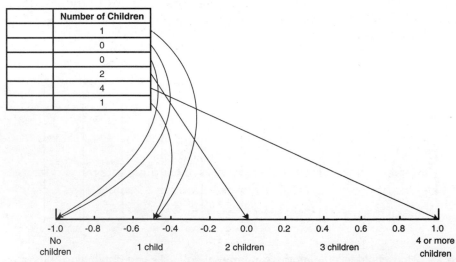

**Figure 7.10**　When codes have an inherent order, they can be mapped onto the unit interval.

The name arises because the sequence of 1s starts on one side and rises to some value, like the mercury in a thermometer; this sequence is then interpreted as a decimal written in binary notation. Thermometer codes are good for things like academic grades and bond ratings, where the difference on one end of the scale is less significant than differences on the other end.

For instance, for many marketing applications, having no children is quite different from having one child. However, the difference between three children and four is rather negligible. Using a thermometer code, the number of children variable might be mapped as follows: 0 (for 0 children), 0.5 (for one child), 0.75 (for two children), 0.875 (for three children), and so on. For categorical variables, it is often easier to keep mapped values in the range from 0 to 1. This is reasonable. However, to extend the range from –1 to 1, double the value and subtract 1.

Thermometer codes are one way of including prior information into the coding scheme. They keep certain codes values close together because you have a sense that these code values should be close. This type of knowledge can improve the results from a neural network—don't make it discover what you already know. Feel free to map values onto the unit interval so that codes close to each other match your intuitive notions of how close they should be.

## Features with Categorical Values

Features with categories are unordered lists of values. These are different from ordered lists, because there is no ordering to preserve and introducing an order is inappropriate. There are typically many examples of categorical values in data, such as:

- Gender, marital status
- Status codes
- Product codes
- Zip codes

Although zip codes look like numbers in the United States, they really represent discrete geographic areas, and the codes themselves give little geographic information. There is no reason to think that 10014 is more like 02116 than it is like 94117, even though the numbers are much closer. The numbers are just discrete names attached to geographical areas.

There are three fundamentally different ways of handling categorical features. The first is to treat the codes as discrete, ordered values, mapping them using the methods discussed in the previous section. Unfortunately, the neural network does not understand that the codes are unordered. So, five codes for marital status ("single," "divorced," "married," "widowed," and "unknown") would be mapped to –1.0, –0.5, 0.0, +0.5, +1.0, respectively. From the perspective of the network, "single" and "unknown" are very far apart, whereas "divorced" and "married" are quite close. For some input fields, this implicit ordering might not have much of an effect. In other cases, the values have some relationship to each other and the implicit ordering confuses the network.

> **WARNING** When working with categorical variables in neural networks, be very careful when mapping the variables to numbers. The mapping introduces an ordering of the variables, which the neural network takes into account, even if the ordering does not make any sense.

The second way of handling categorical features is to break the categories into flags, one for each value. Assume that there are three values for gender (male, female, and unknown). Table 7.3 shows how three flags can be used to code these values using a method called *1 of N Coding*. It is possible to reduce the number of flags by eliminated the flag for the unknown gender; this approach is called *1 of N – 1 Coding*.

Why would we want to do this? We have now multiplied the number of input variables and this is generally a bad thing for a neural network. However, these coding schemes are the only way to eliminate implicit ordering among the values.

The third way is to replace the code itself with numerical data about the code. Instead of including zip codes in a model, for instance, include various census fields, such as the median income or the proportion of households with children. Another possibility is to include historical information summarized at the level of the categorical variable. An example would be including the historical churn rate by zip code for a model that is predicting churn.

> **TIP** When using categorical variables in a neural network, try to replace them with some numeric variable that describes them, such as the average income in a census block, the proportion of customers in a zip code (penetration), the historical churn rate for a handset, or the base cost of a pricing plan.

**Table 7.3**   Handling Gender Using 1 of *N* Coding and 1 of *N* - 1 Coding

| | *N* CODING | | | *N* - 1 CODING | |
| GENDER | GENDER MALE FLAG | GENDER FEMALE FLAG | GENDER UNKNOWN FLAG | GENDER MALE FLAG | GENDER FEMALE FLAG |
| --- | --- | --- | --- | --- | --- |
| Male | +1.0 | -1.0 | -1.0 | +1.0 | -1.0 |
| Female | -1.0 | +1.0 | -1.0 | -1.0 | +1.0 |
| Unknown | -1.0 | -1.0 | +1.0 | -1.0 | -1.0 |

## Other Types of Features

Some input features might not fit directly into any of these three categories. For complicated features, it is necessary to extract meaningful information and use one of the above techniques to represent the result. Remember, the input to a neural network consists of inputs whose values should generally fall between −1 and 1.

Dates are a good example of data that you may want to handle in special ways. Any date or time can be represented as the number of days or seconds since a fixed point in time, allowing them to be mapped and fed directly into the network. However, if the date is for a transaction, then the day of the week and month of the year may be more important than the actual date. For instance, the month would be important for detecting seasonal trends in data. You might want to extract this information from the date and feed it into the network instead of, or in addition to, the actual date.

The address field—or any text field—is similarly complicated. Generally, addresses are useless to feed into a network, even if you could figure out a good way to map the entire field into a single value. However, the address may contain a zip code, city name, state, and apartment number. All of these may be useful features, even though the address field taken as a whole is usually useless.

## Interpreting the Results

Neural network tools take the work out of interpreting the results. When estimating a continuous value, often the output needs to be scaled back to the correct range. For instance, the network might be used to calculate the value of a house and, in the training set, the output value is set up so that $103,000 maps to −1 and $250,000 maps to 1. If the model is later applied to another house and the output is 0.0, then we can figure out that this corresponds to $176,500— halfway between the minimum and the maximum values. This inverse transformation makes neural networks particularly easy to use for estimating continuous values. Often, though, this step is not necessary, particularly when the output layer is using a linear transfer function.

For binary or categorical output variables, the approach is still to take the inverse of the transformation used for training the network. So, if "churn" is given a value of 1 and "no-churn" a value of −1, then values near 1 represent churn, and those near −1 represent no churn. When there are two outcomes, the meaning of the output depends on the training set used to train the network. Because the network learns to minimize the error, the average value produced by the network during training is usually going to be close to the average value in the training set. One way to think of this is that the first pattern the network finds is the average value. So, if the original training set had 50 percent churn and 50 percent no-churn, then the average value the network will produce for the training set examples is going to be close to 0.0. Values higher than 0.0 are more like churn and those less than 0.0, less like churn. If the original training set had 10 percent churn, then the cutoff would more reasonably be –0.8 rather than 0.0 (–0.8 is 10 percent of the way from –1 to 1). So, the output of the network does look a lot like a probability in this case. However, the probability depends on the distribution of the output variable in the training set.

Yet another approach is to assign a confidence level along with the value. This confidence level would treat the actual output of the network as a propensity to churn, as shown in Table 7.4.

For binary values, it is also possible to create a network that produces two outputs, one for each value. In this case, each output represents the strength of evidence that that category is the correct one. The chosen category would then be the one with the higher value, with confidence based on some function of the strengths of the two outputs. This approach is particularly valuable when the two outcomes are not exclusive.

**TIP** Because neural networks produce continuous values, the output from a network can be difficult to interpret for categorical results (used in classification). The best way to calibrate the output is to run the network over a validation set, entirely separate from the training set, and to use the results from the validation set to calibrate the output of the network to categories. In many cases, the network can have a separate output for each category; that is, a *propensity* for that category. Even with separate outputs, the validation set is still needed to calibrate the outputs.

**Table 7.4**  Categories and Confidence Levels for NN Output

| OUTPUT VALUE | CATEGORY | CONFIDENCE |
|---|---|---|
| −1.0 | A | 100% |
| −0.6 | A | 80% |
| −0.02 | A | 51% |
| +0.02 | B | 51% |
| +0.6 | B | 80% |
| +1.0 | B | 100% |

The approach is similar when there are more than two options under consideration. For example, consider a long distance carrier trying to target a new set of customers with three targeted service offerings:

- Discounts on all international calls
- Discounts on all long-distance calls that are not international
- Discounts on calls to a predefined set of customers

The carrier is going to offer incentives to customers for each of the three packages. Since the incentives are expensive, the carrier needs to choose the right service for the right customers in order for the campaign to be profitable. Offering all three products to all the customers is expensive and, even worse, may confuse the recipients, reducing the response rate.

The carrier test markets the products to a small subset of customers who receive all three offers but are only allowed to respond to one of them. It intends to use this information to build a model for predicting customer affinity for each offer. The training set uses the data collected from the test marketing campaign, and codes the propensity as follows: no response $\rightarrow$ −1.00, international $\rightarrow$ −0.33, national $\rightarrow$ +0.33, and specific numbers $\rightarrow$ +1.00. After training a neural network with information about the customers, the carrier starts applying the model.

But, applying the model does not go as well as planned. Many customers cluster around the four values used for training the network. However, apart from the nonresponders (who are the majority), there are many instances when the network returns intermediate values like 0.0 and 0.5. What can be done?

First, the carrier should use a validation set to understand the output values. By interpreting the results of the network based on what happens in the validation set, it can find the right ranges to use for transforming the results of the network back into marketing segments. This is the same process shown in Figure 7.11.

Another observation in this case is that the network is really being used to predict three different things, whether a recipient will respond to each of the campaigns. This strongly suggests that a better structure for the network is to have three outputs: a propensity to respond to the international plan, to the long-distance plan, and to the specific numbers plan. The test set would then be used to determine where the cutoff is for nonrespondents. Alternatively, each outcome could be modeled separately, and the model results combined to select the appropriate campaign.

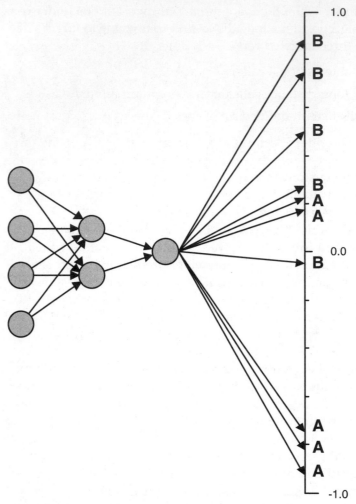

**Figure 7.11**   Running a neural network on 10 examples from the validation set can help determine how to interpret results.

## Neural Networks for Time Series

In many business problems, the data naturally falls into a time series. Examples of such series are the closing price of IBM stock, the daily value of the Swiss franc to U.S. dollar exchange rate, or a forecast of the number of customers who will be active on any given date in the future. For financial time series, someone who is able to predict the next value, or even whether the series is heading up or down, has a tremendous advantage over other investors. Although predominant in the financial industry, time series appear in other areas, such as forecasting and process control. Financial time series, though, are the most studied since a small advantage in predictive power translates into big profits.

Neural networks are easily adapted for time-series analysis, as shown in Figure 7.12. The network is trained on the time-series data, starting at the oldest point in the data. The training then moves to the second oldest point, and the oldest point goes to the next set of units in the input layer, and so on. The network trains like a feed-forward, back propagation network trying to predict the next value in the series at each step.

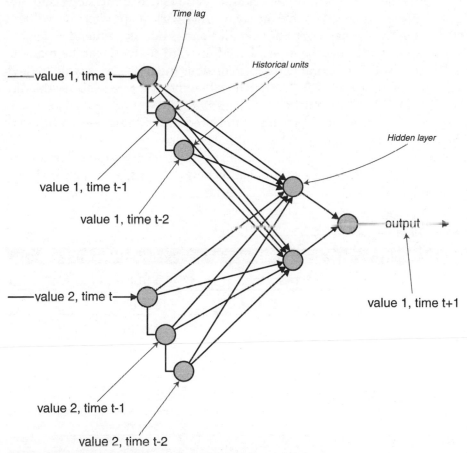

**Figure 7.12**  A time-delay neural network remembers the previous few training examples and uses them as input into the network. The network then works like a feed-forward, back propagation network.

Notice that the time-series network is not limited to data from just a single time series. It can take multiple inputs. For instance, to predict the value of the Swiss franc to U.S. dollar exchange rate, other time-series information might be included, such as the volume of the previous day's transactions, the U.S. dollar to Japanese yen exchange rate, the closing value of the stock exchange, and the day of the week. In addition, non-time-series data, such as the reported inflation rate in the countries over the period of time under investigation, might also be candidate features.

The number of historical units controls the length of the patterns that the network can recognize. For instance, keeping 10 historical units on a network predicting the closing price of a favorite stock will allow the network to recognize patterns that occur within 2-week time periods (since exchange rates are set only on weekdays). Relying on such a network to predict the value 3 months in the future may not be a good idea and is not recommended.

Actually, by modifying the input, a feed-forward network can be made to work like a time-delay neural network. Consider the time series with 10 days of history, shown in Table 7.5. The network will include two features: the day of the week and the closing price.

Create a time series with a time lag of three requires adding new features for the historical, lagged values. (Day-of-the-week does not need to be copied, since it does not really change.) The result is Table 7.6. This data can now be input into a feed-forward, back propagation network without any special support for time series.

**Table 7.5**   Time Series

| DATA ELEMENT | DAY-OF-WEEK | CLOSING PRICE |
| --- | --- | --- |
| 1 | 1 | $40.25 |
| 2 | 2 | $41.00 |
| 3 | 3 | $39.25 |
| 4 | 4 | $39.75 |
| 5 | 5 | $40.50 |
| 6 | 1 | $40.50 |
| 7 | 2 | $40.75 |
| 8 | 3 | $41.25 |
| 9 | 4 | $42.00 |
| 10 | 5 | $41.50 |

**Table 7.6** Time Series with Time Lag

| DATA ELEMENT | DAY-OF-WEEK | CLOSING PRICE | PREVIOUS CLOSING PRICE | PREVIOUS-1 CLOSING PRICE |
|---|---|---|---|---|
| 1 | 1 | $40.25 | | |
| 2 | 2 | $41.00 | $40.25 | |
| 3 | 3 | $39.25 | $41.00 | $40.25 |
| 4 | 4 | $39.75 | $39.25 | $41.00 |
| 5 | 5 | $40.50 | $39.75 | $39.25 |
| 6 | 1 | $40.50 | $40.50 | $39.75 |
| 7 | 2 | $40.75 | $40.50 | $40.50 |
| 8 | 3 | $41.25 | $40.75 | $40.50 |
| 9 | 4 | $42.00 | $41.25 | $40.75 |
| 10 | 5 | $41.50 | $42.00 | $41.25 |

# How to Know What Is Going on Inside a Neural Network

Neural networks are opaque. Even knowing all the weights on all the nodes throughout the network does not give much insight into why the network produces the results that it produces. This lack of understanding has some philosophical appeal—after all, we do not understand how human consciousness arises from the neurons in our brains. As a practical matter, though, opaqueness impairs our ability to understand the results produced by a network.

If only we could ask it to tell us how it is making its decision in the form of rules. Unfortunately, the same nonlinear characteristics of neural network nodes that make them so powerful also make them unable to produce simple rules. Eventually, research into rule extraction from networks may bring unequivocally good results. Until then, the trained network itself is the rule, and other methods are needed to peer inside to understand what is going on.

A technique called *sensitivity analysis* can be used to get an idea of how opaque models work. Sensitivity analysis does not provide explicit rules, but it does indicate the relative importance of the inputs to the result of the network. Sensitivity analysis uses the test set to determine how sensitive the output of the network is to each input. The following are the basic steps:

1. Find the average value for each input. We can think of this average value as the center of the test set.

2. Measure the output of the network when all inputs are at their average value.

3. Measure the output of the network when each input is modified, one at a time, to be at its minimum and maximum values (usually –1 and 1, respectively).

For some inputs, the output of the network changes very little for the three values (minimum, average, and maximum). The network is not *sensitive* to these inputs (at least when all other inputs are at their average value). Other inputs have a large effect on the output of the network. The network is *sensitive* to these inputs. The amount of change in the output measures the sensitivity of the network for each input. Using these measures for all the inputs creates a relative measure of the importance of each feature. Of course, this method is entirely empirical and is looking only at each variable independently. Neural networks are interesting precisely because they can take interactions between variables into account.

There are variations on this procedure. It is possible to modify the values of two or three features at the same time to see if combinations of features have a particular importance. Sometimes, it is useful to start from a location other than the center of the test set. For instance, the analysis might be repeated for the minimum and maximum values of the features to see how sensitive the network is at the extremes. If sensitivity analysis produces significantly different results for these three situations, then there are higher order effects in the network that are taking advantage of combinations of features.

When using a feed-forward, back propagation network, sensitivity analysis can take advantage of the error measures calculated during the learning phase instead of having to test each feature independently. The validation set is fed into the network to produce the output and the output is compared to the predicted output to calculate the error. The network then propagates the error back through the units, not to adjust any weights but to keep track of the sensitivity of each input. The error is a proxy for the sensitivity, determining how much each input affects the output in the network. Accumulating these sensitivities over the entire test set determines which inputs have the larger effect on the output. In our experience, though, the values produced in this fashion are not particularly useful for understanding the network.

**TIP** Neural networks do not produce easily understood rules that explain how they arrive at a given result. Even so, it is possible to understand the relative importance of inputs into the network by using sensitivity analysis. Sensitivity can be a manual process where each feature is tested one at a time relative to the other features. It can also be more automated by using the sensitivity information generated by back propagation. In many situations, understanding the relative importance of inputs is almost as good as having explicit rules.

# Self-Organizing Maps

Self-organizing maps (SOMs) are a variant of neural networks used for undirected data mining tasks such as cluster detection. The Finnish researcher Dr. Tuevo Kohonen invented self-organizing maps, which are also called Kohonen Networks. Although used originally for images and sounds, these networks can also recognize clusters in data. They are based on the same underlying units as feed-forward, back propagation networks, but SOMs are quite different in two respects. They have a different topology and the back propagation method of learning is no longer applicable. They have an entirely different method for training.

## What Is a Self-Organizing Map?

The *self-organizing map* (SOM), an example of which is shown in Figure 7.13, is a neural network that can recognize unknown patterns in the data. Like the networks we've already looked at, the basic SOM has an input layer and an output layer. Each unit in the input layer is connected to one source, just as in the networks for predictive modeling. Also, like those networks, each unit in the SOM has an independent weight associated with each incoming connection (this is actually a property of all neural networks). However, the similarity between SOMs and feed-forward, back propagation networks ends here.

The output layer consists of many units instead of just a handful. Each of the units in the output layer is connected to all of the units in the input layer. The output layer is arranged in a grid, as if the units were in the squares on a checkerboard. Even though the units are not connected to each other in this layer, the grid-like structure plays an important role in the training of the SOM, as we will see shortly.

How does an SOM recognize patterns? Imagine one of the booths at a carnival where you throw balls at a wall filled with holes. If the ball lands in one of the holes, then you have your choice of prizes. Training an SOM is like being at the booth blindfolded and initially the wall has no holes, very similar to the situation when you start looking for patterns in large amounts of data and don't know where to start. Each time you throw the ball, it dents the wall a little bit. Eventually, when enough balls land in the same vicinity, the indentation breaks through the wall, forming a hole. Now, when another ball lands at that location, it goes through the hole. You get a prize—at the carnival, this is a cheap stuffed animal, with an SOM, it is an identifiable cluster.

Figure 7.14 shows how this works for a simple SOM. When a member of the training set is presented to the network, the values flow forward through the network to the units in the output layer. The units in the output layer compete with each other, and the one with the highest value "wins." The reward is to adjust the weights leading up to the winning unit to strengthen in the response to the input pattern. This is like making a little dent in the network.

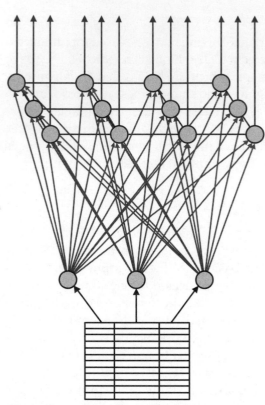

The output units compete with each other for the output of the network.

The output layer is laid out like a grid. Each unit is connected to all the input units, but not to each other.

The input layer is connected to the inputs.

**Figure 7.13** The self-organizing map is a special kind of neural network that can be used to detect clusters.

There is one more aspect to the training of the network. Not only are the weights for the winning unit adjusted, but the weights for units in its immediate neighborhood are also adjusted to strengthen their response to the inputs. This adjustment is controlled by a *neighborliness* parameter that controls the size of the neighborhood and the amount of adjustment. Initially, the neighborhood is rather large, and the adjustments are large. As the training continues, the neighborhoods and adjustments decrease in size. Neighborliness actually has several practical effects. One is that the output layer behaves more like a connected fabric, even though the units are not directly connected to each other. Clusters similar to each other should be closer together than more dissimilar clusters. More importantly, though, neighborliness allows for a group of units to represent a single cluster. Without this neighborliness, the network would tend to find as many clusters in the data as there are units in the output layer—introducing bias into the cluster detection.

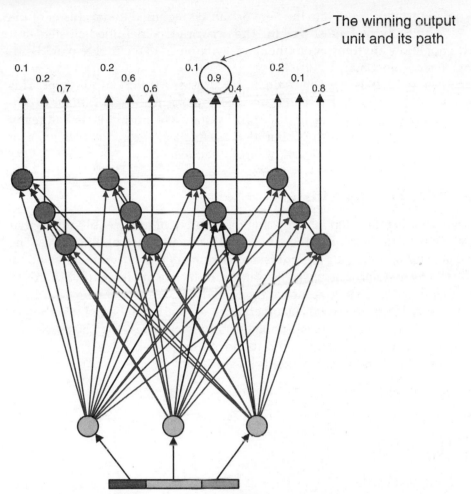

**Figure 7.14**  An SOM finds the output unit that does the best job of recognizing a particular input.

Typically, a SOM identifies fewer clusters than it has output units. This is inefficient when using the network to assign new records to the clusters, since the new inputs are fed through the network to unused units in the output layer. To determine which units are actually used, we apply the SOM to the validation set. The members of the validation set are fed through the network, keeping track of the winning unit in each case. Units with no hits or with very few hits are discarded. Eliminating these units increases the run-time performance of the network by reducing the number of calculations needed for new instances.

Once the final network is in place—with the output layer restricted only to the units that identify specific clusters—it can be applied to new instances. An unknown instance is fed into the network and is assigned to the cluster at the output unit with the largest weight. The network has identified clusters, but we do not know anything about them. We will return to the problem of identifying clusters a bit later.

The original SOMs used two-dimensional grids for the output layer. This was an artifact of earlier research into recognizing features in images composed of a two-dimensional array of pixel values. The output layer can really have any structure—with neighborhoods defined in three dimensions, as a network of hexagons, or laid out in some other fashion.

## Example: Finding Clusters

A large bank is interested in increasing the number of home equity loans that it sells, which provides an illustration of the practical use of clustering. The bank decides that it needs to understand customers that currently have home equity loans to determine the best strategy for increasing its market share. To start this process, demographics are gathered on 5,000 customers who have home equity loans and 5,000 customers who do not have them. Even though the proportion of customers with home equity loans is less than 50 percent, it is a good idea to have equal weights in the training set.

The data that is gathered has fields like the following:

- Appraised value of house
- Amount of credit available
- Amount of credit granted
- Age
- Marital status
- Number of children
- Household income

This data forms a good training set for clustering. The input values are mapped so they all lie between –1 and +1; these are used to train an SOM. The network identifies five clusters in the data, but it does not give any information about the clusters. What do these clusters mean?

A common technique to compare different clusters that works particularly well with neural network techniques is the *average member* technique. Find the most average member of each of the clusters—the center of the cluster. This is similar to the approach used for sensitivity analysis. To do this, find the average value for each feature in each cluster. Since all the features are numbers, this is not a problem for neural networks.

For example, say that half the members of a cluster are male and half are female, and that male maps to –1.0 and female to +1.0. The average member for this cluster would have a value of 0.0 for this feature. In another cluster, there may be nine females for every male. For this cluster, the average member would have a value of 0.8. This averaging works very well with neural networks since all inputs have to be mapped into a numeric range.

> **TIP**   Self-organizing maps, a type of neural network, can identify clusters but they do not identify what makes the members of a cluster similar to each other. A powerful technique for comparing clusters is to determine the center or average member in each cluster. Using the test set, calculate the average value for each feature in the data. These average values can then be displayed in the same graph to determine the features that make a cluster unique.

These average values can then be plotted using parallel coordinates as in Figure 7.15, which shows the centers of the five clusters identified in the banking example. In this case, the bank noted that one of the clusters was particularly interesting, consisting of married customers in their forties with children. A bit more investigation revealed that these customers also had children in their late teens. Members of this cluster had more home equity lines than members of other clusters.

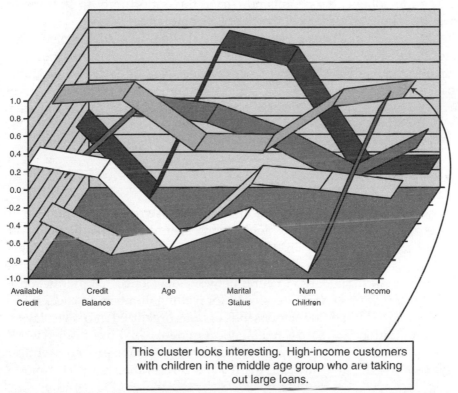

This cluster looks interesting. High-income customers with children in the middle age group who are taking out large loans.

**Figure 7.15**   The centers of five clusters are compared on the same graph. This simple visualization technique (called parallel coordinates) helps identify interesting clusters.

The story continues with the Marketing Department of the bank concluding that these people had taken out home equity loans to pay college tuition fees. The department arranged a marketing program designed specifically for this market, selling home equity loans as a means to pay for college education. The results from this campaign were disappointing. The marketing program was not successful.

Since the marketing program failed, it may seem as though the clusters did not live up to their promise. In fact, the problem lay elsewhere. The bank had initially only used general customer information. It had not combined information from the many different systems servicing its customers. The bank returned to the problem of identifying customers, but this time it included more information—from the deposits system, the credit card system, and so on.

The basic methods remained the same, so we will not go into detail about the analysis. With the additional data, the bank discovered that the cluster of customers with college-age children did actually exist, but a fact had been overlooked. When the additional data was included, the bank learned that the customers in this cluster also tended to have business accounts as well as personal accounts. This led to a new line of thinking. When the children leave home to go to college, the parents now have the opportunity to start a new business by taking advantage of the equity in their home.

With this insight, the bank created a new marketing program targeted at the parents, about starting a new business in their empty nest. This program succeeded, and the bank saw improved performance from its home equity loans group. The lesson of this case study is that, although SOMs are powerful tools for finding clusters, neural networks really are only as good as the data that goes into them.

## Lessons Learned

Neural networks are a versatile data mining tool. Across a large number of industries and a large number of applications, neural networks have proven themselves over and over again. These results come in complicated domains, such as analyzing time series and detecting fraud, that are not easily amenable to other techniques. The largest neural network developed for production is probably the system that AT&T developed for reading numbers on checks. This neural network has hundreds of thousands of units organized into seven layers.

Their foundation is based on biological models of how brains work. Although predating digital computers, the basic ideas have proven useful. In biology, neurons fire after their inputs reach a certain threshold. This model can be implemented on a computer as well. The field has really taken off since the 1980s, when statisticians started to use them and understand them better.

A neural network consists of artificial neurons connected together. Each neuron mimics its biological counterpart, taking various inputs, combining them, and producing an output. Since digital neurons process numbers, the activation function characterizes the neuron. In most cases, this function takes the weighted sum of its inputs and applies an S-shaped function to it. The result is a node that sometimes behaves in a linear fashion, and sometimes behaves in a nonlinear fashion—an improvement over standard statistical techniques.

The most common network is the feed-forward network for predictive modeling. Although originally a breakthrough, the back propagation training method has been replaced by other methods, notably conjugate gradient. These networks can be used for both categorical and continuous inputs. However, neural networks learn best when input fields have been mapped to the range between −1 and +1. This is a guideline to help train the network. Neural networks still work when a small amount of data falls outside the range and for more limited ranges, such as 0 to 1.

Neural networks do have several drawbacks. First, they work best when there are only a few input variables, and the technique itself does not help choose which variables to use. Variable selection is an issue. Other techniques, such as decision trees can come to the rescue. Also, when training a network, there is no guarantee that the resulting set of weights is optimal. To increase confidence in the result, build several networks and take the best one.

Perhaps the biggest problem, though, is that a neural network cannot explain what it is doing. Decision trees are popular because they can provide a list of rules. There is no way to get an accurate set of rules from a neural network. A neural network is explained by its weights, and a very complicated mathematical formula. Unfortunately, making sense of this is beyond our human powers of comprehension.

Variations on neural networks, such as self-organizing maps, extend the technology to undirected clustering. Overall neural networks are very powerful and can produce good models; they just can't tell us how they do it.

# CHAPTER 8

# Nearest Neighbor Approaches: Memory-Based Reasoning and Collaborative Filtering

You hear someone speak and immediately guess that she is from Australia. Why? Because her accent reminds you of other Australians you have met. Or you try a new restaurant expecting to like it because a friend with good taste recommended it. Both cases are examples of decisions based on experience. When faced with new situations, human beings are guided by memories of similar situations they have experienced in the past. That is the basis for the data mining techniques introduced in this chapter.

Nearest neighbor techniques are based on the concept of similarity. Memory-based reasoning (MBR) results are based on analogous situations in the past—much like deciding that a new friend is Australian based on past examples of Australian accents. Collaborative filtering adds more information, using not just the similarities among neighbors, but also their preferences. The restaurant recommendation is an example of collaborative filtering.

Central to all these techniques is the idea of *similarity*. What really makes situations in the past similar to a new situation? Along with finding the similar records from the past, there is the challenge of combining the information from the neighbors. These are the two key concepts for nearest neighbor approaches.

This chapter begins with an introduction to MBR and an explanation of how it works. Since measures of distance and similarity are important to nearest neighbor techniques, there is a section on distance metrics, including a discussion of the meaning of distance for data types, such as free text, that have no obvious geometric interpretation. The ideas of MBR are illustrated through a case study showing how MBR has been used to attach keywords to news stories. The chapter then looks at collaborative filtering, a popular approach to making recommendations, especially on the Web. Collaborative filtering is also based on nearest neighbors, but with a slight twist—instead of grouping restaurants or movies into neighborhoods, it groups the people recommending them.

## Memory Based Reasoning

The human ability to reason from experience depends on the ability to recognize appropriate examples from the past. A doctor diagnosing diseases, a claims analyst flagging fraudulent insurance claims, and a mushroom hunter spotting Morels are all following a similar process. Each first identifies similar cases from experience and then applies what their knowledge of those cases to the problem at hand. This is the essence of memory-based reasoning. A database of known records is searched to find preclassified records similar to a new record. These *neighbors* are used for classification and estimation.

Applications of MBR span many areas:

**Fraud detection.** New cases of fraud are likely to be similar to known cases. MBR can find and flag them for further investigation.

**Customer response prediction.** The next customers likely to respond to an offer are probably similar to previous customers who have responded. MBR can easily identify the next likely customers.

**Medical treatments.** The most effective treatment for a given patient is probably the treatment that resulted in the best outcomes for similar patients. MBR can find the treatment that produces the best outcome.

**Classifying responses.** Free-text responses, such as those on the U.S. Census form for occupation and industry or complaints coming from customers, need to be classified into a fixed set of codes. MBR can process the free-text and assign the codes.

One of the strengths of MBR is its ability to use data "as is." Unlike other data mining techniques, it does not care about the format of the records. It only cares about the existence of two operations: A *distance function* capable of calculating a distance between any two records and a *combination function* capable of combining results from several neighbors to arrive at an answer. These functions are readily defined for many kinds of records, including records with complex or unusual data types such as geographic locations, images, and free text that are usually difficult to handle with other analysis techniques. A case study later in the chapter shows MBR's successful application to the classification of news stories—an example that takes advantage of the full text of the news story to assign subject codes.

Another strength of MBR is its ability to adapt. Merely incorporating new data into the historical database makes it possible for MBR to learn about new categories and new definitions of old ones. MBR also produces good results without a long period devoted to training or to massaging incoming data into the right format.

These advantages come at a cost. MBR tends to be a resource hog since a large amount of historical data must be readily available for finding neighbors. Classifying new records can require processing all the historical records to find the most similar neighbors—a more time-consuming process than applying an already-trained neural network or an already-built decision tree. There is also the challenge of finding good distance and combination functions, which often requires a bit of trial and error and intuition.

## Example: Using MBR to Estimate Rents in Tuxedo, New York

The purpose of this example is to illustrate how MBR works by estimating the cost of renting an apartment in the target town by combining data on rents in several *similar* towns—its nearest neighbors.

MBR works by first identifying neighbors and then combining information from them. Figure 8.1 illustrates the first of these steps. The goal is to make predictions about the town of Tuxedo in Orange County, New York by looking at its neighbors. Not its *geographic* neighbors along the Hudson and Delaware rivers, rather its neighbors based on descriptive variables—in this case, population and median home value. The scatter plot shows New York towns arranged by these two variables. Figure 8.1 shows that measured this way, Brooklyn and Queens are close neighbors, and both are far from Manhattan. Although Manhattan is nearly as populous as Brooklyn and Queens, its home prices put it in a class by itself.

**TIP** Neighborhoods can be found in many dimensions. The choice of dimensions determines which records are close to one another. For some purposes, geographic proximity might be important. For other purposes home price or average lot size or population density might be more important. The choice of dimensions and the choice of a distance metric are crucial to any nearest-neighbor approach.

The first stage of MBR finds the closest neighbor on the scatter plot shown in Figure 8.1. Then the next closest neighbor is found, and so on until the desired number are available. In this case, the number of neighbors is two and the nearest ones turn out to be Shelter Island (which really is an island) way out by the tip of Long Island's North Fork, and North Salem, a town in Northern Westchester near the Connecticut border. These towns fall at about the middle of a list sorted by population and near the top of one sorted by home value. Although they are many miles apart, along these two dimensions, Shelter Island and North Salem are very similar to Tuxedo.

Once the neighbors have been located, the next step is to combine information from the neighbors to infer something about the target. For this example, the goal is to estimate the cost of renting a house in Tuxedo. There is more than one reasonable way to combine data from the neighbors. The census provides information on rents in two forms. Table 8.1 shows what the 2000 census reports about rents in the two towns selected as neighbors. For each town, there is a count of the number of households paying rent in each of several price bands as well as the median rent for each town. The challenge is to figure out how best to use this data to characterize rents in the neighbors and then how to combine information from the neighbors to come up with an estimate that characterizes rents in Tuxedo in the same way.

Tuxedo's nearest neighbors, the towns of North Salem and Shelter Island, have quite different distributions of rents even though the median rents are similar. In Shelter Island, a plurality of homes, 34.6 percent, rent in the $500 to $750 range. In the town of North Salem, the largest number of homes, 30.9 percent, rent in the $1,000 to $1,500 range. Furthermore, while only 3.1 percent of homes in Shelter Island rent for over $1,500, 24.2 percent of homes in North Salem do. On the other hand, at $804, the *median* rent in Shelter Island is above the $750 ceiling of the most common range, while the median rent in North Salem, $1,150, is below the floor of the most common range for that town. If the *average* rent were available, it too would be a good candidate for characterizing the rents in the various towns.

**Table 8.1** The Neighbors

| TOWN | POPULA-TION | MEDIAN RENT | RENT <$500 (%) | RENT $750 (%) | RENT $1000 (%) | RENT $1500 (%) | RENT >$1500 (%) | NO RENT (%) |
|---|---|---|---|---|---|---|---|---|
| Shelter Island | 2228 | $804 | 3.1 | 34.6 | 31.4 | 10.7 | 3.1 | 17 |
| North Salem | 5173 | $1150 | 3 | 10.2 | 21.6 | 30.9 | 24.2 | 10.2 |

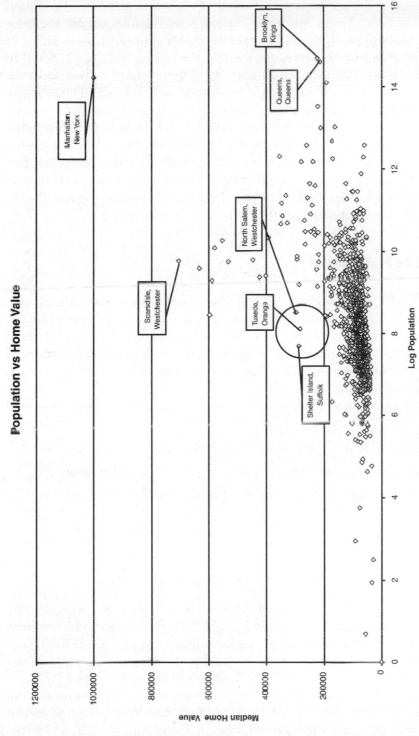

**Figure 8.1**  Based on 2000 census population and home value, the town of Tuxedo in Orange County has Shelter Island and North Salem as its two nearest neighbors.

One possible combination function would be to average the most common rents of the two neighbors. Since only ranges are available, we use the midpoints. For Shelter Island, the midpoint of the most common range is $875. For North Salem, it is $1,250. Averaging the two leads to an estimate for rent in Tuxedo of $1,062.50. Another combination function would pick the point midway between the two median rents. This second method leads to an estimate of $977 for rents in Tuxedo.

As it happens, a plurality of rents in Tuxedo are in the $1,000 to $1,500 range with the midpoint at $1,250. The median rent in Tuxedo is $907. So, averaging the medians slightly overestimates the median rent in Tuxedo and averaging the most common rents slightly underestimates the most common rent in Tuxedo. It is hard to say which is better. The moral is that there is not always an obvious "best" combination function.

## Challenges of MBR

In the simple example just given, the training set consisted of all towns in New York, each described by a handful of numeric fields such as the population, median home value, and median rent. Distance was determined by placement on a scatter plot with axes scaled to appropriate ranges, and the number of neighbors arbitrarily set to two. The combination function was a simple average.

All of these choices seem reasonable. In general, using MBR involves several choices:

1. Choosing an appropriate set of training records
2. Choosing the most efficient way to represent the training records
3. Choosing the distance function, the combination function, and the number of neighbors

Let's look at each of these in turn.

### Choosing a Balanced Set of Historical Records

The training set is a set of historical records. It needs to provide good coverage of the population so that the nearest neighbors of an unknown record are useful for predictive purposes. A random sample may not provide sufficient coverage for all values. Some categories are much more frequent than others and the more frequent categories dominate the random sample.

For instance, fraudulent transactions are much rarer than non-fraudulent transactions, heart disease is much more common than liver cancer, news stories about the computer industry more common than about plastics, and so on.

To achieve balance, the training set should, if possible, contain roughly equal numbers of records representing the different categories.

> **TIP** When selecting the training set for MBR, be sure that each category has roughly the same number of records supporting it. As a general rule of thumb, several dozen records for each category are a minimum to get adequate support and hundreds or thousands of examples are not unusual.

## Representing the Training Data

The performance of MBR in making predictions depends on how the training set is represented. The scatter plot approach illustrated in Figure 8.2 works for two or three variables and a small number of records, but it does not scale well. The simplest method for finding nearest neighbors requires finding the distance from the unknown case to each of the records in the training set and choosing the training records with the smallest distances. As the number of records grows, the time needed to find the neighbors for a new record grows quickly.

This is especially true if the records are stored in a relational database. In this case, the query looks something like:

```
SELECT distance(),rec.category
FROM historical_records rec
ORDER BY 1 ASCENDING;
```

The notation *distance()* fills in for whatever the particular distance function happens to be. In this case, all the historical records need to be sorted in order to get the handful needed for the nearest neighbors. This requires a full-table scan plus a sort—quite an expensive couple of operations. It is possible to eliminate the sort by walking through table and keeping another table of the nearest, inserting and deleting records as appropriate. Unfortunately, this approach is not readily expressible in SQL without using a procedural language.

The performance of relational databases is pretty good nowadays. The challenge with scoring data for MBR is that each case being scored needs to be compared against every case in the database. Scoring a single new record does not take much time, even when there are millions of historical records. However, scoring many new records can have poor performance.

Another way to make MBR more efficient is to reduce the number of records in the training set. Figure 8.2 shows a scatter plot for categorical data. This graph has a well-defined boundary between the two regions. The points above the line are all diamonds and those below the line are all circles. Although this graph has forty points in it, most of the points are redundant. That is, they are not really necessary for classification purposes.

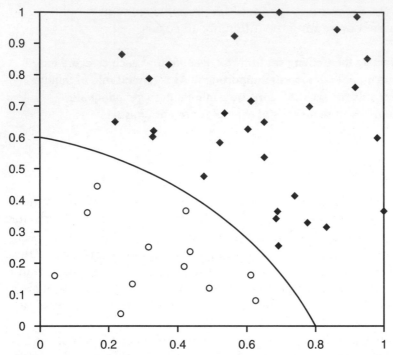

**Figure 8.2**  Perhaps the cleanest training set for MBR is one that divides neatly into two disjoint sets.

Figure 8.3 shows that only eight points in it are needed to get the same results. Given that the size of the training set has such a large influence on the performance of MBR, being able to reduce the size is a significant performance boost.

How can this reduced set of records be found? The most practical method is to look for clusters containing records belonging to different categories. The centers of the clusters can then be used as a reduced set. This works well when the different categories are quite separate. However, when there is some overlap and the categories are not so well-defined, using clusters to reduce the size of the training set can cause MBR to produce poor results. Finding an optimal set of "support records" has been an area of recent research. When such an optimal set can be found, the historical records can sometimes be reduced to the level where they fit inside a spreadsheet, making it quite efficient to apply MBR to new records on less powerful machines.

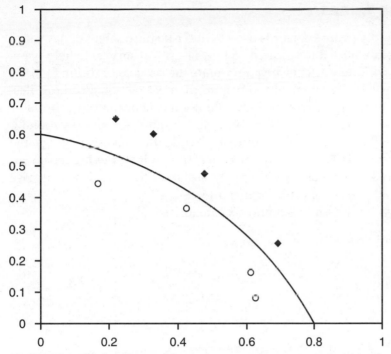

**Figure 8.3**   This smaller set of points returns the same results as in Figure 8.2 using MBR.

## Determining the Distance Function, Combination Function, and Number of Neighbors

The distance function, combination function, and number of neighbors are the key ingredients in using MBR. The same set of historical records can prove very useful or not at all useful for predictive purposes, depending on these criteria. Fortunately, simple distance functions and combination functions usually work quite well. Before discussing these issues in detail, let's look at a detailed case study.

## Case Study: Classifying News Stories

This case study uses MBR to assign classification codes to news stories and is based on work conducted by one of the authors. The results from this case study show that MBR can perform as well as people on a problem involving hundreds of categories and data on a difficult-to-use type of data, free-text.[1]

---

[1]This case study is a summarization of research conducted by one of the authors. Complete details are available in the article "Classifying News Stories using Memory Based Reasoning," by David Waltz, Brij Masand, and Gordon Linoff, in Proceedings, SIGIR '92, published by ACM Press.

## What Are the Codes?

The classification codes are keywords used to describe the content of news stories. These codes are added to stories by a news retrieval service to help users search for stories of interest. They help automate the process of routing particular stories to particular customers and help implement personalized profiles. For instance, an industry analyst who specializes in the automotive industry (or anyone else with an interest in the topic) can simplify searches by looking for documents with the "automotive industry" code. Because knowledgeable experts, also known as editors, set up the codes, the right stories are retrieved. Editors or expert systems have traditionally assigned these codes. This case study investigated the use of MBR for this purpose.

The codes used in this study fall into six categories:

- Government Agency
- Industry
- Market Sector
- Product
- Region
- Subject

The data contained 361 separate codes, distributed as follows in the training set (Table 8.2).

The number and types of codes assigned to stories varied. Almost all the stories had region and subject codes—and, on average, almost three region codes per story. At the other extreme, relatively few stories contained government and product codes, and such stories rarely had more than one such code.

**Table 8.2** Six Types of Codes Used to Classify News Stories

| CATEGORY | # CODES | # DOCS | # OCCURRENCES |
|---|---|---|---|
| Government (G/) | 28 | 3,926 | 4,200 |
| Industry (I/) | 112 | 38,308 | 57,430 |
| Market Sector (M/) | 9 | 38,562 | 42,058 |
| Product (P/) | 21 | 2,242 | 2,523 |
| Region (R/) | 121 | 47,083 | 116,358 |
| Subject (N/) | 70 | 41,902 | 52,751 |

## Applying MBR

This section explains how MBR facilitated assigning codes to news stories for a news service. The important steps were:

1. Choosing the training set
2. Determining the distance function
3. Choosing the number of nearest neighbors
4. Determining the combination function

The following sections discuss each of these steps in turn.

### Choosing the Training Set

The training set consisted of 49,652 news stories, provided by the news retrieval service for this purpose. These stories came from about three months of news and from almost 100 different sources. Each story contained, on average, 2,700 words and had eight codes assigned to it. The training set was not specially created, so the frequency of codes in the training set varied a great deal, mimicking the overall frequency of codes in news stories in general. Although this training set yielded good results, a better-constructed training set with more examples of the less common codes would probably have performed even better.

### Choosing the Distance Function

The next step is choosing the distance function. In this case, a distance function already existed, based on a notion called *relevance feedback* that measures the similarity of two documents based on the words they contain. Relevance feedback, which is described more fully in the sidebar, was originally designed to return documents similar to a given document, as a way of refining searches. The most similar documents are the neighbors used for MBR.

### Choosing the Combination Function

The next decision is the combination function. Assigning classification codes to news stories is a bit different from most classification problems. Most classification problems are looking for the single best solution. However, news stories can have multiple codes, even from the same category. The ability to adapt MBR to this problem highlights its flexibility.

### USING RELEVANCE FEEDBACK TO CREATE A DISTANCE FUNCTION

Relevance feedback is a powerful technique that allows users to refine searches on text databases by asking the database to return documents similar to one they already have. (Hubs and authorities, another method for improving search results on hyperlinked web pages, is described in Chapter 10.) In the course of doing this, the text database scores all the other documents in the database and returns those that are most similar—along with a measure of similarity. This is the relevance feedback score, which can be used as the basis for a distance measure for MBR.

In the case study, the calculation of the relevance feedback score went as follows:

1. Common, non-content-bearing words, such as "it," "and," and "of," were removed from the text of all stories in the training set. A total of 368 words in this category were identified and removed.

2. The next most common words, accounting for 20 percent of the words in the database, were removed from the text. Because these words are so common, they provide little information to distinguish between documents.

3. The remaining words were collected into a dictionary of *searchable terms*. Each was assigned a weight inversely proportional to its frequency in the database. The particular weight was the negative of the base 2 log of the term's frequency in the training set.

4. Capitalized word pairs, such as "United States" and "New Mexico," were identified (automatically) and included in the dictionary of searchable terms.

5. To calculate the relevance feedback score for two stories, the weights of the searchable terms in both stories were added together. The algorithm used for this case study included a bonus when searchable terms appeared in close proximity in both stories.

The relevance feedback score is an example of the adaptation of an already-existing function for use as a distance function. However, the score itself does not quite fit the definition of a distance function. In particular, a score of 0 indicates that two stories have no words in common, instead of implying that the stories are identical. The following transformation converts the relevance feedback score to a function suitable for measuring the "distance" between news stories:

$$d_{\text{classification}} (A,B) = 1 - \frac{\text{score}(A,B)}{\text{score}(A,A)}$$

This is the function used to find the nearest neighbors. Actually, even this is not a true distance function because d(A,B) is not the same as d(B,A), but it works well enough.

**Table 8.3** Classified Neighbors of a Not-Yet-Classified Story

| NEIGHBOR | DISTANCE | WEIGHT | CODES |
|----------|----------|--------|-------|
| 1 | 0.076 | 0.924 | R/FE,R/CA,R/CO |
| 2 | 0.346 | 0.654 | R/FE,R/JA,R/CA |
| 3 | 0.369 | 0.631 | R/FE,R/JA,R/MI |
| 4 | 0.393 | 0.607 | R/FE,R/JA,R/CA |

The combination function used a weighted summation technique. Since the maximum distance was 1, the weight was simply one minus the distance, so weights would be big for neighbors at small distances and small for neighbors at big distances. For example, say the neighbors of a story had the following region codes and weights, shown in Table 8.3.

The total score for a code was then the sum of the weights of the neighbors containing it. Then, codes with scores below a certain threshold value were eliminated. For instance, the score for R/FE (which is the region code for the Far East) is the sum of the weights of neighbors 1, 2, 3, and 4, since all of them contain the R/FE, yielding a score of 2.816. Table 8.4 shows the results for the six region codes contained by at least one of the four neighbors. For these examples, a threshold of 1.0 leaves only three codes: R/CA, R/FE, and R/JA. The particular choice of threshold was based on experimenting with different values and is not important to understanding MBR.

**Table 8.4** Code Scores for the Not-Yet-Classified Story

| CODE | 1 | 2 | 3 | 4 | SCORE |
|------|-----|-----|-----|-----|-------|
| R/CA | 0.924 | 0.654 | 0 | 0.607 | 2.185 |
| R/CO | 0.924 | 0 | 0 | 0 | 0.924 |
| R/FE | 0.924 | 0.654 | 0.631 | 0.607 | 2.816 |
| R/JA | 0 | 0.654 | 0.631 | 0.607 | 1.892 |
| R/MI | 0 | 0.654 | 0 | 0 | 0.624 |

### Choosing the Number of Neighbors

The investigation varied the number of nearest neighbors between 1 and 11 inclusive. The best results came from using more neighbors. However, this case study is different from many applications of MBR because it is assigning multiple categories to each story. The more typical problem is to assign only a single category or code and fewer neighbors would likely be sufficient for good results.

## The Results

To measure the effectiveness of MBR on coding, the news service had a panel of editors review all the codes assigned, whether by editors or by MBR, to 200 stories. Only codes agreed upon by a majority of the panel were considered "correct."

The comparison of the "correct" codes to the codes originally assigned by human editors was interesting. Eighty-eight percent of the codes originally assigned to the stories (by humans) were correct. However, the human editors made mistakes. A total of 17 percent of the codes originally assigned by human editors were incorrect as shown in Figure 8.4.

MBR did not do quite as well. For MBR, the corresponding percentages were 80 percent and 28 percent. That is, 80 percent of the codes assigned by MBR were correct, but the cost was that 28 percent of the codes assigned were incorrect.

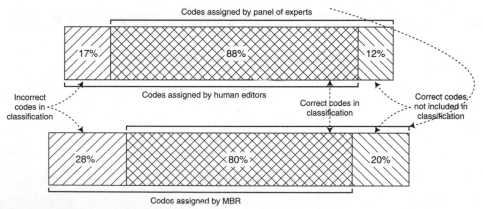

**Figure 8.4** A comparison of results by human editors and by MBR on assigning codes to news stories.

The mix of editors assigning the original codes, though, included novice, intermediate, and experienced editors. The MBR system actually performed as well as intermediate editors and better than novice editors. Also, MBR was using stories classified by the same mix of editors, so the training set was not consistently coded. Given the inconsistency in the training set, it is surprising that MBR did as well as it did. The study was not able to investigate using MBR on a training set whose codes were reviewed by the panel of experts because there were not enough such stories for a viable training set.

This case study illustrates that MBR can be used for solving difficult problems that might not easily be solved by other means. Most data mining techniques cannot handle textual data and assigning multiple categories at the same time is problematic. This case study shows that, with some experimentation, MBR can produce results comparable to human experts. There is further discussion of the metrics used to evaluate the performance of a document classification or retrieval system in the sidebar entitled *Measuring the Effectiveness of Assigning Codes*. This study achieved these results with about two person-months of effort (not counting development of the relevance feedback engine). By comparison, other automated classification techniques, such as those based on expert systems, require many person-years of effort to achieve equivalent results for classifying news stories.

# Measuring Distance

Say your travels are going to take you to a small town and you want to know the weather. If you have a newspaper that lists weather reports for major cities, what you would typically do is find the weather for cities near the small town. You might look at the closest city and just take its weather, or do some sort of combination of the forecasts for, say, the three closest cities. This is an example of using MBR to find the weather forecast. The distance function being used is the geographic distance between the two locations. It seems likely that the Web services that provide a weather forecast for any zip code supplied by a user do something similar.

## What Is a Distance Function?

Distance is the way the MBR measures similarity. For any true distance metric, the distance from point A to point B, denoted by $d(A,B)$, has four key properties:

1. **Well-defined.** The distance between two points is always defined and is a non-negative real number, $d(A,B) \geq 0$.

2. **Identity.** The distance from one point to itself is always zero, so $d(A,A) = 0$.

3. **Commutativity.** Direction does not make a difference, so the distance from A to B is the same as the distance from B to A: d(A,B) = d(B,A). This property precludes one-way roads, for instance.

4. **Triangle Inequality.** Visiting an intermediate point C on the way from A to B never shortens the distance, so d(A,B) ≥ d(A,C) + d(C,B).

For MBR, the points are really records in a database. This formal definition of distance is the basis for measuring similarity, but MBR still works pretty well when some of these constraints are relaxed a bit. For instance, the distance function in the news story classification case study was not *commutative*; that is, the distance from a news story A to another B was not always the same as the distance from B to A. However, the similarity measure was still useful for classification purposes.

What makes these properties useful for MBR? The fact that distance is well-defined implies that every record has a neighbor somewhere in the database—and MBR needs neighbors in order to work. The identity property makes distance conform to the intuitive idea that the most similar record to a given record is the original record itself. Commutativity and the Triangle Inequality make the nearest neighbors local and well-behaved. Adding a new record into the database will not bring an existing record any closer. Similarity is a matter reserved for just two records at a time.

Although the distance measure used to find nearest neighbors is well-behaved, the set of nearest neighbors can have some peculiar properties. For instance, the nearest neighbor to a record B may be A, but A may have many neighbors closer than B, as shown in Figure 8.5. This situation does not pose problems for MBR.

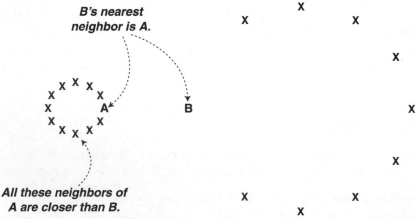

**Figure 8.5**   B's nearest neighbor is A, but A has many neighbors closer than B.

## MEASURING THE EFFECTIVENESS OF ASSIGNING CODES: RECALL AND PRECISION

*Recall* and *precision* are two measurements that are useful for determining the appropriateness of a set of assigned codes or keywords. The case study on coding news stories, for instance, assigns many codes to news stories. Recall and precision can be used to evaluate these assignments.

*Recall* answers the question: "How many of the correct codes did MBR assign to the story?" It is the ratio of codes assigned by MBR that are correct (as verified by editors) to the total number of correct codes on the story. If MBR assigns all available codes to every story, then recall is 100 percent because the correct codes all get assigned, along with many other irrelevant codes. If MBR assigns no codes to any story, then recall is 0 percent.

*Precision* answers the question: "How many of the codes assigned by MBR were correct?" It is the percentage of correct codes assigned by MBR to the total number of codes assigned by MBR. Precision is 100 percent when MBR assigns only correct codes to a story. It is close to 0 percent when MBR assigns all codes to every story.

Neither recall nor precision individually give the full story of how good the classification is. Ideally, we want 100 percent recall and 100 percent precision. Often, it is possible to trade off one against the other. For instance, using more neighbors increases recall, but decreases precision. Or, raising the threshold increases precision but decreases recall. Table 8.5 gives some insight into these measurements for a few specific cases.

**Table 8.5**    Examples of Recall and Precision

| CODES BY MBR | CORRECT CODES | RECALL | PRECISION |
|---|---|---|---|
| A,B,C,D | A,B,C,D | 100% | 100% |
| A,B | A,B,C,D | 50% | 100% |
| A,B,C,D,E,F,G,H | A,B,C,D | 100% | 50% |
| E,F | A,B,C,D | 0% | 0% |
| A,B,E,F | A,B,C,D | 50% | 50% |

The original codes assigned to the stories by individual editors had a recall of 83 percent and a precision of 88 percent with respect to the validated set of correct codes. For MBR, the recall was 80 percent and the precision 72 percent. However, Table 8.6 shows the average across all categories. MBR did significantly better in some of the categories.

*(continued)*

**MEASURING THE EFFECTIVENESS OF ASSIGNING CODES: RECALL AND PRECISION** *(continued)*

**Table 8.6** Recall and Precision Measurements by Code Category

| CATEGORY | RECALL | PRECISION |
|---|---|---|
| Government | 85% | 87% |
| Industry | 91% | 85% |
| Market Sector | 93% | 91% |
| Product | 69% | 89% |
| Region | 86% | 64% |
| Subject | 72% | 53% |

The variation in the results by category suggests that the original stories used for the training set may not have been coded consistently. The results from MBR can only be as good as the examples chosen for the training set. Even so, MBR performed as well as all but the most experienced editors.

## Building a Distance Function One Field at a Time

It is easy to understand distance as a geometric concept, but how can distance be defined for records consisting of many different fields of different types? The answer is, one field at a time. Consider some sample records such as those shown in Table 8.7.

Figure 8.6 illustrates a scatter graph in three dimensions. The records are a bit complicated, with two numeric fields and one categorical. This example shows how to define field distance functions for each field, then combine them into a single record distance function that gives a distance between two records.

**Table 8.7** Five Customers in a Marketing Database

| RECNUM | GENDER | AGE | SALARY |
|---|---|---|---|
| 1 | female | 27 | $ 19,000 |
| 2 | male | 51 | $ 64,000 |
| 3 | male | 52 | $105,000 |
| 4 | female | 33 | $ 55,000 |
| 5 | male | 45 | $ 45,000 |

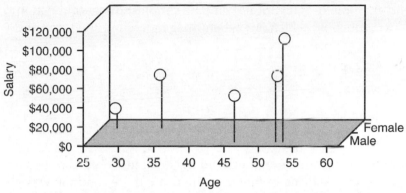

**Figure 8.6**   This scatter plot shows the five records from Table 8.7 in three dimensions—age, salary, and gender—and suggests that standard distance is a good metric for nearest neighbors.

The four most common distance functions for numeric fields are:

- Absolute value of the difference: $|A-B|$
- Square of the difference: $(A-B)^2$
- Normalized absolute value: $|A-B|/(\text{maximum difference})$
- Absolute value of difference of standardized values: $|(A-\text{mean})/(\text{standard deviation}) - (B-\text{mean})/(\text{standard deviation})|$ *which is equivalent to* $|(A-B)/(\text{standard deviation})|$

The advantage of the normalized absolute value is that it is always between 0 and 1. Since ages are much smaller than the salaries in this example, the normalized absolute value is a good choice for both of them—so neither field will dominate the record distance function (difference of standardized values is also a good choice). For the ages, the distance matrix looks like Table 8.8.

**Table 8.8**   Distance Matrix Based on Ages of Customers

|        | 27   | 51   | 52   | 33   | 45   |
|--------|------|------|------|------|------|
| **27** | 0.00 | 0.96 | 1.00 | 0.24 | 0.72 |
| **51** | 0.96 | 0.00 | 0.04 | 0.72 | 0.24 |
| **52** | 1.00 | 0.04 | 0.00 | 0.76 | 0.28 |
| **33** | 0.24 | 0.72 | 0.76 | 0.00 | 0.48 |
| **45** | 0.72 | 0.24 | 0.28 | 0.48 | 0.00 |

Gender is an example of categorical data. The simplest distance function is the "identical to" function, which is 1 when the genders are the same and 0 otherwise:

$d_{gender}$(female, female)   = 0

$d_{gender}$(female, male)   = 1

$d_{gender}$(female, female)   = 1

$d_{gender}$(male, male)   = 0

So far, so simple. There are now three field distance functions that need to merge into a single record distance function. There are three common ways to do this:

- Manhattan distance or summation:
  $d_{sum}(A,B) = d_{gender}(A,B) + d_{age}(A,B) + d_{salary}(A,B)$
- Normalized summation: $d_{norm}(A,B) = d_{sum}(A,B) / max(d_{sum})$
- Euclidean distance:
  $d_{Euclid}(A,B) = sqrt(d_{gender}(A,B)^2 + d_{age}(A,B)^2 + d_{salary}(A,B)^2)$

Table 8.9 shows the nearest neighbors for each of the points using the three functions.

In this case, the sets of nearest neighbors are exactly the same regardless of how the component distances are combined. This is a coincidence, caused by the fact that the five records fall into two well-defined clusters. One of the clusters is lower-paid, younger females and the other is better-paid, older males. These clusters imply that if two records are close to each other relative to one field, then they are close on all fields, so the way the distances on each field are combined is not important. This is not a very common situation.

Consider what happens when a new record (Table 8.10) is used for the comparison.

**Table 8.9** Set of Nearest Neighbors for Three Distance Functions, Ordered Nearest to Farthest

|  | $D_{SUM}$ | $D_{NORM}$ | $D_{EUCLID}$ |
|---|---|---|---|
| 1 | 1,4,5,2,3 | 1,4,5,2,3 | 1,4,5,2,3 |
| 2 | 2,5,3,4,1 | 2,5,3,4,1 | 2,5,3,4,1 |
| 3 | 3,2,5,4,1 | 3,2,5,4,1 | 3,2,5,4,1 |
| 4 | 4,1,5,2,3 | 4,1,5,2,3 | 4,1,5,2,3 |
| 5 | 5,2,3,4,1 | 5,2,3,4,1 | 5,2,3,4,1 |

**Table 8.10** New Customer

| RECNUM | GENDER | AGE | SALARY |
|--------|--------|-----|--------|
| new | female | 45 | $100,000 |

This new record is not in either of the clusters. Table 8.11 shows her respective distances from the training set with the list of her neighbors, from nearest to furthest.

Now the set of neighbors depends on how the record distance function combines the field distance functions. In fact, the second nearest neighbor using the summation function is the farthest neighbor using the Euclidean and vice versa. Compared to the summation or normalized metric, the Euclidean metric tends to favor neighbors where all the fields are relatively close. It punishes Record 3 because the genders are different and are maximally far apart (a distance of 1.00). Correspondingly, it favors Record 1 because the genders are the same. Note that the neighbors for dsum and dnorm are identical. The definition of the normalized distance preserves the ordering of the summation distance—the distances values are just shifted to the range from 0 to 1.

The summation, Euclidean, and normalized functions can also incorporate weights so each field contributes a different amount to the record distance function. MBR usually produces good results when all the weights are equal to 1. However, sometimes weights can be used to incorporate a priori knowledge, such as a particular field suspected of having a large effect on the classification.

## Distance Functions for Other Data Types

A 5-digit American zip code is often represented as a simple number. Do any of the default distance functions for numeric fields make any sense? No. The difference between two randomly chosen zip codes has no meaning. Well, almost no meaning; a zip code does encode location information. The first three digits represent a postal zone—for instance, all zip codes on Manhattan start with "100," "101," or "102."

**Table 8.11** Set of Nearest Neighbors for New Customer

| | 1 | 2 | 3 | 4 | 5 | NEIGHBORS |
|---|---|---|---|---|---|---|
| $d_{sum}$ | 1.662 | 1.659 | 1.338 | 1.003 | 1.640 | 4,3,5,2,1 |
| $d_{norm}$ | 0.554 | 0.553 | 0.446 | 0.334 | 0.547 | 4,3,5,2,1 |
| $d_{Euclid}$ | 0.781 | 1.052 | 1.251 | 0.494 | 1.000 | 4,1,5,2,3 |

Furthermore, there is a general pattern of zip codes increasing from East to West. Codes that start with 0 are in New England and Puerto Rico; those beginning with 9 are on the west coast. This suggests a distance function that approximates geographic distance by looking at the high order digits of the zip code.

- $d_{zip}(A,B) = 0.0$ if the zip codes are identical
- $d_{zip}(A,B) = 0.1$ if the first three digits are identical (e.g., "20008" and "20015"）
- $d_{zip}(A,B) = 0.5$ if the first digits are identical (e.g., "95050" and "98125")
- $d_{zip}(A,B) = 1.0$ if the first digits are not identical (e.g., "02138" and "94704")

Of course, if geographic distance were truly of interest, a better approach would be to look up the latitude and longitude of each zip code in a table and calculate the distances that way (it is possible to get this information for the United States from www.census.gov). For many purposes however, geographic proximity is not nearly as important as some other measure of similarity. 10011 and 10031 are both in Manhattan, but from a marketing point of view, they don't have much else in common, because one is an upscale downtown neighborhood and the other is a working class Harlem neighborhood. On the other hand 02138 and 94704 are on opposite coasts, but are likely to respond very similarly to direct mail from a political action committee, since they are for Cambridge, MA and Berkeley, CA respectively.

This is just one example of how the choice of a distance metric depends on the data mining context. There are additional examples of distance and similarity measures in Chapter 11 where they are applied to clustering.

## When a Distance Metric Already Exists

There are some situations where a distance metric already exists, but is difficult to spot. These situations generally arise in one of two forms. Sometimes, a function already exists that provides a distance measure that can be adapted for use in MBR. The news story case study provides a good example of adapting an existing function, the relevance feedback score, for use as a distance function.

Other times, there are fields that do not appear to capture distance, but can be pressed into service. An example of such a hidden distance field is solicitation history. Two customers who were chosen for a particular solicitation in the past are "close," even though the reasons why they were chosen may no longer be available; two who were not chosen, are close, but not as close; and one that was chosen and one that was not are far apart. The advantage of this metric is that it can incorporate previous decisions, even if the basis for the decisions is no longer available. On the other hand, it does not work well for customers who were not around during the original solicitation; so some sort of neutral weighting must be applied to them

Considering whether the original customers responded to the solicitation can extend this function further, resulting in a solicitation metric like:

- $d_{solicitation}(A, B) = 0$, when A and B both responded to the solicitation
- $d_{solicitation}(A, B) = 0.1$, when A and B were both chosen but neither responded
- $d_{solicitation}(A, B) = 0.2$, when neither A nor B was chosen, but both were available in the data
- $d_{solicitation}(A, B) = 0.3$, when A and B were both chosen, but only one responded
- $d_{solicitation}(A, B) = 0.3$, when one or both were not considered
- $d_{solicitation}(A, B) = 1.0$, when one was chosen and the other was not

Of course, the particular values are not sacrosanct; they are only meant as a guide for measuring similarity and showing how previous information and response histories can be incorporated into a distance function.

# The Combination Function: Asking the Neighbors for the Answer

The distance function is used to determine which records comprise the neighborhood. This section presents different ways to combine data gathered from those neighbors to make a prediction. At the beginning of this chapter, we estimated the median rent in the town of Tuxedo, by taking an average of the median rents in similar towns. In that example, averaging was the combination function. This section explores other methods of canvassing the neighborhood.

## The Basic Approach: Democracy

One common combination function is for the $k$ nearest neighbors to vote on an answer—"democracy" in data mining. When MBR is used for classification, each neighbor casts its vote for its own class. The proportion of votes for each class is an estimate of the probability that the new record belongs to the corresponding class. When the task is to assign a single class, it is simply the one with the most votes. When there are only two categories, an odd number of neighbors should be poled to avoid ties. As a rule of thumb, use $c+1$ neighbors when there are $c$ categories to ensure that at least one class has a plurality.

In Table 8.12, the five test cases seen earlier have been augmented with a flag that signals whether the customer has become inactive.

For this example, three of the customers have become inactive and two have not, an almost balanced training set. For illustrative purposes, let's try to determine if the new record is active or inactive by using different values of $k$ for two distance functions, deuclid and dnorm (Table 8.13).

The question marks indicate that no prediction has been made due to a tie among the neighbors. Notice that different values of $k$ do affect the classification. This suggests using the percentage of neighbors in agreement to provide the level of confidence in the prediction (Table 8.14).

**Table 8.12**   Customers with Attrition History

| RECNUM | GENDER | AGE | SALARY | INACTIVE |
|--------|--------|-----|--------|----------|
| 1 | female | 27 | $19,000 | no |
| 2 | male | 51 | $64,000 | yes |
| 3 | male | 52 | $105,000 | yes |
| 4 | female | 33 | $55,000 | yes |
| 5 | male | 45 | $45,000 | no |
| new | female | 45 | $100,000 | ? |

**Table 8.13**   Using MBR to Determine if the New Customer Will Become Inactive

| | NEIGHBORS | NEIGHBOR ATTRITION | K = 1 | K = 2 | K = 3 | K = 4 | K = 5 |
|--------|-----------|--------------------|-------|-------|-------|-------|-------|
| $d_{sum}$ | 4,3,5,2,1 | Y,Y,N,Y,N | yes | yes | yes | yes | yes |
| $d_{Euclid}$ | 4,1,5,2,3 | Y,N,N,Y,Y | yes | ? | no | ? | yes |

**Table 8.14**   Attrition Prediction with Confidence

| | K = 1 | K = 2 | K = 3 | K = 4 | K = 5 |
|--------|-------|-------|-------|-------|-------|
| $d_{sum}$ | yes, 100% | yes, 100% | yes, 67% | yes, 75% | yes, 60% |
| $d_{Euclid}$ | yes, 100% | yes, 50% | no, 67% | yes, 50% | yes, 60% |

The confidence level works just as well when there are more than two categories. However, with more categories, there is a greater chance that no single category will have a majority vote. One of the key assumptions about MBR (and data mining in general) is that the training set provides sufficient information for predictive purposes. If the neighborhoods of new cases consistently produce no obvious choice of classification, then the data simply may not contain the necessary information and the choice of dimensions and possibly of the training set needs to be reevaluated. By measuring the effectiveness of MBR on the test set, you can determine whether the training set has a sufficient number of examples.

> **WARNING** MBR is only as good as the training set it uses. To measure whether the training set is effective, measure the results of its predictions on the test set using two, three, and four neighbors. If the results are inconclusive or inaccurate, then the training set is not large enough or the dimensions and distance metrics chosen are not appropriate.

## Weighted Voting

Weighted voting is similar to voting in the previous section except that the neighbors are not all created equal—more like shareholder democracy than one-person, one-vote. The size of the vote is inversely proportional to the distance from the new record, so closer neighbors have stronger votes than neighbors farther away do. To prevent problems when the distance might be 0, it is common to add 1 to the distance before taking the inverse. Adding 1 also makes all the votes between 0 and 1.

Table 8.15 applies weighted voting to the previous example. The "yes, customer will become inactive" vote is the first; the "no, this is a good customer" vote is second.

Weighted voting has introduced enough variation to prevent ties. The confidence level can now be calculated as the ratio of winning votes to total votes (Table 8.16).

**Table 8.15**  Attrition Prediction with Weighted Voting

|  | K = 1 | K = 2 | K = 3 | K = 4 | K = 5 |
|---|---|---|---|---|---|
| $d_{sum}$ | **0.749** to 0 | **1.441** to 0 | **1.441** to 0.647 | **2.085** to 0.647 | **2.085** to 1.290 |
| $d_{Euclid}$ | **0.669** to 0 | **0.669** to 0.562 | 0.669 to **1.062** | **1.157** to 1.062 | **1.601** to 1.062 |

**Table 8.16** Confidence with Weighted Voting

|  | 1 | 2 | 3 | 4 | 5 |
|---|---|---|---|---|---|
| $d_{sum}$ | yes, 100% | yes, 100% | yes, 69% | yes, 76% | yes, 62% |
| $d_{Euclid}$ | yes, 100% | yes, 54% | no, 61% | yes, 52% | yes, 60% |

In this case, weighting the votes has only a small effect on the results and the confidence. The effect of weighting is largest when some neighbors are considerably further away than others.

Weighting can also be applied to estimation by replacing the simple average of neighboring values with an average weighted by distance. This approach is used in collaborative filtering systems, as described in the following section.

## Collaborative Filtering: A Nearest Neighbor Approach to Making Recommendations

Neither of the authors considers himself a country music fan, but one of them is the proud owner of an autographed copy of an early Dixie Chicks CD. The Chicks, who did not yet have a major record label, were performing in a local bar one day and some friends who knew them from Texas made a very enthusiastic recommendation. The performance was truly memorable, featuring Martie Erwin's impeccable Bluegrass fiddle, her sister Emily on a bewildering variety of other instruments (most, but not all, with strings), and the seductive vocals of Laura Lynch (who also played a stand-up electric bass). At the break, the band sold and autographed a self-produced CD that we still like better than the one that later won them a Grammy. What does this have to do with nearest neighbor techniques? Well, it is a human example of collaborative filtering. A recommendation from trusted friends will cause one to try something one otherwise might not try.

Collaborative filtering is a variant of memory-based reasoning particularly well suited to the application of providing personalized recommendations. A collaborative filtering system starts with a history of people's preferences. The distance function determines similarity based on overlap of preferences— people who like the same thing are close. In addition, votes are weighted by distances, so the votes of closer neighbors count more for the recommendation. In other words, it is a technique for finding music, books, wine, or anything else that fits into the existing preferences of a particular person by using the judgments of a peer group selected for their similar tastes. This approach is also called *social information filtering*.

Collaborative filtering automates the process of using word-of-mouth to decide whether they would like something. Knowing that lots of people liked something is not enough. *Who* liked it is also important. Everyone values some recommendations more highly than others. The recommendation of a close friend whose past recommendations have been right on target may be enough to get you to go see a new movie even if it is in a genre you generally dislike. On the other hand, an enthusiastic recommendation from a friend who thinks *Ace Ventura: Pet Detective* is the funniest movie ever made might serve to warn you off one you might otherwise have gone to see.

Preparing recommendations for a new customer using an automated collaborative filtering system has three steps:

1. Building a customer profile by getting the new customer to rate a selection of items such as movies, songs, or restaurants.

2. Comparing the new customer's profile with the profiles of other customers using some measure of similarity.

3. Using some combination of the ratings of customers with similar profiles to predict the rating that the new customer would give to items he or she has not yet rated.

The following sections examine each of these steps in a bit more detail.

## Building Profiles

One challenge with collaborative filtering is that there are often far more items to be rated than any one person is likely to have experienced or be willing to rate. That is, profiles are usually sparse, meaning that there is little overlap among the users' preferences for making recommendations. Think of a user profile as a vector with one element per item in the universe of items to be rated. Each element of the vector represents the profile owner's rating for the corresponding item on a scale of –5 to 5 with 0 indicating neutrality and null values for no opinion.

If there are thousands or tens of thousands of elements in the vector and each customer decides which ones to rate, any two customers' profiles are likely to end up with few overlaps. On the other hand, forcing customers to rate a particular subset may miss interesting information because ratings of more obscure items may say more about the customer than ratings of common ones. A fondness for the Beatles is less revealing than a fondness for Mose Allison.

A reasonable approach is to have new customers rate a list of the twenty or so most frequently rated items (a list that might change over time) and then free them to rate as many additional items as they please.

## Comparing Profiles

Once a customer profile has been built, the next step is to measure its distance from other profiles. The most obvious approach would be to treat the profile vectors as geometric points and calculate the Euclidean distance between them, but many other distance measures have been tried. Some give higher weight to agreement when users give a positive rating especially when most users give negative ratings to most items. Still others apply statistical correlation tests to the ratings vectors.

## Making Predictions

The final step is to use some combination of nearby profiles in order to come up with estimated ratings for the items that the customer has not rated. One approach is to take a weighted average where the weight is inversely proportional to the distance. The example shown in Figure 8.7 illustrates estimating the rating that Nathaniel would give to *Planet of the Apes* based on the opinions of his neighbors, Simon and Amelia.

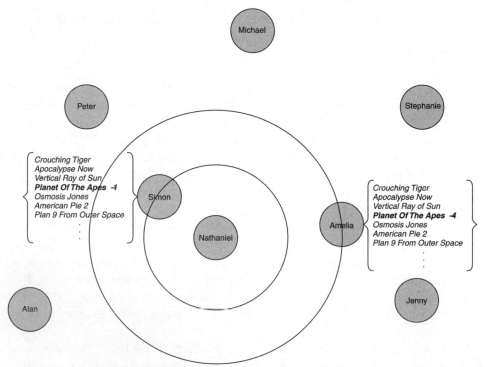

**Figure 8.7**  The predicted rating for *Planet of the Apes* is −2.66.

Simon, who is distance 2 away, gave that movie a rating of –1. Amelia, who is distance 4 away, gave that movie a rating of –4. No one else's profile is close enough to Nathaniel's to be included in the vote. Because Amelia is twice as far away as Simon, her vote counts only half as much as his. The estimate for Nathaniel's rating is weighted by the distance:

(½ (–1) + ¼(–4)) / (½ +¼)= –1.5/0.75= –2.

A good collaborative filtering system gives its users a chance to comment on the predictions and adjust the profile accordingly. In this example, if Nathaniel rents the video of *Planet of the Apes* despite the prediction that he will not like it, he can then enter an actual rating of his own. If it turns out that he really likes the movie and gives it a rating of 4, his new profile will be in a slightly different neighborhood and Simon's and Amelia's opinions will count less for Nathaniel's next recommendation.

## Lessons Learned

Memory based reasoning is a powerful data mining technique that can be used to solve a wide variety of data mining problems involving classification or estimation. Unlike other data mining techniques that use a training set of pre-classified data to create a model and then discard the training set, for MBR, the training set essentially *is* the model.

Choosing the right training set is perhaps the most important step in MBR. The training set needs to include sufficient numbers of examples all possible classifications. This may mean enriching it by including a disproportionate number of instances for rare classifications in order to create a balanced training set with roughly the same number of instances for all categories. A training set that includes only instances of bad customers will predict that all customers are bad. In general, the size of the training set should have at least thousands, if not hundreds of thousands or millions, of examples.

MBR is a $k$-nearest neighbors approach. Determining which neighbors are near requires a distance function. There are many approaches to measuring the distance between two records. The careful choice of an appropriate distance function is a critical step in using MBR. The chapter introduced an approach to creating an overall distance function by building a distance function for each field and normalizing it. The normalized field distances can then be combined in a Euclidean fashion or summed to produce a Manhattan distance.

When the Euclidean method is used, a large difference in any one field is enough to cause two records to be considered far apart. The Manhattan method is more forgiving—a large difference on one field can more easily be offset by close values on other fields. A validation set can be used to pick the best distance function for a given model set by applying all candidates to see which produces better results. Sometimes, the right choice of neighbors depends on modifying the distance function to favor some fields over others. This is easily accomplished by incorporating weights into the distance function.

The next question is the number of neighbors to choose. Once again, investigating different numbers of neighbors using the validation set can help determine the optimal number. There is no right number of neighbors. The number depends on the distribution of the data and is highly dependent on the problem being solved.

The basic combination function, weighted voting, does a good job for categorical data, using weights inversely proportional to distance. The analogous operation for estimating numeric values is a weighted average.

One good application for memory based reasoning is making recommendations. Collaborative filtering is an approach to making recommendations that works by grouping people with similar tastes together using a distance function that can compare two lists user-supplied ratings. Recommendations for a new person are calculated using a weighted average of the ratings of his or her nearest neighbors.

# CHAPTER 9

# Market Basket Analysis and Association Rules

To convey the fundamental ideas of market basket analysis, start with the image of the shopping cart in Figure 9.1 filled with various products purchased by someone on a quick trip to the supermarket. This basket contains an assortment of products—orange juice, bananas, soft drink, window cleaner, and detergent. One basket tells us about what one customer purchased at one time. A complete list of purchases made by all customers provides much more information; it describes the most important part of a retailing business—what merchandise customers are buying and when.

Each customer purchases a different set of products, in different quantities, at different times. Market basket analysis uses the information about what customers purchase to provide insight into who they are and why they make certain purchases. Market basket analysis provides insight into the merchandise by telling us which products tend to be purchased together and which are most amenable to promotion. This information is actionable: it can suggest new store layouts; it can determine which products to put on special; it can indicate when to issue coupons, and so on. When this data can be tied to individual customers through a loyalty card or Web site registration, it becomes even more valuable.

The data mining technique most closely allied with market basket analysis is the automatic generation of association rules. Association rules represent patterns in the data without a specified target. As such, they are an example of undirected data mining. Whether the patterns make sense is left to human interpretation.

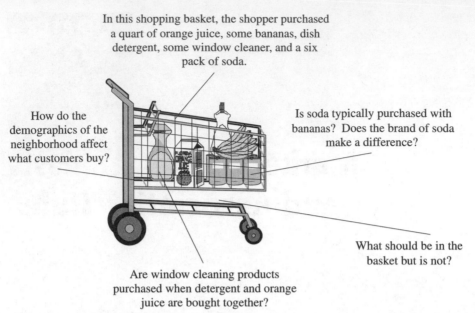

In this shopping basket, the shopper purchased a quart of orange juice, some bananas, dish detergent, some window cleaner, and a six pack of soda.

How do the demographics of the neighborhood affect what customers buy?

Is soda typically purchased with bananas? Does the brand of soda make a difference?

What should be in the basket but is not?

Are window cleaning products purchased when detergent and orange juice are bought together?

**Figure 9.1** Market basket analysis helps you understand customers as well as items that are purchased together.

Association rules were originally derived from point-of-sale data that describes what products are purchased together. Although its roots are in analyzing point-of-sale transactions, association rules can be applied outside the retail industry to find relationships among other types of "baskets." Some examples of potential applications are:

- Items purchased on a credit card, such as rental cars and hotel rooms, provide insight into the next product that customers are likely to purchase.

- Optional services purchased by telecommunications customers (call waiting, call forwarding, DSL, speed call, and so on) help determine how to bundle these services together to maximize revenue.

- Banking services used by retail customers (money market accounts, CDs, investment services, car loans, and so on) identify customers likely to want other services.

- Unusual combinations of insurance claims can be a sign of fraud and can spark further investigation.

- Medical patient histories can give indications of likely complications based on certain combinations of treatments.

Association rules often fail to live up to expectations. In our experience, for instance, they are not a good choice for building cross-selling models in industries such as retail banking, because the rules end up describing previous marketing promotions. Also, in retail banking, customers typically start with a checking account and then a savings account. Differentiation among products does not appear until customers have more products. This chapter covers the pitfalls as well as the uses of association rules.

The chapter starts with an overview of market basket analysis, including more basic analyses of market basket data that do not require association rules. It then dives into association rules, explaining how they are derived. The chapter then continues with ways to extend association rules to include other facets of the market basket analysis.

# Defining Market Basket Analysis

Market basket analysis does not refer to a single technique; it refers to a set of business problems related to understanding point-of-sale transaction data. The most common technique is association rules, and much of this chapter delves into that subject. Before talking about association rules, this section talks about market basket data.

## Three Levels of Market Basket Data

Market basket data is transaction data that describes three fundamentally different entities:

- Customers
- Orders (also called *purchases* or *baskets* or, in academic papers, *item sets*)
- Items

In a relational database, the data structure for market basket data often looks similar to Figure 9.2. This data structure includes four important entities.

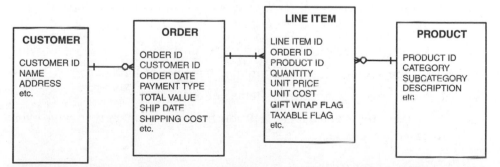

**Figure 9.2** A data model for transaction-level market basket data typically has three tables, one for the customer, one for the order, and one for the order line.

The *order* is the fundamental data structure for market basket data. An order represents a single purchase event by a customer. This might correspond to a customer ordering several products on a Web site or to a customer purchasing a basket of groceries or to a customer buying a several items from a catalog. This includes the total amount of the purchase, the total amount, additional shipping charges, payment type, and whatever other data is relevant about the transaction. Sometimes the transaction is given a unique identifier. Sometimes the unique identifier needs to be cobbled together from other data. In one example, we needed to combine four fields to get an identifier for purchases in a store—the timestamp when the customer paid, chain ID, store ID, and lane ID.

Individual items in the order are represented separately as *line items*. This data includes the price paid for the item, the number of items, whether tax should be charged, and perhaps the cost (which can be used for calculating margin). The item table also typically has a link to a *product reference table*, which provides more descriptive information about each product. This descriptive information should include the product hierarchy and other information that might prove valuable for analysis.

The *customer table* is an optional table and should be available when a customer can be identified, for example, on a Web site that requires registration or when the customer uses an affinity card during the transaction. Although the customer table may have interesting fields, the most powerful element is the ID itself, because this can tie transactions together over time.

Tracking customers over time makes it possible to determine, for instance, which grocery shoppers "bake from scratch"—something of keen interest to the makers of flour as well as prepackaged cake mixes. Such customers might be identified from the frequency of their purchases of flour, baking powder, and similar ingredients, the proportion of such purchases to the customer's total spending, and the lack of interest in prepackaged mixes and ready-to-eat desserts. Of course, such ingredients may be purchased at different times and in different quantities, making it necessary to tie together multiple transactions over time.

All three levels of market basket data are important. For instance, to understand orders, there are some basic measures:

- What is the average number of orders per customer?
- What is the average number of unique items per order?
- What is the average number of items per order?
- For a given product, what is the proportion of customers who have ever purchased the product?

- For a given product, what is the average number of orders per customer that include the item?

- For a given product, what is the average quantity purchased in an order when the product is purchased?

These measures give broad insight into the business. In some cases, there are few repeat customers, so the proportion of orders per customer is close to 1; this suggests a business opportunity to increase the number of sales per customers. Or, the number of products per order may be close to 1, suggesting an opportunity for cross-selling during the process of making an order.

It can be useful to compare these measures to each other. We have found that the number of orders is often a useful way of differentiating among customers; good customers clearly order more often than not-so-good customers. Figure 9.3 attempts to look at the breadth of the customer relationship (the number of unique items ever purchased) by the depth of the relationship (the number of orders) for customers who purchased more than one item. This data is from a small specialty retailer. The biggest bubble shows that many customers who purchase two products do so at the same time. There is also a surprisingly large bubble showing that a sizeable number of customers purchase the same product in two orders. Better customers—at least those who returned multiple times—tend to purchase a greater diversity of goods. However, some of them are returning and buying the same thing they bought the first time. How can the retailer encourage customers to come back and buy more and different products? Market basket analysis cannot answer the question, but it can at least motivate asking it and perhaps provide hints that might help.

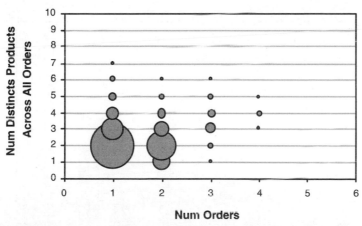

**Figure 9.3**   This bubble plot shows the breadth of customer relationships by the depth of the relationship.

## Order Characteristics

Customer purchases have additional interesting characteristics. For instance, the average order size varies by time and region—and it is useful to keep track of these to understand changes in the business environment. Such information is often available in reporting systems, because it is easily summarized.

Some information, though, may need to be gleaned from transaction-level data. Figure 9.4 breaks down transactions by the size of the order and the credit card used for payment—Visa, MasterCard, or American Express—for another retailer. The first thing to notice is that the larger the order, the larger the average purchase amount, regardless of the credit card being used. This is reassuring. Also, the use of one credit card type, American Express, is consistently associated with larger orders—an interesting finding about these customers.

For Web purchases and mail-order transactions, additional information may also be gathered at the point of sale:

- Did the order use gift wrap?
- Is the order going to the same address as the billing address?
- Did the purchaser accept or decline a particular cross-sell offer?

Of course, gathering information at the point of sale and having it available for analysis are two different things. However, gift giving and responsiveness to cross-sell offers are two very useful things to know about customers. Finding patterns with this information requires collecting the information in the first place (at the call center or through the online interface) and then moving it to a data mining environment.

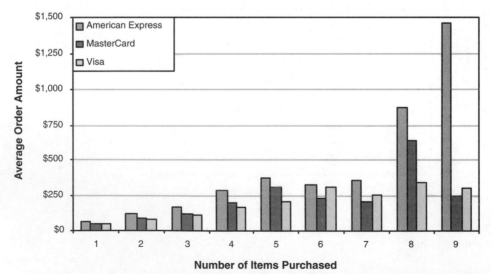

**Figure 9.4**   This chart shows the average amount spent by credit card type based on the number of items in the order for one particular retailer.

## Item Popularity

What are the most popular items? This is a question that can usually be answered by looking at inventory curves, which can be generated without having to work with transaction-level data. However, knowing the sales of an individual item is only the beginning. There are related questions:

- What is the most common item found in a one-item order?
- What is the most common item found in a multi-item order?
- What is the most common item found among customers who are repeat purchasers?
- How has the popularity of particular items changed over time?
- How does the popularity of an item vary regionally?

The first three questions are particularly interesting because they may suggest ideas for growing customer relationships. Association rules can provide answers to these questions, particularly when used with virtual items to represent the size of the order or the number of orders a customer has made.

The last two questions bring up the dimensions of time and geography, which are very important for applications of market basket analysis. Different products have different affinities in different regions—something that retailers are very familiar with. It is also possible to use association rules to start to understand these areas, by introducing virtual items for region and seasonality.

**TIP** Time and geography are two of the most important attributes of market basket data, because they often point to the exact marketing conditions at the time of the sale.

## Tracking Marketing Interventions

As discussed in Chapter 5, looking at individual products over time can provide a good understanding of what is happening with the product. Including marketing interventions along with the product sales over time, as in Figure 9.5, makes it possible to see the effect of the interventions. The chart shows a sales curve for a particular product. Prior to the intervention, sales are hovering at 50 units per week. After the intervention, they peak at about seven or eight times that amount, before gently sliding down over the six or seven weeks. Using such charts, it can be possible to measure the response of the marketing effort.

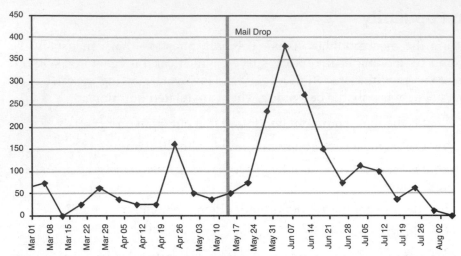

**Figure 9.5** Showing marketing interventions and product sales on the same chart makes it possible to see effects of marketing efforts.

Such analysis does not require looking at individual market baskets—daily or weekly summaries of product sales are sufficient. However, it does require knowing when marketing interventions take place—and sometimes getting such a calendar is the biggest challenge. One of the questions that such a chart can answer is the effect of the intervention. A challenge in answering this question is determining whether the additional sales are incremental or are made by customers who would purchase the product anyway at some later time.

Market basket data can start to answer this question. In addition to looking at the volume of sales after an intervention, we can also look at the number of baskets containing the item. If the number of customers is not increasing, there is evidence that existing customers are simply stocking up on the item at a lower cost.

A related question is whether discounting results in additional sales of other products. Association rules can help answer this question by finding combinations of products that include those being promoted during the period of the promotion. Similarly, we might want to know if the average size of orders increases or decreases after an intervention. These are examples of questions where more detailed transaction level data is important.

## Clustering Products by Usage

Perhaps one of the most interesting questions is what groups of products often appear together. Such groups of products are very useful for making recommendations to customers—customers who have purchased some of the products may be interested in the rest of them (Chapter 8 talks about product recommendations in more detail). At the individual product level, association rules provide some answers in this area. In particular, this data mining technique determines which product or products in a purchase suggest the purchase of other particular products at the same time.

Sometimes it is desirable to find larger clusters than those provided by association rules, which include just a handful of items in any rule. Standard clustering techniques, which are described in Chapter 11, can also be used on market basket data. In this case, the data needs to be pivoted, as shown in Figure 9.6, so that each row represents one order or customer, and there is a flag or a counter for each product purchased. Unfortunately, there are often thousands of different products. To reduce the number of columns, such a transformation can take place at the category level, rather than at the individual product level.

There is typically a lot of information available about products. In addition to the product hierarchy, such information includes the color of clothes, whether food is low calorie, whether a poster includes a frame, and so on. Such descriptions provide a wealth of information, and can lead to useful ad hoc questions:

- Do diet products tend to sell together?
- Are customers purchasing similar colors of clothing at the same time?
- Do customers who purchase framed posters also buy other products?

Being able to answer such questions is often more useful than trying to cluster products, since such directed questions often lead directly to marketing actions.

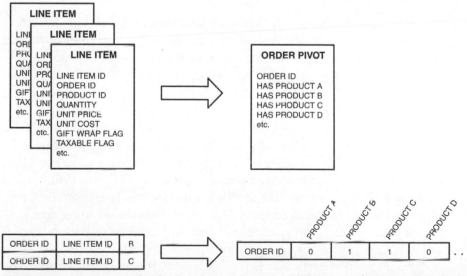

**Figure 9.6**  Pivoting market basket data makes it possible to run clustering algorithms to find interesting groups of products.

# Association Rules

One appeal of association rules is the clarity and utility of the results, which are in the form of rules about groups of products. There is an intuitive appeal to an association rule because it expresses how tangible products and services group together. A rule like, *"if a customer purchases three-way calling, then that customer will also purchase call waiting,"* is clear. Even better, it might suggest a specific course of action, such as bundling three-way calling with call waiting into a single service package.

While association rules are easy to understand, they are not always useful. The following three rules are examples of real rules generated from real data:

- Wal-Mart customers who purchase Barbie dolls have a 60 percent likelihood of also purchasing one of three types of candy bars.

- Customers who purchase maintenance agreements are very likely to purchase large appliances.

- When a new hardware store opens, one of the most commonly sold items is toilet bowl cleaners.

The last two examples are examples that we have actually seen in data. The first is an example quoted in *Forbes* on September 8, 1997. These three examples illustrate the three common types of rules produced by association rules: the *actionable*, the *trivial*, and the *inexplicable*. In addition to these types of rules, the sidebar "Famous Rules" talks about one other category.

## Actionable Rules

*The useful rule contains high-quality, actionable information.* Once the pattern is found, it is often not hard to justify, and telling a story can lead to insights and action. Barbie dolls preferring chocolate bars to other forms of food is not a likely story. Instead, imagine a family going shopping. The purpose: finding a gift for little Susie's friend Emily, since her birthday is coming up. A Barbie doll is the perfect gift. At checkout, little Jacob starts crying. He wants something too—a candy bar fits the bill. Or perhaps Emily has a brother; he can't be left out of the gift-giving festivities. Maybe the candy bar is for Mom, since buying Barbie dolls is a tiring activity and Mom needs some energy. These scenarios all suggest that the candy bar is an impulse purchase added onto that of the Barbie doll.

Whether Wal-Mart can make use of this information is not clear. This rule might suggest more prominent product placement, such as ensuring that customers must walk through candy aisles on their way back from Barbie-land. It might suggest product tie-ins and promotions offering candy bars and dolls together. It might suggest particular ways to advertise the products. Because the rule is easily understood, it suggests plausible causes and possible interventions.

## Trivial Rules

*Trivial results are already known by anyone at all familiar with the business.* The second example ("Customers who purchase maintenance agreements are very likely to purchase large appliances") is an example of a trivial rule. In fact, customers typically purchase maintenance agreements and large appliances at the same time. Why else would they purchase maintenance agreements? The two are advertised together, and rarely sold separately (although when sold separately, it is the large appliance that is sold without the agreement rather than the agreement sold without the appliance). This rule, though, was found after analyzing hundreds of thousands of point-of-sale transactions from Sears. Although it is valid and well supported in the data, it is still useless. Similar results abound: People who buy 2-by-4s also purchase nails; customers who purchase paint buy paint brushes; oil and oil filters are purchased together, as are hamburgers and hamburger buns, and charcoal and lighter fluid.

A subtler problem falls into the same category. A seemingly interesting result—such as the fact that people who buy the three-way calling option on their local telephone service almost always buy call waiting—may be the result of past marketing programs and product bundles. In the case of telephone service options, three-way calling is typically bundled with call waiting, so it is difficult to order it separately. In this case, the analysis does not produce actionable results; it is producing already acted-upon results. Although it is a danger for any data mining technique, market basket analysis is particularly susceptible to reproducing the success of previous marketing campaigns because of its dependence on unsummarized point-of-sale data—exactly the same data that defines the success of the campaign. *Results from market basket analysis may simply be measuring the success of previous marketing campaigns.*

Trivial rules do have one use, although it is not directly a data mining use. When a rule should appear 100 percent of the time, the few cases where it does not hold provide a lot of information about data quality. That is, the exceptions to trivial rules point to areas where business operations, data collection, and processing may need to be further refined.

## Inexplicable Rules

*Inexplicable results seem to have no explanation and do not suggest a course of action.* The third pattern ("When a new hardware store opens, one of the most commonly sold items is toilet bowl cleaner") is intriguing, tempting us with a new fact but providing information that does not give insight into consumer behavior or the merchandise or suggest further actions. In this case, a large hardware company discovered the pattern for new store openings, but could not figure out how to profit from it. Many items are on sale during the store openings, but the toilet bowl cleaners stood out. More investigation might give some explanation: Is the discount on toilet bowl cleaners much larger than for other products? Are they consistently placed in a high-traffic area for store openings but hidden at other times? Is the result an anomaly from a handful of stores? Are they difficult to find at other times? Whatever the cause, it is doubtful that further analysis of just the market basket data can give a credible explanation.

**WARNING** When applying market basket analysis, many of the results are often either *trivial* or *inexplicable*. Trivial rules reproduce common knowledge about the business, wasting the effort used to apply sophisticated analysis techniques. Inexplicable rules are flukes in the data and are not actionable.

## FAMOUS RULES: BEER AND DIAPERS

Perhaps the most talked about association rule ever "found" is the association between beer and diapers. This is a famous story from the late 1980s or early 1990s, when computers were just getting powerful enough to analyze large volumes of data. The setting is somewhere in the midwest, where a retailer is analyzing point of sale data to find interesting patterns.

Lo and behold, lurking in all the transaction data, is the fact that beer and diapers are selling together. This immediately sets marketing minds in motion to figure out what is happening. A flash of insight provides the explanation: beer drinkers do not want to interrupt their enjoyment of televised sports, so they buy diapers to reduce trips to the bathroom. No, that's not it. The more likely story is that families with young children are preparing for the weekend, diapers for the kids and beer for Dad. Dad probably knows that after he has a couple of beers, Mom will change the diapers.

This is a powerful story. Setting aside the analytics, what can a retailer do with this information? There are two competing views. One says to put the beer and diapers close together, so when one is purchased, customers remember to buy the other one. The other says to put them as far apart as possible, so the customer must walk by as many stocked shelves as possible, having the opportunity to buy yet more items. The store could also put higher-margin diapers a bit closer to the beer, although mixing baby products and alcohol would probably be unseemly.

The story is so powerful that the authors noticed at least four companies using the story—IBM, Tandem (now part of HP), Oracle, and NCR Teradata. The actual story was debunked on April 6, 1998 in an article in *Forbes* magazine called "Beer-Diaper Syndrome."

The debunked story still has a lesson. Apparently, the sales of beer and diapers were known to be correlated (at least in some stores) based on inventory. While doing a demonstration project, a sales manager suggested that the demo show something interesting, like "beer and diapers" being sold together. With this small hint, analysts were able to find evidence in the data. Actually, the moral of the story is not about the power of association rules. It is that hypothesis testing can be very persuasive and actionable.

# How Good Is an Association Rule?

Association rules start with transactions containing one or more products or service offerings and some rudimentary information about the transaction. For the purpose of analysis, the products and service offerings are called *items*. Table 9.1 illustrates five transactions in a grocery store that carries five products.

These transactions have been simplified to include only the items purchased. How to use information like the date and time and whether the customer paid with cash or a credit card is discussed later in this chapter.

Each of these transactions gives us information about which products are purchased with which other products. This is shown in a co-occurrence table that tells the number of times that any pair of products was purchased together (see Table 9.2). For instance, the box where the "Soda" row intersects the "OJ" column has a value of "2," meaning that two transactions contain both soda and orange juice. This is easily verified against the original transaction data, where customers 1 and 4 purchased both these items. The values along the diagonal (for instance, the value in the "OJ" column and the "OJ" row) represent the number of transactions containing that item.

**Table 9.1**   Grocery Point-of-Sale Transactions

| CUSTOMER | ITEMS |
|---|---|
| 1 | Orange juice, soda |
| 2 | Milk, orange juice, window cleaner |
| 3 | Orange juice, detergent |
| 4 | Orange juice, detergent, soda |
| 5 | Window cleaner, soda |

**Table 9.2**   Co-Occurrence of Products

|  | OJ | WINDOW CLEANER | MILK | SODA | DETERGENT |
|---|---|---|---|---|---|
| OJ | 4 | 1 | 1 | 2 | 1 |
| Window Cleaner | 1 | 2 | 1 | 1 | 0 |
| Milk | 1 | 1 | 1 | 0 | 0 |
| Soda | 2 | 1 | 0 | 3 | 1 |
| Detergent | 1 | 0 | 0 | 1 | 2 |

This simple co-occurrence table already highlights some simple patterns:

- Orange juice and soda are more likely to be purchased together than any other two items.

- Detergent is never purchased with window cleaner or milk.

- Milk is never purchased with soda or detergent.

These observations are examples of associations and may suggest a formal rule like: *"If a customer purchases soda, then the customer also purchases orange juice."* For now, let's defer discussion of how to find the rule automatically, and instead ask another question. How good is this rule?

In the data, two of the five transactions include both soda and orange juice. These two transactions *support* the rule. The support for the rule is two out of five or 40 percent. Since both the transactions that contain soda also contain orange juice, there is a high degree of *confidence* in the rule as well. In fact, two of the three transactions that contains soda also contains orange juice, so the rule *"if soda, then orange juice"* has a confidence of 67 percent percent. The inverse rule, *"if orange juice, then soda,"* has a lower confidence. Of the four transactions with orange juice, only two also have soda. Its confidence, then, is just 50 percent. More formally, confidence is the ratio of the number of the transactions supporting the rule to the number of transactions where the conditional part of the rule holds. Another way of saying this is that confidence is the ratio of the number of transactions with all the items to the number of transactions with just the "if" items.

Another question is how much better than chance the rule is. One way to answer this is to calculate the *lift* (also called *improvement*), which tells us how much better a rule is at predicting the result than just assuming the result in the first place. Lift is the ratio of the density of the target after application of the left-hand side to the density of the target in the population. Another way of saying this is that lift is the ratio of the records that support the entire rule to the number that would be expected, assuming that there is no relationship between the products (the exact formula is given later in the chapter). A similar measure, the *excess*, is the difference between the number of records supported by the entire rule minus the expected value. Because the excess is measured in the same units as the original sales, it is sometimes easier to work with.

Figure 9.7 provides an example of lift, confidence, and support as provided by Blue Martini, a company that specializes in tools for retailers. Their software system includes a suite of analysis tools that includes association rules.

This particular example shows that a particular jacket is much more likely to be purchased with a gift certificate, information that can be used for improving messaging for selling both gift certificates and jackets.

The ideas behind the co-occurrence table extend to combinations with any number of items, not just pairs of items. For combinations of three items, imagine a cube with each side split into five different parts, as shown in Figure 9.8. Even with just five items in the data, there are already 125 different subcubes to fill in. By playing with symmetries in the cube, this can be reduced a bit (by a factor of six), but the number of subcubes for groups of three items is proportional to the third power of the number of different items. In general, the number of combinations with $n$ items is proportional to the number of items raised to the $n$th power—a number that gets very large, very fast. And generating the co-occurrence table requires doing work for each of these combinations.

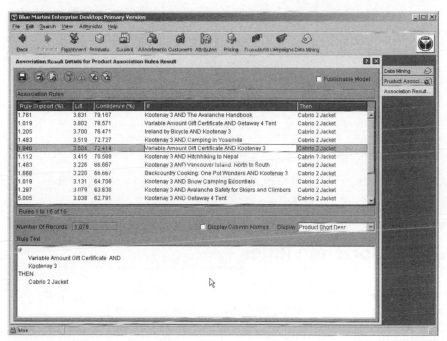

**Figure 9.7** Blue Martini provides an interface that shows the support, confidence, and lift of an association rule.

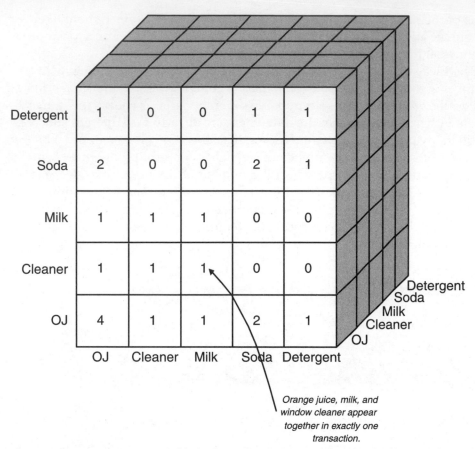

|  | OJ | Cleaner | Milk | Soda | Detergent |
|---|---|---|---|---|---|
| Detergent | 1 | 0 | 0 | 1 | 1 |
| Soda | 2 | 0 | 0 | 2 | 1 |
| Milk | 1 | 1 | 1 | 0 | 0 |
| Cleaner | 1 | 1 | 1 | 0 | 0 |
| OJ | 4 | 1 | 1 | 2 | 1 |

*Orange juice, milk, and window cleaner appear together in exactly one transaction.*

**Figure 9.8**  A co-occurrence table in three dimensions can be visualized as a cube.

## Building Association Rules

This basic process for finding association rules is illustrated in Figure 9.9. There are three important concerns in creating association rules:

- Choosing the right set of items.
- Generating rules by deciphering the counts in the co-occurrence matrix.
- Overcoming the practical limits imposed by thousands or tens of thousands of items.

The next three sections delve into these concerns in more detail.

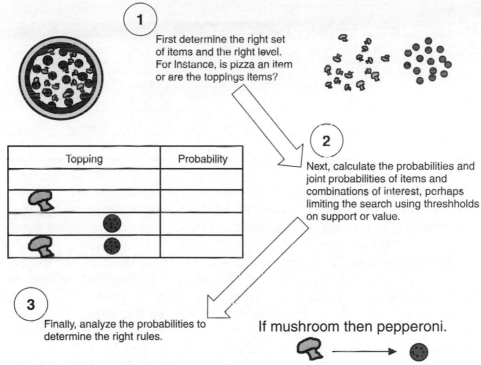

**Figure 9.9** Finding association rules has these basic steps.

## Choosing the Right Set of Items

The data used for finding association rules is typically the detailed transaction data captured at the point of sale. Gathering and using this data is a critical part of applying market basket analysis, depending crucially on the items chosen for analysis. What constitutes a particular item depends on the business need. Within a grocery store where there are tens of thousands of products on the shelves, a frozen pizza might be considered an item for analysis purposes—regardless of its toppings (extra cheese, pepperoni, or mushrooms), its crust (extra thick, whole wheat, or white), or its size. So, the purchase of a large whole wheat vegetarian pizza contains the same "frozen pizza" item as the purchase of a single-serving, pepperoni with extra cheese. A sample of such transactions at this summarized level might look like Table 9.3.

**Table 9.3** Transactions with More Summarized Items

| CUSTOMER | PIZZA | MILK | SUGAR | APPLES | COFFEE |
|----------|-------|------|-------|--------|--------|
| 1 | ✓ | | | | |
| 2 | | ✓ | ✓ | | |
| 3 | ✓ | | | ✓ | ✓ |
| 4 | | ✓ | | | ✓ |
| 5 | ✓ | | ✓ | ✓ | ✓ |

On the other hand, the manager of frozen foods or a chain of pizza restaurants may be very interested in the particular combinations of toppings that are ordered. He or she might decompose a pizza order into constituent parts, as shown in Table 9.4.

At some later point in time, the grocery store may become interested in having more detail in its transactions, so the single "frozen pizza" item would no longer be sufficient. Or, the pizza restaurants might broaden their menu choices and become less interested in all the different toppings. *The items of interest may change over time.* This can pose a problem when trying to use historical data if different levels of detail have been removed.

Choosing the right level of detail is a critical consideration for the analysis. If the transaction data in the grocery store keeps track of every type, brand, and size of frozen pizza—which probably account for several dozen products—then all these items need to map up to the "frozen pizza" item for analysis.

**Table 9.4** Transactions with More Detailed Items

| CUSTOMER | EXTRA CHEESE | ONIONS | PEPPERS | MUSHROOMS | OLIVES |
|----------|--------------|--------|---------|-----------|--------|
| 1 | ✓ | ✓ | | | ✓ |
| 2 | | | ✓ | | |
| 3 | ✓ | ✓ | | ✓ | |
| 4 | | ✓ | | | ✓ |
| 5 | ✓ | | ✓ | ✓ | ✓ |

## Product Hierarchies Help to Generalize Items

In the real world, items have product codes and stock-keeping unit codes (SKUs) that fall into hierarchical categories (see Figure 9.10), called a *product hierarchy* or *taxonomy*. What level of the product hierarchy is the right one to use? This brings up issues such as

- Are large fries and small fries the same product?
- Is the brand of ice cream more relevant than its flavor?
- Which is more important: the size, style, pattern, or designer of clothing?
- Is the energy-saving option on a large appliance indicative of customer behavior?

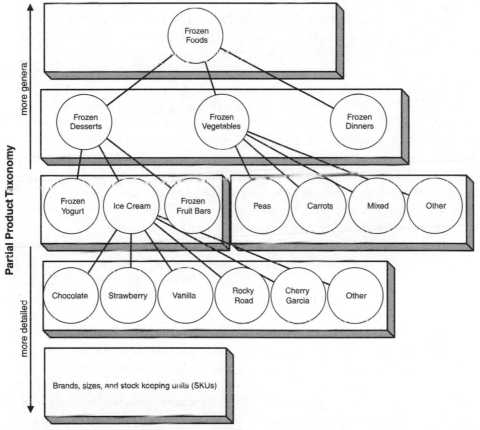

**Figure 9.10**   Product hierarchies start with the most general and move to increasing detail.

The number of combinations to consider grows very fast as the number of items used in the analysis increases. This suggests using items from higher levels of the product hierarchy, "frozen desserts" instead of "ice cream." On the other hand, the more specific the items are, the more likely the results are to be actionable. Knowing what sells with a particular brand of frozen pizza, for instance, can help in managing the relationship with the manufacturer. One compromise is to use more general items initially, then to repeat the rule generation to hone in on more specific items. As the analysis focuses on more specific items, use only the subset of transactions containing those items.

The complexity of a rule refers to the number of items it contains. The more items in the transactions, the longer it takes to generate rules of a given complexity. So, the desired complexity of the rules also determines how specific or general the items should be. In some circumstances, customers do not make large purchases. For instance, customers purchase relatively few items at any one time at a convenience store or through some catalogs, so looking for rules containing four or more items may apply to very few transactions and be a wasted effort. In other cases, such as in supermarkets, the average transaction is larger, so more complex rules are useful.

Moving up the product hierarchy reduces the number of items. Dozens or hundreds of items may be reduced to a single generalized item, often corresponding to a single department or product line. An item like a pint of Ben & Jerry's Cherry Garcia gets generalized to "ice cream" or "frozen foods." Instead of investigating "orange juice," investigate "fruit juices," and so on. Often, the appropriate level of the hierarchy ends up matching a department with a product-line manager; so using categories has the practical effect of finding interdepartmental relationships. Generalized items also help find rules with sufficient support. There will be many times as many transactions supported by higher levels of the taxonomy than lower levels.

Just because some items are generalized does not mean that all items need to move up to the same level. The appropriate level depends on the item, on its importance for producing actionable results, and on its frequency in the data. For instance, in a department store, big-ticket items (such as appliances) might stay at a low level in the hierarchy, while less-expensive items (such as books) might be higher. This hybrid approach is also useful when looking at individual products. Since there are often thousands of products in the data, generalize everything other than the product or products of interest.

**TIP** Market basket analysis produces the best results when the items occur in roughly the same number of transactions in the data. This helps prevent rules from being dominated by the most common items. Product hierarchies can help here. Roll up rare items to higher levels in the hierarchy, so they become more frequent. More common items may not have to be rolled up at all.

## Virtual Items Go beyond the Product Hierarchy

The purpose of virtual items is to enable the analysis to take advantage of information that goes beyond the product hierarchy. Virtual items do not appear in the product hierarchy of the original items, because they cross product boundaries. Examples of virtual items might be designer labels such as Calvin Klein that appear in both apparel departments and perfumes, low-fat and no-fat products in a grocery store, and energy-saving options on appliances.

Virtual items may even include information about the transactions themselves, such as whether the purchase was made with cash, a credit card, or check, and the day of the week or the time of the day the transaction occurred. However, it is not a good idea to crowd the data with too many virtual items. *Only include virtual items when you have some idea of how they could result in actionable information if found in well-supported, high-confidence association rules.*

There is a danger, though. Virtual items can cause trivial rules. For instance, imagine that there is a virtual item for "diet product" and one for "coke product", then a rule might appear like:

*If "coke product" and "diet product" then "diet coke"*

That is, everywhere that <Coke> appears in a basket and <Diet Product> appears in a basket, then <Diet Coke> also appears. Every basket that has Diet Coke satisfies this rule. Although some baskets may have regular coke and other diet products, the rule will have high lift because it is the definition of Diet Coke. When using virtual items, it is worth checking and rechecking the rules to be sure that such trivial rules are not arising.

A similar but more subtle danger occurs when the right-hand side does not include the associated item. So, a rule like:

*If "coke product" and "diet product" then "pretzels"*

probably means,

*If "diet coke" then "pretzels"*

The only danger from having such rules is that they can obscure what is happening.

**TIP** When applying market basket analysis, it is useful to have a hierarchical taxonomy of the items being considered for analysis. By carefully choosing the right levels of the hierarchy, these generalized items should occur about the same number of times in the data, improving the results of the analysis. For specific lifestyle-related choices that provide insight into customer behavior, such as sugar-free items and specific brands, augment the data with virtual items.

### Data Quality

The data used for market basket analysis is generally not of very high quality. It is gathered directly at the point of customer contact and used mainly for operational purposes such as inventory control. The data is likely to have multiple formats, corrections, incompatible code types, and so on. Much of the explanation of various code values is likely to be buried deep in programming code running in legacy systems and may be difficult to extract. Different stores within a single chain sometimes have slightly different product hierarchies or different ways of handling situations like discounts.

Here is an example. The authors were once curious about the approximately 80 department codes present in a large set of transaction data. The client assured us that there were 40 departments and provided a nice description of each of them. More careful inspection revealed the problem. Some stores had IBM cash registers and others had NCR. The two types of equipment had different ways of representing department codes—hence we saw many invalid codes in the data.

These kinds of problems are typical when using any sort of data for data mining. However, they are exacerbated for market basket analysis because this type of analysis depends heavily on the unsummarized point-of-sale transactions.

### Anonymous versus Identified

Market basket analysis has proven useful for mass-market retail, such as supermarkets, convenience stores, drug stores, and fast food chains, where many of the purchases have traditionally been made with cash. Cash transactions are anonymous, meaning that the store has no knowledge about specific customers because there is no information identifying the customer in the transaction. For anonymous transactions, the only information is the date and time, the location of the store, the cashier, the items purchased, any coupons redeemed, and the amount of change. With market basket analysis, even this limited data can yield interesting and actionable results.

The increasing prevalence of Web transactions, loyalty programs, and purchasing clubs is resulting in more and more identified transactions, providing analysts with more possibilities for information about customers and their behavior over time. Demographic and trending information is available on individuals and households to further augment customer profiles. This additional information can be incorporated into association rule analysis using virtual items.

## Generating Rules from All This Data

Calculating the number of times that a given combination of items appears in the transaction data is well and good, but a combination of items is not a rule.

Sometimes, just the combination is interesting in itself, as in the Barbie doll and candy bar example. But in other circumstances, it makes more sense to find an underlying rule of the form:

*if condition, then result.*

Notice that this is just shorthand. If the rule says,

*if Barbie doll, then candy bar*

then we read it as: "if a customer purchases a Barbie doll, then the customer is also expected to purchase a candy bar." The general practice is to consider rules where there is just one item on the right-hand side.

## Calculating Confidence

Constructs such as the co-occurrence table provide information about which combinations of items occur most commonly in the transactions. For the sake of illustration, let's say that the most common combination has three items, A, B, and C. Table 9.5 provides an example, showing the probabilities that items and various combinations are purchased.

The only rules to consider are those with all three items in the rule and with exactly one item in the result:

- If *A* and *B*, then *C*
- If *A* and *C*, then *B*
- If *B* and *C*, then *A*

Because these three rules contain the same items, they have the same support in the data, 5 percent. What about their confidence level? Confidence is the ratio of the number of transactions with all the items in the rule to the number of transactions with just the items in the condition. The confidence for the three rules is shown in Table 9.6.

**Table 9.5** Probabilities of Three Items and Their Combinations

| COMBINATION | PROBABILITY |
|-------------|-------------|
| A | 45.0 % |
| B | 42.5% |
| C | 40.0% |
| A and B | 25.0 % |
| A and C | 20.0 % |
| B and C | 15.0% |
| A and B and C | 5.0% |

**Table 9.6**   Confidence in Rules

| RULE | P(CONDITION) | P(CONDITION AND RESULT) | CONFIDENCE |
|------|-------------|------------------------|------------|
| If A and B then C | 25% | 5% | 0.20 |
| If A and C then B | 20% | 5% | 0.25 |
| If B and C then A | 15% | 5% | 0.33 |

What is confidence really saying? Saying that the rule "*if B and C then A*" has a confidence of 0.33 is equivalent to saying that when B and C appear in a transaction, there is a 33 percent chance that A also appears in it. That is, one time in three A occurs with B and C, and the other two times, B and C appear without A. The most confident rule is the best rule, so the best rule is "*if B and C then A.*"

## Calculating Lift

As described earlier, lift is a good measure of how much better the rule is doing. It is the ratio of the density of the target (using the left hand side of the rule) to density of the target overall. So the formula is:

lift = (p(condition and result) / p (condition) ) / p(result)
    = p(condition and result) / (p(condition) p(result))

When lift is greater than 1, then the resulting rule is better at predicting the result than guessing whether the resultant item is present based on item frequencies in the data. When lift is less than 1, the rule is doing worse than informed guessing. The following table (Table 9.7) shows the lift for the three rules and for the rule with the best lift.

None of the rules with three items shows improved lift. The best rule in the data actually only has two items. When "A" is purchased, then "B" is 31 percent more likely to be in the transaction than if "A" is not purchased. In this case, as in many cases, the best rule actually contains fewer items than other rules being considered.

**Table 9.7**   Lift Measurements for Four Rules

| RULE | SUPPORT | CONFIDENCE | P(RESULT) | LIFT |
|------|---------|------------|-----------|------|
| If A and B then C | 5% | 0.20 | 40% | 0.50 |
| If A and C then B | 5% | 0.25 | 42.5% | 0.59 |
| If B and C then A | 5% | 0.33 | 45% | 0.74 |
| If A then B | 25% | 0.59 | 42.5% | 1.31 |

## The Negative Rule

When lift is less than 1, *negating* the result produces a better rule. If the rule

*if B and C then A*

has a confidence of 0.33, then the rule

*if B and C then NOT A*

has a confidence of 0.67. Since A appears in 45 percent of the transactions, it does NOT occur in 55 percent of them. Applying the same lift measure shows that the lift of this new rule is 1.22 (0.67/0.55), resulting in a lift of 1.33, better than any of the other rules.

## Overcoming Practical Limits

Generating association rules is a multistep process. The general algorithm is:

1. Generate the co-occurrence matrix for single items.
2. Generate the co-occurrence matrix for two items. Use this to find rules with two items.
3. Generate the co-occurrence matrix for three items. Use this to find rules with three items.
4. And so on.

For instance, in the grocery store that sells orange juice, milk, detergent, soda, and window cleaner, the first step calculates the counts for each of these items. During the second step, the following counts are created:

- Milk and detergent, milk and soda, milk and cleaner
- Detergent and soda, detergent and cleaner
- Soda and cleaner

This is a total of 10 pairs of items. The third pass takes all combinations of three items and so on. Of course, each of these stages may require a separate pass through the data or multiple stages can be combined into a single pass by considering different numbers of combinations at the same time.

Although it is not obvious when there are just five items, increasing the number of items in the combinations requires exponentially more computation. This results in exponentially growing run times—and long, long waits when considering combinations with more than three or four items. The solution is *pruning*. Pruning is a technique for reducing the number of items and combinations of items being considered at each step. At each stage, the algorithm throws out a certain number of combinations that do not meet some threshold criterion.

The most common pruning threshold is called *minimum support pruning*. Support refers to the number of transactions in the database where the rule holds. Minimum support pruning requires that a rule hold on a minimum number of transactions. For instance, if there are one million transactions and the minimum support is 1 percent, then only rules supported by 10,000 transactions are of interest. This makes sense, because the purpose of generating these rules is to pursue some sort of action—such as striking a deal with Mattel (the makers of Barbie dolls) to make a candy-bar-eating doll—and the action must affect enough transactions to be worthwhile.

The minimum support constraint has a cascading effect. Consider a rule with four items in it:

*if A, B, and C, then D.*

Using minimum support pruning, this rule has to be true on at least 10,000 transactions in the data. It follows that:

*A must appear in at least 10,000 transactions, and,*
*B must appear in at least 10,000 transactions, and,*
*C must appear in at least 10,000 transactions, and,*
*D must appear in at least 10,000 transactions.*

In other words, minimum support pruning eliminates items that do not appear in enough transactions. The threshold criterion applies to each step in the algorithm. The minimum threshold also implies that:

*A and B must appear together in at least 10,000 transactions, and,*

*A and C must appear together in at least 10,000 transactions, and,*

*A and D must appear together in at least 10,000 transactions,*

*and so on.*

Each step of the calculation of the co-occurrence table can eliminate combinations of items that do not meet the threshold, reducing its size and the number of combinations to consider during the next pass.

Figure 9.11 is an example of how the calculation takes place. In this example, choosing a minimum support level of 10 percent would eliminate all the combinations with three items—and their associated rules—from consideration. This is an example where pruning does not have an effect on the best rule since the best rule has only two items. In the case of pizza, these toppings are all fairly common, so are not pruned individually. If anchovies were included in the analysis—and there are only 15 pizzas containing them out of the 2,000—then a minimum support of 10 percent, or even 1 percent, would eliminate anchovies during the first pass.

The best choice for minimum support depends on the data and the situation. It is also possible to vary the minimum support as the algorithm progresses. For instance, using different levels at different stages you can find uncommon combinations of common items (by decreasing the support level for successive steps) or relatively common combinations of uncommon items (by increasing the support level).

## The Problem of Big Data

A typical fast food restaurant offers several dozen items on its menu, say 100. To use probabilities to generate association rules, counts have to be calculated for each combination of items. The number of combinations of a given size tends to grow exponentially. A combination with three items might be a small fries, cheeseburger, and medium Diet Coke. On a menu with 100 items, how many combinations are there with three different menu items? There are 161,700! This calculation is based on the binomial formula On the other hand, a typical supermarket has at least 10,000 different items in stock, and more typically 20,000 or 30,000.

A pizza restaurant has sold 2000 pizzas, of which:
100 are mushroom only, 150 are pepperoni, 200 are extra cheese
400 are mushroom and pepperoni, 300 are mushroom and extra cheese, 200 are pepperoni and extra cheese
100 are mushroom, pepperoni, and extra cheese.
550 have no extra toppings.

We need to calculate the probabilities for all possible combinations of items.

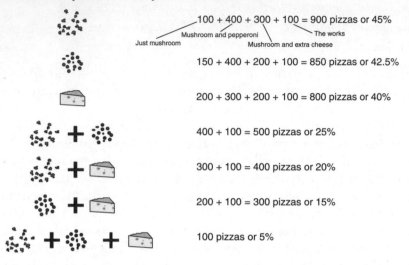

100 + 400 + 300 + 100 = 900 pizzas or 45%
Mushroom and pepperoni          The works
Just mushroom          Mushroom and extra cheese

150 + 400 + 200 + 100 = 850 pizzas or 42.5%

200 + 300 + 200 + 100 = 800 pizzas or 40%

400 + 100 = 500 pizzas or 25%

300 + 100 = 400 pizzas or 20%

200 + 100 = 300 pizzas or 15%

100 pizzas or 5%

There are three rules with all three items:

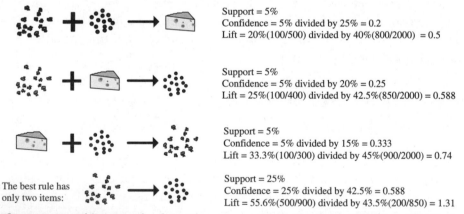

Support = 5%
Confidence = 5% divided by 25% = 0.2
Lift = 20%(100/500) divided by 40%(800/2000) = 0.5

Support = 5%
Confidence = 5% divided by 20% = 0.25
Lift = 25%(100/400) divided by 42.5%(850/2000) = 0.588

Support = 5%
Confidence = 5% divided by 15% = 0.333
Lift = 33.3%(100/300) divided by 45%(900/2000) = 0.74

The best rule has
only two items:

Support = 25%
Confidence = 25% divided by 42.5% = 0.588
Lift = 55.6%(500/900) divided by 43.5%(200/850) = 1.31

**Figure 9.11**  This example shows how to count up the frequencies on pizza sales for market basket analysis.

Calculating the support, confidence, and lift quickly gets out of hand as the number of items in the combinations grows. There are almost 50 million possible combinations of two items in the grocery store and over 100 billion combinations of three items. Although computers are getting more powerful and cheaper, it is still very time-consuming to calculate the counts for this number of combinations. Calculating the counts for five or more items is prohibitively expensive. The use of product hierarchies reduces the number of items to a manageable size.

The number of transactions is also very large. In the course of a year, a decent-size chain of supermarkets will generate tens or hundreds of millions of transactions. Each of these transactions consists of one or more items, often several dozen at a time. So, determining if a particular combination of items is present in a particular transaction may require a bit of effort—multiplied a million-fold for all the transactions.

# Extending the Ideas

The basic ideas of association rules can be applied to different areas, such as comparing different stores and making some enhancements to the definition of the rules. These are discussed in this section.

## Using Association Rules to Compare Stores

Market basket analysis is commonly used to make comparisons between locations within a single chain. The rule about toilet bowl cleaner sales in hardware stores is an example where sales at new stores are compared to sales at existing stores. Different stores exhibit different selling patterns for many reasons: regional trends, the effectiveness of management, dissimilar advertising, and varying demographic patterns in the catchment area, for example. Air conditioners and fans are often purchased during heat waves, but heat waves affect only a limited region. Within smaller areas, demographics of the catchment area can have a large impact; we would expect stores in wealthy areas to exhibit different sales patterns from those in poorer neighborhoods. These are examples where market basket analysis can help to describe the differences and serve as an example of using market basket analysis for directed data mining.

How can association rules be used to make these comparisons? The first step is augmenting the transactions with *virtual items* that specify which group, such as an existing location or a new location, that the transaction comes from. Virtual items help describe the transaction, although the virtual item is not a product or service. For instance, a sale at an existing hardware store might include the following products:

- A hammer
- A box of nails
- Extra-fine sandpaper

**TIP** Adding virtual transactions in to the market basket data makes it possible to find rules that include store characteristics and customer characteristics.

After augmenting the data to specify where it came from, the transaction looks like:

a hammer,

a box of nails,

extra fine sandpaper,

"at existing hardware store."

To compare sales at store openings versus existing stores, the process is:

1. Gather data for a specific period (such as 2 weeks) from store openings. Augment each of the transactions in this data with a virtual item saying that the transaction is from a store opening.

2. Gather about the same amount of data from existing stores. Here you might use a sample across all existing stores, or you might take all the data from stores in comparable locations. Augment the transactions in this data with a virtual item saying that the transaction is from an existing store.

3. Apply market basket analysis to find association rules in each set.

4. Pay particular attention to association rules containing the virtual items.

Because association rules are undirected data mining, the rules act as starting points for further hypothesis testing. Why does one pattern exist at existing stores and another at new stores? The rule about toilet bowl cleaners and store openings, for instance, suggests looking more closely at toilet bowl cleaner sales in existing stores at different times during the year.

Using this technique, market basket analysis can be used for many other types of comparisons:

- Sales during promotions versus sales at other times
- Sales in various geographic areas, by county, standard statistical metropolitan area (SSMA), direct marketing area (DMA), or country
- Urban versus suburban sales
- Seasonal differences in sales patterns

Adding virtual items to each basket of goods enables the standard association rule techniques to make these comparisons.

## Dissociation Rules

A *dissociation rule* is similar to an association rule except that it can have the connector "and not" in the condition in addition to "and." A typical dissociation rule looks like:

*if A and not B, then C.*

Dissociation rules can be generated by a simple adaptation of the basic market basket analysis algorithm. The adaptation is to introduce a new set of items that are the inverses of each of the original items. Then, modify each transaction so it includes an inverse item if, and only if, it does not contain the original item. For example, Table 9.8 shows the transformation of a few transactions. The ¬ before the item denotes the inverse item.

There are three downsides to including these new items. First, the total number of items used in the analysis doubles. Since the amount of computation grows exponentially with the number of items, doubling the number of items seriously degrades performance. Second, the size of a typical transaction grows because it now includes inverted items. The third issue is that the frequency of the inverse items tends to be much larger than the frequency of the original items. So, minimum support constraints tend to produce rules in which all items are inverted, such as:

*if NOT A and NOT B then NOT C.*

These rules are less likely to be actionable.

Sometimes it is useful to invert only the most frequent items in the set used for analysis. This is particularly valuable when the frequency of some of the original items is close to 50 percent, so the frequencies of their inverses are also close to 50 percent.

**Table 9.8**  Transformation of Transactions to Generate Dissociation Rules

| CUSTOMER | ITEMS | CUSTOMER | WITH INVERSE ITEMS |
| --- | --- | --- | --- |
| 1 | {A, B, C} | 1 | {A, B, C} |
| 2 | {A} | 2 | {A, ¬B, ¬C} |
| 3 | {A, C} | 3 | {A, ¬B, C} |
| 4 | {A} | 4 | {A, ¬B, ¬C} |
| 5 | {} | 5 | {¬A, ¬B, ¬C} |

# Sequential Analysis Using Association Rules

Association rules find things that happen at the same time—what items are purchased at a given time. The next natural question concerns sequences of events and what they mean. Examples of results in this area are:

- New homeowners purchase shower curtains before purchasing furniture.

- Customers who purchase new lawnmowers are very likely to purchase a new garden hose in the following 6 weeks.

- When a customer goes into a bank branch and asks for an account reconciliation, there is a good chance that he or she will close all his or her accounts.

Time-series data usually requires some way of identifying the customer over time. Anonymous transactions cannot reveal that new homeowners buy shower curtains before they buy furniture. This requires tracking each customer, as well as knowing which customers recently purchased a home. Since larger purchases are often made with credit cards or debit cards, this is less of a problem. For problems in other domains, such as investigating the effects of medical treatments or customer behavior inside a bank, all transactions typically include identity information.

**WARNING** In order to consider time-series analyses on your customers, there has to be some way of identifying customers. Without a way of tracking individual customers, there is no way to analyze their behavior over time.

For the purposes of this section, a *time series* is an ordered sequence of items. It differs from a transaction only in being ordered. In general, the time series contains identifying information about the customer, since this information is used to tie the different transactions together into a series. Although there are many techniques for analyzing time series, such as ARIMA (a statistical technique) and neural networks, this section discusses only how to manipulate the time-series data to apply the market basket analysis.

In order to use time series, the transaction data must have two additional features:

- A timestamp or sequencing information to determine when transactions occurred relative to each other

- Identifying information, such as account number, household ID, or customer ID that identifies different transactions as belonging to the same customer or household (sometimes called an economic marketing unit)

Building sequential rules is similar to the process of building association rules:

1. All items purchased by a customer are treated as a single order, and each item retains the timestamp indicating when it was purchased.

2. The process is the same for finding groups of items that appear together.

3. To develop the rules, only rules where the items on the left-hand side were purchased before items on the right-hand side are considered.

The result is a set of association rules that can reveal sequential patterns.

## Lessons Learned

Market basket data describes what customers purchase. Analyzing this data is complex, and no single technique is powerful enough to provide all the answers. The data itself typically describes the market basket at three different levels. The order is the event of the purchase; the line-items are the items in the purchase, and the customer connects orders together over time.

Many important questions about customer behavior can be answered by looking at product sales over time. Which are the best selling items? Which items that sold well last year are no longer selling well this year? Inventory curves do not require transaction level data. Perhaps the most important insight they provide is the effect of marketing interventions—did sales go up or down after a particular event?

However, inventory curves are not sufficient for understanding relationships among items in a single basket. One technique that is quite powerful is association rules. This technique finds products that tend to sell together in groups. Sometimes is the groups are sufficient for insight. Other times, the groups are turned into explicit rules—when certain items are present then we expect to find certain other items in the basket.

There are three measures of association rules. Support tells how often the rule is found in the transaction data. Confidence says how often when the "if" part is true that the "then" part is also true. And, lift tells how much better the rule is at predicting the "then" part as compared to having no rule at all.

The rules so generated fall into three categories. Useful rules explain a relationship that was perhaps unexpected. Trivial rules explain relationships that are known (or should be known) to exist. And inexplicable rules simply do not make sense. Inexplicable rules often have weak support.

Market basket analysis and association rules provide ways to analyze item-level detail, where the relationships between items are determined by the baskets they fall into. In the next chapter, we'll turn to link analysis, which generalizes the ideas of "items" linked by "relationships," using the background of an area of mathematics called graph theory.

# Link Analysis

The international route maps of British Airways and Air France offer more than just trip planning help. They also provide insights into the history and politics of their respective homelands and of lost empires. A traveler bound from New York to Mombasa changes planes at Heathrow; one bound for Abidjan changes at Charles de Gaul. The international route maps show how much information can be gained from knowing how things are connected.

Which Web sites link to which other ones? Who calls whom on the telephone? Which physicians prescribe which drugs to which patients? These relationships are all visible in data, and they all contain a wealth of information that most data mining techniques are not able to take direct advantage of. In our ever-more-connected world (where, it has been claimed, there are no more than six degrees of separation between any two people on the planet), understanding relationships and connections is critical. Link analysis is the data mining technique that addresses this need.

Link analysis is based on a branch of mathematics called *graph theory*. This chapter reviews the key notions of graphs, then shows how link analysis has been applied to solve real problems. Link analysis is not applicable to all types of data nor can it solve all types of problems. However, when it can be used, it often yields very insightful and actionable results. Some areas where it has yielded good results are:

- Identifying authoritative sources of information on the World Wide Web by analyzing the links between its pages

- Analyzing telephone call patterns to identify particular market segments such as people working from home

- Understanding physician referral patterns; a referral is a relationship between two physicians, once again, naturally susceptible to link analysis

Even where links are explicitly recorded, assembling them into a useful graph can be a data-processing challenge. Links between Web pages are encoded in the HTML of the pages themselves. Links between telephones are recorded in call detail records. Neither of these data sources is useful for link analysis without considerable preprocessing, however. In other cases, the links are implicit and part of the data mining challenge is to recognize them.

The chapter begins with a brief introduction to graph theory and some of the classic problems that it has been used to solve. It then moves on to applications in data mining such as search engine rankings and analysis of call detail records.

## Basic Graph Theory

Graphs are an abstraction developed specifically to represent relationships. They have proven very useful in both mathematics and computer science for developing algorithms that exploit these relationships. Fortunately, graphs are quite intuitive, and there is a wealth of examples that illustrate how to take advantage of them.

A *graph* consists of two distinct parts:

- *Nodes* (sometimes called *vertices*) are the things in the graph that have relationships. These have names and often have additional useful properties.

- *Edges* are pairs of nodes connected by a relationship. An edge is represented by the two nodes that it connects, so *(A, B)* or *AB* represents the edge that connects A and B. An edge might also have a weight in a *weighted graph*.

Figure 10.1 illustrates two graphs. The graph on the left has four nodes connected by six edges and has the property that there is an edge between every pair of nodes. Such a graph is said to be *fully connected*. It could be representing daily flights between Atlanta, New York, Cincinnati, and Salt Lake City on an airline where these four cities serve as regional hubs. It could also represent four people, all of whom know each other, or four mutually related leads for a criminal investigation. The graph on the right has one node in the center connected to four other nodes. This could represent daily flights connecting Atlanta to Birmingham, Greenville, Charlotte, and Savannah on an airline that serves the Southeast from a hub in Atlanta, or a restaurant frequented by four credit card customers. The graph itself captures the information about what is connected to what. Without any labels, it can describe many different situations. This is the power of abstraction.

A few points of terminology about graphs. Because graphs are so useful for visualizing relationships, it is nice when the nodes and edges can be drawn with no intersecting edges. The graphs in Figure 10.2 have this property. They are *planar* graphs, since they can be drawn on a sheet of paper (what mathematicians call a *plane*) without having any edges intersect. Figure 10.2 shows two graphs that cannot be drawn without having at least two edges cross. There is, in fact, a theorem in graph theory that says that if a graph is nonplanar, then lurking inside it is one of the two previously described graphs.

When a path exists between any two nodes in a graph, the graph is said to be *connected*. For the rest of this chapter, we assume that all graphs are connected, unless otherwise specified. A *path*, as its name implies, is an ordered sequence of nodes connected by edges. Consider a graph where each node represents a city, and the edges are flights between pairs of cities. On such a graph, a node is a city and an edge is a flight segment—two cities that are connected by a nonstop flight. A path is an itinerary of flight segments that go from one city to another, such as from Greenville, South Carolina to Atlanta, from Atlanta to Chicago, and from Chicago to Peoria.

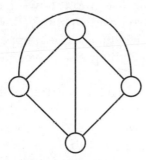

A fully connected graph with four nodes and six edges. In a fully connected graph, there is an edge between every pair of nodes.

A graph with five nodes and four edges.

**Figure 10.1** Two examples of graphs.

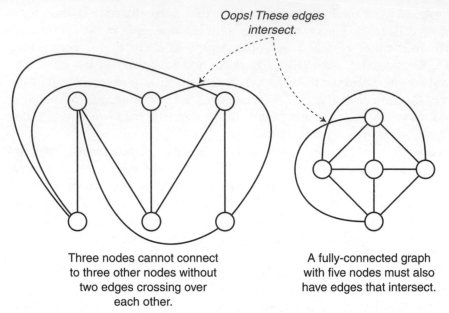

*Oops! These edges intersect.*

Three nodes cannot connect to three other nodes without two edges crossing over each other.

A fully-connected graph with five nodes must also have edges that intersect.

**Figure 10.2** Not all graphs can be drawn without having some edges cross over each other.

Figure 10.3 is an example of a *weighted graph*, one in which the edges have weights associated with them. In this case, the nodes represent products purchased by customers. The weights on the edges represent the *support* for the association, the percentage of market baskets containing both products. Such graphs provide an approach for solving problems in market basket analysis and are also a useful means of visualizing market basket data. This product association graph is an example of an undirected graph. The graph shows that 22.12 percent of market baskets at this health food grocery contain both yellow peppers and bananas. By itself, this does not explain whether yellow pepper sales drive banana sales or vice versa, or whether something else drives the purchase of all yellow fruits and vegetables.

One very common problem in link analysis is finding the shortest path between two nodes. Which is shortest, though, depends on the weights assigned to the edges. Consider the graph of flights between cities. Does shortest refer to distance? To the fewest number of flight segments? To the shortest flight time? Or to the least expensive? All these questions are answered the same way using graphs—the only difference is the weights on the edges.

The following two sections describe two classic problems in graph theory that illustrate the power of graphs to represent and solve problems. Few data mining problems are exactly like these two problems, but the problems give a flavor of how the simple construction of graphs leads to some interesting solutions. They are presented to familiarize the reader with graphs by providing examples of key concepts in graph theory and to provide a stronger basis for discussing link analysis.

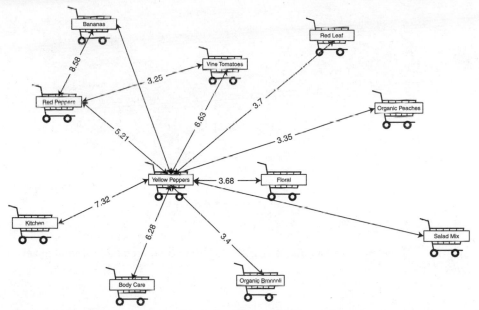

**Figure 10.3**  This is an example of a weighted graph where the edge weights are the number of transactions containing the items represented by the nodes at either end.

## Seven Bridges of Königsberg

One of the earliest problems in graph theory originated with a simple challenge posed in the eighteenth century by the Swiss mathematician Leonhard Euler. As shown in the simple map in Figure 10.4, Königsberg had two islands in the Pregel River connected to each other and to the rest of the city by a total of seven bridges. On either side of the river or on the islands, it is possible to get to any of the bridges. Figure 10.4 shows one path through the town that crosses over five bridges exactly once. Euler posed the question: Is it possible to walk over all seven bridges exactly once, starting from anywhere in the city, without getting wet or using a boat? As an historical note, the problem has survived longer than the name of the city. In the eighteenth century, Königsberg was a prominent Prussian city on the Baltic Sea nestled between Lithuania and Poland. Now, it is known as Kaliningrad, the westernmost Russian enclave, separated from the rest of Russia by Lithuania and Belarus.

In order to solve this problem, Euler invented the notation of graphs. He represented the map of Königsberg as the simple graph with four vertices and seven edges in Figure 10.5. Some pairs of nodes are connected by more than one edge, indicating that there is more than one bridge between them. Finding a route that traverses all the bridges in Königsberg exactly one time is equivalent to finding a path in the graph that visits every edge exactly once. Such a path is called an *Eulerian path* in honor of the mathematician who posed and solved this problem.

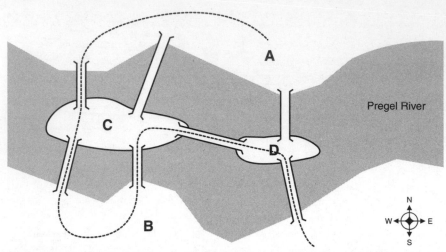

**Figure 10.4**  The Pregel River in Königsberg has two islands connected by a total of seven bridges.

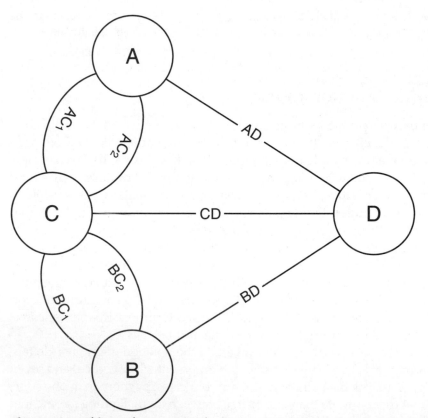

**Figure 10.5**  This graph represents the layout of Königsberg. The edges are bridges and the nodes are the riverbanks and islands.

**WHY DO THE DEGREES HAVE TO BE EVEN?**

Showing that an Eulerian path exists only when the degrees on all nodes are even (except at most two) rests on a simple observation. This observation is about paths in the graph. Consider one path through the bridges:

$A \rightarrow C \rightarrow B \rightarrow C \rightarrow D$

The edges being used are:

$AC_1 \rightarrow BC_1 \rightarrow BC_2 \rightarrow CD$

The edges connecting the intermediate nodes in the path come in pairs. That is, there is an outgoing edge for every incoming edge. For instance, node C has four edges visiting it, and node B has two. Since the edges come in pairs, each intermediate node has an even number of edges in the path. Since an Eulerian path contains all edges in the graph and visits all the nodes, such a path exists only when all the nodes in the graph (minus the two end nodes) can serve as intermediate nodes for the path. This is another way of saying that the degree of those nodes is even.

Euler also showed that the opposite is true. When all the nodes in a graph (save at most two) have an even degree, then an Eulerian path exists. This proof is a bit more complicated, but the idea is rather simple. To construct an Eulerian path, start at any node (even one with an odd degree) and move to any other connected node which has an even degree. Remove the edge just traversed from the graph and make it the first edge in the Eulerian path. Now, the problem is to find an Eulerian path starting at the second node in the graph. By keeping track of the degrees of the nodes, it is possible to construct such a path when there are at most two nodes whose degree is odd.

Euler devised a solution based on the number of edges going into or out of each node in the graph. The number of such edges is called the *degree* of a node. For instance, in the graph representing the seven bridges of Königsberg, the nodes representing the shores both have a degree of three—corresponding to the fact that there are three bridges connecting each shore to the islands. The other two nodes, representing the islands, have degrees of 5 and 3. Euler showed that an Eulerian path exists only when the degrees of all the nodes in a graph are even, except at most two (see technical aside). So, there is no way to walk over the seven bridges of Königsberg without traversing a bridge more than once, since there are four nodes whose degrees are odd.

## Traveling Salesman Problem

A more recent problem in graph theory is the "Traveling Salesman Problem." In this problem, a salesman needs to visit customers in a set of cities. He plans on flying to one of the cities, renting a car, visiting the customer there, then driving to each of other cities to visit each of the rest of his customers. He leaves the car in the last city and flies home. There are many possible routes that the salesman can take. What route minimizes the total distance that he travels while still allowing him to visit each city exactly one time?

The Traveling Salesman Problem is easily reformulated using graphs, since graphs are a natural representation of cities connected by roads. In the graph representing this problem, the nodes are cities and each edge has a weight corresponding to the distance between the two cities connected by the edge. The Traveling Salesman Problem therefore is asking: "What is the shortest path that visits all the nodes in a graph exactly one time?" Notice that this problem is different from the Seven Bridges of Königsberg. We are not interested in simply finding a path that visits all nodes exactly once, but of all possible paths we want the shortest one. Notice that all Eulerian paths have exactly the same length, since they contain exactly the same edges. Asking for the shortest Eulerian path does not make sense.

Solving the Traveling Salesman Problem for three or four cities is not difficult. The most complicated graph with four nodes is a completely connected graph where every node in the graph is connected to every other node. In this graph, 24 different paths visit each node exactly once. To count the number of paths, start at any of nodes (there are four possibilities), then go to any of the other three remaining ones, then to any of the other two, and finally to the last node ($4 * 3 * 2 * 1 = 4! = 24$). A completely connected graph with $n$ nodes has $n!$ (*n factorial*) distinct paths that contain all nodes. Each path has a slightly different collection of edges, so their lengths are usually different. Since listing the 24 possible paths is not that hard, finding the shortest path is not particularly difficult for this simple case.

The problem of finding the shortest path connecting nodes was first investigated by the Irish mathematician Sir William Rowan Hamilton. His study of minimizing energy in physical systems led him to investigate minimizing energy in certain discrete systems that he represented as graphs. In honor of him, a path that visits all nodes in a graph exactly once is called a *Hamiltonian path*.

The Traveling Salesman Problem is difficult to solve. Any solution must consider all of the possible paths through the graph in order to determine which one is the shortest. The number of paths in a completely connected graph grows very fast—as a factorial. What is true for completely connected graphs is true for graphs in general: The number of possible paths visiting all the nodes grows like an exponential function of the number of nodes (although there are a few simple graphs where this is not true). So, as the number of cities increases, the effort required to find the shortest path grows exponentially. Adding just one more city (with associated roads) can result in a solution that takes twice as long—or more—to find.

This lack of scalability is so important that mathematicians have given it a name: NP—where NP means that all known algorithms used to solve the problem scale exponentially—*not* like a *polynomial*. These problems are considered difficult. In fact, the Traveling Salesman Problem is so difficult that it is used for evaluating parallel computers and exotic computing methods—such as using DNA or the mysteries of quantum physics as the basis of computers instead of the more familiar computer chips made of silicon.

All of this graph theory aside, there are pretty good heuristic algorithms for computers that provide reasonable solutions to the Traveling Salesman Problem. The resulting paths are relatively short paths, although they are not guaranteed to be as short as the shortest possible one. This is a useful fact if you have a similar problem. One common algorithm is the greedy algorithm: start the path with the shortest edge in the graph, then lengthen the path with the shortest edge available at either end that visits a new node. The resulting path is generally pretty short, although not necessarily the shortest (see Figure 10.6).

**TIP** Often it is better to use an algorithm that yields good, but not perfect results, instead of trying to analyze the difficulty of arriving at the ideal solution or giving up because there is no guarantee of finding an optimal solution. As Voltaire remarked, *"Le mieux est l'ennemi du bien."* (The best is the enemy of the good.)

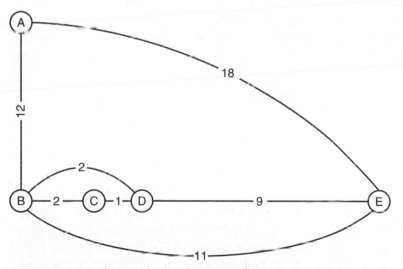

**Figure 10.6** In this graph, the shortest path (ABCDE) has a length of 24, but the greedy algorithm finds a much longer path (CDBEA).

## Directed Graphs

The graphs discussed so far are undirected. In undirected graphs, the edges are like expressways between nodes: they go in both directions. In a directed graph, the edges are like one-way roads. An edge going from A to B is distinct from an edge going from B to A. A directed edge from A to B is an *outgoing edge* of A and an *incoming edge* of B.

Directed graphs are a powerful way of representing data:

- Flight segments that connect a set of cities
- Hyperlinks between Web pages
- Telephone calling patterns
- State transition diagrams

Two types of nodes are of particular interest in directed graphs. All the edges connected to a *source node* are outgoing edges. Since there are no incoming edges, no path exists from any other node in the graph to any of the source nodes. When all the edges on a node are incoming edges, the node is called a *sink node*. The existence of source nodes and sink nodes is an important difference between directed graphs and their undirected cousins.

An important property of directed graphs is whether the graph contains any paths that start and end at the same vertex. Such a path is called a *cycle*, implying that the path could repeat itself endlessly: ABCABCABC and so on. If a directed graph contains at least one cycle, it is called *cyclic*. Cycles in a graph of flight segments, for instance, might be the path of a single airplane. In a call graph, members of a cycle call each other—these are good candidates for a "friends and family–style" promotion, where the whole group gets a discount, or for marketing conference call services.

## Detecting Cycles in a Graph

There is a simple algorithm to detect whether a directed graph has any cycles. This algorithm starts with the observation that if a directed graph has no sink vertices, and it has at least one edge, then any path can be extended arbitrarily. Without any sink vertices, the terminating node of a path is always connected to another node, so the path can be extended by appending that node. Similarly, if the graph has no source nodes, then we can always prepend a node to the beginning of the path. Once the path contains more nodes than there are nodes in the graph, we know that the path must visit at least one node twice. Call this node X. The portion of the path between the first X and the second X in the path is a cycle, so the graph is cyclic.

Now consider the case when a graph has one or more source nodes and one or more sink nodes. It is pretty obvious that source nodes and sink nodes cannot be part of a cycle. Removing the source and sink nodes from the graph, along with all their edges, does not affect whether the graph is cyclic. If the resulting graph has no sink nodes or no source nodes, then it contains a cycle, as just shown. The process of removing sink nodes, source nodes, and their edges is repeated until one of the following occurs:

- No more edges or no more nodes are left. In this case, the graph has no cycles.

- Some edges remain but there are no source or sink nodes. In this case, the graph is cyclic.

If no cycles exist, then the graph is called an *acyclic graph*. These graphs are useful for describing dependencies or one-way relationships between things. For instance, different products often belong to nested hierarchies that can be represented by acyclic graphs. The decision trees described in Chapter 6 are another example.

In an acyclic graph, any two nodes have a well-defined precedence relationship with each other. If node A precedes node B in some path that contains both A and B, then A will precede B in all paths containing both A and B (otherwise there would be a cycle). In this case, we say that A is a *predecessor* of B and that B is a *successor* of A. If no paths contain both A and B, then A and B are *disjoint*. This strict ordering can be an important property of the nodes and is sometimes useful for data mining purposes.

# A Familiar Application of Link Analysis

Most readers of this book have probably used the Google search engine. Its phenomenal popularity stems from its ability to help people find reasonably good material on pretty much any subject. This feat is accomplished through link analysis.

The World Wide Web is a huge directed graph. The nodes are Web pages and the edges are the hyperlinks between them. Special programs called *spiders* or *web crawlers* are continually traversing these links to update maps of the huge directed graph that is the web. Some of these spiders simply index the content of Web pages for use by purely text-based search engines. Others record the Web's global structure as a directed graph that can be used for analysis.

Once upon a time, search engines analyzed only the nodes of this graph. Text from a query was compared with text from the Web pages using techniques similar to those described in Chapter 8. Google's approach (which has now been adopted by other search engines) is to make use of the information encoded in the *edges* of the graph as well as the information found in the *nodes*.

## The Kleinberg Algorithm

Some Web sites or magazine articles are more interesting than others even if they are devoted to the same topic. This simple idea is easy to grasp but hard to explain to a computer. So when a search is performed on a topic that many people write about, it is hard to find the most interesting or authoritative documents in the huge collection that satisfies the search criteria.

Professor Jon Kleinberg of Cornell University came up with one widely adopted technique for addressing this problem. His approach takes advantage of the insight that in creating a link from one site to another, a human being is making a judgment about the value of the site being linked to. Each link to another site is effectively a recommendation of that site. Cumulatively, the independent judgments of many Web site designers who all decide to provide links to the same target are conferring authority on that target. Furthermore, the reliability of the sites making the link can be judged according to the authoritativeness of the sites they link to. The recommendations of a site with many other good recommendations can be given more weight in determining the authority of another.

In Kleinberg's terminology, a page that links to many authorities is a *hub*; a page that is linked to by many hubs is an *authority*. These ideas are illustrated in Figure 10.7 The two concepts can be used together to tell the difference between authority and mere popularity. At first glance, it might seem that a good method for finding authoritative Web sites would be to rank them by the number of unrelated sites linking to them. The problem with this technique is that any time the topic is mentioned, even in passing, by a popular site (one with many inbound links), it will be ranked higher than a site that is much more authoritative on the particular subject though less popular in general. The solution is to rank pages, not by the total number of links pointing to them, but by the number of subject-related hubs that point to them. Google.com uses a modified and enhanced version of the basic Kleinberg algorithm described here.

A search based on link analysis begins with an ordinary text-based search. This initial search provides a pool of pages (often a couple hundred) with which to start the process. It is quite likely that the set of documents returned by such a search does not include the documents that a human reader would judge to be the most authoritative sources on the topic. That is because the most authoritative sources on a topic are not necessarily the ones that use the words in the search string most frequently. Kleinberg uses the example of a search on the keyword "Harvard." Most people would agree that www.harvard.edu is one of the most authoritative sites on this topic, but in a purely content-based analysis, it does not stand out among the more than a million Web pages containing the word "Harvard" so it is quite likely that a text-based search will not return the university's own Web site among its top results. It is very likely, however, that at least a few of the documents returned will contain a link to Harvard's home page or, failing that, that some page that points to one of the pages in the pool of pages will also point to www.harvard.edu.

An essential feature of Kleinberg's algorithm is that it does not simply take the pages returned by the initial text-based search and attempt to rank them; it uses them to construct the much larger pool of documents that point to or are pointed to by any of the documents in the root set. This larger pool contains much more global structure—structure that can be mined to determine which documents are considered to be most authoritative by the wide community of people who created the documents in the pool.

## The Details: Finding Hubs and Authorities

Kleinberg's algorithm for identifying authoritative sources has three phases:

1. Creating the root set
2. Identifying the candidates
3. Ranking hubs and authorities

In the first phase, a *root set* of pages is formed using a text-based search engine to find pages containing the search string. In the second phase, this root set is expanded to include documents that point to or are pointed to by documents in the root set. This expanded set contains the *candidates*. In the third phase, which is iterative, the candidates are ranked according to their strength as *hubs* (documents that have links to many authoritative documents) and *authorities* (pages that have links from many authoritative hubs).

### Creating the Root Set

The root set of documents is generated using a content-based search. As a first step, *stop words* (common words such as "a," "an," "the," and so on) are removed from the original search string supplied. Then, depending on the particular content-based search strategy employed, the remaining search terms may undergo *stemming*. Stemming reduces words to their root form by removing plural forms and other endings due to verb conjugation, noun declension, and so on. Then, the Web index is searched for documents containing the terms in the search string. There are many variations on the details of how matches are evaluated, which is one reason why performing the same search on two text-based search engines yields different results. In any case, some combination of the number of matching terms, the rarity of the terms matched, and the number of times the search terms are mentioned in a document is used to give the indexed documents a score that determines their rank in relation to the query. The top $n$ documents are used to establish the root set. A typical value for $n$ is 200.

### Identifying the Candidates

In the second phase, the root set is expanded to create the set of candidates. The candidate set includes all pages that any page in the root set *links to* along with a subset of the pages that *link to* any page in the root set. Locating pages that link to a particular target page is simple if the global structure of the Web is available as a directed graph. The same task can also be accomplished with an index-based text search using the URL of the target page as the search string.

The reason for using only a subset of the pages that link to each page in the root set is to guard against the possibility of an extremely popular site in the root set bringing in an unmanageable number of pages. There is also a parameter $d$ that limits the number of pages that may be brought into the candidate set by any single member of the root set.

If more than $d$ documents link to a particular document in the root set, then an arbitrary subset of $d$ documents is brought into the candidate set. A typical value for $d$ is 50. The candidate set typically ends up containing 1,000 to 5,000 documents.

This basic algorithm can be refined in various ways. One possible refinement, for instance, is to filter out any links from within the same domain, many of which are likely to be purely navigational. Another refinement is to allow a document in the root set to bring in at most $m$ pages from the same site. This is to avoid being fooled by "collusion" between all the pages of a site to, for example, advertise the site of the Web site designer with a "this site designed by" link on every page.

### Ranking Hubs and Authorities

The final phase is to divide the candidate pages into hubs and authorities and rank them according to their strength in those roles. This process also has the effect of grouping together pages that refer to the same meaning of a search term with multiple meanings—for instance, Madonna the rock star versus the *Madonna and Child* in art history or Jaguar the car versus jaguar the big cat. It also differentiates between authorities on the topic of interest and sites that are simply popular in general. Authoritative pages on the correct topic are not only linked to by many pages, they tend to be linked to by the *same* pages. It is these hub pages that tie together the authorities and distinguish them from unrelated but popular pages. Figure 10.7 illustrates the difference between hubs, authorities, and unrelated popular pages.

Hubs and authorities have a mutually reinforcing relationship. A strong hub is one that links to many strong authorities; a strong authority is one that is linked to by many strong hubs. The algorithm therefore proceeds iteratively, first adjusting the strength rating of the authorities based on the strengths of the hubs that link to them and then adjusting the strengths of the hubs based on the strength of the authorities to which they link.

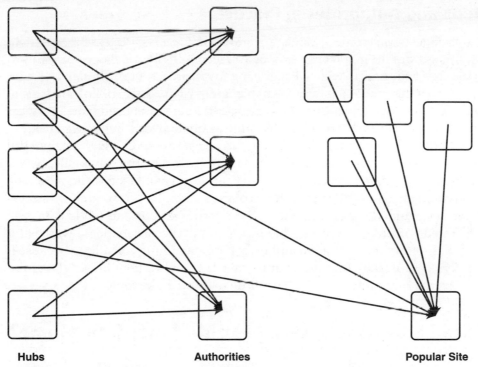

Hubs                    Authorities                    Popular Site

**Figure 10.7**  Google uses link analysis to distinguish hubs, authorities, and popular pages.

For each page, there is a value $A$ that measures its strength as an authority and a value $H$ that measures its strength as a hub. Both these values are initialized to 1 for all pages. Then, the $A$ value for each page is updated by adding up the $H$ values of all the pages that link to them. The $A$ values for each page are then normalized so that the sum of their squares is equal to 1. Then the $H$ values are updated in a similar manner. The $H$ value for each page is set to the sum of the $A$ values of the pages it links to, and the new $H$ values are normalized so that the sum of their squares is equal to 1. This process is repeated until an equilibrium set of $A$ and $H$ values is reached. The pages that end up with the highest $H$ values are the strongest hubs; those with the strongest $A$ values are the strongest authorities.

The authorities returned by this application of link analysis tend to be strong examples of one particular possible meaning of the search string. A search on a contentious topic such as "gay marriage" or "Taiwan independence" yields strong authorities on both sides because the global structure of the Web includes tightly connected subgraphs representing documents maintained by like-minded authors.

## Hubs and Authorities in Practice

The strongest case for the advantage of adding link analysis to text-based searching comes from the market place. Google, a search engine developed at Stanford by Sergey Brin and Lawrence Page using an approach very similar to Kleinberg's, was the first of the major search engines to make use of link analysis to find hubs and authorities. It quickly surpassed long-entrenched search services such as AltaVista and Yahoo! The reason was qualitatively better searches.

The authors noticed that something was special about Google back in April of 2001 when we studied the web logs from our company's site, www.data-miners.com. At that time, industry surveys gave Google and AltaVista approximately equal 10 percent shares of the market for web searches, and yet Google accounted for 30 percent of the referrals to our site while AltaVista accounted for only 3 percent. This is apparently because Google was better able to recognize our site as an authority for data mining consulting because it was less confused by the large number of sites that use the phrase "data mining" even though they actually have little to do with the topic.

# Case Study: Who Is Using Fax Machines from Home?

Graphs appear in data from other industries as well. Mobile, local, and long-distance telephone service providers have records of every telephone call that their customers make and receive. This data contains a wealth of information about the behavior of their customers: when they place calls, who calls them, whether they benefit from their calling plan, to name a few. As this case study shows, link analysis can be used to analyze the records of local telephone calls to identify which residential customers have a high probability of having fax machines in their home.

## Why Finding Fax Machines Is Useful

What is the use of knowing who owns a fax machine? How can a telephone provider act on this information? In this case, the provider had developed a package of services for residential work-at-home customers. Targeting such customers for marketing purposes was a revolutionary concept at the company. In the tightly regulated local phone market of not so long ago, local service providers lost revenue from work-at-home customers, because these customers could have been paying higher business rates instead of lower residential rates. Far from targeting such customers for marketing campaigns, the local telephone providers would deny such customers residential rates—punishing them for behaving like a small business. For this company, developing and selling work-at-home packages represented a new foray into customer service. One question remained. Which customers should be targeted for the new package?

There are many approaches to defining the target set of customers. The company could effectively use neighborhood demographics, household surveys, estimates of computer ownership by zip code, and similar data. Although this data improves the definition of a market segment, it is still far from identifying individual customers with particular needs. A team, including one of the authors, suggested that the ability to find residential fax machine usage would improve this marketing effort, since fax machines are often (but not always) used for business purposes. Knowing who uses a fax machine would help target the work-at-home package to a very well-defined market segment, and this segment should have a better response rate than a segment defined by less precise segmentation techniques based on statistical properties.

Customers with fax machines offer other opportunities as well. Customers that are sending and receiving faxes should have at least two lines—if they only have one, there is an opportunity to sell them a second line. To provide better customer service, the customers who use faxes on a line with call waiting should know how to turn off call waiting to avoid annoying interruptions on fax transmissions. There are other possibilities as well: perhaps owners of fax machines would prefer receiving their monthly bills by fax instead of by mail, saving both postage and printing costs. In short, being able to identify who is sending or receiving faxes from home is valuable information that provides opportunities for increasing revenues, reducing costs, and increasing customer satisfaction.

## The Data as a Graph

The raw data used for this analysis was composed of selected fields from the call detail data fed into the billing system to generate monthly bills. Each record contains 80 bytes of data, with information such as:

- The 10-digit telephone number that originated the call, three digits for the area code, three digits for the exchange, and four digits for the line
- The 10-digit telephone number of the line where the call terminated
- The 10-digit telephone number of the line being billed for the call
- The date and time of the call
- The duration of the call
- The day of the week when the call was placed
- Whether the call was placed at a pay phone

In the graph in Figure 10.8, the data has been narrowed to just three fields: duration, originating number, and terminating number. The telephone numbers are the nodes of the graph, and the calls themselves are the edges, weighted by the duration of the calls. A sample of telephone calls is shown in Table 10.1.

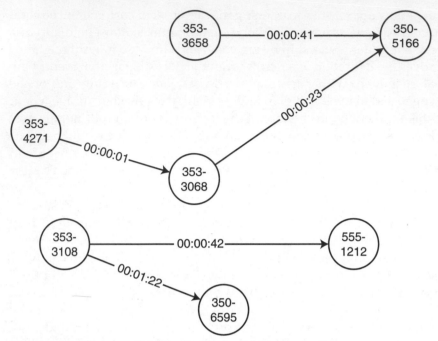

**Figure 10.8** Five calls link together seven telephone numbers.

**Table 10.1** Five Telephone Calls

| ID | ORIGINATING NUMBER | TERMINATING NUMBER | DURATION |
|---|---|---|---|
| 1 | 353-3658 | 350-5166 | 00:00:41 |
| 2 | 353-3068 | 350-5166 | 00:00:23 |
| 3 | 353-4271 | 353-3068 | 00:00:01 |
| 4 | 353-3108 | 555-1212 | 00:00:42 |
| 5 | 353-3108 | 350-6595 | 00:01:22 |

## The Approach

Finding fax machines is based on a simple observation: Fax machines tend to call other fax machines. A set of known fax numbers can be expanded based on the calls made to or received from the known numbers. If an unclassified telephone number calls known fax numbers and doesn't hang up quickly, then there is evidence that it can be classified as a fax number. This simple characterization is good for guidance, but it is an oversimplification. There are actually several types of expected fax machine usage for residential customers:

- *Dedicated fax.* Some fax machines are on dedicated lines, and the line is used only for fax communication.
- *Shared.* Some fax machines share their line with voice calls.
- *Data.* Some fax machines are on lines dedicated to data use, either via fax or via computer modem.

> **TIP** Characterizing expected behavior is a good way to start any directed data mining problem. The better the problem is understood, the better the results are likely to be.

The presumption that fax machines call other fax machines is generally true for machines on dedicated lines, although wrong numbers provide exceptions even to this rule. To distinguish shared lines from dedicated or data lines, we assumed that any number that calls information—411 or 555-1212 (directory assistance services)—is used for voice communications, and is therefore a voice line or a shared fax line. For instance, call #4 in the example data contains a call to 555-1212, signifying that the calling number is likely to be a shared line or just a voice line. When a shared line calls another number, there is no way to know if the call is voice or data. We cannot identify fax machines based on calls to and from such a node in the call graph. On the other hand, these shared lines do represent a marketing opportunity to sell additional lines.

The process used to find fax machines consisted of the following steps:

1. Start with a set of known fax machines (gathered from the *Yellow Pages*).
2. Determine all the numbers that make or receive calls to or from any number in this set where the call's duration was longer than 10 seconds. These numbers are candidates.
   - If the candidate number has called 411, 555-1212, or a number identified as a shared fax number, then it is included in the set of shared voice/fax numbers.
   - Otherwise, it is included in the set of known fax machines.
3. Repeat Steps 1 and 2 until no more numbers are identified.

One of the challenges was identifying wrong numbers. In particular, incoming calls to a fax machine may sometimes represent a wrong number and give no information about the originating number (actually, if it is a wrong number then it is probably a voice line). We made the assumption that such incoming wrong numbers would last a very short time, as is the case with Call #3. In a larger-scale analysis of fax machines, it would be useful to eliminate other anomalies, such as outgoing wrong numbers and modem/fax usage.

The process starts with an initial set of fax numbers. Since this was a demonstration project, several fax numbers were gathered manually from the *Yellow Pages* based on the annotation "fax" by the number. For a larger-scale project, all fax numbers could be retrieved from the database used to generate the *Yellow Pages*. These numbers are only the beginning, the seeds, of the list of fax machine telephone numbers. Although it is common for businesses to advertise their fax numbers, this is not so common for fax machines at home.

## Some Results

The sample of telephone records consisted of 3,011,819 telephone calls made over one month by 19,674 households. In the world of telephony, this is a very small sample of data, but it was sufficient to demonstrate the power of link analysis. The analysis was performed using special-purpose C++ code that stored the call detail and allowed us to expand a list of fax machines efficiently.

Finding the fax machines is an example of a *graph-coloring algorithm*. This type of algorithm walks through the graph and label nodes with different "colors." In this case, the colors are "fax," "shared," "voice," and "unknown" instead of red, green, yellow, and blue. Initially, all the nodes are "unknown" except for the few labeled "fax" from the starting set. As the algorithm proceeds, more and more nodes with the "unknown" label are given more informative labels.

Figure 10.9 shows a call graph with 15 numbers and 19 calls. The weights on the edges are the duration of each call in seconds. Nothing is really known about the specific numbers.

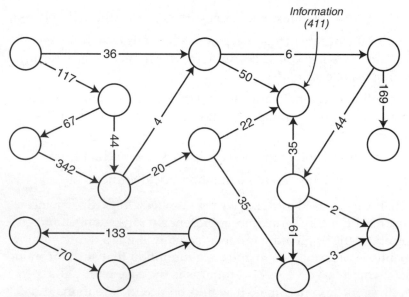

**Figure 10.9**    A call graph for 15 numbers and 19 calls.

Figure 10.10 shows how the algorithm proceeds. First, the numbers that are known to be fax machines are labeled "F," and the numbers for directory assistance are labeled "I." Any edge for a call that lasted less than 10 seconds has been dropped. The algorithm colors the graph by assigning labels to each node using an iterative procedure:

- Any "voice" node connected to a "fax" node is labeled "shared."
- Any "unknown" node connected mostly to "fax" nodes is labeled "fax."

This procedure continues until all nodes connected to "fax" nodes have a "fax" or "shared" label.

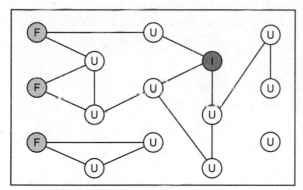

This is the initial call graph with short calls removed and with nodes labeled as "fax," "unknown," and "information."

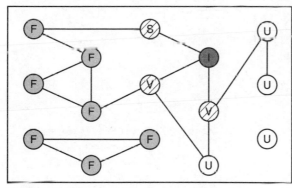

Nodes connected to the initial fax machines are assigned the "fax" label.

Those connected to "information" are assigned the "voice" label.

Those connected to both, are "shared."

The rest are "unknown."

**Figure 10.10** Applying the graph-coloring algorithm to the call graph shows which numbers are fax numbers and which are shared.

## USING SQL TO COLOR A GRAPH

Although the case study implemented the graph coloring using special-purpose C++ code, these operations are suitable for data stored in a relational database. Assume that there are three tables: call_detail, dedicated_fax, and shared_fax. The query for finding the numbers that call a known fax number is:

```
SELECT originating_number
FROM call_detail
WHERE terminating_number IN (SELECT number FROM dedicated_fax)
 AND duration >= 10
GROUP BY originating_number;
```

A similar query can be used to get the calls made by a known fax number. However, this does not yet distinguish between dedicated fax lines and shared fax lines. To do this, we have to know if any calls were made to information. For efficiency reasons, it is best to keep this list in a separate table or view, voice_numbers, defined by:

```
SELECT originating_number
FROM call_detail
WHERE terminating_number in ('5551212', '411')
GROUP BY originating_number;
```

So the query to find dedicated fax lines is:

```
SELECT originating_number
FROM call_detail
WHERE terminating_number IN (SELECT number FROM dedicated_fax)
 AND duration > 9
 AND originating_number NOT IN (SELECT number FROM voice_numbers)
GROUP BY originating_number;
```

and for shared lines it is:

```
SELECT originating_number
FROM call_detail
WHERE terminating_number IN (SELECT number FROM dedicated_fax)
 AND duration > 2
 AND originating_number IN (SELECT number FROM voice_numbers)
GROUP BY originating_number;
```

These SQL queries are intended to show that finding fax machines is possible on a relational database. They are probably not the most efficient SQL statements for this purpose, depending on the layout of the data, the database engine, and the hardware it is running on. Also, if there is a significant number of calls in the database, any SQL queries for link analysis will require joins on very large tables.

# Case Study: Segmenting Cellular Telephone Customers

This case study applies link analysis to cellular telephone calls for the purpose of segmenting existing customers for selling new services.[1] Analyses similar to those presented here were used with a leading cellular provider. The results from the analysis were used for a direct mailing for a new product offering. On such mailings, the cellular company typically measured a response rate of 2 percent to 3 percent. With some of the ideas presented here, it increased its response rate to over 15 percent, a very significant improvement.

## The Data

Cellular telephone data is similar to the call detail data seen in the previous case study for finding fax machines. There is a record for each call that includes fields such as:

- Originating number
- Terminating number
- Location where the call was placed
- Account number of the person who originated the call
- Call duration
- Time and date

Although the analysis did not use the account number, it plays an important role in this data because the data did not otherwise distinguish between business and residential accounts. Accounts for larger businesses have thousands of phones, while most residential accounts have only a single phone.

## Analyses without Graph Theory

Prior to using link analysis, the marketing department used a single measurement for segmentation: minutes of use (MOU), which is the number of minutes each month that a customer uses on the cellular phone. MOU is a useful measure, since there is a direct correlation between MOU and the amount billed to the customer each month. This correlation is not exact, since it does not take into account discount periods and calling plans that offer free nights and weekends, but it is a good guide nonetheless.

The marketing group also had external demographic data for prospective customers. They could also distinguish between individual customers and business accounts. In addition to MOU, though, their only understanding of

---

[1] The authors would like to thank their colleagues Alan Parker, William Crowder, and Ravi Basawi for their contributions to this section.

customer behavior was the total amount billed and whether customers paid the bills in a timely matter. They were leaving a lot of information on the table.

## A Comparison of Two Customers

Figure 10.11 illustrates two customers and their calling patterns during a typical month. These two customers have similar MOU, yet the patterns are strikingly different. John's calls generate a small, tight graph, while Jane's explodes with many different calls. If Jane is happy with her wireless service, her use will likely grow and she might even influence many of her friends and colleagues to switch to the wireless provider.

Looking at these two customers more closely reveals important differences. Although John racks up 150 to 200 MOU every month on his car phone, his use of his mobile telephone consists almost exclusively of two types of calls:

- On his way home from work, he calls his wife to let her know what time to expect him. Sometimes they chat for three or four minutes.

- Every Wednesday morning, he has a 45-minute conference call that he takes in the car on his morning commute.

The only person who has John's car phone number is his wife, and she rarely calls him when he is driving. In fact, John has another mobile phone that he carries with him for business purposes. When driving, he prefers his car phone to his regular portable phone, although his car phone service provider does not know this.

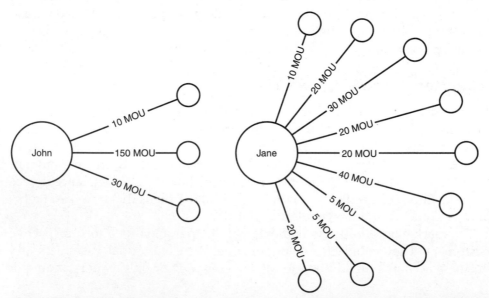

**Figure 10.11** John and Jane have about the same minutes of use each month, but their behavior is quite different.

Jane also racks up about the same usage every month on her mobile phone. She has four salespeople reporting to her that call her throughout the day, often leaving messages on her mobile phone voice mail when they do not reach her in the car. Her calls include calls to management, potential customers, and other colleagues. Her calls, though, are always quite short— almost always a minute or two, since she is usually scheduling meetings. Working in a small business, she is sensitive to privacy and to the cost of the calls so out of habit uses land lines for longer discussions.

Now, what happens if Jane and John both get an offer from a competitor? Who is more likely to accept the competing offer (or *churn* in the vocabulary of wireless telecommunications companies)? At first glance, we might suspect that Jane is the more price-sensitive and therefore the more susceptible to another offer. However, a second look reveals that if changing carriers would require her to change her telephone number it would be a big inconvenience for Jane. (In the United States, number portability has been a long time coming. It finally arrived in November 2003, shortly before this edition was published, perhaps invalidating many existing churn models.) By looking at the number of different people who call her, we see that Jane is quite dependent on her wireless telephone number; she uses features like voicemail and stores important numbers in her cell phone. The number of people she would have to notify is inertia that keeps her from changing providers. John has no such inertia and might have no allegiance to his wireless provider—as long as a competing provider can provide uninterrupted service for his 45-minute call on Wednesday mornings.

Jane also has a lot of *influence*. Since she talks to so many different people, they will all know if she is satisfied or dissatisfied with her service. She is a customer that the cellular company wants to keep happy. But, she is not a customer that traditional methods of segmentation would have located.

## The Power of Link Analysis

Link analysis is played two roles in this analysis of cellular phone data. The first was visualization. The ability to see some of the graphs representing call patterns makes patterns for things like inertia or influence much more obvious. Visualizing the data makes it possible to see patterns that lead to further questions. For this example, we chose two profitable customers considered similar by previous segmentation techniques. Link analysis showed their specific calling patterns and suggested how the customers differ. On the other hand, looking at the call patterns for all customers at the same time would require drawing a graph with hundreds of thousands or millions of nodes and hundreds of millions of edges.

Second, link analysis can apply the concepts generated by visualization to larger sets of customers. For instance, a churn reduction program might avoid targeting customers who have high inertia or be sure to target customers with high influence. This requires traversing the call graph to calculate the inertia or influence for all customers. Such derived characteristics can play an important role in marketing efforts.

Different marketing programs might suggest looking for other features in the call graph. For instance, perhaps the ability to place a conference call would be desirable, but who would be the best prospects? One idea would be to look for groups of customers that all call each other. Stated as a graph problem, this group is a fully connected subgraph. In the telephone industry, these subgraphs are called "communities of interest." A community of interest may represent a group of customers who would be interested in the ability to place conference calls.

## Lessons Learned

Link analysis is an application of the mathematical field of graph theory. As a data mining technique, link analysis has several strengths:

- It capitalizes on relationships.
- It is useful for visualization.
- It creates derived characteristics that can be used for further mining.

Some data and data mining problems naturally involve links. As the two case studies about telephone data show, link analysis is very useful for telecommunications—a telephone call is a link between two people. Opportunities for link analysis are most obvious in fields where the links are obvious such as telephony, transportation, and the World Wide Web. Link analysis is also appropriate in other areas where the connections do not have such a clear manifestation, such as physician referral patterns, retail sales data, and forensic analysis for crimes.

Links are a very natural way to visualize some types of data. Direct visualization of the links can be a big aid to knowledge discovery. Even when automated patterns are found, visualization of the links helps to better understand what is happening. Link analysis offers an alternative way of looking at data, different from the formats of relational databases and OLAP tools. Links may suggest important patterns in the data, but the significance of the patterns requires a person for interpretation.

Link analysis can lead to new and useful data attributes. Examples include calculating an authority score for a page on the World Wide Web and calculating the sphere of influence for a telephone user.

Although link analysis is very powerful when applicable, it is not appropriate for all types of problems. It is not a prediction tool or classification tool like a neural network that takes data in and produces an answer. Many types of data are simply not appropriate for link analysis. Its strongest use is probably in finding specific patterns, such as the types of outgoing calls, which can then be applied to data. These patterns can be turned into new features of the data, for use in conjunction with other directed data mining techniques.

# CHAPTER 11

# Automatic Cluster Detection

The data mining techniques described in this book are used to find meaningful patterns in data. These patterns are not always immediately forthcoming. Sometimes this is because there are no patterns to be found. Other times, the problem is not the lack of patterns, but the excess. The data may contain so much complex structure that even the best data mining techniques are unable to coax out meaningful patterns. When mining such a database for the answer to some specific question, competing explanations tend to cancel each other out. As with radio reception, too many competing signals add up to noise. Clustering provides a way to learn about the structure of complex data, to break up the cacophony of competing signals into its components.

When human beings try to make sense of complex questions, our natural tendency is to break the subject into smaller pieces, each of which can be explained more simply. If someone were asked to describe the color of trees in the forest, the answer would probably make distinctions between deciduous trees and evergreens, and between winter, spring, summer, and fall. People know enough about woodland flora to predict that, of all the hundreds of variables associated with the forest, season and foliage type, rather than say age and height, are the best factors to use for forming clusters of trees that follow similar coloration rules.

Once the proper clusters have been defined, it is often possible to find simple patterns within each cluster. "In Winter, deciduous trees have no leaves so the trees tend to be brown" or "The leaves of deciduous trees change color in the autumn, typically to oranges, reds, and yellows." In many cases, a very noisy dataset is actually composed of a number of better-behaved clusters. The question is: how can these be found? That is where techniques for automatic cluster detection come in—to help see the forest without getting lost in the trees.

This chapter begins with two examples of the usefulness of clustering—one drawn from astronomy, another from clothing design. It then introduces the K-Means clustering algorithm which, like the nearest neighbor techniques discussed in Chapter 8, depends on a geometric interpretation of data. The geometric ideas used in K-Means bring up the more general topic of measures of similarity, association, and distance. These distance measures are quite sensitive to variations in how data is represented, so the next topic addressed is data preparation for clustering, with special attention being paid to scaling and weighting. K-Means is not the only algorithm in common use for automatic cluster detection. This chapter contains brief discussions of several others: Gaussian mixture models, agglomerative clustering, and divisive clustering. (Another clustering technique, self-organizing maps, is covered in Chapter 7 because self-organizing maps are a form of neural network.) The chapter concludes with a case study in which automatic cluster detection is used to evaluate editorial zones for a major daily newspaper.

## Searching for Islands of Simplicity

In Chapter 1, where data mining techniques are classified as directed or undirected, automatic cluster detection is described as a tool for undirected knowledge discovery. In the technical sense, that is true because the automatic cluster detection algorithms themselves are simply finding structure that exists in the data without regard to any particular target variable. Most data mining tasks start out with a preclassified training set, which is used to develop a model capable of scoring or classifying previously unseen records. In clustering, there is no preclassified data and no distinction between independent and dependent variables. Instead, clustering algorithms search for groups of records—the clusters—composed of records similar to each other. The algorithms discover these similarities. It is up to the people running the analysis to determine whether similar records represent something of interest to the business—or something inexplicable and perhaps unimportant.

In a broader sense, however, clustering can be a directed activity because clusters are sought for some business purpose. In marketing, clusters formed for a business purpose are usually called "segments," and customer segmentation is a popular application of clustering.

Automatic cluster detection is a data mining technique that is rarely used in isolation because finding clusters is not often an end in itself. Once clusters have been detected, other methods must be applied in order to figure out what the clusters mean. When clustering is successful, the results can be dramatic: One famous early application of cluster detection led to our current understanding of stellar evolution.

## Star Light, Star Bright

Early in the twentieth century, astronomers trying to understand the relationship between the luminosity (brightness) of stars and their temperatures, made scatter plots like the one in Figure 11.1. The vertical scale measures luminosity in multiples of the brightness of our own sun. The horizontal scale measures surface temperature in degrees Kelvin (degrees centigrade above absolute 0, the theoretical coldest possible temperature).

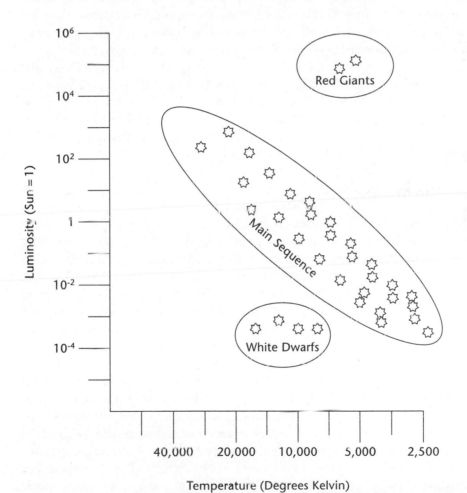

**Figure 11.1** The Hertzsprung-Russell diagram clusters stars by temperature and luminosity.

Two different astronomers, Enjar Hertzsprung in Denmark and Norris Russell in the United States, thought of doing this at about the same time. They both observed that in the resulting scatter plot, the stars fall into three clusters. This observation led to further work and the understanding that these three clusters represent stars in very different phases of the stellar life cycle. The relationship between luminosity and temperature is consistent within each cluster, but the relationship is different between the clusters because fundamentally different processes are generating the heat and light. The 80 percent of stars that fall on the main sequence are generating energy by converting hydrogen to helium through nuclear fusion. This is how all stars spend most of their active life. After some number of billions of years, the hydrogen is used up. Depending on its mass, the star then begins fusing helium or the fusion stops. In the latter case, the core of the star collapses, generating a great deal of heat in the process. At the same time, the outer layer of gasses expands away from the core, and a red giant is formed. Eventually, the outer layer of gasses is stripped away, and the remaining core begins to cool. The star is now a white dwarf.

A recent search on Google using the phrase "Hertzsprung-Russell Diagram" returned thousands of pages of links to current astronomical research based on cluster detection of this kind. Even today, clusters based on the HR diagram are being used to hunt for brown dwarfs (starlike objects that lack sufficient mass to initiate nuclear fusion) and to understand pre–main sequence stellar evolution.

## Fitting the Troops

The Hertzsprung-Russell diagram is a good introductory example of clustering because with only two variables, it is easy to spot the clusters visually (and, incidentally, it is a good example of the importance of good data visualizations). Even in three dimensions, picking out clusters by eye from a scatter plot cube is not too difficult. If all problems had so few dimensions, there would be no need for automatic cluster detection algorithms. As the number of dimensions (independent variables) increases, it becomes increasing difficult to visualize clusters. Our intuition about how close things are to each other also quickly breaks down with more dimensions.

Saying that a problem has many dimensions is an invitation to analyze it geometrically. A *dimension* is each of the things that must be measured independently in order to describe something. In other words, if there are N variables, imagine a space in which the value of each variable represents a distance along the corresponding axis in an N-dimensional space. A single record containing a value for each of the N variables can be thought of as the vector that defines a particular point in that space. When there are two dimensions, this is easily plotted. The HR diagram was one such example. Figure 11.2 is another example that plots the height and weight of a group of teenagers as points on a graph. Notice the clustering of boys and girls.

The chart in Figure 11.2 begins to give a rough idea of people's shapes. But if the goal is to fit them for clothes, a few more measurements are needed! In the 1990s, the U.S. army commissioned a study on how to redesign the uniforms of female soldiers. The army's goal was to reduce the number of different uniform sizes that have to be kept in inventory, while still providing each soldier with well-fitting uniforms.

As anyone who has ever shopped for women's clothing is aware, there is already a surfeit of classification systems (even sizes, odd sizes, plus sizes, junior, petite, and so on) for categorizing garments by size. None of these systems was designed with the needs of the U.S. military in mind. Susan Ashdown and Beatrix Paal, researchers at Cornell University, went back to the basics; they designed a new set of sizes based on the actual shapes of women in the army.[1]

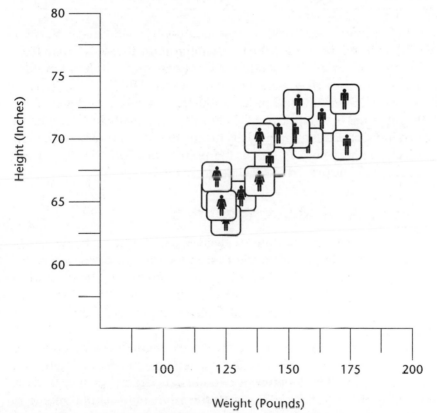

**Figure 11.2**  Heights and weights of a group of teenagers.

[1] Ashdown, Susan P. 1998. "An Investigation of the Structure of Sizing Systems: A Comparison of Three Multidimensional Optimized Sizing Systems Generated from Anthropometric Data," International Journal of Clothing Science and Technology. Vol. 10, #5, pp 324-341.

Unlike the traditional clothing size systems, the one Ashdown and Paal came up with is not an ordered set of graduated sizes where all dimensions increase together. Instead, they came up with sizes that fit particular body types. Each body type corresponds to a cluster of records in a database of body measurements. One cluster might consist of short-legged, small-waisted, large-busted women with long torsos, average arms, broad shoulders, and skinny necks while other clusters capture other constellations of measurements.

The database contained more than 100 measurements for each of nearly 3,000 women. The clustering technique employed was the K-means algorithm, described in the next section. In the end, only a handful of the more than 100 measurements were needed to characterize the clusters. Finding this smaller number of variables was another benefit of the clustering process.

# K-Means Clustering

The K-means algorithm is one of the most commonly used clustering algorithms. The "K" in its name refers to the fact that the algorithm looks for a fixed number of clusters which are defined in terms of proximity of data points to each other. The version described here was first published by J. B. MacQueen in 1967. For ease of explaining, the technique is illustrated using two-dimensional diagrams. Bear in mind that in practice the algorithm is usually handling many more than two independent variables. This means that instead of points corresponding to two-element vectors $(x_1, x_2)$, the points correspond to $n$-element vectors $(x_1, x_2, \ldots, x_n)$. The procedure itself is unchanged.

## Three Steps of the K-Means Algorithm

In the first step, the algorithm randomly selects K data points to be the seeds. MacQueen's algorithm simply takes the first K records. In cases where the records have some meaningful order, it may be desirable to choose widely spaced records, or a random selection of records. Each of the seeds is an embryonic cluster with only one element. This example sets the number of clusters to 3.

The second step assigns each record to the closest seed. One way to do this is by finding the boundaries between the clusters, as shown geometrically in Figure 11.3. The boundaries between two clusters are the points that are equally close to each cluster. Recalling a lesson from high-school geometry makes this less difficult than it sounds: given any two points, A and B, all points that are equidistant from A and B fall along a line (called the perpendicular bisector) that is perpendicular to the one connecting A and B and halfway between them. In Figure 11.3, dashed lines connect the initial seeds; the resulting cluster boundaries shown with solid lines are at right angles to the dashed lines. Using these lines as guides, it is obvious which records are closest to which seeds. In three dimensions, these boundaries would be planes and in $N$ dimensions they would be hyperplanes of dimension $N - 1$. Fortunately, computer algorithms easily handle these situations. Finding the actual boundaries between clusters is useful for showing the process geometrically. In practice, though, the algorithm usually measures the distance of each record to each seed and chooses the minimum distance for this step.

For example, consider the record with the box drawn around it. On the basis of the initial seeds, this record is assigned to the cluster controlled by seed number 2 because it is closer to that seed than to either of the other two.

At this point, every point has been assigned to exactly one of the three clusters centered around the original seeds. The third step is to calculate the centroids of the clusters; these now do a better job of characterizing the clusters than the initial seeds Finding the centroids is simply a matter of taking the average value of each dimension for all the records in the cluster.

In Figure 11.4, the new centroids are marked with a cross. The arrows show the motion from the position of the original seeds to the new centroids of the clusters formed from those seeds.

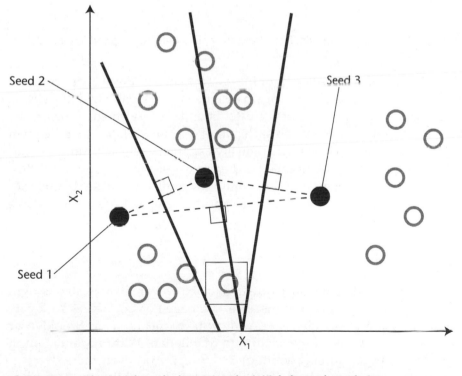

**Figure 11.3**  The initial seeds determine the initial cluster boundaries.

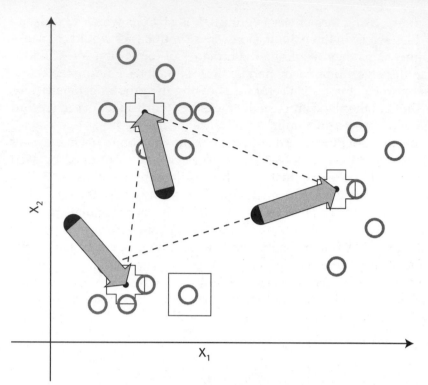

**Figure 11.4**  The centroids are calculated from the points that are assigned to each cluster.

The centroids become the seeds for the next iteration of the algorithm. Step 2 is repeated, and each point is once again assigned to the cluster with the closest centroid. Figure 11.5 shows the new cluster boundaries—formed, as before, by drawing lines equidistant between each pair of centroids. Notice that the point with the box around it, which was originally assigned to cluster number 2, has now been assigned to cluster number 1. The process of assigning points to cluster and then recalculating centroids continues until the cluster boundaries stop changing. In practice, the K-means algorithm usually finds a set of stable clusters after a few dozen iterations.

## What K Means

Clusters describe underlying structure in data. However, there is no one right description of that structure. For instance, someone not from New York City may think that the whole city is "downtown." Someone from Brooklyn or Queens might apply this nomenclature to Manhattan. Within Manhattan, it might only be neighborhoods south of 23rd Street. And even there, "downtown" might still be reserved only for the taller buildings at the southern tip of the island. There is a similar problem with clustering; structures in data exist at many different levels.

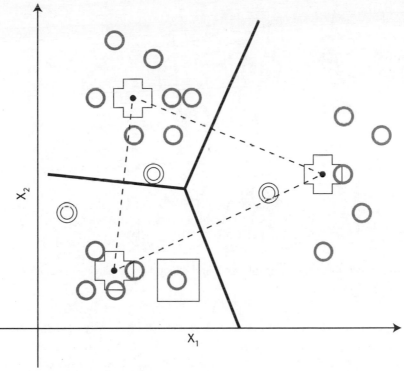

**Figure 11.5**   At each iteration, all cluster assignments are reevaluated.

Descriptions of K-means and related algorithms gloss over the selection of K. But since, in many cases, there is no a priori reason to select a particular value, there is really an outermost loop to these algorithms that occurs during analysis rather than in the computer program. This outer loop consists of performing automatic cluster detection using one value of K, evaluating the results, then trying again with another value of K or perhaps modifying the data. After each trial, the strength of the resulting clusters can be evaluated by comparing the average distance between records in a cluster with the average distance between clusters, and by other procedures described later in this chapter. These tests can be automated, but the clusters must also be evaluated on a more subjective basis to determine their usefulness for a given application. As shown in Figure 11.6, different values of K may lead to very different clusterings that are equally valid. The figure shows clusterings of a deck of playing cards for K = 2 and K = 4. Is one better than the other? It depends on the use to which the clusters will be put.

**Figure 11.6**   These examples of clusters of size 2 and 4 in a deck of playing cards illustrate that there is no one correct clustering.

Often the first time K-means clustering is run on a given set of data, most of the data points fall in one giant central cluster and there are a number of smaller clusters outside it. This is often because most records describe "normal" variations in the data, but there are enough outliers to confuse the clustering algorithm. This type of clustering may be valuable for applications such as identifying fraud or manufacturing defects. In other applications, it may be desirable to filter outliers from the data; more often, the solution is to massage the data values. Later in this chapter there is a section on data preparation for clustering which describes how to work with variables to make it easier to find meaningful clusters.

## Similarity and Distance

Once records in a database have been mapped to points in space, automatic cluster detection is really quite simple—a little geometry, some vector means, *et voilà*! The problem, of course, is that the databases encountered in marketing, sales, and customer support are not about points in space. They are about purchases, phone calls, airplane trips, car registrations, and a thousand other things that have no obvious connection to the dots in a cluster diagram.

Clustering records of this sort requires some notion of *natural association*; that is, records in a given cluster are more *similar* to each other than to records in another cluster. Since it is difficult to convey intuitive notions to a computer, this vague concept of association must be translated into some sort of numeric measure of the degree of similarity. The most common method, but by no means the only one, is to translate all fields into numeric values so that the records may be treated as points in space. Then, if two points are close in the geometric sense, they represent similar records in the database. There are two main problems with this approach:

- Many variable types, including all categorical variables and many numeric variables such as rankings, do not have the right behavior to properly be treated as components of a position vector.

- In geometry, the contributions of each dimension are of equal importance, but in databases, a small change in one field may be much more important than a large change in another field.

The following section introduces several alternative measures of similarity.

## Similarity Measures and Variable Type

Geometric distance works well as a similarity measure for well-behaved numeric variables. A well-behaved numeric variable is one whose value indicates its placement along the axis that corresponds to it in our geometric model. Not all variables fall into this category. For this purpose, variables fall into four classes, listed here in increasing order of suitability for the geometric model.

- Categorical variables
- Ranks
- Intervals
- True measures

*Categorical variables* only describe which of several unordered categories a thing belongs to. For instance, it is possible to label one ice cream pistachio and another butter pecan, but it is not possible to say that one is greater than the other or judge which one is closer to black cherry. In mathematical terms, it is possible to tell that $X \neq Y$, but not whether $X > Y$ or $X < Y$.

*Ranks* put things in order, but don't say how much bigger one thing is than another. The valedictorian has better grades than the salutatorian, but we don't know by how much. If $X$, $Y$, and $Z$ are ranked A, B, and C, we know that $X > Y > Z$, but we cannot define X-Y or Y-Z.

*Intervals* measure the distance between two observations. If it is 56° in San Francisco and 78° in San Jose, then it is 22 degrees warmer at one end of the bay than the other.

*True measures* are interval variables that measure from a meaningful zero point. This trait is important because it means that the ratio of two values of the variable is meaningful. The Fahrenheit temperature scale used in the United States and the Celsius scale used in most of the rest of the world do not have this property. In neither system does it make sense to say that a 30° day is twice as warm as a 15° day. Similarly, a size 12 dress is not twice as large as a size 6, and gypsum is not twice as hard as talc though they are 2 and 1 on the hardness scale. It does make perfect sense, however, to say that a 50-year-old is twice as old as a 25-year-old or that a 10-pound bag of sugar is twice as heavy as a 5-pound one. Age, weight, length, customer tenure, and volume are examples of true measures.

Geometric distance metrics are well-defined for interval variables and true measures. In order to use categorical variables and rankings, it is necessary to transform them into interval variables. Unfortunately, these transformations may add spurious information. If ice cream flavors are assigned arbitrary numbers 1 through 28, it will appear that flavors 5 and 6 are closely related while flavors 1 and 28 are far apart.

These and other data transformation and preparation issues are discussed extensively in Chapter 17.

## Formal Measures of Similarity

There are dozens if not hundreds of published techniques for measuring the similarity of two records. Some have been developed for specialized applications such as comparing passages of text. Others are designed especially for use with certain types of data such as binary variables or categorical variables. Of the three presented here, the first two are suitable for use with interval variables and true measures, while the third is suitable for categorical variables.

### Geometric Distance between Two Points

When the fields in a record are numeric, the record represents a point in n-dimensional space. The distance between the points represented by two records is used as the measure of similarity between them. If two points are close in distance, the corresponding records are similar.

There are many ways to measure the distance between two points, as discussed in the sidebar "Distance Metrics". The most common one is the Euclidian distance familiar from high-school geometry. To find the Euclidian distance between $X$ and $Y$, first find the differences between the corresponding elements of $X$ and $Y$ (the distance along each axis) and square them. The distance is the square root of the sum of the squared differences.

## DISTANCE METRICS

Any function that takes two points and produces a single number describing a relationship between them is a candidate measure of similarity, but to be a true distance metric, it must meet the following criteria:

- ◆ Distance$(X,Y) = 0$ if and only if $X = Y$
- ◆ Distance$(X,Y) \geq 0$ for all $X$ and all $Y$
- ◆ Distance$(X,Y) = $ Distance$(Y,X)$
- ◆ Distance$(X,Y) \leq $ Distance$(X,Z) + $ Distance$(Z,Y)$

These are the formal definition of a distance metric in geometry.

A true distance is a good metric for clustering, but some of these conditions can be relaxed. The most important conditions are the second and third (called identity and commutativity by mathematicians)—that the measure is 0 or positive and is well-defined for any two points. If two records have a distance of 0, that is okay, as long as they are very, very similar, since they will always fall into the same cluster.

The last condition, the Triangle Inequality, is perhaps the most interesting mathematically. In terms of clustering, it basically means that adding a new cluster center will not make two distant points suddenly seem close together. Fortunately, most metrics we could devise satisfy this condition.

## Angle between Two Vectors

Sometimes it makes more sense to consider two records closely associated because of similarities in the way the fields *within* each record are related. Minnows should cluster with sardines, cod, and tuna, while kittens cluster with cougars, lions, and tigers, even though in a database of body-part lengths, the sardine is closer to a kitten than it is to a catfish.

The solution is to use a different geometric interpretation of the same data. Instead of thinking of $X$ and $Y$ as points in space and measuring the distance between them, think of them as *vectors* and measure the *angle* between them. In this context, a vector is the line segment connecting the origin of a coordinate system to the point described by the vector values. A vector has both magnitude (the distance from the origin to the point) and direction. For this similarity measure, it is the direction that matters.

Take the values for length of whiskers, length of tail, overall body length, length of teeth, and length of claws for a lion and a house cat and plot them as single points, they will be very far apart. But if the ratios of lengths of these body parts to one another are similar in the two species, than the vectors will be nearly colinear.

The angle between vectors provides a measure of association that is not influenced by differences in magnitude between the two things being compared (see Figure 11.7). Actually, the sine of the angle is a better measure since it will range from 0 when the vectors are closest (most nearly parallel) to 1 when they are perpendicular. Using the sine ensures that an angle of 0 degrees is treated the same as an angle of 180 degrees, which is as it should be since for this measure, any two vectors that differ only by a constant factor are considered similar, even if the constant factor is negative. Note that the cosine of the angle measures correlation; it is 1 when the vectors are parallel (perfectly correlated) and 0 when they are orthogonal.

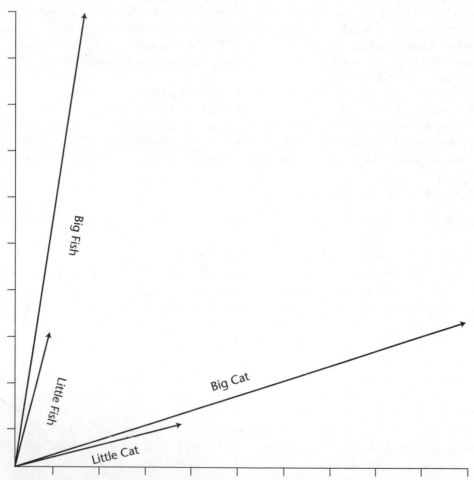

**Figure 11.7**   The angle between vectors as a measure of similarity.

### Manhattan Distance

Another common distance metric gets its name from the rectangular grid pattern of streets in midtown Manhattan. It is simply the sum of the distances traveled along each axis. This measure is sometimes preferred to the Euclidean distance because given that the distances along each axis are not squared, it is less likely that a large difference in one dimension will dominate the total distance.

### Number of Features in Common

When the preponderance of fields in the records are categorical variables, geometric measures are not the best choice. A better measure is based on the degree of overlap between records. As with the geometric measures, there are many variations on this idea. In all variations, the two records are compared field by field to determine the number of fields that match and the number of fields that don't match. The simplest measure is the ratio of matches to the total number of fields.

In its simplest form, this measure counts two null or empty fields as matching. This has the perhaps perverse result that everything with missing data ends up in the same cluster. A simple improvement is to not include matches of this sort in the match count. Another improvement is to weight the matches by the prevalence of each class in the general population. After all, a match on "Chevy Nomad" ought to count for more than a match on "Ford F-150 Pickup."

# Data Preparation for Clustering

The notions of *scaling* and *weighting* each play important roles in clustering. Although similar, and often confused with each other, the two notions are not the same. Scaling adjusts the values of variables to take into account the fact that different variables are measured in different units or over different ranges. For instance, household income is measured in tens of thousands of dollars and number of children in single digits. Weighting provides a relative adjustment for a variable, because some variables are more important than others.

## Scaling for Consistency

In geometry, all dimensions are equally important. Two points that differ by 2 in dimensions $X$ and $Y$ and by 1 in dimension $Z$ are the same distance apart as two other points that differ by 1 in dimension $X$ and by 2 in dimensions $Y$ and $Z$. It doesn't matter what units $X$, $Y$, and $Z$ are measured in, so long as they are the same.

But what if $X$ is measured in yards, $Y$ is measured in centimeters, and $Z$ is measured in nautical miles? A difference of 1 in $Z$ is now equivalent to a difference of 185,200 in $Y$ or 2,025 in $X$. Clearly, they must all be converted to a common scale before distances will make any sense.

Unfortunately, in commercial data mining there is usually no common scale available because the different units being used are measuring quite different things. If variables include plot size, number of children, car ownership, and family income, they cannot all be converted to a common unit. On the other hand, it is misleading that a difference of 20 acres is indistinguishable from a change of \$20. One solution is to map all the variables to a common *range* (often 0 to 1 or –1 to 1). That way, at least the ratios of change become comparable—doubling the plot size has the same effect as doubling income. Scaling solves this problem, in this case by remapping to a common range.

**TIP** It is very important to scale different variables so their values fall roughly into the same range, by normalizing, indexing, or standardizing the values.

Here are three common ways of scaling variables to bring them all into comparable ranges:

- Divide each variable by the range (the difference between the lowest and highest value it takes on) after subtracting the lowest value. This maps all values to the range 0 to 1, which is useful for some data mining algorithms.

- Divide each variable by the mean of all the values it takes on. This is often called "indexing a variable."

- Subtract the mean value from each variable and then divide it by the standard deviation. This is often called *standardization* or "converting to z-scores." A z-score tells you how many standard deviations away from the mean a value is.

Normalizing a single variable simply changes its range. A closely related concept is *vector normalization* which scales all variables at once. This too has a geometric interpretation. Consider the collection of values in a single record or observation as a vector. Normalizing them scales each value so as to make the length of the vector equal one. Transforming all the vectors to unit length emphasizes the differences internal to each record rather than the differences between records. As an example, consider two records with fields for debt and equity. The first record contains debt of \$200,000 and equity of \$100,000; the second, debt of \$10,000 and equity of \$5,000. After normalization, the two records look the same since both have the same ratio of debt to equity.

## Use Weights to Encode Outside Information

Scaling takes care of the problem that changes in one variable appear more significant than changes in another simply because of differences in the magnitudes of the values in the variable. What if we think that two families with the same income have more in common than two families on the same size plot, and we want that to be taken into consideration during clustering? That is where weighting comes in. The purpose of weighting is to encode the information that one variable is more (or less) important than others.

A good place to starts is by standardizing all variables so each has a mean of zero and a variance (and standard deviation) of one. That way, all fields contribute equally when the distance between two records is computed.

We suggest going farther. The whole point of automatic cluster detection is to find clusters that make sense to *you*. If, for your purposes, whether people have children is much more important than the number of credit cards they carry, there is no reason not to bias the outcome of the clustering by multiplying the number of children field by a higher weight than the number of credit cards field. After scaling to get rid of bias that is due to the units, use weights to introduce bias based on knowledge of the business context.

Some clustering tools allow the user to attach weights to different dimensions, simplifying the process. Even for tools that don't have such functionality, it is possible to have weights by adjusting the scaled values. That is, first scale the values to a common range to eliminate range effects. Then multiply the resulting values by a weight to introduce bias based on the business context.

Of course, if you want to evaluate the effects of different weighting strategies, you will have to add another outer loop to the clustering process.

# Other Approaches to Cluster Detection

The basic K-means algorithm has many variations. Many commercial software tools that include automatic cluster detection incorporate some of these variations. Among the differences are alternate methods of choosing the initial seeds and the use of probability density rather than distance to associate records with clusters. This last variation merits additional discussion. In addition, there are several different approaches to clustering, including agglomerative clustering, divisive clustering, and self organizing maps.

## Gaussian Mixture Models

The K-means method as described has some drawbacks:

- It does not do well with overlapping clusters.
- The clusters are easily pulled off-center by outliers.
- Each record is either inside or outside of a given cluster.

*Gaussian mixture models* are a probabilistic variant of K-means. The name comes from the Gaussian distribution, a probability distribution often assumed for high-dimensional problems. The Gaussian distribution generalizes the normal distribution to more than one variable. As before, the algorithm starts by choosing K seeds. This time, however, the seeds are considered to be the means of Gaussian distributions. The algorithm proceeds by iterating over two steps called the estimation step and the maximization step.

The estimation step calculates the *responsibility* that each Gaussian has for each data point (see Figure 11.8). Each Gaussian has strong responsibility for points that are close to its mean and weak responsibility for points that are distant. The responsibilities are be used as weights in the next step.

In the maximization step, a new centroid is calculated for each cluster taking into account the newly calculated responsibilities. The centroid for a given Gaussian is calculated by averaging all the points *weighted by the responsibilities* for that Gaussian, as illustrated in Figure 11.9.

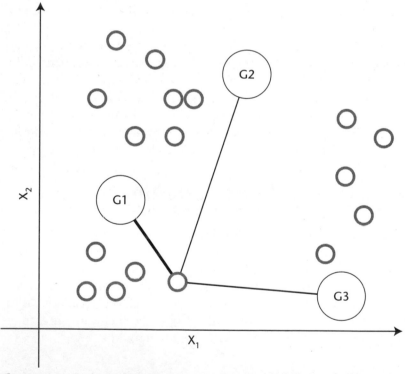

**Figure 11.8** In the estimation step, each Gaussian is assigned some responsibility for each point. Thicker lines indicate greater responsibility.

These steps are repeated until the Gaussians no longer move. The Gaussians themselves can change in shape as well as move. However, each Gaussian is constrained, so if it shows a very high responsibility for points close to its mean, then there is a sharp drop off in responsibilities. If the Gaussian covers a larger range of values, then it has smaller responsibilities for nearby points. Since the distribution must always integrate to one, Gaussians always gets weaker as they get bigger.

The reason this is called a "mixture model" is that the probability at each data point is the sum of a mixture of several distributions. At the end of the process, each point is tied to the various clusters with higher or lower probability. This is sometimes called *soft clustering*, because points are not uniquely identified with a single cluster.

One consequence of this method is that some points may have high probabilities of being in more than one cluster. Other points may have only very low probabilities of being in any cluster. Each point can be assigned to the cluster where its probability is highest, turning this soft clustering into *hard clustering*.

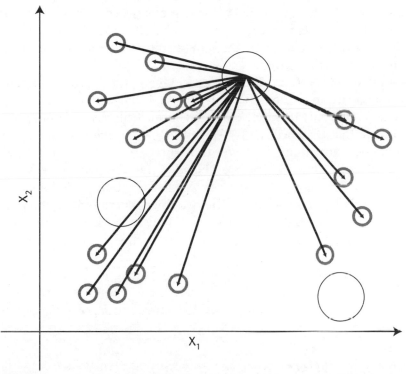

**Figure 11.9**   Each Gaussian mean is moved to the centroid of all the data points weighted by its responsibilities for each point. Thicker arrows indicate higher weights.

# Agglomerative Clustering

The K-means approach to clustering starts out with a fixed number of clusters and allocates all records into exactly that number of clusters. Another class of methods works by agglomeration. These methods start out with each data point forming its own cluster and gradually merge them into larger and larger clusters until all points have been gathered together into one big cluster. Toward the beginning of the process, the clusters are very small and very pure—the members of each cluster are few and closely related. Towards the end of the process, the clusters are large and not as well defined. The entire history is preserved making it possible to choose the level of clustering that works best for a given application.

## An Agglomerative Clustering Algorithm

The first step is to create a *similarity matrix*. The similarity matrix is a table of all the pair-wise distances or degrees of similarity between clusters. Initially, the similarity matrix contains the pair-wise distance between individual pairs of records. As discussed earlier, there are many measures of similarity between records, including the Euclidean distance, the angle between vectors, and the ratio of matching to nonmatching categorical fields. The issues raised by the choice of distance measures are exactly the same as those previously discussed in relation to the K-means approach.

It might seem that with $N$ initial clusters for $N$ data points, $N^2$ measurement calculations are required to create the distance table. If the similarity measure is a true distance metric, only half that is needed because all true distance metrics follow the rule that Distance($X,Y$) = Distance($Y,X$). In the vocabulary of mathematics, the similarity matrix is lower triangular. The next step is to find the smallest value in the similarity matrix. This identifies the two clusters that are most similar to one another. Merge these two clusters into a new one and update the similarity matrix by replacing the two rows that described the parent cluster with a new row that describes the distance between the merged cluster and the remaining clusters. There are now $N-1$ clusters and $N-1$ rows in the similarity matrix.

Repeat the merge step $N-1$ times, so all records belong to the same large cluster. Each iteration remembers which clusters were merged and the distance between them. This information is used to decide which level of clustering to make use of.

## Distance between Clusters

A bit more needs to be said about how to measure distance between clusters. On the first trip through the merge step, the clusters consist of single records so the distance between clusters is the same as the distance between records, a subject that has already been covered in perhaps too much detail. Second and subsequent trips through the loop need to update the similarity matrix with the distances from the new, multirecord cluster to all the others. How do we measure this distance?

As usual, there is a choice of approaches. Three common ones are:

- Single linkage
- Complete linkage
- Centroid distance

In the *single linkage method*, the distance between two clusters is given by the distance between the closest members. This method produces clusters with the property that every member of a cluster is more closely related to at least one member of its cluster than to any point outside it.

Another approach is the *complete linkage method*, where the distance between two clusters is given by the distance between their most distant members. This method produces clusters with the property that all members lie within some known maximum distance of one another.

Third method is the centroid distance, where the distance between two clusters is measured between the centroids of each. The centroid of a cluster is its average element. Figure 11.10 gives a pictorial representation of these three methods.

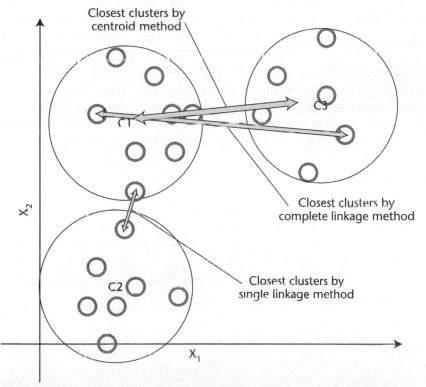

**Figure 11.10**   Three methods of measuring the distance between clusters.

## Clusters and Trees

The agglomeration algorithm creates hierarchical clusters. At each level in the hierarchy, clusters are formed from the union of two clusters at the next level down. A good way of visualizing these clusters is as a tree. Of course, such a tree may look like the decision trees discussed in Chapter 6, but there are some important differences. The most important is that the nodes of the cluster tree do not embed rules describing why the clustering takes place; the nodes simply state the fact that the two children have the minimum distance of all possible clusters pairs. Another difference is that a decision tree is created to maximize the leaf purity of a given target variable. There is no target for the cluster tree, other than self-similarity within each cluster. Later in this chapter we'll discuss divisive clustering methods. These are similar to the agglomerative methods, except that agglomerative methods are build by starting from the leaving and working towards the root whereas divisive methods start at the root and work down to the leaves.

## Clustering People by Age: An Example of Agglomerative Clustering

This illustration of agglomerative clustering uses an example in one dimension with the single linkage measure for distance between clusters. These choices make it possible to follow the algorithm through all its iterations without having to worry about calculating distances using squares and square roots.

The data consists of the ages of people at a family gathering. The goal is to cluster the participants using their age, and the metric for the distance between two people is simply the difference in their ages. The metric for the distance between two clusters of people is the difference in age between the oldest member of the younger cluster and the youngest member of the older cluster. (The one dimensional version of the single linkage measure.)

Because the distances are so easy to calculate, the example dispenses with the similarity matrix. The procedure is to sort the participants by age, then begin clustering by first merging clusters that are 1 year apart, then 2 years, and so on until there is only one big cluster.

Figure 11.11 shows the clusters after six iterations, with three clusters remaining. This is the level of clustering that seems the most useful. The algorithm appears to have clustered the population into three generations: children, parents, and grandparents.

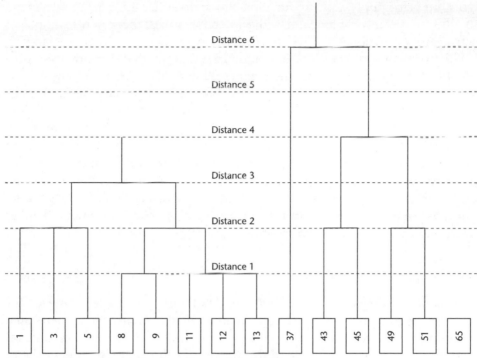

**Figure 11.11**  An example of agglomerative clustering.

## Divisive Clustering

We have already noted some similarities between trees formed by the agglomerative clustering techniques and ones formed by decision tree algorithms. Although the agglomerative methods work from the leaves to the root, while the decision tree algorithms work from the root to the leaves, they both create a similar hierarchical structure. The hierarchical structure reflects another similarity between the methods. Decisions made early on in the process are never revisited, which means that some fairly simple clusters may not be detected if an early split or agglomeration destroys the structure.

Seeing the similarity between the trees produced by the two methods, it is natural to ask whether the algorithms used for decision trees may also be used for clustering. The answer is yes. A decision tree algorithm starts with the entire collection of records and looks for a way to split it into partitions that are *purer*, in some sense defined by a purity function. In the standard decision tree algorithms, the purity function uses a separate variable—the target variable—to make this decision. All that is required to turn decision trees into a clustering algorithm is to supply a purity function chosen to either minimize the average intracluster distance or maximize the intercluster distances. An example of such a purity function is the average distance from the centroid of the parent.

With no change in the purity function, we might say that decision trees provide *directed clustering*; that is, they create clusters of records that are similar with respect to some target variable. For this reason, ordinary decision trees are often a better choice for customer segmentation than the undirected clustering algorithms discussed in this chapter. If the purpose of the customer segmentation is to find customer segments that are loyal or profitable or likely to respond to some particular offer, it makes sense to use one of those variables (or a proxie) as the target for directed clustering. If, on the other hand, the point of the customer segmentation is to stimulate discussion of new product offerings geared to various naturally occurring clusters of customers, than an undirected approach is more appropriate.

## Self-Organizing Maps

Self-organizing maps are a variant of neural networks that have been used for many years in applications such as feature detection in two-dimensional images. More recently, they have been applied successfully for more general clustering applications. There is a discussion of self-organizing networks in Chapter 7.

# Evaluating Clusters

When using the K-means approach to cluster detection, is there a way to determine what value of K finds the best clusters? Similarly, when using a hierarchical approach, is there a test for which level in the hierarchy contains the best clusters? What does it mean to say that a cluster is good?

These questions are important when using clustering in practice. In general terms, clusters should have members that have a high degree of similarity—or, in geometric terms, are close to each other—and the clusters themselves should be widely spaced.

A standard measure of within-cluster similarity is variance (the sum of the squared differences of each element from the mean), so the best set of clusters might be the set whose clusters have tthe lowest variance. However, this measure does not take into account cluster size. A similar measure would be the average variance, the total variance divided by the size of the cluster.

For agglomerative clustering, using variance as a measure does not make sense, since this method always starts out with clusters of one—which, of course, have variance zero. A good measure to use with agglomerative clusters is the difference between the distance value at which it was formed and the distance value at which it is merged into the next level. This is a measure of the durability of the cluster. Strong clusters, like the one linking 1 to 13-year-olds at distance 3 in Figure 11.11, last through many iterations of the algorithm.

A general-purpose measure that works with any form of cluster detection is to take whatever similarity measure or distance metric is used to form the clusters and use it to compare the average distance between members of a cluster and the cluster centroid to the average distance between cluster centroids. This can be done for each cluster individually and for the entire collection of clusters.

**TIP** If there are one or two good clusters along with a number of weaker ones, it may be possible to improve results by removing all members of the strong clusters. The strong clusters are worthy of further analysis anyway, and removing their strong pull may allow new clusters to be detected in the records left behind.

## Inside the Cluster

Clustering often produces one or more strong clusters—rather large clusters where the records are quite similar. The question is, what makes a strong cluster special? What is it about the records in this cluster that causes them to be lumped together? Even more importantly, is it possible to find rules and patterns within this cluster now that the noise from the rest of the database has been reduced?

The easiest way to approach these questions is to take the mean of each variable within the cluster and compare it to the mean of the same variable in the parent population. Rank order the variables by the magnitude of the difference, or better yet, the z-score. Looking at the variables that show the largest difference between the cluster and the rest of the database goes a long way towards explaining what makes the cluster special.

## Outside the Cluster

Clustering can be useful even when only a single cluster is found. When screening for a very rare defect, there may not be enough examples to train a directed data mining model to detect it. One example is testing electric motors at the factory that makes them. Cluster detection methods can be used on a sample containing only good motors to determine the shape and size of the "normal" cluster. When a motor comes along that falls outside the cluster for any reason, it is suspect. This approach has been used in medicine to detect the presence of abnormal cells in tissue samples and in telecommunications to detect calling patterns indicative of fraud.

# Case Study: Clustering Towns

*The Boston Globe* is one of two major dailies serving Boston and the surrounding area of eastern Massachusetts and southern New Hampshire. The *Globe* is the leading circulated newspaper in Boston with daily circulation of over 467,000 in 2003 compared to 243,000 for the *Boston Herald*, the other major daily in town. On Sundays, the *Globe* has circulation of over 705,000. Despite this leading position, in 2003 the *Globe* did not want to stand still. As with many newspapers, it faced declining readership in its core Boston market and strong competition from local papers in the suburban markets where some of its readers have migrated.

In order to compete better with the suburban papers, the *Globe* introduced geographically distinct versions of the paper with specialized editorial content for each of 12 geographically defined zones. Two days a week, readers are treated to a few pages of local coverage for their area. The editorial zones were drawn up using data available to the *Globe*, common sense, and a map, but no formal statistical analysis. There were some constraints on the composition of the editorial zones:

- The zones had to be geographically contiguous so that the trucks carrying the localized editions from the central printing plant in Boston could take sensible routes.

- The zones had to be reasonably compact and contain sufficient population to justify specialized editorial content.

- The editorial zones had to be closely aligned with the geographic zones used to sell advertising.

Within these constraints, the *Globe* wished to design editorial zones that would group similar towns together. Sounds sensible, but which towns are similar? That is the question that *The Boston Globe* brought to us at Data Miners.

## Creating Town Signatures

Before deciding which towns belonged together, there needed to be a way of describing the towns—a town signature with a column for every feature that might be useful for characterizing a town and comparing it with its neighbors. As it happened, Data Miners had worked on an earlier project to find towns with good prospects for future circulation growth that had already defined town signatures. Those signatures, which had been developed for a regression model to predict *Globe* home delivery penetration, turned out to be equally useful for undirected clustering. This is a fairly common occurrence; once a useful set of descriptive attributes has been collected it can be used for all sorts of things. In another example, a long-distance company developed customer signatures based on call detail data in order to predict fraud and later found that the same variables were useful for distinguishing between business and residential users.

> **TIP** Although the time and effort it takes to create a good customer signature can seem daunting, the effort is repaid over time because the same attributes often turn out to be predictive for many different target variables. The oft quoted rule of thumb that 80 percent of the time spent on a data mining project goes into data preparation becomes less true when the data preparation effort can be amortized over several predictive modeling efforts.

## The Data

The town signatures were derived from several sources, with most of the variables coming from town-level U.S. Census data from 1990 and 2001. The census data provides counts of the number of residents by age, race, ethnic group, occupation, income, home value, average commute time, and many other interesting variables. In addition, the *Globe* had household-level data on its subscribers supplied by an outside data vendor as well as circulation figures for each town and subscriber-level information on discount plans, complaint calls, and type of subscription (daily, Sunday, or both).

There were four basic steps to creating the town signatures:

1. Aggregation
2. Normalization
3. Calculation of trends
4. Creation of derived variables

The first step in turning this data into a town signature was to aggregate everything to the town level. For example, the subscriber data was aggregated to produce the total number of subscribers and median subscriber household income for each town.

The next step was to transform counts into percentages. Most of the demographic information was in the form of counts. Even things like income, home value, and number of children are reported as counts of the number of people in predefined bins. Transforming all counts into percentages of the town population is an example of normalizing data across towns with widely varying populations. The fact that in 2001, there were 27,573 people with 4-year college degrees residing in Brookline, Massachusetts is not nearly as interesting as the fact that they represented 47.5 percent of that well-educated town, while the much larger number of people with similar degrees in Boston proper make up only 19.4 percent of the population there.

Each of the scores of variables in the census data was available for two different years 11 years apart. Historical data is interesting because it makes it possible to look at trends. Is a town gaining or losing population? School-age population? Hispanic population? Trends like these affect the feel and character of a town so they should be represented in the signature. For certain factors, such as total population, the absolute trend is interesting, so the ratio of the population count in 2001 to the count in 1990 was used. For other factors such as a town's mix of renters and home owners, the change in the proportion of home owners in the population is more interesting so the ratio of the 2001 home ownership percentage to the percentage in 1990 was used. In all cases, the resulting value is an index with the property that it is larger than 1 for anything that has increased over time and a little less than 1 for anything that has decreased over time.

Finally, to capture important attributes of a town that were not readily discernable from variables already in the signature, additional variables were derived from those already present. For example, both distance and direction from Boston seemed likely to be important in forming town clusters. These are calculated from the latitude and longitude of the gold-domed State House that Oliver Wendell Holmes once called "the hub of the solar system." (Today's Bostonians are not as modest as Justice Holmes; they now refer to the entire city as "the hub of the universe" or simply "the Hub." Headline writers commonly save three letters by using "hub" in place of "Boston" as in the apocryphal "Hub man killed in NYC terror attack.") The online postal service database provides a convenient source for the latitude and longitude for each town. Most towns have a single zip code; for those with more, the coordinates of the lowest numbered zip code were arbitrarily chosen. The distance from the town to Boston was easily calculated from the latitude and longitude using standard Euclidean distance. Despite rumors that have reached us that the Earth is round, we used simple plane geometry for these calculations:

```
distance = sqrt(( hub latitude - town latitude)² + (hub longitude - town
longitude)²)
angle = arctan((hub latitude - town latitude)/(hub longitude - town
longitude))
```

These formulas are imprecise, since they assume that the earth is flat and that one degree of latitude has the same length as one degree of longitude. The area in question is not large enough for these flat Earth assumptions to make much difference. Also note that since these values will only be compared to one another there is no need to convert them into familiar units such as miles, kilometers, or degrees.

## Creating Clusters

The first attempt to build clusters used signatures that describe the towns in terms of both demographics and geography. Clusters built this way could not be used directly to create editorial zones because of the geographic constraint that editorial zones must comprise contiguous towns. Since towns with similar demographics are not necessarily close to one another, clusters based on our signatures include towns all over the map, as shown in Figure 11.12. Weighting could be used to increase the importance of the geographic variables in cluster formation, but the result would be to cause the nongeographic variables to be ignored completely. Since the goal was to find similarities based at least partially on demographic data, the idea of *geographic* clusters was abandoned in favor of *demographic* ones. The demographic clusters could then be used as one factor in designing editorial zones, along with the geographic constraints.

### Determining the Right Number of Clusters

Another problem with the idea of creating editorial zones directly through clustering is that there were business reasons for wanting about a dozen editorial zones, but no guarantee that a dozen good clusters would be found. This raises the general issue of how to determine the right number of clusters for a dataset. The data mining tool used for this clustering effort (MineSet, developed by SGI, and now available from Purple Insight) provides an interesting approach to this problem by combining K-means clustering with the divisive tree approach. First, decide on a lower bound K for the number of clusters. Build K clusters using the ordinary K-means algorithm. Using a fitness measure such as the variance or the mean distance from the cluster center according to whatever distance function is being used, determine which is the worst cluster and split it by forming two clusters from the previous single one. Repeat this process until some upper bound is reached. After each iteration, remember some measure of the overall fitness of the collection of clusters. The measure suggested earlier is the ratio of the mean distance of cluster members from the cluster center to the mean distance between clusters.

It is important to remember that the most important fitness measure for clusters is one that is hard to quantify—the usefulness of the clusters for the intended application. In the cluster tree shown in Figure 11.13, the next iteration of the cluster tree algorithm suggests splitting cluster 2. The resulting clusters have well-defined differences, but they did not behave differently according to any variables of interest to the Globe such as home delivery penetration or subscriber longevity. Figure 11.13 shows the final cluster tree and lists some statistics about each of the four clusters at the leaves.

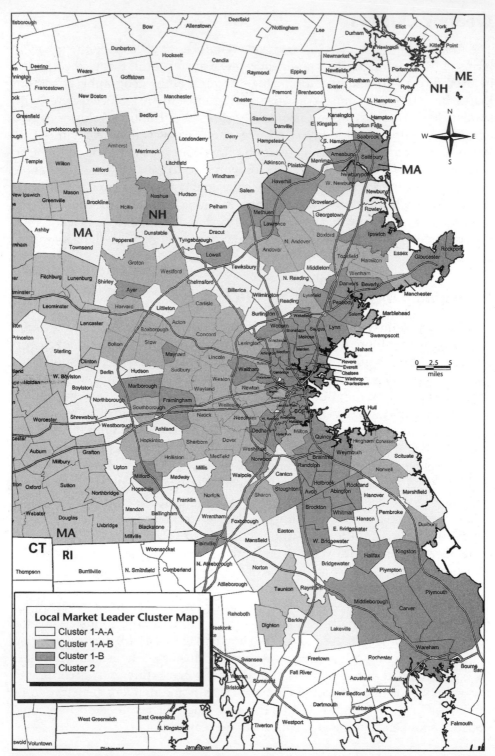

**Figure 11.12** This map shows a demographic clustering of towns in eastern Massachusetts and southern New Hampshire.

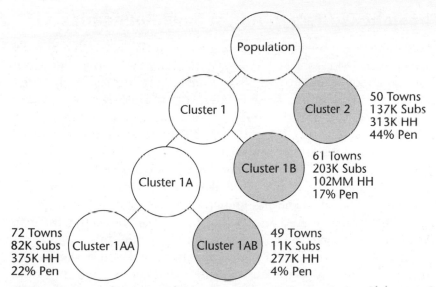

**Figure 11.13** A cluster tree divides towns served by *The Boston Globe* into four distinct groups.

Cluster 2 contains 50 towns with 313,000 households, 137,000 of which subscribe to the daily or Sunday *Globe*. This level of home delivery penetration makes cluster 2 far and away the best cluster. The variables that best distinguish cluster 2 from the other clusters and from the population as a whole are home value and education. This cluster has the highest proportion of any cluster of home values in the top two bins; the highest proportion of people with 4-year college degrees, the highest mean years of education, and the lowest proportion of people in bluecollar jobs. The next best cluster from the point of view of home delivery penetration is Cluster 1AA, which is distinguished by its ordinariness. Its mean values for the most important variables, which in this case are home value and household income, are very close to the overall population means. Cluster 1B is characterized by some of the lowest household incomes, the oldest subscribers, and proximity to Boston. Cluster 1AB is the only cluster characterized primarily by geography. These are towns far from Boston. Not surprisingly, home delivery penetration is very low. Cluster 1AB has the lowest home values of any cluster, but incomes are average. We might infer that people in Cluster 1AB have chosen to live far from the city because they wish to own homes and real estate is less expensive on the outer fringes of suburbia; this hypothesis could be tested with market research.

## Using Thematic Clusters to Adjust Zone Boundaries

The goal of the clustering project was to validate editorial zones that already existed. Each editorial zone consisted of a set of towns assigned one of the four clusters described above. The next step was to manually increase each zone's purity by swapping towns with adjacent zones. For example, Table 11.1 shows that all of the towns in the City zone are in Cluster 1B except Brookline, which is Cluster 2. In the neighboring West 1 zone, all the towns are in Cluster 2 except for Waltham and Watertown which are in Cluster 1B. Swapping Brookline into West 1 and Watertown and Waltham into City would make it possible for both editorial zones to be pure in the sense that all the towns in each zone would share the same cluster assignment. The new West 1 would be all Cluster 2, and the new City would be all Cluster 1B. As can be seen in the map in Figure 11.12, the new zones are still geographically contiguous.

Having editorial zones composed of similar towns makes it easier for the *Globe* to provide sharper editorial focus in its localized content, which should lead to higher circulation and better advertising sales.

**Table 11.1**   Towns in the *City* and *West 1* Editorial Zones

| TOWN | EDITORIAL ZONE | CLUSTER ASSIGNMENT |
| --- | --- | --- |
| Brookline | City | 2 |
| Boston | City | 1B |
| Cambridge | City | 1B |
| Somerville | City | 1B |
| Needham | West 1 | 2 |
| Newton | West 1 | 2 |
| Wellesley | West 1 | 2 |
| Waltham | West 1 | 1B |
| Weston | West 1 | 2 |
| Watertown | West 1 | 1B |

# Lessons Learned

Automatic cluster detection is an undirected data mining technique that can be used to learn about the structure of complex databases. By breaking complex datasets into simpler clusters, automatic clustering can be used to improve the performance of more directed techniques. By choosing different distance measures, automatic clustering can be applied to almost any kind of data. It is as easy to find clusters in collections of news stories or insurance claims as in astronomical or financial data.

Clustering algorithms rely on a similarity metric of some kind to indicate whether two records are close or distant. Often, a geometric interpretation of distance is used, but there are other possibilities, some of which are more appropriate when the records to be clustered contain non-numeric data.

One of the most popular algorithms for automatic cluster detection is K-means. The K-means algorithm is an iterative approach to finding K clusters based on distance. The chapter also introduced several other clustering algorithms. Gaussian mixture models, are a variation on the K-means idea that allows for overlapping clusters. Divisive clustering builds a tree of clusters by successively dividing an initial large cluster. Agglomerative clustering starts with many small clusters and gradually combines them until there is only one cluster left. Divisive and agglomerative approaches allow the data miner to use external criteria to decide which level of the resulting cluster tree is most useful for a particular application.

This chapter introduced some technical measures for cluster fitness, but the most important measure for clustering is how useful the clusters turn out to be for furthering some business goal.

# Knowing When to Worry: Hazard Functions and Survival Analysis in Marketing

Hazards. Survival. These very terms conjure up scary images, whether a shimmering-blue, ball-eating golf hazard or something a bit more frightful from a Stephen King novel, a hatchet movie, or some reality television show. Perhaps such dire associations explain why these techniques are not frequently associated with marketing.

If so, this is a shame. Survival analysis, which is also called time-to-event analysis, is nothing to worry about. Exactly the opposite: survival analysis is very valuable for understanding customers. Although the roots and terminology come from medical research and failure analysis in manufacturing, the concepts are tailor made for marketing. Survival tells us *when* to start worrying about customers doing something important, such as ending their relationship. It tells us which factors are most correlated with the event. Hazards and survival curves also provide snapshots of customers and their life cycles, answering questions such as: "How much should we worry that this customer is going to leave in the near future?" or "This customer has not made a purchase recently; is it time to start worrying that the customer will not return?"

The survival approach is centered on the most important facet of customer behavior: tenure. How long customers have been around provides a wealth of information, especially when tied to particular business problems. How long customers will remain customers in the future is a mystery, but a mystery that past customer behavior can help illuminate. Almost every business recognizes the value of customer loyalty. As we see later in this chapter, a guiding principle of loyalty—that the longer customers stay around, the less likely they are to stop at any particular point in time—is really a statement about hazards.

The world of marketing is a bit different from the world of medical research. For one thing, the consequences of our actions are much less dire: a patient may die from poor treatment, whereas the consequences in marketing are merely measured in dollars and cents. Another important difference is the volume of data. The largest medical studies have a few tens of thousands of participants, and many draw conclusions from a just a few hundred. When trying to determine mean time between failure (MTBF) or mean time to failure (MTTF)—manufacturing lingo for how long to wait until an expensive piece of machinery breaks down—conclusions are often based on no more than a few dozen failures.

In the world of customers, tens of thousands is the lower limit, since customer databases often contain data on millions of customers and former customers. Much of the statistical background of survival analysis is focused on extracting every last bit of information out of a few hundred data points. In data mining applications, the volumes of data are so large that statistical concerns about confidence and accuracy are replaced by concerns about managing large volumes of data.

The importance of survival analysis is that it provides a way of understanding time-to-event characteristics, such as:

- When a customer is likely to leave
- The next time a customer is likely to migrate to a new customer segment
- The next time a customer is likely to broaden or narrow the customer relationship
- The factors in the customer relationship that increase or decrease likely tenure
- The quantitative effect of various factors on customer tenure

These insights into customers feed directly into the marketing process. They make it possible to understand how long different groups of customers are likely to be around—and hence how profitable these segments are likely to be. They make it possible to forecast numbers of customers, taking into account both new acquisition and the decline of the current base. Survival analysis also makes it possible to determine which factors, both those at the beginning of customers' relationships as well as later experiences, have the biggest effect on customers' staying around the longest. And, the analysis can be applied to things other then the end of the customer tenure, making it possible to determine when another event—such as a customer returning to a Web site—is no longer likely to occur.

A good place to start with survival is with visualizing customer retention, which is a rough approximation of survival. After this discussion, we move on to hazards, the building blocks of survival. These are in turn combined into survival curves, which are similar to retention curves but more useful. The chapter ends with a discussion of Cox Proportional Hazard Regression and other applications of survival analysis. Along the way, the chapter provides particular applications of survival in the business context. As with all statistical methods, there is a depth to survival that goes far beyond this introductory chapter, which is consciously trying to avoid the complex mathematics underlying these techniques.

# Customer Retention

Customer retention is a concept familiar to most businesses that are concerned about their customers, so it is a good place to start. Retention is actually a close approximation to survival, especially when considering a group of customers who all start at about the same time. Retention provides a familiar framework to introduce some key concepts of survival analysis such as customer half-life and average truncated customer tenure.

## Calculating Retention

How long do customers stay around? This seemingly simple question becomes more complicated when applied to the real world. Understanding customer retention requires two pieces of information:

- When each customer started
- When each customer stopped

The difference between these two values is the customer tenure, a good measurement of customer retention.

Any reasonable database that purports to be about customers should have this data readily accessible. Of course, marketing databases are rarely simple. There are two challenges with these concepts. The first challenge is deciding on what is a start and stop, a decision that often depends on the type of business and available data. The second challenge is technical: finding these start and stop dates in available data may be less obvious than it first appears.

For subscription and account-based businesses, start and stop dates are well understood. Customers start magazine subscriptions at a particular point in time and end them when they no longer want to pay for the magazine. Customers sign up for telephone service, a banking account, ISP service, cable service, an insurance policy, or electricity service on a particular date and cancel on another date. In all of these cases, the beginning and end of the relationship is well defined.

Other businesses do not have such a continuous relationship. This is particularly true of transactional businesses, such as retailing, Web portals, and catalogers, where each customer's purchases (or visits) are spread out over time—or may be one-time only. The beginning of the relationship is clear—usually the first purchase or visit to a Web site. The end is more difficult but is sometimes created through business rules. For instance, a customer who has not made a purchase in the previous 12 months may be considered lapsed. Customer retention analysis can produce useful results based on these definitions. A similar area of application is determining the point in time after which a customer is no longer likely to return (there is an example of this later in the chapter).

The technical side can be more challenging. Consider magazine subscriptions. Do customers start on the date when they sign up for the subscription? Do customers start when the magazine first arrives, which may be several weeks later? Or do they start when the promotional period is over and they start paying?

Although all three questions are interesting aspects of the customer relationship, the focus is usually on the economic aspects of the relationship. Costs and/or revenue begin when the account starts being used—that is, on the issue date of the magazine—and end when the account stops. For understanding customers, it is definitely interesting to have the original contact date and time, in addition to the first issue date (are customers who sign up on weekdays different from customers who sign up on weekends?), but this is not the beginning of the economic relationship. As for the end of the promotional period, this is really an *initial condition* or *time-zero covariate* on the customer relationship. When the customer signs up, the initial promotional period is known. Survival analysis can take advantage of such initial conditions for refining models.

## What a Retention Curve Reveals

Once tenures can be calculated, they can be plotted on a *retention curve*, which shows the proportion of customers that are retained for a particular period of time. This is actually a cumulative histogram, because customers who have tenures of 3 months are included in the proportions for 1 month and 2 months. Hence, a retention curve always starts at 100 percent.

For now, let's assume that all customers start at the same time. Figure 12.1, for instance, compares the retention of two groups of customers who started at about the same point in time 10 years ago. The points on the curve show the proportion of customers who were retained for 1 year, for 2 years, and so on. Such a curve starts at 100 percent and gradually slopes downward. When a retention curve represents customers who all started at about the same time—as in this case—it is a close approximation to the survival curve.

Differences in retention among different groups are clearly visible in the chart. These differences can be quantified. The simplest measure is to look at retention at particular points in time. After 10 years, for instance, 24 percent of the regular customers are still around, and only about a third of them even make it to 5 years. Premium customers do much better. Over half make it to 5 years, and 42 percent have a customer lifetime of at least 10 years.

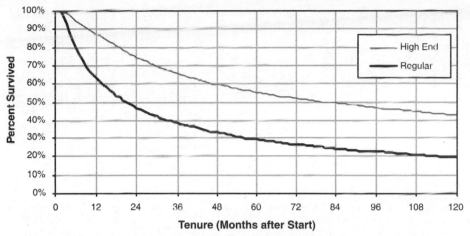

**Figure 12.1** Retention curves show that high-end customers stay around longer.

Another way to compare the different groups is by asking how long it takes for half the customers to leave—the customer half-life (although the statistical term is the *median customer lifetime*). The median is a useful measure because the few customers who have very long or very short lifetimes do not affect it. In general, medians are not sensitive to a few outliers.

Figure 12.2 illustrates how to find the customer half-life using a retention curve. This is the point where exactly 50 percent of the customers remain, which is where the 50 percent horizontal grid line intersects the retention curve. The customer half-life for the two groups shows a much starker difference than the 10-year survival—the premium customers have a median lifetime of close to 7 years, whereas the regular customers have a median a bit under over 2 years.

## Finding the Average Tenure from a Retention Curve

The customer half-life is useful for comparisons and easy to calculate, so it is a valuable tool. It does not, however, answer an important question: "How much, on average, were customers worth during this period of time?" Answering this question requires having an average customer worth per time and an average retention for all the customers. The median cannot provide this information because the median only describes what happens to the one customer in the middle; the customer at exactly the 50 percent rank. A question about average customer worth requires an estimate of the *average* remaining lifetime for all customers.

There is an easy way to find the average remaining lifetime: average customer lifetime during the period is the area under the retention curve. There is a clever way of visualizing this calculation, which Figure 12.3 walks through.

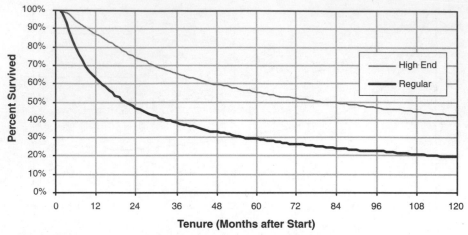

**Figure 12.2**   The median customer lifetime is where the retention curve crosses the 50 percent point.

First, imagine that the customers all lie down with their feet lined up on the left. Their heads represent their tenure, so there are customers of all different heights (or widths, because they are horizontal) for customers of all different tenures. For the sake of visualization, the longer tenured customers lie at the bottom holding up the shorter tenured ones. The line that connects their noses counts the number of customers who are retained for a particular period of time (remember the assumption that all customers started at about the same point in time). The area under this curve is the sum of all the customers' tenures, since every customer lying horizontally is being counted.

Dividing the vertical axis by the total count produces a retention curve. Instead of count, there is a percentage. The area under the curve is the total tenure divided by the count of customers—voilà, the average customer tenure during the period of time covered by the chart.

**TIP**   The area under the customer retention curve is the average customer lifetime for the period of time in the curve. For instance, for a retention curve that has 2 years of data, the area under the curve represents the two-year average tenure.

This simple observation explains how to obtain an estimate of the average customer lifetime. There is one caveat when some customers are still active. The average is really an average for the period of time under the retention curve.

Consider the earlier retention curve in this chapter. These retention curves were for 10 years, so the area under the curves is an estimate of the *average customer lifetime during the first 10 years of their relationship*. For customers who are still active at 10 years, there is no way of knowing whether they will all leave at 10 years plus one day; or if they will all stick around for another century. For this reason, it is not possible to determine the real average until all customers have left.

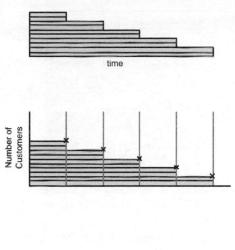

A group of customers with different tenures are stacked on top of each other. Each bar represents one customer.

At each point in time, the edges count the number of customers active at that time.

Notice that the sum of all the areas is the **sum** of all the customer tenures.

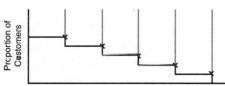

Making the vertical axis a proportion instead of a count produces a curve that looks the same. This is a retention curve

The area under the retention curve is the **average** customer tenure.

**Figure 12.3** Average customer tenure is calculated from the area under the retention curve.

This value, called *truncated mean lifetime* by statisticians, is very useful. As shown in Figure 12.4, the better customers have an average 10-year lifetime of 6.1 years; the other group has an average of 3.7 years. If, on average, a customer is worth, say, $100 per year, then the premium customers are worth $610 – $370 = $240 more than the regular customers during the 10 years after they start, or about $24 per year. This $24 might represent the return on a retention program designed specifically for the premium customers, or it might give an upper limit of how much to budget for such retention programs.

## Looking at Retention as Decay

Although we don't generally advocate comparing customers to radioactive materials, the comparison is useful for understanding retention. Think of customers as a lump of uranium that is slowly, radioactively decaying into lead. Our "good" customers are the uranium; the ones who have left are the lead. Over time, the amount of uranium left in the lump looks something like our retention curves, with the perhaps subtle difference that the timeframe for uranium is measured in billions of years, as opposed to smaller time scales.

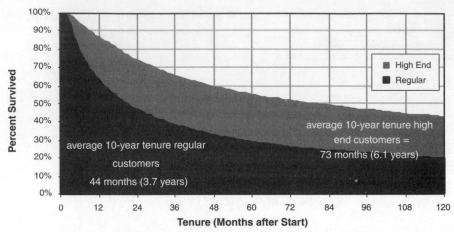

**Figure 12.4**    Average customer lifetime for different groups of customers can be compared using the areas under the retention curve.

One very useful characteristic of the uranium is that we know—or more precisely, scientists have determined how to calculate—exactly how much uranium is going to survive after a certain amount of time. They are able to do this because they have built mathematical models that describe radioactive decay, and these have been verified experimentally.

Radioactive materials have a process of decay described as *exponential* decay. What this means is that the same proportion of uranium turns into lead, regardless of how much time has past. The most common form of uranium, for instance, has a half-life of about 4.5 billion years. So, about half the lump of uranium has turned into lead after this time. After another 4.5 billion years, half the remaining uranium will decay, leaving only a quarter of the original lump as uranium and three-quarters as lead.

**WARNING** Exponential decay has many useful properties for predicting beyond the range of observations. Unfortunately, customers hardly ever exhibit exponential decay.

What makes exponential decay so nice is that the decay fits a nice simple equation. Using this equation, it is possible to determine how much uranium is around at any given point in time. Wouldn't it be nice to have such an equation for customer retention?

It would be very nice, but it is unlikely, as shown in the example in the sidebar "Parametric Approaches Do Not Work."

To shed some light on the issue, let's imagine a world where customers did exhibit exponential decay. For the purposes of discussion, these customers have a half-life of 1 year. Of 100 customers starting on a particular date, exactly 50 are still active 1 year later. After 2 years, 25 are active and 75 have stopped. Exponential decay would make it easy to forecast the number of customers in the future.

## DETERMINING THE AREA UNDER THE RETENTION CURVE

Finding the area under the retention curve may seem like a daunting mathematical effort. Fortunately, this is not the case at all.

The retention curve consists of a series of points; each point represents the retention after 1 year, 2 years, 3 years, and so on. In this case, retention is measured in years; the units might also be days, weeks, or months.

Each point has a value between 0 and 1, because the points represent a proportion of the customers retained up to that point in time.

The following figure shows the retention curve with a rectangle holding up each point. The base of the rectangle has a length of one (measured in the units of the horizontal axis). The height is the proportion retained. The area under the curve is the sum of the areas of these rectangles.

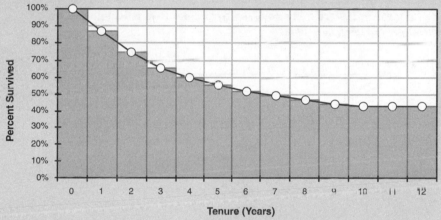

Circumscribing each point with a rectangle makes it clear how to calculate the area under the retention curve.

The area of each rectangle is—base times height—simply the proportion retained. The sum of all the rectangles, then, is just the sum of all the retention values in the curve—an easy calculation in a spreadsheet. *Voilà*, an easy way to calculate the area and quite an interesting observation as well: the sum of the retention values (as percentages) is the average customer lifetime. Notice also that each rectangle has a width of one time unit, in whatever the units are of the horizontal axis. So, the units of the average are also in the units of the horizontal axis.

## PARAMETRIC APPROACHES DO NOT WORK

It is tempting to try to fit some known function to the retention curve. This approach is called *parametric statistics*, because a few parameters describe the shape of the function. The power of this approach is that we can use it to estimate what happens in the future.

The line is the most common shape for such a function. For a line, there are two parameters, the slope of the line and where it intersects the Y-axis. Another common shape is a parabola, which has an additional $X^2$ term, so a parabola has three parameters. The exponential that describes radioactive decay actually has only one parameter, the half-life.

The following figure shows part of a retention curve. This retention curve is for the first 7 years of data.

The figure also shows three best-fit curves. Notice that all of these curves fit the values quite well. The statistical measure of fit is $R^2$, which varies from 0 to 1. Values over 0.9 are quite good, so by standard statistical measures, all these curves fit very, very well.

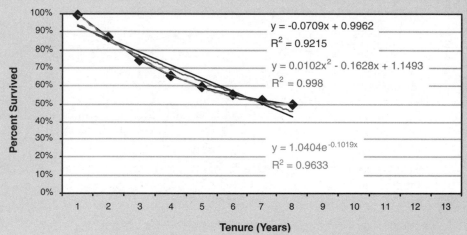

$$y = -0.0709x + 0.9962$$
$$R^2 = 0.9215$$

$$y = 0.0102x^2 - 0.1628x + 1.1493$$
$$R^2 = 0.998$$

$$y = 1.0404e^{-0.1019x}$$
$$R^2 = 0.9633$$

It is easy to fit parametric curves to a retention curve.

The real question, though is not how well these curves fit the data in the range used to define it. We want to know how well these curves work beyond the original 53-week range.

The following figure answers this question. It extrapolates the curves ahead another 5 years. Quickly, the curves diverge from the actual values, and the difference seems to be growing the further out we go.

## PARAMETRIC APPROACHES DO NOT WORK *(continued)*

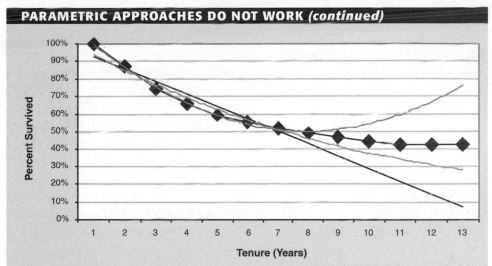

The parametric curves that fit a retention curve do not fit well beyond the range where they are defined.

**Of course, this illustration does not prove that a parametric approach will not work. Perhaps there is some function out there that, with the right parameters, would fit the observed retention curve very well *and continue working beyond the range used to define the parameters*. However, this example does illustrate the challenges of using a parametric approach for approximating survival curves directly, and it is consistent with our experience even when using more data points. Functions that provide a good fit to the retention curve turn out to diverge pretty quickly.**

Another way of describing this is that the customers who have been around for 1 year are going to behave just like new customers. Consider a group of 100 customers of various tenures, 50 leave in the following year, regardless of the tenure of the customers at the beginning of the year—exponential decay says that half are going to leave regardless of their initial tenure. That means that customers who have been around for a while are no more loyal then newer customers. However, it is often the case that customers who have been around for a while are actually *better* customers than new customers. For whatever reason, longer tenured customers have stuck around in the past and are probably a bit less likely than new customers to leave in the future. Exponential decay is a bad situation, because it assumes the opposite: that the tenure of the customer relationship has no effect on the rate that customers are leaving (the worst-case scenario would have longer term customers leaving at consistently higher rates than newer customers, the "familiarity breeds contempt" scenario).

# Hazards

The preceding discussion on retention curves serves to show how useful retention curves are. These curves are quite simple to understand, but only in terms of their data. There is no general shape, no parametric form, no grand theory of customer decay. The data is the message.

Hazard probabilities extend this idea. As discussed here, they are an example of a nonparametric statistical approach—letting the data speak instead of finding a special function to speak for it. Empirical hazard probabilities simply let the historical data determine what is likely to happen, without trying to fit data to some preconceived form. They also provide insight into customer retention and make it possible to produce a refinement of retention curves called survival curves.

## The Basic Idea

A hazard probability answers the following question:

> *Assume that a customer has survived for a certain length of time, so the customer's tenure is t. What is the probability that the customer leaves before t+1?*

Another way to phrase this is: the hazard at time $t$ is the risk of losing customers between time $t$ and time $t+1$. As we discuss hazards in more detail, it may sometimes be useful to refer to this definition. As with many seemingly simple ideas, hazards have significant consequences.

To provide an example of hazards, let's step outside the world of business for a moment and consider life tables, which describe the probability of someone dying at a particular age. Table 12.1 shows this data, for the U.S. population in 2000:

**Table 12.1**  Hazards for Mortality in the United States in 2000, Shown as a Life Table

| AGE | PERCENT OF POPULATION THAT DIES IN EACH AGE RANGE |
|---|---|
| 0–1 yrs | 0.73% |
| 1–4 yrs | 0.03% |
| 5–9 yrs | 0.02% |
| 10–14 yrs | 0.02% |
| 15–19 yrs | 0.07% |
| 20–24 yrs | 0.10% |
| 25–29 yrs | 0.10% |
| 30–34 yrs | 0.12% |

**Table 12.1** *(continued)*

| AGE | PERCENT OF POPULATION THAT DIES IN EACH AGE RANGE |
|---|---|
| 35–39 yrs | 0.16% |
| 40–44 yrs | 0.24% |
| 45–49 yrs | 0.36% |
| 50–54 yrs | 0.52% |
| 55–59 yrs | 0.80% |
| 60–64 yrs | 1.26% |
| 65–69 yrs | 1.93% |
| 70–74 yrs | 2.97% |
| 75–79 yrs | 4.56% |
| 80–84 yrs | 7.40% |
| 85+ yrs | 15.32% |

A life table is a good example of hazards. Infants have about a 1 in 137 chance of dying before their first birthday. (This is actually a very good rate; in less-developed countries the rate can be many times higher.) The mortality rate then plummets, but eventually it climbs steadily higher. Not until someone is about 55 years old does the risk rise as high as it is during the first year. This is a characteristic shape of some hazard functions and is called the *bathtub* shape. The hazards start high, remain low for a long time, and then gradually increase again. Figure 12.5 illustrates the bathtub shape using this data.

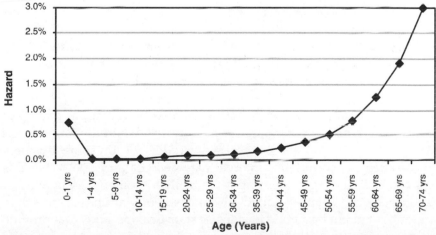

**Figure 12.5** The shape of a bathtub-shaped hazard function starts high, plummets, and then gradually increases again.

The same idea can be applied to customer tenure, although customer hazards are more typically calculated by day, week, or month instead of by year. Calculating a hazard for a given tenure $t$ requires only two pieces of data. The first is the number of customers who stopped at time $t$ (or between $t$ and $t+1$). The second is the total number of customers who could have stopped during this period, also called the *population at risk*. This consists of all customers whose tenure is greater than or equal to $t$, including those who stopped at time $t$. The hazard probability is the ratio of these two numbers, and being a probability, the hazard is always between 0 and 1. These hazard calculations are provided by life table functions in statistical software such as SAS and SPSS. It is also possible to do the calculations in a spreadsheet using data directly from a customer database.

One caveat: In order for the calculation to be accurate, every customer included in the population count must have the opportunity to stop at that particular time. This is a property of the data used to calculate the hazards, rather than the method of calculation. In most cases, this is not a problem, because hazards are calculated from all customers or from some subset based on initial conditions (such as initial product or campaign). There is no problem when a customer is included in the population count up to that customer's tenure, and the customer *could have stopped* on any day before then and still be in the data set.

An example of what not to do is to take a subset of customers who have stopped during some period of time, say in the past year. What is the problem? Consider a customer who stopped yesterday with 2 years of tenure. This customer is included in all the population counts for the first year of hazards. However, the customer could not have stopped during the first year of tenure. The stop would have been more than a year in the past and precluded the customer from being in the data set. Because customers who could not have stopped are included in the population counts, the population counts are too big making the initial hazards too low. Later in the chapter, an alternative method is explained to address this issue.

> **WARNING** To get accurate hazards and survival curves, use groups of customers who are defined only based on initial conditions. In particular, do not define the group based on how or when the members left.

When populations are large, there is no need to worry about statistical ideas such as confidence and standard error. However, when the populations are small—as they are in medical research studies or in some business applications—then the confidence interval may become an issue. What this means is that a hazard of say 5 percent might really be somewhere between 4 percent and 6 percent. When working with smallish populations (say less than a few thousand), it might be a good idea to use statistical methods that provide information about standard errors. For most applications, though, this is not an important concern.

## Examples of Hazard Functions

At this point, it is worth stopping and looking at some examples of hazards. These examples are intended to help in understanding what is happening, by looking at the hazard probabilities. The first two examples are basic, and, in fact, we have already seen examples of them in this chapter. The third is from real-world data, and it gives a good flavor of how hazards can be used to provide an x-ray of customers' lifetimes.

### Constant Hazard

The constant hazard hardly needs a picture to explain it. What it says is that the hazard of customers leaving is exactly the same, no matter how long the customers have been around. This looks like a horizontal line on a graph.

Say the hazard is being measured by days, and it is a constant 0.1 percent. That is, one customer out of every thousand leaves every day. After a year (365 days), this means that about 30.6 percent of the customers have left. It takes about 692 days for half the customers to leave. It will take another 692 days for half of them to leave. And so on, and so on.

The constant hazard means the chance of a customer leaving does not vary with the length of time the customer has been around. This sounds a lot like the exponential retention curve, the one that looks like the decay of radioactive elements. In fact, a constant retention hazard would conform to an exponential form for the retention curve. We say "would" simply because, although this does happen in physics, it does not happen much in marketing.

### Bathtub Hazard

The life table for the U.S. population provided an example of the bathtub-shaped hazard function. This is common in the life sciences, although bathtub shaped curves turn up in other domains. As mentioned earlier, the bathtub hazard initially starts out quite high, then it goes down and flattens out for a long time, and finally, the hazards increase again.

One phenomenon that causes this is when customers are on contracts (for instance, for cell phones or ISP services), typically for 1 year or longer. Early in the contract, customers stop because the service is not appropriate or because they do not pay. During the period of the contract, customers are dissuaded from canceling, either because of the threat of financial penalties or perhaps only because of a feeling of obligation to honor the terms of the initial contract.

When the contract is up, customers often rush to leave, and the higher rate continues for a while because customers have been liberated from the contract.

Once the contract has expired, there may be other reasons, such as the product or service no longer being competitively priced, that cause customers to stop. Markets change and customers respond to these changes. As telephone charges drop, customers are more likely to churn to a competitor than to negotiate with their current provider for lower rates.

## A Real-World Example

Figure 12.6 shows a real-world example of a hazard function, for a company that sells a subscription-based service (the exact service is unimportant). This hazard function is measuring the probability of a customer stopping a given number of weeks after signing on.

There are several interesting characteristics about the curve. First, it starts high. These are customers who sign on, but are not able to be started for some technical reason such as their credit card not being approved. In some cases, customers did not realize that they had signed on—a problem that the authors encounter most often with outbound telemarketing campaigns.

Next, there is an M-shaped feature, with peaks at about 9 and 11 weeks. The first of these peaks, at about 2 months, occurs because of nonpayment. Customers who never pay a bill, or who cancel their credit card charges, are stopped for nonpayment after about 2 months. Since a significant number of customers leave at this time, the hazard probability spikes up.

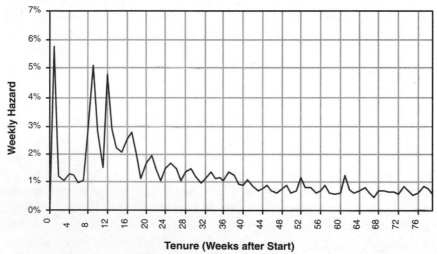

**Figure 12.6**   A subscription business has customer hazard probabilities that look like this.

The second peak in the "M" is coincident with the end of the initial promotion that offers introductory pricing. This promo typically lasts for about 3 months, and then customers have to start paying full price. Many decide that they no longer really want the service. It is quite possible that many of these customers reappear to take advantage of other promotions, an interesting fact not germane to this discussion on hazards but relevant to the business.

After the first 3 months, the hazard function has no more really high peaks. There is a small cycle of peaks, about every 4 or 5 weeks. This corresponds to the monthly billing cycle. Customers are more likely to stop just after they receive a bill.

The chart also shows that there is a gentle decline in the hazard rate. This decline is a good thing, since it means that the longer a customers stays around, the less likely the customer is to leave. Another way of saying this is that customers are becoming more loyal the longer they stay with the company.

## Censoring

So far, this introduction to hazards has glossed over one of the most important concepts in survival analysis: censoring. Remember the definition of a hazard probability, the number of stops at a given time $t$ divided by the population at that time. Clearly, if a customer has stopped before time $t$, then that customer is not included in the population count. This is most basic example of censoring. Customers who have stopped are not included in calculations after they stop.

There is another example of censoring, although it is a bit subtler. Consider customers whose tenure is $t$ but who are currently active. These customers are not included in the population for the hazard for tenure $t$, because the customers might still stop before $t+1$—here today, gone tomorrow. These customers have been dropped out of the calculation for that particular hazard, although they are included in calculations of hazards for smaller values of $t$. Censoring—dropping some customers from some of the hazard calculations—proves to be a very powerful technique, important to much of survival analysis.

Let's look at this with a picture. Figure 12.7 shows a set of customers and what happens at the beginning and end of their relationship. In particular, the end is shown with a small circle that is either open or closed. When the circle is open, the customer has already left and their exact tenure is known since the stop date is known.

A closed circle means that the customer has survived to the analysis date, so the stop date is not yet known. This customer— or in particular, this customer's tenure—is *censored*. The tenure is at least the current tenure, but most likely larger. How much larger is unknown, because that customer's exact stop date has not yet happened.

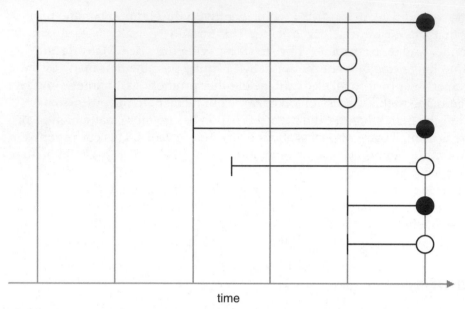

time

**Figure 12.7** In this group of customers who all start at different times, some customers are censored because they are still active.

Let's walk through the hazard calculation for these customers, paying particular attention to the role of censoring. When looking at customer data for hazard calculations, both the tenure and the censoring flag are needed. For the customers in Figure 12.7, Table 12.2 shows this data.

It is instructive to see what is happening during each time period. At any point in time, a customer might be in one of three states: ACTIVE, meaning that the relationship is still ongoing; STOPPED, meaning that the customer stopped during that time interval; or CENSORED, meaning that the customer is not included in the calculation. Table 12.3 shows what happens to the customers during each time period.

**Table 12.2** Tenure Data for Several Customers

| CUSTOMER | CENSORED | TENURE |
|----------|----------|--------|
| 2 | N | 4 |
| 3 | N | 3 |
| 4 | Y | 3 |
| 5 | N | 2 |
| 6 | Y | 1 |
| 7 | N | 1 |

**Table 12.3** Tracking Customers over Several Time Periods

| CUSTOMER | CENSORED | LIFETIME | TIME 0 | TIME 1 | TIME 2 | TIME 3 | TIME 4 | TIME 5 |
|---|---|---|---|---|---|---|---|---|
| 1 | Y | 5 | ACTIVE | ACTIVE | ACTIVE | ACTIVE | ACTIVE | ACTIVE |
| 2 | N | 4 | ACTIVE | ACTIVE | ACTIVE | ACTIVE | STOPPED | CENSORED |
| 3 | N | 3 | ACTIVE | ACTIVE | ACTIVE | STOPPED | CENSORED | CENSORED |
| 4 | Y | 3 | ACTIVE | ACTIVE | ACTIVE | ACTIVE | CENSORED | CENSORED |
| 5 | N | 2 | ACTIVE | ACTIVE | STOPPED | CENSORED | CENSORED | CENSORED |
| 6 | Y | 1 | ACTIVE | ACTIVE | CENSORED | CENSORED | CENSORED | CENSORED |
| 7 | N | 1 | ACTIVE | STOPPED | CENSORED | CENSORED | CENSORED | CENSORED |

**Table 12.4** From Times to Hazards

|         | TIME 0 | TIME 1 | TIME 2 | TIME 3 | TIME 4 | TIME 5 |
|---------|--------|--------|--------|--------|--------|--------|
| ACTIVE   | 7    | 6    | 4    | 3    | 1    | 1    |
| STOPPED  | 0    | 1    | 1    | 1    | 1    | 0    |
| CENSORED | 0    | 0    | 2    | 3    | 5    | 5    |
| HAZARD   | 0%   | 14%  | 20%  | 25%  | 50%  | 0%   |

Notice in Table 12.4 that the censoring takes place one time unit later than the lifetime. That is, Customer #1 survived to Time 5, what happens after that is unknown. The hazard at a given time is the number of customers who are STOPPED divided by the total of the customers who are either ACTIVE or STOPPED.

The hazard for Time 1 is 14 percent, since one out of seven customers stop at this time. All seven customers survived to time 1 and all could have stopped. Of these, only one did. At TIME 2, there are five customers left—Customer #7 has already stopped, and Customer #6 has been censored. Of these five, one stops, for a hazard of 20 percent. And so on. This example has shown how to calculate hazard functions, taking into account the fact that some (hopefully many) customers have not yet stopped.

This calculation also shows that the hazards are highly erratic—jumping from 25 percent to 50 percent to 0 percent in the last 3 days. Typically, hazards do not vary so much. This erratic behavior arises only because there are so few customers in this simple example. Similarly, lining up customers in a table is useful for didactic purposes to demonstrate the calculation on a manageable set of data. In the real world, such a presentation is not feasible, since there are likely to be thousands or millions of customers going down and hundreds or thousands of days going across.

It is also worth mentioning that this treatment of hazards introduces them as conditional probabilities, which vary between 0 and 1. This is possible because the hazards are using time that is in discrete units, such as days or week, a description of time applicable to customer-related analyses. However, statisticians often work with hazard rates rather than probabilities. The ideas are clearly very related, but the mathematics using rates involves daunting integrals, complicated exponential functions, and difficult to explain adjustments to this or that factor. For our purposes, the simpler hazard probabilities are not only easier to explain, but they also solve the problems that arise when working with customer data.

## Other Types of Censoring

The previous section introduced censoring in two cases: hazards for customers after they have stopped and hazards for customers who are still active. There are other useful cases as well. To explain other types of censoring, it is useful to go back to the medical realm.

Imagine that you are a cancer researcher and have found a medicine that cures cancer. You have to run a study to verify that this fabulous new treatment works. Such studies typically follow a group of patients for several years after the treatment, say 5 years. For the purposes of this example, we only want to know if patients die from cancer during the course of the study (medical researchers have other concerns as well, such as the recurrence of the disease, but that does not concern us in this simplified example).

So you identify 100 patients, give them the treatment, and their cancers seem to be cured. You follow them for several years. During this time, seven patients celebrate their newfound health by visiting Iceland. In a horrible tragedy, all seven happen to die in an avalanche caused by a submerged volcano. What is the effectiveness of your treatment on cancer mortality? Just looking at the data, it is tempting to say there is a 7 percent mortality rate. However, this mortality is clearly not related to the treatment, so the answer does not feel right.

And, in fact, the answer is not right. This is an example of *competing risks*. A study participant might live, might die of cancer, or might die of a mountain climbing accident on a distant island. Or the patient might move to Tahiti and drop out of the study. As medical researchers say, such a patient has been "lost to follow-up."

The solution is to censor the patients who exit the study before the event being studied occurs. If patients drop out of the study, then they were healthy to the point in time when they dropped out, and the information acquired during this period can be used to calculate hazards. Afterward there is no way of knowing what happened. They are censored at the point when they exit. If a patient dies of something else, then he or she is censored at the point when death occurs, and the death is not included in the hazard calculation.

**TIP** The right way to deal with competing risks is to develop different sets of hazards for each risk, where the other risks are censored.

Competing risks are familiar in the business environment as well. For instance, there are often two types of stops: voluntary stops, when a customer decides to leave, and involuntary stops, when the company decides a customer should leave—often due to unpaid bills

In doing an analysis on voluntary churn, what happens to customers who are forced to discontinue their relationships due to unpaid bills? If such a customer were forced to stop on day 100, then that customer did not stop voluntarily on days 1–99. This information can be used to generate hazards for voluntary stops. However, starting on day 100, the customer is censored, as shown in Figure 12.8. Censoring customers, even when they have stopped for other reasons, makes it possible to understand different types of stops.

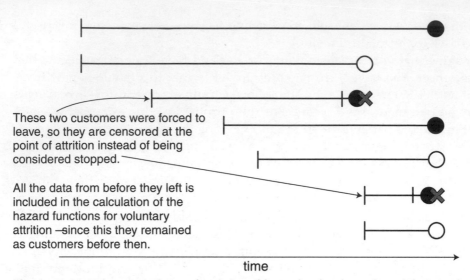

These two customers were forced to leave, so they are censored at the point of attrition instead of being considered stopped.

All the data from before they left is included in the calculation of the hazard functions for voluntary attrition –since this they remained as customers before then.

time

**Figure 12.8** Using censoring makes it possible to develop hazard models for voluntary attrition that include customers who were forced to leave.

# From Hazards to Survival

This chapter started with a discussion of retention curves. From the hazard functions, it is possible to create a very similar curve, called the survival curve. The survival curve is more useful and in many senses more accurate.

## Retention

A retention curve provides information about how many customers have been retained for a certain amount of time. One common way of creating a retention curve is to do the following:

- For customers who started 1 week ago, measure the 1-week retention.
- For customers who started 2 weeks ago, measure the 2-week retention.
- And so on.

Figure 12.9 shows an example of a retention curve based on this approach. The overall shape of this curve looks appropriate. However, the curve itself is quite jagged. It seems odd, for instance, that 10-week retention would be better than 9-week retention, as suggested by this data.

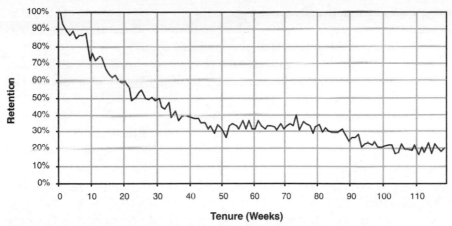

**Figure 12.9**  A retention curve might be quite jagged.

Actually, it is more than odd, it violates the very idea notion of retention. For instance, it opens the possibility that the curve will cross the 50 percent threshold more than once, leading to the odd, and inaccurate, conclusion that there is more than one median lifetime, or that the average retention for customers during the first 10 weeks after they start might be more than the average for the first 9 weeks. What is happening? Are customers being reincarnated?

These problems are an artifact of the way the curve was created. Customers acquired in any given time period may be better or worse than the customers acquired in other time periods. For instance, perhaps 9 weeks ago there was a special pricing offer that brought in bad customers. Customers who started 10 weeks ago were the usual mix of good and bad, but those who started 9 weeks ago were particularly bad. So, there are fewer of the bad customers after 9 weeks than of the better customers after 10 weeks.

The quality of customers might also vary due merely to random variation. After all, in the previous figure, there are over 100 time periods being considered—so, all things being equal, some time periods would be expected to exhibit differences.

A compounding reason is that marketing efforts change over time, attracting different qualities of customers. For instance, customers arriving by different channels often have different retention characteristics, and the mix of customers from different channels is likely to change over time.

## Survival

Hazards give the probability that a customer might stop at a particular point in time. Survival, on the other hand, gives the probability of a customer surviving up to that time. Survival values are calculated directly from the hazards.

At any point in time, the chance that a customer survives to the next unit of time is simply *1 – hazard*, which is called *conditional survival at time t* (it is conditional because it assumes that the customers survived up to time t). Calculating the full survival at a given time requires accumulating all the conditional survivals up to that point in time by multiplying them together. The survival value starts at 1 (or 100 percent) at time 0, since all customers included in analysis survive to the beginning of the analysis.

Since the hazard is always between 0 and 1, the conditional survival is also between 0 and 1. Hence, survival itself is always getting smaller—because each successive value is being multiplied by a number less than 1. The survival curve itself starts at 1, gently goes down, sometimes flattening, perhaps, out but never rising up.

Survival curves make more sense for customer retention purposes than the retention curves described earlier. Figure 12.10 shows a survival curve and its corresponding retention curve. It is clear that the survival curve is smoother, and that it slopes downward at all times. The retention curve bounces all over the place.

The differences between the retention curve and the survival curve may, at first, seem nonintuitive. The retention curve is actually pasting together a whole bunch of different pictures of customers from the past, like a photo collage pieced together from a bunch of different photographs to get a panoramic image. In the collage, the picture in each photo is quite clear. However, the boundaries do not necessarily fit together smoothly. Different pictures in the collage look different, because of differences in lighting or perspective—differences that contribute to the aesthetic of the collage.

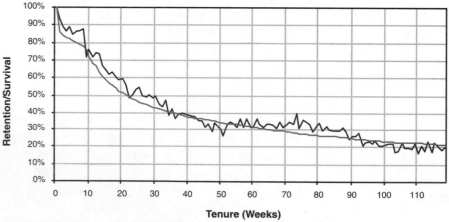

**Figure 12.10**   A survival curve is smoother than a retention curve.

The same thing is happening with retention curves, where customers who start at different points in time have different perspectives. Any given point on the retention curve is close to the actual retention value; however, taken as a whole, it looks jagged. One way to remove the jaggedness is to focus on customers who start at about the same time, as suggested earlier in this chapter. However, this greatly reduces the amount of data contributing to the curve.

**TIP** Instead of using retention curves, use survival curves. That is, first calculate the hazards and then work back to calculate the survival curve.

The survival curve, on the other hand, looks at as many customers as possible, not just the ones who started exactly $n$ time periods ago. The survival at any given point in time $t$ uses information from all customers. The hazard at time $t$ uses information from all customers whose tenure is greater than or equal to that value (assuming all are in the population at risk). Survival, though, is calculated by combining all the information for hazards from smaller values of $t$.

Because survival calculations use all the data, the values are more stable than retention calculations. Each point on a retention curve limits customers to having started at a particular point in time. Also, because a survival curve always slopes downward, calculations of customer half-life and average customer tenure are more accurate. By incorporating more information, survival provides a more accurate, smoother picture of customer retention.

When analyzing customers, both hazards and survival provide valuable information about customers. Because survival is cumulative, it gives a good summary value for comparing different groups of customers: How does the 1-year survival compare among different groups? Survival is also used for calculating customer half-life and mean customer tenure, which in turn feed into other calculations, such as customer value.

Because survival is cumulative, it is difficult to see patterns at a particular point in time. Hazards make the specific causes much more apparent. When discussing some real-world hazards, it was possible to identify events during the customer life cycle that were drivers of hazards. Survival curves do not highlight such events as clearly as hazards do.

The question may also arise about comparing hazards for different groups of customers. It does not make sense to compare average hazards over a period of time. Mathematically, "average hazard" does not make sense. The right approach is to turn the hazards into survival and compare the values on the survival curves.

The description of hazards and survival presented so far differs a bit from how the subject is treated in statistics. The sidebar "A Note about Survival Analysis and Statistics" explains the differences further.

## A NOTE ABOUT SURVIVAL ANALYSIS AND STATISTICS

The discussion of survival analysis in this chapter assumes that time is discrete. In particular, things happen on particular days, and the particular time of day is not important. This is not only reasonable for the problems addressed by data mining, but it is also more intuitive and simplifies the mathematics.

In statistics, though, survival analysis makes the opposite assumption, that time is continuous. Instead of hazard probabilities, statisticians work with hazard rates, which are turned into survival curves by using exponentiation and integration. One difference between a rate and a probability is that the rate can exceed 1, whereas a probability never does. Also, a rate seems less intuitive for many survival problems encountered with customers.

The method for calculating hazards in this chapter is called the life table method, and it works well with discrete time data. A very similar method, called Kaplan-Meier, is used for continuous time data. The two techniques produce almost exactly the same results when events occur at discrete times.

An important part of statistical survival analysis is the estimation of hazards using parameterized regression—trying to find the best functional form for the hazards. This is an alternative approach, calculating the hazards directly from the data.

The parameterized approach has the important advantage that it can more easily include covariates in the process. Later in this chapter, there is an example based on such a parameterized model. Unfortunately, the hazard function rarely follows a form that would be familiar to nonstatisticians. The hazards do such a good job of describing the customer life cycle that it would be shocking if a simple function captured that rich complexity.

We strongly encourage interested readers who have a mathematical or statistical background to investigate the area further.

## Proportional Hazards

Sir David Cox is one of the most cited statisticians of the past century; his work comprises numerous books and over 250 articles. He has received many awards including a knighthood bestowed on him by Queen Elizabeth in 1985. Much of his research centered on understanding hazard functions, and his work has been particularly important in the world of medical research.

His seminal paper was about determining the effect of initial factors (time-zero covariates) on hazards. By assuming that these initial factors have a uniform proportional effect on hazards, he was able to figure out how to measure this effect for different factors. The purpose of this section is to introduce proportional hazards and to suggest how they are useful for understanding customers. This section starts with some examples of why proportional hazards are useful. It then describes an alternative approach before returning to the Cox model itself.

## Examples of Proportional Hazards

Consider the following statement about one risk from smoking: *The risk of leukemia for smokers is 1.53 times greater than for nonsmokers.* This result is a classic example of proportional hazards. At the time of the study, the researchers knew whether someone was or was not a smoker (actually, there was a third group of former smokers, but our purpose here is to illustrate an example). Whether or not someone is a smoker is an example of an initial condition. Since there are only two factors to consider, it is possible to just look at the hazard curves and to derive some sort of average for the overall risk.

Figure 12.11 provides an illustration from the world of marketing. It shows two sets of hazard probabilities, one for customers who joined from a telephone solicitation and the other from direct mail. Once again, how someone became a customer is an example of an initial condition. The hazards for the telemarketing customers are higher; looking at the chart, we might say telemarketing customers are a bit less than twice as risky as direct mail customers. Cox proportional hazard regression provides a way to quantify this.

The two just-mentioned examples use categorical variables as the risk factor. Consider another statement about the risk of tobacco: *The risk of colorectal cancer increases 6.7 percent per pack-year smoked.* This statement differs from the previous one, because it now depends on a continuous variable. Using proportional hazards, it is possible to determine the contribution of both categorical and continuous covariates.

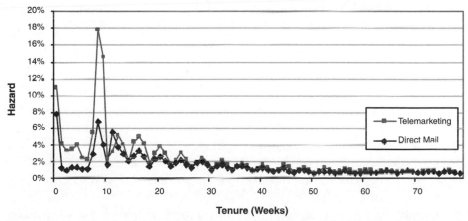

**Figure 12.11**   These two hazard functions suggest that the risk of attrition is about one and a half times as great for customers acquired through telemarketing versus direct mail.

## Stratification: Measuring Initial Effects on Survival

Figure 12.11 showed hazard probabilities for two different groups of customers, one that started via outbound telemarketing campaigns and the other via direct mail campaigns. These two curves clearly show differences between these channels. It is possible to generate a survival curve for these hazards and quantify the difference, using 1-year survival, median survival, or average truncated tenure. This approach to measuring differences among different groups defined by initial conditions is called *stratification* because each group is analyzed independently from other groups. This produces good visualizations and accurate survival values. It is also quite easy, since statistical packages such as SAS and SPSS have options that make it easy to stratify data for this purpose.

Stratification solves the problem of understanding initial effects assuming that two conditions are true. First, the initial effect needs to be a categorical variable. Since the data is being broken into separate groups, some variable, such as channel or product or region, needs to be chosen for this purpose. Of course, it is always possible to use binning to break a continuous variable into discrete chunks.

The second is that each group needs to be fairly big. When starting with lots and lots of customers and only using one variable that takes on a handful of values, such as channel, this is not a problem. However, there may be multiple variables of interest, such as:

- Acquisition channel
- Original promotion
- Geography

Once more than one dimension is included, the number of categories grows very quickly. This means that the data gets spread thinly, making the hazards less and less reliable.

## Cox Proportional Hazards

In 1972, Sir David Cox recognized this problem and he proposed a method of analysis, now known as Cox proportional hazards regression, which overcomes these limitations. His brilliant insight was to find a way to focus on the original conditions and not on the hazards themselves. The question is: What effect do the initial conditions have on hazards? His approach to answering this question is quite interesting.

Fortunately, the ideas are simpler than the mathematics behind his approach. Instead of focusing on hazards, he introduces the idea of partial likelihood. Assuming that only one customer stops at a given time $t$, the partial likelihood at $t$ is the likelihood that exactly that particular customer stopped.

The calculation for the partial likelihood divides whatever function or value represents the hazard for the specific customer that stopped by the sum of all the hazards for all the customers who might have stopped at that time. If all customers had the same hazard rates, then this ratio would be constant (one divided by the population at that point in time). However, the hazards are not constant and hopefully are some function of the initial conditions.

Cox made an assumption that the initial conditions have a constant effect on all hazards, regardless of the time of the hazard. The partial likelihood is a ratio, and the proportionality assumption means that the hazards, whatever they are, appear in both the numerator and denominator multiplied by a complicated expression based on the initial conditions. What is left is a complicated mathematical formula containing the initial conditions. The hazards themselves have disappeared from the partial likelihood; they simply cancel each other out.

The next step is to apply the partial likelihoods of all customers who stop to get the overall likelihood of those particular customers stopping. The product of all these partial likelihoods is an expression that gives the likelihood of seeing exactly the particular set of stopped customers stopping when they did. Conveniently, this likelihood is also expressed only terms of the initial conditions and not in terms of the hazards, which may not be known.

Fortunately, there is an area of statistics called maximum likelihood estimation, which when given a complicated expression for something like this finds the parameter values that make the result most likely. These parameter values conveniently represent the effect of the initial values on the hazards. As an added bonus, the technique works both with continuous and categorical values, whereas the stratification approach only works with categorical values.

## Limitations of Proportional Hazards

Cox proportional hazards regression is very powerful and very clever. However, it has its limitations. In order for all this to work, Cox had to make many assumptions. He designed his approach around continuous time hazards and also made the assumption that only one customer stops at any given time. With some tweaking, implementations of proportional hazards regression usually work for discrete time hazards and handle multiple stops at the same time.

**WARNING** Cox proportional hazards regression ranks and quantifies the effects of initial conditions on the overall hazard function. However, the results are highly dependent on the often dubious assumption that the initial conditions have a constant effect on the hazards over time. Use it carefully.

The biggest assumption in the proportional hazards model is the assumption of proportionality itself. That is, that the effect of the initial conditions on hazards does not have a time component. In practice, this is simply not true. It is rarely, if ever, true that initial conditions have such perfect proportionality, even in the scientific world. In the world of marketing, this is even less likely. Marketing is not a controlled experiment. Things are constantly changing; new programs, pricing, and competition are always arising.

The bad news is that there is no simple algorithm that explains initial conditions, taking into account different effects over time. The good news is that it often does not make a difference. Even with the assumption of proportionality, Cox regression does a good job of determining which covariates have a big impact on the hazards. In other words, it does a good job of explaining what initial conditions are correlated with customers leaving.

Cox's approach was designed only for time-zero covariates, as statisticians call initial values. The approach has been extended to handle events that occur during a customer's lifetime—such as whether they upgrade their product or make a complaint. In the language of statistics, these are time-dependent covariates, meaning that the additional factors can occur at any point during the customer's tenure, not only at the beginning of the relationship. Such factors might be a customer's response to a retention campaign or making complaints. Since Cox's original work, he and other statisticians have extended this technique to include these types of factors.

## Survival Analysis in Practice

Survival analysis has proven to be very valuable for understanding customers and quantifying marketing efforts in terms of customer retention. It provides a way of estimating how long it will be until something occurs. This section gives some particular examples of survival analysis.

### Handling Different Types of Attrition

Businesses that deal with customers have to deal with customers leaving for a variety of reasons. Earlier, this chapter described hazard probabilities and explained how hazards illustrate aspects of the business that affect the customer life cycle. In particular, peaks in hazards coincided with business processes that forced out customers who were not paying their bills.

Since these customers are treated differently, it is tempting to remove them entirely from the hazard calculation. This is the wrong approach. The problem is, which customers to remove is only known *after* the customers have been forced to stop. As mentioned earlier, it is not a good idea to use such knowledge, gained at the end of the customer relationship, to filter customers for analysis.

The right approach is to break this into two problems. What are the hazards for voluntary attrition? What are the hazards for forced attrition? Each of these uses all the customers, censoring the customers who leave due to other factors. When calculating the hazards for voluntary attrition, whenever a customer is forced to leave, the customer is included in the analysis until he or she leaves—at that point, the customer is censored. This makes sense. Up to the point when the customer was forced to leave, the customer did not leave voluntarily.

This approach can be extended for other purposes. Once upon a time, the authors were trying to understand different groups of customers at a newspaper, in particular, how survival by acquisition channel was or was not changing over time. Unfortunately, during one of the time periods, there was a boycott of the newspaper, raising the overall stop levels during that period. Not surprisingly, the hazards went up and survival decreased during this time period.

Is there a way to take into account these particular stops? The answer is "yes," because the company did a pretty good job of recording the reasons why customers stopped. The customers who boycotted the paper were simply censored on the day they stopped—as they say in the medical world, these customers were lost to follow-up. By censoring, it was possible to get an accurate estimate of the overall hazards without the boycott.

## When Will a Customer Come Back?

So far, the discussion of survival analysis has focused on the end of the customer relationship. Survival analysis can be used for many things besides predicting the probability of bad things happening. For instance, survival analysis can be used to estimate when customers will return after having stopped.

Figure 12.12 shows a survival curve and hazards for reactivation of customers after they deactivate their mobile telephone service. In this case, the hazard is the probability that a customer returns a given number of days after the deactivation.

There are several interesting features in these curves. First, the initial reactivation rate is very high. In the first week, more than a third of customers reactivate. Business rules explain this phenomenon. Many deactivations are due to customers not paying their bills. Many of these customers are just holding out until the last minute—they actually intend to keep their phones; they just don't like paying the bill. However, once the phone stops working, they quickly pay up.

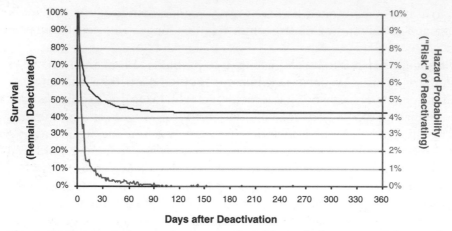

**Figure 12.12** Survival curve (upper curve) and hazards (lower curve) for reactivation of mobile telephone customers.

After 90 days, the hazards are practically zero—customers do not reactivate. Once again, the business processes provide guidance. Telephone numbers are reserved for 90 days after customers leave. Normally, when customers reactivate, they want to keep the same telephone number. After 90 days, the number may have been reassigned, and the customer would have to get a new telephone number.

This discussion has glossed over the question of how new (reactivated) customers were associated with the expired accounts. In this case, the analysis used the telephone numbers in conjunction with an account ID. This pretty much guaranteed that the match was accurate, since reactivated customers retained their telephone numbers and billing information. This is very conservative but works for finding reactivations. It does not work for finding other types of winback, such as customers who are willing to cycle through telephone numbers in order to get introductory discounts.

Another approach is to try to identify individuals over time, even when they are on different accounts. For businesses that collect Social Security numbers or driver's license numbers as a regular part of their business, such identifying numbers can connect accounts together over time. (Be aware that not everyone who is asked to supply this kind of identifying information does so accurately.) Sometimes matching names, addresses, telephone numbers, and/or credit cards is sufficient for matching purposes. More often, this task is outsourced to a company that assigns individual and household IDs, which then provide the information needed to identify which new customers are really former customers who have been won back.

Studying initial covariates adds even more information. In this case, "initial" means whatever is known about the customer at the point of deactivation. This includes not only information such as initial product and promotion, but also customer behavior before deactivating. Are customers who complain a lot more or less likely to reactivate? Customers who roam? Customers who pay their bills late?

This example shows the use of hazards to understand a classic time-to-event question. There are other questions of this genre amenable to survival analysis:

- When customers start on a minimum pricing plan, how long will it be before they upgrade to a premium plan?

- When customers upgrade to a premium plan, how long will it be before they downgrade?

- What is the expected length of time between purchases for customers, given past customer behavior and the fact that different customers have different purchase periods?

One nice aspect of using survival analysis is that it is easy to ask about the effects of different initial conditions—such as the number of times that a customer has visited in the past. Using proportional hazards, it is possible to determine which covariates have the most effect on the desired outcome, including which interventions are most and least likely to work.

## Forecasting

Another interesting application of survival analysis is forecasting the number of customers into the future, or equivalently, the number of stops on a given day in the future. In the aggregate, survival does a good job of estimating how many customers will stick around for a given length of time.

There are two components to any such forecast. The first is a model of existing customers, which can take into account various covariates during the customer's life cycle. Such a model works by applying one or more survival models to all customers. If a customer has survived for 100 days, then the probability of stopping tomorrow is the hazard at day 100. To calculate the chance of stopping the day after tomorrow, first assume that the customer does not stop tomorrow and then does stop on day 101. This is the conditional survival (one minus the hazard—the probability of not stopping) at day 100 times the hazard for day 101. Applying this to all customer tenures, it is possible to forecast stops of existing customers in the future.

Figure 12.13 shows such a forecast for stops for 1 month, developed by survival expert Will Potts. Also shown are the actual values observed during this period. The survival-based forecast proves to be quite close to what is actually happening. By the way, this particular survival estimate used a parametric model on the hazards rather than empirical hazard rates; the model was able to take into account the day of the week. This results in the weekly cycle of stops evident in the graph.

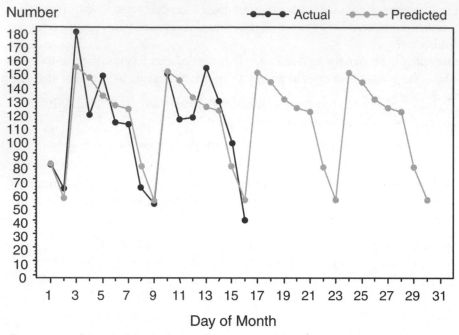

**Figure 12.13** Survival analysis can also be used for forecasting customer stops.

The second component of a customer-level forecast is a bit more difficult to calculate. This component is the effect of new customers on the forecast, and the difficulty is not technical. The challenge is getting estimates for new starts. Fortunately, there are often budget forecasts that contain new starts, sometimes broken down by product, channel, or geography. It is possible to refine the survival models to take into account these effects. Of course, the forecast is only as accurate as the budget. The upside, though, is that the forecast, based on survival techniques, can be incorporated into the process of managing actual levels against budgeted levels.

The combination of these components—stop forecasts for existing customers and stop forecasts for new customers—makes it possible to develop estimates of customer levels into the future. The authors have worked with clients who have taken these forecasts forward years. Because the models for new customers included the acquisition channel, the forecasting model made it possible to optimize the future acquisition channel mix.

## Hazards Changing over Time

One of the more difficult issues in survival analysis is whether the hazards themselves are constant or whether they change over time. The assumption in scientific studies is that hazards do not change. The goal of scientific survival analysis is to obtain estimates of the "real" hazard in various situations.

This assumption may or may not be true in marketing. Certainly, working with this assumption, survival analysis has proven its worth with customer data. However, it is interesting to consider the possibility that hazards may be changing over time. In particular, if hazards do change, that gives some insight into whether the market place and customers are getting better or worse over time.

One approach to answering this question is to base hazards on customers who are stopping rather than customers who are starting, especially, say, customers who have stopped in each of the past few years. In other words, were the hazards associated with customers who stopped last year significantly different from the hazards associated with customers who stopped the previous year? Earlier, this chapter warned that calculating hazards for a set of customers chosen by their stop date does not produce accurate hazards. How can we overcome this problem?

There is a way to calculate these hazards, although this has not yet appeared in standard statistical tools. This method uses time windows on the customers to estimate the hazard probability. Remember the definition of the empirical hazard probability: the number of customers who stopped at a particular time divided by the number of customers who could have stopped at that time. Up to now, all customers have been included in the calculation. The idea is to restrict the customers only to those who could have stopped during the period in question.

As an example, consider estimating the hazards based on customers who stopped in 2003. Customers who stopped in 2003 were either active on the first day of 2003 or were new customers during the year. In either case, customers only contribute to the population count starting at whatever their tenure was on the first day of 2003 (or 0 for new starts).

Let's consider the calculation of the 1-day hazard probability. What is the population of customers who could have stopped with 1 day of tenure and also have the stop in 2003? Only customers that started between December 31, 2002 and December 30, 2003 could have a 1-day stop in 2003. So, the calculation of the 1-day hazard uses all stops in 2003 where the tenure was 1 day as the total for stops. The population at risk consists of customers who started between December 31, 2002 and December 30, 2003. As another example, the 365-day hazard would be based on a population count of customers who started in 2002.

The result is an estimate of the hazards based on stops during a particular period of time. For comparison purposes, survival proves to be more useful than the hazards themselves. Figure 12.14 provides an example, showing that survival is indeed decreasing over the course of several years. The changes in survival are small. However, the calculations are based on hundreds of thousands of customers and do represent a decline in customer quality.

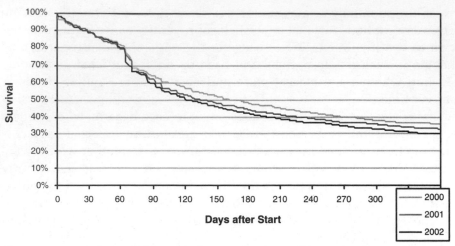

**Figure 12.14**  A time-window technique makes it possible to see changes in survival over time.

## Lessons Learned

Hazards and survival analysis are designed for understanding customers. This chapter introduced hazards as the conditional probability of a customer leaving at a given point in time. This treatment of survival analysis is unorthodox in terms of statistics, which prefers an approach based on continuous rates rather than discrete time probabilities. However, this treatment is more intuitive for analyzing customers.

Hazards are like an x-ray of the customer life cycle. The related idea of survival, which is the proportion of customers who survive up to a particular point in time, makes it possible to compare different groups of customers and to translate results into dollars and cents. When there are enough customers (and usually there are), stratifying the customers by building a separate curve for each group provides a good comparison. It is possible to use other measures, such as the survival at a particular point in time, the customer half-life, and the average tenure, to better understand customers.

One of the key concepts in survival analysis is censoring. This means that some customers are dropped from the analysis. The idea of censoring can be extended to understand competing risks, such as voluntary versus forced attrition. Censoring also makes it possible to discard certain outcomes, such as a one-time boycott, without adversely biasing overall results.

One of the most powerful aspects of hazards is the ability to determine which factors, at the onset, are responsible for increasing or decreasing the hazards. In addition to stratifying customers, there is another technique, Cox proportional hazards regression, which has proven its worth since the 1970s and continues to be extended and improved upon.

Survival analysis has many applications beyond measuring the probability of customers leaving. It has been used for forecasting customer levels, as well as for predicting other types of events during the customer life cycle. It is a very powerful tool, seemingly designed specifically for understanding customers and their life cycles.

# CHAPTER 13

# Genetic Algorithms

Like memory-based reasoning and neural networks, genetic algorithms are based on an analogy to biological processes. Evolution and natural selection have, over the course of millions of years, resulted in adaptable, specialized species that are highly suited to their environments. Evolution optimizes the fitness of individuals over succeeding generations by propagating the genetic material in the fittest individuals of one generation to the next generation.

Genetic algorithms apply the same idea to problems where the solution can be expressed as an optimal "individual" and the goal is to maximize the "fitness" of individuals. Many problems can be described in this way; the challenge is encoding the problem in the right fashion. For instance, one application of genetic algorithms is to the training of neural networks. An individual is then a set of values for the weights inside the network; the fitness of an individual is the accuracy of the neural network having those weights on the training set. The training proceeds in an evolutionary way, by having more fit individuals propagate their weights to succeeding generations. Less fit individuals—and their genetic material—do not survive. Although chance plays a significant role in the survival of any particular individual, over a larger population there are enough examples of different types of individuals for natural selection to propagate the genetic material that produces the fittest individuals.

Genetic algorithms, which are also called evolutionary algorithms, have been applied to optimization problems in various industries, including complex scheduling problems, resource optimization in large factories, and classification problems involving complex data types. They have also been used in combination with other data mining algorithms, including determining the best topology for neural networks, determining the scoring function for memory-based reasoning, and, as already mentioned, optimizing weights in neural networks. However, genetic algorithms are not commonly found in general data mining packages.

---

**OPTIMIZATION**

Optimization problems have three features:

♦ A set of parameters (which for GAs are called *genomes* or *chromosomes*)

♦ A function that combines the parameters into a single value (the *fitness function*)

♦ A set of constraints on the parameters (for GAs these are incorporated into the fitness function)

The goal is to find the parameters that maximize or minimize the fitness function, subject to the constraints. Searching through all combinations of parameters that meet the constraints is too cumbersome for even the most advanced computers; even for a small number of parameters, the number of combinations is too large to search.

Genetic algorithms are one approach to solving such problems, but not the only one. When the fitness function satisfies some specific mathematical conditions, then differential calculus can be used to find the optimal solution. Although few functions in practice are differentiable, calculus also includes ideas for estimating solutions in other cases. The conjugate-gradient method for training neural networks is based on such ideas, as is the "solver" capability in Excel.

Another approach arises with linear programming problems. These are problems where the fitness function is linear and all the constraints are also linear. These constraints are often met in resource allocation problems, such as:

> A company produces widgets in a set of factories. Each factory has a capacity, a cost of production, and a cost for transporting widgets to customers. How many widgets should each factory produce to satisfy customer demand at minimal cost?

The standard method for solving such problems is called the Simplex method, and it is computationally efficient. Such problems have been solved with thousands of variables. Further information on linear programming type problems is available on the linear programming FAQ at www-unix.mcs.anl.gov/otc/Guide/faq/linear-programming-faq.html.

Another approach is called simulated annealing. This uses an analogy to a physical process: some liquids cool and form crystalline patterns as they cool. The crystal minimizes certain types of energy, and this happens across the entire crystal. Scientists studying physical properties are the most common users of simulated annealing.

The first work on genetic algorithms dates back to the late 1950s, when biologists and computer scientists worked together to model the mechanisms of evolution on early computers. A bit later, in the early 1960s, Professor John Holland and his colleagues at the University of Michigan applied this work on computerized genetics—chromosomes, genes, alleles, and fitness functions—to optimization problems. In 1967, one of Holland's students, J. D. Bagley, coined the term *genetic algorithms* in his graduate thesis to describe the optimization technique. At the time, many researchers were uncomfortable with genetic algorithms because of their dependence on random choices during the process of evolving a solution; these choices seemed arbitrary and unpredictable. In the 1970s, Prof. Holland developed a theoretical foundation for the technique. His theory of schemata gives insight into why genetic algorithms work—and intriguingly suggests why genetics itself creates successful, adaptable creatures such as ourselves.

In the world of data mining and data analysis, the use of genetic algorithms has not been as widespread as the use of other techniques. Data mining focuses on tasks such as classification and prediction, rather than on optimization. Although many data mining problems can be framed as optimization problems, this is not the usual description. For instance, a typical data mining problem might be to predict the level of inventory needed for a given item in a catalog based on the first week of sales, characteristics about the items in the catalog, and its recipients. Rephrasing this as an optimization problem turns it into something like "what function best fits the inventory curve for predictive purposes." Applying statistical regression techniques is one way to find the function. Feeding the data into a neural network is another way of estimating it. Using genetic algorithms offers another possibility. The aside "Optimization" discusses other methods designed specifically for this purpose.

This chapter covers the background of genetics on computers, and introduces the schema mechanism invented by John Holland to explain why genetic algorithms work. It talks about two case studies, one in the area of resource optimization and the other in the area of classifying email messages. Although few commercial data mining products include genetic algorithms (GAs), more specialized packages do support the algorithms. They are an important and active area of research and may become more widely used in the future.

## How They Work

The power of genetic algorithms comes from their foundation in biology, where evolution has proven capable of adapting life to a multitude of environments (see sidebar "Simple Overview of Genetics"). The success of mapping the template for the human genome—all the common DNA shared by human individuals—is just the beginning. The human genome has been providing knowledge for advances in many fields, such as medical research, biochemistry, genetics, and even anthropology. Although interesting, human genomics is fortunately beyond the scope of knowledge needed to understand genetic algorithms. The language used to describe the computer technique borrows heavily from the biological model, as discussed in the following section.

## Genetics on Computers

A simple example helps illustrate how genetic algorithms work: trying to find the maximum value of a simple function with a single integer parameter $p$. The function in this example is the parabola (which looks like an upside-down "U") defined by $31p - p^2$ where $p$ varies between 0 and 31 (see Figure 13.1). The parameter $p$ is expressed as a string of 5 bits to represent the numbers from 0 to 31; this bit string is the genetic material, called a *genome*. The fitness function peaks at the values 15 and 16, represented as *01111* and *10000*, respectively. This example shows that genetic algorithms are applicable even when there are multiple, dissimilar peaks.

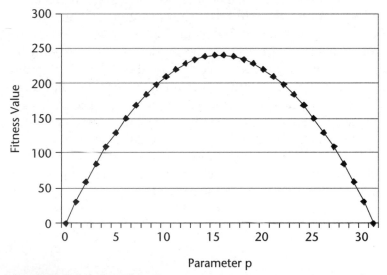

**Figure 13.1**   Finding the maximum of this simple function helps illustrate genetic algorithms.

GAs work by evolving successive generations of genomes that get progressively more and more *fit*; that is, they provide better solutions to the problem. In nature, fitness is simply the ability of an organism to survive and reproduce. On a computer, evolution is simulated with the following steps:

1. Identify the genome and fitness function.
2. Create an initial generation of genomes.
3. Modify the initial population by applying the operators of genetic algorithms.
4. Repeat Step 3 until the fitness of the population no longer improves.

The first step is setting up the problem. In this simple example, the genome consists of a single, 5-bit gene for the parameter $p$. The fitness function is the parabola. Over the course of generations, the fitness function is going to be maximized.

For this example, shown in Table 13.1, the initial generation consists of four genomes, randomly produced. A real problem would typically have a population of hundreds or thousands of genomes, but that is impractical for illustrative purposes. Notice that in this population, the average fitness is 122.5—pretty good, since the actual maximum is 240, but evolution can improve it.

The basic algorithm modifies the initial population using three operators—selection, then crossover, then mutation—as illustrated in Figure 13.2. These operators are explained in the next three sections.

**Table 13.1** Four Randomly Generated Genomes

| GENOME | P | FITNESS |
|--------|---|---------|
| 10110 | 22 | 198 |
| 00011 | 3 | 84 |
| 00010 | 2 | 58 |
| 11001 | 25 | 150 |

**generation n**　　　　**generation n + 1**

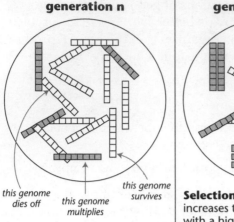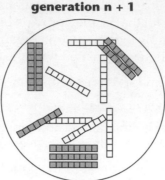

*this genome dies off*　*this genome multiplies*　*this genome survives*

**Selection** keeps the size of the population constant but increases the fitness of the next generation. Genomes with a higher fitness (darker shading) proliferate and genomes with lighter shading die off.

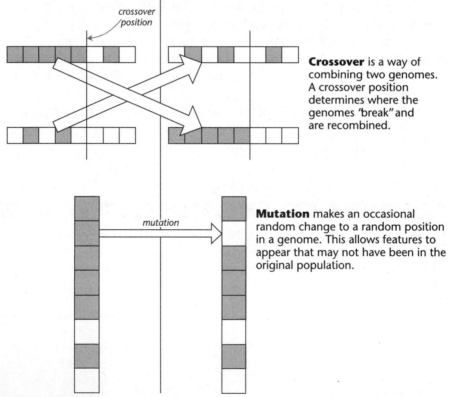

*crossover position*

**Crossover** is a way of combining two genomes. A crossover position determines where the genomes "break" and are recombined.

*mutation*

**Mutation** makes an occasional random change to a random position in a genome. This allows features to appear that may not have been in the original population.

**Figure 13.2**　The basic operators in genetic algorithms are selection, crossover, and mutation.

## SIMPLE OVERVIEW OF GENETICS

Life depends on proteins, which consist of sequences of 20 basic units called amino acids. The chromosomes in the nucleus of a cell are strands of DNA (deoxyribonucleic acid) that carry the blueprints for the proteins needed by the cell. The 23 chromosomes in each human cell together are the genome for that individual. In general, the genomes of different individuals in a species are very similar to each other; however, there are some individual differences.

The DNA in the genome encodes these blueprints for the amino acids sequences using strands of nucleotides. These nucleotides constitute the four letters of the genetic alphabet:

- ◆ A, adenine
- ◆ C, cytosine
- ◆ G, guanine
- ◆ T, thymine

Triplets of nucleotides represent the 20 amino acids. For instance, the amino acid called methionine corresponds to the triplet ATG. Another amino acid, lysine, has two "spellings": AAA and AAG. So, if a strand of DNA contains the following letters:

ATGAAGATGCGA

then it decodes into a protein containing four amino acids: methionine, ATG; lysine, AAG; methionine, ATG; followed by arginine, CGA (see figure). This description intentionally glosses over the details of the actual biochemical mechanism that turns the blueprints into proteins, but it provides a high-level outline of the mapping from genetic information in DNA to the building blocks of proteins.

A biological example of encoding is the mapping from nucleotides in DNA to amino acids in protein.

In this simplified model, the process of evolution works as follows. The proteins produced by the representations in the DNA express themselves as features of the living organism, such as blue eyes, five fingers, the structure of the brain, a long trunk, and so on. Genes can express themselves in damaging ways, causing the resulting organism to die. Healthy organisms survive to produce offspring and pass their DNA to the next generation. In higher-level animals, the DNA is actually combined with the DNA from another survivor during sexual replication, using a technique called crossover. Sometimes, mistakes are made in passing genes from one generation to the next—these are mutations. The combination of all these processes over the course of many generations results in organisms highly adapted to their environment: the process of evolution.

*(continued)*

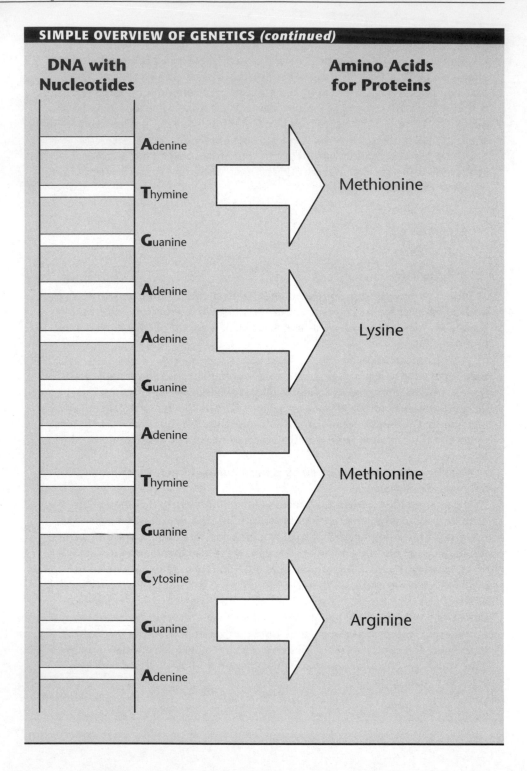

## SIMPLE OVERVIEW OF GENETICS *(continued)*

**DNA with Nucleotides**

**Amino Acids for Proteins**

**A**denine
**T**hymine
**G**uanine

→ Methionine

**A**denine
**A**denine
**G**uanine

→ Lysine

**A**denine
**T**hymine
**G**uanine

→ Methionine

**C**ytosine
**G**uanine
**A**denine

→ Arginine

## Selection

The selection step is analogous to the process of natural selection where only the fittest individuals in the population survive to pass their genetic material on to the next generation. Unlike nature, though, the size of the population remains constant from one generation to the next, so there is no chance of the population becoming extinct (which would clearly not be the optimum solution!). The chance of a genome surviving to the next generation is proportional to its fitness value—the better the fitness value relative to other genomes, the more copies that survive to the next generation. Table 13.2 shows the ratio of the fitness of the four genomes to the population fitness. This ratio determines the number of copies of each genome expected in the next generation.

The expected number of copies is a fraction, but the number of genomes in the population is never fractional. Survival is based on choosing the genomes in a random way proportional to their fitness. A random number is generated between 0 and 1, and this random number is used to determine whether a copy of a genome survives or not. Using the example from Table 13.2, if the first random number is less than 0.404, then genome 10110 would be chosen; if it is between 0.404 and 0.576 (40.4% + 17.1%), the genome 00011 would be chosen, and so on. More random numbers are generated until the next generation has the right number of genomes. Using a random number generator converts the fractional probabilities to whole number approximations, and it also allows some genomes with low fitness to survive.

Applying selection to the original four genomes yields the survivors shown in Table 13.3. Notice that in general this procedure produces more copies of the fitter genomes and fewer of the less fit. One of the less fit, *00011*, has not survived this round of selection, but there are two copies of *10110*, the fittest. And, the average fitness of the population has increased from 122.5 to 151.0.

**Table 13.2**   Using Fitness for Selection

| GENOME | POPULATION FITNESS | % OF TOTAL EXPECTED FITNESS | COPIES |
|--------|--------------------|-----------------------------|--------|
| 10110 | 198 | 40.4% | 1.62 |
| 00011 | 84 | 17.1% | 0.69 |
| 00010 | 58 | 11.8% | 0.47 |
| 11001 | 150 | 30.6% | 1.22 |

**Table 13.3** The Population after Selection

| GENOME | P | FITNESS |
|--------|-----|---------|
| 10110  | 22  | 198     |
| 11001  | 25  | 150     |
| 00010  | 2   | 58      |
| 10110  | 22  | 198     |

## Crossover

The next operator applied to the surviving genomes is crossover. Crossover, which occurs in nature, creates two new genomes from two existing ones by gluing together pieces of each one. As shown in Figure 13.2, crossover starts with two genomes and a random position. The first part of one genome swaps places with the first part of the second. For instance, starting with the two genomes *10110* and *00010* and using a crossover position between the second and third position works as follows:

10 | 1 1 0

00 | 0 1 0

The result of crossover is (the genes from the second genome are underlined):

10 | 0 1 0

00 | 1 1 0

The resulting genomes, called children, each have a piece of their chromosomes inherited from each of their parents. Applying crossover to the population proceeds by selecting pairs of genomes and flipping a coin to determine whether they split and swap. This probability is the crossover probability, denoted by $p_c$. If they do cross over, then a random position is chosen and the children of the original genomes replace them in the next generation. A value of 0.5 for the crossover probability (corresponding to a coin toss) generally produces good results. In the example, the two genomes *10110* and *00010* are chosen for crossover, and the position is between the second and third genes (Table 13.4). Notice that after selection and crossover, the average fitness of the population has gone from 122.5 to 183.0. This is a significant improvement after only one generation.

**Table 13.4**  The Population after Selection and Crossover

| GENOME | P | FITNESS |
|--------|-----|---------|
| 10010 | 18 | 234 |
| 11001 | 25 | 150 |
| 00110 | 6 | 150 |
| 10110 | 22 | 198 |

## Mutation

The final operation is mutation. Mutation rarely occurs in nature and is the result of miscoded genetic material being passed from a parent to a child. The resulting change in the gene may represent a significant improvement in fitness over the existing population, although more often than not, the results are harmful. Selection and crossover do a good job of searching the space of possible genomes, but they depend on initial conditions and randomness that might conspire to prevent certain valuable combinations from being considered in succeeding generations. Mutation provides the additional input. The mutation rate is quite small in nature and is usually kept quite low for genetic algorithms—no more than one mutation or so per generation is a reasonable bound. For the example at hand, when a mutation occurs, the bit changes from a 0 to a 1 or from a 1 to a 0.

Assume that there is one mutation in this generation, occurring in the second genome at position 3. Table 13.5 shows the population of genomes after such a mutation. Notice that this mutation, like many mutations, is destructive: The fitness of the genome affected by the mutation decreased from 150 to 58, the average fitness of the population decreased from 183.0 to 160.0, and the resulting genome is unlikely to survive to the next generation. This is not unusual. The primary modus operandi of genetic algorithms is selection and crossover. Mutation is very much a second-order effect that helps avoid premature convergence to a local optimum. When the initial population provides good coverage of the space of possible combinations, succeeding generations move quickly toward the optimal solution by means of selection and crossover. Changes introduced by mutation are likely to be destructive and do not last for more than a generation or two. Yet, despite the harmful mutation in this example, the second generation is a considerable improvement over the original population.

**Table 13.5**   The Population after Selection, Crossover, and Mutation

| GENOME | P | FITNESS |
|--------|-----|---------|
| 10010 | 18 | 234 |
| 11101 | 29 | 58 |
| 00110 | 6 | 150 |
| 10110 | 22 | 198 |

The basis of genetic algorithms is the continual improvement of the fitness of the population by means of selection, crossover, and mutation as genes are passed from one generation to the next. After a certain number of generations—typically several dozen or hundred—the population evolves to a near-optimal solution. Genetic algorithms do not always produce the exact optimal solution, but they do a very good job of getting close to the best solution. In data mining, where exact solutions may not be feasible, being close to the best solution still yields actionable results.

## Representing Data

The previous example illustrated the basic mechanisms of applying genetic algorithms to the optimization of a simple function, $31p - p^2$. Since the example was trying to maximize a particular function, the function itself served as the fitness function. The genomes were quite easy to create, because the function had one parameter, a 5-bit integer that varied between 0 and 31. This genome contained a single gene, representing the parameter, and consisting of a sequence of 5 binary bits. The choice of representation using binary sequences is not accidental. As explained later in the section on schemata, genetic algorithms work best on binary representations of data—a highly convenient circumstance, since computers themselves work most efficiently on binary data.

Genetic algorithms are different from other data mining and optimization techniques in that they manipulate the patterns of bits in the genomes and do not care at all about the values represented by the bits—only the fitness function knows what the patterns really mean. One requirement for the fitness function is the ability to transform any genome into a fitness value. This requirement does not seem particularly onerous, because computers are used to working with data in bits. However, some patterns of bits may violate constraints imposed on the problem. When the genome violates such constraints, then the fitness is set to a minimum. That is, testing for constraints in the fitness function incorporates constraints into the solution.

For instance, the previous example had a constraint that the value be between 0 and 31. This was made implicitly true by using 5 bits to represent the genome. What if there were 8 bits? In this case, the fitness function would look like:

- $31 - p^2$ when $0 <= p <= 31$
- 0 otherwise

The general rule here is to include a minimum fitness value for any bit patterns that do not make sense or that violate problem constraints. Such patterns may not be in the original population, but they might appear because of crossover and mutation.

**TIP** The fitness function is defined on the genome, a sequence of bits. It must be able to understand any pattern of 1s and 0s in the bits. When a particular pattern of bits does not make sense, then the fitness function should return a very low value—so the pattern does not get passed on to succeeding generations.

## Case Study: Using Genetic Algorithms for Resource Optimization

One area where genetic algorithms have proven quite successful is in problems involving scheduling resources subject to a wide range of constraints. These types of problems involve competition for limited resources, while adhering to a complex set of rules that describe relationships. The key to these problems is defining a fitness function that incorporates all the constraints into a single fitness value. These problems are outside the range of what we have been considering as traditional data mining problems; however, they are interesting and illustrate the power of genetic algorithms.

An example of such a problem is the assignment of 40 medical residents to various duties in an outpatient clinic, as faced by Dr. Ed Ewen at the Medical Center of Delaware. The clinic is open 7 days a week, and the residents are assigned to one particular day of the week through an entire year, regardless of their other duties. The best assignment balances several different goals:

- The clinic must have staff at all times.
- The clinic should have a balance of first-, second-, and third-year residents.
- Third-year residents see eight patients per day, second-year residents see six, and first-year residents see four.

So far, this problem is not so complicated. However, each resident spends 4 weeks on a rotation in a given part of the hospital, such as the intensive care ward, the oncology unit, or a community hospital. These rotations impose some other constraints:

- Senior residents do not go to the clinic when they are assigned to the medical intensive care rotation, but all other residents do.

- Junior residents do not go to the clinic when they are assigned to the cardiac care rotation, but all other residents do.

- No more than two residents from the intensive care rotation can be assigned to the clinic on the same day.

- No more than three residents from other rotations can be assigned to the clinic on the same day.

As an example of problems that may arise, consider that during one rotation, five residents are assigned to the clinic on a particular day. During the next rotation, the senior is on the medical intensive care rotation and the two juniors are on the cardiac care rotation. Now there are only two residents left at the clinic—and this is insufficient for clinic operations.

The genetic algorithms approach recognizes that there is probably no perfect solution to this problem, but that some assignments of residents to days of the week are clearly better than others. Dr. Ewen recognized that he could capture the "goodness" of a schedule using a fitness function. Actually, the function that Dr. Ewen used was an anti-fitness function—the higher the value, the worse the schedule. This function imposed penalties for violating the constraints:

- For each day when the clinic has fewer than three residents, an amount is added—a larger amount the bigger the size of the deficit.

- For each day when there are no seniors in the clinic, a small amount is added.

- For each day when fewer than three residents are left on a rotation, a large amount is added to the fitness function.

- And so on.

Setting up a spreadsheet with these functions, Dr. Ewen tried to minimize the functions to get the best assignment. His initial assignments had scores in the range of 130 to 140. After several hours of work, he was able to reduce the score to 72. Pretty good.

However, he had available a genetic algorithms package from the Ward Systems Group (www.wardsystems.com) that plugs into Excel spreadsheets. He started with a population of 100 randomly generated assignments, none of which were very good. After 80 generations, the package lowered the score to 21—considerably better than he was able to do by hand.

This example gives a good feeling for optimization problems where genetic algorithms are applicable. They differ from most data mining problems because they are more rule-oriented than data-oriented. The key to solving these problems is to incorporate the constraints into a single fitness function to be optimized (either by finding a maximum or a minimum). The resulting fitness function might be highly nonlinear, making it difficult to optimize using other techniques. As we will see, the same techniques adapt to situations featuring larger amounts of data.

**TIP** Genetic algorithms are a good tool when there are more rules than data in the problem (although they are useful in other areas as well). These types of scheduling problems often involve competition for limited resources subject to complex relationships that describe resources and their users.

## Schemata: Why Genetic Algorithms Work

At first sight, there is nothing sacrosanct in the selection, crossover, and mutation operators introduced earlier in this chapter. Why, for instance, does crossover choose only one intermediate point instead of two or more? Why do low mutation rates produce better results? The fact that nature behaves this way is not sufficient justification if multiple crossover points would produce better results more quickly or if a high mutation rate would work better.

For solving problems that yield actionable results, the fact that genetic algorithms have worked well in practice may be sufficient justification for continuing to use them as they are. However, it is still comforting to know that the technique has a theoretical foundation. Prof. Holland developed his theory of schemata processing in the early 1970s to explain why selection, crossover, and mutation work so well in practice. Readers interested in using genetic algorithms for some of their problems are particularly well advised to understand schemata, even if the genetic algorithms are buried inside tools they are using, since this understanding explains both the power and the limits of the technique.

A *schema*, which comes from the Greek word meaning "form" or "figure," is simply a representation of the patterns present in a genome. Schemata (the plural is formed from the Greek root) are represented as sequences of symbols. The 1s and 0s (called the *fixed positions*) of genomes are augmented by an asterisk, *, that matches either a 0 or a 1. The relationship between a schema and a genome is simple. A genome matches a schema when the fixed positions in the schema match the corresponding positions in the genome. An example should make this quite clear; the following schema:

10**

matches all of the following four genomes because they all have four symbols, beginning with a *1* followed by a *0*:

1 0 0 0

1 0 0 1

1 0 1 1

1 0 1 0

The *order* of a schema is the number of fixed positions that it contains. For instance, the order of *1*10111* is 6, of ****1010**1* is 5, and of *0**************** is 1. The *defining length* of a schema is the distance between the outermost fixed positions. So, the defining length of *1*10111* is 6 (counting from the left, $7 - 1$), of ****1010**1* is 6 ($10 - 4$) and of *0**************** is 0 ($1 - 1$).

Now, let us look at fitness functions in terms of schemata. If the genome *000* survives from one generation to the next, then the schema *0*** has also survived, as have **0*, ***0, *00, 0*0, 00*, and ****. The fitness of a particular schema, then, is the average fitness of all the genomes that match the schema in a given population. For instance, the fitness of the schema *0*** is the average fitness of the genomes *000, 001, 010*, and *011* since the schema survives when these genomes survive, at least considering only the selection operator. Consider two schemata from the previous example using the fitness function $31p - p^2$, *10*** and *00***. One genome in the initial population matches *10***, so its fitness is 176. The two genomes matching *00**** have fitness values of 87 and 58. The first schema is fitter than the second. And, in fact, in the next generation there is only one genome matching *00**** and there are two matching *10***. The fitter schema has survived and proliferated; the less fit is disappearing.

A geometric view of schemata is sometimes helpful for understanding them. Consider the eight possible genomes of length three: *000, 001, 010, 011, 100, 101, 110,* and *111*. These lie at the corners of a unit cube, as shown in Figure 13.3. Schemata then correspond to the edges and faces of the cube. The edges are the schemata of order 2 and the faces of order 1. As genetic algorithms are processing different genomes; they are also processing schemata, visualized by these features on a cube. The population covers pieces of the cube trying to find the corners with the best fitness, and the schemata provide information about large regions of the possible solutions. This geometric perspective generalizes to higher dimensions, where the selection, crossover, and mutation operators correspond to cuts through hypercubes in some higher-dimension space that is a bit harder to visualize

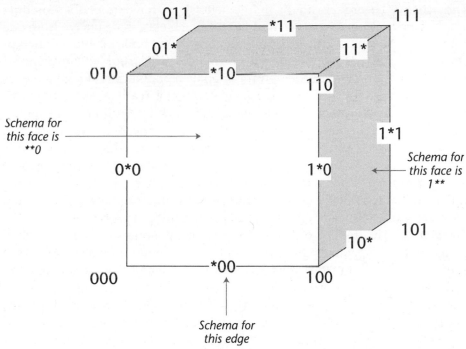

**Figure 13.3**   A cube is a useful representation of schemata on 3 bits. The corners represent the genomes, the edges represent the schemata of order 2, the faces, the schemata of order 1, and the entire cube, the schema of order 0.

Consider the schema, $1^{***}1$. This is also quite fit in the original population, with a fitness of 150. There is one genome that matches it in the original population and the same one in the next generation. This schema has survived only because the genome containing it did not cross over with another genome. A crossover would likely have destroyed it. Compare this to $10^{***}$ that survived a crossover. The shorter the defining length of a schema, the more likely it will be to survive from one generation to another. So, even longer schemata that are very fit are likely to be replaced by shorter, but fit, cousins. Using more complicated crossover techniques, such as making two cuts, changes the behavior entirely. With more complicated techniques, the defining length is no longer useful, and Holland's results on schemata do not necessarily hold.

Holland rigorously proved these two observations and summed them up in the Schema Theorem (also called the Fundamental Theorem of Genetic Algorithms): short, low-order schemata with above-average fitness increase in population from one generation to the next. In other words, short, low-order schemata are the building blocks that genetic algorithms are working on. From one generation to the next, the fittest building blocks survive and mix with each other to produce fitter and fitter genomes.

The Schema Theorem explains that genetic algorithms are really searching through the possible schemata to find fit building blocks that survive from one generation to the next. A natural question is how many building blocks are typically being processed? We will spare the reader the details, but Holland showed that the number of schemata being processed by a population of $n$ genomes is proportional to $n^3$. This means that each generation is really evaluating $n^3$ different schemata, even though it is only doing work on $n$ different genomes. Holland calls this property *implicit parallelism*. The computational effort for a genetic algorithm is proportional to the size of the population, and in this effort, the algorithm is usefully processing a number of schemata proportional to $n^3$. The property of implicit parallelism should not be confused with explicit parallelism that is available when running genetic algorithms on a distributed network of workstations or on a computer with multiple processors.

The Schema Theorem gives us insight into why genomes work better when there are only two symbols (*0*s and *1*s) in the representation. Finding the best building blocks requires processing as many schemata as possible from one generation to the next. For two symbols, the number of different genomes of a given length is $2^{length}$ and the number of different schemata is $3^{length}$. Roughly, the number of unique schemata being processed by a single genome is about $1.5^{length}$. Now, what happens if there are more symbols in the alphabet, say by adding 2 and 3? Now the number of genomes of a given length is $4^{length}$, and the number of different schemata is $5^{length}$ (because the asterisk adds one more symbol). Although there are more schemata, the number of schemata corresponding to a given genome is only $1.25^{length}$. As the number of symbols increases, the relative number of schemata decreases. Another way of looking at this is to consider the schema *00. If there are only two letters in the alphabet, then only two genomes process this schema, *000* and *100*. If there are four letters, then there are four genomes: *000, 100, 200,* and *300*. Since genetic algorithms are trying to find the best schemata using a given population size, the additional genomes do not help the search.

Schemata are the building blocks of the solutions, and using only two symbols allows the maximum number of schemata to be represented in a given population size. These estimates are not exact, but they are suggestive. More rigorous treatment confirms the result that an alphabet of two symbols is optimal from the point of view of processing schemata.

## More Applications of Genetic Algorithms

Genetic algorithms have been used to solve some real problems. This section talks about two applications of genetic algorithms. The first is their application to neural networks and the second is their application to predictive modeling.

## Application to Neural Networks

Neural networks and genetic algorithms are natural allies. One of the strengths of genetic algorithms is their ability to work on *black boxes*—that is, on problems where the fitness function is available but the details of the calculations are not known. The use of genetic algorithms to train neural networks is a good example, although this method of training is not common.

Figure 13.4 illustrates a simple neural network with three input nodes, a hidden layer with two nodes, and a single output node. The key to making the network work well is adjusting the weights on its edges so that the output produces the right answer for appropriate inputs. Chapter 7 discussed the nature of the functions inside the nodes and how standard training algorithms proceed. For the current discussion, all we need is that the network can produce an output for any given set of weights and inputs. The weights are real numbers, and there is a training set that includes inputs and the corresponding correct output.

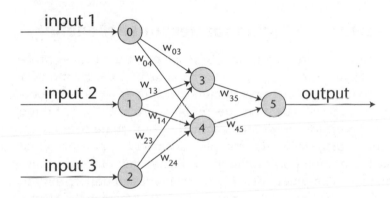

Without really even understanding how a neural network works, the weights can be gathered into a genome so a genetic algorithm can optimize them.

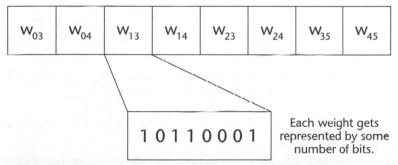

**Figure 13.4**   A neural network is described by weights that genetic algorithms can optimize.

The first problem faced is to determine what a genome looks like. The genome consists of all the weights in the network glommed together. What is the fitness function? The fitness function creates a network using the weights and then applies this model to the training set. The fitness function then compares the predicted output of this neural network to the actual output; hence, the fitness function is defined as the overall error of the neural network with those weights on the training set. The genetic algorithm proceeds by minimizing this function.

Another application to neural networks is determining the topology of the network—how many nodes should be in the hidden layer and what activation functions should be used. Different topologies can be described using different sets of weights, and then the genetic algorithms can proceed to find the best ones. In this case, the fitness function creates the network described by the genome, and then trains the network using standard training methods, and the error from the best network is used for the fitness function. This is an example of genetic algorithms being used to evolve optimal solutions for a complicated problem.

## Case Study: Evolving a Solution for Response Modeling

A more interesting use of genetic algorithms is to solve a real business problem. Direct feedback from customers is a powerful source of information for businesses. When a customer makes a complaint, the company has an opportunity to make a good impression by fixing the problem promptly or, if it is too late for that, by making up for the problem somehow. For some companies, such as product goods manufacturers, complaints provide dates of actual product use—a bit of additional information to add to manufacturing and shipping dates. Customer complaints also hand companies an opportunity to improve processes so that they have fewer dissatisfied customers in the future.

In our work building retention models for mobile phone companies, we have seen situations where customers who make calls to customer service are more loyal than other customers. Apparently, responding to the expressed needs of customers can make them happier and more loyal, especially when the response is prompt and appropriate. At another mobile phone company, calls to customer service indicated a higher probability of churn, due no doubt to the long wait periods at their call centers.

This case study talks about classifying complaints for routing complaints versus compliments, using the ideas of genetic algorithms.

### Business Context

The custom service department of a major international airline processes many customer comments, which arrive via several channels:

- Response cards included in the in-flight magazine
- Comment forms on the airline's Web site
- Telephone calls to the customer service center
- Cards, letters, and email messages

Different comments have different priorities for responses. Compliments, for example, may result in an automated "thank you for being a loyal customer" type of message. On the other hand, all complaints need at least to be acknowledged, and many complaints require follow-up action. The sooner the company responds, the better the chance of keeping a perhaps valuable, but disgruntled, customer.

Airline personnel spend significant amounts of time analyzing customer comments, first sorting them into complaints and other comments, and then routing the complaints to the appropriate group for follow-up. When customers are already upset about lost baggage, canceled flights, rude treatment, or lousy food, a slow or inappropriate response only makes things worse. This particular airline decided to reduce the time it took to respond to a complaint by automating the initial categorization of comments. Their approach evolved a solution using software from Genalytics (www.genalytics.com), a software company in Newburyport, MA.

## Data

All customer comments end up in a comment database, regardless of the channel they come in by. This database includes both fixed fields describing the comment and the actual text itself. A complete customer comment record has the following fields:

- Date
- Source (email, comment card, telephone contact, letter, other)
- Flight number
- Class of service
- Departure airport
- Destination airport
- Mileage account number
- Organization receiving comment
- Names of involved airline employee(s) if mentioned
- Free-text comments

Some records are missing data for some fields. Comments coming in through the call center are usually filled in correctly, because the call-center reps are trained to fill in all the fields. However, left to themselves, customers may not fill in all the fields when sending a comment card or email message.

The first step is preprocessing the text. The company preprocesses the comments to correct certain spelling errors and to create a large number of derived variables about the content (is the word "food" present? is the word "meal" present? and so on). Such derived variables are created for every word in the database that occurs more than some threshold number of times across all messages and is not a very common word such as "of" or "the." Some of the new variables convey metadata about the comment, such as its size in bytes and the number of distinct words in contains. Together, these variables form the comment header. The comment itself is not used, instead the various derived variables are used.

### The Data Mining Task: Evolving a Solution

The data mining task was to come up with a model that takes as input a large number of variables describing each customer comment and somehow combine them to come up with a classification. The specific task was to classify comment signatures based on whether or not they are complaints. There are several ways of approaching this, such as using decision trees or clustering. In this case, though, the company evolved a solution.

Solving a problem with genetic algorithms requires genomes and a fitness function. The genomes are based on the preprocessed comments, one genome per comment. First, a few more fields are added for interaction variables, such as whether both "baggage" and "JFK" are mentioned or whether both "food" and "chicken" are mentioned. The header, metadata variables and interaction variables form the comment signature, as shown in Figure 13.5.

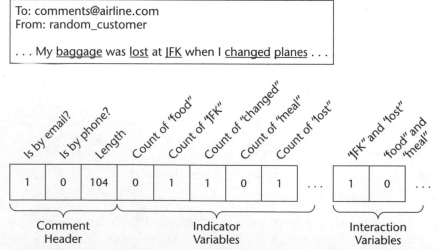

**Figure 13.5**  The comment signature describes the text in the comment.

The comment signature is not the genome, but it is related to it. Instead, the genome is a set of weights corresponding to each variable in the signature (along with an additional weight called a bias). It is possible to multiply the weights in the genome times the corresponding fields in the comment signature to obtain a prediction for the comment being a complaint, as shown in Figure 13.6. This is the fitness function for a single comment signature. The full fitness function applies this to all the comment signatures in the training set.

The Genalytics System creates a random population of genomes. These genomes generally have most of the weights set to low values, and just a few set to high values. That is, the initial population consists of genomes that are specialized for the simplest features in the comment signature. Although the initial population performed very poorly, its use of selection, crossover, and mutation lead to better and better solutions. After tens of thousands of generations, the final model was able to classify 85 percent of the records correctly—enough to speed up the airline's complaint processing. The chart in Figure 13.7 shows the improvement in the fitness function in succeeding generations.

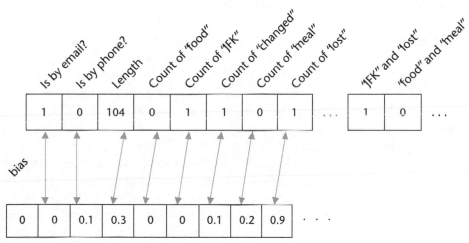

**Figure 13.6** The genome has a weight for each field in the comment signature, plus an additional weight called a bias.

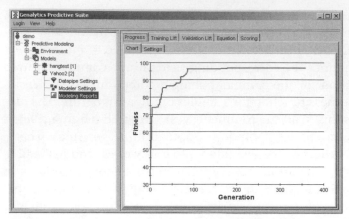

**Figure 13.7** The Genalytics system shows the progress of the training and how the fitness function improves with each generation.

# Beyond the Simple Algorithm

Researchers have been pushing the bounds on genetic algorithms in several directions. Some of these enhancements are refinements to the basic algorithm; others modify the algorithm to provide a better model of genetic activity in the natural world. This work is often performed under the rubric of machine learning, an area of current artificial intelligence research that aims to enable computers to learn in ways analogous to humans. Companies such as Genalytics are starting to apply these evolutionary techniques to marketing.

The simple genetic algorithm previously described has room for improvement in several areas. One of the inefficiencies in the algorithm is the fact that entire populations are replaced from one generation to the next. This is a gross oversimplification of what happens in nature. Instead of replacing an entire population, some researchers have worked with overlapping populations that can grow in size. They have introduced the notion of *crowding* to determine which existing members should be targeted for replacement. When applied naively, this tends to result in very fast convergence, often to suboptimal solutions, because all the less fit genomes are replaced before they have an opportunity to reproduce—and the less fit genomes sometimes have something to offer. To get around this, the targets for replacement often come from subsets of the population that exhibit high degrees of similarity.

The issue of overly fast convergence is actually a problem for the simple genetic algorithm because the goal of finding the globally optimal solution is easily confused by locally optimal solutions. Overly fast convergence often suggests that the search is being limited. To get around this, the various probabilities for crossover and mutation are often set high initially, then slowly decreased from one generation to the next. Or, an initial population is allowed to grow before shrinking in size as the fitness becomes more consistent across the population.

The genomes discussed so far consist of only a single strand of genes. Didn't we learn back in high school that DNA consists of two intertwining strands in a helix structure? And what happened to those other concepts buried back in this high-school past, such as recessive and dominant genes? The genetics used so far is based on the simplest chromosomes found in nature, single-stranded, or *haploid* chromosomes. These tend to be found in uncomplicated, single-cell organisms. In more complex organisms, the chromosomes are two-stranded, or *diploid*, as in our own DNA.

The algorithmic characteristics of diploid chromosomes are much the same as haploid chromosomes, since diploid chromosomes can be treated as two chromosomes tied together. The actual algorithm proceeds in much the same way: Selection, crossover, and mutation are the same. The difference is that now there are two alleles for each gene (two possible values) instead of one. When they match, there is no problem. When they do not, which does the fitness function use? In the language of genetics, this is asking which of the alleles is *expressed*. For instance, when an allele for blue eyes pairs up with an allele for brown eyes, the brown eyes "win"; that is, they are expressed instead of the blue eyes. (Actually, eye color is a bit more complicated than this simple example, but this is useful for explanatory purposes.) Researchers have solved this problem by including information about dominance in the alleles themselves. The details of this mechanism are beyond the scope of this book. The interested reader is referred to Goldberg's classic book *Genetic Algorithms in Search, Optimization, and Machine Learning (1989,* Addison-Wesley, ISBN 0201157675)

Why we should care about diploid structures? Geneticists have long wondered why two-stranded chromosomes predominate in nature, when single-stranded ones are simpler. They believe that the two-stranded structure allows an organism to "remember" a gene that was useful in another environment, but has become less useful in the current environment. In terms of GA, this suggests that these are useful in cases where the environment—or fitness function—is changing over time. In the real world, this may prove to be quite useful. An example of a changing fitness function would be a function that tried to determine the price of bonds over time. The goodness of a given bond price depends on factors not under control of the algorithm, such as the rate of inflation. The "fitness" function can take this into account by changing over time to incorporate estimates of inflation.

# Lessons Learned

Genetic algorithms are a very powerful optimization technique. Optimization is not at the heart of data mining, but it can solve interesting and important problems. In fact, some data mining algorithms, such as neural networks, depend on optimization "under the hood."

The key to the power of genetic algorithms is that they depend on only two things. First is the genome and the second the fitness function. The fitness function makes sense of the genome, by producing a value from what looks like a random set of bits. The genome encodes the problem; often it consists of a set of weights on some equation. Genetic algorithms work on a wide variety of fitness functions, making it possible to encode many different types of problems that are not easily handled by other means.

The process of evolution starts with a random population and then applies three transformation steps. The first is selection, which means that more fit genomes survive from one generation to another. This corresponds to natural selection. The second is crossover, where two genomes swap pieces and is analogous to a similar natural process. The third is mutation, where some values are changed randomly. Mutations are usually quite rare both in nature and in genetic algorithms.

The application of these three processes produces a new generation, whose average fitness should be greater than the original. As more and more generations are created, the population moves to an optimal solution. These processes have a theoretical foundation, based on schemata. This theory explains how genetic algorithms move toward a solution.

Genetic algorithms have been applied to practical problems, often to resource optimization problems. However, they can even be used for predictive modeling and classification, as explained in the case study on classifying comments made to an airline.

# CHAPTER 14

# Data Mining throughout the Customer Life Cycle

The purpose of data mining is to help businesses realize value from their most important asset: customers. Earlier chapters have talked about the algorithms and methodology for making data mining successful. This chapter turns from the specific technology to customers. The next three chapters continue this theme, stepping away from technical algorithms to talk about the data and the systems environment needed to exploit data mining.

For almost any business, customers are the critical asset. Yet, they are elusive, because of the wide variety of different relationships that change over time. Different industries have different definitions of customers. Within an industry, different competitors have different approaches to managing these relationships. Some focus on quality of service, some on convenience, some on price, and some on other aspects of the relationship. No two businesses have exactly the same definition of a customer, nor treat customers the same way throughout the relationship.

The purpose of data mining is to complement other customer service initiatives, not to replace them. Customer interactions take place through many channels—through direct mail pieces, through call centers, face-to-face, via advertising. Now that the "click and mortar" way of doing business is becoming standard, most businesses provide an online interface to their customers. The Web, with its new capabilities for interacting with customers, has the potential to provide a wealth of customer behavior data that can be turned into a new window on the customer relationship. It is ironic that a technology that has largely replaced human-to-human interactions is allowing companies to treat their customers more personally.

This brings us back to the customer and to the customer life cycle. This chapter strives to put data mining into focus with the customer at the center. It starts with an overview of different types of customer relationships, then goes into the details of the customer life cycle as it relates to data mining. The chapter provides examples of how customers are defined in various industries and some of the issues in deciding when the customer relationship begins and when it ends. The focal point is the customer and the ongoing relationship that customers have with companies.

## Levels of the Customer Relationship

One of the major goals of data mining is to understand customers and the relationships that customers have with an organization. A good place to start understanding them better is by using the different levels of customer relationships and what customers are telling us through their behavior.

Customers generate a wealth of behavioral information. Every payment made, every call to customer service, every click on the Web, every transaction provides information about what each customer does, and when, and which interventions are working and which are not. The Web is a particularly rich source of information. CNN does not know who is viewing or paying attention to their cable news program. *The New York Times* does not know which parts of the paper each subscriber reads. On the Web, though, cnn.com and nytimes.com have a much better indication of readers' interests. Connecting this source of information back to individuals over time is challenging (not to mention the challenge of connecting readers interests to advertising over time).

Customers are not all created equal. Nor should all customers be treated equally, since some are clearly more valuable than others. Figure 14.1 shows a continuum of customer relationships, from the perspective of the amount of investment worthy of each relationship. Some customers merit very deep and intimate relationships centered around people. Other customers are too numerous and, individually, not valuable enough to maintain individual relationships. For this group, we need technology to help make the relationship more intimate. The third group is perhaps the most challenging, because they are in between those who merit real intimacy and those who merit feigned intimacy. This group often includes small businesses as well as indirect relationships. The sidebar "No Customer Relationship" talks about another situation, companies that do not know about their end users and do not need to.

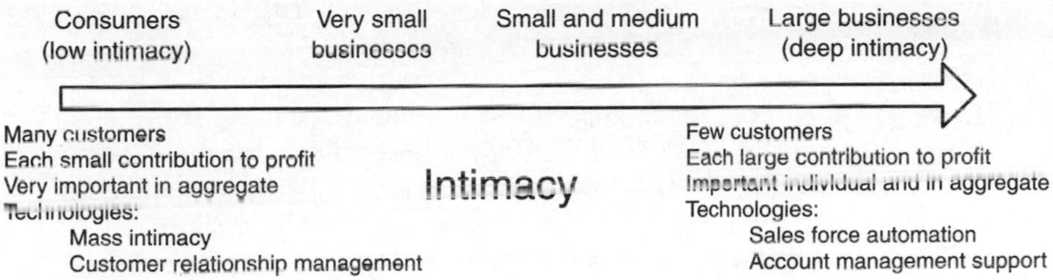

| Consumers<br>(low intimacy) | Very small<br>businesses | Small and medium<br>businesses | Large businesses<br>(deep intimacy) |
|---|---|---|---|

Many customers
Each small contribution to profit
Very important in aggregate
Technologies:
    Mass intimacy
    Customer relationship management

Intimacy

Few customers
Each large contribution to profit
Important individual and in aggregate
Technologies:
    Sales force automation
    Account management support

**Figure 14.1** Intimacy in customer relationships generally increases as the size of the account increases.

## Deep Intimacy

Customers who are worth a deep intimate relationship are usually large organizations—business customers. These customers are big enough to devote dedicated resources, in the form of account managers and account teams. The relationship is usually some sort of business-to-business relationship. One-off products and services characterize these relationships, making it difficult to compare different customers, because each customer has a set of unique products.

An example is the branding triumvirate of McDonald's, Coca-Cola, and Disney. McDonald's is the largest retailer of Coke products worldwide. When Disney has special promotions in fast food restaurants for children's movies, McDonald's gets first dibs at distributing the toys inside their Happy Meals. And when Disney characters (at least the good guys!) drink soda or open the refrigerator—Coke products are likely to be there. Coke also has exclusive arrangements with Disney, so Disney serves Coke products at its theme parks, in its hotels, and on its cruises. There are hundreds of people working together to make this branding triumvirate work. Data mining, with even the most advanced algorithms on even the fastest computers, is not going to replace these people—nor will this process be automated in the conceivable future.

On the other hand, even large account teams and individual managers can benefit from analysis, particularly around sales force automation tools. Data mining analysis can help such groups work better, by providing an understanding of what is really going on. Data can still help find some useful answers: which McDonald's are particularly good at selling which soft drinks? Where are product placements resulting in higher sales? What is the relationship between weather and drink consumption at theme parks versus hotels? And so on.

## NO CUSTOMER RELATIONSHIP

The streets of Tokyo are lined with ubiquitous convenience stores that are much like 7-11s or corner convenience stores in Manhattan. These stores carry a small array of products, mostly food, including freshly made lunches. There are three companies that dominate this market, Lawsons, Seven-Eleven Japan, and Family Mart, the third largest of which processes about 20 million transactions each day. Given that the population of Japan is a bit over 120 million, this means that, on average, every Japanese person purchases something from one of these stores every other day. That is a phenomenal amount of consumer interaction.

Dive a bit more deeply into the business. About the only thing these companies know about their customers is that almost everyone who lives in Japan is at least an occasional buyer. Transactions are almost exclusively cash-based, so the companies have no way to tie a customer to a series of transactions over time and in different stores.

The strength of these companies is really in distribution and payments. On the distribution side, they are able to make three deliveries each day to the stores, guaranteeing that lunchtime sushi is fresh and the produce hasn't wilted. Many people also use the stores near their homes to pay their bills with cash, something that is very convenient in a cash-dominated society. Combining these two businesses, some of the stores are becoming staging points for orders, made through catalogs or over the Web. Customers can pay for and pick up goods in their friendly, neighborhood convenience store.

Japanese convenience stores are an extreme example of businesses that know very little about their end users. Packaged good manufacturers are another example, because they do not own the retailing relationship. Manufacturers only know when they have shipped goods to warehouses. End-user information is still important, but the behavior is not sitting in their databases, it is in the database of disparate retailers. To find out about customer behavior, they might:

♦ Use industry-wide panels of customers to see how products are used

♦ Use surveys to find out about customers and when and how they use the products

♦ Build relationships with retailers to get access to the point-of-sale data

♦ Listen to the data they are collecting, via complaints and compliments on the Web, in call centers, and through the mail

Distribution data does still have tremendous value, giving an idea of what is being sold when and where. Inside lurks information about which advertising messages should go where and which products are more popular—and data mining can be used for these things.

On the business-to-business side, even large financial institutions can benefit from understanding customers. One of the largest banks in the world wanted to analyze foreign exchange transactions to determine which clients would benefit from taking out a loan in one currency and repaying it in another rather than taking out the loan in one currency and exchanging the proceeds up front. The goal was to provide better products for the clients and a longer-term relationship. However, people are then needed to interpret and act on these results.

Although the deep relationship is often associated with large businesses, this is not always the case. Private banking groups in retail banks work with high net-worth individuals, and give them highly personalized service— usually with a named banker managing their relationship. When a private banking customer wants a loan or to make an investment, that person simply calls his or her private banker. Private banking groups have traditionally been highly profitable, so profitable that they can get away with almost anything. The private banking group at one large bank was able to violate corporate information technology standards, bringing in Macintosh computers and AS400s, when the standards for the rest of the bank were Windows and Unix. The private bank could get away with it; they were that profitable.

Also, just having large businesses as customers does not mean that each customers necessarily merits such close attention. Directories, whether on the Web or on yellow pages, have many business customers, but almost all are treated equally. Although the customers include many large businesses, each listing brings in a small amount of revenue so few are worth additional effort.

## Mass Intimacy

At the other extreme is the mass intimacy relationship. Companies that are serving a mass market typically have hundreds of thousands, or millions, or tens of millions of customers. Although most customers would love to have the attention of dedicated staff for all their needs, this is simply not economically feasible. Companies would have to employ armies of people to work with customers, and the incremental benefit would not make up for the cost.

This is where data mining fits in particularly well with customer relationship management. Many customer interactions are fully automated, especially on the Web. This has the advantage of being highly scalable; however, it comes at a loss of intelligence and warmth in the customer relationship. Using technology to make the relationship stronger is a multipronged effort:

- Staff who work directly with customers (whether face-to-face, through call centers, or via Web-enabled interfaces) must be trained to treat customers respectfully, while at the same time trying to expand the relationship using enhanced information about customers.

- Automated systems need to be flexible, so different messages can be directed to different customers. This clearly applies on the Web, but it also applies to billing inserts, cashier receipts, background scripts read while customers are on hold, and so on.

- Both staff and automated systems that work with customers need to be able to respond to new practices and new messages. Sometimes, these new approaches come from the good ideas of staff. Sometimes, they come from careful analysis and data mining. Sometimes, from a combination of the two.

This is an extension of the virtuous cycle of data mining. Learning—whether accomplished through algorithms or through people—needs to be acted upon. Rolling out results is as necessary as getting them in the first place. Success involves working with call centers and training personnel who come in contact with customers. Customer interactions over the Web have the advantage that they are already automated, making it possible to complete the virtuous cycle electronically. People are still involved in the process to manage and validate the results. However, the Web makes it possible to obtain data, analyze it, act on the results, and measure the effects without ever leaving the electronic medium.

The goal of customer understanding can conflict with the goal of efficient channel operation. One large mobile telephone company in the United States, for instance, tried asking customers for their email addresses when they called in with service related questions. Having the email address has many benefits. For one thing, future service questions could be handled over the Web at a lower cost than through the call center. It also opens the possibility for occasional marketing messages, cross-sell, and retention opportunities. However, because the questions added several seconds to the average call length, the call center stopped asking. For the call center, getting on to the next call was more important than enhancing the relationship with each customer.

**WARNING** Privacy is a major concern, particularly for individual customers. However, it is peripheral to data mining itself. To a large extent, the concern is more about companies sharing data with each other rather than about a single company using data mining on its own to understand customer behavior. In some jurisdictions, it may be illegal to use information collected for operational purposes for another purpose such as marketing or improving customer relationships.

Mass intimacy also brings up the issue of privacy, which has become a major concern with the growth of the Web. To the extent that we are studying customer behavior, the data sources are the transactions between the customer and the company—data that companies typically can use for business purposes such as CRM (although there are some legal exceptions even to this). The larger concern is when companies sell information about individuals. Although such data may be useful when purchased, or may be a valuable source of revenue, it is not a necessary part of data mining.

## In-between Relationships

The in-between relationship is perhaps the most challenging. These are the customers who are not big enough to warrant their own account teams, but are big enough to require specialized products and services. These may be small and medium-sized businesses. However, there are other groups, such as so-called "mass affluent" banking customers, who do not have quite enough assets to merit private banking yet who still do want special attention.

These customers often have a wider array of products, or at least of pricing mechanisms—discounts for volume purchases, and so on—than mass intimacy customers. They also have more intense customer service demands, having dedicated call centers and Web sites. There are often account specialists who are responsible for dozens or hundreds of these relationships at the same time. These specialists do not always give equal attention to all customers. One use of data mining is in spreading best practices—finding what has been working and has not been working and spreading this information.

When there are tens of thousands of customers, it is also possible to use data mining directly to find patterns that distinguish good customers from bad, and for determining the next product to sell to a particular customer. This use is very similar to the mass intimacy case.

## Indirect Relationships

Indirect relationships are another type of customer relationship, where intermediate agents broker the relationship with end users. For instance, insurance companies sell their products through agents, and it is often the agent that builds the relationship with the customer. Some are captive agents that only sell one company's policies; others offer an assortment of products from different companies.

Such agent relationships pose a business challenge. For instance, an insurance company once approached Data Miners, Inc. to build a model to determine which policyholders were likely to cancel their policies. Before starting the project, the company realized what would happen if such a model were put in place. Armed with this information, agents would switch high-risk policyholders to other carriers—accelerating the loss of these accounts rather than preventing it. This company did not go ahead with the project. Perhaps part of the problem was a lack of imagination in figuring out appropriate interventions. The company could have provided special incentives to agents to keep customers who were at risk—a win-win situation for everyone involved. In such agent-based relationships, data mining can be used not only to understand customers but also to understand agents.

Indirection occurs in other areas as well. For instance, mutual fund companies sell retirement plans through employers. The first challenge is getting the employer to include the funds in the plan. The second is getting employees to sign up for the right funds. Ditto for many health care plans at large companies in the United States.

Product manufacturers have a similar problem. Telephone handset manufacturers such as Motorola, Nokia, and Ericsson, would like to develop a loyal customer base, so customers continue to return to them handset after handset. Automobile manufacturers have similar goals. Pharmaceutical companies have traditionally marketed to the doctors who prescribe drugs rather then the people who use them, although drugs such as Viagra are now also being marketed to consumers. Another good example of a campaign for a product sold indirectly is the "Intel Inside" campaign on personal computers—a mark of quality meant to build brand loyalty for a chip that few computer users ever actually see. However, Intel has precious little information on the people and companies whose desktops are adorned with their logo.

## Customer Life Cycle

When thinking about customers, it is easy to think of them as static, unchanging entities that compose "the market." However, this is not really accurate. Customers are people (or organizations of people), and they change over time. Understanding these changes is an important part of the value of data mining.

These changes are called the customer life cycle. In fact, there are two customer life cycles of interest, as shown in Figure 14.2. The first are life stages. For an individual, this refers to life events, such as graduating from high school, having kids, getting a job, and so on. For a business customer, the life cycle often refers to the size or maturity of the business. The second customer life cycle is the life cycle of the relationship itself. These two life cycles are fairly independent of each other, and both are very important for business.

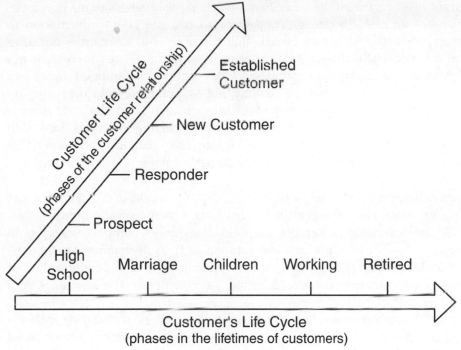

**Figure 14.2**   There are two customer life cycles.

## The Customer's Life Cycle: Life Stages

The customer's life cycle consists of events external to the customer relationship that represent milestones in the life of each individual customer. These milestones consist of events large and small, familiar to everyone.

The perspective of the customer's life stages is useful because people—even business people—understand these events and how they affect individual customers. For instance, moving is a significant event. When people move, they often purchase new furniture, subscribe to the local paper, open a new bank account, and so on. Knowing who is moving is useful for targeting such individuals, especially for furniture dealers, newspapers, and banks (among others). This is true for many other life events as well, from graduating from high school and college, to getting married, having children, changing jobs, retiring, and so on. Understanding these life stages enables companies to define products and messages that resonate with particular groups of people.

For a small business, this is not a problem. A wedding gown shop specializes in wedding gowns; such a business grows not because women get married more often, but through recommendations. Similarly, moving companies do not need to encourage their recent customers to relocate; they need to bring in new customers.

Larger businesses, on the other hand, rarely have business plans that focus exclusively on one life stage. They want to use life stage information to develop products and enhance marketing messages, but there are some complications. The first is that customers' particular circumstances are usually not readily available in corporate databases. One solution is to augment databases with purchased information. Of course, such appended data elements are never available for every customer, and, although such appended data is readily available in the United States, it may not be available in jurisdictions with different privacy laws. And, such external sources of data indicate events that have occurred in the past, making the customer's current life stage a matter of inference.

Even when customers go out of their way to provide useful information, companies often simply forget it. For instance, when customers move, they provide the new address to replace the old. How many companies keep both addresses? And how many of these companies then determine whether the customer is moving up or moving down, by using appended demographics or census data to measure the wealth of the neighborhood? The answer is very few, if any.

Similarly, many women change their names when they get married and provide such information to the companies they do business with. At some point after two people wed, the couple starts to combine their finances, for instance by having one checking account instead of two. Most companies do not record when a customer changes her name, losing the opportunity to provide targeted messaging for changing financial circumstances.

In practice, managing customer relationships based on life stages is difficult:

- It is difficult to identify events in a timely manner.
- Many events are one-time, or very rare.
- Life stage events are generally unpredictable and out of your control.

These shortcomings do not render them useless, by any means, because life stages provide a critical understanding of how to reach customers with a particular message. Advertisers, for instance, are likely to include different messages, depending on the target audience of the medium. However, in the interest of developing long-term relationships with customers, we want to ask if there is a way to improve on the use of the customer's life cycle.

## Customer Life Cycle

The customer life cycle provides another dimension to understanding customers. This focuses specifically on the business relationship, based on the observation that the customer relationship evolves over time. Although each business is different, the customer relationship places customers into five major phases, as shown in Figure 14.3:

- *Prospects* are people in the target market who are not yet customers.

- *Responders* are prospects who have exhibited some interest, for instance, by filling out an application or registering on a Web site.

- *New customers* are responders who have made a commitment, usually an agreement to pay, such as having made a first purchase, having signed a contract, or having registered at a site with some personal information.

- *Established customers* are those new customers who return, for whom the relationship is hopefully broadening or deepening.

- *Former customers* are those who have left, either as a result of voluntary attrition (because they have defected to a competitor or no longer see value in the product), forced attrition (because they have not paid their bills), or expected attrition (because they are no longer in the target market, for instance, because they have moved).

The precise definition of the phases depends on each particular business. For an e-media site, for instance, a prospect may be anyone on the Web; a responder, someone who has visited the site; a new customer, someone who has registered; and an established customer a repeat visitor. Former customers are those who have not returned within some length of time that depends on the nature of the site. For other businesses, the definitions might be quite different. Life insurance companies, for instance, have a target market. Responders are those who fill out an application—and then often have their blood taken for blood tests. New customers are those applicants who are accepted, and established customers are those who pay their premiums for insurance payments.

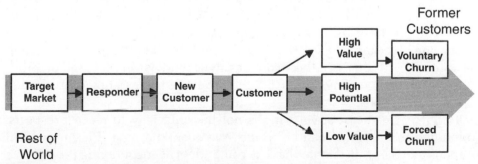

**Figure 14.3**   The customer life cycle progresses through different stages.

## Subscription Relationships versus Event-Based Relationships

Another dimension of the customer life-cycle relationship is the commitment inherent in a transaction. Consider the following ways of being a telephone customer:

- Making a call at a payphone
- Purchasing a prepaid telephone card for a set number of minutes
- Buying a prepaid mobile telephone
- Choosing a long distance carrier
- Buying a postpay mobile phone with no fixed term contract
- Buying a mobile phone with a contract

The first three are examples of event-based relationships. The last three are examples of subscription-based relationships. The next two sections explore the characteristics of these relationships in more detail.

**TIP** An ongoing billing relationship is a good sign of an ongoing subscription relationship. Such ongoing customer relationships offer the opportunity for engaging in a dialog with customers in the course of business activities.

### Event-Based Relationships

Event-based relationships are one-time commitments on the part of the customer. The customer may or may not return. In the above examples, the telephone company may not have much information at all about the customer, especially if the customer paid in cash. Such anonymous transactions still have information; however, there is clearly little opportunity for providing direct messages to customers who have provided no contact information.

When event-based relationships predominate, companies usually communicate with prospects by broadcasting messages widely (for instance in media advertising, free standing inserts, Web ads, and the like) rather than targeting messages at individuals. In these cases, analytic work is very focused on product, geography, and time, because these are three things known about customers' transactions.

Of course, broadcast advertising is not the only way to reach prospects. Couponing through the mail or on the Web is another way. Pharmaceutical companies in the United States have become adept at encouraging prospective customers to call in to get more information—while the company gathers a bit of information about the caller.

Sometimes, event-based relationships imply a business-to-business relationship with an intermediary. Once again, pharmaceutical companies provide an example, since much of their marketing budget is spent on medical providers, encouraging them to prescribe certain drugs.

## Subscription-Based Relationships

Subscription-based relationships provide more natural opportunities to understand customers. In the list given earlier, the last three examples all have ongoing billing relationships where customers have agreed to pay for a service over time. A subscription relationship offers the opportunity for future cash flow (the stream of future customer payments) and many opportunities for interacting with each customer.

For the purposes of this discussion, subscription-based relationships are those where there is a continuous relationship with a customer over time. This may take the form of a billing relationship, but it also might take the form of a retailing affinity card or a registration at a Web site.

In some cases, the billing relationship is a subscription of some sort, which leaves little room to up-sell or cross-sell. So, a customer who has subscribed to a magazine may have little opportunity for an expanded relationship. Of course, there is some opportunity. The magazine customer could purchase a gift subscription or buy branded products. However, the future cash flow is pretty much determined by the current composition of products.

In other cases, the ongoing relationship is just a beginning. A credit card may send a bill every month; however, nothing charged, nothing owed. A long-distance provider may charge a customer every month, but it may only be for the monthly minimum. A cataloger sends catalogs to customers, but most will not make a purchase. In such cases, usage stimulation is an important part of the relationship.

Subscription-based relationships have two key events—the beginning and end of the relationship. When these events are well defined, then survival analysis (Chapter 12) is a good candidate for understanding the duration of the relationship. However, sometimes defining the end of the relationship is difficult:

- A credit card relationship may end when a customer has no balance and has made no transactions for a specified period of time (such as 3 months or 6 months).

- A catalog relationship may end when a customer has not purchased from the catalog in a specified period of time (such as 18 months).

- An affinity card relationship may end when a customer has not used the card for a specified period of time (such as 12 months).

Even when the relationship is quite well understood, there may be some tricky situations. Should the end date of the relationship be the date of customer contact or the date the account is closed? Should customers who fail to pay their last bill be considered the same as customers who were stopped for nonpayment?

These situations are meant as guidelines for understanding the customer relationship. It is worthwhile to map out the different stages of customer interactions. Figure 14.4 shows different elements of customer experience for newspaper subscription customers. These customers basically have the following types of interactions:

- Starting the subscription via some channel

- Changing the product (weekday to 7-day, weekend to 7-day, 7-day to weekday, 7-day to weekend)

- Suspending delivery (typically for a vacation)

- Complaining

- Stopping the subscription (either voluntarily or forced)

In a subscription-based relationship, it is possible to understand the customer over time, gathering all these disparate types of events into a single picture of the customer relationship.

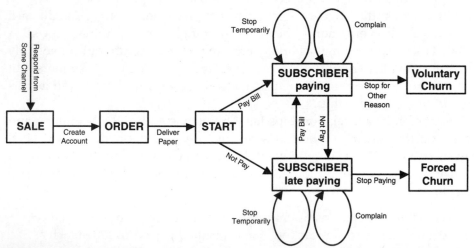

**Figure 14.4**   (Simplified) customer experience for newspaper subscribers includes several different types of interactions.

# Business Processes Are Organized around the Customer Life Cycle

The customer life cycle describes customers in terms of the length and depth of their relationship. Business processes move customers from one phase of the life cycle to the next, as shown in Figure 14.5. Looking at these business processes is valuable, because this is precisely what businesses want to do: make customers more valuable over time. In this section, we look at these different processes and the role that data mining plays in them.

## Customer Acquisition

Customer acquisition is the process of attracting prospects and turning them into customers. This is often done by advertising and word of mouth, as well as by targeted marketing. Data mining can and does play an important role in acquisition. Chapter 5, for instance, has an interesting example of using expected values derived from chi-square to highlight differences in acquisition among different regions. Such descriptive analyses can suggest best practices to spread through different regions.

There are three important questions with regards to acquisition, which are investigated in this section: Who are the prospects? When is a customer acquired? What is the role of data mining?

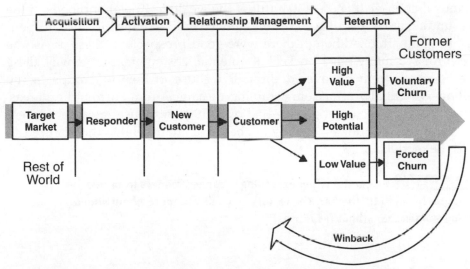

**Figure 14.5**   Business processes are organized around the customer life cycle.

## Who Are the Prospects?

Understanding who prospects are is quite important because messages should be targeted to an audience of prospects. From the perspective of data mining, one of the challenges is using historical data when the prospect base changes. Here are three typical reasons why care must be used when doing prospecting:

- Geographic expansion brings in prospects, who may or may not be similar to customers in the original areas.
- Changes to products, services, and pricing may bring in different target audiences.
- Competition may change the prospecting mix.

These are the types of situations that bring up the question: Will the past be a good predictor of the future? In most cases, the answer is "yes," but the past has to be used intelligently.

The following story is an example of the care that needs to be taken. One company in the New York area had a large customer base in Manhattan and was looking to expand into the suburbs. They had done direct mail campaigns focused on Manhattan, and built a model set derived from responders to these campaigns. What is important for this story is that Manhattan has a high concentration of very expensive neighborhoods, so the model set was biased toward the wealthy. That is, both the responders and nonresponders were much wealthier than the average inhabitant of the New York area.

When the model was extended to areas outside Manhattan, what areas did the model choose? It chose a handful of the wealthiest neighborhoods in the surrounding areas, because these areas looked most like the historical responders in Manhattan. Although there were good prospects in these areas, the model missed many other pockets of potential customers. By the way, these other pockets were discovered through the use of control groups in the mailing—essentially a random sampling of names from surrounding areas. Some areas in the control groups had quite high response rates; these were wealthy areas, but not as wealthy as the Manhattan neighborhoods used to build the model.

**WARNING** Be careful when extending response models from one geographic area to another. The results may tell you more about similar geographies than about response.

## When Is a Customer Acquired?

There is usually an underlying process in the acquisition of customers; the details of the process depend on the particular industry, but there are some general steps:

- Customers respond in some way and on some date. This is the "sale" date.

- In an account-based relationship, the account is created. This is the "account open date."

- The account is used in some fashion.

Sometimes, all these things happen at the same time. However, there are invariably complications—bad credit card numbers, misspelled addresses, buyer's remorse, and so on. The result is that there may be several dates that correspond to the acquisition date.

Assuming that all relevant dates are available, which is the best to use? That depends on the particular purpose. For instance, after a direct mail drop or an email drop, it might be interesting to see the response curve to know when responses are expected to come in, as shown in Figure 14.6. For this purpose, the sale date is most important date, because it indicates customer behavior and the question is about customer behavior. Whatever might cause the account open date to be delayed is not of interest.

A different question would have a different answer. For comparing the response of different groups, for instance, the account open date might be more important. Prospects who register a "sale" but whose account never opens should be excluded from such an analysis. This is also true in applications where the goal is forecasting the number of customers who are going to open accounts.

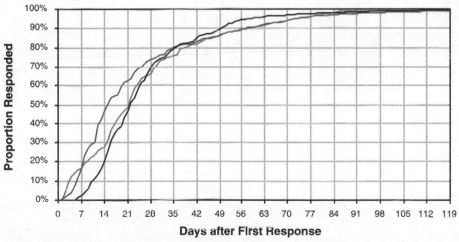

**Figure 14.6** These response curves for three direct mail campaigns show that 80 percent of the responses came within 5 to 6 weeks.

## What Is the Role of Data Mining?

Available data limits the role that predictive modeling can play. Predictive modeling is used for channels such as direct mail and telemarketing, where the cost of contact is relatively high. The goal is to limit the contacts to prospects that are more likely respond and become good customers. Data available for such endeavors falls into three categories:

- Source of prospect
- Appended individual/household data
- Appended demographic data at a geographic level (typical census block or census block group)

The purpose here is to discuss prospecting from the perspective of data mining. A good place to begin is with an outline of a typical acquisition strategy. Companies that use direct mail or outbound telemarketing purchase lists. Some lists are historically very good, so they would be used in their entirety. For names from less expensive lists, one set of models is based on appended demographics, when such demographics are available at the household level. When such demographics are not available, neighborhood demographics are used instead in a different set of models.

One of the challenges in direct marketing is the echo effect—prospects may be reached by one channel but come in through another. For instance, a company might send a group of prospects an email message. Instead of responding to the email on the Web, some respondents might call a call center. Or customers may receive an advertising message or direct mail, yet respond through the Web site. Or an advertising campaign may encourage responses through several different channels at the same time. Figure 14.7 shows an example of the echo effect, as shown by the correlation between two channels, inbound calls and direct mail. Another challenge is the funneling effect during customer activation described in the next section.

**WARNING** The echo effect may artificially under- or overestimate the performance of channels, because customers inspired by one channel may be attributed to another.

## Customer Activation

Once a prospect has exhibited an interest, there is some sort of activation process. This may be as simple as a customer filling out a registration form on a Web site. Or, it might involve a more lengthy approval process, such as a credit check. Or, it could be a bit more onerous, as in the example of life insurance companies who often want to perform an underwriting exam that might include taking blood samples before setting rates. In general, activation is an operational process, more focused on business needs than analytic needs.

As an operational process, customer activation may seem to have little to do with data mining. There are two very important interactions, though. The first is that activation provides a view of new customers at the point when they join. This is a very important perspective on the customer, and, as a data source, it needs to be preserved. Both the initial conditions and subsequent changes are of interest.

**TIP** Customer activation provides the initial conditions of the customer relationship. Such initial conditions are often useful predictors of long term customer behavior.

Activation is also important because it narrows it further refines the customer base. This is a funneling effect, as shown in Figure 14.8. This process is for a newspaper subscription, a familiar process analogous to many similar processes. It basically has the following steps:

**The Sale.** A prospect shows interest in getting a subscription, by providing address and payment information, either on the Web, on a call, or on a mail-in response card.

**The Order.** An account is created, which includes a preliminary verification on the address and payment information.

**The Subscription.** The paper is actually physically delivered, requiring further verification of the address and special delivery instructions.

**The Paid Subscription.** The customer pays for the paper.

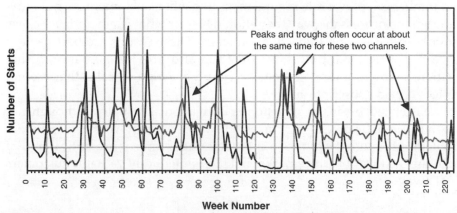

**Figure 14.7** Correlation between two channels over time suggests that one channel may be leaking into another or something external is affecting both channels.

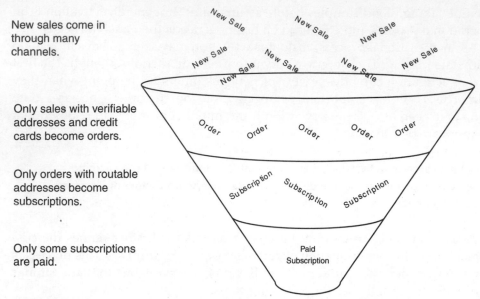

New sales come in through many channels.

Only sales with verifiable addresses and credit cards become orders.

Only orders with routable addresses become subscriptions.

Only some subscriptions are paid.

**Figure 14.8** The customer activation process funnel eliminates responders at each step of the activation process.

Each of these steps loses some customers, perhaps only a few percent perhaps more. For instance, credit cards may be invalid, have improper expiration dates, or not match the delivery address. The customer may live outside the delivery region. The deliverers may not understand special delivery instructions. The address may be in an apartment building that does not allow access, or the customer may simply not pay. Most of these are operational considerations (the exception is whether or not the customer pays), and they illustrate the kinds of operational concerns and processes involved with customer activation.

Data mining can play a role in understanding when customers are not moving through the process the way they should be—or what characteristics cause a customer to fail during the activation stage. These results are best used to improve the operational processes. They can also provide guidance during acquisition, by highlighting strategies that are bringing in sales that are not converted to paid subscriptions.

For Web-related businesses, customer activation is usually, although not always, an automatic process that takes little time. When it works well, there is no problem. Although it can take a short amount of time, it is a critical part of the customer acquisition process. When it fails, potentially valuable customers are kept away.

## Relationship Management

Once a prospect has become a customer, the goal is to increase the customer's value. This usually entails the following activities:

**Up-Selling.** Having the customer buy premium products and services.

**Cross-Selling.** Broadening the customer relationship, such as having customers buy CDs, plane tickets, and cars, in addition to books.

**Usage Stimulation.** Ensuring that the customer comes back for more, for example, by ensuring that customers see more ads or uses their credit card for more purchases.

These three activities are very amenable to data mining, particularly predictive modeling that can determine which customers are the best targets for which messages. This type of predictive modeling often determines the course of action for customers, as discussed in Chapter 3. However, there is a challenge of providing customers the right marketing messages, without inundating them with too many or contradictory messages.

Although telephone calls and mail solicitations are bothersome, unwanted email messages (often called *spam*) tend to have a more negative effect on the customer relationship. One reason may be that customers are often paying for their Internet connection or for the disk space for email. Another reason may be that this mail may arrive at work, rather than at home. Then there is the problem of spam that includes annoying pop-up ads. And, of course, such email has often been quite unsolicited, offending people who do not want to receive solicitations for gambling, money laundering, Viagra, sex sites, debt reduction, illegal pyramid marketing schemes, and the like.

Because email is abused so often, even legitimate companies who are communicating with bona fide customers run the risk of being associated with the dubious ones. This is a danger, and in fact suggests that customer contact needs to be broader than email.

Another danger for companies that offer many products and services is getting the right message across. Customers do not necessarily want choice; customers simply want you to provide what they want. Making customers find the one thing that interests them in a barrage of marketing communication does not do a good job of getting the message across. For this reason, it is useful to focus messages to each customer on a small number of products that are likely to interest that customer. Of course, each customer has a different potential set. Data mining plays a key role here in finding these associations.

## Retention

Customer retention is one of the areas where predictive modeling is applied most often. There are two approaches for looking at customer retention. The first is the survival analysis approach described in Chapter 12, which attempts to understand customer tenure. Survival analysis assigns a probability that a customer is going to leave after some period of time.

## AN ENGINE FOR CHURN FORECASTING

Forecasting customer stops and customer levels plays an important role in businesses, particularly for planning future budgets and marketing endeavors. A forecast provides an expect value (or set of expected values), that can be used for comparing what actually happened to what was expected. This is a natural application of data mining, particularly survival analysis.

The following figure shows what a forecasting engine looks like.

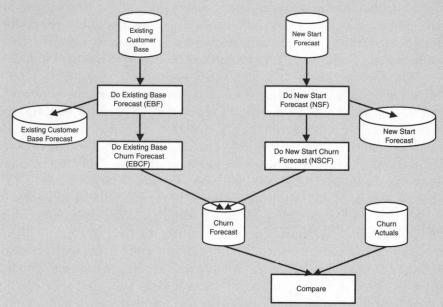

A forecasting engine uses data mining to predict customer levels (and hence churn) as well a providing explanations in the form of deviations from the expected.

There are five important inputs:

*Effective Date*. All numbers before this date are actuals; all numbers after this date are forecasts.

*Forecast Dimensions*. These are attributes of customers, such as product, geography, and the channel used for developing the forecast.

*New Starts*. This is a list of new starts broken down by the forecast dimensions after the effective date.

*Active Customers*. This is a list of all customers active on the effective date, including the forecast dimensions for each customer.

*Actual Churn*. These are actual stops broken into forecast dimensions; these are used for comparisons for explanatory purposes. This is not available when the forecast is being developed, but is used later.

The forecast is then broken into the following pieces. The *existing base forecast* (EBF) determines the probability of each *active customer* being active on given dates in the future; this forecast is a direct application of survival analysis. The *new start forecast* (NSF) determines the contribution to the future base from *new starts*. That is, these are the new starts who are active on future dates. This is a direct application of survival analysis with a twist, because every day, new customers are starting: $NSF(t) =$ One Day Survival of $NSF(t - 1)$ + New Starts$(t)$.

The churn forecast is easily derived from the EBF and NSF. The existing base churn forecast (EBCF) is the number of churners on a given day in the future from the existing base. This is the difference in survival on successive days: $EBCF(t) = EBF(t) - EBF(t + 1)$. The new start churn forecast (NSCF) is the number of churners on a given day in the future from the new starts. This is a little trickier to calculate, because we have to take into account new starts: $NSCF(t) =$ $NSF(t - 1) -$ One Day Survival of $NSF(t - 1)$. The churn forecast is the sum of these, $CF(t) = EBCF(t) + NSCF(t)$.

All of the pieces of the forecast typically use forecast dimensions. The result is that the forecast can be compared to actuals, making it possible to explain the results in terms understandable and useful to the business.

The power of survival analysis is that it focuses on what is often the most important determinant of retention, customer tenure. Customers who have been around for a long time are usually more likely to stay around longer. However, survival analysis can also take into account other factors, through several enhancements to the basic technique. When there is a lot of data, different factors can be investigated independently, using a process called *stratification*. When there are many other factors, then parametric modeling and proportional hazards modeling provides a similar capability (these are not discussed in detail in this book). In either case, it is possible to get an idea of customers' remaining tenures. This is useful not only for retention interventions, but also for customer lifetime value calculations and for forecasting numbers of customers, as discussed in the sidebar "An Engine for Churn Forecasting."

An alternative approach is to predict who is going to leave for some small amount of time in the future. This is more of a traditional predictive modeling problem, where we are looking for patterns in similar data from the past. This approach is particularly useful for focused marketing interventions. Knowing who is going leave in the near future makes the marketing campaign more focused, so more money can be invested in saving each customer.

## Winback

Once customers have left, there is still the possibility that they can be lured back. Winback tries to bring back valuable customers, by providing them with incentives, products, and pricing promotions.

Winback tends to depend more on operational strategies than on data analysis. Sometimes it is possible to determine why customers left. However, the winback strategies need to begin as part of the retention efforts themselves. Some companies, for instance, have specialized "save teams." Customers cannot leave without talking to a person who is trained in trying to retain them. In addition to saving customers, save teams also do a good job of tracking the reasons why customers are leaving—information that can be very valuable to future efforts to keep customers.

Data analysis can sometimes help determine why customers are leaving, particularly when customer service complaints can be incorporated into operational data. However, trying to lure back disgruntled customers is quite hard. The more important effort is trying to keep them in the first place with competitive products, attractive offers, and useful services.

## Lessons Learned

Customers, in all their forms, are central to business success. Some are big and very important; these merit specialized relationships. Others are small and very numerous. This is the sweet spot for data mining, because data mining can help provide mass intimacy where it is too expensive to have personal relationships with everyone all the time. Some are in between, requiring a balance between these approaches.

Subscription-based relationships are a good model for customer relationships in general because there is a well-defined beginning and end to the relationship. Each customer has his or her own life cycle defined by events—marriage, graduation, children, moving, changing jobs, and so on. These can be useful for marketing, but suffer from the problem that companies do not know when they occur.

The customer life cycle, in contrast, looks at customers from the perspective of their business relationship. First, there are prospects, who are activated to become new customers. New customers offer opportunities for up-selling, cross-selling, and usage stimulation. Eventually all customers leave, making retention an important data mining application both for marketing and forecasting. And once customers have left, they may be convinced to return through winback strategies. Data mining can enhance all these business opportunities.

As more of the world is technology-driven, more and more data is available, particularly about customer behavior. Data mining seeks to use all this data to advantage, by summarizing data and applying algorithms that produce meaningful results even on large data sets.

In the midst of all this technology, though, the customer relationship still maintains its central position. After all, customers—because they provide revenue—are the one thing that businesses need to remain successful, year after year. Eventually, other funding sources dry up. No computer ever made a purchase from Amazon; no software ever paid for a Pez dispenser on eBay; no cell phone ever made an airline or restaurant reservation. There are always people, individually or collectively, on the other end.

# CHAPTER 15

# Data Warehousing, OLAP, and Data Mining

Since the introduction of computers into data processing centers in the 1960s, just about every operational system in business has been computerized. These automated systems run companies, spewing out large amounts of data along the way. This automation has changed how we do business and how we live: ATM machines, adjustable rate mortgages, just-in-time inventory control, online retailing, credit cards, Google, overnight deliveries, and frequent flier/buyer clubs are a few examples of how computer-based automation has opened new markets and revolutionized existing ones. This is not a new story; it has been going on for decades.

In a typical company, such systems create vast amounts of data spread through scads of disparate systems, from general ledgers to sales force automation systems, from inventory control to electronic data interchange (EDI), and so on. Data about specific parts of a business is there—lots and lots of data, somewhere, in some form. Data is available but not information—*and not the right information at the right time*. The goal of data warehouses is to make the right information available at the right time. Data warehousing is the process of bringing together disparate data from throughout an organization for decision-support purposes.

A data warehouse serves as a decision-support system of record, making it possible to reconcile reports because they have the same underlying source. Such a system not only reduces the need to explain disparate results, but also provides consistent views of the business across business units and time. We believe that, over time, informed decisions lead to better bottom-line results over time, and data warehouses help managers make informed decisions. Decision support, as used here, is an intentionally ambiguous concept. It can be as rudimentary as getting production reports to front-line managers every week. It can be as complex as sophisticated modeling of prospective customers using neural networks to determine which message to offer. It can be and is just about everything in between.

Data warehousing is a natural ally of data mining. Data mining seeks to find actionable patterns in data and therefore has a firm requirement for clean and consistent data. Much of the effort behind data mining endeavors is in the steps of identifying, acquiring, and cleansing the data. A well-designed corporate data warehouse is a valuable ally. Better yet, if the design of the data warehouse includes support for data mining applications, the warehouse facilitates and catalyzes data mining efforts. The two technologies work together to deliver value. Data mining fulfills some of the promise of data warehousing by converting an essentially inert source of clean and consistent data into actionable information.

There is also a technological component to this relationship. Apart from the ability of users to run multiple jobs at the same time, most software, including data mining and statistical software, does not take advantage of the multiple processors and multiple disks available on the fastest servers. Relational database management systems (RDBMS), the heart of most data warehouses, are parallel-enabled and can take advantage of all of a system's resources for processing a single query. Even more importantly, users do not need to be aware of this fact, since the interface, some variant on SQL, remains the same. A database running on a powerful server can be a powerful asset for processing large amounts of data, as is the case when summarizing transactions at the customer level.

As useful as data warehousing is, such systems are not prerequisite for data mining and data analysis. Statisticians, actuaries, and analysts have been using statistical packages for decades—and achieving good results with their analyses—without the benefit of a well-designed centralized warehouse. This process can continue to be useful. Because of the need for consistent, accurate, and timely data to support business units, data warehousing has become increasingly important for any kind of decision support or information analysis.

This chapter is focused on data warehousing as part of the virtuous cycle of data mining, as a valuable and often critical component in supporting all four phases of the cycle: identifying opportunities, analyzing data, applying information, and measuring results. It is not a how-to guide for building a warehouse—there are many books already devoted to that subject, and we heartily recommend Ralph Kimball's *The Data Warehouse Toolkit* (Wiley, 2002) and Bill Inmon's *Building the Data Warehouse* (Wiley, 2002).

The chapter starts with a discussion of the different types of data that are available, and then discusses data warehousing requirements from the perspective of data mining. It then shows a typical data warehousing architecture and variants on this theme. The chapter next turns to Online Analytic Processing (OLAP), an alternative approach to the normalized data warehouse. The final discussion covers the role of data mining in these environments. As with much that has to do with data mining, however, the place to start is with data.

## The Architecture of Data

There are many different flavors of information represented on computers. Different levels of data represent different types of abstraction, as shown in Figure 15.1.

- Transaction data
- Operational summary data
- Decision-support summary data
- Schema
- Metadata
- Business rules

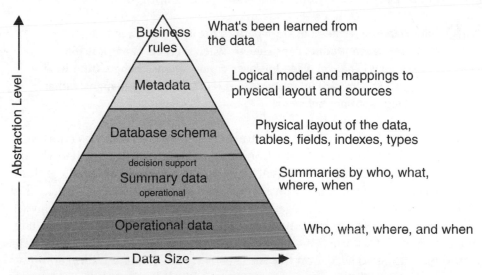

**Figure 15.1**  A hierarchy of data and its descriptions helps users navigate around a data warehouse. As data gets more abstract, it generally gets less voluminous.

The level of abstraction is an important characteristic of data used in data mining. In a well-designed system, it should be possible to drill down through these levels of abstraction to obtain the base data that supports a summarization or a business rule. The lower levels of the pyramid are more voluminous and tend to be the stuff of databases. The upper levels are smaller and tend to be the stuff of computer programs. All these levels are important, because we do not want to analyze the detailed data to merely produce what should already be known.

## Transaction Data, the Base Level

Every product purchased by a customer, every bank transaction, every Web page visit, every credit card purchase, every flight segment, every package, every telephone call is recorded in some operational system. Every time a new customer opens an account or pays a bill, there should be a record of the transaction somewhere, providing information about who, what, where, when, and how much. Such transaction-level data is the raw material for understanding customer behavior. It is the eyes and ears of the enterprise.

Unfortunately, over time operational systems change because of changing business needs. Fields may change their meaning over time. Important data is simply rolled off and deleted. Change is constant, in response to the introduction of new products, expanding numbers of customers, acquisitions, reorganizations, and new technology. The fact that operational data changes over time has to be part of any robust data warehousing approach.

**TIP** Data warehouses need to store data so the information is compatible over time, even when product lines change, when markets change, when customer segments change, when business organizations change. Otherwise, data mining is likely to pick up patterns that represent these changes, rather than underlying customer behavior.

The amount of data gathered from transactional systems can be enormous. A single fast food restaurant sells hundreds of thousands of meals over the course of a year. A chain of supermarkets can have tens or hundreds of thousands of transactions a day. A large bank processes millions of checks and credit card purchases a day. Large Web sites have millions of hits each day (in 2003, Google was already handling over 250 million searches each day). A telephone company has tens or even hundreds of millions of completed calls every day. A large ad server on the Web keeps track of over a billion ad views every day. Even with the price of disk space falling, storing all these transactions requires a significant investment. For reference, it is worth remembering that a day has 86,400 seconds, so a million transactions a day is really an average of about 12 transactions per second all day (and 250 million searches amounts to close to 3,000 searches per second!)—with peaks several times higher.

Because of the large data volumes, there is often a reluctance to store transaction-level data in a data warehouse. From the perspective of data mining, this is a shame, since the transactions best describe customer behavior.

## Operational Summary Data

Operational summaries play the same role as transactions; the difference being that operational summaries are derived from transactions. The most common examples are billing systems, which summarize transactions, usually into monthly or four-week bill cycles. These summaries are customer-facing and often result in other transactions, such as bill payments. In some cases, operational summaries may include fields that are summarized to enhance the company's understanding of its customers rather than for operational purposes. For instance, Chapter 4 described how AT&T used call detail records to calculate a "bizocity" score, indicating how businesslike a telephone number's calling pattern appears. The records of each call are discarded, but the score is kept up to date.

There is a distinction between operational summary data and transaction data, because summaries are for a period of time and transactions represent events. Consider the amount paid by a subscription customer. In a billing system, amount paid is a summary for the billing period. A payment history table instead provides detail on every payment transaction. For most customers, the monthly summary and payment transactions are very similar. However, two payments might arrive during the same billing period. The more detailed payment information might be useful for insight into customer payment patterns.

## Decision-Support Summary Data

Decision-support summary data is the data used for making decisions about the business. The financial data used to run a company provides an example of decision-support summary data; this is often considered to be the cleanest data for decision making. Another example is the data warehouses and data marts whose purpose is to provide a decision-support system of record at the customer level. Maintaining decision-support summary data is the purpose of the data warehouse.

Generally, it is a bad idea to use the same system for analytic and operational purposes, since operational purposes need to take precedence, resulting in a system that is optimized for operations and not decision support. Financial systems are not generally designed for understanding customers, because they are designed for accounting purposes. Making customer summaries balance exactly to the general ledger is highly complex and usually not worth the effort. One of the goals of data warehousing is to provide consistent definitions and layouts so similar reports produce similar results, no matter which business user is producing them or when they are produced. This chapter is mostly concerned with this level of abstraction.

In one sense, summaries seem to destroy information as they aggregate things. For this reason, different summaries are useful for different purposes. Point-of-sale transactions may capture every can of sardines that goes over the scanner, but only summaries begin to describe the shopper's behavior in terms of her habitual time of day to shop and the proportion of her dollars spent in the canned food department. In this case, the customer summary seems to be creating information.

**WARNING** Do not expect customer-level data warehouse information to balance exactly against financial systems (although the two systems should be close). Although theoretically possible, such balancing can prove very difficult and distract from the purpose of the data warehouse.

## Database Schema

So far, the discussion has been on data. The structure of data is also important—what data is stored, where it is stored, what is not stored, and so on. The sidebar "What is a relational database?" explains the key ideas behind relational databases, the most common systems for storing large amounts of data.

No matter how the data is stored, it is important to distinguish between two ways of describing the storage. The *physical schema* describes the layout in the technical detail needed by the underlying software. An example is the "CREATE TABLE" statement in SQL. A *logical schema*, on the other hand, describes the data in a way more accessible to end users. The two are not necessarily the same, nor even similar, as shown in Figure 15.2.

**WARNING** The existence of fields in a database does not mean that the data is actually present. It is important to understand every field used for data mining, and not to assume that a field populated correctly just because it exists. Skepticism is your ally.

An analogy might help to understand the utility of the physical and logical schemas. The logical schema describes things in a way that is familiar to business users. This would be analogous to saying that a house is ranch style, with four bedrooms, three baths, and a two-car garage. The physical schema goes into more detail about how it is laid out. The foundation is reinforced concrete, 4 feet deep; the slab is 1,500 square feet; the walls are concrete block; and so on. The details of construction, although useful and complete, may not help a family find the right house.

Logical Model

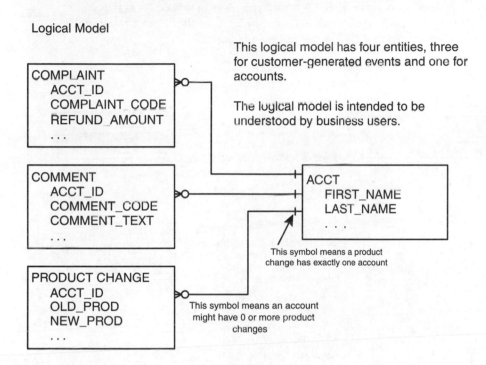

This logical model has four entities, three for customer-generated events and one for accounts.

The logical model is intended to be understood by business users.

This symbol means a product change has exactly one account

This symbol means an account might have 0 or more product changes

Physical Model

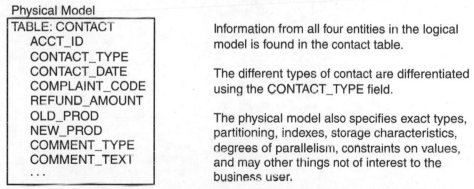

Information from all four entities in the logical model is found in the contact table.

The different types of contact are differentiated using the CONTACT_TYPE field.

The physical model also specifies exact types, partitioning, indexes, storage characteristics, degrees of parallelism, constraints on values, and may other things not of interest to the business user.

**Figure 15.2**  The physical and logical schema may not be related to each other.

## WHAT IS A RELATIONAL DATABASE?

One of the most common ways to store data is in a relational database management system (RDBMS). The basis of relational databases starts with research by E. F. Codd in the early 1970s on the properties of a special type of set composed of tuples—what we would call rows in tables. From this, he derived a relational algebra consisting of operations that form a relational algebra, which are depicted in the following figure:

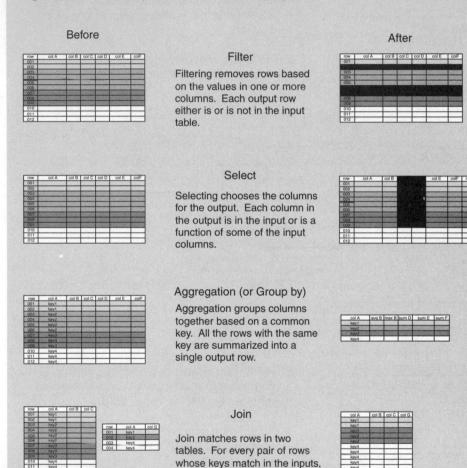

### Filter

Filtering removes rows based on the values in one or more columns. Each output row either is or is not in the input table.

### Select

Selecting chooses the columns for the output. Each column in the output is in the input or is a function of some of the input columns.

### Aggregation (or Group by)

Aggregation groups columns together based on a common key. All the rows with the same key are summarized into a single output row.

### Join

Join matches rows in two tables. For every pair of rows whose keys match in the inputs, a new row is created in the output.

Relational databases have four major querying operations.

These operations are in addition to set operations, such as union and intersection. In nonscientific terminology, these relational operations are:

*Filter* a given set of rows based on the values in the rows.

*Select* a given set of columns and perform basic operations on them.

*Group* rows together and aggregate values in the columns.

*Join* two tables together based on the values in the columns.

Interestingly, the relational operations do not include sorting (except for output purposes). These operations specify *what* can be done with tuples, not *how* it gets done. In fact, relational databases often use sorting for grouping and joining operations; however, there are non-sort-based algorithms for these operations as well.

SQL, developed by IBM in the 1980s, has become the standard language for accessing relational databases and implements these basic operations. Because SQL supports subqueries (that is, using the results of one query as a table in another query), it is possible to express some very complex data manipulations.

A common way of representing the database structure is to use an entity-relationship (E-R) diagram. The following figure is a simple E-R diagram with five entities and four relationships among them. In this case, each entity corresponds to a separate table with columns corresponding to the attributes of the entity. In addition, columns represent the relationships between tables in the database; such columns are called *keys* (either foreign or primary keys). Explicitly storing keys in the database tables using a consistent naming convention facilitates finding one's way around the database.

One nice feature of relational databases is the ability to design a database so that any given data item appears in exactly one place—with no duplication. Such a database is called a *normalized* database. Knowing exactly where each data item is located is highly efficient in theory, since updating any field requires modifying only one row in one table. When a normalized database is well-designed and implemented, there is no redundant data, out-of-date data, or invalid data.

An important idea behind normalization is creating reference tables. Each reference table logically corresponds to an entity, and each has a key used for looking up information about the entity. In a normalized database, the "join" operation is used to lookup values in reference tables.

Relational databases are a powerful way of storing and accessing data. However, much of their design is focused on updating the data and handling large numbers of transactions. Data mining is interested in combining data together to spot higher level patterns. Typically, data mining uses many queries, each of which requires several joins, several aggregations, and subqueries—a veritable army of killer queries.

*(continued)*

## WHAT IS A RELATIONAL DATABASE? *(continued)*

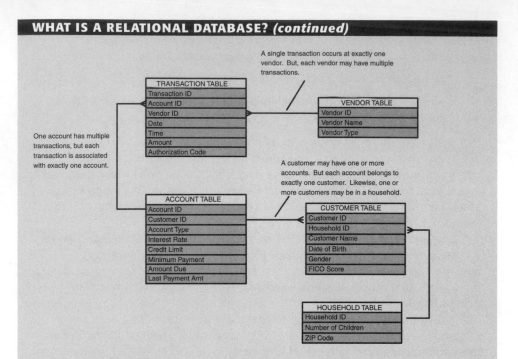

A single transaction occurs at exactly one vendor. But, each vendor may have multiple transactions.

**TRANSACTION TABLE**
- Transaction ID
- Account ID
- Vendor ID
- Date
- Time
- Amount
- Authorization Code

**VENDOR TABLE**
- Vendor ID
- Vendor Name
- Vendor Type

One account has multiple transactions, but each transaction is associated with exactly one account.

A customer may have one or more accounts. But each account belongs to exactly one customer. Likewise, one or more customers may be in a household.

**ACCOUNT TABLE**
- Account ID
- Customer ID
- Account Type
- Interest Rate
- Credit Limit
- Minimum Payment
- Amount Due
- Last Payment Amt

**CUSTOMER TABLE**
- Customer ID
- Household ID
- Customer Name
- Date of Birth
- Gender
- FICO Score

**HOUSEHOLD TABLE**
- Household ID
- Number of Children
- ZIP Code

An E-R diagram can be used to show the tables and fields in a relational database. Each box shows a single table and its columns. The lines between them show relationships, such as 1-many, 1-1, and many-to-many. Because each table corresponds to an entity, this is called a *physical design*.

Sometimes, the physical design of a database is very complicated. For instance, the TRANSACTION TABLE might actually be split into a separate table for each month of transactions. In this case, the above E-R diagram is still useful; it represents the *logical* structure of the data, as business users would understand it.

An entity relationship diagram describes the layout of data for a simple credit card database.

**With respect to data mining, relational databases (and SQL) have some limitations. First, they provide little support for time series. This makes it hard to figure out from transaction data such things as the second product purchased, the last three promos a customer responded to, or the ordering of events; these can require very complicated SQL. Another problem is that two operations often eliminate fields inadvertently. When a field contains a missing value (NULL) then it automatically fails any comparison, even "not equals".**

> Also, the default join operation (called an inner join) eliminates rows that do not match, which means that customers may inadvertently be left out of a data pull. The set of operations in SQL is not particularly rich, especially for text fields and dates. The result is that every database vendor extends standard SQL to include slightly different sets of functionality.

Database schema can also illuminate unusual findings in the data. For instance, we once worked with a file of call detail records in the United States that had city and state fields for the destination of every call. The file contained over two hundred state codes—that is a lot of states. What was happening? We learned that the city and state fields were never used by operational systems, so their contents were automatically suspicious—data that is not used is not likely to be correct. Instead of the city and state, all location information was derived from zip codes. These redundant fields were inaccurate because the state field was written first and the city field, with 14 characters, was written second. Longer city names overwrote the state field next to it. So, "WEST PALM BEACH, FL" ended up putting the "H" in the state field, becoming "WEST PALM BEAC, HL," and "COLORADO SPRINGS, CO" became "COLORADO SPRIN, GS." Understanding the data layout helped us figure out this interesting but admittedly uncommon problem.

## Metadata

Metadata goes beyond the database schema to let business users know what types of information are stored in the database. This is, in essence, documentation about the system, including information such as:

- The values legally allowed in each field
- A description of the contents of each field (for instance, is the start date the date of the sale or the date of activation)
- The date when the data was loaded
- An indication of how recently the data has been updated (when after the billing cycle does the billing data land in this system?)
- Mappings to other systems (the status code in table A is the status code field in table B in such-and-such source system)

When available, metadata provides an invaluable service. When not available, this type of information needs to be gleaned, usually from friendly database administrators and analysts—a perhaps inefficient use of everyone's time. For a data warehouse, metadata provides discipline, since changes to the warehouse must be reflected in the metadata to be communicated to users. Overall, a good metadata system helps ensure the success of a data warehouse by making users more aware of and comfortable with the contents. For data miners, metadata provides valuable assistance in tracking down and understanding data.

## Business Rules

The highest level of abstraction is business rules. These describe why relationships exist and how they are applied. Some business rules are easy to capture, because they represent the history of the business—what marketing campaigns took place when, what products were available when, and so on. Other types of rules are more difficult to capture and often lie buried deep inside code fragments and old memos. No one may remember why the fraud detection system ignores claims under $500. Presumably there was a good business reason, but the reason, the business rule, is often lost once the rule is embedded in computer code.

Business rules have a close relationship to data mining. Some data mining techniques, such as market basket analysis and decision trees, produce explicit rules. Often, these rules may already be known. For instance, learning that conference calling is sold with call waiting may not be interesting, since this feature is only sold as part of a bundle. Or a direct mail model response model that ends up targeting only wealthy areas may reflect the fact that the historical data used to build the model was biased, because the model set only had responders in these areas.

Discovering business rules in the data is both a success and a failure. Finding these rules is a successful application of sophisticated algorithms. However, in data mining, we want actionable patterns and such patterns are not actionable.

## A General Architecture for Data Warehousing

The multitiered approach to data warehousing recognizes that data needs come in many different forms. It provides a comprehensive system for managing data for decision support. The major components of this architecture (see Figure 15.3) are:

- *Source systems* are where the data comes from.
- Extraction, transformation, and load (ETL) move data between different data stores.

- The *central repository* is the main store for the data warehouse.
- The *metadata repository* describes what is available and where.
- *Data marts* provide fast, specialized access for end users and applications.
- *Operational feedback* integrates decision support back into the operational systems.
- *End users* are the reason for developing the warehouse in the first place.

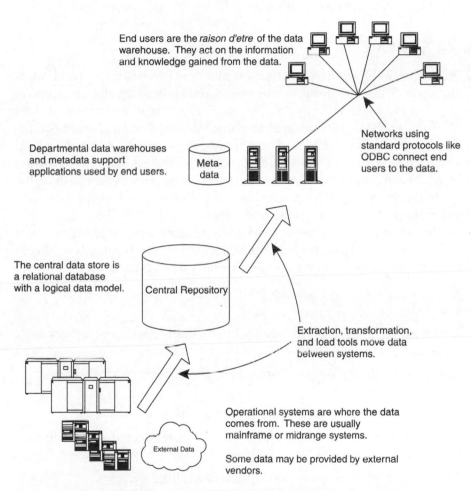

End users are the *raison d'etre* of the data warehouse. They act on the information and knowledge gained from the data.

Networks using standard protocols like ODBC connect end users to the data.

Departmental data warehouses and metadata support applications used by end users.

Meta-data

The central data store is a relational database with a logical data model.

Central Repository

Extraction, transformation, and load tools move data between systems.

External Data

Operational systems are where the data comes from. These are usually mainframe or midrange systems.

Some data may be provided by external vendors.

**Figure 15.3** The multitiered approach to data warehousing includes a central repository, data marts, end-user tools, and tools that connect all these pieces together.

One or more of these components exist in virtually every system called a data warehouse. They are the building blocks of decision support throughout an enterprise. The following discussion of these components follows a data-flow approach. The data is like water. It originates in the source systems and flows through the components of the data warehouse ultimately to deliver information and value to end users. These components rest on a technological foundation consisting of hardware, software, and networks; this infrastructure must be sufficiently robust both to meet the needs of end users and to meet growing data and processing requirements.

## Source Systems

Data originates in the source systems, typically operational systems and external data feeds. These are designed for operational efficiency, not for decision support, and the data reflects this reality. For instance, transactional data might be rolled off every few months to reduce storage needs. The same information might be represented in different ways. For example, one retail point-of-sale source system represented returned merchandise using a "returned item" flag. That is, except when the customer made a new purchase at the same time. In this case, there would be a negative amount in the purchase field. Such anomalies abound in the real world.

Often, information of interest for customer relationship management is not gathered as intended. Here, for instance, are six ways that business customers might be distinguished from consumers in a telephone company:

- Using a customer type indicator: "B" or "C," for business versus consumer.

- Using rate plans: Some are only sold to business customers; others to consumers.

- Using acquisition channels: Some channels are reserved for business, others for consumers.

- Using number of lines: 1 or 2 for consumer, more for business.

- Using credit class: Businesses have a different set of credit classes from consumers.

- Using a model score based on businesslike calling patterns

(Needless to say, these definitions do not always agree.) One challenge in data warehousing is arriving at a consistent definition that can be used across the business. The key to achieving this is metadata that documents the precise meaning of each field, so everyone using the data warehouse is speaking the same language.

Gathering the data for decision support stresses operational systems since these systems were originally designed for transaction processing. Bringing the data together in a consistent format is almost always the most expensive part of implementing a data warehousing solution.

The source systems offer other challenges as well. They generally run on a wide range of hardware, and much of the software is built in-house or highly customized. These systems are commonly mainframe and midrange systems and generally use complicated and proprietary file structures. Mainframe systems were designed for holding and processing data, not for sharing it. Although systems are becoming more open, getting access to the data is always an issue, especially when different systems are supporting very different parts of the organization. And, systems may be geographically dispersed, further contributing to the difficulty of bringing the data together.

## Extraction, Transformation, and Load

Extraction, transformation, and load (ETL) tools solve the problem of gathering data from disparate systems, by providing the ability to map and move data from source systems to other environments. Traditionally, data movement and cleansing have been the responsibility of programmers, who wrote special-purpose code as the need arose. Such application-specific code becomes brittle as systems multiply and source systems change.

Although programming may still be necessary, there are now products that solve the bulk of the ETL problems. These tools make it possible to specify source systems and mappings between different tables and files. They provide the ability to verify data, and spit out error reports when loads do not succeed. The tools also support looking up values in tables (so only known product codes, for instance, are loaded into the data warehouse). The goal of these tools is to describe where data comes from and what happens to it—not to write the step-by-step code for pulling data from one system and putting it into another. Standard procedural languages, such as COBOL and RPG, focus on each step instead of the bigger picture of what needs to be done. ETL tools often provide a metadata interface, so end users can understand what is happening to "their" data during the loading of the central repository.

This genre of tools is often so good at processing data that we are surprised that such tools remain embedded in IT departments and are not more generally used by data miners. *Mastering Data Mining* has a case study from 1998 on using one of these tools from Ab Initio, for analyzing hundreds of gigabytes of call detail records—a quantity of data that would still be challenging to analyze today.

## Central Repository

The central repository is the heart of the data warehouse. It is usually a relational database accessed through some variant of SQL.

One of the advantages of relational databases is their ability to run on powerful, scalable machines by taking advantage of multiple processors and multiple disks (see the side bar "Background on Parallel Technology"). Most statistical and data mining packages, for instance, can run multiple processing threads at the same time. However, each thread represents one task, running on one processor. More hardware does not make any given task run faster (except when other tasks happen to be interfering with it). Relational databases, on the other hand, can take a single query and, in essence, create multiple threads all running at the same time for one query. As a result, data-intensive applications on powerful computers often run more quickly when using a relational database than when using non-parallel enabled software—and data mining is a very data-intensive application.

A key component in the central repository is a logical data model, which describes the structure of the data inside a database in terms familiar to business users. Often, the data model is confused with the physical layout (or schema) of the database, but there is a critical difference between the two. The purpose of the physical layout is to maximize performance and to provide information to database administrators (DBAs). The purpose of the logical data model is to communicate the contents of the database to a wider, less technical audience. The business user must be able to understand the logical data model—entities, attributes, and relationships. The physical layout is an implementation of the logical data model, incorporating compromises and choices along the way to optimize performance.

When embarking on a data warehousing project, many organizations feel compelled to develop a comprehensive, enterprise-wide data model. These efforts are often surprisingly unsuccessful. The logical data model for the data warehouse does not have to be quite as uncompromising as an enterprise-wide model. For instance, a conflict between product codes in the logical data model for the data warehouse can be (but not necessarily should be) resolved by including both product hierarchies—a decision that takes 10 minutes to make. In an enterprise-wide effort, resolving conflicting product codes can require months of investigations and meetings.

> **TIP** Data warehousing is a process. Be wary of any large database called a data warehouse that does not have a process in place for updating the system to meet end user needs. Such a data warehouse will eventually fade into disuse, because end users needs are likely to evolve, but the system will not.

## BACKGROUND ON PARALLEL TECHNOLOGY

Parallel technology is the key to scalable hardware, and it comes in two flavors: symmetric multiprocessing systems (SMPs) and massively parallel processing systems (MPPs), both of which are shown in the following figure. An SMP machine is centered on a *bus*, a special network present in all computers that connects processing units to memory and disk drives. The bus acts as a central communication device, so SMP systems are sometimes called *shared everything*. Every processing unit can access all the memory and all the disk drives. This form of parallelism is quite popular because an SMP box supports the same applications as uniprocessor boxes—and some applications can take advantage of additional hardware with minimal changes to code. However, SMP technology has its limitations because it places a heavy burden on the central bus, which becomes saturated as the processing load increases. Contention for the central bus is often what limits the performance of SMPs. They tend to work well when they have fewer than 10 to 20 processing units.

MPPs, on the other hand, behave like separate computers connected by a very high-speed network, sometimes called a switch. Each processing unit has its own memory and its own disk storage. Some nodes may be specialized for processing and have minimal disk storage, and others may be specialized for storage and have lots of disk capacity. The bus connecting the processing unit to memory and disk drives never gets saturated. However, one drawback is that some memory and some disk drives are now local and some are remote—a distinction that can make MPPs harder to program. Programs designed for one processor can always run on one processor in an MPP—but they require modifications to take advantage of all the hardware. MPPs are truly scalable so long as the network connecting the processors can supply more bandwidth, and faster networks are generally easier to design than faster buses. There are MPP-based computers with thousands of nodes and thousands of disks.

Both SMPs and MPPs have their advantages. Recognizing this, the vendors of these computers are making them more similar. SMP vendors are connecting their SMP computers together in clusters that start to resemble MPP boxes. At the same time, MPP vendors are replacing their single-processing units with SMP units, creating a very similar architecture. However, regardless of how powerful the hardware is, software needs to be designed to take advantage of these machines. Fortunately, the largest database vendors have invested years of research into enabling their products to do so.

*(continued)*

**BACKGROUND ON PARALLEL TECHNOLOGY *(continued)***

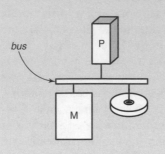

### Uniprocessor

A simple computer follows the architecture laid out by Von Neumann. A processing unit communicates to memory and disk over a local bus. (Memory stores both data and the executable program.) The speed of the processor, bus, and memory limits performance and scalability.

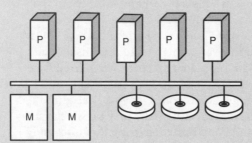

### SMP

The symmetric multiprocessor (SMP) has a shared-everything architecture. It expands the capabilities of the bus to support multiple processors, more memory, and a larger disk. The capacity of the bus limits performance and scalability. SMP architectures usually max out with fewer than 20 processing units.

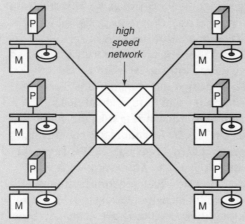

high speed network

### MPP

The massively parallel processor (MMP) has a shared-nothing architecture. It introduces a high-speed network (also called a switch) that connects independent processor/memory/disk components. MPP architectures are very scalable but fewer software packages can take advantage of all the hardware.

Parallel computers build on the basic Von Neumann uniprocessor architecture. SMP and MPP systems are scalable because more processing units, disk drives, and memory can be added to the system.

Data warehousing is a process for managing the decision-support system of record. A process is something that can adjust to users' needs as they are clarified and change over time. A process can respond to changes in the business as needs change over time. The central repository itself is going to be a brittle, little-used system without the realization that as users learn about data and about the business, they are going to want changes and enhancements on the time scale of marketing (days and weeks) rather than on the time scale of IT (months).

## Metadata Repository

We have already discussed metadata in the context of the data hierarchy. It can also be considered a component of the data warehouse. As such, the metadata repository is an often overlooked component of the data warehousing environment. The lowest level of metadata is the database schema, the physical layout of the data. When used correctly, though, metadata is much more. It answers questions posed by end users about the availability of data, gives them tools for browsing through the contents of the data warehouse, and gives everyone more confidence in the data. This confidence is the basis for new applications and an expanded user base.

A good metadata system should include the following:

- The annotated logical data model. The annotations should explain the entities and attributes, including valid values.
- Mapping from the logical data model to the source systems.
- The physical schema.
- Mapping from the logical model to the physical schema.
- Common views and formulas for accessing the data. What is useful to one user may be useful to others.
- Load and update information.
- Security and access information.
- Interfaces for end users and developers, so they share the same description of the database.

In any data warehousing environment, each of these pieces of information is available somewhere—in scripts written by the DBA, in email messages, in documentation, in the system tables in the database, and so on. A metadata repository makes this information available to the users, in a format they can readily understand. The key is giving users access so they feel comfortable with the data warehouse, with the data it contains, and with knowing how to use it.

## Data Marts

Data warehouses do not actually do anything (except store and retrieve data effectively). Applications are needed to realize value, and these often take the form of data marts. A data mart is a specialized system that brings together the data needed for a department or related applications. Data marts are often used for reporting systems and slicing-and-dicing data. Such data marts often use OLAP technology, which is discussed later in this chapter. Another important type of data mart is an exploratory environment used for data mining, which is discussed in the next chapter.

Not all the data in data marts needs to come from the central repository. Often specific applications have an exclusive need for data. The real estate department, for instance, might be using geographic information in combination with data from the central repository. The marketing department might be combining zip code demographics with customer data from the central repository. The central repository only needs to contain data that is likely to be shared among different applications, so it is just one data source—usually the dominant one—for data marts.

## Operational Feedback

Operational feedback systems integrate data-driven decisions back into the operational systems. For instance, a large bank may develop cross-sell models to determine what product next to offer a customer. This is a result of a data mining system. However, to be useful this information needs to go back into the operational systems. This requires a connection back from the decision-support infrastructure into the operational infrastructure.

Operational feedback offers the capability to complete the virtuous cycle of data mining very quickly. Once a feedback system is set up, intervention is only needed for monitoring and improving it—letting computers do what they do best (repetitive tasks) and letting people do what they do best (spot interesting patterns and come up with ideas). One of the advantages of Web-based businesses is that they can, in theory, provide such feedback to their operational systems in a fully automated way.

## End Users and Desktop Tools

The end users are the final and most important component in any data warehouse. A system that has no users is not worth building. These end users are analysts looking for information, application developers, and business users who act on the information.

### Analysts

Analysts want to access as much data as possible to discern patterns and create ad hoc reports. They use special-purpose tools, such as statistics packages, data mining tools, and spreadsheets. Often, analysts are considered to be the primary audience for data warehouses.

Usually, though, there are just a few technically sophisticated people who fall into this category. Although the work that they do is important, it is difficult to justify a large investment based on increases in their productivity. The virtuous cycle of data mining comes into play here. A data warehouse brings together data in a cleansed, meaningful format. The purpose, though, is to spur creativity, a very hard concept to measure.

Analysts have very specific demands on a data warehouse:

- The system has to be responsive. Too much of the work of analysis is in the form of answering urgent questions in the form of ad hoc analysis or ad hoc queries.

- Data needs to be consistent across the database. That is, if a customer started on a particular date, then the first occurrence of a product, channel, and so on should be exactly on that date.

- Data needs to be consistent across time. A field that has a particular meaning now should have the same meaning going back in time. At the very least, differences should be well documented.

- It must be possible to drill down to customer level and preferably to the transaction level detail to verify values in the data warehouse and to develop new summaries of customer behavior.

Analysts place a heavy load on data warehouses, and need access to consistent information in a timely manner.

### Application Developers

Data warehouses usually support a wide range of applications (in other words, data marts come in many flavors). In order to develop stable and robust applications, developers have some specific needs from the data warehouse.

First, the applications they are developing need to be shielded from changes in the structure of the data warehouse. New tables, new fields, and reorganizing the structure of existing tables should have a minimal impact on existing applications. Special application-specific views on the data help provide this assurance. In addition, open communication and knowledge about what applications use which attributes and entities can prevent development gridlock.

Second, the developers need access to valid field values and to know what the values mean. This is the purpose of the metadata repository, which provides documentation on the structure of the data. By setting up the application to verify data values against expected values in the metadata, developers can circumvent problems that often appear only after applications have rolled out.

The developers also need to provide feedback on the structure of the data warehouse. This is one of the principle means of improving the warehouse, by identifying new data that needs to be included in the warehouse and by fixing problems with data already loaded. Since real business needs drive the development of applications, understanding the needs of developers is important to ensure that a data warehouse contains the data it needs to deliver business value.

The data warehouse is going to change and applications are going to continue to use it. The key to delivering success is controlling and managing the changes. The applications are for the end users. The data warehouse is there to support their data needs—not vice versa.

### Business Users

Business users are the ultimate devourers of information derived from the corporate data warehouse. Their needs drive the development of applications, the architecture of the warehouse, the data it contains, and the priorities for implementation.

Many business users only experience the warehouse through printed reports, static online reports, or spreadsheets—basically the same way they have been gathering information for a long time. Even these users will experience the power of having a data warehouse as reports become more accurate, more consistent, and easier to produce.

More important, though, are the people who use the computers on their desks and are willing to take advantage of direct access to the data warehousing environment. Typically, these users access intermediate data marts to satisfy the vast majority of their information needs using friendly, graphical tools that run in their familiar desktop environment. These tools include off-the-shelf query generators, custom applications, OLAP interfaces, and report generation tools. On occasion, business users may drill down into the central repository to explore particularly interesting things they find in the data. More often, they will contact an analyst and have him or her do the heavier analytic work.

Business users also have applications built for specific purposes. These applications may even incorporate some of the data mining techniques discussed in previous chapters. For instance, a resource scheduling application might include an engine that optimizes the schedule using genetic algorithms. A sales forecasting application may have built-in survival analysis models. When embedded in an application, the data mining algorithms are usually quite well hidden from the end user, who cares more about the results than the algorithms that produced them.

## Where Does OLAP Fit In?

The business world has been generating automated reports to meet business needs for many decades. Figure 15.4 shows a range of common reporting capabilities. The oldest manual methods are the mainframe report-generation tools whose output is traditionally printed on green bar paper or green screens. These mainframe reports automate paper-based methods that preceded computers. Producing such reports is often the primary function of IS departments. Even minor changes to the reports require modifying code that sometimes dates back decades. The result is a lag between the time when a user requests changes and the time when he or she sees the new information that is measured in weeks and months. This is old technology that organizations are generally trying to move away from, except for the lowest-level reports that summarize specific operational systems.

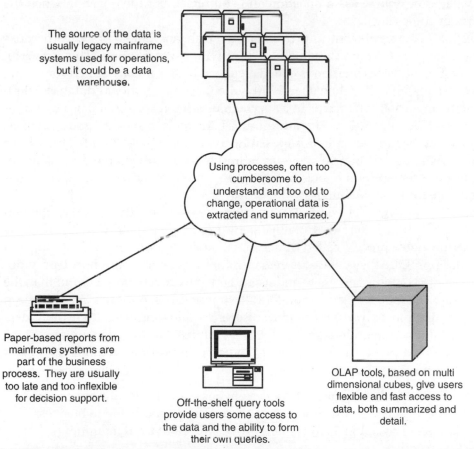

The source of the data is usually legacy mainframe systems used for operations, but it could be a data warehouse.

Using processes, often too cumbersome to understand and too old to change, operational data is extracted and summarized.

Paper-based reports from mainframe systems are part of the business process. They are usually too late and too inflexible for decision support.

Off-the-shelf query tools provide users some access to the data and the ability to form their own queries.

OLAP tools, based on multi dimensional cubes, give users flexible and fast access to data, both summarized and detail.

**Figure 15.4**  Reporting requirements on operational systems are typically handled the same way they have been for decades. Is this the best way?

In the middle are off-the-shelf query generation packages that have become popular for accessing data in the past decade. These generate queries in SQL and can talk to local or remote data sources using a standard protocol, such as the Open Database Connectivity (ODBC) standard. Such reports might be embedded in a spreadsheet, accessed through the Web, or through some other reporting interface. With a day or so of training, business analysts can usually generate the reports that they need. Of course, the report itself is often running as an SQL query on an already overburdened database, so response times are measured in minutes or hours, when the queries are even allowed to run to completion. These response times are much faster than the older report-generation packages, but they still make it difficult to exploit the data. The goal is to be able to ask a question and still remember the question when the answer comes back.

OLAP is a significant improvement over ad hoc query systems, because OLAP systems design the data structure with users in mind. This powerful and efficient representation is called a cube, which is ideally suited for slicing and dicing data. The cube itself is stored either in a relational database, typically using a star schema, or in a special multidimensional database that optimizes OLAP operations. In addition, OLAP tools provide handy analysis functions that are difficult or impossible to express in SQL. If OLAP tools have one downside, it is that business users start to focus only on the dimensions of data represented by the tool. Data mining, on the other hand, is particularly valuable for creative thinking.

Setting up the cube requires analyzing the data and the needs of the end users, which is generally done by specialists familiar with the data and the tool, through a process called dimensional modeling. Although designing and loading an OLAP system requires an initial investment, the result provides informative and fast access to end users, generally much more helpful than the results from a query-generation tool. Response times, once the cube has been built, are almost always measured in seconds, allowing users to explore data and drill down to understand interesting features that they encounter.

OLAP is a powerful enhancement to earlier reporting methods. Its power rests on three key features:

- First, a well-designed OLAP system has a set of relevant dimensions—such as geography, product, and time—understandable to business users. These dimensions often prove important for data mining purposes.

- Second, a well-designed OLAP system has a set of useful measures relevant to the business.

- Third, OLAP systems allow users to slice and dice data, and sometimes to drill down to the customer level.

**TIP** Quick response times are important for getting user acceptance of reporting systems. When users have to wait, they may forget the question that they asked. Interactive response times as experienced by end users should be in the range of 3–5 seconds.

These capabilities are complementary to data mining, but not a substitute for it. Nevertheless, OLAP is a very important (perhaps even the most important) part of the data warehouse architecture because it has the largest number of users.

## What's in a Cube?

A good way to approach OLAP is to think of data as a cube split into subcubes, as shown in Figure 15.5. Although this example uses three dimensions, OLAP can have many more; three dimensions are useful for illustrative purposes. This example shows a typical retailing cube that has one dimension for time, another for product, and a third for store. Each subcube contains various measures indicating what happened regarding that product in that store on that date, such as:

- Total number of items sold
- Total value of the items
- Total amount of discount on the items
- Inventory cost of the items

The measures are called *facts*. As a rule of thumb, dimensions consist of categorical variables and facts are numeric. As users slice and dice the data, they are aggregating facts from many different subcubes. The dimensions are used to determine exactly which subcubes are used in the query.

Even a simple cube such as the one described above is very powerful. Figure 15.6 shows an example of summarizing data in the cube to answer the question "On how many days did a particular store not sell a particular product?" Such a question requires using the store and product dimension to determine which subcubes are used for the query. This question only looks at one fact, the number of items sold, and returns all the dates for which this value is 0. Here are some other questions that can be answered relatively easily:

- What was the total number of items sold in the past year?
- What were the year over year sales, by month, of stores in the Northeast?
- What was the overall margin for each store in November? (Margin being the price paid by the customer minus the inventory cost.)

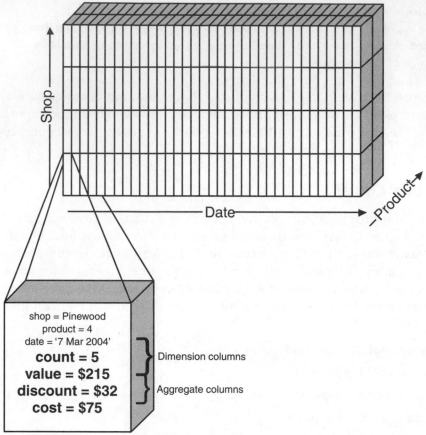

shop = Pinewood
product = 4
date = '7 Mar 2004'
**count = 5**
**value = $215**
**discount = $32**
**cost = $75**

Dimension columns

Aggregate columns

**Figure 15.5** The cube used for OLAP is divided into subcubes. Each subcube contains the key for that subcube and summary information for the data falls into that subcube.

Of course, the ease of getting a report that can answer one of these questions depends on the particular implementation of the reporting interface. However, even for ad hoc reporting, accessing the cube structure can prove much easier than accessing a normalized relational database.

## Three Varieties of Cubes

The cube described in the previous section is an example of a summary data cube. This is a very common example in OLAP. However, not all cubes are summary cubes. And, a data warehouse may contain many different cubes for different purposes.

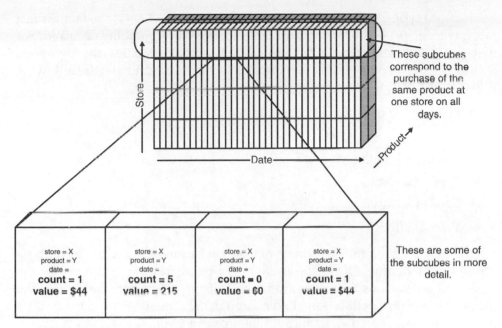

These subcubes correspond to the purchase of the same product at one store on all days.

| store = X<br>product = Y<br>date =<br>**count = 1**<br>**value = $44** | store = X<br>product = Y<br>date =<br>**count = 5**<br>**value = 215** | store = X<br>product = Y<br>date =<br>**count = 0**<br>**value = $0** | store = X<br>product = Y<br>date =<br>**count = 1**<br>**value = $44** |
|---|---|---|---|

These are some of the subcubes in more detail.

The answer to the question is the number of subcubes where **count** is not equal to **0**.

**Figure 15.6** On how many days did store *X* not sell any product *Y*?

Another type of cube represents individual events. These cubes contain the most detailed data related to customer interactions, such as calls to customer service, payments, individual bills, and so on. The summaries are made by aggregating events across the cube. Such event cubes typically have a customer dimension or something similar, such as an account, Web cookie, or household, which ties the event back to the customer. A small number of dimensions, such as the customer ID, date, and event type are often sufficient for identifying each subcube. However, an event cube often has several other dimensions, which provide more detailed information and are important for aggregating data. The facts in such a table often contain dollar amounts and counts.

Event cubes are very powerful. Their use is limited because they rapidly become very big—the database tables representing them can have millions, hundreds of millions, or even billions of rows. Even with the power of OLAP and parallel computers, such cubes require a bit of processing time for routine queries. Nonetheless, event cubes are particularly valuable because they make it possible to "drill down" from other cubes—to find the exact set of events used for calculating a particular value.

The third type of cube is a variant on the event cube. This is the factless fact table, whose purpose is to represent the evidence that something occurred. For instance, there might be a factless fact table that specifies the prospects included in a direct mail campaign. Such a fact table might have the following dimensions:

- Prospect ID (perhaps a household ID)
- Source of the prospect name
- Target date of the mailing
- Type of message
- Type of creative
- Type of offer

This is a case where there may not be any numeric facts to store about the individual name. Of course, there might be interesting attributes for the dimensions—such as the promotional cost of the offers and the cost of the names. However, this data is available through the dimensions and hence does not need to be repeated at the individual prospect level.

Regardless of the type of fact table, there is one cardinal rule: any particular item of information should fall into exactly one subcube. When this rule is violated, the cube cannot easily be used to report on the various dimensions. A corollary of this rule is that when an OLAP cube is being loaded, it is very important to keep track of any data that has unexpected dimensional values. Every dimension should have an "other" category to guarantee that all data makes it in.

**TIP** When choosing the dimensions for a cube, be sure that each record lands in exactly one subcube. If you have redundant dimensions—such as one dimension for date and another for day of the week—then the same record will land in two or more subcubes. If this happens, then the summarizations based on the subcubes will no longer be accurate.

Apart from the cardinal rule that each record inserted into the cube should land in exactly one subcube, there are three other things to keep in mind when designing effective cubes:

- Determining the facts
- Handling complex dimensions
- Making dimensions conform across the data warehouse

These three issues arise when trying to develop cubes, and resolving them is important to making the cubes useful for analytic purposes.

## *Facts*

Facts are the measures in each subcube. The most useful facts are *additive*, so they can be combined together across many different subcubes to provide responses to queries at arbitrary levels of summarization. Additive facts make it possible to summarize data along any dimension or along several dimensions at one time—which is exactly the purpose of the cube.

Examples of additive facts are:

- Counts
- Counts of variables with a particular value
- Total duration of time (such as spent on a web site)
- Total monetary values

The total amount of money spent on a particular product on a particular day is the sum of the amount spent on that product in each store. This is a good example of an additive fact. However, not all facts are additive. Examples include:

- Averages
- Unique counts
- Counts of things shared across different cubes, such as transactions

Averages are not a very interesting example of a nonadditive fact, because an average is a total divided by a count. Since each of these is additive, the average can be derived after combining these facts.

The other examples are more interesting. One interesting question is how many unique customers did some particular action. Although this number can be stored in a subcube, it is not additive. Consider a retail cube with the date, store, and product dimensions. A single customer may purchase items in more than one store, or purchase more than one item in a store, or make purchases on different days. A field containing the number of unique customers has information about one customer in more than one subcube, violating the cardinal rule of OLAP, so the cube is not going to be able to report on unique customers.

A similar thing happens when trying to count numbers of transactions. Since the information about the transaction may be stored in several different subcubes (since a single transaction may involve more than one product), counts of transactions also violate the cardinal rule. This type of information cannot be gathered at the summary level.

Another note about facts is that not all numeric data is appropriate as a fact in a cube. For instance, age in years is numeric, but it might be better treated as a dimension rather than a fact. Another example is customer value. Discrete ranges of customer value are useful as dimensions, and in many circumstances more useful than trying to include customer value as a fact.

When designing cubes, there is a temptation to mix facts and dimensions by creating a count or total for a group of related values. For instance:

- Count of active customers of less than 1-year tenure, between 1 and 2 years, and greater than 2 years

- Amount credited on weekdays; amount credited on weekends

- Total for each day of the week

Each of these suggests another dimension for the cube. The first should have a customer tenure dimensions that takes at least three values. The second appeared in a cube where the time dimension was by month. These facts suggest a need for daily summaries, or at least for separating weekdays and weekends along a dimension. The third suggests a need for a date dimension at the granularity of days.

### Dimensions and Their Hierarchies

Sometimes, a single column seems appropriate for multiple dimensions. For instance, OLAP is a good tool for visualizing trends over time, such as for sales or financial data. A specific date in this case potentially represents information along several dimensions, as shown in Figure 15.7:

- Day of the week
- Month
- Quarter
- Calendar year

One approach is to represent each of these as a different dimension. In other words, there would be four dimensions, one for the day of the week, one for the month, one for the quarter, and one for the calendar year. The data for January 2004, then would be the subcube where the January dimension intersects the 2004 dimension.

This is not a good approach. Multidimensional modeling recognizes that time is an important dimension, and that time can have many different attributes. In addition to the attributes described above, there is also the week of the year, whether the date is a holiday, whether the date is a work day, and so on. Such attributes are stored in reference tables, called dimension tables. Dimension tables make it possible to change the attributes of the dimension without changing the underlying data.

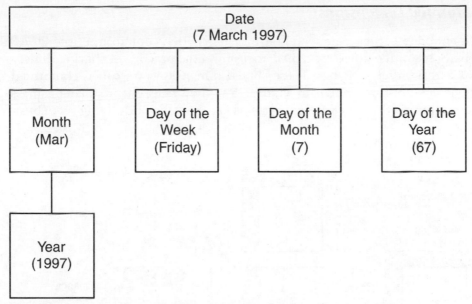

**Figure 15.7** There are multiple hierarchies for dates.

**WARNING** Do not take shortcuts when designing the dimensions for an OLAP system. These are the skeleton of the data mart, and a weak skeleton will not last very long.

Dimension tables contain many different attributes describing each value of the dimension. For instance, a detailed geography dimension might be built from zip codes and include dozens of summary variables about the zip codes. These attributes can be used for filtering ("How many customers are in high-income areas?"). These values are stored in the dimension table rather than the fact table, because they cannot be aggregated correctly. If there are three stores in a zip code, a zip code population fact would get added up three times—multiplying the population by three.

Usually, dimension tables are kept up to date with the most recent values for the dimension. So, a store dimension might include the current set of stores with information about the stores, such as layout, square footage, address, and manager name. However, all of these may change over time. Such dimensions are called slowly changing dimensions, and are of particular interest to data mining because data mining wants to reconstruct accurate histories. Slowly changing dimensions are outside the scope of this book. Interested readers should review Ralph Kimball's books.

## Conformed Dimensions

As mentioned earlier, data warehouse systems often contain multiple OLAP cubes. Some of the power of OLAP arises from the practice of sharing dimensions across different cubes. These shared dimensions are called conformed dimensions and are shown in Figure 15-8; they help ensure that business results reported through different systems use the same underlying set of business rules.

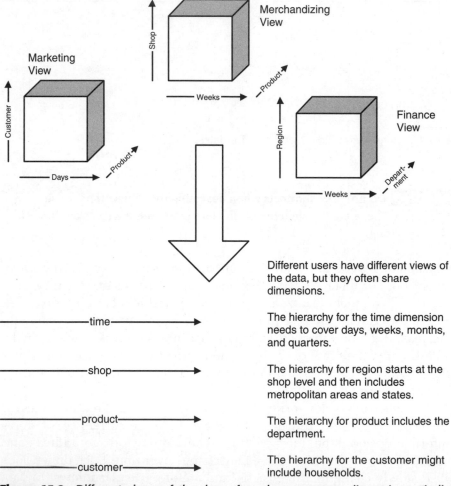

Different users have different views of the data, but they often share dimensions.

The hierarchy for the time dimension needs to cover days, weeks, months, and quarters.

The hierarchy for region starts at the shop level and then includes metropolitan areas and states.

The hierarchy for product includes the department.

The hierarchy for the customer might include households.

**Figure 15.8** Different views of the data often share common dimensions. Finding the common dimensions and their base units is critical to making data warehousing work well across an organization.

A good example of a conformed dimension is the calendar dimension, which keeps track of the attributes of each day. A calendar dimension is so important that it should be a part of every data warehouse. However, different components of the warehouse may need different attributes. For instance, a multinational business might include sets of holidays for different countries, so there might be a flag for "United States Holiday," "United Kingdom Holiday," "French Holiday," and so on, instead of an overall holiday flag. January 1st is a holiday in most countries; however, July 4th is mostly celebrated in the United States.

One of the challenges in building OLAP systems is designing the conformed dimensions so that they are suitable for a wide variety of applications. For some purposes geography might be best described by city and state; for another, by county; for another, by census block group; and for another by zip code. Unfortunately, these four descriptions are not fully compatible, since there can be several small towns in a zip code, and there are five counties in New York City. Multidimensional modeling helps resolve such conflicts.

## Star Schema

Cubes are easily stored in relational databases, using a denormalized data structure called the *star schema*, developed by Ralph Kimball, a guru of OLAP. One advantage of the star schema is its use of standard database technology to achieve the power of OLAP.

A star schema starts with a *central fact table* that corresponds to facts about a business. These can be at the transaction level (for an event cube), although they are more often low-level summaries of transactions. For retail sales, the central fact table might contain daily summaries of sales for each product in each store (shop-SKU-time). For a credit card company, a fact table might contain rows for each transaction by each customer or summaries of spending by product (based on card type and credit limit), customer segment, merchant type, customer geography, and month. For a diesel engine manufacturer interested in repair histories, it might contain each repair made on each engine or a daily summary of repairs at each shop by type of repair.

Each row in the central fact table contains some combination of keys that makes it unique. These keys are called *dimensions*. The central fact table also has other columns that typically contain numeric information specific to each row, such as the amount of the transaction, the number of transactions, and so on. Associated with each dimension are auxiliary tables called *dimension tables*, which contain information specific to the dimensions. For instance, the dimension table for date might specify the day of the week for a particular date, its month, year, and whether it is a holiday.

In diagrams, the dimension tables are connected to the central fact table, resulting in a shape that resembles a star, as shown in Figure 15.9.

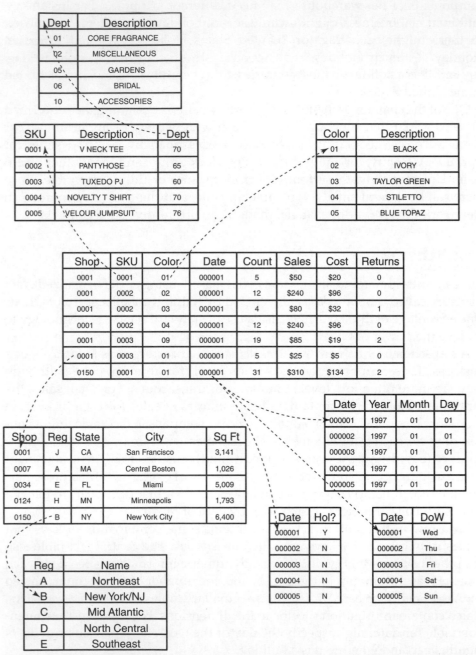

**Figure 15.9** A star schema looks more like this. Dimension tables are conceptually nested, and there may be more than one dimension table for a given dimension.

In practice, star schemas may not be efficient for answering all users' questions, because the central fact table is so large. In such cases, the OLAP systems introduce summary tables at different levels to facilitate query response. Relational database vendors have been providing more and more support for star schemas. With a typical architecture, any query on the central fact table would require multiple joins back to the dimension tables. By applying standard indexes, and creatively enhancing indexing technology, relational databases can handle these queries quite well.

## OLAP and Data Mining

Data mining is about the successful exploitation of data for decision-support purposes. The virtuous cycle of data mining, described in Chapter 2, reminds us that success depends on more than advanced pattern recognition algorithms. The data mining process needs to provide feedback to people and encourage using information gained from data mining to improve business processes. The data mining process should enable people to provide input, in the form of observations, hypotheses, and hunches about what results are important and how to use those results.

In the larger context of data exploitation, OLAP clearly plays an important role as a means of broadening the audience with access to data. Decisions once made based on experience and educated guesses can now be based on data and patterns in the data. Anomalies and outliers can be identified for further investigation and further modeling, sometimes using the most sophisticated data mining techniques. For instance, a user might discover that a particular item sells better at a particular time during the week through the use of an OLAP tool. This might lead to an investigation using market basket analysis to find other items purchased with that item. Market basket analysis might suggest an explanation for the observed behavior—more information and more opportunities for exploiting the information.

There are other synergies between data mining and OLAP. One of the characteristics of decision trees discussed in Chapter 6 is their ability to identify the most informative features in the data relative to a particular outcome. That is, if a decision tree is built in order to predict attrition, then the upper levels of the tree will have the features that are the most important predictors for attrition. Well, these predictors might be a good choice for dimensions using an OLAP tool. Such analysis helps build better, more useful cubes. Another problem when building cubes is determining how to make continuous dimensions discrete. The nodes of a decision tree can help determine the best breaking point for a continuous value. This information can be fed into the OLAP tool to improve the dimension.

One of the problems with neural networks is the difficulty of understanding the results. This is especially true when using them for undirected data mining, as when using SOM networks to detect clusters. The SOM identifies clusters, but cannot explain what the clusters mean.

OLAP to the rescue! The data can now be enhanced with a predicted cluster, as well as with other information about customers, such as demographics, purchase history, and so on. This is a good application for a cube. Using OLAP—with information about the clusters included as a dimension—makes it possible for end users to explore the clusters and to determine features that distinguish them. The dimensions used for the OLAP cube should include the inputs to the SOM neural network, along with the cluster identifier, and perhaps other descriptive variables. There is a tricky data conversion problem because the neural networks require continuous values scaled between –1 and 1, and OLAP tools prefer discrete values. For values that were originally discrete, this is no problem. For continuous values, various binning techniques solve the problem.

As these examples show, OLAP and data mining complement each other. Data mining can help build better cubes by defining appropriate dimensions, and further by determining how to break up continuous values on dimensions. OLAP provides a powerful visualization capability to help users better understand the results of data mining, such as clustering and neural networks. Used together, OLAP and data mining reinforce each other's strengths and provide more opportunities for exploiting data.

# Where Data Mining Fits in with Data Warehousing

Data mining plays an important role in the data warehouse environment. The initial returns from a data warehouse come from automating existing processes, such as putting reports online and giving existing applications a clean source of data. The biggest returns are the improved access to data that can spur innovation and creativity—and these come from new ways of looking at and analyzing data. This is the role of data mining—to provide the tools that improve understanding and inspire creativity based on observations in the data.

A good data warehousing environment serves as a catalyst for data mining. The two technologies work together as partners:

- Data mining thrives on large amounts of data and the more detailed the data, the better—data that comes from a data warehouse.

- Data mining thrives on clean and consistent data—capitalizing on the investment in data cleansing tools.

- The data warehouse environment enables hypothesis testing and simplifies efforts to measure the effects of actions taken—enabling the virtuous cycle of data mining.

- Scalable hardware and relational database software can offload the data processing parts of data mining.

There is, however, a distinction between the way data mining looks at the world and the way data warehousing does. Normalized data warehouses can store data with time stamps, but it is very difficult to do time-related manipulations—such as determining what event happened just before some other event of interest. OLAP introduces a time dimension. Data mining extends this even further by taking into account the notion of "before" and "after." Data mining learns from data (the "before"), with the purpose of applying these findings to the future (the "after"). For this reason, data mining often puts a heavy load on data warehouses. These are complementary technologies, supporting each other as discussed in the next few sections.

## Lots of Data

The traditional approach to data analysis generally starts by reducing the size of the data. There are three common ways of doing this: summarizing detailed transactions, taking a subset of the data, and only looking at certain attributes. The reason for reducing the size of the data was to make it possible to analyze the data on the available hardware and software systems. When properly done, the laws of statistics come into play, and it is possible to choose a sample that behaves roughly like the rest of the data.

Data mining, on the other hand, is searching for trends in the data and for valuable anomalies. It is often trying to answer different types of questions from traditional statistical analysis, such as "what product is this customer most likely to purchase next?" Even if it is possible to devise a model using a subset of data, it is necessary to deploy the model and score all customers, a process that can be very computationally intensive.

Fortunately, data mining algorithms are often able to take advantage of large amounts of data. When looking for patterns that identify rare events—such as having to write-off customers because they failed to pay—having large amounts of data ensures that there is sufficient data for analysis. A subset of the data might be statistically relevant in total, but when you try to decompose it into other segments (by region, by product, by customer segment), there may be too little data to produce statistically meaningful results.

Data mining algorithms are able to make use of lots of data. Decision trees, for example, work very well, even when there are dozens or hundreds of fields in each record. Link analysis requires a full complement of the data to create a graph. Neural networks can train on millions of records at a time. And, even though the algorithms often work on summaries of the detailed transactions (especially at the customer level), what gets summarized can change from one run to the next. Prebuilding the summaries and discarding the transaction data locks you into only one view of the business. Often the first result from using such summaries is a request for some variation on them.

## Consistent, Clean Data

Data mining algorithms are often applied to gigabytes of data combined from several different sources. Much of the work in looking for actionable information actually takes place when bringing the data together—often 80 percent or more of the time allocated to a data mining project is spent bringing the data together—especially when a data warehouse is not available. Subsequent problems, such as matching account numbers, interpreting codes, and house-holding, further delay the analysis. Finding interesting patterns is often an iterative process that requires going back to the data to get additional data elements. Finally, when interesting patterns are found, it is often necessary to repeat the process on the most recent data available.

A well-designed and well-built data warehouse can help solve these problems. Data is cleaned once, when it is loaded into the data warehouse. The meaning of fields is well defined and available through the metadata. Incorporating new data into analyses is as easy as finding out what data is available through the metadata and retrieving it from the warehouse. A particular analysis can be reapplied on more recent data, since the warehouse is kept up to date. The end result is that the data is cleaner and more available—and that the analysts can spend more time applying powerful tools and insights instead of moving data and pushing bytes.

## Hypothesis Testing and Measurement

The data warehouse facilitates two other areas of data mining. Hypothesis testing is the verification of educated guesses about patterns in the data. Do tropical colors really sell better in Florida than elsewhere? Do people tend to make long-distance calls after dinner? Are the users of credit cards at restaurants really high-end customers? All of these questions can be expressed rather easily as queries on the appropriate relational database. Having the data available makes it possible to ask questions and find out quickly what the answers are.

**TIP** The ability to test hypotheses and ideas is a very important aspect of data mining. By bringing the data together in one place, data warehouses enable answering in-depth, complicated questions. One caveat is that such queries can be expensive to run, falling into the killer query category.

Measurement is the other area where data warehouses have proven to be very valuable. Often when marketing efforts, product improvements, and so forth take place, there is limited feedback on the degree of success achieved. A data warehouse makes it possible to see the results and to find related effects. Did sales of other products improve? Did customer attrition increase? Did calls to customer service decrease? And so on. Having the data available makes it possible to understand the effects of an action, whether the action was spurred by data mining results or by something else.

Of particular value in terms of measurement is the effect of various marketing actions on the longer-term customer relationship. Often, marketing campaigns are measured in terms of response. While response is clearly a dimension of interest, it is only one. The longer term behavior of customers is also of interest. Did an acquisition campaign bring in good customers or did the newly acquired customers leave before they even paid? Did an upsell campaign stick, or did customers return to their previous products? Measurement enables an organization to learn from its mistakes and to build on its successes.

## Scalable Hardware and RDBMS Support

The final synergy between data mining and data warehousing is on the systems level. The same scalable hardware and software that makes it possible to store and query large databases provides a good system for analyzing data. Chapter 17 talks about building the customer signature. Often, the best place to build the signature is in the central repository or, failing that, in a data mart with similar amounts of data.

There is also the question of running data mining algorithms in parallel, taking further advantage of the powerful machines. This is often not necessary, because actually building models represents a small part of the time devoted to data mining—preparing the data and understanding the results are much more important. Databases, such as Oracle and Microsoft SQL Server, are increasingly providing support for data mining algorithms, which enables such algorithms to run in parallel.

## Lessons Learned

Data warehousing is not a system but a process that can greatly benefit data mining and data analysis efforts. From the perspective of data mining, the most important functionality is the ability to recreate accurate snapshots of history. Another very important facet is support for ad hoc reporting. In order to learn from data, you need to know what really happened.

A typical data warehousing system contains the following components:

- The source systems provide the input into the data warehouse.

- The extraction , transformation, and load tools clean the data and apply business rules so that new data is compatible with historical data.

- The central repository is a relational database specifically designed to be a decision-support system of record.

- The data marts provide the interface to different varieties of users with different needs.

- The metadata repository informs users and developers about what is inside the data warehouse.

One of the challenges in data warehousing is the massive amount of data that must be stored, particularly if the goal is to keep all customer interactions. Fortunately, computers are sufficiently powerful that the question is more about budget than possibility. Relational databases can also take advantage of the most powerful hardware, parallel computers.

Online Analytic Processing (OLAP) is a powerful part of data warehousing. OLAP tools are very good at handling summarized data, allowing users summarize information along one or several dimensions at one time. Because these systems are optimized for user reporting, they often have interactive response times of less than 5 seconds.

Any well-designed OLAP system has time as a dimension, making it very useful for seeing trends over time. Trying to accomplish the same thing on a normalized data warehouse requires very complicated queries that are prone to error. To be most useful, OLAP systems should allow users to drill down to detail data for all reports. This capability ensures that all data is making it into the cubes, as well as giving users the ability to spot important patterns that may not appear in the dimensions.

As we have pointed out throughout this chapter, OLAP complements data mining. It is not a substitute for it. It provides better understanding of data, and the dimensions developed for OLAP can make data mining results more actionable. However, OLAP does not automatically find patterns in data.

OLAP is a powerful way to distribute information to many end users for advanced reporting needs. It provides the ability to let many more users base their decisions on data, instead of on hunches, educated guesses, and personal experience. OLAP complements undirected data mining techniques such as clustering. OLAP can provide the insight needed to find the business value in the identified clusters. It also provides a good visualization tool to use with other methods, such as decision trees and memory-based reasoning.

Data warehousing and data mining are not the same thing; however, they do complement each other, and data mining applications are often part of the data warehouse solution.

# CHAPTER 16

# Building the Data Mining Environment

*In the Big Rock Candy Mountains,*
*There's a land that's fair and bright,*
*Where the handouts grow on bushes*
*And you sleep out every night.*
*Where the boxcars all are empty*
*And the sun shines every day*
*And the birds and the bees*
*And the cigarette trees*
*The lemonade springs*
*Where the bluebird sings*
*In the Big Rock Candy Mountains.*

Twentieth century hoboes had a vision of utopia, so why not twenty-first century data miners? For us, the vision is one of a company that puts the customer at the center of its operations and measures its actions by their effect on long-term customer value. In this ideal organization, business decisions are based on reliable information distilled from vast quantities of customer data. Needless to say, data miners—the people with the skills to turn all that data into the information needed to run the company—are held in great esteem.

This chapter starts with a utopian vision of a truly customer-centric organization with the ideal data mining environment to produce the information on which all decisions are based. Having a description of what the ideal data mining environment would look like is helpful for establishing more realistic near term goals. The chapter then goes on to look at the various components of the data mining environment—the staff, the data mining infrastructure, and the data mining software itself. Although we may not be able to achieve all elements of the utopian vision, we can use the vision to help create an environment suitable for successful data mining work.

# A Customer-Centric Organization

Despite the familiar cliché that the customer is king, in most companies customers are not treated much like royalty. One reason is that most businesses are not organized around customers; they are organized around products. Supermarkets, for example, have long been able to track the inventory levels of tens of thousands of products in order to keep the shelves well stocked, and they are able to calculate the profit margin on any item. But, until recently, these same stores knew nothing about individual customers—not their names, nor how many trips per month they make, nor what time of day they tend to shop, nor whether they use coupons, nor if they have children, nor what percent of the household's shopping is done in this store, nor how close they live—nothing. We don't mean to pick on supermarkets. Banks have been organized around loans; telephone companies have been organized around switches; airlines have been organized around operations. None have known much (or cared much) about customers.

In all of these industries, technology now makes it possible to shift the focus to customers. Such a shift is not easy; in fact, it is nothing short of revolutionary. By combining point-of-sale scanner data with a loyalty card program, a grocery retailer can, with a lot of effort, learn who is buying what and when they buy it, which customers are price-sensitive and which ones like to try new products, which ones like to bake from scratch and which ones prefer prepared meals, and so on. A telephone company can figure out who is making business calls and who is primarily chatting with friends. An online music store can make individualized recommendations of new music.

The harder challenge is being able to make effective use of this new ability to see customers in data. A truly customer-centric organization would be happy to continue offering an unprofitable service if the customers who use the loss-generating service spend more in other areas and therefore increase the profitability of the company as a whole. A customer-centric company does not have to ask the same questions every time a customer calls in. A customer-centric company judges a marketing campaign on the value customers generate over their lifetimes rather than on the initial response rate.

Becoming truly customer-centric means changing the corporate culture and the way everyone from top managers to call-center operators are rewarded. As long as each product line has a manager whose compensation is tied to the amount and margin of product sold, the company will remain focused on products rather than customers. In other words, the company is paying its managers to focus on products, and the managers are doing their jobs. In the ideal customer-centric organization, everyone is rewarded for increasing customer value and understands that this requires learning from each customer interaction and the ability to use what has been learned to serve customers better. As a result, the company records every interaction with its customers and keeps an extensive historical record of these interactions.

# An Ideal Data Mining Environment

The ideal context for data mining is an organization that appreciates the value of information. Bringing together customer data from all of the many places where it is originally collected and putting it into a form suitable for data mining is a difficult and expensive process. It will only happen in an organization that understands how valuable that data is once it can be properly exploited. Information is power. A learning organization values progress and steady improvement; such an organization wants and invests in accurate information. Remember that the producers of information always have real power to determine what data is available and when. They are not passive consumers of a take-it-or-leave-it data warehouse, they have the power to determine what data is available, although collecting such data might mean changing operational procedures.

## The Power to Determine What Data Is Available

In the ideal data mining environment, the importance of data analysis is recognized and its results are shared across the organization. Marketing people instinctively regard every campaign as a controlled experiment, even when that means not including some customers in a promising campaign because those customers are part of a control group. Designers of operational systems instinctively keep track of all customer transactions, including nonbillable ones such as customer service inquiries, bank account balance inquiries, or visits to particular sections of the company Web site. Everyone expects that customer interactions from different channels can be identified as involving the same customer, even when some happen at an ATM, some in a bank branch, some over the phone, and some on the Web.

In such an environment, an analyst at a telephone company trying to understand the relationship between quality of wireless telephone service and churn has no trouble getting customer-level data on dropped calls and other failures. The analyst can also readily see a customer's purchase history even though some purchases were made in stores, some through the mail-order catalog, and some on the Web. It is similarly easy to determine, for each of a customer's calls to customer service, the duration of the call and whether the call was handled by a human representative or stayed in the IVR, and in the latter case, what path was followed through the prompts. Best of all, when the required data is not readily available, there is a team of people whose job it is to make it available—even when that means redesigning an application form, reprogramming an automated switch—or simply loading the data correctly in the first place.

## The Skills to Turn Data into Actionable Information

The ideal data mining environment is staffed by people whose superior skills in data processing and data mining are only surpassed by their intimate understanding of how the business operates and its goals for the future. The data mining group includes database experts, programmers, statisticians, data miners, and business analysts, all working together to ensure that business decisions are based on accurate information. This team of people has the communication skills to spread whatever they may learn to the appropriate parts of the organization, whether that is marketing, operations, management, or strategy

## All the Necessary Tools

The ideal data mining environment includes sufficient computing power and database resources to support the analysis of the most detailed level of customer transactions. It includes software for manipulating all that data and creating model sets from it. And, of course, it includes a rich collection of data mining software so that all the techniques from Chapters 5–13 can be applied.

# Back to Reality

Readers will not be shocked to learn that we have never seen the ideal data mining environment just described. We have, however, worked with many companies that are moving in the right direction. These companies are taking steps to transform themselves into customer-centric organizations. They are building data mining groups. They are gathering customer data from operational systems and creating a single customer view. Many of them are already reaping substantial benefits.

## Building a Customer-Centric Organization

The first component of the utopian vision that opened the chapter was a truly customer-centric organization. In terms of data, one of the hardest parts of building a customer-centric organization is establishing a single view of the customer shared across the entire enterprise that informs every customer interaction. The flip side of this challenge is establishing a single image of the company and its brand across all channels of communication with the customer, including retail stores, independent dealers, the Web site, the call centers, advertising, and direct marketing. The goal is not only to make more informed decisions; the goal is to improve the customer experience in a measurable way. In other words, the customer strategy has both *analytic* and *operational* components. This book is more concerned with the analytic component, but both are critical to success.

**TIP** Building a customer-centric organization requires a strategy with both analytic and operational components. Although this book is about the analytical component, the operational component is also critical.

Building a customer-centric organization requires centralizing customer information from a variety of sources in a single data warehouse, along with a set of common definitions and well-understood business processes describing the source of the data. This combination makes it possible to define a set of *customer metrics* and business rules used by all groups to monitor the business and to measure the impact of changing market conditions and new initiatives.

The centralized store of customer information is, of course, the data warehouse described in the previous chapter. As shown in Figure 16.1, there is two-way traffic between the operational systems and the data warehouse. Operational systems supply the raw data that goes into the data warehouse, and the warehouse in turn supplies customer scores, decision rules, customer segment definitions, and action triggers to the operational system. As an example, the operational systems of a retail Web site capture all customer orders. These orders are then summarized in a data warehouse. Using data from the data warehouse, association rules are created and used to generate cross-sell recommendations that are sent back to the operational systems. The end result: a customer comes to the site to order a skirt and ends up with several pairs of tights as well.

## Creating a Single Customer View

Every part of the organization should have access to a single shared view of the customer and present the customer with a single image of the company. In practical terms that means sharing a single customer profitability model, a single payment default risk model, a single customer loyalty model, and shared definitions of such terms as *customer start*, *new customer*, *loyal customer*, and *valuable customer*.

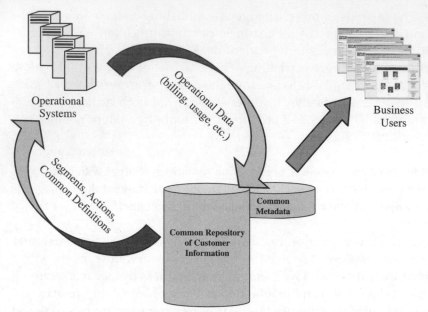

**Figure 16.1**  A customer-centric organization requires centralized customer data.

It is natural for different groups to have different definitions of these terms. At one publication, the circulation department and the advertising sales department have different views on who are the most valuable customers because the people who pay the highest subscription prices are not necessarily the people of most interest to the advertisers. The solution is to have an advertising value and a subscription value for each customer, using ideas such as advertising fitness introduced in Chapter 4.

At another company, the financial risk management group considers a customer "new" for the first 4 months of tenure, and during this initial *probationary period* any late payments are pursued aggressively. Meanwhile, the customer loyalty group considers the customer "new" for the first 3 months and during this *welcome period* the customer is treated with extra care. So which is it: a honeymoon or a trial engagement? Without agreement within the company, the customer receives mixed messages.

For companies with several different lines of business, the problem is even trickier. The same company may provide Internet service and telephone service, and, of course, maintain different billing, customer service, and operational systems for the two services. Furthermore, if the ISP was recently acquired by the telephone company, it may have no idea what the overlap is between its existing telephone customers and its newly acquired Internet customers.

## Defining Customer-Centric Metrics

On September 24, 1929, Lieutenant James H. Doolittle of the U.S. Army Air Corps made history by flying "blind" to demonstrate that with the aid of newly invented instruments such as the artificial horizon, the directional gyroscope, and the barometric altimeter, it was possible to fly a precise course even with the cockpit shrouded by a canvas hood. Before the invention of the artificial horizon, pilots flying into a cloud or fog bank would often end up flying upside down. Now, thanks to all those gauges in the cockpit, we calmly munch pretzels, sip coffee, and revise spreadsheets in weather that would have grounded even Lieutenant Doolittle. Good business metrics are just as crucial to keeping a large business flying on the proper course.

Business metrics are the signals that tell management which levers to move and in what direction. Selecting the *right* metrics is crucial because a business tends to become what it is measured by. A business that measures itself by the number of customers it has will tend to sign up new customers without regard to their expected tenure or prospects for future profitability. A business that measures itself by market share will tend to increase market share at the expense of other goals such as profitability. The challenge for companies that want to be customer-centric is to come up with realistic customer-centric measures. It sounds great to say that the company's goal is to increase customer loyalty; it is harder to come up with a good way to measure that quality in customers. Is merely having lasted a long time a sign of loyalty? Or should loyalty be defined as being resistant to offers from competitors? If the latter, how can it be measured?

Even seemingly simple metrics such as *churn* or *profitability* can be surprisingly hard to pin down. When does churn actually occur:

- On the day phone service is actually deactivated?
- On the day the customer first expressed an intention to deactivate?
- At the end of the first billing cycle after deactivation?
- On the date when the telephone number is released for new customers?

Each of these definitions plays a role in different parts of a telephone business. For wireless subscribers on a contract, these events may be far apart. And, which churn events should be considered voluntary? Consider a subscriber who refuses to pay in order to protest bad service and is eventually cut off; is that voluntary or involuntary churn? What about a subscriber who stops voluntarily and then doesn't pay the final amount owed? These questions do not have a right answer; they do suggest the subtleties of defining the customer relationship.

As for profitability, which customers are considered profitable depends a great deal on how costs are allocated.

## Collecting the Right Data

Once metrics such as *loyalty*, *profitability*, and *churn* have been properly defined, the next step is to determine the data needed to calculate them correctly. This is different from simply approximating the definition using whatever data happens to be available. Remember, in the ideal data mining environment, the data mining group has the power to determine what data is made available!

Information required for managing the business should drive the addition of new tables and fields to the data warehouse. For example, a customer-centric company ought to be able to tell which of its customers are profitable. In many companies this is not possible because there is not enough information available to sensibly allocate costs at the customer level. One of our clients, a wireless phone company, approached this problem by compiling a list of questions that would have to be answered in order to decide what it costs to provide service to a particular customer. They then determined what data would be required to answer those questions and set up a project to collect it.

The list of questions was long, and included the following:

- How many times per year does the customer call customer care?
- Does the customer pay bills online, by check, or by credit card?
- What proportion of the customer's airtime is spent roaming?
- On which outside networks does the customer roam?
- What is the contractual cost for these networks?
- Are the customer's calls to customer care handled by the IVR or by human operators?

Answering these cost-related questions required data from the call-center system, the billing system , and a financial system. Similar exercises around other important metrics revealed a need for call detail data, demographic data, credit data, and Web usage data.

## From Customer Interactions to Learning Opportunities

A customer-centric organization maintains a learning relationship with its customers. Every interaction with a customer is an opportunity for learning, an opportunity that can be siezed when there is good communication between data miners and the various customer-facing groups within the company.

Almost any action the company takes that affects customers—a price change, a new product introduction, a marketing campaign—can be designed so that it is also an experiment to learn more about customers. The results of these experiments should find their way into the data warehouse, where they will be available for analysis. Often the actions themselves are suggested by data mining.

As an example, data mining at one wireless company showed that having had service suspended for late payment was a predictor of both *voluntary* and *involuntary* churn. That late payment is a predictor of later nonpayment is hardly a surprise, but the fact that late payment (or the company's treatment of late payers) was a predictor of voluntary churn seemed to warrant further investigation.

The observation led to the hypothesis that having had their service suspended lowers a customers' loyalty to the company and makes it more likely that they will take their business elsewhere when presented with an opportunity to do so. It was also clear from credit bureau data that some of the late payers were financially able to pay their phone bills. This suggested an experiment: Treat low-risk customers differently from high-risk customers by being more patient with their delinquency and employing gentler methods of persuading them to pay before suspending them. A controlled experiment tested whether this approach would improve customer loyalty without unacceptably driving up bad debt. Two similar cohorts of low-risk, high-value customers received different treatments. One was subjected to the "business as usual" treatment, while the other got the kinder, gentler treatment. At the end of the trial period, the two groups were compared on the basis of retention and bad debt in order to determine the financial impact of switching to the new treatment. Sure enough, the kinder, gentler treatment turned out to be worthwhile for the lower risk customers—increasing payment rates and slightly increasing long term tenure.

## Mining Customer Data

When every customer interaction is generating data, there are endless opportunities for data mining. Purchasing patterns and usage patterns can be mined to create customer segments. Response data can be mined to improve the targeting of future campaigns. Multiple response models can be combined into best next offer models. Survival analysis can be employed to forecast future customer attrition. Churn models can spot customers at risk for attrition. Customer value models can identify the customers worth keeping.

Of course, all this requires a data mining group and the infrastructure to support it.

## The Data Mining Group

The data mining group is specifically responsible for building models and using data to learn about customers—as opposed to leading marketing efforts, devising new products, and so on. That is, this group has technical responsibilities rather than business responsibilities.

We have seen data mining groups located in several different places in the corporate hierarchy:

- Outside the company as an outsourced activity
- As part of IT
- As part of marketing, customer relationship management, or finance organization
- As an interdisciplinary group whose members still belong to their home departments

Each of these structures has certain benefits and drawbacks, as discussed below.

## Outsourcing Data Mining

Companies have varying reasons for considering outsourcing data mining. For some, data mining is only an occasional need and so not worth investing in an internal group. For others, data mining is an ongoing requirement, but the skills required seem so different from the ones currently available in the company that building this expertise from scratch would be very challenging. Still others have their customer data hosted by an outside vendor and feel that the analysis should take place close to the data.

### Outsourcing Occasional Modeling

Some companies think they have little need for building models and using data to understand customers. These companies generally fall into one of two types. The first are the companies with few customers, either because the company is small or because each customer is very large. As an example, the private banking group at a typical bank may serve a few thousand customers, and the account representatives personally know their clients. In such an environment, data mining may be superfluous, because people are so intimately involved in the relationship.

However, data mining can play a role even in this environment. In particular, data mining can make it possible to understand best practices and to spread them. For instance, some employees in the private bank may do a better job in some way (retaining customers, encouraging customers to recommend friends, family members, colleagues, and so on). These employees may have best practices that should be spread through the organization.

**TIP** Data mining may be unncessary for companies where dedicated staff maintain deep and personal long-term relationships with their customers.

Data mining may also seem unimportant to rapidly growing companies in a new market. In this situation, customer acquisition drives the business, and advertising, rather than direct marketing, is the principal way of attracting new customers. Applications for data mining in advertising are limited, and, at this stage in their development, companies are not yet focused on customer relationship management and customer retention. For the limited direct marketing they do, outsourced modeling is often sufficient.

Wireless communications, cable television, and Internet service providers all went through periods of exponential growth that have only recently come to an end as these markets matured (and before them, wired telephones, life insurance, catalogs, and credit cards went through similar cycles). During the initial growth phases, understanding customers may not be a worthwhile investment—an additional cell tower, switch, or whatever may provide better return. Eventually, though, the business and the customer base grow to a point where understanding the customers takes on increased importance. In our experience, it is better for companies to start early along the path of customer insight, rather than waiting until the need becomes critical.

## Outsourcing Ongoing Data Mining

Even when a company has recognized the need for data mining, there is still the possibility of outsourcing. This is particularly true when the company is built around customer acquisition. In the United States, credit bureaus and household data suppliers are happy to provide modeling as a value added service with the data they sell. There are also direct marketing companies that handle everything from mailing lists to fulfillment—the actual delivery of products to customers. These companies often offer outsourced data mining.

Outsourcing arrangements have financial advantages for companies. The problem is that customer insight is being outsourced as well. A company that relies on outsourcing customers analytics runs the risk that customer understanding will be lost between the company and the vendor.

For instance, one company used direct mail for a significant proportion of its customer acquisition and outsourced the direct mail response modeling work to the mailing list vendors. Over the course of about 2 years, there were several direct mail managers in the company and the emphasis on this channel decreased. What no one had realized was that direct mail was driving acquisition that was being credited to other channels. Direct mail pieces could be filled in and returned by mail, in which case the new acquisition was credited to direct mail. However, the pieces also contained the company's URL and a free phone number. Many prospects who received the direct mail found it more convenient to respond by phone or on the Web, often forgetting to provide the special code identifying them as direct mail prospects. Over time, the response attributed to direct mail decreased, and consequently the budget for direct mail decreased as well. Only later, when decreased direct mail led to decreased responses in other channels, did the company realize that ignoring this echo effect had caused them to make a less-than-optimal business decision.

## Insourcing Data Mining

The modeling process creates more then models and scores; it also produces insights. These insights often come during the process of data exploration and data preparation that is an important part of the data mining process. For that reason, we feel that any company with ongoing data mining needs should develop an in-house data mining group to keep the learning in the company.

### Building an Interdisciplinary Data Mining Group

Once the decision has been made to bring customer understanding in-house, the question is where. In some companies, the data mining group has no permanent home. It consists of a group of people seconded from their usual jobs to come together to perform data mining. By its nature, such an arrangement seems temporary and often it is the result of some urgent requirement such as the need to understand a sudden upsurge in customer defaults. While it lasts, such a group can be very effective, but it is unlikely to last very long because the members will be recalled to their regular duties as soon as a new task requires their attention.

### Building a Data Mining Group in IT

A possible home is in the systems group, since this group is often responsible for housing customer data and for running customer-facing operational systems. Because the data mining group is technical and needs access to data and powerful software and servers, the IT group seems like a natural location. In fact, analysis can be seen as an extension of providing databases and access tools and maintaining such systems.

Being part of IT has the advantage that the data mining group has access to hardware and data as needed, since the IT group has these technical resources and access to data. In addition, the IT group is a service organization with clients in many business units. In fact, the business units that are the "customers" for data mining are probably already used to relying on IT for data and reporting.

On the other hand, IT is sometimes a bit removed from the business problems that motivate customer analytics. Since very slight misunderstandings of the business problems can lead to useless results, it is very important that people from the business units be very closely involved with any IT-based data mining projects.

### Building a Data Mining Group in the Business Units

The alternative to putting the data mining group where the data and computers are is to put it close to the problems being addressed. That generally means the marketing group, the customer relationship management group (where such a thing exists), or the finance group. Sometimes there are several small data mining groups, one in each of several business units. A group in finance building credit risk models and collections models, one in marketing building response models, and one in CRM building cross-sell models and voluntary churn models.

The advantages and disadvantages of this approach are the inverse of those for putting data mining in IT. The business units have a great understanding of their own business problems, but may still have to rely on IT for data and computing resources. Although either approach can be successful, on balance we prefer to see data mining centered in the business units.

## What to Look for in Data Mining Staff

The best data mining groups are often eclectic mixes of people. Because data mining has not existed very long as a separately named activity, there are few people who can claim to be trained data miners. There are data miners who used to be physicists, data miners who used to be geologists, data miners who used to be computer scientists, data miners who used to be marketing managers, data miners who used to be linguists, and data miners who are still statisticians.

This makes lunchtime conversation in a data mining group fairly interesting, but it doesn't offer much guidance for hiring managers. The things that make good data miners better than mediocre ones are hard to teach and impossible to automate: good intuition, a feel for how to coax information out of data, and a natural curiosity.

No one indivdiual is likely to have all the skills required for completing a data mining project. Among them, the team members should cover the following:

- Database skills (SQL, if the data is stored in relational databases)
- Data transformation and programming skills (SAS, SPSS, S-Plus, PERL, other programming languages, ETL tools)
- Statistics
- Machine learning skills
- Industry knowledge in the relevant industry
- Data visualization skills
- Interviewing and requirements-gathering skills
- Presentation, writing, and communication skills

A new data mining group should include someone who has done commercial data mining before—preferably in the same industry. If necessary, this expertise can be provided by outside consultants.

# Data Mining Infrastructure

In companies where data mining is merely an exploratory activity, useful data mining can be accomplished with little infrastructure. A desktop workstation with some data mining software and access to the corporate databases is likely to be sufficient. However, when data mining is central to the business, the data mining infrastructure must be considerably more robust. In these companies, updating customer profiles with new model scores either on a regular schedule such as once a month or, in some cases with each new transaction, is part of the regular production process of the data warehouse. The data mining infrastructure must provide a bridge between the exploratory world where models are developed and the production world where models are scored and marketing campaigns run.

A production-ready data mining environment must be able to support the following:

- The ability to access data from many sources and bring the data together as customer signatures in a data mining model set.

- The ability to score customers using already created models from the model library on demand.

- The ability to manage hundreds of model scores over time.

- The ability to manage scores or hundreds of models developed over time.

- The ability to reconstruct a customer signature for any point in a customer's tenure, such as immediately before a purchase or other interesting event.

- The ability to track changes in model scores over time.

- The ability to publish scores, rules, and other data mining results back to the data warehouse and to other applications that need them.

The data mining infrastructure is logically (and often physically) split into two pieces supporting two quite different activities: mining and scoring. Each task presents a different set of requirements.

## The Mining Platform

The mining platform supports software for data manipulation along with data mining software embodying the data mining techniques described in this book, visualization and presentation software, and software to enable models to be published to the scoring environment.

Although we have already touched on a few integration issues, others to consider include:

- Where in the client/server hierarchy is the software to be installed?

- Will the data mining software require its own hardware platform? If so, will this introduce a new operating system into the mix?

- What software will have to be installed on users' desktops in order to communicate with the package?

- What additional networking, SQL gateways, and middleware will be required?

- Does the data mining software provide good interfaces to reporting and graphics packages?

The purpose of the mining platform is to support exploration of the data, mining, and modeling. The system should be devised with these activities in mind, including the fact that such work requires much processing and computing power. The data mining software vendor should be able to provide specifications for a data mining platform adequate for the anticipated dataset sizes and expected usage patterns.

## The Scoring Platform

The scoring platform is where models developed on the mining platform are applied to customer records to create scores used to determine future treatments. Often, the scoring platform is the customer database itself, which is likely to be a relational database running on a parallel hardware platform.

In order to score a record, the record must contain, or the scoring platform must be able to calculate, the same features that went into the model. These features used by the model are rarely in the raw form in which they occur in the data. Often, new features have been created by combining existing variables in various ways, such as taking the ratio of one to another and performing transformations such as binning, summing, and averaging. Whatever was done to calculate the features used when the model was created must now be done for every record to be scored. Since there may be hundreds of millions of transactional records, it matters how this is done. When the volume of data is large, so is the data processing challenge.

Scoring is not complete until the scores reside on a customer database somewhere accessible to the software that will be used to select customers for inclusion in marketing campaigns. If Web log or call detail or point-of-sale scanner data needed as a model input resides in flat files on one system, and the customer marketing database resides on another system but the two are accurate as of different dates, this too can be a data processing challenge.

## One Example of a Production Data Mining Architecture

Web retailing is an industry that has gone farther than most in routinely incorporating data mining and scoring into the operational environment. Many Web retailers update a customer's profile with every transaction and use model scores to determine what to display and what to recommend. The architecture described here is from Blue Martini, a company that supplies software for mining-ready retail Web sites. The example it provides of how data mining can be made an integral part of a company's operations is not restricted to Web retailing. Many companies could benefit from a similar architecture.

### Architectural Overview

The Blue Martini architecture is designed to support the differing needs of marketers, merchandisers, and, not least, data miners. As shown in Figure 16.2, it has three modules for three different types of users. For merchandisers, this architecture supports multiple product hierarchies and tools for controlling collections and promotions. For marketers there are tools for making controlled experiments to track the effectiveness of various messages and marketing rules. For data miners, there is integrated modeling software and relief from having to create customer signatures by hand from dozens of different Web server and application logs. The architecture is what Ralph Kimball and Richard Merz would call a data Webhouse, made up of several special-purpose data marts with different schemas, all using common field definitions and shared metadata.

Customers at a Web store interact with pages generated as needed from a database that includes product information and the page templates. The contents of the page are driven by rules. Some of these rules are business rules entered by managers. Others are generated automatically and then edited by professional merchandisers.

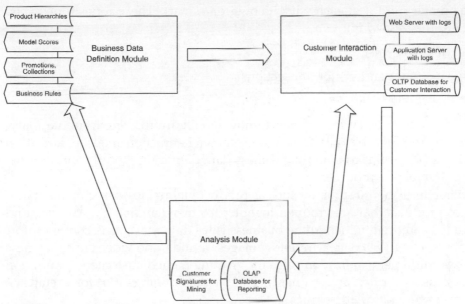

**Figure 16.2** Blue Martini provides a good example of an IT architecture for data mining–driven Web retailing.

Generating pages from a database has many advantages. First it makes it possible to enforce a consistent look and feel across the Web site. Such standard interfaces help customers navigate through the site. Using a database also makes it possible to make global changes quickly, such as updating prices for a sale. Another feature is the ability to store templates in different languages and currencies, so the site can be customized for users in different counties. From the data mining perspective, a major advantage is that all customer interactions are logged in the database.

User interactions are managed through a collection of data marts. Reporting and mining are centered on a customer behavior data mart that includes information derived from the user interaction, product, and business-rule data marts. The complicated extract and transformation logic required to create customer signatures from transaction data is part of the system—a great simplification for anyone who has ever tried massaging Web logs to get information about customers.

## Customer Interaction Module

This architecture includes the databases and software needed to support merchandising, customer interaction, reporting, and mining as well as customer-centric marketing in the form of personalization. The Blue Martini system has three major modules, each with its own data mart. These repositories keep track of the following:

- Business rules
- Customer and visitor transactions
- Customer behavior

The customer behavior data mart, shown in Figure 16.2 as part of the analysis module, is fed by data from the customer interaction module, and it, in turn, supplies rules to both the business data definition module and the customer interaction module.

Merchandising information such as product hierarchies, assortments (families of products that are grouped together for merchandising purposes), and price lists are maintained in the business rules data mart, as is content information such as Web page templates, images, sounds, and video clips. Business rules include personalization rules for greeting named customers, promotion rules, cross-sell rules, and so on. Much of the data mining effort for a retail site goes into generating these rules.

The customer interaction module is the part of the system that touches customers directly by processing all the customer transactions. The customer interaction module is responsible for maintaining users' sessions and context. This module implements the actual Web store and collects any data that may be wanted for later analysis. The customer transaction data mart logs business events such as the following:

- Customer adds an item to the basket.
- Customer initiates check-out process.
- Customer completes check-out process.
- Cross-sell rule is triggered, and recommendation is made.
- Recommended link is followed.

The customer interaction module supports marketing experiments by implementing control groups and keeping track of multiple rules. It has detailed knowledge of the content it serves and can track many things that are not tracked in the Web server logs. The customer interaction module collects data that allows both products and customers to be tracked over time.

## Analysis Module

The database that supports the customer interaction module, like most online transaction processing systems, is a relational database designed to support quick transaction processing. Data destined for the analytic module must be extracted and transformed to support the structures suitable for mining and reporting. Data mining requires flat signature tables with one row per customer or item to be studied. This means transformations that flatten product hierarchies so that, for example, the same transaction might generate one flag indicating that the customer bought French wine, another that he or she bought a wine from the Burgundy region, and a third indicating that the wine was from the Beaujolais district in Burgundy. Other data must be rolled up from order files, billing files, and session logs that contain multiple transactions per customer. Typical values derived this way include total spending by category, average order amount, difference between this customer's average order and the mean average order, and the number of days since the customer last made a purchase.

Reporting is done from a multidimensional database that allows retrospective queries at various levels. Data mining and OLAP are both part of the analysis module, although they answer different kinds of questions. *OLAP queries* are used to answer questions such as these:

- What are the top-selling products?
- What are the worst-selling products?
- What are the top pages viewed?
- What are conversion rates by brand name?
- What are the top referring sites by visit count?
- What are the top referring sites by dollar sales?
- How many customers abandoned market baskets?

*Data mining* is used to answer more complicated questions such as these:

- What are the characteristics of heavy spenders? Does this user fit the profile?
- What promotion should be offered to this customer?
- What is the likelihood that this customer will return within 1 month?
- What customers should we worry about because they haven't visited the site recently?
- Which products are associated with customers who spend the most money?
- Which products are driving sales of which other products?

In Figure 16.2, the arrow labeled "build data warehouse" connects the customer interaction module to the analysis module and represents all the transformations that must occur before either data mining or reporting can be done properly. Two more arrows, labeled "deploy results," show the output of the analysis module being shipped back to the business data definition and customer interaction modules. Yet another arrow, labeled "stage data," shows how the business rules embedded in the business definition module feed into the customer interacting module.

What is appealing about this architecture is the way that it facilitates the virtuous cycle of data mining by allowing new knowledge discovered through data mining to be fed directly to the systems that interact with customers.

# Data Mining Software

One of the ways that the data mining world has changed most since the first edition of this book came out is the maturity of data mining software products. Robustness, usability, and scalability have all improved significantly. The one thing that may have decreased is the number of data mining software vendors as tiny boutique software firms have been pushed aside by larger, more established companies. As stated in the first edition, it is not reasonable to compare the merits of particular products in a book intended to remain useful beyond the shelf-life of the current versions of these products. Although the products are changing—and hopefully improving—over time, the criteria for evaluating them have not changed: Price, availability, scalability, support, vendor relationships, compatibility, and ease of integration all factor into the selection process.

## Range of Techniques

As must be clear by now, there is no single data mining technique that is applicable in all situations. Neural networks, decision trees, market basket analysis, statistics, survival analysis, genetic algorithms, memory-based reasoning, link analysis, and automatic cluster detection all have a place. As shown in the case studies, it is not uncommon for two or more of these techniques to be applied in combination to achieve results beyond the reach of any single method.

Be sure that the software selected is powerful enough to support the data and goals needed for the organization. It is a good idea to have software a bit more advanced than the analysts' abilities, so people can try out new things that they might not otherwise think of trying. Having multiple techniques available in a single set of tools is useful, because it makes it easier to combine and compare different techniques. At the same time, having several different products makes sense for a larger group, since different products have different strengths—even when they support the same underlying functionality. Some are better at presenting results; some are better at developing scores; some are more intuitive for novice users.

Assess the range of data mining tasks to be addressed and decide which data mining techniques will be most valuable. If you have a single application in mind, or a family of closely related applications, then it is likely that you

---

**QUESTIONS TO ASK WHEN SELECTING DATA MINING SOFTWARE**

The following list of questions is designed to help select the right data mining software for your company. We present the questions as an unordered list. The first thing you should do is order the list according to your own priorities. These priorities will necessarily be different from case to case, which is why we have not attempted to rank them for you. In some environments, for example, there is an established standard hardware supplier and platform-independence is not an issue, while in other environments it is of paramount concern so different divisions can use the package or in anticipation of a future change in hardware.

- ◆ What is the range of data mining techniques offered by the vendor?
- ◆ How scalable is the product in terms of the size of the data, the number of users, the number of fields in the data, and its use of the hardware?
- ◆ Does the product provide transparent access to databases and files?
- ◆ Does the product provide multiple levels of user interfaces?
- ◆ Does the product generate comprehensible explanations of the models it generates?
- ◆ Does the product support graphics, visualization, and reporting tools?
- ◆ Does the product interact well with other software in the environment, such as reporting packages, databases, and so on?
- ◆ Can the product handle diverse data types?
- ◆ Is the product well documented and easy to use?
- ◆ What is the availability of support, training, and consulting?
- ◆ How well will the product fit into the existing computing environment?
- ◆ Does the vendor have credible references?

Once you have determined which of these questions are most important to your organization, use them to assess candidate software packages by interviewing the software vendors or by enlisting the aid of an independent data mining consultant.

---

will be able to select a single technique and stick with it. If you are setting up a data mining lab environment to handle a wide range of data mining applications, you will want to look for a coordinated suite of tools.

## Scalability

Data mining provides the greatest benefit when the data to be mined is large and complex. But, data mining software is likely to be demonstrated on small, sample datasets. Be sure that the data mining software being considered can handle the anticipated data volume—and then perhaps a bit more to take into account future growth (data does not grow smaller over time). The scalability aspect of data mining is important in three ways:

- Transforming the data into customer signatures requires a lot of I/O and computing power.
- Building models is a repetitive and very computationally expensive.
- Scoring models requires complex data transformations.

For exploring and transforming data, the most readily available scalable software are relational databases. These have been designed to take advantage of multiple processors and multiple disks for handling a single database query. Another class of software, the extraction, transformation, and load tools (ETL) used to create databases may also be scalable and useful for data mining. However, most programming languages do not scale; they only support single processors and single disks for handling a single task. When there is a lot of data that needs to be combined, the most scalable solution to handling the data is often found at this level.

Building models and exploring data require software that runs fast enough and on large enough quantities of data. Some data mining tools only work on data in memory, so the volume of data is limited by available memory. This has the advantage that algorithms run faster. On the other hand there are limits. In practice, this was a problem when available memory was measured in megabytes; the gigabytes of memory available even on a typical workstation ameliorate the problem. Often, the data mining environment puts multiuser data mining servers on a powerful server close to the data. This is a good solution. As workstations become more powerful, building the models locally is also a viable solution. In either case, the goal is to run the models on hundreds of thousands or millions of rows in a reasonable amount of time. A data mining environment should encourage users to understand and explore the data, rather than expending effort sampling it down to make it fit in.

The scoring environment is often the most complex, because it require transforming the data and running the models at the same time—preferably with a minimal amount of user interaction. Perhaps the best solution is when data mining software can both read and write to relational databases, making it possible to use the database for scalable data manipulation and the data mining tool for efficient model building.

## Support for Scoring

The ability to write to as well as read from a database is desirable when data mining is used to develop models used for scoring. The models may be developed using samples extracted from the master database, but once developed, the models will score every record in the database.

The value of a response model decreases with time. Ideally, the results of one campaign should be analyzed in time to affect the next one. But, in many organizations there is a long lag between the time a model is developed and the time it can be used to append scores to a database; sometimes the time is measured in weeks or months. The delay is caused by the difficulty of moving the scoring model, which is often developed on a different computer from the database server, into a form that can be applied to the database. This might involve interpreting the output of a data mining tool and writing a computer program that embodies the rules that make up the model.

The problem is even worse when the database is actually stored at a third facility, such as that of a list processor. The list processor is unlikely to accept a neural network model in the form of C source code as input to a list selection request. Building a unified model development and scoring framework requires significant integration effort, but if scoring large databases is an important application for your business, the effort will be repaid.

## Multiple Levels of User Interfaces

In many organizations, several different communities of users use the data mining software. In order to accommodate their differing needs, the tool should provide several different user interfaces:

- A graphical user interface (GUI) for the casual user that has reasonable default values for data mining parameters.
- Advanced options for more skilled users.
- An ability to build models in batch mode (which could be provided by a command line interface).
- An applications program interface (API) so that predictive modeling can be built into applications

The GUI for a data mining tool should not only make it easy for users to build models, it should be designed to encourage best practices such as ensuring that model assessment is performed on a hold-out set and that the target variables for predictive models come from a later timeframe than the inputs. The user interface should include a help system, with context-sensitive help. The user interface should provide reasonable default values for such things as the minimum number of records needed to support a split in a decision tree or the number of nodes in the hidden layer of a neural network to improve the chance of success for casual users. On the other hand, the interface should make it easy for more knowledgeable users to change the defaults. Advanced users should be able to control every aspect of the underlying data mining algorithms.

## Comprehensible Output

Tools vary greatly in the extent to which they explain themselves. Rule generators, tree visualizers, Web diagrams, and association tables can all help.

Some vendors place great emphasis on the visual representation of both data and rules, providing three-dimensional data terrain maps, geographic information systems (GIS), and cluster diagrams to help make sense of complex relationships. The final destination of much data mining work is reports for management, and the power of graphics should not be underestimated for convincing non-technical users of data mining results. A data mining tool should make it easy to export results to commonly available reporting an analysis packages such as Excel and PowerPoint.

## Ability to Handle Diverse Data Types

Many data mining software packages place restrictions on the kinds of data that can be analyzed. Before investing in a data mining software package, find out how it deals with the various data types you want to work with.

Some tools have difficulty using categorical variables (such as model, type, gender) as input variables and require the user to convert these into a series of yes/no variables, one for each possible class. Others can deal with categorical variables that take on a small number of values, but break down when faced with too many. On the target field side, some tools can handle a binary classification task (good/bad), but have difficulty predicting the value of a categorical variable that can take on several values.

Some data mining packages on the market require that continuous variables (income, mileage, balance) be split into ranges by the user. This is especially likely to be true of tools that generate association rules, since these require a certain number of occurrences of the same combination of values in order to recognize a rule.

Most data mining tools cannot deal with text, although such support is starting to appear. If the text strings in the data are standardized codes (state, part number), this is not really a problem, since character codes can easily be converted to numeric or categorical ones. If the application requires the ability to analyze free text, some of the more advanced data mining tool sets are starting to provide support for this capability.

## Documentation and Ease of Use

A well-designed user interface should make it possible to start mining right away, even if mastery of the tool requires time and study. As with any complex software, good documentation can spell the difference between success and frustration. Before deciding on a tool, ask to look over the manual. It is very important that the product documentation fully describes the algorithms used, not just the operation of the tool. Your organization should not be basing decisions on techniques that are not understood. A data mining tool that relies on any sort of proprietary and undisclosed "secret sauce" is a poor choice.

## Availability of Training for Both Novice and Advanced Users, Consulting, and Support

It is not easy to introduce unfamiliar data mining techniques into an organization. Before committing to a tool, find out the availability of user training and applications consulting from the tool vendor or third parties.

If the vendor is small and geographically remote from your data mining locations, customer support may be problematic. The Internet has shrunk the planet so that every supplier is just a few keystrokes away, but it has not altered the human tendency to sleep at night and work in the day; time zones still matter.

### Vendor Credibility

Unless you are already familiar with the vendor, it is a good idea to learn something about its track record and future prospects. Ask to speak to references who have used the vendor's software and can substantiate the claims made in product brochures.

We are not saying that you should not buy software from a company just because it is new, small, or far away. Data mining is still at the leading edge of commercial decision-support technology. It is often small, start-up companies that first understand the importance of new techniques and successfully bring them to market. And paradoxically, smaller companies often provide better, more enthusiastic support since the people answering questions are likely to be some people who designed and built the product.

## Lessons Learned

The ideal data mining environment consists of a customer-centric corporate culture and all the resources to support it. Those resources include data, data miners, data mining infrastructure, and data mining software. In this ideal data mining environment, the need for good information is ingrained in the corporate culture, operational procedures are designed with the need to gather good data in mind, and the requirements for data mining shape the design of the corporate data warehouse.

Building the ideal environment is not easy. The hardest part of building a customer-centric organization is changing the culture and how to accomplish that is beyond the scope of this book. From a purely data perspective, the first step is to create a single customer view that encompasses all the relationships the company has with a customer across all channels. The next step is to create customer-centric metrics that can be tracked, modeled, and reported.

Customer interactions should be turned into learning opportunities whenever possible. In particular, marketing communications should be set up as controlled experiments. The results of these experiments are input for data mining models used for targeting, cross-selling, and retention.

There are several approaches to incorporating data mining into a company's marketing and customer relationship management activities. Outsourcing is a possibility for companies with only occasional modeling needs. When there is an ongoing need for data mining, it is best done internally so that insights produced during mining remain within the company rather than with an outside vendor.

A data mining group can be successful in any of several locations within the company organization chart. Locating the group in IT puts it close to data and technical resources. Locating it within a business unit puts it close to the business problems. In either case, it is important to have good communication between IT and the business units.

Choosing software for the data mining environment is important. However, the success of the data mining group depends more on having good processes and good people than on the particular software found on their desktops.

# CHAPTER 17

# Preparing Data for Mining

As a translucent amber fluid, gasoline—the power behind the transportation industry—barely resembles the gooey black ooze pumped up through oil wells. The difference between the two liquids is the result of multiple steps of refinement that distill useful products from the raw material.

Data preparation is a very similar process. The raw material comes from operational systems that have often accumulated crud, in the form of eccentric business rules and layers of system enhancements and fixes, over the course of time. Fields in the data are used for multiple purposes. Values become obsolete. Errors are fixed on an ongoing basis, so interpretations change over time. The process of preparing data is like the process of refining oil. Valuable stuff lurks inside the goo of operational data. Half the battle is refinement. The other half is converting its energy to a useful form—the equivalent of running an engine on gasoline.

The proliferation of data is a feature of modern business. Our challenge is to make sense of the data, to refine the data so that the engines of data mining can extract value. One of the challenges is the sheer volume of data. A customer may call the call center several times a year, pay a bill once a month, turn the phone on once a day, make and receive phone calls several times a day. Over the course of time, hundreds of thousands or millions of customers are generating hundreds of millions of records of their behavior. Even on today's computers, this is a lot of data processing. Fortunately, computer systems have become powerful enough that the problem is really one of having an adequate budget for buying hardware and software; technically, processing such vast quantities of data is possible.

Data comes in many forms, from many systems, and in many different types. Data is always dirty, incomplete, sometimes incomprehensible and incompatible. This is, alas, the real world. And yet, data is the raw material for data mining. Oil starts out as a thick tarry substance, mixed with impurities. It is only by going through various stages of refinement that the raw material becomes usable—whether as clear gasoline, plastic, or fertilizer. Just as the most powerful engines cannot use crude oil as a fuel, the most powerful algorithms (the engines of data mining) are unlikely to find interesting patterns in unprepared data.

After more than a century of experimentation, the steps of refining oil are quite well understood—better understood than the processes of preparing data. This chapter illustrates some guidelines and principles that, based on experience, should make the process more effective. It starts with a discussion of what data should look like once it has been prepared, describing the customer signature. It then dives into what data actually looks like, in terms of data types and column roles. Since a major part of successful data mining is in the derived variables, ideas for these are presented in some detail. The chapter ends with a look at some of the difficulties presented by dirty data and missing values, and the computational challenge of working with large volumes of commercial data.

# What Data Should Look Like

The place to start the discussion on data is at the end: what the data should look like. All data mining algorithms want their inputs in tabular form—the rows and columns so common in spreadsheets and databases. Unlike spreadsheets, though, each column must mean the same thing for all the rows.

Some algorithms need their data in a particular format. For instance, market basket analysis (discussed in Chapter 9) usually looks at only the products purchased at any given time. Also, link analysis (see Chapter 10) needs references between records in order to connect them. However, most algorithms, and especially decision trees, neural networks, clustering, and statistical regression, are looking for data in a particular format called the *customer signature*.

## The Customer Signature

The customer signature is a snapshot of customer behavior that captures both current attributes of the customers and changes in behavior over time. Like a signature on a check, each customer's signature is theoretically unique—capturing the unique characteristics of the individual. Unlike a signature on a check, though, the customer signature is used for analysis and not identification; in fact, often customer signatures have no more identifying information than a string of seemingly random digits representing a household, individual, or account number. Figure 17.1 shows that a customer signature is simply a row of data that represents the customer and whatever might be useful for data mining.

This column is an ID field where the value is different in every column. It is ignored for data mining purposes.

This column is from the customer information file.

This column is the target, what we want to predict.

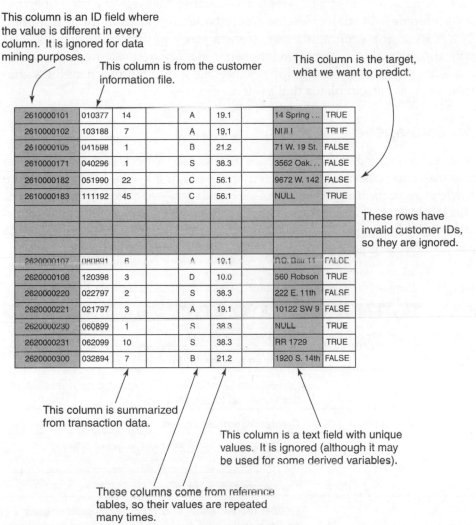

These rows have invalid customer IDs, so they are ignored.

This column is summarized from transaction data.

This column is a text field with unique values. It is ignored (although it may be used for some derived variables).

These columns come from reference tables, so their values are repeated many times.

**Figure 17.1** Each row in the customer signature represents one customer (the unit of data mining) with fields describing that customer.

It is perhaps unfortunate that there is no big database sitting around with up-to-date customer signatures, ready for all modeling applications. Such a system might at first sight seem very useful. However, the lack of such a system is an opportunity because modeling efforts require understanding data. No single customer signature works for all modeling efforts, although some customer signatures work well for several applications

The "customer" in customer signature is the unit of data mining. This book focuses primarily on customers, so the unit of data mining is typically an account, an individual, or a household. There are other possibilities. Chapter 11 has a case study on clustering towns—because that was the level of action for developing editorial zones for a newspaper. Acquisition modeling often takes place at the geographic level, census block groups or zip codes. And applications outside customer relationship management are even more disparate. *Mastering Data Mining*, for instance, has a case study where the signatures are press runs in plants that print magazines.

## The Columns

The columns in the data contain values that describe aspects of the customer. In some cases, the columns come directly from existing business systems; more often, the columns are the result of some calculation—so called *derived variables*.

Each column contains values. The *range* refers to the set of allowable values for that column. Table 17.1 shows range characteristics for typical types of data used for data mining.

**Table 17.1**  Range Characteristics for Typical Types of Data Used for Data Mining

| VARIABLE TYPE | TYPICAL RANGE CHARACTERISTICS |
|---|---|
| Categorical variables | List of acceptable values |
| Numeric | Minimum and maximum values |
| Dates | Earliest and latest dates, often latest date is less than or equal to current date |
| Monetary amounts | Greater than or equal to 0 |
| Durations | Greater than or equal to 0 (or perhaps strictly greater than 0) |
| Binned or quantiled values | The number of quantiles |
| Counts | Greater than or equal to 0 (or perhaps greater than or equal to 1) |

Histograms, such as those in Figure 17.2, shows how often each value or range of values occurs in some set of data. The vertical axis is a count of records, and the horizontal axis is the values in the column. The shape of this histogram shows the *distribution* of the values (strictly speaking, in a distribution, the counts are divided by the total number of records so the area under the curve is one). If we are working with a sample, and the sample is randomly chosen, then the distribution of values in the subset should be about the same as the distribution in the original data.

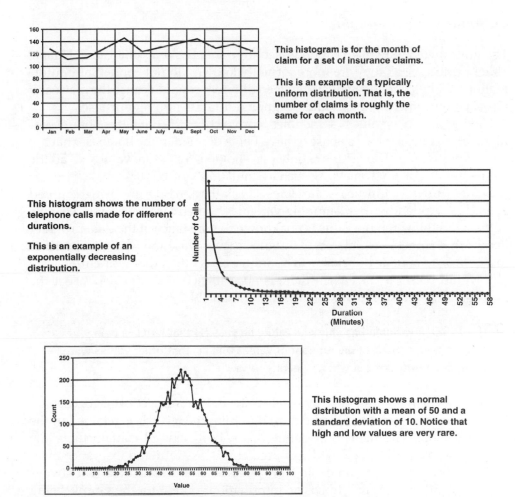

This histogram is for the month of claim for a set of insurance claims.

This is an example of a typically uniform distribution. That is, the number of claims is roughly the same for each month.

This histogram shows the number of telephone calls made for different durations.

This is an example of an exponentially decreasing distribution.

This histogram shows a normal distribution with a mean of 50 and a standard deviation of 10. Notice that high and low values are very rare.

**Figure 17.2**   Histograms show the distribution of data values.

The distribution of the values provides important insights into the data. It shows which values are common and which are less common. Just looking at the distribution of values brings up questions—such as why an amount is negative or why some categorical values are not present. Although statisticians tend to be more concerned with distributions than data miners, it is still important to look at variable values. Here, we illustrate some special cases of distributions that are important for data mining purposes, as well as the special case of variables synonymous with the target.

### Columns with One Value

The most degenerate distribution is a column that has only one value. Unary-valued columns, as they are more formally known, do not contain any information that helps to distinguish between different rows. Because they lack any information content, they should be ignored for data mining purposes.

Having only one value is sometimes a property of the data. It is not uncommon, for instance, for a database to have fields defined in the database that are not yet populated. The fields are only placeholders for future values, so all the values are uniformly something such as "null" or "no" or "0."

Before throwing out unary variables, check that NULLs are being counted as values. Appended demographic variables sometimes have only a single value or NULL when the value is not known. For instance, if the data provider knows that someone is interested in golf—say because the person subscribes to a golfing magazine or belongs to a country club—then the "golf-enthusiast" flag would be set to "Y."When there is no evidence, many providers set the flag to NULL—meaning unknown—rather than "N."

> **TIP** When a variable has only one value, be sure (1) that NULL is being included in the count of the number of values and (2) that other values were not inadvertently left out when selecting rows.

Unary-valued columns also arise when the data mining effort is focused on a subset of customers, and the field used to filter the records is retained in the resulting table. The fields that define this subset may all contain the same value. If we are building a model to predict the loss-ratio (an insurance measure) for automobile customers in New Jersey, then the state field will always have "NJ" filled in. This field has no information content for the sample being used, so it should be ignored for modeling purposes.

### Columns with Almost Only One Value

In "almost-unary" columns, almost all the records have the same value for that column. There may be a few outliers, but there are very few. For example, retail data may summarize all the purchases made by each customer in each department. Very few customers may make a purchase from the automotive department of a grocery store or the tobacco department of a department store. So, almost all customers will have a $0 for total purchases from these departments.

Purchased data often comes in an "almost-unary" format, as well. Fields such as "people who collect porcelain dolls" or "amount spent on greens fees" will have a null or $0 value for all but very few people. Or, some data, such as survey data, is only available for a very small subset of the customers. These are all extreme examples of data skew, shown in Figure 17.3.

The big question with "almost-unary" columns is, "When can they be ignored?" To justify ignoring them, the values must have two characteristics. First, almost all the records must have the same value. Second, there must be so few records with a different value, that they constitute a negligible portion of the data.

What is a negligible portion of the data? It is a group so small that even if the data mining algorithms identified it perfectly, the group would be too small to be significant.

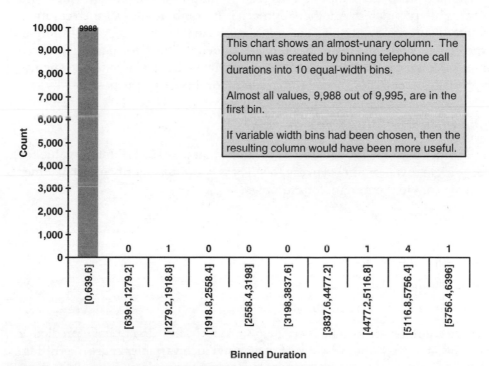

**Figure 17.3** An almost-unary field, such as the bins produced by equal-width bins in this case, is useless for data mining purposes

Before ignoring a column, though, it is important to understand why the values are so heavily skewed. What does this column tell us about the business? Perhaps few people ever buy automotive products because only a handful of the stores in question even sell them. Identifying customers as "automotive-product-buyers," in this case, may not be useful.

In other cases, an event might be rare for other reasons. The number of people who cancel their telephone service on any given day is negligible, but over time the numbers accumulate. So the cancellations need to be accumulated over a longer time period, such as a month, quarter, or year. Or, the number of people who collect porcelain dolls may be very rare in itself, but when combined with other fields, this might suggest an important segment of collectors.

The rule of thumb is that, even if a column proves to be very informative, it is unlikely to be useful for data mining if it is almost-unary. That is, fully understanding the rows with different values does not yield actionable results. As a general rule of thumb, if 95 to 99 percent of the values in the column are identical, the column—in isolation—is likely to be useless without some work. For instance, if the column in question represents the target variable for a model, then stratified sampling can create a sample where the rare values are more highly populated. Another approach is to combine several such columns for creating derived variables that might prove to be valuable. As an example, some census fields are sparsely populated, such as those for particular occupations. However, combining some of these fields into a single field—such as "high status occupation"—can prove useful for modeling purposes.

## Columns with Unique Values

At the other extreme are categorical columns that take on a different value for every single row—or almost every row. These columns identify each customer uniquely (or close enough), for example:

- Customer name
- Address
- Telephone number
- Customer ID
- Vehicle identification number

These columns are also not very helpful. Why? They do not have predictive value, because they uniquely identify each row. Such variables cause overfitting.

One caveat—which will be investigated later in this chapter. Sometimes these columns contain a wealth of information. Lurking inside telephone numbers and addresses is important geographical information. Customers' first names give an indication of gender. Customer numbers may be sequentially assigned, telling us which customers are more recent—and hence show up as important variables in decision trees. These are cases where the important features (such as geography and customer recency) should be extracted from the fields as derived variables. However, data mining algorithms are not yet powerful enough to extract such information from values; data miners need to do the extraction.

### Columns Correlated with Target

When a column is too highly correlated with the target column, it can mean that the column is just a synonym. Here are two examples:

- "Account number is NULL" may be synonymous with failure to respond to a marketing campaign. Only responders opened accounts and were assigned account numbers.

- "Date of churn is not NULL" is synonymous with having churned.

Another danger is that the column reflects previous business practices. For instance, the data may show that all customers with call forwarding also have call waiting. This is a result of product bundling; call forwarding is sold in a product bundle that always includes call waiting. Or the data may show that almost all customers reside in the wealthiest areas, because this where customer acquisition campaigns in the past were targeted. This illustrates that data miners need to know historical business practices. Columns synonymous with the targets should be ignored.

**TIP** An easy way to find columns synonymous with the target is to build decision trees. The decision tree will choose one synonymous variable, which can then be ignored. If the decision tree tool lets you see alternative splits, then all such variables can be found at once.

## Model Roles in Modeling

Columns contain data with data types. In addition, columns have roles with respect to the data mining algorithms. Three important roles are:

**Input columns.** These are columns that are used as input into the model.

**Target column(s).** This column or set of columns is only used when building predictive models. These are what is interesting, such as propensity to buy a particular product, likelihood to respond to an offer, or probability of remaining a customer. When building undirected models, there does not need to be a target.

**Ignored columns.** These are columns that are not used.

Different tools have different names for these roles. Figure 17.4 shows how a column is removed from consideration in Angoss Knowledge Studio.

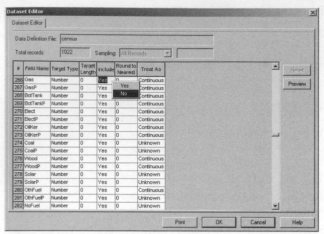

**Figure 17.4**  Angoss Knowledge Studio supports several model roles, such as ignoring a column when building a model.

**TIP**  Ignored columns play a very important role in clustering. Since ignored columns are not used to build the clusters, their distribution in the clusters can be very informative. By ignoring columns such as customer profitability or response flags, we can see how these "ignored" columns are distributed in the clusters. And we might just discover something very interesting about customer profit or responders.

There are some more advanced roles as well, which are used under specific circumstances. Figure 17.5 shows the many model roles available in SAS Enterprise Miner. These model roles include:

**Identification column.** These are columns that uniquely identify each row. In general, these columns are ignored for data mining purposes, but are important for scoring.

**Weight column.** This is a column that specifies a "weight" to be applied to each row. This is a way of creating a weighted sample by including the weight in the data.

**Cost column.** The cost column specifies a cost associated with a row. For instance, if we are building a customer retention model, then the "cost" might include an estimate of each customer's value. Some tools can use this information to optimize the models that they are building.

The additional model roles available in the tool are specific to SAS Enterprise Miners.

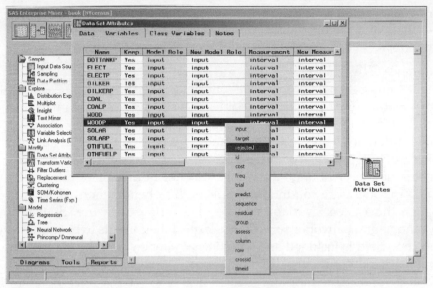

**Figure 17.5**   SAS Enterprise Miner has a wide range of available model roles.

## Variable Measures

Variables appear in data and have some important properties. Although databases are concerned with the type of variables (and we'll return to this topic in a moment), data mining is concerned with the *measure* of variables. It is the measure that determines how the algorithms treat the values. The following measures are important for data mining:

- *Categorical* variables can be compared for equality but there is no meaningful ordering. For example, state abbreviations are categorical. The fact that Alabama is next to Alaska alphabetically does not mean that they are closer to each other than Alabama and Tennessee, which share a geographic border but appear much further apart alphabetically.

- *Ordered* variables can be compared with equality and with greater than and less than. Classroom grades, which range from A to F, are an example of ordered values.

- *Interval* variables are ordered and support the operation of subtraction (although not necessarily any other mathematical operation such as addition and multiplication). Dates and temperatures are examples of intervals.

■ *True numeric* variables are interval variables that support addition and other mathematical operations. Monetary amounts and customer tenure (measured in days) are examples of numeric variables.

The difference between true numerics and intervals is subtle. However, data mining algorithms treat both of these the same way. Also, note that these measures form a hierarchy. Any ordered variable is also categorical, any interval is also categorical, and any numeric is also interval.

There is a difference between measure and data type. A numeric variable, for instance, might represent a coding scheme—say for account status or even for state abbreviations. Although the values look like numbers, they are really categorical. Zip codes are a common example of this phenomenon.

Some algorithms expect variables to be of a certain measure. Statistical regression and neural networks, for instance, expect their inputs to be numeric. So, if a zip code field is included and stored as a number, then the algorithms treat its values as numeric, generally not a good approach. Decision trees, on the other hand, treat all their inputs as categorical or ordered, even when they are numbers.

Measure is one important property. In practice, variables have associated types in databases and file layouts. The following sections talk about data types and measures in more detail.

## Numbers

Numbers usually represent quantities and are good variables for modeling purposes. Numeric quantities have both an ordering (which is used by decision trees) and an ability to perform arithmetic (used by other algorithms such as clustering and neural networks). Sometimes, what looks like a number really represents a code or an ID. In such cases, it is better to treat the number as a categorical value (discussed in the next two sections), since the ordering and arithmetic properties of the numbers may mislead data mining algorithms attempting to find patterns.

There are many different ways to transform numeric quantities. Figure 17.6 illustrates several common methods:

**Normalization.** The resulting values are made to fall within a certain range, for example, by subtracting the minimum value and dividing by the range. This process does not change the form of the distribution of the values. Normalization can be useful when using techniques that perform mathematical operations such as multiplication directly on the values, such as neural networks and K-means clustering. Decision trees are unaffected by normalization, since the normalization does not change the order of the values.

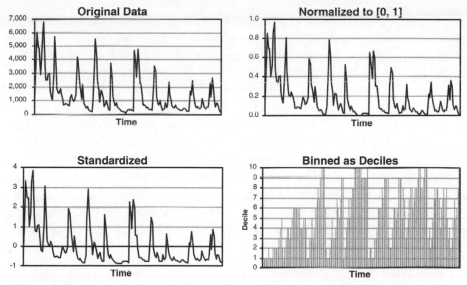

**Figure 17.6** Normalization, standardization, and binning are typical ways to transform a numeric variable.

**Standardization.** This transforms the values into the number of standard deviations from the mean, which gives a good sense of how unexpected the value is. The arithmetic is easy—subtract the average value and divide by the standard deviation. These standardized values are also called *z-scores*. As with normalization, standardization does not affect the ordering, so it has no effect on decision trees.

**Equal-width binning.** This transforms the variables into ranges that are fixed in width. The resulting variable has roughly the same distribution as the original variable. However, binning values affects all data mining algorithms.

**Equal-height binning.** This transforms the variables into *n*-tiles (such as quintiles or deciles) so that the same number of records falls into each bin. The resulting variable has a uniform distribution.

Perhaps unexpectedly, binning values can improve the performance of data mining algorithms. In the case of neural networks, binning is one of several ways of reducing the influence of outliers, because all outliers are grouped together into the same bin. In the case of decision trees, binned variables may result in child nodes having more equal sizes at high levels of the tree (that is, instead of one child getting 5 percent of the records and the other 95 percent, with the corresponding binned variable one might get 20 percent and the other 80 percent). Although the split on the binned variables is not optimal, subsequent splits may produce better trees.

## Dates and Times

Dates and times are the most common examples of interval variables.. These variables are very important, because they introduce the time element into data analysis. Often, the importance of date and time variables is that they provide sequence and timestamp information for other variables, such as cause and resolution of the last complaint call.

Because there is a myriad of different formats, working with dates and time stamps can be difficult. Excel has fifteen different date formats prebuilt for cells, and the ability to customize many more. One typical internal format for dates and times is as a single number—the number of days or seconds since some date in the past. When this is the case, data mining algorithms treat dates as numbers. This representation is adequate for the algorithms to detect what happened earlier and later. However, it misses other important properties, which are worth adding into the data:

- Time of day
- Day of the week, and whether it is a workday or weekend
- Month and season
- Holidays

In his book *The Data Warehouse Toolkit* (Wiley, 2002), Ralph Kimball strongly recommends that a calendar be one of the first tables built for a data warehouse. We strongly agree with this recommendation, since the attributes of the calendar are often important for data mining work.

One challenge when working with dates and times is time zones. Especially in the interconnected world of the Web, the time stamp is generally the time stamp from the server computer, rather than the time where the customer is. It is worth remembering that the customer who is visiting the Web site repeatedly in the wee hours of the morning might actually be a Singapore lunchtime surfer rather than a New York night owl.

## Fixed-Length Character Strings

Fixed-length character strings usually represent categorical variables, which take on a known set of values. It is always worth comparing the actual values that appear in the data to the list of legal values—to check for illegal values, to verify that the field is always populated, and to see which values are most and least frequent.

Fixed-length character strings often represent codes of some sort. Helpfully, there are often reference tables that describe what these codes mean. The reference tables can be particularly useful for data mining, because they provide hierarchies and other attributes that might not be apparent just looking at the code itself.

Character strings do have an ordering—the alphabetical ordering. However, as the earlier example with Alabama and Alaska shows, this ordering might be useful for librarians, but it is less useful for data miners. When there is a sensible ordering, it makes sense to replace the codes with numbers. For instance, one company segmented customers into three groups: NEW customers with less than 1 year of tenure, MARGINAL customers with between 1 and 2 years, and CORE customers with more than 2 years. These categories clearly have an ordering. In practice, one way to incorporate the ordering would be to map the groups into the numbers 1, 2, and 3. A better way would be to include that actual tenure for data mining purposes, although reports could still be based on the tenure groups.

Data mining algorithms usually perform better when there are fewer categories rather than more. One way to reduce the number of categories is to use attributes of the codes, rather than the codes themselves. For instance, a mobile phone company is likely to have customers with hundreds of different handset equipment codes (although just a few popular varieties will account for the vast bulk of customers). Instead of using each model independently, include features such as handset weight, original release date of the handset, and the features it provides.

Zip codes in the United States provide a good example of a potentially useful variable that takes on many values. One way to reduce the number of values is to use only the first three characters (digits). These are the sectional center facility (SCF), which is usually at the center of a county or large town. They maintain most of the geographic information in the zip code but at a higher level. Even though the SCF and zip codes are numbers, they need to be treated as codes. One clue is that the leading "0" in the zip code is important—the zip code of Data Miners, Inc. is 02114, and it would not make sense without the leading "0".

Some businesses are regional; consequently almost all customers are located in a small number of zip codes. However, there still may be many other customers spread thinly in many other places. In this case, it might be best to group all the rare values into a single "other" category. Another and often better approach, is to replace the zip codes with information about the zip code. There could be several items of information, such as median income and average home value (from the census bureau), along with penetration and response rate to a recent marketing campaign. Replacing string values with descriptive numbers is a powerful way to introduce business knowledge into modeling.

**TIP**  Replacing categorical variables with numeric summaries of the categories—such as product penetration within a zip code—improves data mining models and solves the problem of working with categoricals that have too many values.

Neural networks and K-means clustering are examples of algorithms that want their inputs to be intervals or true numerics. This poses a problem for strings. The naïve approach is to assign a number to each value. However, the numbers have additional information that is not present in the codes, such as ordering. This spurious ordering can hide information in the data. A better approach is to create a set of flags, called *indicator variables*, for each possible value. Although this increases the number of variables, it eliminates the problem of spurious ordering and improves results. Neural network tools often do this automatically.

In summary, there are several ways to handle fixed-length character strings:

- If there are just a few values, then the values can be used directly.

- If the values have a useful ordering, then the values can be turned into rankings representing the ordering.

- If there are reference tables, then information describing the code is likely to be more useful.

- If a few values predominate, but there are many values, then the rarer values can be grouped into an "other" category.

- For neural networks and other algorithms that expect only numeric inputs, values can be mapped to indicator variables.

A general feature of these approaches is that they incorporate domain information into the coding process, so the data mining algorithms can look for unexpected patterns rather than finding out what is already known.

### IDs and Keys

The purpose of some variables is to provide links to other records with more information. IDs and keys are often stored as numbers, although they may also be stored as character strings. As a general rule, such IDs and keys should not be used directly for modeling purposes.

A good example of a field that should generally be ignored for data mining purposes are account numbers. The irony is that such fields may improve models, because account numbers are not assigned randomly. Often, they are assigned sequentially, so older accounts have lower account numbers; possibly they are based on acquisition channel, so all Web accounts have higher numbers than other accounts. It is better to include the relevant information explicitly in the customer signature, rather than relying on hidden business rules.

In some cases, IDs do encode meaningful information. In these cases, the information should be extracted to make it more accessible to the data mining algorithms. Here are some examples.

*Telephone numbers* contain country codes, area codes, and exchanges—these all contain geographical information. The standard 10-digit number in North

American starts with a three-digit area code followed by a three-digit exchange and a four-digit line number. In most databases, the area code provides good geographic information. Outside North America, the format of telephone numbers differs from place to place. In some cases, the area codes and telephone numbers are of variable length making it more difficult to extract geographic information.

*Uniform product codes* (Type A UPC) are the 12-digit codes that identify many of the products passed in front of scanners. The first six digits are a code for the manufacturer, the next five encode the specific product. The final digit has no meaning. It is a check digit used to verify the data.

*Vehicle identification numbers* are the 17-character codes inscribed on automobiles that describe the make, model, and year of the vehicle. The first character describes the country of origin. The second, the manufacturer. The third is the vehicle type, with 4 to 8 recording specific features of the vehicle. The 10th is the model year; the 11th is the assembly plant that produced the vehicle. The remaining six are sequential production numbers.

*Credit card numbers* have 13 to 16 digits. The first few digits encode the card network. In particular, they can distinguish American Express, Visa, Master-Card, Discover, and so on. Unfortunately, the use of the rest of the numbers depends on the network, so there are no uniform standards for distinguishing gold cards from platinum cards, for instance. The last digit, by the way, is a check digit used for rudimentary verification that the credit card number is valid. The algorithm for check digit is called the Luhn Algorithm, after the IBM researcher who developed it.

*National ID numbers* in some countries (although not the United States) encode the gender and data of birth of the individual. This is a good and accurate source of this demographic information, when it is available.

## Names

Although we want to get to know the customers, the goal of data mining is not to actually meet them. In general, names are not a useful source of information for data mining. There are some cases where it might be interesting to classify names according to ethnicity (such as Hispanic names or Asian names) when trying to reach a particular market or by gender for messaging purposes. However, such efforts are at best very rough approximations and not widely used for modeling purposes.

## Addresses

Addresses describe the geography of customers, which is very important for understanding customer behavior. Unfortunately, the post office can understand many different variations on how addresses are written. Fortunately, there are service bureaus and software that can standardize address fields.

One of the most important uses of an address is to understand when two addresses are the same and when they are different. For instance, is the delivery address for a product ordered on the Web the same as the billing address of the credit card? If not, there is a suggestion that the purchase is a gift (and the suggestion is even stronger if the distance between the two is great and the giver pays for gift wrapping!).

Other than finding exact matches, the entire address itself is not particularly useful; it is better to extract useful information and present it as additional fields. Some useful features are:

- Presence or absence of apartment numbers
- City
- State
- Zip code

The last three are typically stored in separate fields. Because geography often plays such an important role in understanding customer behavior, we recommend standardizing address fields and appending useful information such as census block group, multi-unit or single unit building, residential or business address, latitude, longitude, and so on.

### Free Text

Free text poses a challenge for data mining, because these fields provide a wealth of information, often readily understood by human beings, but not by automated algorithms. We have found that the best approach is to extract features from the text intelligently, rather than presenting the entire text fields to the computer.

Text can come from many sources, such as:

- Doctors' annotations on patient visits
- Memos typed in by call-center personnel
- Email sent to customer service centers
- Comments typed into forms, whether Web forms or insurance forms
- Voice recognition algorithms at call centers

Sources of text in the business world have the property that they are ungrammatical and filled with misspellings and abbreviations. Human beings generally understand them, but it is very difficult to automate this understanding. Hence, it is quite difficult to write software that automatically filters spam even though people readily recognize spam.

Our recommended approach is to look for specific features by looking for specific substrings. For instance, once upon a time, a Jewish group was boycotting a company because of the company's position on Israel. Memo fields typed in by call-center service reps were the best source of information on why customers were stopping. Unfortunately, these fields did not uniformly say "Cancelled due to Israel policy." In fact, many of the comments contained references to "Isreal," "Is rael," "Palistine" [sic], and so on. Classifying the text memos required looking for specific features in the text (in this case, the presence of "Israel," "Isreal," and "Is rael" were all used) and then analyzing the result.

### Binary Data (Audio, Image, Etc.)

Not surprisingly, there are other types of data that do not fall into these nice categories. Audio and images are becoming increasingly common. And data mining tools do not generally support them.

Because these types of data can contain a wealth of information, what can be done with them? The answer is to extract features into derived variables. However, such feature extraction is very specific to the data being used and is outside the scope of this book.

## Data for Data Mining

Data mining expects data to be in a particular format:

- All data should be in a single table.
- Each row should correspond to an entity, such as a customer, that is relevant to the business.
- Columns with a single value should be ignored.
- Columns with a different value for every column should be ignored—although their information may be included in derived columns.
- For predictive modeling, the target column should be identified and all synonymous columns removed.

Alas, this is not how data is found in the real world. In the real world, data comes from source systems, which may store each field in a particular way. Often, we want to replace fields with values stored in reference tables, or to extract features from more complicated data types. The next section talks about putting this data together into a customer signature.

# Constructing the Customer Signature

Building the customer signature, especially the first time, is a very incremental process. At a minimum, customer signatures need to be built at least two times—once for building the model and once for scoring it. In practice, exploring data and building models suggests new variables and transformations, so the process is repeated many times. Having a repeatable process simplifies the data mining work.

The first step in the process, shown in Figure 17.7, is to identify the available sources of data. After all, the customer signature is a summary, at the customer level, of what is known about each customer. The summary is based on available data. This data may reside in a data warehouse. It might equally well reside in operational systems and some might be provided by outside vendors. When doing predictive modeling, it is particularly important to identify where the target variable is coming from.

The second step is identifying the customer. In some cases, the customer is at the account level. In others, the customer is at the individual or household level. In some cases, the signature may have nothing to do with a person at all. We have used signatures for understanding products, zip codes, and counties, for instance, although the most common use is for accounts and households.

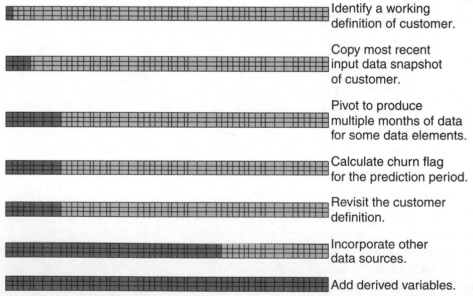

Identify a working definition of customer.

Copy most recent input data snapshot of customer.

Pivot to produce multiple months of data for some data elements.

Calculate churn flag for the prediction period.

Revisit the customer definition.

Incorporate other data sources.

Add derived variables.

**Figure 17.7** Building customer signatures is an iterative process; start small and work through the process step-by-step, as in this example for building a customer signature for churn prediction.

Once the customer has been identified, data sources need to be mapped to the customer level. This may require additional lookup tables—for instance, to convert accounts into households. It may not be possible to find the customers in the available data. Such a situation requires revisiting the customer definition.

The key to building customer signatures is to start simple and build up. Prioritize the data sources by the ease with which they map to the customer. Start with the easiest one, and build the signature using it. You can use a signature before all the data is put into it. While awaiting more complicated data transformations, get your feet wet and understand what is available. When building customer signatures out of transactions, be sure to get all the transactions associated with a particular customer.

## Cataloging the Data

The data mining group at a mobile telecommunications company wants to develop a churn model in-house. This churn model will predict churn for one month, given a one-month lag time. So, if the data is available for February, then the churn prediction is for April. Such a model provides time for gathering the data and scoring new customers, since the February data is available sometime in March.

At this company, there are several potential sources of data for the customer signatures. All of these are kept in a data repository with 18 months of history. Each file is an end-of-the-month snapshot—basically a dump of an operational system into a data repository.

The UNIT_MASTER file contains a description of every telephone number in service and a snapshot of what is known about the telephone number at the end of the month. Examples of fields in this file are the telephone number, billing account, billing plan, handset model, last billed date, and last payment.

The TRANS_MASTER file contains every transaction that occurs on a particular telephone number during the course of the month. These are account-level transactions, which include connections, disconnections, handset upgrades, and so on.

The BILL_MASTER file describes billing information at the account level. Multiple handsets might be attached to the same billing account—particularly for business customers and customers on family billing plans.

Although other sources of data were available in the company, these were not immediately highlighted for use for the customer signature. One source, for instance, was the call detail records—a record of every telephone call—that is useful for predicting churn. Although this data was eventually used by the data mining group, it was not part of this initial effort.

## Identifying the Customer

The data is typical of the real world. Although the focus might be on one type of customer or another, the data has multiple groups. The sidebar "Residential Versus Business Customers" talks about distinguishing between these two segments.

The business problem being addressed in this example is churn. As shown in Figure 17.8, the customer data model is rather complex, resulting in different options for the definition of customer:

- Telephone number
- Customer ID
- Billing account

This being the real world, though, it is important to remember that these relationships are complex and change over time. Customers might change their telephone numbers. Telephones might be added or removed from accounts. Customers change handsets, and so on. For the purposes of building the signature, the decision was to use the telephone number, because this was how the business reported churn.

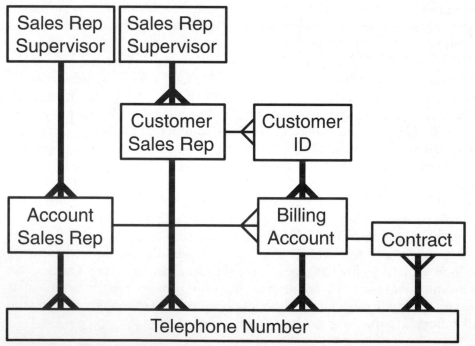

**Figure 17.8**   The customer model is complicated and takes into account sales, billing, and business hierarchy information.

## RESIDENTIAL VERSUS BUSINESS CUSTOMERS

Often data mining efforts focus on one type of customer—such as residential customers or small businesses. However, data for all customers is often mixed together in operational systems and data warehouses. Typically, there are multiple ways to distinguish between these types of customers:

♦ Often there is a customer type field, which has values like "residential" and "small business."

♦ There might be a sales hierarchy; some sales channels are business-only while others are residential-only.

♦ Some billing plans are only for businesses; others are only for residential customers.

♦ There might be business rules, so any customer with more than two lines is considered business.

These examples illustrate the fact that there are typically several different rules for distinguishing between different types of customers. Given the opportunity to be inconsistent, most data sources will not fail. The different rules select different subsets of customers.

Is this a problem? That depends on the particular model being worked on. The hope is that the rules are all very close, so the customers included (or missed) by one rule are essentially the same as those included by the others. It is important to investigate whether or not this is true, and when the rules disagree.

What usually happens in practice is that one of the rules is predominant, because that is the way the business is organized. So, although the customer type might be interesting, the sales hierarchy is probably more important, since it corresponds to people who have responsibility for different customer segments.

The distinction between businesses and residences is important for prospects as well as customers. A long-distance telephone company sees many calls traversing its network that were originated by customers of other carriers. Their switches create call detail records containing the originating and destination telephone numbers. Any domestic number that does not belong to an existing customer belongs to a prospect. One long-distance company builds signatures to describe the behavior of the unknown telephone numbers over time by tracking such things as how frequently the number is seen, what times of day and days of the week it is typically active, and the typical call duration. Among other things, this signature is used to score the unknown telephone numbers for the likelihood that they are businesses because business and residential customers are attracted by different offers.

One simplification would be to focus only on customers whose accounts have only one telephone number. Since the purpose is to build a model for residential customers, this was a good way of simplifying the data model for getting started. If the purpose were to build a model for business customers, a better choice for the customer level would be the billing account level, since business customers often turn handsets and telephone numbers on and off. However, churn in this case would mean the cancelation of the entire account, rather than the cancelation of a single telephone number. These two situations are the same for those residential customers who have only one line.

## First Attempt

The first attempt to build the customer signature needs to focus on the simplest data source. In this case, the simplest data source is the UNIT_MASTER file, which conveniently stores data at the telephone number level, the level being used for the customer signature.

It is worth pointing out two problems with this file and the customer definition:

- Customers may change their telephone number.
- Telephone numbers may be reassigned to new customers.

These problems will be addressed later; the first customer signature is at the telephone number level to get started. The process used to build the signature has four steps: identifying the time frames, creating a recent snapshot, pivoting columns, and calculating the target.

### Identifying the Time Frames

The first attempt at building the customer signature needs to take into account the time frame for the data, as discussed in Chapter 3. Figure 17.9 shows a model time chart for this data. The ultimate model set should have more than one time frame in it. However, the first attempt focuses on only one time frame.

The time frame defined churn during 1 month—August. All of the input data come from at least 1 month before. The cutoff date is June 30, in order to provide 1 month of latency.

### Taking a Recent Snapshot

The most recent snapshot of data is defined by the cutoff date. These fields in the signature describe the most recent information known about a customer before he or she churned (or did not churn).

| | Jan | Feb | Mar | Apr | May | Jun | Jul | Aug | Sep | Oct | Nov |
|---|---|---|---|---|---|---|---|---|---|---|---|
| SCORE | | | | | | 4 | 3 | 2 | 1 | | P |
| MODEL SET | | | | 4 | 3 | 2 | 1 | | P | | |
| MODEL SET | | | 4 | 3 | 2 | 1 | | P | | | |

**Figure 17.9** A model time chart shows the time frame for the input columns and targets when building a customer signature.

This is a set of fields from the UNIT_MASTER file for June—fields such as the handset type, billing plan, and so on. It is important to keep the time frame in mind when filling the customer signature. It is a good idea to use a naming convention to avoid confusion. In this case, all the fields might have a suffix of "_01," indicating that they are from the most recent month of input data.

> **TIP** Use a naming convention when building the customer signature to indicate the time frame for each variable. For instance, the most recent month of input data would have a "_01" suffix; the month before, "_02"; and so on.

At this point, presumably not much is known about the fields, so descriptive information is useful. For instance, the billing plan might have a description, monthly base, per-minute cost, and so on. All of these features are interesting and of potential value for modeling—so it is reasonable to bring them into the model set. Although descriptions are not going to be used for modeling (codes are much better), they help the data miners understand the data.

## Pivoting Columns

Some of the fields in UNIT_MASTER represent data that is reported in a regular time series. For instance, bill amount has a value for every month, and each of these values needs to be put into a separate column. These columns come from different UNIT_MASTER records, one for June, one for May, one for April, and so on. Using a naming convention, the fields would be, for example:

- Last_billed_amount_01 for June (which may already be in the snapshot)
- Last_billed_amount_02 for May
- Last_billed_amount_03 for April

At this point, the customer signature is starting to take shape. Although the input fields only come from one source, the appropriate fields have been chosen as input and aligned in time.

## Calculating the Target

A customer signature for predictive modeling would not be useful without a target variable. Since the customer signature is going to be used for churn modeling, the target needs to be whether or not the customer churned in August. This is in the account status field for the August UNIT_MASTER record. Note that only customers who were active on or before June 30 are included in the model set. A customer that starts in July and cancels in August is not included.

## Making Progress

Although quite rudimentary, the customer signature is ready for use in a model set. Having a well-defined time frame, a target variable, and input variables, it is functional, even if minimally so. Although useful and a place to get started, the signature is missing a few things.

First, the definition of customer does not take into account changes in telephone numbers. The TRANS_MASTER file solves this problem, because it keeps track of these types of changes on customers' accounts. To fix the definition of customer requires creating a table, which has the original telephone number on the account (with perhaps a counter, since a telephone number can actually be reused). A typical row in this table would have the following columns:

- Telephone Number
- Effective Date
- End Date
- Unique Customer Identifier

With this table, the customer identifier can be used instead of the telephone number, so the customer signatures are robust with respect to changes in telephone number.

Another shortcoming of the customer signature is its reliance on only one data source. Additional data sources should be added in, one at a time, to build a richer signature of customer behavior. The model set only has one time frame of data. Additional time frames make models that are more stable. This customer signature also lacks derived variables, which are the subject of much of the rest of this chapter.

## Practical Issues

There are some practical issues encountered when building customer signatures. Customer signatures often bring together the largest sources of data and perform complex operations on them. This becomes an issue in terms of computing resources. Although the resulting model set probably has at most tens or hundreds of megabytes, the data being summarized could be thousands of times larger. For this reason, it is often a good idea to do as much of the processing as possible in relational databases, because these can take advantage of multiple processors and multiple disks at the same time.

Although the resulting queries are complicated, much of the work of putting together the signatures can be done in SQL or in the database's scripting language. This is useful not only because it increases efficiency, but also because the code then resides in only one place—reducing the possibility of error and increasing the ability to find bugs when they occur. Alternatively, the data can be extracted from the source and pieced together. Increasingly, data mining tools are becoming better at manipulating data. However, this generally requires some amount of programming, in a language such as SAS, SPSS, S-Plus, or Perl. The additional processing not only adds time to the effort, but it also introduces a second level where bugs might creep in.

It is important when creating signatures to realize that data mining is an iterative process that often requires rebuilding the signature. A good approach is to create a template for pulling one time frame of data from the data sources, and then to do multiple such pulls to create the model set. For the score set, the same process can be used, since the score set closely resembles the model set.

# Exploring Variables

Data exploration is critically intertwined with the data mining process. In many ways, data mining and data exploration are complementary ways of achieving the same goal. Where data mining tends to highlight the interesting algorithms for finding patterns, data exploration focuses more on presenting data so that people can intuit the patterns. When it comes to communicating results, pretty pictures that *show* what is happening are often much more effective than dry tables of numbers. Similarly, when preparing data for data mining, seeing the data provides insight into what is happening, and this insight can help improve models.

## Distributions Are Histograms

The place to start when looking at data is with histograms of each field; histograms show the distribution of values in fields. Actually, there is a slight difference between histograms and distributions, because histograms count occurrences, whereas distributions are normalized. However, for our purposes, the similarities are much more important—histograms and distributions (or strictly speaking, the density function associated with the distribution) have similar shapes; it is only the scale of the Y-axis that changes.

Most data mining tools provide the ability to look at the values that a single variable takes on as a histogram. The vertical axis is the number of times each value occurs in the sample; the horizontal axis shows the various values.

Numeric variables are often binned when creating histograms. For the purpose of exploring the variables, these bins should be of equal width and not of equal height. Remember that equal-height binning creates bins that all contain the same number of values. Bins containing similar numbers of records are useful for modeling; however, they are less useful for understanding the variables themselves.

## Changes over Time

Perhaps the most revealing information becomes apparent when the time element is incorporated into a histogram. In this case, only a single value of a variable is used. The chart shows how the frequency of this value changes over time.

As an example, the chart in Figure 17.10 shows fairly clearly that something happened during one March with respect to the value "DN." This type of pattern is important. In this case, the "DN" represents duplicate accounts that needed to be canceled when two different systems were merged. In fact, we stumbled across the explanation only after seeing such a patterns and asking questions about what was happening during this time period.

The top chart shows the raw values, and that can be quite useful. The bottom one shows the standardized values. The curves in the two charts have the same shape; the only difference is the vertical scale. Remember that standardizing values converts them into the number of standard deviations from the mean, so values outside the range of –2 to 2 are unusual; values less then –3 or greater than 3 should be very rare. Visualizing the same data shows that the peaks are many standard deviations outside expected values—and 14 standard deviations is highly suspect. The likelihood of this happening randomly is so remote that the chart suggests that something external is affecting the variable—something external like the one-time even of merging of two computer systems, which is how the duplicate accounts were created.

Creating one cross-tabulation by time is not very difficult. Unfortunately, however, there is not much support in data mining tools for this type of diagram. They are easy to create in Excel or with a bit of programming in SAS, SPSS, S-Plus, or just about any other programming language. The challenge is that many such diagrams are needed—one for each value taken on by each categorical variable. For instance, it is useful to look at:

- Different types of accounts opened over time.
- Different reasons why customers stop over time.
- Performance of certain geographies over time.
- Performance of different channels over time.

Because these charts explicitly go back in time, they bring up issues of what happened when. They can be useful for spotting particularly effective combinations that might not otherwise be obvious—such as "oh, our Web banner click-throughs go up after we do email campaigns."

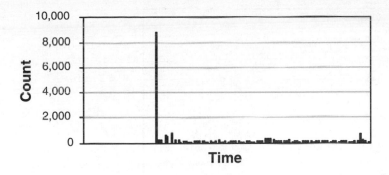

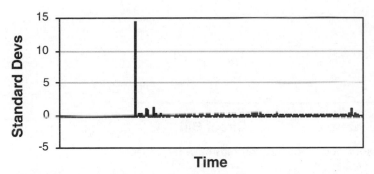

**Figure 17.10** This histogram suggests that something unusual was happening with this stop code. The top diagram is the raw data; in the bottom one, the values are standardized.

## Crosstabulations

Looking at variables over time is one example of a cross-tabulation. In general, cross-tabulations show how frequently two variables occur with respect to each other. Figure 17.11 shows a cross-tabulation between two variables, channel and credit card payment. The size of the bubble shows the proportion of customers starting in the channel with that payment method. This is the same data shown in Table 17.2.

Cross-tabulations without time show static images rather than trends. This is useful, but trend information is usually even more useful.

**Table 17.2** Cross Tabulation of Channels by Payment Method

|  | CREDIT CARD | DIRECT BILL |
|---|---|---|
| DM | 69,126 | 51,481 |
| TM | 50,105 | 249,208 |
| WEB | 67,830 | 29,608 |

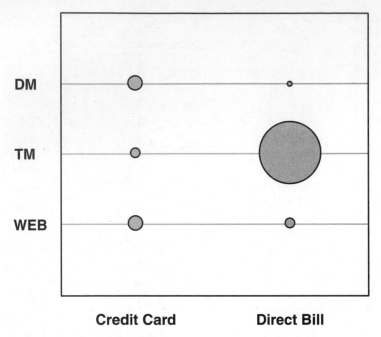

**Figure 17.11** Cross-tabulations show relationships between variables.

## Deriving Variables

There have been many examples of derived variables in this chapter and throughout this book. Such variables are predigested, making it easier for data mining algorithms to incorporate them into models. Perhaps more important, derived variables make it possible to incorporate domain knowledge into the data mining process. Put the domain information into the data so that the data mining algorithms can use it to find patterns.

Because adding variables is central to any successful data mining project, it is worth looking at the six basic ways that derived variables are calculated in a bit of detail. These six methods are:

- Extracting features from a single value
- Combining values within a record (used, among other things, for capturing trends)
- Looking up auxiliary information in another table
- Pivoting time-dependent data into multiple columns
- Summarizing transactional records
- Summarizing fields across the model set

The following sections discuss these methods, giving examples of derived variables and highlighting important points about computing them.

## Extracting Features from a Single Value

Computationally, parsing values is a very simple operation because all the data needed is present in a single value. Even though it is so simple, it is quite useful, as these examples show:

- Calculating the day of the week from a date
- Extracting the credit card issuer code from a credit card number
- Taking the SCF (first three digits) of a zip code
- Determining the vehicle manufacturer code from the VIN
- Adding a flag when a field is missing

These operations generally require rudimentary operations that data mining tools should be able to handle. Unfortunately, many statistical tools focus more on numeric data types than on the strings, dates, and times often encountered in business data—so string operations and date arithmetic can be difficult. In such cases, these variables may need to be added during a preprocessing phase or as data is extracted from data sources.

## Combining Values within a Record

As with the extraction of features from a single value, combining values within a record is computationally simple—instead of using one variable, there are several variables. Most data mining tools support adding derived variables that combine values from several fields, particularly for numeric fields. This can be very useful, for adding ratios, sums, averages, and so on. Such derived values are often more useful for modeling purposes than the raw data because these variables start to capture underlying customer behavior. Date fields are often combined. Taking the difference of two dates to calculate duration is an especially common and useful example.

It is not usually necessary to combine string fields, unless the fields are somehow related. For instance, it might be useful to combine a "credit card payment flag" with a "credit card type," so there is one field representing the payment type.

## Looking Up Auxiliary Information

Looking up auxiliary information is a more complicated process than the previous two calculations. A lookup is an example of joining two tables together (to use relational database terminology), with the simplifying assumption that one table is big and the other table is relatively small.

When the lookup table is small enough, such as Table 17.3, which describes the mapping between initial digits of a credit card number and the credit card type, then a simple formula can suffice for the lookup.

The more common situation is having a secondary table or file with the information. This table might, for instance, contain:

■ Populations and median household incomes of zip codes (usefully provided for downloading for the United States by the U.S. Census Bureau at www.census.gov)

■ Hierarchies for product codes

■ Store type information about retail locations

Unfortunately data mining tools do not, as a rule, make it easy to do lookups without programming. Tools that do provide this facility, such as I-Miner from Insightful, usually require that both tables be sorted by the field or fields used for the lookup; an example of this is shown in Figure 17.12. This is palatable for one such field, but it is cumbersome when there are many different fields to be looked up. In general, it is easier to do these lookups outside the tool, especially when the lookup tables and original data are both coming from databases.

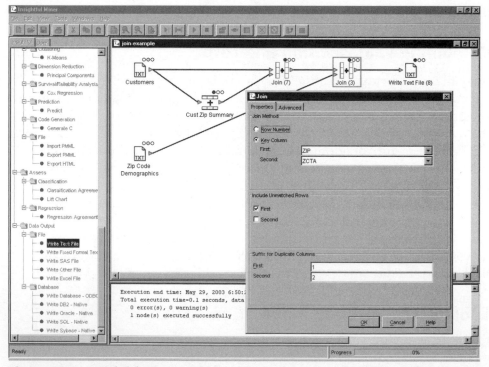

**Figure 17.12** Insightful Miner enables users to use and create lookup tables from the graphical user interface.

Sometimes, the lookup tables already exist. Other times, they must be created as needed. For instance, one useful predictor of customer attrition is the historical attrition rate by zip code. To add this to a customer signature requires calculating the historical attrition rate for each zip code and then using the result as a lookup table.

**WARNING** When using database joins to look up values in a lookup table, always use a left outer join to ensure that no customer rows are lost in the process! An outer join in SQL looks like:

```
SELECT c.*, l.value
FROM (customer c left outer join lookup l on c.code = l.code)
```

**Table 17.3**  Credit Card Prefixes

| CARD TYPE | PREFIX | LENGTH |
|---|---|---|
| MasterCard | 51 | 16 |
| MasterCard | 52 | 16 |
| MasterCard | 53 | 16 |
| MasterCard | 54 | 16 |
| MasterCard | 55 | 16 |
| Visa | 4 | 13 |
| Visa | 4 | 16 |
| American Express | 34 | 15 |
| American Express | 37 | 15 |
| Diners Club | 300 | 14 |
| Diners Club | 301 | 14 |
| Diners Club | 302 | 14 |
| Diners Club | 303 | 14 |
| Diners Club | 304 | 14 |
| Diners Club | 305 | 14 |
| Discover | 6011 | 16 |
| enRoute | 2014 | 15 |
| enRoute | 2149 | 15 |
| JCB | 3 | 16 |
| JCB | 2131 | 15 |
| JCB | 1800 | 15 |

## Pivoting Regular Time Series

Data about customers is often stored at a monthly level, where each month has a separate row of data. For instance, billing data is often stored this way, since most subscription-based companies bill customers once a month. This data is an example of a regular time series, because the data occurs at fixed, defined intervals. Figure 17.13 illustrates the process needed to put this data into a customer signature. The data must be pivoted, so values that start out in rows end up in columns.

This is generally a cumbersome process, because neither data mining tools nor SQL makes it easy to do pivoting. Data mining tools generally require programming for pivoting. To accomplish this, the customer file needs to be sorted by customer ID, and the billing file needs to be sorted by the customer ID and the billing date. Then, special-purpose code is needed to calculate the pivoting columns. In SAS, proc TRANSPOSE is used for this purpose. The sidebar "Pivoting Data in SQL" shows how it is done in SQL.

Most businesses store customer data on a monthly basis, usually by calendar month. Some industries, though, show strong weekly cyclical patterns, because customers either do or do not do things over the weekend. For instance, Web sites might be most active during weekdays, and newspaper subscriptions generally start on Mondays or Sundays.

Such weekly cycles interfere with the monthly data, because some months are longer than others. Consider a Web site where most activity is on weekdays. Some months have 20 weekdays; others have up to 23 (not including holidays). The difference between successive months could be 15 percent, due solely to the difference in the number of weekdays. To take this into account, divide the monthly activity by the number of weekdays during the month, to get an "activity per weekday." This only makes sense, though, when there are strong weekly cycles.

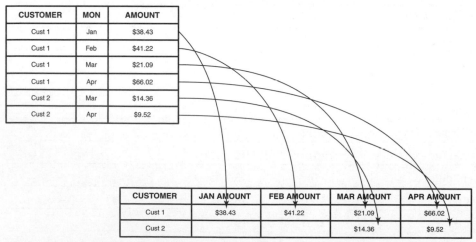

**Figure 17.13** Pivoting a field takes values stored in one or more rows for each customer and puts them into a single row for each customer, but in different columns.

## PIVOTING DATA IN SQL

SQL does not have great support for pivoting data (although some databases may have nonstandard extensions with this capability). However, when using standard SQL it is possible to pivot data.

Assume that the data consists of billing records and that each has a sequential billing number assigned to it. The first billing record has a "1," the second "2," and so on. The following SQL fragment shows how to pivot this data:

```
SELECT customer_id,
       sum(case when bill_seq = 1 then bill_amt end) as bill_1,
       sum(case when bill_seq = 2 then bill_amt end) as bill_2,
       sum(case when bill_seq = 3 then bill_amt end) as bill_3,
       . . .
FROM billing
GROUP BY customer_id
```

One problem with this fragment is that different customers have different numbers of billing periods. However, the query can only take a fixed number. When a customer has fewer billing periods than the query wants, then the later periods are filled with NULLs.

Actually, this code fragment is not generally what is needed for customer signatures because the signature wants the most recent billing periods—such as the last 12 or 24. For customers who are active, this is the most recent period. However, for customers who have stopped, this requires considering their stop date instead. The following code fragment takes this into account:

```
SELECT customer_id,
       sum(case when trunc(months_between(bill_date, cutoff) = 1
                then bill_amt else 0 end) as bill_1,
       sum(case when trunc(months_between(bill_date, cutoff) = 2
                then bill_amt else 0 end) as bill_2,
       . . .
FROM billing b,
     (select customer_id,
             (case when status = 'ACTIVE' then sysdate
                  else stop_date end) as cutoff
      from customer) c
where b.customer_id = c.customer_id
GROUP BY customer_id
```

This code fragment does use some extensions to SQL for the date calculations (these are expressed as Oracle functions in this example). However, most databases have similar functions.

The above code is an example of a killer query, because it is joining a big table (the customer table) with an even bigger table (the customer billing table) and then doing a grouping operation. Fortunately, modern databases can take advantage of multiple processors and multiple disks to perform this query in a reasonable amount of time.

## Summarizing Transactional Records

Transactional records are an example of an irregular time series—that is, the records can occur at any point in time. Such records are generated by customer interactions, as is the case with:

- Automated teller machine transactions
- Telephone calls
- Web site visits
- Retail purchases

There are several challenges when working with irregular time series. First, the transaction volumes are very, very large. Working with such voluminous data requires sophisticated tools and powerful computers. Second, there is no standard way of working with them. The regular time series data has a natural way of pivoting. For irregular time series, it is necessary to determine how best to summarize the data.

One way is to transform the irregular time series into regular time series and then to pivot the series. For instance, calculate the number of calls per month or the amount withdrawn from ATMs each month, and then pivot the sums by month. When working with transactions, these calculations can be more complex, such as the number of calls longer than 10 minutes or the number of withdrawals less than $50. These specialized summaries can be quite useful. More complicated examples that describe customer behavior are provided just after the next section.

Another approach is to define a set of data transformations that are run on the transactional data as it is being collected. This is an approach taken in the telecommunications industry, where the volume of data is vast. Some variables may be as simple as minutes of use, others may be a complex as a score for whether the calling number is a business or residence. This approach hard-codes the calculations, and such calculations are hard to change. Although such variables can be useful, a more flexible environment for summarizing transactional data is strategically more useful.

## Summarizing Fields across the Model Set

The last method for deriving variables is summarizing values across fields in the customer signature itself. There are several examples of such fields:

- Binning values into equal sized bins requires calculating the breakpoints for the bins.
- Standardizing a value (subtracting the mean and dividing by the standard deviation) requires calculating the mean and standard deviation for the field and then doing the calculation.

- Ranking a value (so the smallest value has a value of 1, the second smallest 2, and so on) requires sorting all the values to get the ranking.

Although these are complicated operations, they are performed directly on the model set. Data mining tools provide support for these operations, especially for binning numeric values, which is the most important of the three.

One type of binning that would be very useful is not readily available. This is binning for codes based on frequency. That is, it would be useful to keep all codes that have at least, say, 1,000 instances in the model set and to place all other codes in a single "other" category. This is useful for working with outliers, such as the many old and unpopular handsets that show up in mobile telephone data although few customers use them. One way to handle this is to identify the handsets to keep and to add a new field "handset for analysis" that keeps these handsets and places the rest into an "other" category. A more automated way is to create a lookup table to map the handsets. However, perhaps a better way is to replace the handset ID itself with information such as the date the handset was released, its weight, and the features it uses—information that is probably available in a lookup table already.

# Examples of Behavior-Based Variables

The real power of derived variables comes from the ability to summarize customer behaviors along known dimensions. This section builds on the ideas already presented and gives three examples of useful behavior-based variables.

## Frequency of Purchase

Once upon a time, catalogers devised a clever method for characterizing customer behavior using three dimensions—recency, frequency, and monetary value. RFM, which relies on these three variables, has been used at least since the 1970s. Of these three descriptions of customer behavior, recency is usually the most predictive, but frequency is the most interesting. Recency simply means the length of time since a customer made a purchase. Monetary value is traditionally the total amount purchased (although we have found the average purchase value more useful since the total is highly correlated with frequency).

In traditional RFM analysis, frequency is just the number of purchases. However, a simple count does not do a good job of characterizing customer behavior. There are other approaches to determining frequency, and these can be applied to other areas not related to catalog purchasing—frequency of complaints, frequency of making international telephone calls, and so on. The important point is that customers may perform an action at irregular intervals, and we want to characterize this behavior pattern because it provides potentially useful information about customers.

One method of calculating frequency would be to take the length of time indicated by the historical data and divide it by the number of times the customer made a purchase. So, if the catalog data goes back 6 years and a customer made a single purchase, then that frequency would be once every 6 years.

Although simple, this approach misses an important point. Consider two customers:

- John made a purchase 6 years ago and has received every catalog since then.

- Mary made a purchase last month when she first received the catalog.

Does it make sense that both these customers have the same frequency? No. John more clearly has a frequency of no more than once every 6 years. Mary only had the opportunity to make one purchase in the past month, so her frequency would more accurately be described as once per month. The first point about frequency is that it should be measured from the first point in time that a customer had an opportunity to make a purchase.

There is another problem. What we really know about John and Mary is that their frequencies are no more than once every 6 years and no more than once per month, respectively. Historically, one observation does not contain enough information to deduce a real frequency. This is really a time to event problem, such as those discussed in Chapter 12.

Our goal here is to characterize frequency as a derived variable, rather than predict the next event (which is best approached using survival analysis). To do this, let's assume that there are two or more events, so the average time between events is the total span of time divided by the number of events minus one, as shown in Figure 17.14. This provides the average time between events for the period when the events occurred.

There is no perfect solution to the question of frequency, because customer events occur irregularly and we do not know what will happen in the future—the data is censored. Taking the time span from the first event to the most recent event runs into the problem that customers whose events all took place long ago may have a high frequency. The alternative is to take the time since the first event, in essence pretending that the present is an event. This is unsatisfying, because the next event is not known, and care must be taken when working with censored data. In practice, taking the number of events since the first event could have happened and dividing by the total span of time (or the span when the customer was active) is the best solution.

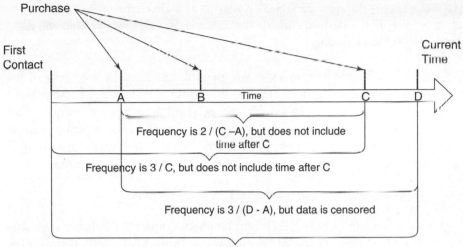

**Figure 17.14**   There is no perfect way to estimate frequency, but these four ways are all reasonable.

## Declining Usage

In telecommunications, one significant predictor of churn is declining usage—customers who use services less and less over time are more likely to leave than other customers. Customers who have declining usage are likely to have many variables indicating this:

- Billing measures, such as recent amounts spent are quite small.
- Usage measures, such as recent amounts used are quite small or always at monthly minimums.
- Optional services recently have no usage.
- Ratios of recent measures to older measures are less than 1, often significantly less than one, indicating recent usage is smaller than historical usage.

The existence of so many different measures for the same underlying behavior suggests a situation where a derived variable might be useful to capture the behavior in a single variable. The goal is to incorporate as much information as possible into a "declining usage" indicator.

> **TIP**  When many different variables all suggest a single customer behavior, then it is likely that a derived variable that incorporates this information will do a better job for data mining.

Fortunately, mathematics provides an elegant solution, in the form of the best fit line, as shown in Figure 17.15. The goodness of fit is described by the $R^2$ statistic, which varies from 0 to 1, with values near 0 being poor fit and values near 1 being very good. The slope of the line provides the average rate of increase or decrease in some variable over time. In statistics, this slope is called the beta function and is calculated according to the following formula:

```
Sum of (x-average(x))*(y-average(y)) / sum((x-average(x))²)
```

To give an example of how this might be used, consider the following data for the customer shown in the previous figure. Table 17.4 walks through the calculation for a typical customer.

**Table 17.4**  Example of Calculating the Slope for a Time Series

| MONTH (X –VALUE) | X – AVG(X) | (X – AVG (X))^2 | Y (FROM CUST A) | Y – AVG(Y) | (X – AVG(X)) * (Y – AVG(Y)) |
|---|---|---|---|---|---|
| 1 | −5.5 | 30.25 | 53.47 | 3.19 | −17.56 |
| 2 | −4.5 | 20.25 | 46.61 | −3.67 | 16.52 |
| 3 | −3.5 | 12.25 | 47.18 | −3.10 | 10.84 |
| 4 | −2.5 | 6.25 | 49.54 | −0.74 | 1.85 |
| 5 | −1.5 | 2.25 | 48.71 | −1.57 | 2.35 |
| 6 | −0.5 | 0.25 | 52.04 | 1.76 | −0.88 |
| 7 | 0.5 | 0.25 | 48.45 | −1.83 | −0.91 |
| 8 | 1.5 | 2.25 | 54.16 | 3.88 | 5.83 |
| 9 | 2.5 | 6.25 | 54.47 | 4.19 | 10.47 |
| 10 | 3.5 | 12.25 | 53.69 | 3.42 | 11.95 |
| 11 | 4.5 | 20.25 | 45.93 | −4.35 | −19.59 |
| 12 | 5.5 | 30.25 | 49.10 | −1.18 | −6.51 |
| TOTAL | | 143 | | | 14.36 |
| SLOPE | | | | | 0.1004 |

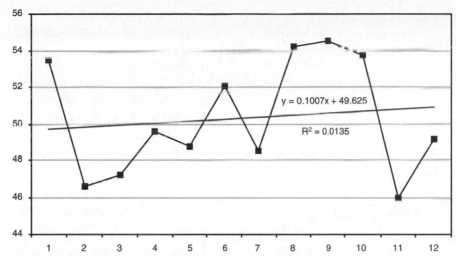

**Figure 17.15**  The slope of the line of best fit provides a good measure of changes over time.

This example shows a very typical use for calculating the slope—finding the slope over the previous year's usage or billing patterns. The tabular format shows the calculation in a way most suitable for a spreadsheet. However, many data mining tools provide a function to calculate beta values directly from a set of variables in a single row. When such a function is not available, it is possible to express it using more basic arithmetic functions.

Although monthly data is often the most convenient for such calculations, remember that different months have different numbers of days. This issue is particularly significant for businesses that have strong weekly cycles. Some months have five full weekends, for instance, while others only have four. Different months have between 20 and 23 working days (not including holidays). These differences can account for up to 25 percent of the difference between months. When working with data that has such cycles, it is a good idea to calculate the "average per weekend" or "average per working day" to see how the chosen measure is changing over time.

> **TIP** When working with data that has weekly cycles but must be reported by month, consider variables such as "average per weekend day" or "average per work day" so that comparisons between months are more meaningful.

## Revolvers, Transactors, and Convenience Users: Defining Customer Behavior

Often, business people can characterize different groups of customers based on their behavior over time. However, translating an informal business description into a form useful for data mining is challenging. Faced with such a challenge, the best response is to determine measures of customer behavior that match the business understanding.

This example is about a credit card group at a major retail bank, which has found that profitable customers come in three flavors:

- *Revolvers* are customers who maintain large balances on their credit cards. These are highly profitable customers because every month they pay interest on large balances.

- *Transactors* are customers who have high balances every month, but pay them off. These customers do not pay interest, but the processing fee charged on each transaction is an important source of revenue. One component of the transaction fee is based on a percentage of the transaction value.

- *Convenience users* are customers who periodically charge large amounts, for vacations or large purchases, for example, and then pay them off over several months. Although not as profitable as revolvers, they are lower risk, while still paying significant amounts of interest.

The marketing group believes that these three types of customers are motivated by different needs. So, understanding future customer behavior would allow future marketing campaigns to send the most appropriate message to each customer segment. The group would like to predict customer behavior 6 months in the future.

The interesting part of this example is not the prediction, but the definition of the segments. The training set needs examples where customers are already classified into the three groups. Obtaining this classification proves to be a challenge.

## Data

The data available for this project consisted of 18 months of billing data, including:

- Credit limit
- Interest rate
- New charges made during each month
- Minimum payment
- Amount paid
- Total balance in each month
- Amount paid in interest and related charges each month

The rules for these credit cards are typical. When a customer has paid off the balance, there is no interest on new charges (for 1 month). However, when there is an outstanding balance, then interest is charged on both the balance and on new charges. What does this data tell us about customers?

## Segmenting by Estimating Revenue

Estimated revenue is a good way of understanding the value of customers. (By itself, this value does not provide much insight into customer behavior, so it is not very useful for messaging.) Basing customer value on revenue alone assumes that the costs for all customers are the same. This is not true, but it is a useful approximation, since a full profitability model is quite complicated, difficult to develop, and beyond the scope of this example.

Table 17.5 illustrates 1 month of billing for six customers. The last column is the estimated revenue, which has two components. The first is the amount of interest paid. The second is the transaction fee on new transactions, which is estimated to be 1 percent of the new transaction volume for this example.

**Table 17.5**   Six Credit Card Customers and 1 Month of Data

| | CREDIT LIMIT | RATE | NEW CHARGES | BEGINNING BALANCE | MIN PAYMENT | AMOUNT PAID | INTEREST | TRANSACTION REVENUE | EST. REVENUE |
|---|---|---|---|---|---|---|---|---|---|
| Customer 1 | $500 | 14.9% | $50 | $400 | $15 | $15 | $4.97 | $0.50 | $5.47 |
| Customer 2 | $5,000 | 4.9% | $0 | $4,500 | $135 | $135 | $18.38 | $0.00 | $18.38 |
| Customer 3 | $6,000 | 11.9% | $100 | $3,300 | $99 | $1,000 | $32.73 | $1.00 | $33.73 |
| Customer 4 | $10,000 | 14.9% | $2,500 | $0 | $0 | $75 | $0.00 | $25.00 | $25.00 |
| Customer 5 | $8,000 | 12.9% | $6,500 | $0 | $0 | $6,500 | $0.00 | $65.00 | $65.00 |
| Customer 6 | $5,000 | 17.9% | $0 | $4,500 | $135 | $135 | $67.13 | $0.00 | $67.13 |

Estimated revenue is a good way to compare different customers with a single number. The table clearly shows that someone who rarely uses the credit card (Customer 1) has very little estimated revenue. On the other hand, those who make many charges or pay interest create a larger revenue stream.

However, estimated revenue does not differentiate between different types of customers. In fact, a transactor (Customer 5) has very high revenue. So, does a revolver who has no new charges (Customer 6). This example shows that estimated revenue has little relationship to customer behavior. Frequent users of the credit card and infrequent users both generate a lot of revenue. And this is to be expected, since there are different types of profitable customers.

The real world is more complicated than this simplified example. Each customer has a risk of bankruptcy, where the outstanding balance must be written off. Different types of cards have different rules. For instance, many co-branded cards have the transaction fee going to the co-branded institution. And, the cost of servicing different customers varies, depending on whether the customer uses customer service, disputes charges, pays bills online, and so on.

In short, estimating revenue is a good way of understanding which customers are valuable. But, it does not provide much insight into customer behavior.

## Segmentation by Potential

In addition to actual revenue, each customer has a potential revenue. This is the maximum amount of revenue that the customer could possibly bring in each month. The maximum revenue is easy to calculate. Simply assume that the entire credit line is used either in new charges (hence transaction revenue) or in carry-overs (hence interest revenue). The greater of these is the potential revenue.

Table 17.6 compares the potential revenue with the actual revenue for the same six customers during one month. This table shows some interesting characteristics. Some not-so-profitable customers are already saturating their potential. Without increasing their credit limits or interest rate, it is not possible to increase their value.

**Table 17.6** Potential of Six Credit Card Customers

| | CREDIT LIMIT | RATE | INTEREST | TRANSACTION | POTENTIAL REVENUE | ACTUAL | POTENTIAL |
|---|---|---|---|---|---|---|---|
| Customer 1 | $500 | 14.9% | $6.21 | $5.00 | $6.21 | $5.47 | 88% |
| Customer 2 | $5,000 | 4.9% | $20.42 | $50.00 | $50.00 | $18.38 | 37% |
| Customer 3 | $6,000 | 11.9% | $59.50 | $60.00 | $60.00 | $33.73 | 56% |
| Customer 4 | $10,000 | 14.9% | $124.17 | $100.00 | $124.17 | $25.00 | 20% |
| Customer 5 | $8,000 | 12.9% | $86.00 | $80.00 | $86.00 | $65.00 | 76% |
| Customer 6 | $5,000 | 17.9% | $74.58 | $50.00 | $74.58 | $67.13 | 90% |

There is another aspect of comparing actual revenue to potential revenue; it normalizes the data. Without this normalization, wealthier customers appear to have the most potential, although this potential is not fully utilized. So, the customer with a $10,000 credit line is far from meeting his or her potential. In fact, it is Customer 1, with the smallest credit line, who comes closest to achieving his or her potential value. Such a definition of value eliminates the wealth effect, which may or may not be appropriate for a particular purpose.

### Customer Behavior by Comparison to Ideals

Since estimating revenue and potential does not differentiate among types of customer behavior, let's go back and look at the definitions in more detail. First, what is it inside the data that tells us who is a revolver? Here are some definitions of a revolver:

- Someone who pays interest every month
- Someone who pays more than a certain amount of interest every month (say, more than $10)
- Someone who pays more than a certain amount of interest, almost every month (say, more than $10 in 80 percent of the months)

All of these have an ad hoc quality (and the marketing group had historically made up definitions similar to these on the fly). What about someone who pays very little interest, but does pay interest every month? Why $10? Why 80 percent of the months? These definitions are all arbitrary, often the result of one person's best guess at a definition at a particular time.

From the customer perspective, what is a revolver? It is someone who only makes the minimum payment every month. So far, so good. For comparing customers, this definition is a bit tricky because the minimum payments change from month to month and from customer to customer.

Figure 17.16 shows the actual and minimum payments made by three customers, all of whom have a credit line of $2,000. The revolver makes payments that are very close to the minimum payment each month. The transactor makes payments closer to the credit line, but these monthly charges vary more widely, depending on the amount charged during the month. The convenience user is somewhere in between. Qualitatively, the shapes of the curves provide insight into customer behavior.

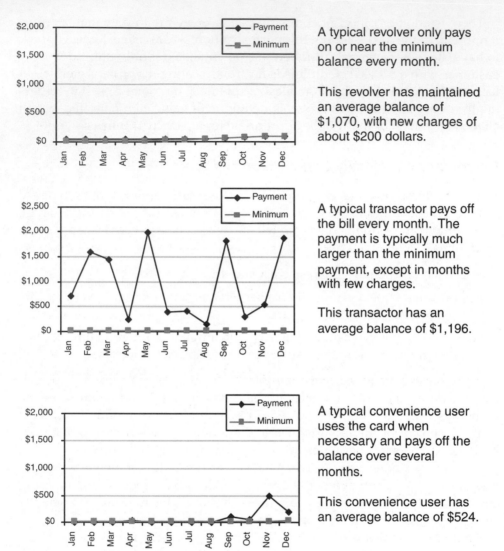

A typical revolver only pays on or near the minimum balance every month.

This revolver has maintained an average balance of $1,070, with new charges of about $200 dollars.

A typical transactor pays off the bill every month. The payment is typically much larger than the minimum payment, except in months with few charges.

This transactor has an average balance of $1,196.

A typical convenience user uses the card when necessary and pays off the balance over several months.

This convenience user has an average balance of $524.

**Figure 17.16**    These three charts show actual and minimum payments for three credit card customers with a credit line of $2,000.

Manually looking at shapes is an inefficient way to categorize the behavior of several million customers. Shape is a vague, qualitative notion. What is needed is a score. One way to create a score is by looking at the area between the "minimum payment" curve and the actual "payment" curve. For our purposes, the area is the sum of the differences between the payment and the minimum. For the revolver, this sum is $112; for the convenience user, $559.10; and for the transactor, a whopping $13,178.90.

This score makes intuitive sense. The lower it is, the more the customer looks like a revolver. However, the score does not work for comparing two cardholders with different credit lines. Consider an extreme case. If a cardholder has a credit line of $100 and was a perfect transactor, then the score would be no more than $1,200. And yet an imperfect revolver with a credit line of $2,000 has a much larger score.

The solution is to normalize the value by dividing each month's difference by the total credit line. Now, the three scores are 0.0047, 0.023, and 0.55, respectively. When the normalized score is close to 0, the cardholder is close to being a perfect revolver. When it is close to 1, the cardholder is close to being a perfect transactor. Numbers in between represent convenience users. This provides a revolver-transactor score for each customer, with convenience users falling in the middle.

This score for customer behavior has some interesting properties. Someone who never uses their card would have a minimum payment of 0 and an actual payment of 0. These people look like revolvers. That might not be a good thing. One way to resolve this would be to include the estimated revenue potential with the behavior score, in effect, describing the behavior using two numbers.

Another problem with this score is that as the credit line increases, a customer looks more and more like a revolver, unless the customer charges more. To get around this, the ratios could instead be the monthly balance to the credit line. When nothing is owed and nothing paid, then everything has a value of 0.

Figure 17.17 shows a variation on this. This score uses the ratio of the amount paid to the minimum payment. It has some nice features. Perfect revolvers now have a score of 1, because their payment is equal to the minimum payment. Someone who does not use the card has a score of 0. Transactors and convenience users both have scores higher than 1, but it is hard to differentiate between them.

This section has shown several different ways of measuring the behavior of a customer. All of these are based on the important variables relevant to the customer and measurements taken over several months. Different measures are more valuable for identifying various aspects of behavior.

## The Ideal Convenience User

The measures in the previous section focused on the extremes of customer behavior, as typified by revolvers and transactors. Convenience users were just assumed to be somewhere in the middle. Is there a way to develop a score that is optimized for the ideal convenience user?

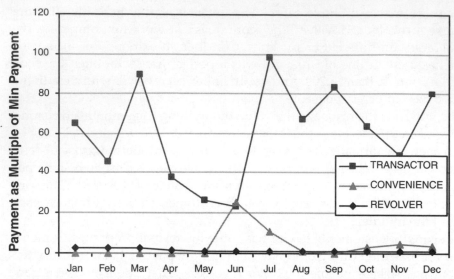

**Figure 17.17** Comparing the amount paid as a multiple of the minimum payment shows distinct curves for transactors, revolvers, and convenience users.

First, let's define the ideal convenience user. This is someone who, twice a year, charges up to his or her credit line and then pays the balance off over 4 months. There are few, if any, additional charges during the other 10 months of the year. Table 17.7 illustrates the monthly balances for two convenience users as a ratio of their credit lines.

This table also illustrates one of the main challenges in the definition of convenience users. The values describing their behavior have no relationship to each other in any given month. They are out of phase. In fact, there is a fundamental difference between convenience users on the one hand and transactors and revolvers on the other. Knowing that someone is a transactor exactly describes their behavior in any given month—they pay off the balance. Knowing that someone is a convenience user is less helpful. In any given month, they may be paying nothing, paying off everything, or making a partial payment.

**Table 17.7** Monthly Balances of Two Convenience Users Expressed as a Percentage of Their Credit Lines

|       | JAN | FEB | MAR | APR | MAY | JUN | JUL | AUG | SEP | NOV | DEC |
|-------|-----|-----|-----|-----|-----|-----|-----|-----|-----|-----|-----|
| Conv1 | 80% | 60% | 40% | 20% | 0%  | 0%  | 0%  | 60% | 30% | 15% | 70% |
| Conv2 | 0%  | 0%  | 83% | 50% | 17% | 0%  | 67% | 50% | 17% | 0%  | 0%  |

Does this mean that it is not possible to develop a measure to identify convenience users? Not at all. The solution is to sort the 12 months of data by the balance ratio and to create the convenience-user measure using the sorted data.

Figure 17.18 illustrates this process. It shows the two convenience users, along with the profile of the ideal convenience user. Here, the data is sorted, with the largest values occurring first. For the first convenience user, month 1 refers to January. For the second, it refers to March.

Now, using the same idea of taking the area between the ideal and the actual produces a score that measures how close a convenience user is to the ideal. Notice that revolvers would have outstanding balances near the maximum for all months. They would have high scores, indicating that they are far from the ideal convenience user. For convenience users, the scores are much smaller.

This case study has shown several different ways of segmenting customers. All make use of derived variables to describe customer behavior. Often, it is possible to describe a particular behavior and then to create a score that measures how each customer's behavior compares to the ideal.

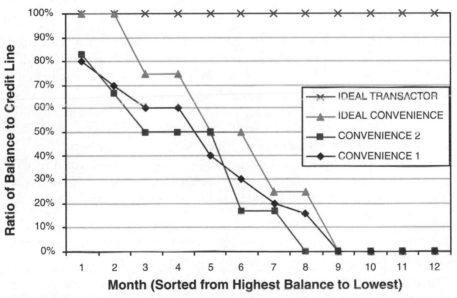

**Figure 17.18** Comparison of two convenience users to the ideal, by sorting the months by the balance ratio.

# The Dark Side of Data

Working with data is a critical part of the data mining process. What does the data mean? There are many ways to answer this question—through written documents, in database schemas, in file layouts, through metadata systems, and, not least, via the database administrators and systems analysis who know what is really going on. No matter how good the documentation, the real story lies in the data.

There is a misconception that data mining requires perfect data. In the world of business analysis, the perfect is definitely the enemy of the sufficiently good. For one thing, exploring data and building models highlights data issues that are otherwise unknown. Starting the process with available data may not result in the best models, but it does start a process that can improve over time. For another thing, waiting for perfect data is often a way of delaying a project so that nothing gets done.

This section covers some of the important issues that make working with data a sometimes painful process.

## Missing Values

Missing values refer to data that should be there but is not. In many cases, missing values are represented as NULLs in the data source, making it easy to identify them. However, be careful: NULL is sometimes an acceptable value. In this case, we say that the value is empty rather than missing, although the two look the same in source data. For instance, the stop code of an account might be NULL, indicating that the account is still active. This information, which indicates whether data is censored or not, is critical for survival analysis.

Another time when NULL is an acceptable value is when working with overlay data describing demographics and other characteristics of customers and prospects. In this case, NULL often has one of two meanings:

- There is not enough evidence to indicate whether the field is true for the individual. For instance, lack of subscriptions to golfing magazines suggests the person is not a golfer, but does not prove it.

- There is no matching record for the individual in the overlay data.

**TIP** When working with ovelay data, it is useful to replace NULLs with alternative values, one meaning that the record does not match and the other meaning that the value is unknown.

It is worth distinguishing between these situations. One way is to separate the data where the records do not match, creating two different model sets. The other is to replace the NULL values with alternative values, indicating whether the failure to match is at the record level or the field level.

Because customer signatures use so much aggregated data, they often contain "0" for various features. So, missing data in the customer signatures is not the most significant issue for the algorithms. However, this can be taken too far. Consider a customer signature that has 12 months of billing data. Customers who started in the past 12 months have missing data for the earlier months. In this case, replacing the missing data with some arbitrary value is not a good idea. The best thing is to split the model set into two pieces—those with 12 months of tenure and those who are more recent.

When missing data is a problem, it is important to find its cause. For instance, one database we encountered had missing data for customers' start dates. With further investigation, it turned out that these were all customers who had started and ended their relationship prior to March 1999. Subsequent use of this data source focused on either customers who started after this date or who were active on this date. In another case, a transaction table was missing a particular type of transaction before a certain date. During the creation of the data warehouse, different transactions were implemented at different times. Only carefully looking at crosstabulations of transaction types by time made it clear that one type was implemented much later than the rest.

In another case, the missing data in a data warehouse was just that—missing because the data warehouse had failed to load it properly. When there is such a clear cause, the database should be fixed, especially since misleading data is worse than no data at all.

One approach to dealing with missing data is to try to fill in the values—for example, with the average value or the most common value. Either of these substitutions changes the distribution of the variable and may lead to poor models. A more clever variation of this approach is to try to calculate the value based on other fields, using a technique such as regression or neural networks. We discourage such an approach as well, unless absolutely necessary, since the field no longer means what it is supposed to mean.

**WARNING** One of the worst ways to handle missing values is to replace them with some "special" value such as 9999 or –1 that is supposed to stick out due to its unreasonableness. Data mining algorithms will happily use these values as if they were real, leading to incorrect results.

Usually data is missing for systematic reasons, as in the new customers scenario mentioned earlier. A better approach is to split the model set into parts, eliminating the missing fields from one data set. Although one data set has more fields, neither will have missing values.

It is also important to understand whether the data is going to be missing in the future. Sometimes the right approach is to build models on records that have complete data (and hope that these records are sufficiently representative of all records) and to have someone fix the data sources, eliminating this headache in the future.

## Dirty Data

Dirty data refers to fields that contain values that might look correct, but are not. These can often be identified because such values are outliers. For instance, once upon a time, a company thought that it was very important for their call-center reps to collect the birth dates of customers. They thought it was so important that the input field on the screen was mandatory. When they looked at the data, they were surprised to see that more than 5 percent of their customers were born in 1911; and not just in 1911, but on November 11th. It turns out that not all customers wanted to share their birth date, so the call-center reps quickly learned that typing six "1"s was the quickest way to fill the field (the day, month, and year eachtook two characters). The result: many customers with the exact same birthday.

The attempt to collect accurate data often runs into conflict with efforts to manage the business. Many stores offer discounts to customers who have membership cards. What happens when a customer does not have a card? The business rules probably say "no discount." What may really happen is that a store employee may enter a default number, so that customer can still qualify. This friendly gesture leads to certain member numbers appearing to have exceptionally high transaction volumes.

One company found several customers in Elizabeth, NJ with the zip code 07209. Unfortunately, the zip code does not exist, which was discovered when analyzing the data by zip code and appending zip code information. The error had not been discovered earlier because the post office can often figure out how to route incorrectly addressed mail. Such errors can be fixed by using software or an outside service bureau to standardize the address data.

What looks like dirty data might actually provide insight into the business. A telephone number, for instance, should consist only of numbers. The billing system for one regional telephone company stored the number as a string (this is quite common actually). The surprise was several hundred "telephone numbers" that included alphabetic characters. Several weeks (!) after being asked about this, the systems group determined that these were essentially calling card numbers, not attached to a telephone line, that were used only for third-party billing services.

Another company used media codes to determine how customers were acquired. So, media codes starting with "W" indicated that customers came from the Web, "D" indicated response to direct mail, and so on. Additional characters in the code distinguished between particular banner ads and particular email campaigns. When looking at the data, it was surprising to discover Web customers starting as early as the 1980s. No, these were not bleeding-edge customers. It turned out that the coding scheme for media codes was created in October 1997. Earlier codes were essentially gibberish. The solution was to create a new channel for analysis, the "pre-1998" channel.

**WARNING** Wthe most pernicious data problem are the ones you don't know about. For this reason, data mining cannot be performed in a vacuum; input from business people and data analysts are critical for success.

All of these cases are examples where dirty data could be identified. The biggest problems in data mining, though, are the unknown ones. Sometimes, data problems are hidden by intervening systems. In particular, some data warehouse builders abhor missing data. So, in an effort to clean data, they may impute values. For instance, one company had more than half their loyal customers enrolling in a loyalty program in 1998. The program has been around longer, but the data was loaded into the data warehouse in 1998. Guess what? For the participants in the initial load, the data warehouse builders simply put in the current date, rather than the date when the customers actually enrolled.

The purpose of data mining is to find patterns in data, preferably interesting, actionable patterns. The most obvious patterns are based on how the business is run. Usually, the goal is to gain an understanding of customers more than an understanding of how the business is run. To do this, it is necessary to understand what was happening when the data was created.

## Inconsistent Values

Once upon a time, computers were expensive, so companies did not have many of them. That time is long past, and there are now many systems for many different purposes. In fact, most companies have dozens or hundreds of systems, some on the operational side, some on the decision-support side. In such a world, it is inevitable that data in different systems does not always agree.

One reason that systems disagree is that they are referring to different things. Consider the start date for mobile telephone service. The order-entry system might consider this the date that customer signs up for the service. An operational system might consider it the date that the service is activated. The billing system might consider it the effective date of the first bill. A downstream decision-support system might have yet another definition. All of these dates should be close to each other. However, there are always exceptions. The best solution is to include all these dates, since they can all shed light on the business. For instance, when are there long delays between the time a customer signs up for the service and the time the service actually becomes effective? Is this related to churn? A more common solution is to choose one of the dates and call that the start date.

Another reason has to do with the good intentions of systems developers. For instance, a decision-support system might keep a current snapshot of customers, including a code for why the customer stopped. One code value might indicate that some customers stopped for nonpayment; other code values might represent other reasons—going to a competitor, not liking the service, and so on. However, it is not uncommon for customers who have stopped voluntarily to not pay their last bill. In this data source, the actual stop code was simply overwritten. The longer ago that a customer stopped, greater the chance that the original stop reason was subsequently overwritten when the company determines—at a later time—that a balance is owed. The problem here is that one field is being used for two different things—the stop reason and nonpayment information. This is an example of poor data modeling that comes back to bite the analysts.

A problem that arises when using data warehouses involves the distinction between the initial loads and subsequent incremental loads. Often, the initial load is not as rich in information, so there are gaps going back in time. For instance, the start date may be correct, but there is no product or billing plan for that date. Every source of data has its peculiarities; the best advice is to get to know the data and ask lots of questions.

# Computational Issues

Creating useful customer signatures requires considerable computational power. Fortunately, computers are up to the task. The question is more which system to use. There are several possibilities for doing the transformation work:

- Source system, typically in databases of some sort (either operational or decision support)
- Data extraction tools (used for populating data warehouses and data marts)
- Special-purpose code (such as SAS, SPSS, S-Plus, Perl)
- Data mining tools

Each of these has its own advantages and disadvantages.

## Source Systems

Source systems are usually relational databases or mainframe systems. Often, these systems are highly restricted, because they have many users. Such source systems are not viable platforms for performing data transformations. Instead, data is dumped (usually as flat files) from these systems and manipulated elsewhere.

In other cases, the databases may be available for ad hoc query use. Such queries are useful for generating customer signatures because of the power of relational databases. In particular, databases make it possible to:

- Extract features from individual fields, even when these fields are dates and strings

- Combine multiple fields using arithmetic operations
- Look up values in reference tables
- Summarize transactional data

Relational databases are not particularly good at pivoting fields, although as shown earlier in this chapter, they can be used for that as well.

On the downside, expressing transformations in SQL can be cumbersome, to say the least, requiring considerable SQL expertise. The queries may extend for hundreds of lines, filled with subqueries, joins, and aggregations. Such queries are not particularly readable, except by whoever constructed them. These queries are also killer queries, although databases are becoming increasingly powerful and able to handle them. On the plus side, databases do take advantage of parallel hardware, a big advantage for transforming data.

## Extraction Tools

Extraction tools (often called ETL tools for extract-transform-load) are generally used for loading data warehouses and data marts. In most companies, business users do not have ready access to these tools, and most of their functionality can be found in other tools. Extraction tools are generally on the expensive side because they are intended for large data warehousing projects.

In *Mastering Data Mining* (Wiley, 1999), we discuss a case study using a suite of tools from Ab Initio, Inc., a company that specializes in parallel data transformation software. This case study illustrates the power of such software when working on very large volumes of data, something to consider in an environment where such software might be available.

## Special-Purpose Code

Coding is the tried-and-true way of implementing data transformations. The choice of tool is really based on what the programmer is most familiar with and what tools are available. For the transformations needed for a customer signature, the main statistical tools all have sufficient functionality.

One downside of using special-purpose code is that it adds an extra layer to the data transformation process. Data must still be extracted from source systems (one possible source of error) and then passed through code (another source of error). It is a good idea to write code that is well documented and reusable.

## Data Mining Tools

Increasingly, data mining tools have the ability to transform data within the tool. Most tools have the ability to extract features from fields and to combine multiple fields in a row, although the support for non-numeric data types varies from tool to tool and release to release. Some tools also support summarizations within the customer signature, such as binning variables (where the binning breakpoints are determined first by looking at the entire set of data) and standardization.

However, data mining tools are generally weak on looking up values and doing aggregations. For this reason, the customer signature is almost always created elsewhere and then loaded into the tool. Tools from leading vendors allow the embedding of programming code inside the tool and access to databases using SQL. Using these features is a good idea because such features reduce the number of things to keep track of when transforming data.

## Lessons Learned

Data is the gasoline that powers data mining. The goal of data preparation is to provide a clean fuel, so the analytic engines work as efficiently as possible. For most algorithms, the best input takes the form of customer signatures, a single row of data with fields describing various aspects of the customer. Many of these fields are input fields, a few are targets used for predictive modeling.

Unfortunately, customer signatures are not the way data is found in available systems—and for good reason, since the signatures change over time. In fact, they are constantly being built and rebuilt, with newer data and newer ideas on what constitutes useful information.

Source fields come in several different varieties, such as numbers, strings, and dates. However, the most useful values are usually those that are added in. Creating derived values may be as simple as taking the sum of two fields. Or, they may require much more sophisticated calculations on very large amounts of data. This is particularly true when trying to capture customer behavior over time, because time series, whether regular or irregular, must be summarized for the signature.

Data also suffers (and causes us to suffer along with it) from problems— missing values, incorrect values, and values from different sources that disagree. Once such problems are identified, it is possible to work around them. The biggest problems are the unknown ones—data that looks correct but is wrong for some reason.

Many data mining efforts have to use data that is less than perfect. As with old cars that spew blue smoke but still manage to chug along the street, these efforts produce results that are good enough. Like the vagabonds in Samuel Beckett's play *Waiting for Godot*, we can choose to wait until perfection arrives. That is the path to doing nothing; the better choice is to plow ahead, to learn, and to make incremental progress.

# CHAPTER 18

# Putting Data Mining to Work

You've reached the last chapter of this book, and you are ready to start putting data mining to work for your company. You are convinced that when data mining has been woven into the fabric of your organization, the whole enterprise will benefit from an increased understanding of its customers and market, from better-focused marketing, from more-efficient utilization of sales resources, and from more-responsive customer support. You also know that there is a big difference between understanding something you have read in a book and actually putting it into practice. This chapter is about how to bridge that gap.

At Data Miners, Inc., the consulting company founded by the authors of this book, we have helped many companies through their first data mining projects. Although this chapter focuses on a company's first foray into data mining, it is really about how to increase the probability of success for any data mining project, whether the first or the fiftieth. It brings together ideas from earlier chapters and applies them to the design of a data mining pilot project. The chapter begins with general advice about integrating data mining into the enterprise. It then discusses how to select and implement a successful pilot project. The chapter concludes with the story of one company's initial data mining effort and its success.

# Getting Started

The full integration of data mining into a company's customer relationship management strategy is a large and daunting project. It is best approached incrementally, with achievable goals and measurable results along the way. The final goal is to have data mining so well integrated into the decision-making process that business decisions use accurate and timely customer information as a matter of course. The first step toward achieving this goal is demonstrating the real business value of data mining by producing a measurable return on investment from a manageable pilot or proof-of-concept project. The pilot should be chosen to be valuable in itself and to provide a solid basis for the business case needed to justify further investment in analytical CRM.

In fact, a pilot project is not that different from any other data mining project. All four phases of the virtuous cycle of data mining are represented in a pilot project albeit with some changes in emphasis. The proof of concept is limited in budget and timeframe. Some problems with data and procedures that would ordinarily need to be fixed may only be documented in a pilot project.

**TIP**  A pilot project is a good first step in the incremental effort to revolutionize a business using data mining.

Here are the topic sentences for a few of the data mining pilot projects that we have collaborated on with our clients:

- Find 10,000 high-end mobile telephone customers customers who are most likely to churn in October in time for us to start an outbound tele-marketing campaign in September.

- Find differences in the shopping profiles of Hispanic and non-Hispanic shoppers in Texas with respect to ready-to-eat cereals, so we can better direct our Spanish-language advertising campaigns.

- Guide our expansion plans by discovering what our best customers have in common with one another and locate new markets where similar customers can be found.

- Build a model to identify market research segments among the customers in our corporate data warehouse, so we can target messages to the right customers

- Forecast the expected level of debt collection for the next several months, so we can manage to a plan.

These examples show the diversity of problems that data mining can address. In each case, the data mining challenge is to find and analyze the appropriate data to solve the business problem. However, this process starts by choosing the right demonstration project in the first place.

## What to Expect from a Proof-of-Concept Project

When the proof-of-concept project is complete, the following are available:

- A prototype model development system (which might be outsourced or might be the kernel of the production system)
- An evaluation of several data mining techniques and tools (unless the choice of tool was foreordained)
- A plan for modifying business processes and systems to incorporate data mining
- A description of the production data mining environment
- A business case for investing in data mining and customer analytics

Even when the decision has already been made to invest in data mining, the proof-of-concept project is an important way to step through the virtuous cycle of data mining for the first time. You should expect challenges and hiccups along the way, because such a project is touching several different parts of the organization—both technical and operational—and needs them to work together in perhaps unfamiliar ways.

## Identifying a Proof-of-Concept Project

The purpose of a proof-of-concept project is to validate the utility of data mining while managing risk. The project should be small enough to be practical and important enough to be interesting. A successful data mining proof-of-concept project is one that leads to actions with measurable results. To find candidates for a proof of concept, study the existing business processes to identify areas where data mining could provide tangible benefits with results that can be measured in dollars. That is, the proof of concept should create a solid business case for further integration of data mining into the company's marketing, sales, and customer-support operations.

A good way to attract attention and budget dollars to a project is to use data mining to meet a real business need. The most convincing proof-of-concept projects focus on areas that are already being measured and evaluated analytically, and where there is already an acknowledged need for improvement. Likely candidates include:

- Response models
- Default risk models
- Attrition models
- Usage models
- Profitability models

These are areas where there is a well-defined link between improved accuracy of predictions and improved profitability. With some projects, it is easy to act on the data mining results. This is not to say that pilot projects with a focus on increased insight and understanding without any direct link to the bottom line cannot be successful. They are, however, harder to build a business case for.

Potential users of new information are often creative and have good imaginations. During interviews, encourage them to imagine ways to develop true learning relationships with customers. At the same time, make an inventory of available data sources, identifying additional fields that may be desirable or required. Where data is already being warehoused, study the data dictionaries and database schemas. When the source systems are operational systems, study the record layouts that will be supplying the data and get to know the people who are familiar with how the systems process and store information.

As part of the proof-of-concept selection process, do some initial profiling of the available records and fields to get a preliminary understanding of relationships in the data and to get some early warnings of data problems that may hinder the data mining process. This effort is likely to require some amount of data cleansing, filtering, and transformation.

Once several candidate projects have been identified, evaluate them in terms of the ability to act on the results, the usefulness of the potential results, the availability of data, and the level of technical effort. One of the most important questions to ask about each candidate project is "how will the results be used?" As illustrated by the example in the sidebar "A Successful Proof of Concept?" a common fate of data mining pilot projects is to be technically successful but underappreciated because no one can figure out what to do with the results.

There are certainly many examples of successful data mining projects that originated in IT. Nevertheless, when the people conducting the data mining are not located in marketing or some other group that communicates directly with customers, sponsorship or at least input from such a group is important for a successful project. Although data mining requires interaction with databases and analytic software, it is not primarily an IT project and should rarely be attempted in isolation from the owners of the business problem being addressed.

**TIP** A data mining pilot project may be based in any of several groups within the company, but it must always include active participation from the group that feels ownership of the business problem to be addressed.

Marketing campaigns make good proof-of-concept projects because in most companies there is already a culture of measuring the results of such campaigns. A controlled experiment showing a statistically significant improvement in response to a direct mail, telemarketing, or email campaign is easily translated into dollars. The best way to prove the value of data mining is with

## A SUCCESSFUL PROOF OF CONCEPT?

A data mining proof of concept project can be technically successful, yet disappointing overall. In one example, a cellular telephone company launched a data mining project to gain a better understanding of customer churn. The project succeeded in identifying several customer segments with high churn risk. With the groups identified, the company could offer these customers incentives to stay. So far, the project seems like a good proof-of-concept that returns actionable results.

The data mining models found one group of high-risk customers, consisting of subscribers whose calling behavior did not match their rate plans. One subgroup of these customers were on rate plans with low monthly fees, and correspondingly few included minutes. Such plans make sense for people who use their phones infrequently, such as the "safety user" who leaves a telephone in the car's glove compartment, rarely turning it on but more secure in the knowledge that the phone is available for emergencies. When such users change their telephone habits (as sometimes happens once they realize the usefulness of a mobile phone), they end up using more minutes than are included in their plan, paying high per minute charges for the overage.

The company declared the data mining project a success because the groups that the model identified as high risk were tracked and did in fact leave in droves. However, nothing was done because the charter of the group sponsoring the data mining project was to explore new technologies rather than manage customer relationships. In a narrow sense, the project was indeed successful. It proved the concept that data mining could identify customers at high risk for churn. In a broader sense, the organization was not ready for data mining, so it could not successfully act on the results.

There is another organizational challenge with these customers. As long as they remain, the mismatched customers are quite profitable, paying for expensive overcalls or on a too-expensive rate plan. Moving them to a rate plan that saved them money ("right-planning" them) might very well decrease churn but also decrease profitability. Which is more important, churn or profitability? Data mining often raises as many questions as it answers, and the answers to some questions depend on business strategy more than on data mining results.

a demonstration project that goes beyond evaluating models to actually measuring the results of a campaign based on the models. Where that is not possible, careful thought must be given to how to attach a dollar value to the results of the demonstration project. In some cases, it is sufficient to test the new models derived from data mining against historical data.

## Implementing the Proof-of-Concept Project

Once an appropriate business problem has been selected, the next step is to identify and collect data that can be transformed into actionable information. Data sources have already been identified as part of the process of selecting the proof-of-concept project. The next step is to extract data from those sources and transform it into customer signatures, as described in the previous chapter. Designing a good customer signature is tricky the first few times. This is an area where the help of experienced data miners can be valuable.

In addition to constructing the initial customer signature, there needs to be a prototype data exploration and model development environment. This environment could be provided by a software company or data mining consultancy, or it can be constructed in-house as part of the pilot project. The data mining environment is likely to consist of a data mining software suite installed on a dedicated analytic workstation. The model development environment should be rich enough to allow the testing of a variety of data mining techniques. Chapter 16 has advice on selecting data mining software and setting up a data mining environment. One of the goals of the proof-of-concept project is to determine which techniques are most effective in addressing the particular business problem being tackled.

Using the prototype data mining system involves a process of refining the data extraction requirements and interfaces between the environment and the existing operational and decision-support computing environments. Expect this to be an iterative process that leads to a better understanding of what is needed for the future data mining environment. Early data mining results will suggest new modeling approaches and refinements to the customer signature.

When the prototype data mining environment has been built, use it to build predictive models to perform the initial high-payback task identified when the proof-of-concept project was defined. Carefully measure the performance of the models on historical data.

It is entirely feasible to accomplish the entire proof-of-concept project without actually building a prototype data mining environment in-house by using external facilities. There are advantages and disadvantages to this approach. On the positive side, a data mining consultancy brings insights gained through experience working with data from other companies to the problem at hand. It is unlikely that anyone on your own staff has the knowledge and experience with the broad range of data mining tools and techniques that specialists can bring to bear. On the negative side, you and your staff will not learn as much about the data mining process if consultants do all the actual data mining work. Perhaps the best compromise is to put together a team that includes outside consultants along with people from the company.

### Act on Your Findings

The next step is to measure the results of modeling. In some case, this is best done using historical data (preferably an out-of-time sample for a good comparison). Another possibility that requires more cooperation from other groups is to set up a controlled experiment comparing the effects of the actions taken based on data mining with the current baseline. Such a controlled experiment is particularly valuable in a company that already has a culture of doing such experiments.

Finally, use the results of modeling (whether from historical testing or an actual experiment) to build a business case for integrating data mining into the business operations on a permanent basis.

Sometimes, the result of the pilot project is insight into customers and the market. In this case, success is determined more subjectively, by providing insight to business people. Although this might seem the easier proof-of-concept project, it is quite challenging to find results in a span of weeks that make a favorable impression on business people with years of experience.

Many data mining proof-of-concept projects are not ambitious because they are designed to assess the technology rather than the results of its application. It is best when the link between better models and better business results is not hypothetical, but is demonstrated by actual results. Statisticians and analysts may be impressed by theoretical results; senior management is not.

A graph showing the lift in response rates achieved by a new model on a test dataset is impressive; however, new customers gained because of the model are even more impressive.

## Measure the Results of the Actions

It is important to measure both the effectiveness of the data mining models themselves and the actual impact on the business of the actions taken as a result of the models' predictions.

Lift is an appropriate way to measure the effectiveness of the models themselves. Lift measures the change in concentration of records of some particular type (such as responders or defaulters) relative to model scores. To measure the impact on the business requires more information. If the pilot project builds a response model, keep track of the following costs and benefits:

- What is the fixed cost of setting up the campaign and the model that supports it?
- What is the cost per recipient of making the offer?
- What is the cost per respondent of fulfilling the offer?
- What is the value of a positive response?

The last item seems obvious, but is often overlooked. We have seen more than one data mining initiative get bogged down because, although it was shown that data mining could reach more customers, there was no clear model of what a new customer was worth and therefore no clear understanding of the benefits to be derived.

Although the details of designing a good marketing test are beyond the scope of this book, it is important to control for both the efficacy of the data mining model and the efficacy of the offer or message employed. This can be accomplished by tracking the response of four different groups:

- Group A, selected to receive the offer by the data mining model
- Group B, selected at random to receive the same offer
- Group C, also selected at random, that does not get the offer
- Group D, selected by the model to receive the offer, but does not get it.

If the model does a good job of finding the right customers, group A will respond at a significantly higher rate than group B. If the offer is effective, group B will respond at a higher rate than group C. Sometimes, a model does a good job of finding responders for an ineffective offer. In such a case, groups A and D have similar response rates. Each pair-wise comparison answers a different question, as shown in Figure 18.1.

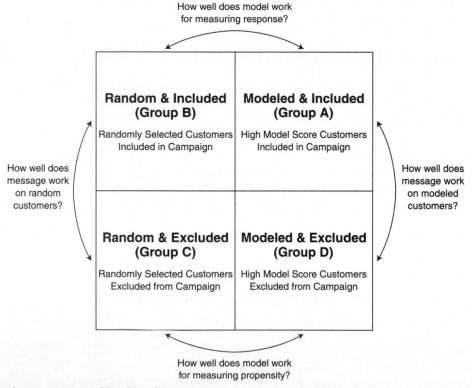

**Figure 18.1** Tracking four different groups makes it possible to determine both the effect of the campaign and the effect of the model.

This latter situation does occur. One Canadian bank used a model to pick customers who should be targeted with a direct mail campaign to open investment accounts. The people picked by the model did, in fact, open investment accounts at a higher rate than other customers—whether or not they received the promotional material. In this case there is a simple reason. The bank had flooded its customers with messages about investment accounts—advertising, posters in branches, billing inserts, and messages when customers called in and were put on hold. Against this cacophony of messages, the direct mail piece was redundant.

# Choosing a Data Mining Technique

The choice of which data mining technique or techniques to apply depends on the particular data mining task to be accomplished and on the data available for analysis. Before deciding on a data mining technique, first translate the business problem to be addressed into a series of data mining tasks and understand the nature of the available data in terms of the content and types of the data fields.

## Formulate the Business Goal as a Data Mining Task

The first step is to take a business goal such as "improve retention" and turn it into one or more of the data mining tasks from Chapter 1. As a reminder, the six basic tasks addressed by the data mining techniques discussed in this book are:

- Classification
- Estimation
- Prediction
- Affinity grouping
- Clustering
- Profiling and description

One approach to the business goal of improving retention is to identify the subscribers who are likely to cancel, figure out why, and make them some kind of offer that addresses their concerns. For the strategy to be successful, subscribers who are likely to cancel must be identified and assigned to groups according to their presumed reasons for leaving. An appropriate retention offer can then be designed for each group.

Using a model set that contains examples of customers who have canceled along with examples of those who have not, many of the data mining techniques discussed in this book are capable of labeling each customer as more or less likely to churn. The additional requirement to identify separate segments of subscribers at risk and understand what motivates each group to leave suggests the use of decision trees and clever derived variables.

Each leaf of the decision tree has a label, which in this case would be "not likely to churn" or "likely to churn." Each leaf in the tree has different proportions of the target variables; this proportion of churners that can be used as a churn score. Each leaf also has a set of rules describing who ends up there. With skill and creativity, an analyst may be able to turn these mechanistic rules into comprehensible reasons for leaving that, once understood, can be counteracted. Decision trees often have more leaves than desired for the purpose of developing special offers and telemarketing scripts. To combine leaves, into larger groups, take whole branches of the tree as the groups, rather than single leaves.

Note that our preference for decision-tree methods in this case stems from the desire to understand the reasons for attrition and our desire to treat subgroups differentially. If the goal were simply to do the best possible job of predicting the subscribers at risk, without worrying about the reasons, we might select a different approach. Different business goals suggest different data mining techniques. If the goal were to estimate next month's minutes of use for each subscriber, neural networks or regression would be better choices. If the goal were to find naturally occurring customer segments an undirected clustering technique or profiling and hypothesis testing would be appropriate.

## Determine the Relevant Characteristics of the Data

Once the data mining tasks have been identified and used to narrow the range of data mining methods under consideration, the characteristics of the available data can help to refine the selection further. In general terms, the goal is to select the data mining technique that minimizes the number and difficulty of the data transformations that must be performed in order to coax good results from the data.

As discussed in the previous chapter, some amount of data transformation is always part of the data mining process. The raw data may need to be summarized in various ways, data encodings must be rationalized, and so forth. These kinds of transformations are necessary regardless of the technique chosen. However, some kinds of data pose particular problems for some data mining techniques.

### Data Type

Categorical variables are especially problematic for data mining techniques that use the numeric values of input variables. Numeric variables of the kind that can be summed and multiplied play to the strengths of data mining techniques, such as regression, K-means clustering, and neural networks, that are based on arithmetic operations. When data has many categorical variables, then decision trees are quite useful, although association rules and link analysis may be appropriate in some cases.

## Number of Input Fields

In directed data mining applications, there should be a single target field or dependent variable. The rest of the fields (except for those that are either clearly irrelevant or clearly dependent on the target variable) are treated as potential inputs to the model. Data mining methods vary in their ability to successfully process large numbers of input fields. This can be a factor in deciding on the right technique for a particular application.

In general, techniques that rely on adjusting a vector of weights that has an element for each input field run into trouble when the number of fields grows very large. Neural networks and memory-based reasoning share that trait. Association rules run into a different problem. The technique looks at all possible combinations of the inputs; as the number of inputs grows, processing the combinations becomes impossible to do in a reasonable amount of time.

Decision-tree methods are much less hindered by large numbers of fields. As the tree is built, the decision-tree algorithm identifies the single field that contributes the most information at each node and bases the next segment of the rule on that field alone. Dozens or hundreds of other fields can come along for the ride, but won't be represented in the final rules unless they contribute to the solution.

**TIP** When faced with a large number of fields for a directed data mining problem, it is a good idea to start by building a decision tree, even if the final model is to be built using a different technique. The decision tree will identify a good subset of the fields to use as input to a another technique that might be swamped by the original set of input variables.

## Free-Form Text

Most data mining techniques are incapable of directly handling free-form text. But clearly, text fields often contain extremely valuable information. When analyzing warranty claims submitted to an engine manufacturer by independent dealers, the mechanic's free-form notes explaining what went wrong and what was done to fix the problem are at least as valuable as the fixed fields that show the part numbers and hours of labor used.

One data mining technique that can deal with free text is memory-based reasoning, one of the nearest neighbor methods discussed in Chapter 8. Recall that memory-based reasoning is based on the ability to measure the *distance* from one record to all the other records in a database in order to form a neighborhood of similar records. Often, finding an appropriate distance metric is a stumbling block that makes it hard to apply the technique, but researchers in the field of information retrieval have come up with good measures of the distance between two blocks of text. These measurements are based on the overlap in vocabulary between the documents, especially of uncommon words and proper nouns. The ability of Web search engines to find appropriate articles is one familiar example of text mining.

As described in Chapter 8, memory-based reasoning on free-form text has also been used to classify workers into industries and job categories based on written job descriptions they supplied on the U.S. census long form and to add keywords to news stories.

## Consider Hybrid Approaches

Sometimes, a combination of techniques works better than any single approach. This may require breaking down a single data mining task into two or more subtasks. The automotive marketing example from Chapter 2 is a good example. Researchers found that the best way of selecting prospects for a particular car model was to first use a neural network to identify people likely to buy a car, then use a decision tree to predict the particular model each car buyer would select.

Another example is a bank that uses three variables as input to a credit solicitation decision. The three inputs are estimates for:

- The likelihood of a response
- The projected first-year revenue from this customer
- The risk of the new customer defaulting

These tasks vary considerably in the amount of relevant training data likely to be available, the input fields likely to be important, and the length of time required to verify the accuracy of a prediction. Soon after a mailing, the bank knows exactly who responded because the solicitation contains a deadline after which responses are considered invalid. A whole year must pass before the estimated first-year revenue can be checked against the actual amount, and it may take even longer for a customer to "go bad." Given all these differences, it is not be surprising that a different data mining techniques may turn out to be best for each task.

## How One Company Began Data Mining

Over the years, the authors have watched many companies make their first forays into data mining. Although each company's situation is unique, some common themes emerge. At each company there was someone responsible for the data mining project who truly believed in the power and potential of analytic customer relationship management, often because he or she had seen it in action in other companies. This leader was not usually a technical expert, and frequently did not do any of the actual technical work. He or she functioned as an evangelist to build the data mining team and secure sponsorship for a data mining pilot.

The successful efforts crossed corporate boundaries to involve people from both marketing and information technology. The teams were usually quite small—often consisting of only 4 or 5 people—yet included people who understood the data, people who understood the data mining techniques, people who understood the business problem to be addressed, and at least one person with experience applying data mining to business problems. Sometimes several of these roles were combined in one person.

In all cases, the initial data mining pilot project addressed a problem of real importance to the organization—one where the value of success would be recognized. Some of the best pilot projects were designed to measure the usefulness of data mining by looking at the results of the *actions* suggested by the data mining effort.

One of the companies, a wireless service provider, agreed to let us describe its data mining pilot project.

## A Controlled Experiment in Retention

In 1996, Comcast Cellular was a wireless phone service provider in a market of 7.5 million people in a three-state area centered around Philadelphia. In 1999, Comcast Cellular was absorbed by SBC and is now part of Cingular, but at the time this pilot study took place, it was a regional service provider facing tough competition from fast-growing national networks. Increasing competition meant that subscribers were faced with many competing offers, and each month a significant proportion of the customer base switched to a competing service. This churn, as it is called in the industry, was very disturbing because even though new subscribers easily outnumbered the defectors, the acquisition cost for a new customer was often in the $500 to $600 range. There is a detailed discussion of churn in Chapter 4.

With even more competitors, poised to enter its market, Comcast Cellular wanted to reach out to existing subscribers with a proactive effort to ensure their continued happiness. The difficulty was knowing which customers were at risk and for what reasons. For any retention campaign, it is important to understand which customers are at risk because a retention offer costs the company money. It doesn't make sense to offer an inducement to customers who are likely to remain anyway. It is equally important to understand what motivates different customer segments to leave, since different retention offers are appropriate for different segments. An offer of free night and weekend minutes may be very attractive to customers who use their phones primarily to keep in touch with friends, but of little interest to business users.

The pilot project was a three-way partnership between Comcast, a group of data mining consultants (including the authors), and a telemarketing service bureau.

- Comcast supplied data and expertise on its own business practices and procedures.

- The data mining consultants developed profiles of likely defectors based on usage patterns in call detail data.

- The telemarketing service bureau worked with Comcast to use the profiles to develop retention offers for an outbound telemarketing campaign.

This description focuses on the data mining aspect of the combined effort. The goal of the data mining effort was to identify groups of subscribers with an unusually high likelihood to cancel their subscriptions in the next 60 days. The data mining tool employed used a rule induction algorithm similar to decision trees to create segments of high-risk customers described by simple rules. The plan was to include these high-risk customers in telemarketing campaigns aimed at retaining them. The retention offers were to be tailored to different customer segments discovered through data mining. The experimental design allowed for the comparison of three groups:

- Group A consists of customers judged by the model to be high risk for whom no intervention was performed.

- Group B consists of customers judged by the model to be high risk for whom some intervention was performed.

- Group C is representative of the general population of customers.

The study design is illustrated in Figure 18.2. Our hope, of course, was that group A would suffer high attrition compared to groups B and C, proving that both the model and the intervention were effective.

Here the project ran into a little trouble. The first difficulty was that although the project included a budget for outbound telemarketing calls to the people identified as likely to cancel, there was neither budget nor authorization to actually *offer* anything to the people being called. Another problem was a technical problem in the call center. It was not possible to transfer a dissatisfied customer directly over to the customer service group at the phone company to resolve particular problems outside the scope of the retention effort (such as mistakes on bills). Yet another problem was that although the customer database included a home phone number for each customer, only about 75 percent of them turned out to be correct.

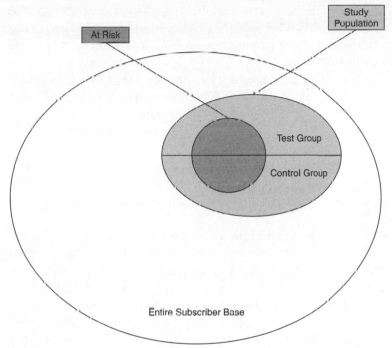

**Figure 18.2**   Study design for the analytic customer relationship marketing test.

In the end, the outbound telemarketing company simply called people from the test and control groups and asked them a series of questions designed to elicit their level of satisfaction and volunteered to refer any problems reported to customer service. Despite this rather lame intervention, 60-day retention was significantly better for the test group than for the control group. Apparently, just showing that the company cared enough to call was enough to decrease churn.

## The Data

In the course of several interviews with the client, we identified two sources of data for use in the pilot. The first source was a customer profile database that had already been set up by a database marketing company. This database contained summary information for each subscriber including the billing plan, type of phone, local minutes of use by month, roaming minutes of use by month, number of calls to and from each identified cellular market in the United States, and dozens of other similar fields.

The second source was call detail data collected from the wireless switches. Each time a mobile phone is switched on, it begins a two-way conversation with nearby cell sites. The cell sites relay data from the telephone such as the serial number and phone type to a central switching office. Computers at the switching office figure out which cell site the phone should be talking to at the moment and send a message back to the phone telling it which cell it is using and what frequency to tune to.

When the subscriber enters a phone number and presses the send button, the number is relayed to the central switch, which in turn sets up the call over regular land lines or relays it to the cell closest to another wireless subscriber. Every switch generates a call detail record that includes the subscriber ID, the originating number, the number called, the originating cell, the call duration, the call termination reason, and so on. These call detail records were used to generate a behavioral profile of each customer, including such things as the number of distinct numbers called and the proportion of calls by time of day and day of week.

The pilot project used 6 months of data for around 50,000 subscribers some of whom canceled their accounts and some of whom did not. Our original intention was to merge the two data sources so that a given subscriber's data from the marketing database (billing plan, tenure, type of phone, total minutes of use, home town, and so on) would be linked to the detail records for each of his or her calls. That way, a single model could be built based on independent variables from both sources. For technical reasons, this proved difficult, so due to time and budgetary constraints we ended up building two separate models, one based on the marketing data and one based on call detail data.

The marketing data was already summarized at the customer level and stored in an easily accessible database system. Getting the call detail data into a usable form was more challenging. Each switch had its own collection of reel-to-reel tapes like the ones used to represent computers in 1960s movies. These tapes were continuously recycled so that a 90-day moving window was always current with the tapes from 90 days earlier being used to record the current day's calls. Since eight tapes were written every day, we found ourselves looking at over 700 tape reels, each of which had to be loaded individually by hand into a borrowed 9-track tape drive. Once loaded, the call detail data, which was written in an arcane format unique to the switching equipment, needed extensive preprocessing in order to be made ready for analysis. The 70 million call detail records were reduced to 10 million by filtering out records that did not relate to calls to or from the churn model population of around.

Even before predictive modeling began, simple profiling of the call detail data suggested many possible avenues for increasing profitability. Once call detail was available in a queryable form, it became possible to answer questions such as:

- Are subscribers who make many short calls more or less loyal than those who make fewer, longer calls?

- Do dropped calls lead to calls to customer service?

- What is the size of a subscriber's "calling circle" for both mobile-to-mobile and mobile-to-fixed-line calling?
- How does a subscriber's usage vary from hour to hour, month to month, and weekday to weekend?
- Does the subscriber call any radio station call-in lines?
- How often does a subscriber call voice mail?
- How often does a subscriber call customer service?

The answers to these and many other questions suggested a number of marketing initiatives to stimulate cellular phone use at particular times and in particular ways. Furthermore, as we had hoped, variables built around measures constructed from the call detail, such as size of calling circle, proved to be highly predictive of churn.

## The Findings

Data mining isolated several customer segments at high risk for churn. Some of these were more actionable than others. For example, it turned out that subscribers who, judging by where their calls entered the network, commuted to New York were much more likely to churn than subscribers who commuted to Philadelphia. This was a coverage issue. Customers who lived in the Comcast coverage area and commuted to New York, found themselves roaming (making use of another company's network) for most of every work day. The billing plans in effect at that time made roaming very expensive. Commuters to Philadelphia remained within the Comcast coverage area for their entire commute and work day and so incurred no roaming charges. This problem was not very actionable because neither changing the coverage area nor changing the rules governing rate plans was within the power of the sponsors of the study, although the information could be used by other parts of the business.

A potentially more actionable finding was that customers whose calling patterns did not match their rate plan were at high risk for churn. There are two ways that a customer's calling behavior may be inappropriate for his or her rate plan. One segment of customers pays for more minutes than they actually use. Arguably, a wireless company might be able to increase the lifetime value of these customers by moving them to a lower rate plan. They would be worth less each month, but might last longer. The only way to find out for sure would be with a marketing test. After all, customers might accept the offer to pay less each month, but still churn at the same rate. Or, the rate of churn might be lowered, but not enough to make up for the loss in near-term revenue.

The other type of mismatch between calling behavior and rate plan occurs when subscribers sign up for a low-cost rate plan that does not include many minutes of use and find themselves frequently using more minutes than the plan allows. Since the extra minutes are charged at a high rate, these customers end up paying higher bills than they would on a more expensive rate plan with more included minutes. Moving these customers to a higher-rate plan would save them some money, while also increasing the amount of revenue from the fixed portion of their monthly bill.

## The Proof of the Pudding

Comcast was able to make a direct cost/benefit analysis of the combined data mining and telemarketing action plan. Armed with this data, Comcast was able to make an informed decision to invest in future data mining efforts. Of course, the story does not really end there; it never does.

The company was faced with a whole new set of questions based on the data that comes back from the initial study. New hypotheses were formed and tested. The response data from the telemarketing effort became fodder for a new round of knowledge discovery. New product ideas and service plans were tried out. Each round of data mining started from a higher base because the company knew its customers better. That is the virtuous cycle of data mining.

# Lessons Learned

In a business context, the successful introduction of data mining requires using data mining techniques to address a real business challenge. For companies that are just getting started with analytical customer relationship management, integrating data mining can be a daunting task. A proof-of-concept project is a good way to get started. The proof of concept should create a solid business case for further integration of data mining into the company's marketing, sales, and customer-support operations. This means that the project should be in an area where it is easy to link improved understanding gained through data mining with improved profitability.

The most successful proof-of-concept projects start with a well-defined business problem, and use data related to that problem to create a plan of action. The action is then carried out in a controlled manner and the results carefully analyzed to evaluate the effectiveness of the action taken. In other words, the proof of concept should involve one full trip around the virtuous cycle of data mining. If this initial project is successful, it will be the first of many. The primary lesson from this chapter is also an important lesson of the book as a whole: data mining techniques only become useful when applied to meaningful problems. Data mining is a technical activity that requires technical expertise, but its success is measured by its effect on the business.

# Index